Lecture Notes in Computer Science 2848

Edited by G. Goos, J. Hartmanis, and J. van Leeuwen

T0226167

Springer
Berlin
Heidelberg
New York
Hong Kong
London
Milan
Paris
Tokyo

Faith Ellen Fich (Ed.)

Distributed Computing

17th International Conference, DISC 2003
Sorrento, Italy, October 1-3, 2003
Proceedings

Springer

Series Editors

Gerhard Goos, Karlsruhe University, Germany
Juris Hartmanis, Cornell University, NY, USA
Jan van Leeuwen, Utrecht University, The Netherlands

Volume Editor

Faith Ellen Fich
Department of Computer Science
University of Toronto
10 King's College Road, Toronto, Ontario
Canada M5S 3G4
E-mail: fich@cs.toronto.edu

Cataloging-in-Publication Data applied for

A catalog record for this book is available from the Library of Congress.

Bibliographic information published by Die Deutsche Bibliothek
Die Deutsche Bibliothek lists this publication in the Deutsche Nationalbibliografie;
detailed bibliographic data is available in the Internet at <http://dnb.ddb.de>.

CR Subject Classification (1998): C.2.4, C.2.2, F.2.2, D.1.3, F.1.1, D.4.4-5

ISSN 0302-9743
ISBN 3-540-20184-X Springer-Verlag Berlin Heidelberg New York

Springer-Verlag Berlin Heidelberg New York
a member of BertelsmannSpringer Science+Business Media GmbH

http://www.springer.de

© Springer-Verlag Berlin Heidelberg 2003
Printed in Germany

Typesetting: Camera-ready by author, data conversion by PTP Berlin GmbH
Printed on acid-free paper   SPIN: 10958551   06/3142   5 4 3 2 1 0

Preface

DISC, the International Symposium on DIStributed Computing, is an annual conference for the presentation of research on the theory, design, analysis, implementation, and application of distributed systems and networks. DISC 2003 was held on October 1–3, 2003 in Sorrento, Italy.

There were 91 regular papers submitted to DISC this year. These were read and evaluated by the program committee members, assisted by external reviewers. The quality of submissions was high and we were unable to accept many deserving papers. Twenty-five papers were selected by the program committee to be included in these proceedings. It is expected that these papers will be submitted, in a more polished form, to fully refereed scientific journals.

The Best Student Paper Award was selected from among the accepted papers that were not co-authored by any program committee members. This year, the award was given to Ittai Abraham for the paper "Probabilistic Quorums for Dynamic Systems", co-authored with Dahlia Malkhi.

The support of the University of Salerno, Italy and, in particular, its Dipartimento di Informatica ed Applicazioni is gratefully acknowledged. The review process and the preparation of this volume were done using CyberChair. I also thank Denise Lobo for her excellent help with these matters.

October 2003   Faith Ellen Fich

Organizing Committee

Luigi Catuogno, University of Salerno, Italy
Stelvio Cimato, University of Salerno, Italy
Roberto De Prisco, University of Salerno, Italy
    and Akamai Technologies, USA (Chair)
Barbara Masucci, University of Salerno, Italy

DISC 2003 was sponsored by the University of Salerno, Italy and, in particular, its Dipartimento di Informatica ed Applicazioni.

Steering Committee

Faith Ellen Fich, University of Toronto, Canada
Shay Kutten, Technion, Israel
Dahlia Malkhi, The Hebrew University of Jerusalem, Israel
Marios Mavronicolas, University of Cyprus, Cyprus
Michel Raynal, Irisa, France (Chair)
Alex Shvartsman, University of Connecticut, USA (Vice-chair)
Jennifer Welch, Texas A&M University, USA

Program Committee

Hagit Attiya, Technion, Israel
Bernadette Charron-Bost, École Polytechnique Palaiseau,
France
Angela Demke Brown, University of Toronto, Canada
Roberto De Prisco, University of Salerno, Italy and Akamai Technologies, USA
Danny Dolev, Hebrew University, Israel
Faith Ellen Fich, University of Toronto, Canada (Chair)
Rachid Guerraoui, École Polytechnique Fédérale de Lausanne, Switzerland
Lisa Higham, University of Calgary, Canada
Colette Johnen, Université de Paris-Sud, France
Mirosław Kutyłowski, Wroclaw University of Technology, Poland
David Peleg, Weizmann Institute, Israel
Rüdiger Reischuk, Universität zu Lübeck, Germany
Eric Ruppert, York University, Canada
Nir Shavit, Tel Aviv University, Israel
Ion Stoica, University of California, Berkeley, USA
Amin Vahdat, Duke University, USA

External Reviewers

Ittai Abraham
Daniel Adkins
Micah Adler
Adnan Agbaria
Marcos Aguilera
Jan Arpe
Vincenzo Auletta
Amir Bar-Or
Wolfgang Bein
Allan Borodin
Stéphane Boucheron
Sébastien Cantarell
Luigi Catuogno
Arindam Chakraborty
Subhendu Chattopadhyay
Chirdeep Chhabra
Bogdan Chlebus
Stelvio Cimato
Alan Covington
Ariel Daliot
Partha Dutta
Jeff Edmonds
Panagiota Fatourou
Hugues Fauconnier
Mikhail Fomitchev
Pierre Fraigniaud
Clemente Galdi
Felix Gärtner
Leszek Gąsieniec
Philippe Gauron
Maciej Gębala
Brighten Godfrey
Marcin Gogolewski
Garth Goodson

Sidath Handurukande
David Hay
Danny Hendler
Ryan Huebsch
Kleoni Ioannidou
LillAnne Jackson
Andreas Jakoby
Tomasz Jurdziński
Yaniv Kaplan
Marcin Karpiński
Jalal Kawash
Idit Keidar
Roger Khazan
Marcin Kik
Petr Kouznetsov
Darek Kowalski
Łukasz Krzywiecki
Jarosław Kutyłowski
Edya Ladan
Karthik
   Lakshminarayanan
Hyonho Lee
Fabrice Le Fessant
Ron Levy
Jorg Liebeherr
Maciej Liskiewicz
Boon Thau Loo
Victor Luchangco
Dahlia Malkhi
Bodo Manthey
Angelo Monti
Shlomo Moran
Marcin Mucha
Alessandro Panconesi

Paolo Penna
Nihal Pekergin
Giuseppe Persiano
Franck Petit
Umberto Ferraro Petrillo
Laurence Pilard
Bastian Pochon
Sergio Rajsbaum
Ananth Rajagopala Rao
David Ratajczak
Sylvia Ratnasami
Adolfo Rodriquez
Bartłomiej Różański
Brigitte Rozoy
Wojciech Rutkowski
André Schiper
Ori Shalev
Ilya Shnayderman
Kamil Skalski
Lakshminarayanan
   Subramanian
Sébastien Tixeuil
Kashi Vishwanath
Hagen Völzer
Jianping Wang
Lixiao Wang
Paweł Wlaź
Avishai Wool
Jay Wylie
Haifeng Yu
Idan Zach
Paweł Zalewski
Marcin Zawada

Table of Contents

Resilient Consensus for Infinitely Many Processes

(Extended Abstract)

Michael Merritt[1] and Gadi Taubenfeld[2]

[1] AT&T Labs, 180 Park Ave., Florham Park, NJ 07932, USA.
mischu@research.att.com
[2] School of computer science, the Interdisciplinary Center,
P.O.Box 167, Herzliya 46150, Israel. tgadi@idc.ac.il

Abstract. We provide results for implementing resilient consensus for a (countably) infinite collection of processes.

- For a known number of faults, we prove the following equivalence result: For every $t \geq 1$, there is a t-resilient consensus object for infinitely many processes if and only if there is a t-resilient consensus object for $t + 1$ processes.
- For an unknown or infinite number of faults, we consider whether an infinite set of wait-free consensus objects, capable of solving consensus for any finite collection of processes, suffice to solve wait-free consensus for infinitely many processes. We show that this implication holds under an assumption precluding runs in which the number of simultaneously active processes is not bounded, leaving the general question open.

All the proofs are constructive and several of the constructions have adaptive time complexity. (Reduced to the finite domain, some improve on the time complexity of known results.) Furthermore, we prove that the constructions are optimal in some space parameters by providing tight simultaneous-access and space lower bounds. Finally, using known techniques, we draw new conclusions on the universality of resilient consensus objects in the infinite domain.

1   Introduction

We explore the solvability of consensus when the number of processes which may participate is countably infinite. The investigation broadens our understanding of the limits of fault-tolerant computation. Recent work has investigated the the design of algorithms assuming no a priori bound on the number of processes [ASS02,CM02,GMT01,MT00]. Moreover, these assume that the number of active processes may be infinite (in infinite runs). The primary motivation for such an investigation is to understand the limits of distributed computation. While in practice the number of processes will always be finite, algorithms designed for an infinite number of processes may scale well: their time complexity may depend on the actual contention and not on the total number of processes.

F.E. Fich (Ed.): DISC 2003, LNCS 2848, pp. 1–15, 2003.
© Springer-Verlag Berlin Heidelberg 2003

1.1   Basic Concepts

A factor in designing algorithms where the number of processes is unknown is the concurrency level, the maximum number of processes that may be active simultaneously. (That is, processes participating in the algorithm at the same instant of time. This is often called point contention. A weaker possible definition of concurrency, often called interval contention, is not considered here.) Following [MT00,GMT01], we distinguish between the following concurrency levels:

- finite: There is a finite bound (denoted by c) on the maximum number of processes that are simultaneously active, over all runs.
- bounded: In each run, there is a finite bound on the maximum number of processes that are simultaneously active. (But there is no finite bound over all runs.)
- unbounded: In each run, the number of processes that are simultaneously active is finite but can grow without bound.

Notice that although an infinite number of processes may take steps in the same run, we assume that the concurrency in any single state is finite.

Time complexity is computed using the standard model, in which each primitive operation on a shared object is assumed to take no more than one time unit. An algorithm is adaptive to process contention if the time complexity of processes' operations is bounded by a function of the number of processes active before and concurrently with those operations. It is adaptive to operation contention if the time complexity of processes' operations is bounded by a function of the number of operations active before and concurrently with those operations. (The term contention sensitive was first used to describe such algorithms [MT93], but later the term adaptive become commonly used.)

Each shared object presents a set of operations. For example, x.op denotes operation op on object x. For each such operation x.op on x, there is an associated access control list, denoted $ACL(x.op)$, which is the set of processes allowed to invoke that operation. Each operation execution begins with an invocation by a process in the operation's ACL, and remains pending until a response is received by the invoking process. The ACLs for two different operations on the same object can differ, as can the ACLs for the same operation on two different objects. A process not in the ACL for x.op cannot invoke x.op.

A process may be either correct or faulty. Correct processes are constrained to obey their specifications. A faulty processes follows its protocol up to a certain point and then stops. (I.e., no Byzantine faults.) We generally use t to denote the maximum number of faulty processes, and throughout the rest of the paper, we assume that $t \geq 1$. For any object x, we say x is t-resilient if any operation invocation when executed by a correct process, eventually completes in any run in which at most t processes fail. An object is wait-free if it can tolerate any number of faults.

Next we define some of the objects used in this paper. An atomic register x, is a linearizable object with two operations: x.read and x.write(v) where $v \neq \perp$. An x.read that occurs before the first x.write() returns $\perp$. An x.read that occurs after an x.write() returns the value written in the last preceding x.write() operation. (Throughout, atomic registers are assumed to be wait-free, and with no limits on the number of processes that may access them simultaneously.)

A (binary) consensus object x, is a linearizable object with one operation: x.propose(v), where $v \in \{0, 1\}$, satisfying: (1) In any run, the x.propose() operation returns the same value, called the consensus value, to every correct process that invokes it. (2) In any finite run, if the consensus value is v, then some process invoked x.propose(v).

Many abstract objects support read operations: operations which return information about the state of the object, without constraining its future behavior (c.f. [Her91]). Atomic registers (and some other abstract objects) also support write() operations: operations that do not return a value, and which constrain future object behavior independently of the state in which they are invoked. These operations have long been known to be weak synchronization primitives [LA87, Her91]. Since we are focusing here on strong synchronization such as consensus, we define an operation to be powerful if it is neither a read nor a write() operation. for an object (or object type) x, we define $\text{ACL}_{pow}(x)$ to be the union of $\text{ACL}(x.\text{op})$ for all powerful operations x.op of x.

An object specification also constrains another property: the access complexity, $\text{Access}(x)$, a bound on the number of distinct processes that may invoke powerful operations in any well-formed run. Obviously, $\text{Access}(x) \leq |\text{ACL}_{pow}(x)|$. An object x is softwired for n processes if $\text{ACL}_{pow}(x)$ is the set of all processes (which in this paper is infinite) and $\text{Access}(x) = n$. An object x is hardwired for n processes if $\text{Access}(x) = |\text{ACL}_{pow}(x)| = n$.

For $u \geq n > t$, we denote by (u, n, t)-cons a consensus object x that is t-resilient, has $\text{Access}(x) = n$, and $|\text{ACL}_{pow}(x)| = u$. That is, x is a t-resilient consensus object in which in any well-formed run, at most n processes taken from a fixed universe of u processes access it. Thus, $(t+1, t+1, t)$-cons is hardwired and wait-free for $t+1$ processes, more generally (n, n, t) is t-resilient and hardwired for n processes, (∞, n, t)-cons is t-resilient and softwired for n processes, (∞, ∞, t)-cons is t-resilient consensus for an infinite number of processes, and (∞, ∞, ∞)-cons is wait-free consensus for an infinite number of processes.

For sets of object types x and y, the notation $x \Rightarrow y$ (or $y \Leftarrow x$) means that it is possible to implement all the objects of type x using any number of objects of type y and atomic registers. The notation $x \Leftrightarrow y$ means that both $x \Rightarrow y$ and $x \Leftarrow y$.

1.2   Summary of Results

We show how to implement t-resilient (and wait-free) consensus objects for infinitely many processes from consensus objects for finitely many processes. Furthermore, we provide tight simultaneous-access and space bounds for these implementations. Simultaneous-access measures the maximum number of processes that are allowed to simultaneously invoke operations, other than atomic reads and writes, on the same primitive object.

Number of faults is known. We show that for every $t \geq 1$: there is a t-resilient consensus object for infinitely many processes iff there is a hardwired t-resilient consensus object for $t + 1$ processes:

- $\forall t \geq 1 : [(t+1, t+1, t)\text{-cons} \Leftrightarrow (\infty, t+1, t)\text{-cons} \Leftrightarrow (\infty, \infty, t)\text{-cons}]$.

Number of faults is not known. For an unknown or infinite number of faults, we consider whether an infinite set of wait-free consensus objects, capable of solving consensus for any finite collection of processes, suffice to solve wait-free consensus for infinitely many processes. We show that this implication holds under an assumption precluding runs with unbounded concurrency, leaving the general question open:

- $[\forall t \geq 0 : (t+1, t+1, t)\text{-cons}] \Leftrightarrow (\infty, \infty, \infty)\text{-cons}$ in runs with bounded concurrency.

This result, enables to implement wait-free consensus for infinitely many processes (assuming bounded concurrency) from any known solution for wait-free consensus (deterministic or randomized) for only finitely many processes.

A lower bound. We show that,

- any implementation of a t-resilient consensus object for any number (finite or infinite) of processes and $t \geq 1$ must use: for every set of processes T where $|T| = t + 1$, at least one object on which the $t + 1$ processes in T, can simultaneously invoke powerful operations.

This result demonstrates the optimality (in terms of the number of strong objects) of our constructions. Finally, using known techniques, we draw new conclusions on the universality of resilient consensus objects in the infinite domain.

1.3   Related Work

We mention below previous work that specifically investigates models with infinitely many processes.

Computing with infinitely many processes has previously been investigated in models with communication primitives stronger than read/write or studying problems such as mutual exclusion that do not admit wait-free solution [MT00]. In [GMT01], wait-free computation using only atomic registers is considered. It is shown that bounding concurrency reveals a strict hierarchy of computational models, of which unbounded concurrency is the weakest model. Nevertheless, it is demonstrate that adaptive versions of many interesting problems (collect, snapshot, renaming) are solvable even in the unbounded concurrency model.

Randomized consensus algorithms for infinitely many processes has been explored in [ASS02]. The strongest result is a wait-free randomized algorithm using only atomic registers. Also, it is stated that standard universal constructions based on consensus continue to work with infinitely many processes with only slight modifications. In [CM02], active disk paxos protocol is implemented for infinitely many processes. The solution facilitates a solution to the consensus problem with an unbounded number of processes. The solution is based on a collection of a finite number of read-modify-write objects with faults, that emulates a new reliable shared memory abstraction called a ranked register.

1.4   Overview of the Paper

The next two sections describe constructions of wait-free and t-resilient consensus for infinitely many processes, from objects for finitely many processes. They address softwired and hardwired base objects, and constructions of softwired from hardwired. Interestingly, several of these constructions match the bounds imposed by the results in Section 4. (Indeed, these bounds guided their discovery.) In addition, several of the constructions presented are adaptive to process or operation contention. In two cases, these lead to improvements of known results for finitely many processes, supporting the intuition that algorithms for infinitely many processes will lead to adaptive and efficient algorithms for the finite case, cf.[GMT01]. The third section following presents and discusses lower bounds, and the final section discusses the universality of resilient consensus objects in the infinite domain.

2   A Strong Equivalence for t-Resilience

The major result of this section is a strong equivalence between hardwired t-resilient consensus and t-resilient consensus for an infinite number of processes:

Theorem 1. $\forall t \geq 1 : [(t+1,t+1,t)\text{-cons} \Leftrightarrow (\infty,\infty,t)\text{-cons}]$.
This theorem extends an equivalence result for finitely many processes alluded to by Chandra et al[CHJT94]: $\forall n > t \geq 1 : [(t+1,t+1,t)\text{-cons} \Leftrightarrow (n,n,t)\text{-cons}]$. Theorem 1 together with observations that (∞,∞,t)-cons objects are universal for t-resilient objects (Corollary 4), implies the universality of the (seemingly) restrictive $(t+1,t+1,t)$-cons objects, even for infinitely many processes.

Theorem 1 is a corollary of the major results of the next two subsections: Theorem 2 in the first subsection shows $(\infty,t+1,t)$-cons $\Leftrightarrow (\infty,\infty,t)$-cons, and Theorem 4 in the second subsection shows that $(t+1,t+1,t)$-cons $\Leftrightarrow (\infty,t+1,t)$-cons. (Note that the arrows from right to left are all trivial.)

2.1   Constructing t-Resilient Consensus from Softwired Consensus for $t+1$ Processes

This subsection presents a construction implementing t-resilient consensus for an infinite number of processes from softwired consensus for $t+1$ processes:
Theorem 2. $\forall t \geq 1 : [(\infty,t+1,t)\text{-cons} \Leftrightarrow (\infty,\infty,t)\text{-cons}]$.
This theorem is a consequence of the two lemmas that follow: The first implements t-resilient consensus using test&sets, the second shows how to implement the test&sets from $(\infty,2,1)$-cons. (The latter are trivial to implement from $(\infty,t+1,t)$-cons.)

Implementing (∞, ∞, t)-cons from $(\infty, t+1, t)$-cons and test&sets

Given a single $(\infty, t+1, t)$-cons object, C, the challenge to implement t-resilient consensus, or (∞, ∞, t)-cons, is to reduce the infinite set of potentially active processes to at most $t+1$, each invoking a separate operation instance on the base object. The algorithm below uses a separate test&set primitive for each of the $t+1$ potential invocations on C.

The linearizable test&set primitive supports a single parameter-less operation, *test*. Runs of instances of the this object are well-formed iff no two invocations take the same process identifier as argument. The implementation is trivially wait-free, and in failure-free, well-formed runs, the invocation linearized first returns 1, and the remainder return 0. Moreover, once an invocation returns 0, the set of invocations that may return 1 is finite. It follows that in general runs, if an invocation returns 0 and no other invocation returns 1, there is a failed process with an invocation that is pending forever. By (∞, ∞, ∞)-test&set we denote such an object which supports wait-free *test* operation invocations by infinitely many processes, with any number of crash faults.

Lemma 1. There is an implementation of (∞, ∞, t)-cons using one $(\infty, t+1, t)$-cons object, $t+1$ (∞, ∞, ∞)-test&set objects, and one register.

Proof. The implementation in Figure 1 uses $t+1$ instances, $E_1, ..., E_{t+1}$, of (∞, ∞, ∞)-test&set objects. Each instance E_j is used to select a process to access the softwired $(\infty, t+1, t)$-cons object C. Processes move through these object instances in order, each process i invoking test_i on E_1, and moving on to E_2,... if it loses. (That is, if the invocation returns 0.) A process that loses in all $t+1$ test&set objects knows that there are $t+1$ non-empty, disjoint sets of processes contending for those objects. At least one such set contains only correct processes, so it is safe to wait for the consensus value (from C) to be announced via the *Announce* register. Hence, all correct processes either win a test&set and access C, or read the consensus value in *Announce*. □

Reduced to the finite case, the construction in Figure 1 is very similar to a simulation construction in Chandra, et al[CHJT94]. The focus of Chandra et al is for a model in which non-faulty processes must participate, a model we define in Section 4 as *participation required*. This assumption introduces considerable complexity that is the major focus of that paper. Figure 1 indicates that the complex construction and special assumptions needed for the simulation can be greatly simplified when participation is not required. (In the case that participation is required, the relationship between wait-free and t-resilient consensus for infinitely many processes remains essentially unexplored. Given the anomalies and complexities of this model for finitely many proceses (such as the special case $t=1$, [LH00]), there may be surprises here.)

Implementing test&set objects from $(\infty, 2, 1)$-cons

Lemma 2. (∞, ∞, ∞)-test&set can be implemented from a register and infinitely many $(\infty, 2, 1)$-cons objects.

propose$_i$(u: boolean), returns boolean   /* Code of invocation i. */
Shared:
    $E_1..E_{t+1}$: (∞, ∞, ∞)-test&set objects.
    C: $(\infty, t+1, t)$-cons.
    Announce: register, initially $\perp$.
Local:
    level: integer, initially 1.

```
1    while (level ≤ t + 1) do
2        if invoke(test, i, E_level) then              /* If won E_level,  */
3            Announce := invoke(propose,u,C)            /* propose u to C,   */
4            return(Announce)                     /* set Announce and return, */
5        else level := level + 1                    /* else move to next level. */
        fi
     od                                      /* If lost all t + 1 levels, */
6    while (Announce = ⊥) do skip od       /* spin on Announce and return. */
7    return(Announce)
```

Fig. 1. Implementing (∞, ∞, t)-cons from $(\infty, t+1, t)$-cons and test&sets.

Proof. The simple construction in Figure 2 implements a (∞, ∞, ∞)-test&set object from the infinite array $B[1..\infty]$ of $(\infty, 2, 1)$-cons objects and a single doorway bit.

The implementation is quite simple: it treats the $(\infty, 2, 1)$-cons object instances $B[1..\infty]$ as an unbalanced infinite binary tree, where the left child of tree node $B[i]$ is the process that invokes test$_i$, and the right child of $B[i]$ is the contending process (if any) that wins at node $B[i+1]$. Contenders entering as the left child propose the value 0, those from the right propose 1, and each "wins" the node if their proposed value is returned. A familiar 'doorway' bit ensures that the invocation of the eventual test&set winner is concurrent with or precedes the invocation of any test&set loser.

In this construction, an invocation of *invoke*(test,i,E) requires at most i operations on the embedded consensus objects–by balancing the tree, as in the adaptive tournament tree of Attiya and Bortnikov [AB00], previously adapted to infinite arrivals by Aspnes, Shah, and Shah [ASS02], this time complexity can be easily reduced to $O(log(i))$. These time bounds have a nice consequence: if processes first invoke a renaming algorithm adaptive to process contention, and use the resulting name in the test&set algorithm (invoking the test operation indexed by the new name), the entire construction will be adaptive to process contention. Indeed, there is a one-shot linearizable, wait-free renaming object, (∞, ∞, ∞)-rename, adaptive to process contention, for infinitely many processes using registers [GMT01]. This renaming object supports the operation rename, which invoked by process k returns a positive integer i as a new name, where i is linear in the number of invocations to the object. (And distinct invocations return distinct names.)   □

```
test_i, returns boolean                              /* Code of invocation i. */
Shared:
    doorway: boolean, initially 0.
    B[1..∞]: array of (∞, 2, 1)-cons.
Local:
    step: index to B
    result: boolean
1   if doorway then return(0) else doorway := 1 fi
2   step := i
3   result := ¬(invoke(propose,0,B[step]))
4   while ((step ≠ 1) and (result = 1)) do
5       step := step − 1                             /* Step up in tree B. */
6       result := invoke(propose,1,B[step])
    od
7   return(result)                                   /* True iff won path to root in B. */
```

Fig. 2. Implementing (∞, ∞, ∞)-test&set from $(\infty, 2, 1)$-cons.

Theorem 3. There is an implementation of (∞, ∞, t)-cons, adaptive to process contention, using registers, one $(\infty, t+1, t)$-cons object, and infinitely many $(\infty, 2, 1)$-cons objects.

Since $(\infty, t+1, t)$-cons trivially implements $(\infty, 2, 1)$-cons, Theorem 2 follows.

2.2 Constructing Softwired Consensus from Hardwired

Next we show that it is possible to replace softwired consensus objects with hardwired consensus objects:

Theorem 4. $\forall t \geq 1 : [(t+1, t+1, t)\text{-cons} \Leftrightarrow (\infty, t+1, t)\text{-cons}]$.

This theorem extends known results for the finite case [CHJT94,BGA94]: $\forall n > t \geq 1 : [(t+1, t+1, t)\text{-cons} \Leftrightarrow (n, t+1, t)\text{-cons}]$. (These constructions for the finite case do not extend to the infinite. As we remark below, our constructions are adaptive and more efficient when applied to the finite case.)

Theorem 4 follows from:

Theorem 5. There is an implementation of $(\infty, t+1, t)$-cons, adaptive to process contention, using registers and for every set of processes T, where $|T| \leq t+1$, one $(|T|, |T|, |T|-1)$-cons object, $C[T]$, such that $ACL_{pow}(C[T].propose()) = T$.

Proof. The construction uses the fact that there is a long-lived, linearizable, wait-free snapshot object, (∞, ∞, ∞)-snap, for infinitely many processes using registers [GMT01], and which is adaptive to operation contention. Such a snapshot object supports two operations: write, which invoked by process i updates a variable v_i, and a scan which returns the (finite) set of all pairs (i, v_i) such that a write to v_i is linearized before the scan.

Since we are implementing a $(\infty, t+1, t)$-cons object, out of infinitely many processes at most $t+1$ may eventually participate. (Its access complexity is $t+1$.) However, the identity of the participating processes are not known in advance.

```
propose_i(u: boolean), returns boolean              /* Code of invocation i. */
Shared:
     C[T]: for every set T of at most t + 1 processes, (|T|,|T|,|T − 1|)-cons.
     S: snapshot object with fields
           level: integer, initially 0,
           value: {⊥, 0, 1}, initially ⊥.
     Result: {⊥, 0, 1}, initially ⊥.
Local:
     snap, oldsnap: finite sets of (process, (level, value)) tuples, initially empty
     toggle: boolean, iniitally 0,
     result: boolean
0    if (Result ≠ ⊥) then return(Result)
1    invoke(write, i, (0, ⊥), S)
2    snap := invoke(scan_i, S)
3    while (participants(snap) ≠ participants(oldsnap)) do
4         result := invoke(propose_i, max(snap, u), C[participants(snap)])
5         invoke(write, i, (|participants(snap)|, result), S)
6         oldsnap := snap
7         snap := invoke(scan_i, S)
     od
8    Result := result
9    return(result)
```

Fig. 3. Implementing $(\infty, t + 1, t)$-cons from $(t + 1, t + 1, t)$-cons.

The algorithm in Figure 3 uses a snapshot object S in which each variable v_i has two fields, $v_i.level$, a natural number, and $v_i.value \in \{\bot, 0, 1\}$. In the write operation by process i, denoted by $invoke(\text{write}, i, (a, b), S)$, a is written to $v_i.level$ and b to $v_i.value$.

If a scan operation returns a set s, define and $val \in \{0, 1\}$, then define:

- $participants(s)$ to be the set of all indices i such that (i, v_i) is in s.
- $max(s, val)$ to be val if there is no tuple (i, v) in s such that $v.value \neq \bot$, and otherwise to be the value of a $v.value$ such that $v.level \geq u.level$ for all (j, u) in s with $u.value \neq \bot$.

Since at most $t + 1$ processes participate, eventually the while loop will terminate. Also, because all snapshots of the same size contain the same set of participants, the agreement property of the consensus objects $C[S]$ guarantee that $u.level = w.level$ implies $u.value = w.value$.

Take any complete run α (in which all correct participating processes terminate), and let k be the minimum such that some invocation, $cons_i$, exits the while loop after taking two successive snapshots of size k. We claim that all terminating invocations return the last value r written by $cons_i$ to $v_i.value$. This claim follows from a stronger claim: that in α if any process invokes $propose(u)$ on an object $C[S]$ with $|S| > k$, then $u = r$, and that in any state of α, if $u.level \geq k$ then $u.value$ is either $\bot$ or r. The proof of this claim is by induction on the size of sets S for which processes invoke **propose** operations on $C[S]$, from k to $t + 1$. By the argument above, if $u.level = k$ then $u.value = r$, and the basis follows.

Now suppose the claim holds for all values from k to $k' - 1$. If no process invokes **propose** on an object $C[S]$ with $|S| = k'$, then no $u.level$ is ever k' and the induction follows.

Suppose to the contrary that a non-empty set of processes invoke **propose** on an object $C[S]$ with $|S| = k'$, and hence also the result of these invocations may be written to some $u.value$. (By the argument above, all such operations return the same value.)

Some of these processes may propose the non-$\bot$ value from some w such that $w.level = k'$, hence taking as input to $C[S]$ the result from a previous **propose** operation on $C[S]$. But a non-empty subset of processes see only $w.level$ values smaller than k'. Since these processes see a set of participants of size $k' > k$, they also see that $v_i.k$ is set to k. Hence, they will propose to the consensus object $C[S]$ a non-$\bot$ value of some $w.value$ with $w.level$ at least k but less than k', which by induction is r.

Note that any correct (hence termination) invocation either sees a value set in the *Result* register, or enters and exits the while loop on line 3. The *Result* register is only set by invocations that exit the same while loop, so it suffices to consider the values of *result* in the latter invocations when they exit the while loop. By definition, all such invocations see at least k participants, and by the claim above, $result = r$.

Finally, note that the number of invocations to the embedded snapshot object by any process is linear in the process contention. Since the snapshot is adaptive to operation contention, the entire construction is adaptive to process contention.

$\square$

As noted at the beginning of this section, using this construction from hardwired objects, the $(\infty, t + 1, t)$-cons object in Figure 1 can be replaced with hardwired objects. Moreover, the softwired $(\infty, 2, 1)$-cons objects embedded in the test&set objects can also be replaced with hardwired objects, proving the next result. (The simultaneous access complexity of the construction is $t + 1$ and hence it matches the lower bound of Section 4.)

Theorem 6. There is an implementation of (∞, ∞, t)-cons, adaptive to process contention, using registers and one $(|T|, |T|, |T| - 1)$-cons for every set of processes T where $|T| \leq t + 1$, and infinitely many $(2, 2, 1)$-cons objects.

Designed for an infinite number of processes, this construction is more efficient than previous constructions when the number of processes is finite. Prior constructions have complexity exponential in n and t [CHJT94,BGA94]:

Corollary 1. There is an implementation of (n, n, t)-cons, adaptive to process contention, using registers, one $(|T|, |T|, |T| - 1)$-cons for every set of processes T where $|T| \leq t + 1$, and $O(tn^3)$ $(2, 2, 1)$-cons objects.

(We note that a non-adaptive version of this construction, without renaming, uses only $O(tn^2)$ $(2, 2, 1)$-cons objects.)

If $n > t$, (n, n, t)-cons objects trivially implement $(t+1, t+1, t)$-cons. Hence, Theorem 6 and Corollary 1 establish the equivalence of t-resilient and wait-free consensus for both infinite and finite numbers of processes.

These are strong equivalences compared to the similar result for finite numbers of processes alluded to by Chandra et al[CHJT94], which requires the base objects in the wait-free construction to be wait-free and soft-wired, so that the n processes can "simulate" them. Our constructions run these objects as black boxes, and need no such assumptions.

3   The Number of Faults Is Not Known or May Be Infinite

A major open question is the relationship between t-resilient consensus and wait-freedom for infinitely many processes: The result $[\forall t \geq 0 : (t + 1, t + 1, t)\text{-cons}]$ $\Leftarrow (\infty, \infty, \infty)$-cons is trivial, but what of the other direction? The major result of this section shows the converse, but only in runs with bounded concurrency:

Theorem 7. $[\forall t \geq 1 : (t + 1, t + 1, t)\text{-cons}] \Leftrightarrow (\infty, \infty, \infty)$-cons in runs with bounded concurrency.

This theorem is a corollary of the following result:

Theorem 8. There are implementations of (∞, ∞, ∞)-cons for bounded concurrency, using registers and either:

1. for every resilience bound t, $t \geq 1$, one $(\infty, t + 1, t)$-cons object, or
2. for every finite set of processes T, one $(|T|, |T|, |T| - 1)$-cons object.

Proof. Focusing on the second part of the theorem, as in Theorem 5, we use the construction from Figure 3, but adding as shared objects hardwired $(|T|, |T| - 1)$-cons objects $C[T]$ for every finite set T (not just for those with $|T|$ bounded by $t + 1$).

Termination of the while loop is assured by the bounded concurrency assumption: the *Result* register blocks more than a finite number of invocations from entering the while loop. Otherwise the proof is identical. (The *Result* register and lines 0 and 8 were not necessary for the previous case, where the number of invocations was bounded by a known t.)

The first part of the theorem simply substitutes a single $(\infty, t + 1, t)$-cons object in place of the (infinitely many) hardwired objects for sets of size $t+1$.   □

As noted, it is an interesting open question whether the bounded concurrency assumption is necessary in Theorem 7, or can it be replaced with unbounded concurrency. An interesting weaker question is also open: whether consensus for unbounded concurrency can be implemented from the set $\{(t + 1, t + 1, t)\text{-cons} : t \geq 1\}$, for a finite but unknown number of faults.

4   Lower Bounds: The Simultaneous-Access Theorem

We first state a general theorem establishing a necessary condition for implementing consensus in shared memory systems. (The proof is a detailed case analysis along the lines of previous proofs, cf [FLP85,LA87]. Space constraints preclude inclusion of details.) We show that when at most t processes may crash, the consensus problem is only solvable in systems containing "enough" shared objects on which "enough" processes can simultaneously invoke powerful operations. The theorem shows that there is a tradeoff between simultaneous-access and space complexity: when more processes are allowed to access the same object simultaneously, fewer objects may suffice to implement consensus.

We use the notation ℓ-participation to mean that at least ℓ processes must participate. The two extreme cases are: (1) participation is not required (i.e., 1-participation), and (2) participation is required. Participation not required is usually assumed when solving resource allocation problems or when requiring a high degree of concurrency, and is most natural for systems with infinitely many potential participants. (It also has simpler compositional properties in t-resilient constructions than does the participation required model, in which for example, embedded objects must be shown to be accessed by sufficiently many processes to assure invocation termination.)

For any object x, we say x is t-resilient assuming ℓ-participation, if any operation invocation when executed by a correct process, eventually completes in any run in which each of at least ℓ processes participates and in which at most t processes fail.

Theorem 9 (The Simultaneous Access Theorem). In any implementation of a t-resilient consensus object for any number (finite or infinite) of processes, assuming ℓ-participation and $t \geq 1$, for *every* set of processes L where $|L| = max(\ell, t + 1)$ there is *some* set $T \subseteq L$ where $|T| = t + 1$, such that for some object o, all the processes in T can *simultaneously* invoke powerful operations on o.

We explicitly state two interesting special cases:

Theorem 10. Any implementation of a (∞, ∞, t)-cons where $t \geq 1$, must use,

- when participation is required, for *some* set of processes T where $|T| = t+1$, at least one object on which the $t+1$ processes in T can simultaneously invoke powerful operations, and
- when participation is not required, for *every* set of processes T where $|T| = t+1$, at least one object on which the $t+1$ processes in T can simultaneously invoke powerful operations.

The last requirement may be satisfied by having just one object, whose access control list includes all the processes, and on which every subset of $t+1$ processes can simultaneously invoke powerful operations. The following observations follow from the last theorem.

Corollary 2. Any implementation of (∞, ∞, t)-cons where $t \geq 1$, from registers and t'-resilient consensus objects where $t' \leq t$, requires at least:

- When participation is required, one $(u, t + 1, t)$-cons for some $u > t$.
- When participation is not required, for every set of processes T where $|T| = t + 1$, a $(u, t + 1, t)$-cons for some $u > t$, which all the processes in T can access.

Corollary 3. Any implementation of a wait-free consensus object for infinitely many processes from registers and wait-free consensus objects for finitely many processes requires, for every positive integer number k, $(u, t + 1, t)$-cons for some $u > t \geq k$.

5 Universal Constructions for Infinitely Many Processes

Earlier work on fault-tolerant distributed computing provide techniques (called universal constructions) to transform sequential specifications of arbitrary shared objects into wait-free concurrent implementations that use universal objects [Her91,Plo89,JT92]. Plotkin showed that sticky bits are universal [Plo89], and independently, Herlihy proved the universality of consensus objects [Her91]. Herlihy also classified shared objects by their consensus number: that is, the maximum number of processes that can reach consensus using multiple instances of the object and read/write registers [Her91]. In their work on randomized consensus for infinitely many processes, Aspnes, Shah, and Shah mention simple modifications to Herlihy's universal construction for crash faults [Her91] to accommodate the case that that the number of participating processes may be infinite [ASS02]. As in [MMRT03], it is also possible to generalize the definition of t-resilient object for which this construction is valid. (Herlihy's universal construction is wait-free for fixed n and implements any object with a sequential specification. In a t-resilient setting, objects with inherently concurrent behaviors may be extremely useful. For example, once $t + 1$ active processes have been identified, algorithms can safely wait for one of these (necessarily correct) processes to announce the result of a computation–as in the algorithm in Figure 1.) Due to space constraints, we omit the full details of this generalization, and assuming some familiarity with Herlihy's construction, outline our interpretation of the changes alluded to by Aspnes et al [ASS02], before stating their consequences for our setting.

The key idea of Herlihy's universal construction for n processes is for each process to first announce its next invocation to a single-writer shared register, then to compete (using consensus) to thread (a binary encoding of) its id to a sequence of such ids. The state of the object can be inferred by reading this sequence of threaded process ids, then mapping those via the shared register to a sequence of invocations. To ensure every process invocation is eventually threaded, each process helps others by threading another process before terminating.

Specifically, to implement the jth invocation by process i, a description of the invocation is first written in the shared register Announce$[i][j]$. Process i contends with the other processes to thread this invocation (and that of another invocation by process k during the helping stage) by adding a binary encoding of i (correspondingly, k) to Sequence[1...], of process-id's, where each Sequence[k] is a $\lceil \log(n) \rceil$ string of $(n, n-1)$-cons objects.

As suggested by Aspnes, Shah, and Shah [ASS02], the first modification necessary is to specify Sequence[k] as a consensus object over an infinite set of values. Using an unbalanced, infinite binary tree, with binary consensus objects as internal nodes, the values tracing a path from leaf to root encodes the corresponding input, extending binary consensus to an infinitary domain.

The second modification necessary is to carefully specify the order in which processes help other invocations–and to ensure that each invocations looks to help a pending invocation (if one exists) earlier in that order, before it seeks to thread its own id. The simplest choice is for processes to invoke adaptive renaming for each invocation, so that the j'th invocation by process i is mapped to a new unique name k, bounded by a function of the previous and concurrent invocations. The values of i and j can be recorded in the k'th entry of a new array, $Name\_to\_invocation[k]$. This way, each invocation has a finite number of preceding invocations in the order. Once a process i announces it's j'th invocation, the (finite) number of pending invocations may be threaded ahead of it, together with the finite number of invocations that precede it in this order (only of course if they are invoked). After this, any other invocation will choose to help this one.

Corollary 4. W e have the following, assuming infinitely m any processes and $t \geq 1$:

1. $(\infty, t+1, t)$-cons objects are universal for t-resilient objects.
2. $(t+1, t+1, t)$-cons objects are universal for t-resilient objects.
3. The infinite set of objects $\{(\infty, t+1, t)\text{-cons}\}$ is universal for wait-free, bounded concurrency objects.
4. The infinite set of objects $\{(t+1, t+1, t)\text{-cons}\}$ is universal for wait-free, bounded concurrency objects.

Proof. The first part of the corollary follows by implementing the consensus objects in Sequence using Corollary 3, the second using Theorem 5. The last two parts follow from Theorem 8.

We note also that the referenced corollary and theorems, together with the use of renaming, support implementations that are adaptive to operation contention. □

References

[ASS02]   J. Aspnes, G. Shah, and J. Shah, Wait-free consensus with infinite arrivals. In *Proc. 34th Annual Symp. on Theory of Computing*, 524–533, May 2002.
[AB00]   H. Attiya and V. Bortnikov, Adaptive and efficient mutual exclusion. In *Proc. 19th ACM Symp. on Principles of Distributed Computing*, 91–100, July 2000.

[BGA94]   E. Borowsky, E. Gafni, and Y. Afek. Consensus power makes (some) sense! In *Proc. 13th ACM Symp. on Principles of Distributed Computing*, 363–372, August 1994.

[CHJT94]   T. Chandra, V. Hadzilacos, P. Jayanti, and S. Toueg, Wait-freedom vs. *t*-resiliency and the robustness of wait-free hierarchies. In *Proc. 13th ACM Symp. on Principles of Distributed Computing*, 334–343, August 1994. Expanded version:
           www.cs.toronto.edu/ vassos/research/list-of-publications.html.

[CM02]   G. Chocker and D. Malkhi. Active disk paxos with infinitely many processes. In *Proc. 21th ACM Symp. on Principles of Distributed Computing*, 78–87, July 2002.

[FHS98]   F. Fich, M. Herlihy, and N. Shavit, On the Space Complexity of Randomized Synchronization. *Journal of the ACM*, 45(5):843–862, September 1998.

[FLP85]   M.J. Fischer, N.A. Lynch, and M.S. Paterson. Impossibility of distributed consensus with one faulty process. *Journal of the ACM*, 32(2):374–382, April 1985.

[GMT01]   E. Gafni, M. Merritt, and G. Taubenfeld. The concurrency hierarchy, and algorithms for unbounded concurrency. In *Proc. 20th ACM Symp. on Principles of Distributed Computing*, 161–169, August 2001.

[HW90]   M.P. Herlihy and J.M. Wing. Linearizability: A correctness condition for concurrent objects. *ACM Transactions on Programming Languages and Systems* 12(3):463–492, July 1990.

[Her91]   M.P. Herlihy. Wait-free synchronization. *ACM Transactions on Programming Languages and Systems* 13(1):124–149, January 1991.

[JT92]   P. Jayanti and S. Toueg, Some results on the impossibility, universality and decidability of consensus, In *Proc. 6th Int. Workshop on Distributed Algorithms, (WDAG'92)* LNCS 647, 69–84. Springer Verlag, November 1992.

[LH00]   W.K. Lo and V. Hadzilacos. On the power of shared objects to implement one-resilient consensus. *Distributed Computing* 13(4):219–238, 2000.

[LA87]   M.C. Loui and H. Abu-Amara. Memory requirements for agreement among unreliable asynchronous processes. *Advances in Computing Research*, 4:163–183, 1987.

[MMRT03]   D. Malkhi, M. Merritt, M. Reiter, and G. Taubenfeld. Objects shared by Byzantine processes. *Distributed Computing* 16(1):37–48, 2003. Also in: *Proc.14th International Symposium on Distributed Computing (DISC 2000)*, LNCS 1914, 345–359, 2000.

[MT93]   M. Merritt and G. Taubenfeld. Speeding Lamport's fast mutual exclusion algorithm. *Information Processing Letters*, 45:137–142, 1993. (Also published as an AT&T technical memorandum, May 1991.)

[MT00]   M. Merritt and G. Taubenfeld. Computing with infinitely many processes. *Proceedings of the 14th International Symposium on Distributed Computing* LNCS 1914, 164–178. Springer Verlag, October 2000.

[Plo89]   S.A. Plotkin. Sticky bits and universality of consensus. In *Proc. 8th ACM Symp. on Principles of Distributed Computing*, 159–175, August 1989.

Uniform Solvability with a Finite Number of MWMR Registers

(Extended Abstract)

Marcos K. Aguilera[1], Burkhard Englert[2], and Eli Gafni[3]

[1] HP Labs Systems Research Center, 1501 Page Mill Road, Mail Stop 1250
Palo Alto, CA 94304
aguilera@hpl.hp.com

[2] University of California Los Angeles, Dept. of Mathematics
Los Angeles, CA 90095-1555
englert@math.ucla.edu

[3] University of California Los Angeles, Dept. of Computer Science
Los Angeles, CA 90095-1596
eli@cs.ucla.edu.

Abstract. This paper introduces a new interesting research question concerning tasks. The weak-test-and-set task has a uniform solution that requires only two Multi-Writer Multi-Reader (MWMR) registers. Recently it was shown that if we take the long-lived version and require a step complexity that is adaptive to interval contention then, like mutual exclusion, no solution with finitely many MWMR registers is possible. Here we show that there are simple tasks which provably cannot be solved uniformly with finitely many MWMR registers. This opens up the research question of when a task is uniformly solvable using only finitely many MWMR registers.

1 Introduction

A uniform protocol[10,12,26,29] is one that does not use information about the number of processors in the system. Such protocols, by definition, must work with any arbitrary, but finite, number of participants. They are important in dynamic settings in which we do not want to force an upper bound on the number of participating processors. One of the simplest non-trivial uniform protocols is a splitter [31,33], which requires only two shared registers, and can be directly used to achieve a very weak form of mutual exclusion, in which (1) safety is always guaranteed: no two processors enter the critical section, (2) liveness is guaranteed only in solo executions: if a processor runs alone then it enters the critical section, and (3) no re-entry in the critical section is possible (one-shot).[1]

Uniform protocols, however, are usually built on top of one-shot adaptive collect [20], which is implemented by an infinite binary tree of splitters. Can

---

[1] There are protocols to "reset" the splitter to allow re-entry, but these protocols are not uniform.

F.E. Fich (Ed.): DISC 2003, LNCS 2848, pp. 16–29, 2003.

one-shot collect be accomplished with a finite number of MWMR registers? It is known that mutual exclusion among n processors requires n shared registers [21], and hence admits no uniform implementations with bounded memory. The proof of this result relies heavily on the long-lived (reusable) nature of mutual exclusion. More recently, [1] has studied another variant of mutual exclusion called weak-test-and-set. Roughly speaking, weak-test-and-set satisfies properties (1) and (2) above, but it allows re-entry after a processor has left the critical section, so that weak-test-and-set is a long-lived (reusable) object. [1] shows that weak-test-and-set has no uniform wait-free implementations with finitely many MWMR registers. Like with mutual exclusion, the result relies heavily on the long-lived nature of weak-test-and-set. For example, as observed above, a "one-shot" version of weak-test-and-set has a trivial uniform wait-free implementation using a splitter, i.e., using a finite number of Multi-Writer Multi-Reader (MWMR) registers. In this paper we show that long-livedness, accompanied with the requirement that complexity adapt to interval-contention [2,3,4,5,7,8,9,11,13, 15,17,18,19,22,28,32,34], is not the only requirement that precludes a solution in finite space. To do so, we introduce a new task [27] that is a simple generalization of the one-shot weak-test-and-set. Roughly speaking, a task assigns a finite set of possible output tuples for each possible set of participating processors. The generalized weak- test-and-set task is specified as follows: The set of processors $p_0, p_1, p_2, \ldots$ is a priori partitioned into classes. The output tuple for a set of participating processors that all belong to the same class is all 1's. Otherwise an output tuple for a participating set of mixed classes of processors consists of 0's and 1's with no two processors of different classes outputting 1.

There is a very simple uniform solution to this task: a participating processor registers its name and uses collect [14] to obtain the set of all registered processors. If the set has more than one class then the processor outputs 0, else it outputs 1. This protocol works, but requires an unbounded number of shared MWMR registers. If we are limited to finitely many MWMR registers, we show that the weak-test-and-set task has no uniform wait-free implementation. This opens up the interesting research question of characterizing what tasks are uniformly solvable in finite space! Furthermore, we show that this impossibility relies heavily on two assumptions: (1) that the cardinality of classes is not uniformly bounded, and (2) that the number of classes is infinite. In fact, we show that if we relax any of these assumptions, that is, if (!1) there is a single upper bound on the number of processors in all classes or (!2) there are only finitely many classes, then the generalized weak-test-and-set task has a uniform solution with finitely many registers. (Note that neither (!1) nor (!2) means that the system has finitely many processors).

Obviously, since collect solves the generalized weak-test-and-set, it cannot be implemented with only finitely many MWMR registers.

Related Work

Uniform protocols, i.e., protocols that do not require a priori knowledge of the number of processors in the system, have been studied, particularly in the context of ring protocols (e.g. [12,29]). Adaptive protocols, i.e. protocols whose step complexity is a function of the size of the participating set, have been studied in [4,5,6,16,22,32]. Adaptive protocols that only use the number n of processors to bound their space complexity can be easily modified into a uniform protocol that uses unbounded memory by replacing n with ∞. Long-lived adaptive protocols that assume some huge upper bound N on the number of processors, but require the complexity of the protocol to be a function of the concurrency have been studied in [2,3,7,8,9,17,18,19,20,28,33].

As we mentioned before, the weak-test-and-set object is defined in [1]. It is a long-lived object, rather than a single-shot task. Our generalized weak-test-and-set task degenerates to a single-shot version of weak-test-and-set when there is only one processor per class.

Generalized weak-test-and-set is related to group mutual exclusion [30], much in the same way that weak-test-and-set is related to mutual exclusion. Group mutual exclusion is a generalization of mutual exclusion in which multiple processors may enter the critical section simultaneously, provided they are part of the same group. It allows a processor to block if the critical section is occupied by processors from another group. This is quite different from generalized weak-test-and-set, which admits non-blocking solutions. Moreover, group mutual exclusion is a long-lived problem, which needs to concern itself with reentry into the critical section, whereas the generalized weak-test-and-set task is single shot.

The covering technique used in our impossibility proof with finitely many MWMR registers first appeared in [21] to show some bounds on the number of registers necessary for mutual exclusion. However, the proof in [21] inherently relies on the long-lived nature of mutual exclusion: it makes processors execute mutual exclusion multiple times, while leaving some harmful residue for each execution. In this way, after a large number of executions, the protocol must finally fail. In our proof, we deal with tasks, which are inherently single-shot, and so we require a different approach to get a contradiction in a single execution. Fich, Herlihy and Shavit [25] gave an $\Omega(\sqrt{n})$ lower bound on the number of multiwriter multi-reader registers needed for randomized consensus. This also shows non-uniformity for a one-shot task using only MWMR registers. Generalized weak test-and-set, however, is a task that is much simpler and can hence be solved much more easily than randomized consensus. Their [25] covering construction relies heavily on the fact that processors need to agree on a decision. In our case, this is not required. Processors can leave by simply outputting 0, whenever they see any processor from a different group. As we will show in Section 5.1, there is, for example, a very simple implementation of generalized weak test-and-set if the number of groups is less or equal than the number of MWMR registers and each group is possibly infinite, i.e. with infinitely many processors and finitely many MWMR registers.

2   Model

We consider an asynchronous shared memory system with registers, in which a set Π of processors can communicate with each other by writing to and reading from a finite number of registers. Registers are Multi-Writer Multi-Reader (MWMR), meaning that they can be read and written by any processor in the system, and they can hold values in $\mathbf{N} = \{1, 2, \ldots\}$. For some of our results, we also consider Single-Writer Multi-Reader (SWMR) registers and, in fact, without loss of generality, we assume that each processor has at most one such register to which it can write (and it can be read by any processor).

The correctness condition for concurrent accesses to registers is linearizability.

The set Π of processors that m ay participate is countably infinite and, in fact, we assume that $\Pi = \mathbf{N}$. Elements of Π are called processor id's. Not all processors actually run simultaneously; in fact, in each run, only a finite number of them execute. These are called the set of participating processors or simply participants. Protocols running in our model are uniform: they do not know a priori the number of participants or a bound on this number.

Processors may fail by crashing. A processor that does not crash is called correct. We consider wait-free protocols, that is, protocols that guarantee that correct processors always make progress, regardless of the behavior of other processors (e.g., even when other processors have crashed).

2.1   Tasks

Traditionally, a task is defined to be a function from inputs to sets of outputs. However, for our model with infinitely many processors, we assume without loss of generality that the processor id and the input have been coalesced together and we call both of them the processor id. Hence, we define a task T to be a function that maps finite subsets S of processors to sets of outputs, where each output is a map from S to $\mathbf{N}$, that is $T(S) \in 2^{S \to \mathbf{N}}$. Intuitively, $T(S)$ is the set of all possible outcomes when S is the set of participating processors. Each outcome $f \in T(S)$ is a mapping $f : S \to \mathbf{N}$ that indicates the output of each processor in S.

A protocol solves a task T if, whenever S is the set of participating processors, there exists a mapping $f \in T(S)$ so that every correct processor p outputs $f(p)$. Note that tasks are inherently "short-lived": there is only one execution of a task in a run of the system.

We say that a protocol for a task is adaptive [2,3,4,5,7,8,9,11,15,17,18,19,20, 22,28,34] if the number of steps (read/write operations) taken by each processor is bounded by a function of the contention. To strengthen our impossibility results, we use a very weak notion of contention: we define contention to be the number of participants from the beginning of the run until the processor outputs a value.

3   The Generalized Weak Test-and-Set Task

Roughly speaking, in the generalized weak test-and-set task, processors are a priori partitioned into classes, and the goal is for processors in at most one of the classes to "win", that is, to output 1. All other processors must output 0. In order to avoid trivial solutions where every processor always outputs 0, we also require that if all participants belong to the same class then they all output 1.

More precisely, the following two properties must be satisfied:

– All participants that output 1 belong to the same class;
– If all participants belong to the same class then they all output 1.

4   Impossibility Results

4.1   Impossibility with Finitely Many Registers

In this section, we show that there is no uniform solution for the generalized weak test-and-set task with finitely many shared registers (either MWMR or SWMR). Without loss of generality, we assume that all the registers are MWMR. In the next section, we strengthen our impossibility result to allow an infinite number of SWMR registers (and still a finite number of MWMR registers), but we assume that the protocol is adaptive.

Theorem 1. There is no uniform wait-free implementation of the generalized weak-test-and-set task in a system with finitely many shared registers.

We show the theorem by contradiction: assume there is such an implementation that uses only k registers $r_1, \ldots, r_k$.

Definition 1. A register configuration is a k-tuple containing the state of each register in the system.

Note that this notion only makes sense at times when all of the registers have only one possible linearization (e.g., it does not make sense if there is an outstanding write). This will always be the case in the states that we consider.

We now progressively construct many runs $R_1, R_2, \ldots$ such that in R_i, all processors belong to the same class C_i. As we shall see, we will build a run $R_{i,j}$ that is a mix of R_i and R_j (for infinitely many $j \neq i \in \mathbf{N}$). Since all processors in R_i belong to class C_i and all processors in R_j belong to C_j, where $C_i \cap C_j = \emptyset$ for all $i \neq j \in \mathbf{N}$, the id's of processors in R_i are always different from the ones in R_j. In this way, the processors running in $R_{i,j}$ are the disjoint union of the processors in R_i and R_j.

In each run R_i, we start bignum$_0$ processors from class C_i and let them execute solo, one after the other, until they are about to write to their first register. Throughout this proof bignum$_h$ and bignum$'_h$ are large numbers to be determined later (for every $h \in \mathbf{N}$).

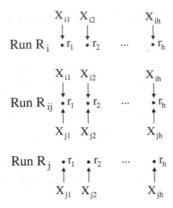

Fig. 1. Situation at the end of phase h of the inductive construction. Each set X_{ik} (resp. X_{jk}) represents a large number of processors from class i (resp. class j) that are about to write to register r_k. In run R_i (resp. R_j) there are only processors from class i (resp. class j), and run R_{ij} has the union of processors from R_i and R_j.

Our construction proceeds in phases that we construct inductively. We begin with phase 0 of the construction:

Since there are only finitely many registers, we can pick an infinite subset $R_{j_1}, R_{j_2}, \ldots$ of the runs $R_1, R_2, \ldots$ such that at least bignum $'_0$ processors in each run cover the same register, call it r_1. To avoid cluttering up notation, we will call these runs $R_1, R_2, \ldots$ rather than $R_{j_1}, R_{j_2}, \ldots$

Now for every $i \neq j \in \mathbf{N}$, we can construct another run $R_{i,j}$ as a combination of R_i and R_j, that is, processors in R_i and R_j run solo, one after the other in some irrelevant order, until they are about to write to r_1. Note that for every $i \neq j$, all runs R_i and $R_{i,j}$ have the same register configuration, since no processor has yet written to any registers.

In phase 1, we extend R_i by starting bignum $_1$ new processors (processors that have not executed before) from class C_i and letting them run solo, one after the other, until they either (a) terminate or (b) they cover a register different from r_1 (if they attempt to write to r_1, we let them do so and let them continue execute until they cover a register different from r_1).

We now show inductively for any phase $1 \leq h \leq k$ that (a) cannot happen in phase h.

Claim . For all $1 \leq h \leq k$, $i \in \mathbf{N}$, no processor executing steps in phase h of run R_i will terminate in phase h.

Proof. We proceed inductively to build phase h of the construction from phase $h-1$. At the end of phase $h-1$, we have runs R_i and $R_{i,j}$ (for all $i \neq j \in \mathbf{N}$) such that (1) in R_i there is a large number of processors covering $r_1, r_2, \ldots, r_{h-1}$, (2) each processor in R_i and in R_j have the same state as in $R_{i,j}$. See Figure 1.

To ensure that R_i and $R_{i,j}$ have the same register configuration, we pick in both runs processors (one for each register) that cover each of $r_1, r_2, \ldots, r_{h-1}$, and let them execute one step. We do so for R_i (we will get back to $R_{i,j}$ below). Then, in R_i we start bignum $_{h-1}$ new processors from class C_i and let them run solo, one after the other, until they either (a) terminate or (b) they cover a register different from $r_1, r_2, \ldots, r_{h-1}$.

We now show that no processor can terminate in phase h (i.e. that (a) cannot happen):

By way of contradiction, assume that a processor p terminates before writing to a register different from $r_1, r_2, \ldots, r_{h-1}$. Then p must output 1 by property (1) of the generalized test-and-set task, since in R_i all processors are from class C_i. Moreover, in $R_{i,j}$ we can execute the same processors that executed one step in R_i to overwrite $r_1, r_2, \ldots, r_{h-1}$, and then let p execute. Then, p will behave exactly as in R_i; hence p outputs 1 in $R_{i,j}$. Now pick processors in R_j that cover $r_1, r_2, \ldots, r_{h-1}$ (one for each register) and let them all execute one step (overwriting the contents of $r_1, r_2, \ldots, r_{h-1}$). Do the same in $R_{i,j}$. We can now start a new processor in $R_{i,j}$ from class C_j and let it execute until completion. Such a processor will behave as if it were running in R_j and hence will decide 1 in $R_{i,j}$. This violates property (2) of the generalized test-and-set task and shows the claim.   □

Now since there are only finitely many registers, we can pick an infinite subset $R_{j_1}, R_{j_2}, \ldots$ of the runs $R_1, R_2, \ldots$ such that at least bignum $'_{h-1}$ processors cover the same register, call it r_h. To avoid cluttering up notation, we will call these runs $R_1, R_2, \ldots$ rather than $R_{j_1}, R_{j_2}, \ldots$

We now extend $R_{i,j}$ by "pasting" runs R_i and R_j one after the other (Note that, since in both runs we begin by allowing for each register $r_1, r_2, \ldots, r_{h-1}$, one processor covering each such register to complete its write, it does not matter which run comes first, say R_i as follows.) In $R_{i,j}$ we allow the same processors that executed one step in R_i to execute the same step in $R_{i,j}$ and to overwrite $r_1, r_2, \ldots, r_{h-1}$. Then we start bignum $_{h-1}$ new processors from class C_i and let them run solo. Such processors will behave exactly as in R_i and, after doing so, processors in R_i will have the same state in both R_i and $R_{i,j}$.

We then paste R_j in the same manner. Thus, we have (1) in R_i there is a large number of processors covering $r_1, r_2, \ldots, r_h$, and (2) each processor in R_i or R_j have the same state as in $R_{i,j}$. This concludes phase h.

By carrying out these constructions until phase $h = k+1$ (recall that k is the number of registers), we get a contradiction because a processor will be executing forever (by Claim 4.1, the processor cannot terminate before it attempts to write to a register different from $r_1, r_2, \ldots, r_k$, but unfortunately there is no such register).

4.2   Infinitely Many SWMR Registers

We will now show that our impossibility result holds for adaptive implementations even if we allow processors to use an infinite number of SWMR registers (but finite number of MWMR registers). Without loss of generality, we assume that each processor has one SWMR register assigned to it. In this case the runs constructed in Theorem 1 might not be valid anymore since in $R_{i,j}$ processors from R_i might read the SWMR register of a processor from R_j and not write to r_1 ($r_1, ..., r_{h-1}$ respectively) anymore and instead terminate with 0. Moreover, processors from R_i in $R_{i,j}$ might read the SWMR register of a processor from R_j causing them to terminate. Note, however, that in R_i and R_j itself, we do not need to worry about covering processors being discovered through their SWMR registers. As long as processors from say R_i do not "discover" any processor from R_j in $R_{i,j}$ they are still forced to write to a new MWMR register. Note, moreover, that in $R_{i,j}$ there are no traces of the processors covering the MWMR registers $r_1, ..., r_{h-1}$ in any MWMR register that could "point" a processor say from R_i to the SWMR registers of a processor from R_j.

To avoid these problems, we use a technique first presented by Afek, Boxer and Touitou [1]. We prevent processors whose SWMR registers are later read from taking part in the constructed runs. So, at any given state in a run $R_{i,j}$, if processor p from R_i (R_j) reads the SWMR register of processor q from R_j (R_i) and q is participating and currently covering one of the MWMR registers, then we construct another run in which q is replaced by another processor q'. Processor p will still read the same SWMR registers, i.e. of q and not of q'. Let $R_{i,j}$ be the run in which q is participating and $R'_{i,j}$ be the run in which q' is participating. As in [1], the behavior of q and q' is somewhat equivalent, i.e. they are both writing and covering the same MWMR registers in $R_{i,j}$ and $R'_{i,j}$. A processor like q' always exists because: (1) There is a large enough set of processors to select q' from since only a bounded number of processors participated in the run so far and we are able to choose from infinitely many processors. (2) Processor p can perform only a bounded number of read operations - exactly a function of the number of processors that performed steps so far.

During all the runs $R_{i,j}$, some i, j, previously constructed, we maintain a large enough set of "equivalent" runs. These runs allow us to replace the run at any given point in which we enter a dangerous state, i.e. a state where a processor from one class reads the SWMR register of a participating processor from another class.

Definition 2. Let p be a processor participating in run R_i. W e say that a state s in run $R_{i,j}$ is i-transparent for p, if there is a run segment starting at s in which p takes steps that p cannot distinguish from a run segment in R_i.

Definition 3. Two runs $R_{i,j}$ and $R'_{i,j}$ are equivalent with respect to a set of processors G from R_i (R_j) if (1) the state at the end of both runs $R_{i,j}$ and $R'_{i,j}$ is i-transparent (j-transparent) with respect to G, (2) the MWMR registers $r_1, ..., r_h$ covered in $R_{i,j}$ and $R'_{i,j}$ are the same and they are covered by processors from the same classes and (3) if processor $p \in G$ participating in R_i (R_j) participates in both $R_{i,j}$ and $R'_{i,j}$ then p cannot distinguish between the two.

When constructing a run $R_{i,j}$ in the proof, whenever a covering processor q from R_i (R_j), that we selected to participate in the run is discovered by a processor from R_j (R_i) we need to replace it by a processor q' from R_i (R_j) that cannot be discovered.

We achieve this by considering an equivalent run in which q' takes steps instead of q. Note that if we remove q from $R_{i,j}$ we also automatically remove it from R_i.

Theorem 2. There is no uniform adaptive wait-free implementation of the generalized weak-test-and-set task in a system with finitely many M W M R registers and infinitely many SW M R registers.

Proof. We proceed as in the proof of Theorem 1: We progressively construct many runs $R_1, R_2, \ldots$ such that in R_i, all processors belong to the same class C_i. We will build a run $R_{i,j}$ that is a mix of R_i and R_j (for infinitely many $j \neq i \in \mathbf{N}$). In this way, the processors running in $R_{i,j}$ are the disjoint union of the processors in R_i and R_j.

In each run R_i, we start bignum $_0$ processors from class C_i and let them execute solo, one after the other, until they are about to write to their first register. As before, bignum $_h$ and bignum $'_h$ are large numbers to be determined later (for every $h \in \mathbf{N}$).

The construction proceeds in phases that we construct inductively. We begin with phase 0 of the construction:

Since there are only finitely many registers, we can pick an infinite subset $R_{j_1}, R_{j_2}, \ldots$ of the runs $R_1, R_2, \ldots$ such that at least bignum $'_0$ processors in each run cover the same register, call it r_1. To avoid cluttering up notation, we will call these runs $R_1, R_2, \ldots$ rather than $R_{j_1}, R_{j_2}, \ldots$.

Now for every $i \neq j \in \mathbf{N}$, we can construct another run $R_{i,j}$ as a combination of R_i and R_j, that is, processors in R_i and R_j run solo, one after the other in some irrelevant order, until they are about to write to r_1. Note that for every $i \neq j$, all runs R_i and $R_{i,j}$ have the same register configuration, since no processor has yet written to any registers.

In phase 1, we extend R_i by starting bignum $_1$ new processors (processors that have not executed before) from class C_i and letting them run solo, one after the other, until they either (a) terminate or (b) they cover a register different from r_1 (if they attempt to write to r_1, we let them do so and continue executing). We show inductively for any phase $1 \leq h \leq k$ that (a) cannot happen in phase h.

Claim. For all $1 \leq h \leq k$, $i \in \mathbf{N}$, no processor executing steps in phase h of run R_i will terminate in phase h.

Note that this is the inductive claim from Theorem 1. The proof of this claim, however, might not be valid anymore, since in each phase $1 \leq h \leq k$, a participating processor p in $R_{i,j}$ might read the SWMR register of a processor q from class C_j and immediately output 0. To avoid this problem, we construct in each phase h of the construction for each $i \neq j \in \mathbf{N}$, i.e. each $R_{i,j}$ a run $R'_{i,j}$ that is equivalent to $R_{i,j}$. In the new run $R'_{i,j}$ we remove active processors that are later "discovered" by other active processors, i.e. any processor covering a register, whose SWMR register is later read by another participating processor, has been removed in $R'_{i,j}$. So, for each participating processor p that reads the SWMR register of participating processors $q_0, ..., q_n$ (from class C_j), we replace in $R'_{i,j}$, $q_0, ..., q_n$ with processors $q'_0, ..., q'_n$ from class C_j. Hence in $R'_{i,j}$ the processors $q'_0, ..., q'_n$ take steps instead of $q_0, ..., q_n$ and no participating processor reads the SWMR register of $q'_0, ..., q'_n$. Intuitively, we construct such a new run $R'_{i,j}$ that is equivalent to $R_{i,j}$ by repeating the construction of the current run from the beginning. In the new run we remove participating processors from R_j (R_i) that are later discovered from processors in R_i (R_j). We replace them with other processors that are from R_j (R_i) that are not discovered and whose behavior is equivalent

It remains to show that there are always such replacement processors q'. This follows from the fact that (1) in any given phase a processor is allowed to read at most a bounded (by a function of the number of processors that performed any steps up to this stage) number of SWMR registers. By the generalized weak test-and-set task specification, a participating processor cannot perform at any given stage an unbounded search of all (infinitely) many SWMR registers, since it would then possibly enter a deadlocked state. (2) Only a finite number of processors participated up to any given stage. This means, we are always able to select all needed processors q' from an infinite set of processors. (Note, that this might require us to adjust bignum $_h$ for each phase h such that we always are able to chose q' from sufficiently many processors.)

Hence we obtain a construction where no processor reads the SWMR register of any other participating processor. Such a construction has the properties of the run in Theorem 1. Hence the proof of the claim follows. As in the proof of Theorem 1, this proves the theorem.   □

5   Possibility Results

The following two possibility results prove that our impossibility result for an implementation with a constant number of MWMR registers relies heavily on the following two assumptions: (1) that there are infinitely many classes of processors, and (2) that there is no finite bound b on the number of processors that are in the same class. In fact, we now provide uniform implementation with finitely many MWMR registers when either (!1) there is a single upper bound on the number of processors in all classes or (!2) there are only finitely many classes.

5.1   Number of Classes Is Finite

To implement generalized weak-test-and-set with a finite number k of classes of processors (where each class can have an infinite number of processors), we simply assign a MWMR register to each class. All MWMR registers initially contain ⊥. A processor executing the generalized weak-test-and-set algorithm $\mathcal{A}$ simply first writes 1 to the MWMR register corresponding to its class and then scans all other MWMR registers. If it sees 1 only in the MWMR register assigned to its class, it outputs 1. Otherwise, it outputs 0.

Theorem 3. *Algorithm $\mathcal{A}$ is an implementation of the generalized weak-test-and-set task with finitely many classes of processors using only a constant number of MWMR registers.*

Proof. Let C be a class of processors. Since all processors in C write the same value (1) to the same MWMR register and since this value once written is never changed, the processors in C, for each of the finitely many such classes C, emulate a single writer. Hence the claim follows.   □

5.2   Number of Processors in Each Class Is Uniformly Bounded

Assume there is an upper bound $b < \infty$ on the size of each class C of processors (but there may be an infinite number of classes). We now provide an implementation $\mathcal{B}$ of generalized weak-test-and-set using only a constant number of MWMR registers.

The implementation uses splitters in a way described by Attiya, Fouren and Gafni [20]. A splitter is defined as follows: A processor entering a splitter exits with either stop, left or right. It is guaranteed that if a single processor enters the splitter, then it obtains stop, and if two or more processors enter it, then there are two processors that obtain different values. Implementation $\mathcal{B}$ uses a complete binary tree of depth $b + 1$. Each vertex of the tree contains a splitter. As in the adaptive collect algorithm of Attiya, Fouren and Gafni [20], a processor acquires a vertex v; from this point on the processor stores its values in $v.val$.

A processor moves down the tree according to the values obtained in the splitters along the path: If it receives left it moves to the left child; if it receives right, it moves to the right child. A processor marks each vertex it accesses by raising a flag associated with the vertex; a vertex is marked if its flag is raised. The processor acquires a vertex v when it obtains stop at the splitter associated with v; then it writes its id and class identifier into $v.id$. A processor that acquired a vertex then as in [20], by traversing the part of the tree containing marked vertices, in DFS order, collects the values written in the marked vertices. If it sees a processor from a different class than its own, it outputs 0, else 1.

If a processor p executing this implementation reaches a leaf of the tree, i.e. depth $b + 1$, without acquiring a vertex, it immediately outputs 0. Since the bound on the membership of the class of processors is b, there must be at least one processor participating that does not have the same initial value as p.

Theorem 4. *Algorithm $\mathcal{B}$ is an implementation of the generalized weak-test-and-set task with a bounded by b number of processors in each class of processors using only a constant number of MWMR registers.*

Proof. Immediate.   □

6   Conclusion

Afek et al [1] showed that a long-lived task requires an infinite number of MWMR registers in case there is no a priori bound to the number of the participating processors. We have extended this result showing that the long-liveness is not necessarily the crucial ingredient that raises the need for infinite memory. This raises the interesting question on when such a memory is really required. Another way of extending the result in [1] is to notice that the proof there actually requires the concurrency to exceed the number of MWMR registers. What if we do not have an a priori bound on the concurrency? Can we nevertheless use a fortiori a finite number of MWMR registers? I.e., can splitters be reused in a uniform protocol? We conjecture they cannot—a conjecture that if proven will make the research area of adaptive algorithms a bit less appealing.

Acknowledgement. We are thankful to the DISC referees for valuable comments.

References

1. Y. Afek, P. Boxer and D. Touitou. Bounds on the shared memory requirements for long-lived and adaptive objects. In *Proc. of 20th Annual ACM Symp. on Principles of Distributed Computing*, pp. 81–89, 2000.
2. Y. Afek, H. Attiya, A. Fouren, G. Stupp and D. Touitou. Long-Lived Renaming made adaptive. *Proc. of 18th Annual ACM Symp. on Principles of Distributed Computing*: pp. 91–103, 1999.
3. Y. Afek, H. Attiya, G. Stupp and D. Touitou. Adaptive long-lived renaming using bounded memory. *Proc. of the 40th IEEE Ann. Symp. on Foundations of Computer Science*, pp. 262–272, 1999.
4. Y. Afek, D. Dauber and D. Touitou. Wait-free made fast. *Proc. of the 27th Ann. ACM Symp. on Theory of Computing*: pp. 538–547, 1995.
5. Y. Afek and M. Merritt. Fast, wait-free $(2k-1)$-renaming. In *Proc. of the 18th Ann. ACM Symp. on Principles of Distributed Computing*, pp. 105–112, 1999.
6. Y. Afek, M. Merritt, G. Taubenfeld and D. Touitou. Disentangling multi-object operations. In *Proc. of 16th Annual ACM Symp. on Principles of Distributed Computing*, pp. 111–120, 1997.
7. Y. Afek, G. Stupp and D. Touitou. Long lived adaptive collect with applications. *Proc. of the 40th IEEE Ann. Symp. on Foundations of Computer Science*, pp. 262–272, 1999.
8. Y. Afek, G. Stupp and D. Touitou. Long lived adaptive splitter and applications. Unpublished manuscript, 1999.
9. Y. Afek, G. Stupp and D. Touitou. Long lived and adaptive atomic snapshot and immediate snapshot. *Proc. of the 19th Ann. ACM Symp. on Principles of Distributed Computing*, pp. 71–80, 2000.
10. M.K. Aguilera, B. Englert and E. Gafni. On using network attached disks as shared memory. *To appear in Proc.of the 22nd Ann. ACM Symp. on Principles of Distributed Computing*, 2003.

11. J. Anderson and Y.-J. Kim. Adaptive mutual exclusion with local spinning. *Proceedings of the 14th International Conference, DISC 2000*, pp. 29–43, 2000.
12. D. Angluin. Local and global properties in networks of processors. In *Proceedings of the 12th ACM Symposium on Theory of Computing*, pp. 82–93, 1980.
13. J. Aspnes, G. Shah and J. Shah. Wait free consensus with infinite arrivals. *Proc. of the 34th Annual ACM Symposium on the Theory of Computing*, pp. 524–533, 2002.
14. J. Aspnes and O. Waarts. Modular competitiveness for distributed algorithms. In *Proc. 28th ACM Symp. Theory of Comp.*, pp. 237–246, 1996.
15. H. Attiya and V. Bortnikov. Adaptive and efficient mutual exclusion. In *Proceedings of the 19th Annual ACM Symposium on Principles of Distributed Computing*, pp. 91–100, 2000.
16. H. Attiya and E. Dagan. Universal operations: Unary versus binary. In *Proc. 15th Annual ACM Symp. on Principles of Distributed Computing*, pp. 223–232, 1996.
17. H. Attiya and A. Fouren. Adaptive wait-free algorithms for lattice agreement and renaming. In *Proc. 17th Annual ACM Symp. on Principles of Distributed Computing*, pp. 277–286, 1998.
18. H. Attiya and A. Fouren. Adaptive long-lived renaming with read and write operations. Technical Report 0956, Faculty of Computer Science, Technion, Haifa, 1999. http://www.cs.technion.ac.il/ hagit/pubs/tr0956.ps.gz.
19. H. Attiya and A. Fouren. Algorithms adaptive to point contention. *JACM*, 2001, submitted for publication.
20. H. Attiya, A. Fouren and E. Gafni. An adaptive collect algorithm with applications. *Distributed Computing*, 15(2), pp. 87–96, 2002.
21. J. Burns and N. Lynch. Bounds on shared memory for mutual exclusion. *Information and Computation* 107(2):pp. 171–184, 1993.
22. M. Choy and A.K. Singh. Adaptive solutions to the mutual exclusion problem. *Distributed Computing*, 8(1), pp. 1–17, 1994.
23. P. Fatourou, F. Fich and E. Ruppert. Space-optimal multi-writer snapshot objects are slow. *Proc. 21st Annual ACM Symp. on Principles of Distributed Computing*, pp. 13–20, 2002.
24. P. Fatourou, F. Fich and E. Ruppert. A tight lower bound for space-optimal implementations of multi-writer snapshots. *Proc. 35th Annual ACM Symp. on Theory of Computing*, pp. 259–268, 2003.
25. F. Fich, M. Herlihy and N. Shavit. On the space complexity of randomized synchronization. *JACM* 45(5), pp. 843–862, 1998.
26. E. Gafni. A simple algorithmic characterization of uniform solvability. *Proceedings of the 43rd Annual IEEE Symposium on Foundations of Computer Science*, pp. 228–237, 2002.
27. M. Herlihy and N. Shavit. The topological structure of asynchronous computability. *JACM* 46(6), pp. 858–923, 1999.
28. M. Inoue, S. Umetani, T. Masuzawa and H. Fujiwara. Adaptive long-lived $O(k^2)$ renaming with $O(k^2)$ steps. *Proceedings of the 15th International Conference on Distributed Computing*, pp. 123–135, 2001.
29. A. Itai and M. Rodeh. Symmetry breaking in distributed networks. *Information and Computation*, 88(1): pp. 60–87, 1990.
30. Y.-J. Joung. Asynchronous group mutual exclusion (extended abstract). In *Proceedings of the 17th Annual ACM Symposium on Principles of Distributed Computing*, pp.51–60, 1998.
31. L. Lamport. A fast mutual exclusion algorithm. *ACM Transactions on Computer Systems*, 5(1): pp. 1–11, 1987.

32. M. Merritt and G. Taubenfeld. Speeding Lamport's fast mutual exclusion algorithm. *Information Processing Letters*, 45: pp. 137–142, 1993.
33. M. Moir and J. H. Anderson. Wait-free algorithms for fast, long-lived renaming. *Sci. Comput. Programming*, 25(1): pp. 1–39, 1995.
34. G.L. Peterson. Time efficient adaptive mutual exclusion algorithms. Unpublished manuscript, 2001.

Timing-Based Mutual Exclusion with Local Spinning*

(Extended Abstract)

Yong-Jik Kim and James H. Anderson

Department of Computer Science
University of North Carolina at Chapel Hill
{kimy,anderson}@cs.unc.edu

Abstract. We consider the time complexity of shared-memory mutual exclusion algorithms based on reads, writes, and comparison primitives under the remote-memory-reference (RMR) time measure. For asynchronous systems, a lower bound of $\Omega(\log N / \log \log N)$ RMRs per critical-section entry has been established in previous work, where N is the number of processes. In this paper, we show that lower RMR time complexity is attainable in semi-synchronous systems in which processes may execute *delay* statements. When assessing the time complexity of delay-based algorithms, the question of whether delays should be counted arises. We consider both possibilities. Also of relevance is whether delay durations are upper-bounded. (They are lower-bounded by definition.) Again, we consider both possibilities. For each of these possibilities, we present an algorithm with either $\Theta(1)$ or $\Theta(\log \log N)$ time complexity. For the cases in which a $\Theta(\log \log N)$ algorithm is given, we establish matching $\Omega(\log \log N)$ lower bounds.

1 Introduction

Recent work on shared-memory mutual exclusion has focused on the design of algorithms that minimize interconnect contention through the use of *local spinning*. In local-spin algorithms, all busy waiting is by means of read-only loops in which one or more "spin variables" are repeatedly tested. Such variables must be either locally cacheable or stored in a local memory module that can be accessed without an interconnection network traversal. The former is possible on cache-coherent (CC) machines, while the latter is possible on distributed shared-memory (DSM) machines.

In this paper, several results concerning the time complexity of local-spin mutual exclusion algorithms are given. Time complexity is defined herein using the *remote-memory-reference (RMR) measure* [8]. Under this measure, an algorithm's time complexity is defined as the total number of RMRs required in the worst case by one process to enter and then exit its critical section. An algorithm may have different RMR time complexities on CC and DSM machines, because variable locality is dynamically determined on CC machines and statically on DSM machines (see [7]).

In this paper, we consider mutual exclusion algorithms based on reads, writes, and comparison primitives such as *test-and-set* and *compare-and-swap* (CAS). A *comparison primitive* is an atomic operation on a shared variable v that is expressible using the following pseudo-code.

---

* Work supported by NSF grant CCR 0208289.

$compare\_and\_fg(v, old, new)$
  $temp := v;$
  if $v = old$ **then** $v := f(old, new)$ **fi**;
  return $g(temp, old, new)$

For example, CAS can be specified by defining $f(old, new) = new$ and $g(temp, old, new) = old$.

In earlier work, Cypher [11] established a time-complexity lower bound of $\Omega(\log \log N/ \log \log \log N)$ RMRs for any asynchronous N-process mutual exclusion algorithm based on reads, writes, and comparison primitives. In recent work [5], we presented for this class of algorithms a substantially improved lower bound of $\Omega(\log N/ \log \log N)$ RMRs, which is within a factor of $\Theta(\log \log N)$ of being optimal, since algorithms based only on reads and writes with $\Theta(\log N)$ RMR time complexity are known [22].[1] The proofs of these lower bounds use the ability to "stall" some processes for arbitrarily long durations, and hence are not applicable to *semi-synchronous systems*, in which the time required to execute a statement is upper-bounded.

A number of interesting "timing-based" mutual exclusion algorithms have been devised in recent years in which such bounds are exploited, and processes have the ability to delay their execution [2, 4, 16, 17]. Such algorithms are the focus of this paper. We exclusively consider the *known-delay* model [4, 16, 17], in which there is a known upper bound, denoted Δ, on the time required to read or write a shared variable.[2] For simplicity, all process delays are assumed to be implemented via the statement $delay(\Delta)$. (Longer delays can be obtained by concatenating such statements; we will use $delay(c \cdot \Delta)$ as a shorthand for c such statements in sequence.)

In prior work on timing-based algorithms, the development of algorithms that are fast in the *absence* of contention has been the main focus. In fact, to the best of our knowledge, all timing-based algorithms previously proposed use non-local busy-waiting. Hence, these algorithms have unbounded RMR time complexity under contention.

Contributions. In this paper, we present time-complexity bounds for timing-based algorithms under the known-delay model in which all busy-waiting is by local spinning. (Our results are summarized in Table 1, which is explained below.) Under this model, the class of algorithms considered in this paper can be restricted somewhat with no loss of generality. In particular, comparison primitives can be implemented in constant time from reads and writes by using delays [3, 19]. Thus, it suffices to consider only timing-based algorithms based on reads and writes. In the rest of the paper, all claims are assumed to apply to this class of algorithms, unless noted otherwise.

When assessing the RMR time complexity of timing-based algorithms, the question of whether delays should be counted arises. Given that Δ is necessarily at least the duration of one RMR, it may make sense to count delays. Accordingly, we define the *RMR-Δ*

---

[1] In contrast, several $\Theta(1)$ algorithms are known that are based on noncomparison primitives (*e.g.*, [6, 9, 12, 18]). We do not consider such algorithms in this paper.

[2] Equivalently, statement executions can be considered to take place instantaneously (*i.e.*, atomically), with consecutive statement executions of the same process occurring at most Δ time units apart. We adopt this model in our lower bound proof. The known-delay model differs from the *unknown-delay* model [2], wherein the upper bound Δ is unknown *a priori*, and hence, cannot be used directly in an algorithm.

Table 1. Summary of results. Each entry gives a time-complexity figure that is shown to be optimal.

	RMR Time Complexity		RMR-Δ Time Complexity
Arch.	Delays Bounded	Delays Unbounded	Delays Bounded/Unbounded
DSM	$\Theta(1)$ {ALG. DSM}	$\Theta(1)$ {ALG. DSM}	$\Theta(1)$ {ALG. DSM}
CC	$\Theta(1)$ {ALG. CC}	$\Theta(\log \log N)$ {ALG. T, Thm. 3}	$\Theta(\log \log N)$ {ALG. T, Thm. 2}

time complexity of an algorithm to be the total number of RMRs and $delay(\Delta)$ statements required in the worst case by one process to enter and then exit its critical section. (Note that this measure includes the total delay duration as well as the number of delay statements, since Δ is fixed for a given system.)

On the other hand, one might argue that delays should be ignored when assessing time complexity, just like local memory references. For completeness, we consider this possibility as well by also considering the standard RMR measure (which ignores delays). One limitation of the RMR measure is that it allows algorithms with long delays to be categorized as having low time complexity. For this reason, we view the RMR-Δ measure as the better choice.

As we shall see, the exact semantics assumed of the statement $delay(\Delta)$ is of relevance as well. It is reasonable to assume that a process is delayed by *at least* Δ time units when invoking this statement. However, it is not clear whether a specific upper bound on the delay duration should be assumed. For completeness, we once again consider both possibilities.

Our results are summarized in Table 1. The headings "Delays Bounded/Unbounded" indicate whether delay durations are assumed to be upper bounded. Each table entry gives a time-complexity figure that is shown to be optimal by giving an algorithm, and for the $\Theta(\log \log N)$ entries, a lower bound. Due to space constraints, ALGORITHMS DSM and CC, as well as one of our lower bounds, are presented only in the full version of this paper [14]. The main conclusion to be drawn from these results is the following: *in semi-synchronous systems in which delay statements are supported, substantially smaller RMR time complexity is possible than in asynchronous systems when devising mutual exclusion algorithms using reads, writes, and comparison primitives, regardless of how one resolves the issues of whether to count delays and how to define the semantics of the delay statement.*

In the following sections, we present ALGORITHM T, a $\Theta(\log \log N)$ algorithm, and a matching $\Omega(\log \log N)$ lower bound for CC machines under the RMR-Δ measure.

2   A $\Theta(\log \log N)$ Algorithm

In this section, we describe ALGORITHM T (for "tree"), illustrated in Fig. 3, in which each process executes $\Theta(\log \log N)$ RMRs and $\Theta(\log \log N)$ delay statements in order to enter and then exit its critical section. Upper bounds on delays are not required.

ALGORITHM T is constructed by combining smaller instances of a mutual exclusion algorithm in a binary arbitration tree. A similar approach has been used in algorithms in which each tree node represents an instance of a two-process mutual exclusion algorithm [13, 22]. If each node takes $\Theta(1)$ time, then $\Theta(\log N)$ time is required for a process to enter (and then exit) its critical section.

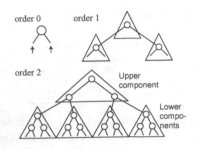

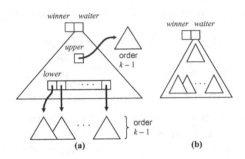

Fig. 1. Structure of arbitration trees used in ALGORITHM T. A tree of order $k > 0$ has an upper component and $2^{2^{k-1}}$ lower components, each of order $k - 1$.

Fig. 2. Structure of an arbitration tree of *TreeType*, of order k. **(a)** A "verbose" depiction, showing dynamic links for its components. **(b)** A simplified version.

In order to obtain a faster algorithm, we give the tree an additional structure, as follows. For the sake of simplicity, we assume that $N = 2^{2^K}$ holds for some integer $K > 0$. (Otherwise, we add "dummy processes" to the nearest such number. Since $\log \log 2^{2^K} = K$, such padding increases the algorithm's time complexity by only a constant factor.) We say that a binary arbitration tree has *order* k if it has 2^k (non-leaf) levels and 2^{2^k} leaves, as shown in Fig. 1. A tree of order zero is a two-process mutual exclusion algorithm. A tree T of order $k > 0$ is divided into the top 2^{k-1} levels and the bottom 2^{k-1} levels: the top levels constitute a single tree of order $k - 1$, and the bottom levels, $2^{2^{k-1}}$ distinct trees of order $k - 1$. (This structure is rather similar to the van Emde Boas tree [21], which implements a $\Theta(\log \log u)$-time search structure over a fixed set of integers in the range $1..u$.) We call these subtrees T's *components*. Thus, T consists of a single *upper component* and $2^{2^{k-1}}$ *lower components*, where the root node of each lower component corresponds to a leaf node of the upper component. These components are linked into T dynamically by pointers, so a process can exchange a particular component S with another tree S' (of order $k - 1$) in $\Theta(1)$ time.

We also say that tree S is a *constituent* of tree T if either S is T or S is a constituent of another component of T. Associated with each tree T is a field called *winner*, which is accessed by CAS operations. (As noted earlier, CAS can be implemented in $\Theta(1)$ time using delays [3, 19].) A process p attempts to establish $T.winner = p$ by invoking CAS, in which case it is said to have *acquired* T. The structure of an arbitration tree explained thus far is depicted in Fig. 2. (The *waiter* field is explained later.)

Arbitration tree and waiting queue. We start with a high-level overview of ALGO-RITHM T. A tree T_0 of order K and N leaves is used, in which each process is statically assigned to a leaf node. The algorithm is constructed by recursively combining instances of a mutual exclusion algorithm for each component of T_0. The process that wins the outermost instance of the algorithm (*i.e.*, that associated with T_0) enters its critical section.

Note that, for each process p, its path from its leaf up to the root in T_0 is contained in two components, namely, some lower component L_i and the upper component U. To enter its critical section, p attempts to acquire both components on this path (by invoking CAS on $L_i.winner$, and then on $U.winner$). If p acquires both components, then it may enter its critical section, by invoking *ExecuteCS*. As explained shortly, p may also be "promoted" to its critical section after failing to acquire either tree. (In that case, p may

```
TreeType = record
    order: 0..K;
    upper: pointer to TreeType;
    lower: array[0..(2^{2^{order-1}} - 1)] of
        pointer to TreeType;
    winner, waiter: (⊥, 0..N - 1)
end

shared variables
    T_0: (a tree with order K);
    Spin: array[0..N - 1] of boolean;
    Promoted: (⊥, 0..N - 1) initially ⊥;
    WaitingQueue: queue of {0..N - 1}
        initially empty;

process p ::    /* 0 ≤ p < N */

while true do
0:  Noncritical Section;

1:  Spin[p] := false;
2:  AccessTree(&T_0, p);
3:  TryToPromote();
4:  Signal()      /* open the barrier */
od

procedure TryToPromote()
/* promote a waiting process (if any) */
5:  q := Promoted;
6:  if (q = p) ∨ (q = ⊥) then
7:      next := Dequeue(WaitingQueue);
8:      Promoted := next;
9:      if next ≠ ⊥ then
10:         Spin[next] := true fi
    fi

procedure ExecuteCS(side: 0, 1)
11: if side = 1 then await Spin[p] fi;
12: Entry_2(side);
13: Critical Section;
14: Wait();      /* wait at the barrier */
15: Exit_2(side)
```

```
procedure AccessTree(
    ptrT: pointer to TreeType, pos: 0..N - 1)
16: k := ptrT -> order;
17: if k = 0 then               /* base case */
18:     ptrT -> waiter := p;
19:     ExecuteCS(1);
20:     return
    fi;

21: indx := ⌊pos/2^{2^{k-1}}⌋;
22: ptrL := ptrT -> lower[indx];
23: if CAS(ptrL -> winner, ⊥, p) ≠ ⊥ then
24:     AccessTree(ptrL, pos mod 2^{2^{k-1}});
                /* recurse into the lower component */
25:     return
    fi;

26: ptrU := ptrT -> upper;
27: if CAS(ptrU -> winner, ⊥, p) ≠ ⊥ then
28:     AccessTree(ptrU, indx)
                /* recurse into the upper component */
    else
29:     if ptrT = &T_0 then
30:         ExecuteCS(0)
        else
31:         ptrT -> waiter := p;
32:         ExecuteCS(1)
        fi;

        /* update the upper component */
33:     ptrC := GetCleanTree(k - 1);
34:     ptrT -> upper := ptrC;
35:     delay(Δ_0);
36:     Enqueue(WaitingQueue, ptrU -> waiter)
    fi;

        /* update the lower component */
37: ptrC := GetCleanTree(k - 1);
38: ptrT -> lower[indx] := ptrC;
39: delay(Δ_0);
40: Enqueue(WaitingQueue, ptrL -> waiter)
```

Fig. 3. ALGORITHM T, unbounded space version. (Each private variable used in *AccessTree* is assumed to be on the call stack.)

have acquired only L_i, or neither L_i nor U.) To arbitrate between these two possibilities, an additional two-process mutual exclusion algorithm is invoked inside *ExecuteCS* (lines 12 and 15 in Fig. 3), which can be easily implemented in $\Theta(1)$ time [22]. Promoted processes invoke *ExecuteCS(side)* with *side* = 1, and other processes with *side* = 0. In any case, p later resets any component(s) it has acquired.

The algorithm also uses a serial waiting queue, named *WaitingQueue*, which is accessed only within exit sections. A "barrier" mechanism (lines 4 and 14) is used that ensures that multiple processes do not execute their exit sections concurrently. As a result, *WaitingQueue* can be implemented as a sequential data structure, in which each operation takes $\Theta(1)$ time. When a process p, inside its exit section, discovers another waiting process q, p adds q to the waiting queue. In addition, p dequeues a process r from the queue (if the queue is nonempty), and "promotes" r to its critical section (lines 5–10).

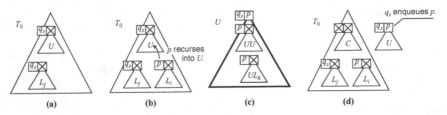

Fig. 4. An example of recursive execution. The left-side boxes represent the *winner* field; the right-side ones, *waiter*. **(a)** A process q_s acquires both L_j and U and performs a regular (non-promoted) entry. **(b)** Process p acquires L_i, but fails to acquire U. **(c)** p recurses into U, acquires its two components UL_k and UU, and becomes U's primary waiter. (Note that the tree depicted here is U, not T_0.) **(d)** Process q_s, in its exit section, updates $T_0.upper$ to point to a clean tree, C, delays itself, and enqueus p onto *WaitingQueue*.

The barrier is specified by two procedures `Wait` and `Signal`. Since executions of `Wait` are serialized by `Entry`$_2$ and `Exit`$_2$, we can easily implement these procedures in $O(1)$ time. In CC machines, `Wait` can be defined as "**await** *Flag*; *Flag* := *false*" and `Signal` as "*Flag* := *true*," where *Flag* is a shared boolean variable. In DSM machines, a slightly more complicated implementation is required, which can be found in [14].

Recursive execution. We now consider the case that a process p fails to acquire both of its components of T_0. (Until we consider the exit section below, p is assumed to be defined as such.) Assume that p fails to acquire S (which may be either L_i or U), because some other process q_s has already acquired it. The case for $S = U$ is illustrated in Fig. 4. In this case, p recurses into S (we say that p "enters" S), and executes an identical mutual exclusion algorithm, except for one difference: if p acquires both components of S along its path inside S (which we denote by SL_k and SU, respectively), then instead of entering its critical section, it writes its identity into another field *waiter* of S (Fig. 4(c)). We say that p is the *primary waiter* of S in this case. If p still fails to acquire both SL_k and SU, then it recurses further into the component it failed to acquire. Therefore, we have:

Property 1 A process p that enters a tree S ($\neq T_0$) eventually becomes the primary waiter of some constituent S' of S.

Once p becomes a primary waiter, it stops and waits until it is promoted by some other process.

After p enters S, it tries to acquire SL_k in $\Theta(1)$ steps. If p succeeds, then it tries to acquire SU in $\Theta(1)$ steps. Otherwise, some other process r has already acquired SL_k. That process will eventually attempt to acquire SU in $\Theta(1)$ steps, unless it has already done so. Since the first process to attempt to acquire SU succeeds, we have the following.

Property 2 If some process enters a tree S, then some process becomes S's primary waiter in $\Theta(1)$ steps, that is, in $O(\Delta)$ time.

Inside its exit section, process q_s (which has acquired S) first delays itself by $\Delta_0 = \Theta(\Delta)$ time, and then examines its path in order to discover other waiting processes (Fig. 4(d)). In particular, for each component q_s has acquired (including S), q_s determines if that component has a primary waiter. Thus:

Property 3 If a process q acquires a tree S, then q enqueues S's primary waiter (if any) in q's exit section.

As explained shortly, p may enter S only before q_s finishes its delay. Because p has entered S, by Property 2, q_s's delay ensures that q_s indeed finds a primary waiter of S.

If p is the primary waiter of S, then q_s enqueues p onto the waiting queue; otherwise, q_s enqueues the primary waiter of S, which eventually executes its exit section and examines the components of S it has acquired. Continuing in this manner, every process that stopped inside S, including p, is eventually enqueued onto the waiting queue. Thus, p eventually enters its critical section.

Exit-section execution. We now consider the exit section of a process p. As explained before, the barrier mechanism ensures that exit-section executions are serialized. For each component S of T_0 that is acquired by p (which may be L_i or U), p updates T_0's pointer for S so that it now points a "clean" tree C, as shown in Fig. 4(d). We assume the existence of a function $GetCleanTree$, which returns a pointer to a previously unused tree of a given order. (This results in unbounded space complexity. Space can be bounded by recycling used trees, as shown in [14].) Note that some process may still be executing inside S, which is now unlinked from T_0.

As explained above, after unlinking S, p delays itself by Δ_0, and thus ensures that if any process has entered S (the "old" component), then some process has become its primary waiter. p then checks for the primary waiter of S, and enqueues the waiter if it exists.

From the discussion so far, it is clear that the mutual exclusion algorithm at each tree T of order k incurs $\Theta(1)$ RMR-Δ time complexity, plus the time required for a recursive invocation at some component (of order $k - 1$) of T. (Note that p may recurse into either L_i or U, but not both.) Thus, $\Theta(k)$ RMR-Δ time complexity is incurred at T, and $\Theta(K) = \Theta(\log \log N)$ at T_0.

A version of ALGORITHM T with bounded space is presented in detail in [14]. From ALGORITHM T, we have the following theorem.

Theorem 1. *The mutual exclusion problem can be solved with* $\Theta(\log \log N)$ *RMR-Δ (or RMR) time complexity on CC or DSM machines in the known-delay model.* $\square$

3   Lower Bound: System Model

In this section, we present the model of a shared-memory system used in our lower-bound proof. Due to space limitations, we only prove the lower bound in Table 1 pertaining to the RMR-Δ measure. Our system model is similar to that used in [5, 8].

Shared-memory systems. A *shared-memory system* $\mathcal{S} = (C, P, V)$ consists of a set of computations C, a set of processes P, and a set of variables V. A *computation* is a finite sequence of timed events. A *timed event* is a pair (e, t), where e is an event and t is a nonnegative real value, specifying the time e is executed. An *event* e, executed by a process $p \in P$, has the form of $[p, \mathsf{Op}, \ldots]$. We call Op the *operation* of event e, denoted $op(e)$. Op can be one of the following: read(v), write(v), or delay, where v is a variable in V. For brevity, we sometimes use e_p to denote an event executed by process p. The following assumption formalizes requirements regarding the atomicity of events.

Atomicity Property: Each event e_p is one of the following.

- $e_p = [p, \text{read}(v), \alpha]$. In this case, e_p reads the value α from v. We call e_p a *read event*.
- $e_p = [p, \text{write}(v), \alpha]$. In this case, e_p writes the value α to v. We call e_p a *write event*.
- $e_p = [p, \text{delay}]$. In this case, e_p delays p by a fixed amount Δ, defined so that each event execution finishes in Δ time. We call e_p a *delay event*. $\qquad\qquad\square$

In a computation, event timings must appear in nondecreasing order. (When multiple events are executed at the same time, their effect is determined by the order they appear in a computation.) The value of variable v at the end of computation H, denoted $value(v, H)$, is the last value written to v in H (or the initial value of v if v is not written in H). The last event to write to v in H is denoted $writer\_event(v, H)$,[3] and the process that executes the event is denoted $writer(v, H)$. If v is not written by any event in H, then we let $writer(v, H) = \bot$ and $writer\_event(v, H) = \bot$. The execution time of the last event of H is denoted $last(H)$.

We use $\langle (e, t), \ldots \rangle$ to denote a computation that begins with the event e executed at time t, $\langle \rangle$ to denote the empty computation, and $H \circ G$ to denote the computation obtained by concatenating computations H and G. For a computation H and a set of processes Y, $H \mid Y$ denotes the subcomputation of H that contains all events of processes in Y. A computation H is a Y-*computation* iff $H = H \mid Y$. For simplicity, we abbreviate these definitions when applied to a singleton set of processes (*e.g.*, $H \mid p$ instead of $H \mid \{p\}$).

Mutual exclusion systems. We now define a special kind of shared-memory system, namely mutual exclusion systems, which are our main interest.

A *mutual exclusion system* $\mathcal{S} = (C, P, V)$ is a shared-memory system that satisfies the following properties. Each process $p \in P$ has an auxiliary variable $stat_p$ that ranges over $\{ncs, entry, exit\}$. The variable $stat_p$ is initially ncs and is accessed only by the following events: $Enter_p = [p, \text{write}(stat_p), entry]$, $CS_p = [p, \text{write}(stat_p), exit]$, and $Exit_p = [p, \text{write}(stat_p), ncs]$. We call these events *transition events*. These events represent the start of p's entry section, p's critical-section execution, and the end of p's exit section, respectively.

We henceforth assume each computation contains at most one $Enter_p$ event for each process p, because this is sufficient for our proof. The remaining requirements of a mutual exclusion system are as follows.

Definition: For a computation H, we define $\text{Act}(H)$, the set of *active processes* in H, as $\{p \in P : value(stat_p, H) \text{ is } entry \text{ or } exit\}$. $\qquad\qquad\square$

Exclusion: At most one process may be enabled to execute CS_p after any $H \in C$.

Progress (Livelock freedom): Given $H \in C$, if some process is active after H, then H can be extended by events of active processes so that some such process p eventually executes either CS_p or $Exit_p$.

Cache-coherent systems. On cache-coherent systems, some variable accesses may be handled locally, without causing interconnect traffic. In order to apply our lower bound to such systems, we do not count every read/write event, but only critical events, as defined below. As shown in [5, 14], the number of critical events by any process is an asymptotic lower bound for the number of events (by that process) that incur interconnect traffic in

---

[3] Although our definition of an event allows multiple instances of the same event, we assume that such instances are distinguishable from each other.

systems with any combinations of write-through/write-back and write-invalidate/write-update caching schemes.

Definition: Let e_p be an event in $H \in C$, and let $H = F \circ \langle e_p \rangle \circ \cdots$, where F is a subcomputation of H. We say that e_p is a *cache-miss event* in H if one of the following conditions holds: **(i)** it is the first read of a variable v by p; **(ii)** it writes a variable v such that $writer(v, F) \neq p$.   □

Definition: We say that an event e_p is *critical* iff one of the following conditions holds. **(i)** e_p accesses $stat_p$. (In this case, e_p is called a *transition event*.) **(ii)** e_p is a delay event. **(iii)** e_p is a cache-miss event.   □

Transition events are defined as critical because this allows us to combine certain cases in the proofs that follow. Since a process executes only three transition events per critical-section execution, this has no asymptotic impact.

Note that the above definition of a cache-miss event depends on the particular computation that contains the event, specifically the prefix of the computation preceding the event. Therefore, when saying that an event is (or is not) a cache-miss event or a critical event, the computation containing the event must be specified.

Properties of computations. The timing requirements of a mutual exclusion system are captured by requiring the following for each $H \in C$.

T1: For any two timed events (e_p, t) and (f_q, t') in H, if e_p precedes f_q, then $t \leq t'$ holds.

T2: For any timed event (e_p, t) in H, if $e_p \neq Exit_p$ and if $last(H) > t + \Delta$, then e_p is not the last event in $H \mid p$.

T3: For any two consecutive timed events (e_p, t) and (f_p, t') in $H \mid p$, the following holds:

$$\begin{cases} t' = t + \Delta, & \text{if } e_p \text{ is a delay event,} \\ t + \Delta_c \leq t' \leq t + \Delta, & \text{if } e_p \text{ is a cache-miss event,} \\ t \leq t' \leq t + \Delta, & \text{otherwise,} \end{cases}$$

where Δ_c is a lower bound (less than Δ) on the duration of a cache-miss event.

Note that T3 allows noncritical events to execute arbitrarily fast. If this were not the case, then a "free" delay statement that is not counted when assessing time complexity could be implemented by repeatedly executing noncritical events (*e.g.*, by reading a dummy variable). In fact, our model allows noncritical events that take zero duration. (Thus, our proof does not apply to completely synchronous systems.) We could have instead required them to have durations lower-bounded by an arbitrarily small positive constant, at the expense of more complicated bookkeeping in our proofs.

On the other hand, cache-miss events take some duration between Δ_c and Δ, and hence our lower bound applies to systems with both upper and lower bounds on the execution time of such events. All delay events are assumed to have an exact duration of Δ. Thus, the issue of whether delays are upper bounded does not arise in our proof.

We assume the following standard properties for computations: changing only the timings of a valid computation leaves it valid (provided that T1–T3 are preserved); a prefix of a valid computation is also valid; a process determines its next event only based on its execution history; and reading a variable returns the value last written to it, or its initial value if it has not been written.

4   Lower Bound: Proof Sketch

Our lower-bound proof focuses on a special class of computations called "regular" computations. A regular computation consists of events of two groups of processes, "invisible processes" and "visible processes." Informally, only a visible process may be known to other processes. Each invisible process is in its entry section, competing with other (invisible and visible) processes. A visible process may be in any section.

At the end of this section, a detailed overview of the proof is given. Here, we give cursory overview, so that the definition of a regular computation will make sense. Initially, we start with a regular computation in which all the processes in P are invisible. The proof proceeds by inductively constructing longer regular computations, until the desired lower bound is attained. At the mth induction step, we consider a regular computation H_m with n invisible processes and at most m visible processes. The regularity condition defined below ensures that *no participating process has knowledge of any other process that is invisible*. Thus, we can "erase" any invisible process (*i.e.*, remove its events from the computation) and still get a valid computation.

After H_m, some invisible processes may be "blocked" due to knowledge of visible processes — that is, they may start repeatedly reading variables read previously, not executing any critical event until visible processes take further steps. In order to construct a longer computation H_{m+1}, we need a "sufficient" number of unblocked processes. As shown later, it is possible to extend H_m to obtain a computation A by letting visible processes execute some further steps (and by possibly erasing some invisible processes) such that, after A, enough invisible processes are unblocked.

To construct H_{m+1}, we append to A one next critical event for each such unblocked process. Since these next critical events may introduce information flow, some invisible processes may need to be erased to ensure regularity. Sometimes erasing alone does not leave enough active processes for the next induction step. This may happen only if some variable v exists that is accessed by "many" of the critical events we are trying to append. In that case, we erase processes accessing other variables and then apply the "covering" strategy: we add the last process to write to v to the set of visible processes. All subsequent reads of v must read the value written by this process, and hence information flow from invisible processes is prevented. Thus, we can construct. H_{m+1}.

The induction continues until the desired lower bound of $\Omega(\log \log N)$ critical events is achieved. This basic proof strategy of erasing and covering has been used previously to prove several other lower bounds for concurrent systems ([1, 5, 10, 15, 20] — see also [7]). Note that, in asynchronous systems, we can "stall" *all* invisible processes until all visible processes finish execution. Thus, blocked processes pose no problem. However, this is clearly impossible in semi-synchronous systems, resulting in additional complications (*e.g.*, finding enough unblocked processes). We now define the regularity condition.

Definition: Let $S = (C, P, V)$ be a mutual exclusion system. We say that $H \in C$ is *regular* iff there exist two disjoint sets of processes, $\text{Inv}(H)$, the set of *invisible processes*, and $\text{Vis}(H)$, the set of *visible processes*, satisfying $\text{Inv}(H) \cup \text{Vis}(H) = \{p \in P: H \mid p \neq \langle \rangle\}$, such that the following conditions hold.

- **R1:** If a process p writes to a variable v, and if another process q reads *that* value from v, then p is visible (*i.e.*, $p \in \text{Vis}(H)$).

- **R2:** If a variable v is accessed by more than one process in H and if H contains a write to v, then $writer(v, H) \in \mathrm{Vis}(H)$ holds.[4]
- **R3:** Every invisible process is in its entry section.
- **R4:** If two events e_p and f_p access a variable v, and if some process writes v in between, then some visible process writes v between e_p and f_p. (This condition is used to show that the property of being a critical event is preserved after erasing some invisible processes.) □

Detailed proof overview. Initially, we start with a regular computation H_1, where $\mathrm{Inv}(H_1) = P$, $\mathrm{Vis}(H_1) = \{\}$, and each process has one critical event, executed at time 0. We then inductively show that other longer computations exist, the last of which establishes our lower bound. Each computation is obtained by covering some variable and/or erasing some processes.

At the mth induction step, we consider a computation $H = H_m$ in which each process in $\mathrm{Inv}(H)$ executes m critical events, $|\mathrm{Vis}(H)| \le m$, and each active process executes its last event at the same time $t = t_m$. Furthermore, we assume

$$\log \log n = \Theta(\log \log N) \quad \text{and} \quad m = O(\log \log N), \tag{1}$$

where $n = |\mathrm{Inv}(H)|$. We construct a regular computation $G = H_{m+1}$ such that $\mathrm{Act}(G)$ consists of $\Omega(\sqrt{n}/(\log \log N)^2)$ processes, each of which executes $m + 1$ critical events in G. (To see why (1) is reasonable, note that $\log \log n$ is initially $\log \log N$ and decreases by $\Theta(1)$ at each induction step.) The construction method is explained below. For now, we assume that all n invisible processes are unblocked. At the end of this section, we explain how to adjust the argument if this is not the case.

Definition: If H is a regular computation, then a process $p \in \mathrm{Inv}(H)$ is *blocked after H* iff there exists no p-computation A such that A contains a critical event (in $H \circ A$) and $H \circ A \in C$ holds. □

Due to the Exclusion property, each unblocked process (except at most one) executes a critical event *before* entering its critical section. We call these events "next" critical events, and denote the corresponding set of processes by Y. We consider three cases, based on the variables accessed by these next critical events.

Case 1: Delay events. If there exist $\Omega(\sqrt{n})$ processes that have a next critical event that is a delay event, then we erase all other invisible processes and append these delay events. Since a delay event does not cause information flow, the resulting computation is regular. (Such delays may force visible processes to take steps. We explain how to handle this after Case 3.)

In the remaining two cases, we can assume that $\Theta(n)$ next critical events are critical reads or writes.

Case 2: Erasing strategy (Fig. 5). Assume that there exist $\Omega(\sqrt{n})$ distinct variables that are accessed by some next critical events. For each such variable v, we select one process whose next critical event accesses v. Let Y' be the set of selected processes. Since

---

[4] Note that R2 is not a consequence of R1. For example, consider a case in which a process $q = writer(v, H)$ writes v *after* another process p reads v.

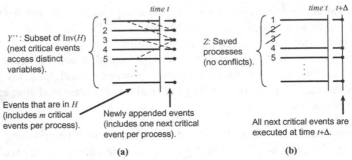

Fig. 5. Erasing strategy. Here and in later figures, black circles ($\bullet$) respresent critical events.

we have at most m visible processes, and since each visible process executes at most $\log \log N$ critical events in H (otherwise, our lower bound is achieved), they collectively access at most $m \log \log N$ distinct variables. We erase processes in Y' that access these variables. By (1), we have $m \log \log N = o(\sqrt{n})$, so we still have $\Omega(\sqrt{n})$ processes left. Let Y'' be the subset of Y' that is not erased (Fig. 5(a)). We now eliminate remaining possible conflicts among processes in Y'' by constructing a "conflict graph" $\mathcal{G}$ as follows.

Each process p in Y'' is considered a vertex in $\mathcal{G}$. By induction, p has m critical events in H. If such an event accesses the same variable as the next critical event of some other process q, then introduce the edge $\{p, q\}$.

Since the next critical events of processes in Y'' access distinct variables, each process generates at most m edges. By applying Turán's theorem (see [14]), we can find a subset $Z \subseteq Y''$ with no conflicts such that $|Z| = \Omega(\sqrt{n}/m)$. By retaining Z and erasing all other invisible processes, we can eliminate all conflicts (Fig. 5(b)) and construct G.

Case 3: Covering strategy. Assume that the next critical events collectively access $O(\sqrt{n})$ distinct variables. Since there are $\Theta(n)$ next critical reads/writes, some variable v is accessed by $\Omega(\sqrt{n})$ next critical events. Let Y_v be the set of these processes. First, we retain Y_v and erase all other invisible processes. Let the resulting computation be H'. We then arrange the next critical events of Y_v by placing all writes before all reads, and letting all writes and reads execute at time $t + \Delta$. In this way, the only information flow among processes in Y_v is that from the "last writer" of v, denoted p_{LW}, to any subsequent reader (of v). We then add p_{LW} to the set of visible processes, i.e., $p_{\mathrm{LW}} \in \mathrm{Vis}(G)$ holds. Thus, no invisible process is known to other processes, and we can construct G.

Finally, after any of the three cases, we let each active visible process execute one more event (critical or noncritical), so that it "keeps pace" with the invisible processes and preserves T2 and T3. Each such event may cause a conflict with at most one invisible process, so we erase at most m more invisible processes, which is $o(\sqrt{n}/m)$, by (1).

From the discussion so far, we have the following lemma.

Lemma 1. *Let H be a regular computation satisfying the following: $n = |\mathrm{Inv}(H)|$, each $p \in \mathrm{Inv}(H)$ has exactly m critical events in H and is unblocked after H, $|\mathrm{Vis}(H)| \leq m$, and each active process executes its last event at time t.*

Then, there exists a regular computation G satisfying the following: $|\mathrm{Inv}(G)| = \Omega(\sqrt{n}/m)$, each $p \in \mathrm{Inv}(G)$ has exactly $m + 1$ critical events in G, $|\mathrm{Vis}(G)| \leq m + 1$, and each active process in G executes its last event at time $t + \Delta$. $\qquad\Box$

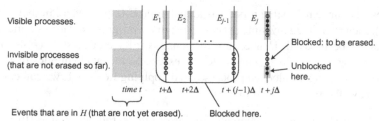

Fig. 6. Finding unblocked processes. In this figure, black and white circles (●, ○) respresent critical and noncritical events, and shaded boxes represent computations made of possibly many events.

Finding unblocked processes. We now explain how we can find "enough" unblocked invisible processes. Consider $F = H \mid \text{Vis}(H)$, a computation obtained by erasing all invisible processes. It can be easily shown that F is a regular computation in C. Let the processes in $\text{Vis}(H)$ execute in "lockstep," *i.e.*, let each process in $\text{Vis}(H)$ execute exactly one event per each interval of length Δ. By extending F in such a way until all visible processes finish execution, we have an extension $F \circ D = F \circ D_1 \circ D_2 \cdots \circ D_{k'}$, where each D_j contains exactly one event by each process in $\text{Vis}(H)$, executed at time $t + j\Delta$. Since we allow noncritical events to take zero time, if a segment D_j (where $j < k'$) consists of only noncritical events, then we can "merge" it into the next segment and create a segment of length Δ. Continuing in this way, we can define an extension $F \circ E = F \circ E_1 \circ E_2 \circ \cdots \circ E_k$, such that: **(i)** D and E consist of the same sequence of events (only event timings are different); **(ii)** every event in E_j is executed at time $t + j\Delta$; **(iii)** every E_j (except perhaps the last one) contains some critical event; **(iv)** any critical event in E_j is the last event by that process in E_j.

If E contains more than $m \log \log N$ critical events, then some visible process executes more than $\log \log N$ critical events in E, and hence our lower bound is achieved. Thus, assume otherwise. By (iii), we have $k \leq m \log \log N + 1$.

For each E_j, starting with E_1, we do the following to find n' invisible processes that are unblocked simultaneously, where $n' = n/(k + 1) - m$. We first append the *noncritical* events of E_j. It can be shown that noncritical events do not cause information flow. After that, we determine how many invisible processes are unblocked. If n' or more such processes are unblocked, then we can erase all blocked invisible processes and construct G by applying Lemma 1, as depicted in Fig. 6. Otherwise, we erase the *unblocked* invisible processes, and let each remaining (blocked) invisible process execute one noncritical event, in order to keep pace. (See $E_1, \ldots, E_{j-1}$ of Fig. 6.) Finally, we append the critical events of E_j. By (iv), each visible process may execute at most one critical event in E_j. Thus, E_j has at most m critical events. If some critical event reads a variable written by an invisible process, then we erase that invisible process to prevent information flow. Thus, we can append the critical events in E_j, erase at most m invisible processes, and preserve regularity. We then repeat the same procedure for the next segment E_{j+1}, and so on.

Note that we erase at most $n' + m = n/(k + 1)$ invisible processes to append each E_j. It is clear that either we find n' invisible unblocked processes (after appending $E_1 \circ \cdots \circ E_j$, for some $0 \leq j \leq k$), or we append all of E. However, in the latter case, we have erased at most $kn/(k + 1)$ invisible processes. Thus, at least $n/(k + 1)$ invisible processes remain after E. Moreover, since each such process may only know of visible processes, and since no visible process is active after E (*i.e.*, they are in their noncritical sections), each remaining invisible process must make progress toward its critical section, *i.e.*, it cannot be blocked. Hence, in either case, we have at least $n/(k+1) - m = \Omega(n/(m \log \log N))$ unblocked invisible processes. (Note that (1) implies $m = o(n/k)$.) Therefore, by erasing all blocked processes and applying Lemma 1, we can construct G. Thus, we have the following lemma.

Lemma 2. *Let H be a regular computation satisfying the following: $n = |\mathrm{Inv}(H)|$, each $p \in \mathrm{Inv}(H)$ has exactly m critical events in H, $|\mathrm{Vis}(H)| \leq m$, and each active process executes its last event at time t.*

Then, there exists a regular computation G satisfying the following: $|\mathrm{Inv}(G)| = \Omega(\sqrt{n}/(\log \log N)^2)$, $|\mathrm{Vis}(G)| \leq m + 1$, each $p \in \mathrm{Inv}(G)$ has exactly $m + 1$ critical events in G, and each active process executes its last event at time t', for some $t' > t$. $\square$

By applying Lemma 2 inductively, we have the following.

Theorem 2. *For any mutual exclusion system $S = (C, P, V)$, there exists a computation in which a process incurs $\Omega(\log \log N)$ RMR-Δ time complexity in order to enter and then exit its critical section.* $\square$

As shown in [14], the above lower bound can be adapted for the RMR measure, provided delays are unbounded. Thus, we have the following.

Theorem 3. *For any mutual exclusion system $S = (C, P, V)$ with unbounded delays, there exists a computation in which a process incurs $\Omega(\log \log N)$ RMR time complexity in order to enter and then exit its critical section.*

5   Concluding Remarks

To the best of our knowledge, this paper is the first work on timing-based mutual exclusion algorithms in which all busy-waiting is by local spinning. Our specific interest has been to determine whether lower RMR time complexity is possible (for mutual exclusion algorithms based on reads, writes, and comparison primitives) in semi-synchronous systems with delays. We have shown that this is indeed the case, regardless of whether delays are assumed to be counted when assessing time complexity, and whether delay values are assumed to be upper bounded. For each system model and time measure that arises by resolving these issues, we have presented an algorithm that is asymptotically time-optimal. Interestingly, under the RMR measure with unbounded delays, DSM machines allow provably lower time complexity than CC machines. In contrast to this situation, it is usually the case that designing efficient local-spin algorithms is easier for CC machines than for DSM machines.

References

1. Y. Afek, P. Boxer, and D. Touitou. Bounds on the shared memory requirements for long-lived and adaptive objects. In *Proceedings of the 19th Annual ACM Symposium on Principles of Distributed Computing*, pages 81–89. ACM, July 2000.

2. R. Alur, H. Attiya, and G. Taubenfeld. Time-adaptive algorithms for synchronization. In *Proceedings of the 26th Annual ACM Symposium on Theory of Computing*, pages 800–809. ACM, May 1994.
3. R. Alur and G. Taubenfeld. How to share an object: A fast timing-based solution. In *Proceedings of the 5th IEEE Symposium on Parallel and Distributed Processing*, pages 470–477. IEEE, 1993.
4. R. Alur and G. Taubenfeld. Fast timing-based algorithms. *Distributed Computing*, 10(1):1–10, 1996.
5. J. Anderson and Y.-J. Kim. An improved lower bound for the time complexity of mutual exclusion. In *Proceedings of the 20th Annual ACM Symposium on Principles of Distributed Computing*, pages 90–99. ACM, August 2001.
6. J. Anderson and Y.-J. Kim. Local-spin mutual exclusion using fetch-and-ϕ primitives. In *Proceedings of the 23rd IEEE International Conference on Distributed Computing Systems*, pages 538–547. IEEE, May 2003.
7. J. Anderson, Y.-J. Kim, and T. Herman. Shared-memory mutual exclusion: Major research trends since 1986. *Distributed Computing*, 2003 (to appear).
8. J. Anderson and J.-H. Yang. Time/contention tradeoffs for multiprocessor synchronization. *Information and Computation*, 124(1):68–84, January 1996.
9. T. Anderson. The performance of spin lock alternatives for shared-memory multiprocessors. *IEEE Transactions on Parallel and Distributed Systems*, 1(1):6–16, January 1990.
10. J. Burns and N. Lynch. Mutual exclusion using indivisible reads and writes. In *Proceedings of the 18th Annual Allerton Conference on Communication, Control, and Computing*, pages 833–842, 1980.
11. R. Cypher. The communication requirements of mutual exclusion. In *Proceedings of the Seventh Annual Symposium on Parallel Algorithms and Architectures*, pages 147–156, June 1995.
12. G. Graunke and S. Thakkar. Synchronization algorithms for shared-memory multiprocessors. *IEEE Computer*, 23:60–69, June 1990.
13. J. Kessels. Arbitration without common modifiable variables. *Acta Informatica*, 17:135–141, 1982.
14. Y.-J. Kim and J. Anderson. Timing-based mutual exclusion with local spinning. Manuscript, July 2003. Available from http://www.cs.unc.edu/~anderson/papers.html.
15. Y.-J. Kim and J. Anderson. A time complexity bound for adaptive mutual exclusion. In *Proceedings of the 15th International Symposium on Distributed Computing*, October 2001.
16. L. Lamport. A fast mutual exclusion algorithm. *ACM Transactions on Computer Systems*, 5(1):1–11, February 1987.
17. N. Lynch and N. Shavit. Timing based mutual exclusion. In *Proceedings of the 13th IEEE Real-Time Systems Symposium*, pages 2–11. IEEE, December 1992.
18. J. Mellor-Crummey and M. Scott. Algorithms for scalable synchronization on shared-memory multiprocessors. *ACM Transactions on Computer Systems*, 9(1):21–65, February 1991.
19. S. Ramamurthy, M. Moir, and J. Anderson. Real-time object sharing with minimal support. In *Proceedings of the 15th Annual ACM Symposium on Principles of Distributed Computing*, pages 233–242. ACM, May 1996.
20. E. Styer and G. Peterson. Tight bounds for shared memory symmetric mutual exclusion. In *Proceedings of the 8th Annual ACM Symposium on Principles of Distributed Computing*, pages 177–191. ACM, August 1989.
21. P. van Emde Boas. Preserving order in a forest in less than logarithmic time and linear space. *Information Processing Letters*, 6(3):80–82, June 1977.
22. J.-H. Yang and J. Anderson. A fast, scalable mutual exclusion algorithm. *Distributed Computing*, 9(1):51–60, August 1995.

On the Uncontended Complexity of Consensus

Victor Luchangco[1], Mark Moir[1], and Nir Shavit[2]

[1] Sun Microsystems Laboratories, 1 Network Drive, Burlington, MA 01803
[2] The School of Computer Science, Tel Aviv University, Tel Aviv 69978, Israel

Abstract. Lock-free algorithms are not required to guarantee a bound on the number of steps an operation takes under contention, so we cannot use the usual worst-case analysis to quantify them. A natural alternative is to consider the worst-case time complexity of operations executed in the more common *uncontended* case.

Many state-of-the-art lock-free algorithms rely on compare-and-swap (CAS) or similar operations with high consensus number to allow effective interprocess coordination. Given the fundamental nature of consensus operations to interprocess coordination, and the fact that instructions such as CAS are usually significantly more costly than simple loads and stores, it seems natural to consider a complexity measure that counts the number of operations with higher consensus number.

In this paper we show that, despite its natural appeal, such a measure is not useful. We do so by showing that one can devise a wait-free implementation of the universal compare-and-swap operation, with a "fast path" that requires only a constant number of loads and stores when the CAS is executed without contention, and uses a hardware CAS operation only if there is contention. Thus, at least in theory, any CAS-based algorithm can be transformed into one that does not invoke *any* CAS operations along its uncontended "fast path", so simply counting the number of such operations invoked in this case is meaningless.

1 Introduction

Compare-and-swap (CAS)—an operation with infinite consensus number in the wait-free/lock-free hierarchy [9]—has been used in implementing numerous non-blocking data structures and operations. Recently, it has been used to implement non-blocking work-stealing deques [1,8], linked lists [6,23], hash tables [23,26], NCAS [7,10], and software transactional memories [14]. The implementations of these data structures adopt an optim istic approach, in which an operation completes quickly in the absence of contention but may incur a significant performance penalty when it encounters contention. The assumption in this approach is that contention is generally low, so most operations will complete without incurring the penalty.

Some useful non-blocking progress conditions, such as lock-freedom and the recently proposed obstruction-freedom condition [12], are not required to provide a worst-case bound on operation time complexity in the contended case. Therefore, standard worst-case analysis is not applicable to such algorithms. An alternative is to count the various types of synchronization operations executed in the

F.E. Fich (Ed.): DISC 2003, LNCS 2848, pp. 45–59, 2003.

presumably common uncontended executions, extending an approach taken by Lamport [19], who counted the number of loads and stores on the uncontended "fast path" of a mutual exclusion algorithm.

The cost of executing a hardware CAS operation has been estimated to be anywhere from 3 to 60 times higher than that of a simple load or store, depending on the architecture [2,17], and this relative cost is expected to grow [16]. Thus, it is natural to consider a complexity measure that counts the number of CAS operations invoked on the uncontended path.

This paper shows that, however natural, such a complexity measure is not useful. We achieve this by presenting a linearizable, wait-free implementation of a shared variable that supports load, store[1] and CAS operations that do not invoke expensive hardware synchronization operations (such as CAS) in the uncontended case. We call our implementation fast-CAS.

Fast-CAS variables implemented using our algorithm can be allocated and deallocated dynamically. Unlike many non-blocking algorithms, our algorithm is population-oblivious [13]; that is, it does not require knowledge of a bound on the number of threads that access it. When there are V fast-CAS variables and T threads, our algorithm requires $O(T + V)$ space. Therefore, the incremental space overhead for each new variable and each new thread is constant.

The key to our fast-CAS implementation is the understanding that one can build a mechanism to detect contention and default to using hardware CAS only in that case, in a way that allows for a fast-path consensus mechanism that uses only a constant number of multi-writer shared registers when there is no contention. We explain this construction in stages, first exposing the intricacies of building a wait-free one-shot fast-path consensus algorithm (Section 3), and then presenting our reusable fast-path CAS implementation in detail (Section 4).

Our fast-CAS object is widely applicable because it fully complies with the semantics of a shared variable on which atomic load, store, and CAS operations can be performed repeatedly. As such, it can be used as a "black box" in any CAS-based algorithm in the literature. Thus, it implies the following theorem:

Any CAS-based concurrent algorithm, blocking or non-blocking, can be transformed to one that does not invoke hardware CAS operations if there is no contention.

Though our algorithm is widely applicable, it should be viewed primarily as a theoretical result, as it is unlikely to provide performance benefits in the common shared-memory multiprocessor architectures in which we are most interested (the "fast" part of the name relates more to the motivation than to the end result). Our fast-CAS implementation—which requires up to six loads and four stores in the absence of contention—is likely to be at least as expensive as invoking a hardware CAS operation on such architectures. Moreover, the algorithm depends

---

[1] In this paper, we show only how to implement load and CAS operations; store is a straightforward extension of CAS.

on sequential consistency [18] for correctness, and must therefore be augmented with expensive memory barrier operations on many modern architectures.[2]

Nevertheless, our result implies that it is never necessary to invoke a hardware CAS operation if there is no contention, regardless of the non-blocking progress condition considered. This has important consequences both for the search for a separation between novel consistency conditions such as obstruction-freedom [12] and stronger progress properties in modern shared-memory multiprocessors [9], and for guiding our thinking when designing and evaluating non-blocking algorithms. Specifically, it shows that what we and others have considered to be a natural measure—the number of CAS operations invoked by an uncontended operation—is not a useful measure for either purpose.

Unrelated Work

Because CAS can be used to implement wait-free consensus, while loads and stores alone are not sufficient, our result may seem counterintuitive to some readers familiar with various impossibility results and lower bounds in the literature. In particular, using the bivalency proof technique of Fischer, Lynch and Paterson [5], Loui and Abu-Amara [20] showed that no deterministic, wait-free algorithm can implement consensus using only loads and stores. Furthermore, Fich, Herlihy and Shavit [4] showed that even nondeterministic consensus algorithms require $\Omega(\sqrt{T})$ space per consensus object for implementations from historyless objects, where T is the number of participants. In contrast, our algorithm is wait-free and deterministic, uses only constant space per fast-CAS variable, and uses only loads and stores in the uncontended case.

This apparent contradiction can be resolved by understanding that the bad executions at the core of these impossibility proofs rely on interleaving the steps of multiple threads. Therefore, these results do not apply to our algorithm, which can use CAS in these contended executions.

Organization of this paper: Section 2 presents some preliminaries. In Section 3, we illustrate the intuition behind the key ideas in our CAS implementation by presenting a much simpler one-shot wait-free consensus algorithm. Then, in Section 4, we present our fast-CAS implementation in detail. We sketch a linearizability proof in Section 5. Concluding remarks appear in Section 6.

2   Preliminaries

The correctness condition we consider for our implementations is that of linearizability [15]. Informally, a linearizable implementation of an object that supports a set of operations guarantees that every execution of every operation can be considered to take effect at a unique point between its invocation and response,

---

[2] In simple performance experiments conducted with the help of Ori Shalev, our fast-CAS implementation performed slightly worse than hardware CAS.

such that the sequence of operations taken in the order of these points is consistent with the sequential specification of the implemented operations.

For the purposes of presentation, we consider a shared-memory multiprocessor system that supports linearizable load, store, and compare-and-swap (CAS) instructions for accessing memory. A CAS(a,e,n) instruction takes three parameters: an address a, an expected value e, and a new value n. If the value currently stored at address a matches the expected value e, then CAS stores the new value n at address a and returns true; we say that the CAS succeeds in this case. Otherwise, CAS returns false and does not modify the memory; we say that the CAS fails in this case.

3   One-Shot Consensus

Before presenting our fast-CAS implementation in detail, we first illustrate the key idea behind this algorithm by presenting a simple wait-free consensus algorithm. In the consensus problem [5], each process begins with an input value, and each process that terminates must decide on a value. It is required that every process that decides on a value decides the same value, and that this value is the input value of at least one process.

```
shared variables              val_t propose(val) {
    val_t V;   // value        1: if splitter()
    bool C;    // contention    2:     V = val;
    val_t D;   // decision value 3:     if ¬C return val;
                               else
initially                      4:     C = true;
    ¬C ∧                       5:     if V ≠ ⊥
    D = ⊥ ∧                    6:         val = V;
    V = ⊥                      7: CAS(&D,⊥,val);
                               8: return D;
```

Fig. 1. Simple wait-free consensus algorithm.

Our simple consensus algorithm, shown in Fig. 1, has the property that if a single process p executes the entire algorithm without any other process starting to execute it, then p reaches a decision using only read and write operations. The high-level intuition about how this is achieved is the same as for several read-write-based consensus algorithms in the literature. Specifically, if p runs for long enough without any other process starting to execute, then p writes information sufficient for other processes that run later to determine that p has already decided on its own value, and then determines that no other process has yet begun executing. In this case, p can return its own input value; processes that run later will determine that it has done so, and return the same value.

From results mentioned in Section 1, we know that read-write-based consensus algorithms cannot guarantee termination in bounded time in all executions. Some such algorithms (e.g., the algorithm of Saks, Shavit and Woll [25]) use randomization to provide termination with high probability. The algorithm in Fig. 1 takes a different approach: in case of contention, it employs a CAS operation to reach consensus. Below we briefly explain our algorithm and how it avoids the use of CAS in the absence of contention, and employs CAS to ensure that every process reaches a decision within a bounded number of steps in the face of contention.

Central to our consensus algorithm is the use of a "splitter"[3] function. The splitter function has the following properties:

1. if one process completes executing the splitter function before any other process starts, then that process "wins" the splitter (i.e., the function returns true); and
2. at most one process wins the splitter.

In addition to the shared variables used to implement the splitter function, the algorithm employs three other shared variables. V is used by the process (if any) that wins the splitter to record its input value. C is used by processes that detect contention by losing the splitter to indicate to any process that wins the splitter that contention has been detected. D is used by processes that detect contention to determine a consensus decision. C is initialized to false, and V and D are both initialized to ⊥, a special value that is assumed not to be the input value of any process.

Consider what happens if process p runs alone. By Property 1 above, p wins the splitter (line 1), writes its input value to V (line 2), and then—because no other process is executing—reads false from C and returns p's input value. By Property 2, any subsequent process q loses the splitter, sets C to true (line 4), and then reads V. Because p completed before q started, q sees p's input value (which is not ⊥) in V, changes its input value to that value (line 6), and attempts to CAS it into D (line 7). Because all such processes behave the same way, whether q's CAS succeeds or not, q returns p's input value, which it reads from D (line 8).

Now suppose no process runs alone. If all processes return from line 8, it is easy to see that they all return the same value. If any process p returns from line 3, then it won the splitter, so all other processes lose the splitter and return from line 8. Furthermore, p writes its input value to V before any process executes line 4, so all other processes see p's input value in V on line 5 and, as explained above, return it from line 8.

In the algorithm presented in Fig. 1, all processes except possibly one invoke a CAS operation. We can modify this algorithm so that, provided one process completes before any other starts, none of the processes invoke CAS: Any process

---

[3] Several variations on Lamport's "fast path" mechanism for mutual exclusion [19] have been used in wait-free renaming algorithms, beginning with the work of Moir and Anderson [24]. These mechanisms have come to be known as *splitters* in the renaming literature [3].

that would have returned from line 3 first writes its input value into D, and before invoking CAS, all processes check whether D = ⊥, and if not, they instead return the value found. Thus, this algorithm can replace a consensus object (or a CAS variable that changes value at most once) in any non-blocking algorithm without changing the asymptotic time or space complexity of the algorithm. However, again, we do not believe such a substitution is likely to provide a performance benefit in practice in current architectures; the immediate value of our results is in their implications about useful complexity measures of non-blocking algorithms, and in guiding results that attempt to establish a separation between non-blocking progress conditions.

4   Wait-Free CAS Implementation

The one-shot consensus algorithm described in the previous section illustrates the basic idea behind the fast-CAS implementation presented in this section: we use a splitter to detect the simple uncontended case, and then use a hardware CAS operation to recover when contention complicates matters. However, because the CAS implementation is long-lived, supporting multiple changes of value, it is more complicated. The first step towards supporting multiple changes is showing that the splitter can be reset and reused in the absence of contention. However, after contention has been encountered, we still have to allow value changes, and also when the contention dies down, we want to be able to again avoid the use of the hardware CAS operation.

These goals are achieved by introducing a level of indirection: we associate with each implemented variable a fixed location which, at any point in time, contains a pointer to a memory block; we call this block the currentblock for that variable. Each block contains a value field V; under "normal" circumstances, the V field of the current block contains the abstract value of the implemented variable. A block is active when it becomes current, and remains active and current as long as there is no contention. While the current block is active, operations can complete by acting only on that block without using CAS or any other strong synchronization primitives. When there is contention, an operation may make the current block inactive, which prevents the abstract value from changing while that block remains current. Once inactive, a block remains inactive. Therefore, an operation that wishes to change the abstract value when the current block is inactive must replace the block (using CAS) with a new active block.[4]

Data Structures

The structure of a block and C-like pseudocode for WFRead and WFCAS are shown in Fig. 2. For simplicity, we present the code for a single location L; it is straightforward to modify our code to support multiple locations.

---

[4] As discussed later, this operation invokes CAS even it executes alone. However, once the current block is replaced with an active block, no subsequent operation invokes CAS until contention is again detected.

```
struct blk_s {
    pidtype X;    // splitter
    bool Y;       //   variables
    val_t V;      //   value
    bool C;       // contention
    val_t D;      // decision value
} blk_t
```

initially For some b,

$$L = b \land$$
$$\neg b \to Y \land$$
$$\neg b \to C \land$$
$$b \to D = \bot \land$$
$$b \to V = \text{initial value}$$

```
val_t decide(blk_t *b) {
1:  v = b→V;
2:  CAS(&b→D,⊥,v);
3:  return b→D;
}
```

```
blk_t *get_new_block(val_t nv) {
4:  nb = malloc(sizeof(blk_t));
5:  nb→Y = false;
6:  nb→C = false;
7:  nb→D = ⊥;
8:  nb→V = nv;
9:  return nb;
}
```

```
val_t WFRead() {
10: blk_t *b = L;
11: val_t v = b→V;
12: if (¬b→C) return v;              R1
13: return decide(b);                R2
}
```

```
bool WFCAS(val_t ev, val_t nv) {
14: if (ev == nv) return WFRead()==ev;   C1
15: blk_t *b = L;
16: b→X = p;
17: if (b→Y) goto 27;
18: b→Y = true;
19: if (b→X ≠ p) goto 27;
20: v = b→V;
21: if (b→C) goto 28;
22: if (v ≠ ev)
        b→Y = false;
        return false;                C2
23: b→V = nv;
24: if (b→C)
25:     if (decide(b) == nv) return true;   C3
        goto 28;
26: b→Y = false;
        return true;                 C4
27: b→C = true;
28: if (decide(b) ≠ ev) return false;   C5
29: nb = get_new_block(nv);
30: return CAS(&L,b,nb);             C6
}
```

Fig. 2. Wait-free implementation of WFRead and WFCAS. Statement labels indicate atomicity assumptions for proof, as explained in Section 5.

A block b has five fields: The C field indicates whether the block is active ($b \to C$ holds when b is inactive, i.e., contention has been detected since b became current), and the V field of the current block contains the abstract value while that block is active. The D field is used to determine the abstract value while the block is current but inactive. (The D field is initialized to $\bot$, a special value that is not L's initial value, nor passed to any WFCAS operation.) The X and Y fields are used to implement the splitter that is used to detect contention (the splitter code is included explicitly in lines 16 to 19). For this algorithm, winning the splitter is interpreted as reaching line 20; recall that a process always wins the splitter if there is no contention. If the splitter does detect contention, then the operation branches to line 27, where it makes the block inactive.

Below we describe the WFCAS and WFRead operations in more detail. These descriptions are sufficient to understand our algorithm, but do not consider all cases. We sketch a formal correctness proof in Section 5.

The WFCAS Operation

A WFCAS operation whose expected and new values are equal is trivially reduced
to a WFRead operation (discussed below); WFCAS simply invokes WFRead in this
case (line 14). This is not simply an optimization; it is needed for wait-freedom,
as explained later. Henceforth, assume the expected and new values differ.

Suppose a WFCAS operation reads b when it executes line 15—that is, b is
the current block at this time—and then goes through the splitter of block b
(lines 16 to 19), reaching line 20, and reads v from $b{\rightarrow}V$. As long as b is the
current block, the splitter guarantees that until this operation resets the splitter
(by setting $b{\rightarrow}Y$ to false in line 22 or 26), no other operation executes lines 20
to 26 (see Lemma 1 in Section 5).

If b is active throughout this operation's execution (checked on lines 21
and 24), then $b{\rightarrow}V$ contains the abstract value during that interval, so the operation can operate directly on $b{\rightarrow}V$. Specifically, if $b{\rightarrow}V$ does not contain the
operation's expected value, the operation resets the splitter, and returns false
(line 22). Otherwise, the operation stores its new value in $b{\rightarrow}V$ (line 23). Because
the splitter guarantees that no other process writes $b{\rightarrow}V$ before the operation
completes, this store changes the abstract value from the operation's expected
value to its new value (assuming b remains active throughout the operation).

If, after writing $b{\rightarrow}V$, the operation discovers that b is no longer active
(line 24), then it does not know if its store succeeded in changing the abstract
value because the store may have occurred before or after b became inactive; no
process can ascertain the order of these events. Instead, processes that find (or
make) the current block inactive use a simple agreement protocol (by invoking
decide(b) in line 25 or 28) to determine the value that is the abstract value from
the moment that b becomes inactive until b is replaced as the current block; we
call this the decision value of b. Processes make this determination by attempt-
ing to change $b{\rightarrow}D$ from the special value $\perp$ to a non-$\perp$ value read from $b{\rightarrow}V$
(line 1). This is achieved using a CAS operation (line 2), so that all processes
determine the same decision value (line 3) for block b.

The decision value of block b is crucial to the correctness of our algorithm;
we must ensure that it is chosen such that the abstract value changes when
b becomes inactive if and only if a WFCAS operation executing at that point,
with expected and new values corresponding to the abstract values immediately
before and after the change, is considered to have taken effect at that point.

As described above, the tricky case occurs when a WFCAS operation by some
process p stores its new value to $b{\rightarrow}V$—where b is the block it determined to
be current when it executed line 15—and then determines at line 24 that b has
become inactive.

If p's store occurs before b becomes inactive, then the abstract value changes
at the store, and so the WFCAS operation must return true. This is ensured by
our algorithm because the decision value of b is a value read from $b{\rightarrow}V$ after b
becomes inactive, and the splitter ensures that no other value is stored into $b{\rightarrow}V$
after p's store and before p's operation completes (Lemma 1).

On the other hand, if p's store occurs after b becomes inactive then the abstract value does not change at the time of the store because, as stated above, from the time b becomes inactive until b is no longer current, the abstract value is the decision value of b. However, if the decision value of b is p's new value, then p cannot determine the relative order of p's store and b becoming inactive. Therefore, p returns true (line 25) in this case too, which is correct because the abstract value changes from p's expected value to p's new value when b becomes inactive. (The properties of the splitter and the test in line 22 together ensure that the abstract value is p's expected value immediately before b becomes inactive in this case.)

Otherwise, the decision value of b is not p's new value (so p does not return true from line 25). In this case, we argue that the decision value of b is the abstract value immediately before b becomes inactive; that is, the abstract value does not change when b becomes inactive. To see why, first observe that p executes the store only after determining that $b \rightarrow V$ is its expected value (line 22). Recall that the splitter guarantees that no process changes $b \rightarrow V$ between p executing statement 20 and the completion of p's operation (Lemma 1). Thus, because the decision value of b is a value read from $b \rightarrow V$ after b becomes inactive, this decision value can only be p's expected value or p's new value.

Recall that, once the current block becomes inactive, the abstract value cannot change until that block is replaced as the current block, as described next.

If a WFCAS operation finds that b is inactive and it has not changed the abstract value—that is, either the test on line 21 succeeds or the one on line 25 fails—then the operation invokes decide(b) to determine the decision value of b (line 28). This value is the abstract value from the time b became inactive until b is replaced as the current block, and thus, in particular, it is the abstract value at some time during the execution of this operation. If the decision value is not the operation's expected value, the operation returns false (line 28).

Otherwise, the operation prepares a new active block with its new value in the V field (line 29), and attempts to replace b with this new block using CAS (line 30). If the CAS succeeds, then the abstract value changes from the decision value of b, which is the operation's expected value, to the value in the V field of the new block, which is the operation's new value, so the operation returns true. If the CAS fails, then at some point during the execution of this operation, another WFCAS operation replaced b with its own block, whose V field contains that operation's new value, which is not the decision value of b (because that operation's expected value is the decision value of b, and is not, by the test on line 14, the operation's new value). Therefore, immediately after b is replaced, the abstract value differs from the decision value of b, which is the expected value of the WFCAS operation that failed to replace b, so that operation can return false.

The WFRead Operation

It is now easy to see how a WFRead operation works. It first reads L to find the current block (line 10), and then it reads the V field of that block (line 11). If that block is active afterwards, then the value read was the abstract value when line 11 executed, so the operation returns that value (line 12). Otherwise, it returns the decision value of that block (line 13). If the block was active when the operation read L, then its decision value was the abstract value when the block became inactive. Otherwise, its decision value was the abstract value at the time L was read in line 10.

Space Overhead

At any point in time, our algorithm requires one fixed location and one block—the current block—for each fast-CAS variable. In addition, deallocation of blocks that were previously current may be prevented because slow threads may still access them in the future, and some blocks may have been allocated but not (yet) made current. (The determination of when a block can be safely freed can be made using a non-blocking memory management scheme such as the one described in [11].) Each one of these additional blocks is associated with at least one thread, and each thread is associated with at most one block. Therefore, the total space requirement of our algorithm when used to implement V variables for T threads is $O(T + V)$; that is, there is a constant additional space cost for each new fast-CAS variable and each new thread.

A Note on Contention

As we have stated, if there is no contention, the WFRead and WFCAS operations do not invoke CAS. However, if there is contention, some operations may invoke CAS—even operations that do not execute concurrently with that contention. For example, a pair of concurrent WFCAS operations can leave the algorithm in a state in which the current block is no longer active; in this case, a later WFCAS operation that executes alone will have to execute a CAS in order to install a new block. Unless contention arises again later, all subsequent operations will again complete without invoking CAS.

5 Linearizability Proof Sketch

In this section, we sketch a proof that our algorithm is a linearizable implementation of WFRead and WFCAS. In the full paper, we present a complete and more detailed proof [21]. Specifically, given any execution history, we assign each operation a linearization point between its invocation and response such that the value returned by each operation is consistent with a sequential execution in which the operations are executed in the order of their linearization points.

To simplify the proof, we consider only complete execution histories (i.e., histories in which every operation invocation has a corresponding response). Because the algorithm is wait-free, the linearizability of all complete histories implies the linearizability of all histories. We assume that every newly allocated block has never been allocated before, which is equivalent to assuming an environment that provides garbage collection. Also, because blocks are not accessed before initialization, we can assume that they already contain the values they will be initialized with before they are allocated and initialized. Thus, for this proof, initialization is a no-op. Finally, we assume that any sequence of instructions starting from one statement label in Fig. 2 and ending immediately before the next statement label is executed atomically, except when that statement calls `decide` or `WFRead`, in which case the actions of the invoked procedure occur before (and not atomically with) the action of the statement that invokes that procedure.

Throughout the proof, references to "any block" or "all blocks" are quantified only over those blocks that are at some time installed as the current block (i.e., the block pointed to by L); those that are never installed are accessed only during initialization and so are of no concern.

All blocks evolve in a similar way, as shown in Fig. 3. Specifically, for any block b, initially and until b is installed, $\neg b{\to}C$ and $b{\to}D = \perp$ hold. Because $b{\to}C$ and $b{\to}D$ are changed only by lines 27 and 2 respectively, $b{\to}C$ and $b{\to}D = v$ for any $v \neq \perp$ are stable properties.[5] Furthermore, we have the following properties:

1. $b{\to}D$ is set to a non-$\perp$ value by the first execution, if any, of line 2 within an invocation of `decide`(b);
2. whenever `decide`(b) is invoked, $b{\to}C$ already holds; and
3. some invocation of `decide`(b) (i.e., the one on line 28) completes before b is replaced as the current block (in line 30).

Recall that b is active if $L = b$ and $\neg b{\to}C$. We say that b is deciding if it is inactive and $b{\to}D = \perp$, and that b is decided if $b{\to}D \neq \perp$. Following the discussion above, a block is active when it is installed, and must become deciding and then decided before it is replaced. For any block b, at most one non-$\perp$ value is written into $b{\to}D$; this value is returned by every invocation of `decide`(b).

Let $\delta_C(b)$ be the event, if any, that makes b inactive, $\delta_D(b)$ be the event, if any, that makes b decided, and $dv(b)$ be the non-$\perp$ value, if any, that is written into $b{\to}D$. For any block b other than the final block (i.e., the block that is current at the end of the execution history), $\delta_C(b)$, $\delta_D(b)$ and $dv(b)$ are well-defined. If the final block is made inactive, it is decided before the operation that made it inactive completes, so because we are considering only complete histories, either δ_C, δ_D and $dv(b)$ are all defined for the final block, or none of them are.

If b is the current block (i.e., $L = b$), the abstract value of L is

$$AV \equiv \begin{cases} b{\to}V & \text{if } \neg b{\to}C \text{ holds (i.e., } b \text{ is active)} \\ dv(b) & \text{otherwise.} \end{cases}$$

Note that $dv(b)$ is defined whenever $b{\to}C$ holds. While b is active, $AV = b{\to}V$; while b is current but inactive (either deciding or decided), $AV = dv(b)$.

Linearization Points

Below we specify the linearization point for each operation. We categorize operations by the statement from which they return, using the labels shown in Fig. 2.

---

[5] That is, if either property holds in any state, it holds in all subsequent states.

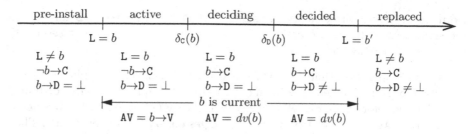

Fig. 3. The evolution of block b. $\delta_C(b)$ and $\delta_D(b)$ are the events that change $b{\to}C$ and $b{\to}D$; $dv(b)$ is the decision value of block b; and AV is the abstract value (see text).

In some cases, we have further subcases. We use $o.k$ to denote the execution by operation o of line k, and $o.\mathtt{x}$ to denote the value of the o's local variable $\mathtt{x}$ after it is set (an operation sets each local variable at most once).

R1 (returns $o.\mathtt{v}$) Linearize to $o.11$.
R2 (returns $dv(o.\mathtt{b})$), $o.\mathtt{b}$ decided at $o.10$ Linearize to $o.10$.
R2 (returns $dv(o.\mathtt{b})$), $o.\mathtt{b}$ not decided at $o.10$ Linearize to $\delta_D(o.\mathtt{b})$.
C1 Linearize to the linearization point of the WFRead invoked on line 14.
C2 (returns *false*) Linearize to $o.20$.
C3 (returns *true*), $o.\mathtt{b}$ is active at $o.23$ Linearize to $o.23$.
C3 (returns *true*), $o.\mathtt{b}$ is not active at $o.23$ Linearize to $\delta_C(o.\mathtt{b})$.
C4 (returns *true*) Linearize to $o.23$
C5 (returns *false*), $o.\mathtt{b}$ is decided at $o.15$ Linearize to $o.15$.
C5 (returns *false*), $o.\mathtt{b}$ is not decided at $o.15$ Linearize to $\delta_D(o.\mathtt{b})$.
C6, returns *true* Linearize to $o.30$.
C6, returns *false* Sometime between $o.15$ and $o.30$, $o.\mathtt{b}$ is replaced as the current block. If $dv(o.\mathtt{b}) \neq o.\mathtt{ev}$ then linearize the operation immediately before $o.\mathtt{b}$ is replaced; otherwise, linearize it immediately after $o.\mathtt{b}$ is replaced.

We first consider the operations that do not change the abstract value. With one exception, it is easy to see, using Fig. 3, that the abstract value is consistent with the operation executing atomically at its linearization point. For example, if WFRead returns from R1, then $o.\mathtt{b}$ is active at $o.12$, so it is also active at the operation's linearization point $o.11$; at this point $\mathtt{AV} = o.\mathtt{b}{\to}\mathtt{V} = o.\mathtt{v}$, as required.

The exception is when a WFCAS operation returns *false* from C6. In this case, some other WFCAS operation o' replaced $o.\mathtt{b}$ with $o'.\mathtt{nb}$, and because of the tests on lines 14 and 28, $o'.\mathtt{nv} \neq dv(o.\mathtt{b})$. $\mathtt{AV} = dv(o.\mathtt{b})$ holds immediately before $o.\mathtt{b}$ is replaced, which is o's linearization point if $dv(o.\mathtt{b}) \neq o.\mathtt{ev}$. Otherwise, o's linearization point is immediately after $o.\mathtt{b}$ is replaced, when $\mathtt{AV} = o'.\mathtt{nv} \neq o.\mathtt{ev}$.

If a WFCAS operation o returns *true* from C6, the CAS on line 30 succeeds. Thus, immediately before $o.30$, $o.\mathtt{b}$ is current and decided, so $\mathtt{AV} = dv(o.\mathtt{b}) = o.\mathtt{ev}$ (see line 28), and immediately after $o.30$, $\mathtt{AV} = o.\mathtt{nb}{\to}\mathtt{V} = o.\mathtt{nv}$.

For the final cases (when a WFCAS operation returns from C3 or C4), we use the following lemma, which says that at most one process has won (and not subsequently reset) the splitter of a block.

Lemma 1. *For any block b, in any state of the history, there exists at most one process p such that $p.b = b$ and p has reached line 20 but has not subsequently completed its WFCAS operation.*

A WFCAS operation that returns from C3 or C4 has won the splitter for o.b. Because o.b→V is changed only by line 23, Lemma 1 implies that after o.20 until immediately before o.23, o.b→V = o.v, which is o.ev (see line 22). If o.b is active at o.23, then AV = o.b→V at o.23, which changes o.b→V from o.ev to o.nv. Thus, if a WFCAS operation o returns from C4 (Fig. 3 and the test at line o.24 imply that o.b is active at o.23 in this case), or if it returns from C3 and o.b is active at o.23, then o is correctly linearized at o.23. If the operation returns from C3 and o.b is not active at o.23, then it is linearized to δ_C(o.b), which occurs between o.21 and o.23. Immediately before δ_C(o.b), AV = o.b→V = o.ev, and immediately after δ_C(o.b), AV = dv(o.b), which is o.nv (see line 25). Thus, AV changes from o.ev to o.nv at δ_C(o.b).

Finally, we argue that AV changes only at the linearization points of WFCAS operations that return true. This is the trickiest part of the proof, and depends heavily on the observation the decision value of a block b must have been in b→V while b was deciding.

Lemma 2. *If dv(b) is defined, then b→V = dv(b) at some point between $\delta_C(b)$ and $\delta_D(b)$.*

There are only three ways in which AV may change:

L changes Only a successful CAS on line 30 changes L, which is done by a WFCAS operation that returns true.

b→V changes while b is active Only o.23 for some WFCAS operation o changes b→V. If b is active when o.24 is executed, then o returns from C4. Otherwise, $\delta_C(b)$ occurs after o.23, so Lemma 1 implies that b→V = o.nv from $\delta_C(b)$ until o completes. Because o invokes decide(b) in this case, $\delta_D(b)$ occurs before o completes, so by Lemma 2, dv(b) = o.nv. Thus, o returns true from C3, and is linearized to o.23 in this case.

b→C changes while b is current and b→V $\neq$ $\boldsymbol{dv}(b)$ Only line 27 changes b→C; this event is $\delta_C(b)$. By Lemma 2, dv(b) is stored by some process p into b→V after $\delta_C(b)$. Because b is inactive when p executes line 23, its subsequent test on line 24 succeeds. Therefore, p's operation returns true from C3 in this case. The linearization point of p's WFCAS operation is defined to be $\delta_C(b)$ in this case, as required.

6   Concluding Remarks

We have shown how to implement a linearizable shared variable supporting constant-time read and CAS operations that do not invoke synchronization primitives in the absence of contention. It is straightforward to extend our algorithm to also support a store operation with the same property.

Because of the number of loads and stores performed by our algorithm—even in the absence of contention—it is not clear that our algorithm would ever provide a performance improvement in practice. Nonetheless, our results have important implications for the way we measure non-blocking algorithms and for the study of the differences between various non-blocking progress conditions. Specifically, they show that any non-blocking algorithm (including wait-free ones) that uses CAS can be transformed to one that does not invoke CAS in the absence of contention. Thus, the measure of the number of CAS's invoked in the absence of contention should not be used when comparing algorithms and is also not useful for establishing a separation between obstruction-freedom and stronger progress conditions.

It is interesting to note that the abstract value of the implemented fast-CAS location in a particular state cannot always be determined simply by examining that state (because the abstract value in some states is determined by the decision value of the current block, which is only determined in the future by invoking decide). This means that a formal automata-based proof would require a backward simulation, rather than a more straightforward forward simulation [22].

Given the negative results with respect to establishing a separation between obstruction-freedom and stronger non-blocking progress conditions, relevant future work includes seeking alternative ways to achieve such a separation.

Acknowledgments. We are grateful to Ori Shalev for help with preliminary performance experiments, and to Simon Doherty for useful discussions.

References

1. N. S. Arora, R. D. Blumofe, and C. G. Plaxton. Thread scheduling for multiprogrammed multiprocessors. In *Proceedings of the 10th Annual ACM Symposium on Parallel Algorithms and Architectures*, pages 119–129, 1998.
2. B. N. Bershad. Practical considerations for non-blocking concurrent objects. In *Proceedings 13th IEEE International Conference on Distributed Computing Systems*, pages 264–273, 1993.
3. H. Buhrman, J. Garay, J. Hoepman, and M. Moir. Long-lived renaming made fast. In *Proceedings of the 14th Annual ACM Symposium on Principles of Distributed Computing*, pages 194–203, 1995.
4. F. Fich, M. Herlihy, and N. Shavit. On the space complexity of randomized synchronization. *Journal of the ACM*, 45(5):843–862, 1998.
5. M. Fischer, N. Lynch, and M. Paterson. Impossibility of distributed consensus with one faulty process. *Journal of the ACM*, pages 374–382, 1985.
6. T. L. Harris. A pragmatic implementation of non-blocking linked lists. In *Proceedings of the 15th International Symposium on Distributed Computing*, 2001.
7. T. L. Harris, K. Fraser, and I. A. Pratt. A practical multi-word compare-and-swap operation. In *Proceedings of 16th International Symposium on DIStributed Computing*, 2002.
8. D. Hendler and N. Shavit. Non-blocking steal-half work queues. In *Proceedings of the 21st Annual ACM Symposium on Principles of Distributed Computing*, pages 280–289, 2002.

9. M. Herlihy. Wait-free synchronization. *ACM Transactions on Programming Languages and Systems*, 13(1):124–149, 1991.
10. M. Herlihy, V. Luchangco, and M. Moir. Obstruction-free software NCAS and transactional memory. Unpublished manuscript, 2002.
11. M. Herlihy, V. Luchangco, and M. Moir. The repeat offender problem: A mechanism for supporting lock-free dynamic-sized data structures. In *Proceedings of the 16th International Symposium on DIStributed Computing*, 2002. A improved version of this paper is in preparation for journal submission; please contact authors.
12. M. Herlihy, V. Luchangco, and M. Moir. Obstruction-free synchronization: Double-ended queues as an example. In *Proceedings of the 23rd International Conference on Distributed Computing Systems*, 2003.
13. M. Herlihy, V. Luchangco, and M. Moir. Space- and time-adaptive nonblocking algorithms. In *Proceedings of Computing: The Australasian Theory Symposium (CATS)*, 2003.
14. M. Herlihy, V. Luchangco, M. Moir, and W. N. Scherer III. Software transactional memory of dynamic-sized data structures. In *Proceedings of the 22nd Annual ACM Symposium on Principles of Distributed Computing*, 2003.
15. M. Herlihy and J. Wing. Linearizability: A correctness condition for concurrent objects. *ACM Transactions on Programming Languages and Systems*, 12(3):463–492, 1990.
16. K. Kawachiya, A. Koseki, and T. Onodera. Lock reservation: Java locks can mostly do without atomic operations. In *Proceedings of the ACM Conference on Object-Oriented Programming, Systems, Languages, and Applications (OOPSLA)*, pages 130–141, 2002.
17. A. LaMarca. A performance evaluation of lock-free synchronization protocols. In *Proceedings of the 13th Annual ACM Symposium on Principles of Distributed Computing*, pages 130–140, Los Angeles, CA, 1994.
18. L. Lamport. How to make a multiprocessor computer that correctly executes multiprocessor programs. *IEEE Transactions on Computers*, C-28(9):690–691, 1979.
19. L. Lamport. A fast mutual exclusion algorithm. *ACM Transactions on Computer Systems*, 5(1):1–11, 1987.
20. M. C. Loui and H. H. Abu-Amara. Memory requirements for agreement among unreliable asynchronous processes. In F. P. Preparata, editor, *Advances in Computing Research*, volume 4, pages 163–183. JAI Press, 1987.
21. V. Luchangco, M. Moir, and N. Shavit. On the uncontended complexity of consensus. In preparation, 2002.
22. N. Lynch and F. Vaandrager. Forward and backward simulations – part I: Untimed systems. *Information and Computation*, 121(2):214–233, 1995.
23. M. M. Michael. High performance dynamic lock-free hash tables and list-based sets. In *Proceedings of the 14th Annual ACM Symposium on Parallel Algorithms and Architectures*, pages 73–82, 2002.
24. M. Moir and J. Anderson. Wait-free algorithms for fast, long-lived renaming. *Science of Computer Programming*, 25:1–39, 1995. A preliminary version appeared in *Proceedings of the 8th International Workshop on Distributed Algorithms*, 1994, pp. 141–155.
25. M. Saks, N. Shavit, and H. Woll. Optimal time randomized consensus — making resilient algorithms fast in practice. In *Proceedings of the Second Annual ACM-SIAM Symposium on Discrete algorithms*, pages 351–362, 1991.
26. O. Shalev and N. Shavit. Split-ordered lists — lock-free resizable hash tables. In *Proceedings of the 22nd Annual ACM Symposium on Principles of Distributed Computing*, 2003.

Probabilistic Quorums for Dynamic Systems
(Extended Abstract)*

Ittai Abraham and Dahlia Malkhi

School of Engineering and Computer Science,
The Hebrew University of Jerusalem, Israel.
{ittaia,dalia}@cs.huji.ac.il

Abstract. A quorum system is a set of sets such that every two sets in the quorum system intersect. Quorum systems may be used as a building block for performing updates and global queries on a distributed, shared information base. An ε-intersecting quorum system is a distribution on sets such that every two sets from the distribution intersect with probability $1 - \varepsilon$. This relaxation of consistency results in a dramatic improvement of the load balancing and resilience of quorum systems, making the approach especially attractive for scalable and dynamic settings.

In this paper we assume a dynamic model where nodes constantly join and leave the system. A quorum chosen at time s must evolve and transform as the system grows/shrinks in order to remain viable. For such a dynamic model, we introduce dynamic ε-intersecting quorum systems. A dynamic ε-intersecting quorum system ensures that in spite of arbitrary changes in the system population, any two evolved quorums intersect with probability $1 - \varepsilon$.

1 Introduction

Consider the following natural information-sharing problem. Participants wish to publicize certain data items, and be able to access the whole information base with search queries. In order to balance the load of updates and queries among the participants, quorums may be used for reading and for writing. Quorums enhance the load balance and availability, and provide flexibility in tuning between read costs and writes costs. However, quorum systems are defined over a universe known to all participants, requiring each process to maintain knowledge of all the other participants.

We aim for a scalable and dynamic information-sharing solution, in which maintaining global knowledge of the system configuration is prohibitive. More concretely, we allow each participant to maintain connections with, and even knowledge of, only a constant number of other members. This restriction stems both from our vision of having ubiquitous, low-memory devices participate in Internet resource sharing applications; and from the desire to keep the amount of state that needs to be updated at reconfiguration very low.

---

* Full version appears as Leibnitz Center TR 2003-32, The Hebrew University [3].

F.E. Fich (Ed.): DISC 2003, LNCS 2848, pp. 60–74, 2003.
© Springer-Verlag Berlin Heidelberg 2003

Our focus on scale and dynamism of information-sharing systems is supported by the stellar popularity of recent resource sharing applications like Gnutella. In these systems, users make available certain data items, like music clips or software, and the system supports global querying of the shared information. Gnutella supports global querying through a probabilistic depth-bounded multicast. This approach is effective, yet ad hoc.

We devise techniques for the information sharing problem, capable of dealing with high decentralization and dynamism exhibited in Internet-scale applications. Our approach is based on the probabilistic quorum systems (PQSs) of Malkhi et al. in [18]. We extend the treatment of PQSs to cope with scalability and high dynamism in the following ways. First, we allow each participant only partial knowledge of the full system, and avoid maintaining any global information of the system size and its constituents. To this end, we develop a theory of PQSs whose individual member selection probability is non-uniform. We demonstrate a realization of such a non-uniform PQS that is fully adapted for the dynamic and scalable settings we aim for. The second extension of PQSs we address is to evolve quorums as the system grows/shrinks in order for them to remain viable. We provide both a formal definition of quorum evolution and the algorithms to realize it.

We first remind the reader of PQSs and motivate their use. The PQSs of Malkhi et al. [18] are an attractive approach for sharing information in a large network. Using a PQS, each participant can disseminate new updates to shared data by contacting a subset (a probabilistic quorum) of $k\sqrt{n}$ processes chosen uniformly at random, where n is the size of the system and k is a reliability parameter. Likewise, participants query data from such quorums. Intuitively, analysis similar to the famous "birthday paradox" (e.g., see [6]) shows that each pair of update/query quorums intersect with probability $1 - e^{-k^2/2}$. The result is that with arbitrarily good probability a query obtains up to date information, and with a small calculated risk it might obtain stale data.

The benefit of the PQS approach is tremendous: Publicizing information and global querying are done each with only a $O(1/\sqrt{n})$ fraction of the participants. At the same time, PQSs maintain availability in face of as many as $O(n)$ faults. In deterministic approaches these two features are provably impossible to achieve simultaneously (see [21]). Indeed, PQSs have been employed in diverse and numerous settings. To name just a few deployments, PQSs were used for designing probabilistic distributed emulations of various shared objects [14,15]; they were used for constructing persistent shared objects in the Phalanx and Fleet systems [16,17]; and they were employed for maintaining tracking data in mobile ad-hoc networks [10].

Now we get to why we need new PQSs. The prevalent PQS construction [18] is not adequate precisely for the kind of scalable and dynamic settings for which PQSs are most beneficial. First, it requires global and precise knowledge of the system size 'n'. Second, it hinges on the ability of each participant to select other processes uniformly at random. And third, it does not indicate what should happen to a quorum that stores data at time s, as the system grows/shrinks.

Our goal is to maintain a PQS that copes with dynamism so that every pair of quorums intersect with the desired probability $1 - \varepsilon$ despite any number of system reconfigurations. To this end, we introduce the notion of dynamic PQSs. This notion captures the need for quorums to evolve as the system changes, and requires pairs of evolved quorums to intersect with probability $1-\varepsilon$. We present a dynamic PQS construction that works without maintaining any global knowledge of the system size or its participants. Our approach incurs a reasonable price per system reconfiguration.

It is worth noting that independently and simultaneously to our work, Naor and Wieder [20] sought solutions in dynamic settings for maintaining **deterministic** quorum systems. Compared with strict quorum systems, PQSs are natural for dynamic and non-structured environments: Finding members can be done in parallel and efficiently, and replacing failed members is trivial.

Technical approach: We first consider the problem of establishing probabilistic quorums in a setting in which full knowledge of the system by each member is not desirable. After that, we address quorum evolution.

Consider a system in which each process is linked to only a small number of other processes. Clearly, a quorum establishment operation initiated at some process must somehow walk the links in the system in search of unknown members. There are indeed some recent dynamic networks that support random walks. The works of [22,7,24] assume a-priori known bound on the network size, whereas we do not place any bound on network growth. A different approach is taken in the AntWalk system [23], that necessitates periodic, global "re-mixing" of the links of old members with those of the new processes that arrived. We consider the price of this approach too heavy for Internet wide applications.

The first step in our solution to avoid the globalization pitfall is to introduce a non-uniform PQS as follows. Let us have any probability distribution $p : S \to [0..1]$ over individual member selection. We define the flat access strategy $f(p, m)$ as the quorum selection distribution obtained by selecting m members according to p. We show that a quorum system with the access strategy $f(p, k\sqrt{n})$ is an $e^{-k^2/2}$-intersecting PQS.

It is left to show how to realize a process selection distribution p in dynamic settings and how to preserve it in evolving quorums. Our approach makes use of recent advances in overlay networks for peer-to-peer applications. Specifically, our design employs a dynamic routing graph based on the dynamic approximation of the de Bruijn network introduced in [1] [1]. This dynamic graph has w.h.p. a constant-degree, logarithmic routing complexity, and logarithmic mixing time. Thus, random walks are rapidly mixing to a stationary distribution p. This means that using a logarithmic number of messages, each process can find other participants with selection probability p.

The dynamic graph allows to estimate the size of the network n with a constant error factor. Using this estimation, the flat access strategy $f(p, k\sqrt{n})$ is approximated by performing roughly $k\sqrt{n}$ random walks of $\log(n)$ steps each.

---

[1]   The dynamic De Bruijn construction appeared independently also in [19,8,13].

We obtain at any instant in time an $e^{-k^2/2}$-intersecting PQS. Accessing quorums is done in $\log(n)$ rounds of communication.

Finally, we need to describe how to evolve quorums as the system grows. We devise an evolution strategy that grows the quorums along with the system's growth automatically and distributively. We prove that our evolution technique keeps quorums sufficiently large, as well as maintains the individual member selection distribution p. The cost of our maintenance algorithm is w.h.p. a constant number of random walks per system reconfiguration. Each single walk incurs a logarithmic number of messages and a state change in one process.

To summarize, the results of our construction is a scalable information sharing mechanism based on dynamic PQSs. The construction maintains $1 - \varepsilon$ intersection probability in any dynamic setting, without central coordination or global knowledge. The system achieves the following performance measures with high probability: The cost of a member addition (join) is a logarithmic number of messages, and a state-change in a constant number of members. Further, the advantage of using PQSs is stressed in the time required for accessing a quorum. The $O(\sqrt{n})$ random selections can be branched concurrently from the initiator to its neighbors, then their neighbors, and so on. Hence, quorum selection is done in $O(\log n)$ communication rounds. Regardless of system growth, the load incurred by information maintenance and update processing on individual members is balanced up to a constant factor.

2   Problem Definition

We consider a (potentially infinite) universe W of possible processes. The system consists of a dynamic subset of processes taken from W that evolves over time as processes join and leave the system. For purposes of reasoning about the system, we use a logical discrete time-scale $T = \{0, 1, \dots\}$. At each time-step $i \in T$ there exists a set $U(i)$ of processes from W that are considered members of the system at that time. Each time-step i consists of a single event $e(i)$, which is one of the following: Either a process joins the system, or a process leaves the system. For each time step $t > 0$, the partial history of events uniquely determines the universe $U = U(t)$ consisting of all the processes that joined the system minus those that have left.

Focusing on a fixed time step $t > 0$ for now, we first recall the relevant definitions from [18]. A set system Q over a universe U is a set of subsets of U. A (strict) quorum system Q over a universe U is a set system over U such that for every $Q, Q' \in Q$, $Q \cap Q' \neq \emptyset$. Each $Q \in Q$ is called a quorum. An access strategy ac for a set system Q specifies a probability distribution on the elements of Q. That is, $ac : Q \to [0, 1]$ satisfies $\sum_{Q \in Q} ac(Q) = 1$. We are now ready to state the definition of probabilistic quorum systems:

Definition 1 (ϵ-intersecting quorum system[18]). Let Q be a set system, let ac be an access strategy for Q, and let $0 < \epsilon < 1$ be given. The tuple $\langle Q, ac \rangle$ is an ϵ-intersecting quorum system if $\Pr[Q \cap Q' \neq \emptyset] \geq 1 - \epsilon$, where the probability is taken with respect to the strategy ac.

We now proceed to define time-evolving quorums. We first define an evolution strategy as follows:

Definition 2 (Evolution strategy). For every $t \in T$, let $\mathcal{Q}(t)$ be a set system over the system $U(t)$. An evolution strategy ev_t specifies a probability distribution on the elements of $\mathcal{Q}(t)$ for each given element of $\mathcal{Q}(t-1)$. Formally, $ev_t : \mathcal{Q}(t-1) \times \mathcal{Q}(t) \to [0,1]$ satisfies

$$\forall Q' \in \mathcal{Q}(t-1) : \sum_{Q \in \mathcal{Q}(t)} ev_t(Q', Q) = 1 \ .$$

Thus, $ev_t(Q', Q)$ for $Q' \in \mathcal{Q}(t-1)$ and $Q \in \mathcal{Q}(t)$ indicates the probability that Q' evolves into Q.

The access strategies over $U(1), U(2), \ldots$ together with an evolution strategy determine the probability that a certain subset occurs as the evolution of any previously created quorum. The following definition captures this distribution:

Definition 3 (Evolving probability distribution). For every time step $i \in T$, let $\langle \mathcal{Q}(i), ac_i \rangle$ be a probabilistic quorum system and ev_i be an evolution strategy. The evolving probability distribution $p_t^s : \mathcal{Q}(t) \to [0,1]$ for quorums created at time s that evolved up to time t, for $t \geq s$, is defined recursively as follows:

$$\forall Q \in \mathcal{Q}(t) : p_t^s(Q) = \begin{cases} ac_s(Q) & t = s, \\ \sum\limits_{Q' \in \mathcal{Q}(t-1)} p_{(t-1)}^s(Q') ev_t(Q', Q) & t > s. \end{cases} \tag{1}$$

Our goal is to devise a mechanism for maintaining ε-intersecting probabilistic quorums in each $U(t)$, and to evolve quorums that maintain information (such as updates to data) so that their evolution remains ε-intersecting with quorums in later time steps. Any two quorums created at times s and t will evolve in a manner that at any later time r, their intersection probability remains $1 - \varepsilon$. This is captured in the following definition:

Definition 4 (Dynamic ϵ-intersecting probabilistic quorum system). For every time step $i > 0$, let $\langle \mathcal{Q}(i), ac_i \rangle$ be a probabilistic quorum system and ev_i be an evolution strategy. Let $0 < \epsilon < 1$ be given. Then $\langle \mathcal{Q}(i), ac_i, ev_i \rangle$ is a dynamic ϵ-intersecting quorum system if for all $r \geq s \geq t > 0, Q, Q' \in \mathcal{Q}(r)$:

$$\Pr[Q \cap Q' \neq \emptyset] \geq 1 - \epsilon$$

where the probability is taken over the choices of Q and Q', distributed respectively according to $Q \sim p_r^s$ and $Q' \sim p_r^t$.

2.1   Performance Measures

Driven by our goal to maintain quorums in very large and dynamic environments, such as Internet-wide peer-to-peer applications, we identify the following four performance measures. First, we have the complexity of handling join/leave events, measured in terms of messages and the number of processes that must incur a state-change. Second, we consider the complexity of accessing a quorum, measured both in messages and in communication rounds (assuming that in each communication round, a process can exchange messages once with all of its links). These two measures reflect the complexity incurred by linking processes in the system to each other and of the searching over the links. Our goal is to keep the join/leave message complexity logarithmic, and the number of state-changes constant per reconfiguration. We strive to maintain quorum access in a logarithmic number of rounds.

Additionally, we consider two traditional measures that were defined to assess the quality of probabilistic quorum systems [21,18]: The load inflicted on processes is the fraction of total updates/queries they must receive. The degree of resilience is the amount of failures tolerable by the service. The reader is referred to [21,18] for the precise definition of these measures. Our goals with respect to the latter two measures are to preserve the good performance of PQSs in static settings. Specifically, we wish for the load to be $O(1/\sqrt{n})$ and the resilience to be $O(n)$.

3   Non-uniform Probabilistic Quorum Systems

In this section, we extend the treatment of probabilistic quorum systems of [18] to constructions that employ non-uniform member selection.

Let S be a system containing n members (e.g., $S = U(t)$ for some $t > 0$). Let $p(s)$ be any distribution over the members $s \in S$. We first define a flat non-uniform selection strategy that chooses members according to p until a certain count is reached.

Definition 5 (Flat access strategy). The flat access strategy $f(p, m) : 2^S \rightarrow [0,1]$ as follows: for $Q \in 2^S$, $f(p, m)(Q)$ equals the probability of obtaining the set Q by repeatedly choosing m times (with repetitions) from the universe S using the distribution p.

The flat strategy $f(p, m)$ strictly generalizes the known access strategy for PQSs in which members are chosen repeatedly m times using a uniform distribution. In the Lemma below, we obtain a generalized probabilistic quorum system with non-uniform member selection.

Lemma 1. The construction $\langle 2^S, f(p, k\sqrt{n}) \rangle$ is an $(e^{-k^2/2})$-intersecting quorum system.

Proof. Consider two sets $Q, Q' \sim f(p, k\sqrt{n})$. For every $s \in S$ denote an indicator variable x_s that equals 1 if $s \in Q \cap Q'$, and equals 0 otherwise. Thus, $E[\sum_{s \in S} x_s] = k^2 n p^2(s)$. By the Cauchy-Schwartz inequality, we have $\sum_{s \in S} p^2(s) \frac{1}{n} \geq \left(\sum_{s \in S} p(s) \frac{1}{n} \right)^2$. Combining the above: $E(\sum_{s \in S} x_s) = k^2 n \sum_{s \in S} p^2(s) \geq k^2$.

We now wish to apply Chernoff bounds to bound the deviation from the mean. Since the x_s's are dependent, we cannot apply the bounds directly. Rather, we define i.i.d. random variables $y_s \sim x_s$. Clearly, $E[\sum_s y_s] = E[\sum_s x_s]$. Due to a result by Hoeffding [12], we have: $Pr[Q \cap Q' = \emptyset] = Pr[\sum_{s \in S} x_s = 0] \leq Pr[\sum_{s \in S} y_s = 0] < \cdot e^{-k^2/2}$.

Finally, note that implementing $f(p, k\sqrt{n})$ requires global knowledge of n, which is difficult in a dynamic setting. The remaining of this paper is devoted to approximating f, i.e., we show how to (roughly) maintain a non-uniform flat quorum access strategy and how to evolve quorums, over a dynamic system.

4   Non-uniform Probabilistic Quorums in Dynamic Systems

4.1   The Dynamic Graph

A key component in the construction is a dynamic routing graph among the processes. The graph allows processes to search for other processes during quorum selection. Denote $G(t) = \langle V(t), E(t) \rangle$ a directed graph representing the system at time t as follows. $V(t)$ is the set of processes $U(t)$ at time point $t > 0$. There is a directed edge $(u, v) \in E(t)$ if u knows v and can communicate directly with it. Henceforth, we refer to system participants as processes or as nodes interchangeably.

Driven by the need to maintain the goals stated above in Section 2.1, we wish to maintain a dynamic graph $G(t)$ with the following properties: (1) Small constant degree (so as to maintain constant join/leave complexity). (2) Logarithmic routing complexity (so as to maintain a reasonable quorum selection cost). (3) Rapid mixing time, so that we can maintain a fixed individual selection distribution using a small number of steps from each node.

We choose to employ for $G(t)$ a routing graph that approximates a de Bruijn routing graph. In the de Bruijn [5], a node $\langle a_1, \ldots, a_k \rangle$ has an edge to the two nodes $\langle a_2, \ldots, a_k, 0/1 \rangle$ (shift, then set the last bit). We employ a dynamic approximation of the De Bruijn graph that was introduced in [1]. This dynamic graph has w.h.p. a constant-degree, logarithmic routing complexity, and logarithmic mixing time.

The dynamic graph is constructed dynamically as follows. We assume that initially, G_1 has two members that bootstrap the system, whose id's are 0 and 1. The graph linking is a dynamic de Bruijn linking, defined as follows:

Definition 6 (Dynamic de Bruijn linking). We say that a graph has a dynamic de Bruijn linking if each node whose id is $\langle a_1, \ldots, a_k \rangle$ has an edge to each node whose id is $\langle a_2, \ldots, a_k \rangle$ or whose id is a prefix thereof, or whose id has any postfix in addition to it.

Joining and the leaving of members is done as follows:

Join: When a node u joins the system, it chooses some member node v and "splits" it. That is, let $\hat{v} = \langle a_1, \ldots, a_k \rangle$ be the identifier v has before the split. Then u uniformly chooses $i \in \{0, 1\}$, obtains identifier $u.id = \langle a_1, \ldots, a_k, i \rangle$ and v changes its identifier to $v.id = \langle a_1, \ldots, a_k, (1 - i) \rangle$. The links to and from v and u are updated so as to maintain the dynamic de Bruijn linking.

Leave: When a node u leaves the system, it finds a pair of 'twin' nodes $\langle a_1, \ldots, a_k, 0 \rangle$, $\langle a_1, \ldots, a_k, 1 \rangle$. If u is not already one of them, it uniformly chooses $i \in \{0, 1\}$, swaps with $\langle a_1, \ldots, a_k, i \rangle$, and $\langle a_1, \ldots, a_k, i \rangle$ leaves.

When a twin $\langle a_1, \ldots, a_k, i \rangle$ leaves, its twin $\langle a_1, \ldots, a_k, (1 - i) \rangle$ changes its identifier to $\langle a_1, \ldots, a_k \rangle$. The links to and from $\langle a_1, \ldots, a_k \rangle$ are updated so as to maintain the dynamic de Bruijn linking.

Definition 7 (Level). For a node v with id $\langle a_1, \ldots, a_k \rangle$. Define its level as $\ell(v) = k$.

Definition 8 (Global gap). The global gap of a graph $G(t)$ is $\max_{v,u \in V(t)} |\ell(v) - \ell(u)|$.

For a more general definition of these dynamic graphs, and an analysis of their properties see [1]. Techniques for maintaining w.h.p. constant-bound on the global gap in dynamic graphs such as $G(t)$ are presented in [1] and independently in [4] with logarithmic per join/leave cost. In [19] techniques are presented for maintaining a global gap of $C = 2$ with linear cost per join/leave. From here on, we assume that w.h.p. a constant bound C on the global gap is maintained.

If the global gap is small, then a node can estimate the size of the network by examining its own level. This is stated in the following lemma:

Lemma 2. Let $G(t)$ be a dynamic de Bruijn graph with global gap C. Then for all $u \in V(t) : 2^{\ell(u)-C} \le |V(t)| \le 2^{\ell(u)+C}$.

4.2 Quorum Selection

For a node u to establish a read or a write quorum, it initiates $k\sqrt{2^{\ell(u)+2C}}$ random walk messages. When a node u initiates a random walk it creates a message M with a hop-count $\ell(u)$, an id $u.id$, and appends any payload A to it, i.e., $M = \langle \ell(u), u.id, A \rangle$. Each node (including u) that receives a message $\langle j, id, A \rangle$ with a non zero hop-count $j > 0$, forwards a message $M' = \langle j-1, id, A \rangle$, randomly to one of its outgoing edges. If $(u, v) \in E$ then the probability that u forwards the message to v is:

$$\Pr[u \text{ forwards to } v] = \frac{1}{2^{\max\{\ell(v)-\ell(u)+1,1\}}} \tag{2}$$

By induction on the splits and merges of the dynamic graph it is clear that the above function (Equation 2) is a well defined probability function.

We call the node that receives a message with hop-count 0 the destination of the message. As a practical matter, it should be clear that a destination node opens the message payload and executes any operation associated with it, such as updating data or responding to a query. These matters are specific to the application, and are left outside the scope of this paper.

4.3   Analysis of Quorum Selection

Let $G(t)$ be a dynamic graph on n nodes. Recall the probability distribution of message forwarding as defined in Section 4.2, Equation 2. We represent this distribution using a weighted adjacency $(n \times n)$-matrix $M(t)$ as follows:

$$m_{v,u} = \Pr[u \text{ forwards to } v] = \begin{cases} \frac{1}{2^{\max\{\ell(v)-\ell(u)+1,1\}}} & (u,v) \in E(t), \\ 0 & \text{otherwise.} \end{cases}$$

The main result we pursue, namely, that our construction realizes a non-uniform PQS, stems from the two propositions below. Due to space limitations, most proofs are omitted; the full version of the paper [3] contains all proofs.

Theorem 1. The stationary distribution of $M(t)$ is the vector x, such that $\forall v \in V(t)$, $x_v = \frac{1}{2^{\ell(v)}}$

For every $t > 0$, denote $x(t)$ as the stationary distribution on $M(t)$. We now show that the random walk algorithm described in Section 4.2 chooses nodes according to $x(t)$.

Theorem 2. The mixing time of a random walk on $M(t)$ starting from a node of level k is k.

The theorems above together imply that our graph maintenance algorithm together with our random walk quorum selection strategy implement a non-uniform selection strategy over the members of $V(t)$, where the probability of choosing $v \in V(t)$ is $1/2^{\ell(v)}$.

As an immediate consequence of the propositions above, we have our main theorem as follows:

Theorem 3. For a system S on a dynamic graph with global gap C, the quorum selection strategy as described above forms a e^{-k^2}-intersecting probabilistic quorum system.

Proof. The theorem follows from the fact that by assumption, each quorum access includes at least $k\sqrt{2^{\ell(u)+2C}} \geq k\sqrt{n}$ independent selections, each one done according to the distribution $x(t)$.

5   Quorum Evolution

In this section we describe the evolution algorithm for maintaining dynamic ε-intersecting quorum systems. For such a construction, quorums need to evolve along with the growth of the system in order to maintain their intersection properties. This property must be maintained in spite of any execution sequence of join and leave events that may be given by an adversary.

One trivial solution would be to choose new quorums instead of the old ones each time the network's size multiplies. Such a solution has a major drawback, it requires a global overhaul operation that may affect all the system at once. Even if we consider amortized costs, this process requires to change the state of $\sqrt{|V|}$ nodes for some join events. In contrast, our evolution scheme w.h.p. resorts only to local increments for each join or leave event, each causing only a constant number of nodes to change their state.

The intuition for our algorithm comes from the following simple case. Suppose the network is totally balanced, i.e., all nodes have the same level m, and a quorum with $2^{m/2}$ data entries is randomly chosen. Further assume that after a series of join events, the network's size multiplies by 4 and all nodes have level $m+2$. Our evolution algorithm works as follows in this simple scenario. Each time a node splits, each data entry stored on the split node randomly chooses which sibling to move to. In addition, if the node that splits has an even level then each of its data entries also creates one more duplicate data entry and randomly assigns it to a new node. Thus the number of data entries doubles from $2^{m/2}$ to $2^{(m+2)/2}$ and each data entry is randomly distributed on the network.

Our evolution algorithm simulates this behavior on approximately balanced networks. Thus, its success relies on the fact that the global gap of the dynamic graph w.h.p. is at most C. In order to avoid fractions, we set the bound C on the global gap to be an even number.

5.1   Informal Description of the Evolution Algorithm

Recall that a join (respectively, leave) event translates to a split (respectively, merge) operation on the dynamic graph. We now explain how the random walk algorithm is enhanced, and what actions are taken when a split or a merge operation occurs.

We divide the levels of the graph into phases of size C, all the levels $(i-1)C+1,\ldots,iC$ belong to phase iC. When a node in phase iC wants to establish a quorum, it sends $k2^{(i+1)C/2}$ random walk messages. Each such message also contains the *phase* of the sender which is iC.

When two nodes are merged, the data entries are copied to the parent node. If the parent node is later split, we want each data entry to go to the sibling it originally came from. Otherwise, the distribution of the data entry's location will be dependent on the execution sequence. Thus, each data entry also stores all the random choices it has made as a sequence of random bits called *dest*. When an entry is first created, *dest* is set to the id of the node that the data entry is in.

When a node of level i is split into two nodes of level $i + 1$, there are two possibilities: Either $|dest| \geq i + 1$ and the data entry moves according to the (i+1)th bit of $dest$. Otherwise, the data entry randomly chooses which one of the two sibling to move to, and it records this decision by adding the appropriate bit to $dest$.

The number of data entries is increased only when a data entry is split on a node whose level is a multiple of C. If a data entry with phase iC is involved in a split operation on a node with level iC then $2^{C/2} - 1$ new data entries with phase $(i + 1)C$ are created. These data entries are randomly distributed using the random walk algorithm.

Additionally, whenever a random walk message from a node in phase jC arrives to a node u with phase $(j + 1)C$, we simulate as if the message first arrived at an ancestor node of level jC that is a prefix of u, and later this ancestor node had undergone some split operations. Thus, if a phase $(j + 1)C$ node receives a message with hop count 0 initiated by a node in phase jC then, in addition to storing the data entry, the node also creates $2^{2/C} - 1$ new data entries with phase $(j + 1)C$. This simulation technique is recursively expanded to cases where a node in phase $(j + \ell)C$ receives a message initiated by a node in phase jC.

5.2   Evolution Algorithm

Enhanced random walk: Denote $phase(i) = C\lceil i/C \rceil$. When a node u initiates a random walk it creates a message M with a hop-count $\ell(u)$, phase $phase(\ell(u))$, id $u.id$, and payload A to it, i.e., $M = \langle \ell(u), phase(\ell(u)), u.id, A \rangle$. Each node that receives a message $\langle j, ph, id, A \rangle$ with a non zero hop-count $j > 0$, forwards a message $M' = \langle j - 1, ph, id, A \rangle$, randomly to one of its outgoing edges v with probability $\Pr[u \text{ forwards to } v] = \frac{1}{2^{\max\{\ell(v) - \ell(u) + 1, 1\}}}$.

Nodes store information as a data entry of the form $(dest, ph, id, A)$, where $dest$ is a sequence of bits that describes the location of the entry, ph is the phase, id is the identity of the quorum initiator, and A is the payload.

When node w receives a message $M = \langle 0, ph, id, A \rangle$ it stores the data entry $(w.id, ph, id, A)$. If $phase(\ell(w)) > ph$ then for every i such that $\lceil ph/C \rceil < i \leq \lceil \ell(w)/C \rceil$, w sends $2^{C/2} - 1$ messages of the form $\langle \ell(w), iC, id, A \rangle$.

Create: A node u creates a quorum by initiating $k2^{(phase(\ell(u))+C)/2}$ enhanced random walk messages.

Split: Suppose node u wants to enter the system, and $v = \langle a_1, \ldots, a_k \rangle$ is the node to be split into nodes $\langle a_1, \ldots, a_k, 0 \rangle$ and $\langle a_1, \ldots, a_k, 1 \rangle$. For every data entry (d, ph, id, A) held in v do the following. If $|d| \geq k + 1$ then store (d, ph, id, A) at node $\langle a_1, \ldots, a_k, dest_{k+1} \rangle$ where $dest_i$ is the ith bit of $dest$. Otherwise, if $|d| < k + 1$ then with uniform probability choose $i \in \{0, 1\}$ and send to node $\langle a_1, \ldots, a_k, i \rangle$ the message $\langle 0, ph, id, A \rangle$. Node $\langle a_1, \ldots, a_k, i \rangle$ will handle this message using the enhanced random walk algorithm (in particular, if the split has crossed a phase boundary, it will generate $2^{C/2} - 1$ new data replicas).

Merge: Suppose node u wants to leave the system, and the twin nodes $\langle a_1, \ldots, a_k, 0 \rangle$, $\langle a_1, \ldots, a_k, 1 \rangle$ are the nodes that merge into node $v = \langle a_1, \ldots, a_k \rangle$. If u and one of the twins swap their ids then they also swap the data entries that they hold. After the swap, the merged node $v = \langle a_1, \ldots, a_k \rangle$ copies all the data entries that the nodes with ids $\langle a_1, \ldots, a_k, 0 \rangle$, $\langle a_1, \ldots, a_k, 1 \rangle$ held.

5.3 Analysis of Quorum Evolution

Given a network $G(t)$ on n nodes, we seek to show that the evolved quorum's distribution is at least as good as the flat access scheme $f(x(t), k\sqrt{n})$. So we must show a set of data entries that are independently distributed, whose size is at least $k\sqrt{n}$. Note that the existence of some of the data entries is dependent on the execution history. Therefore, it is not true that all data entries are independently distributed. However, we use a more delicate argument in which we analyze the size of a subset of the data entries whose existence is independent of the execution sequence.

The main result we pursue is that a non-uniform PQS is maintained despite any system reconfiguration, and is given in the Theorem below. The following two lemmas are crucial for proving it. Their proofs are in [3].

Lemma 3. For any time t, data entry D, the distribution of D's location on $V(t)$ is $x(t)$.

Definition 9. Denote $L(t)$ as the lowest phase on $G(t)$, $L(t) = \min_{v \in V(t)} phase(\ell(v))$.

Lemma 4. Let $t > 0$, and let the dynamic graph $G(t)$ have global gap C. Consider any quorum initiated by a node u at phase i with payload A. If $L(t) \geq i$ then the number of data entries of the form (d, ph, u, A) such that $ph \leq L(t)$ is exactly $k2^{((L(t)+C)/2}$.

Theorem 4. On dynamic networks with global gap C, the evolution algorithm maintains a dynamic $e^{k^2/2}$-intersecting quorum system.

Proof. By Lemma 3 the locations of all data entries of all quorums are distributed by $x(t)$, the stationary distribution of $M(t)$. Consider a quorum initiated at a phase i node. If $L(t) < i$ then the initial $k2^{(i+C)/2} \geq k\sqrt{|V(t)|}$ data entries suffice. If $L(t) \geq i$ then by Lemma 4 every quorum has $k2^{(L(t)+C)/2}$ entries whose existence is independent of the execution history. Since the network has global gap of C, then $k2^{(L(t)+C)/2} \geq k\sqrt{|V(t)|}$. Thus at any time t, the evolving probability distribution p_t^r of the above subset of data entries of any quorum, for any establishment time r, is a flat access strategy $f(x(t), m)$ in which $m \geq k\sqrt{|V(t)|}$. By Lemma 1 this access scheme forms an $e^{k^2/2}$-intersecting quorum system as required.

Our construction implements, for any history of events, access strategies and an evolution strategy that maintains the evolving probability distribution p_t^r as a flat access strategy on $V(t)$ using the distribution $x(t)$ with more than $\sqrt{|V(t)|}$ independent choices. Thus, at any time t, all quorums (both newly established and evolved) are ε-intersecting.

6   Performance Analysis

Our protocols hinge on the network balancing algorithms we employ, e.g., from [1], and on their ability to maintain the bound C on the global level gap. We note that the network construction of [1] incurs a constant number of state-changes per join/leave and a logarithmic number of messages. It maintains the global gap bound C w.h.p. Below, the analysis stipulates that the global gap C is maintained, and calculates additional costs incurred by our algorithm.

Join/leave complexity. When a new process joins the system, it may cause a split of a node whose level is a multiple of C. In that case, we allocate a constant number of new data entries, that incur a constant number of random walks. Thus, the message cost is $O(\log(n))$ and the number of processes incurring a change in their state is constant. Leave events generate one message and a state change to one process.

Quorum access complexity. When selecting a quorum, we initiate $O(\sqrt{n})$ random walks. For efficiency, a process may dispatch multiple walks on each of its links, and have them branch repeatedly. The total number of communication rounds needed for all walks to reach their (random) targets is $O(\log(n))$, and the total number of messages is $O(\sqrt{n}\log(n))$.

Load and Resilience. The load on each process during quorum selection at time t is $O(1/\sqrt{n})$. As the system grows, the load above continues to hold. However, if the system dramatically diminishes, the relative fraction of data entries could grow, causing high load on processes. Naturally, a practical system must deploy garbage collection mechanisms in order to preserve resources. The discussion of garbage collection is left outside the scope of this paper.

Because only $k2^C\sqrt{n}$ processes need be available in order for some (high quality) quorum to be available, the fault tolerance is $n - k2^C\sqrt{n} + 1 = \Omega(n)$. Finally, it is not hard to derive that the failure probability F_p, i.e., the probability that no high-quality quorum is available when process failures occur with individual i.i.d. probability p, is at most $e^{-\Omega(n)}$, for $p \leq 1 - 2\frac{k2^C}{\sqrt{n}} - \delta$. This failure probability is optimal [21].

7   Discussion

In this paper we assumed the read-write ratio to be roughly equal. It is possible to extend the techniques of this paper to differentiate between read-quorums and write-quorums, and achieve better performance. Given any read-write ratio, instead of having all operations select $cn^{1/2}$ nodes, read operations select cn^{α} nodes, and write operations select $cn^{1-\alpha}$ nodes for some predetermined $0 < \alpha < 1$.

We presented a system with a constant $1 - \varepsilon$ intersection probability. In the AntWalk system [23], $\sqrt{n \log n}$ processes are randomly chosen thus leading to intersection with high probability. Our quorum selection and evolution algorithm can be modified along similar lines to achieve a high probability dynamic intersecting quorum system.

Our analysis is sketched in a model in which changes are sequential. While we believe our construction to be efficient in much stronger settings, where a large number of changes may occur simultaneously, it is currently an open problem to provide a rigorous analysis.

The fault tolerance analysis concerns the robustness of the data which the system stores against $O(n)$ failures. While the data will not be lost due to such catastrophic failure, clearly our constant degree network, which is used to access the data, may disconnect. Network partitioning can be reduced by robustifing the network through link replication. But unless each node has $O(n)$ links, $O(n)$ failures will disconnect any network. Once the network is partitioned, the problem of rediscovering the network's nodes is addressed in [11,2]. When the network is reconnected, the dynamic de-Bruijn can be reconstructed. After recovering from this catastrophic failure, the system will maintain consistency, since the information itself was not lost.

References

1. I. Abraham, B. Awerbuch, Y. Azar, Y. Bartal, D. Malkhi and E. Pavlov. A Generic Scheme for Building Overlay Networks in Adversarial Scenarios. In *International Parallel and Distributed Processing Symposium* (IPDPS 2003), April 2003, Nice, France.

2. I. Abraham, D. Dolev. Asynchronous Resource Discovery. In proceedings of *the 22nd ACM Symposium on Principles of Distributed Computing* (PODC 2003). June 2003.

3. I. Abraham and D. Malkhi. Probabilistic Quorums for Dynamic Systems. Leibnitz Center TR 2003-32, School of Computer Science and Engineering, The Hebrew University, June 2003. http://leibniz.cs.huji.ac.il/tr/acc/2003/HUJI-CSE-LTR-2003-32_dpq11.ps

4. M. Adler, E. Halperin, R. Karp and V. Vazirani. A stochastic process on the hypercube with applications to peer to peer networks. In *The 35th Annual ACM Symposium on Theory of Computing* (STOC), 2003.

5. N. G. de Bruijn. A combinatorial problem, Konink. Nederl. Akad. Wetersh. Verh. Afd. Natuurk. Eerste Reelss, A49 (1946), pp. 758–764.

6. W. Feller. *An Introduction to Probability Theory and Its Applications, volume 1.* John Wiley & Sons, New York, 3rd edition, 1967.

7. A. Fiat and J. Saia. Censorship resistant peer-to-peer content addressable networks. In *Proceedings of the 13th ACM-SIAM Symposium on Discrete Algorithms*, 2002.

8. P. Fraigniaud and P. Gauron. The Content-Addressable Network D2B. Technical Report 1349, LRI, Univ. Paris-Sud, France, January 2003.

9. http://gnutella.wego.com.

10. Z. J. Haas and B. Liang. Ad hoc mobility management with randomized database groups. In *Proceedings of the IEEE Internation Conference on Communications*, June 1999.

11. M. Harchol-Balter, T. Leighton, and D. Lewin. Resource Discovery in Distributed Networks. In *Proc. 15th ACM Symp. on Principles of Distributed Computing*, May 1999, pp. 229–237.

12. W. Hoeffding. Probability inequalities for sums of bounded random variables. *Journal of the American Statistical Association* 58(301):13–30, 1963.

13. F. Kaashoek and D. R. Karger. Koorde: A Simple Degree-optimal Hash Table. In *2nd International Workshop on Peer-to-Peer Systems* (IPTPS '03), February 2003, Berkeley, CA.

14. H. Lee and J. L. Welch. Applications of Probabilistic Quorums to Iterative Algorithms. In *Proceedings of 21st International Conference on Distributed Computing Systems* (ICDCS-21), Pages 21–28. April, 2001.

15. H. Lee and J. L. Welch. Randomized Shared Queues. Brief announcement in *Twentieth ACM Symposium on Principles of Distributed Computing* (PODC 2001).

16. D. Malkhi, M. Reiter. Secure and Scalable Replication in Phalanx. Proceedings of the 17th IEEE Symposium on Reliable Distributed Systems (SRDS '98), October 1998, Purdue University, West Lafayette, Indiana, pages 51–60.

17. D. Malkhi and M. Reiter. An Architecture for Survivable Coordination in Large Distributed Systems. IEEE Transactions on Knowledge and Data Engineering, 12(2):187–202, April 2000.

18. D. Malkhi, M. Reiter, A. Wool and R. Wright. Probabilistic quorum systems. The Information and Computation Journal 170(2):184–206, November 2001.

19. M. Naor and U. Weider. Novel architectures for P2P applications: the continuous-discrete approach. In proceedings pf *Fifteenth ACM Symposium on Parallelism in Algorithms and Architectures (SPAA 2003)*, June 2003.

20. M. Naor and U. Wieder. Scalable and Dynamic Quorum Systems. In proceedings of *the 22nd ACM Symposium on Principles of Distributed Computing (PODC 2003)*, June 2003.

21. M. Naor and A. Wool. The load, capacity and availability of quorum systems. *SIAM Journal of Computing*, 27(2):423–447, April 1998.

22. G. Pandurangan, P. Raghavan and E. Upfal. Building low-diameter p2p networks. In *Proceedings of the 42nd Annual IEEE Symposium on the Foundations of Computer Science (FOCS)*, 2001.

23. D. Rataczjak. Decentralized Dynamic Networks. M. Eng. Thesis Proposal, MIT, May 2000.

24. J. Saia, A. Fiat, S. Gribble, A. Karlin, and S. Saroiu. Dynamically Fault-Tolerant Content Addressable Networks, In *Proceedings of the 1st International Workshop on Peer-to-Peer Systems (IPTPS '02)*, March 2002, Cambridge, MA USA

Efficient Replication of Large Data Objects

Rui Fan and Nancy Lynch

MIT Computer Science and Artificial Intelligence Laboratory,
200 Technology Square,
Cambridge, MA USA 02139
{rfan,lynch}@theory.lcs.mit.edu

Abstract. We present a new distributed data replication algorithm tailored especially for large-scale read/write data objects such as files. The algorithm guarantees atomic data consistency, while incurring low latency costs. The key idea of the algorithm is to maintain copies of the data objects separately from information about the locations of up-to-date copies. Because it performs most of its work using only the location information, our algorithm needs to access only a few copies of the actual data; specifically, only one copy during a read and only $f + 1$ copies during a write, where f is an assumed upper bound on the number of copies that can fail. These bounds are optimal. The algorithm works in an asynchronous message-passing environment. It does not use additional mechanisms such as group communication or distributed locking. It is suitable for implementation in WANs as well as LANs. We also present two lower bounds on the costs of data replication. The first lower bound is on the number of low-level writes required during a read operation on the data. The second bound is on the minimum space complexity of a class of efficient replication algorithms. These lower bounds suggest that some of the techniques used in our algorithm are necessary. They are also of independent interest.

1 Introduction

Data replication is an important technique for improving the reliability and scalability of data services. To be most useful, data replication should be transparent to the user. Thus, while there exist multiple physical copies of the data, users should only see one logical copy, and user operations should appear to execute atomically on the logical copy.

To maintain atomicity, existing replication algorithms typically use locks [4], embed physical writes to the data within a logical read [3,14], or assume powerful network primitives such as group communication [2]. However, such techniques have adverse effects on performance [8], and practical systems either sacrifice their consistency guarantees [12], or rely on master copies [15] or use very few replicas.

This paper presents an algorithm which deals with the performance penalty of data replication by taking advantage of the fact that, in a typical application requiring replication, such as a file system, the size of the objects being replicated

F.E. Fich (Ed.): DISC 2003, LNCS 2848, pp. 75–91, 2003.

is often much larger than the size of the metadata (such as tags or pointers) used by the algorithm. In this situation, it is efficient to perform more cheap operations on the metadata in order to avoid expensive operations on the data itself.

Our algorithm replicates a single data item supporting read and write operations, and guarantees that the operations appear to happen atomically. The normal case[1] communication cost is nearly constant for a read operation, and nearly linear in f for a write, where f is an upper bound on the number of replica failures. The latency for a read and write are both nearly constant. Here, we measure the communication and latency costs in terms of the number of data items accessed, and ignore the number of metadata items accessed, as the former term is dominant.[2] Our algorithm runs on top of any reliable, asynchronous message passing network. It tolerates high latency and network instability, and therefore is appropriate in both LAN and WAN settings.

The basic idea of the algorithm is to separately store copies of the data in *replica servers*, and information about where the most up-to-date copies are located in *directory servers*. We call this layered replication approach *Layered Data Replication (LDR)*. Roughly speaking, to read the data, a client first reads the directories to find the set of up-to-date replicas, then reads the data from one of the replicas. To write, a client first writes its data to a set of replicas, then informs the directories that these replicas are now up-to-date.

In addition to our replication algorithm, we prove two lower bounds on the costs of replication. The first lower bound shows that in any atomically consistent replication algorithm, clients must sometimes write to at least f replicas during a logical read, where f is the number of replicas that can fail. The second lower bound shows that for a *selfish* atomic replication algorithm, *i.e.*, one in which clients do not "help" each other, the replicas need to have memory which is proportional to the maximum number of clients that can concurrently write. In addition to their independent interest, these lower bounds help explain some of the techniques *LDR* uses, such as writing to the directories during a read, and sometimes storing multiple copies of the data in a replica.

Our paper is organized as follows. Section 2 describes related work on data replication. Section 3 formally defines our model and problem. Section 4 describes the *LDR* algorithm, while Sections 5 and 6 prove its correctness, and analyzes and compares its performance to other replication algorithms. Section 7 presents our lower bounds. Finally, Section 8 concludes.

2   Related Work

There has been extensive work on database replication [4,15,5,2]. Algorithms that guarantee strong consistency usually rely on locking and commit protocols [4]. Practical systems usually sacrifice consistency for performance [12], or rely on master copies [5] or group communication [2]. In our work, we do not consider

---

[1] *I.e.*, when there are no failures.

[2] The amount of metadata accessed is also not large.

transactions, only individual read/write operations on a single object. Therefore, we can avoid the use of locks, commit protocols and group communication, while still guaranteeing strong consistency.

Directory-based replication is also used in file systems, such as Farsite [1]. However, this system focuses more on tolerating Byzantine failures and providing file-system semantics, and their replication algorithm and analysis is less formal and precise than ours.

Our use of directory servers bears similarities to the *witness replicas* of [16] and the *ghost replicas* of [18]. These replicas store only the version number of the latest write, and are cheap to access. We extend these ideas by storing the locations of up-to-date replicas in directories, allowing *LDR* to access the minimum copies of the actual data. In addition, since our replicas are not used in voting, we can replicate the data in arbitrary sets of (at least $f + 1$) replicas, instead of only in quorums. This allows optimizations on replica placement, which can further enhance *LDR*'s performance. Lastly, while [16] and [18] still need external concurrency control mechanisms, *LDR* does not.

Directory-based cache-coherence protocols [17] are used in distributed shared memory systems, and are in spirit similar to our work. However, these algorithms are not directly comparable to *LDR*, since the assumptions and requirements in the shared memory setting are quite different from ours.

The algorithm used to maintain consistency among the directories is based on the weighted voting algorithm of [7] and the shared memory emulation algorithms of [3] and [14]. One can apply [3] and [14] directly for data replication. However, doing so is expensive, because these algorithms read and write the data to a quorum of replicas in each client read or write operation. The client read operation is especially slow compared to *LDR*, since *LDR* only accesses the data from one replica during a read.

Theorem 10.4 of [9] is similar in spirit to our first bound. It shows that in a wait-free simulation of a single-writer, multi-reader register using single-writer, single-reader registers, a reader must sometimes write. In contrast, our lower bound considers arbitrary processes simulating a multi-reader, multi-writer register, and shows that a reader must sometimes write to at least f processes, where f is the number of processes allowed to fail.

3   Specification

3.1   Model

Let x be the data object we are replicating. x takes values in a set V, and has default value v_0. x can be read and written to. To replicate multiple objects, we run multiple instances of *LDR*. However, we do not support transactions, *i.e.*, single operations that both read and write, or access multiple objects.

LDR is based on the client-server model. Each client and server is modeled by an I/O automaton [13]. The communication between clients and servers is modeled by a standard reliable, FIFO asynchronous network.

3.2   Interface, Assumptions, and Guarantees

The clients receive external input actions to read and write to x. Upon receiving an input, a client interacts with the servers to perform the requested action. To distinguish the input actions that read/write x from the low-level reads and writes which clients perform on the servers, we sometimes call the former *logical* or *client* reads/writes, and the latter *physical* reads/writes.

Let $\mathcal{C}$ be the set of *client endpoints*. For every $i \in \mathcal{C}$, client i has *invocations* (input actions) $read_i$ (resp., $write(v)_i$) to read (resp., write v to) x, and *corresponding responses* (output actions) $read - ok(*)_i$ (resp., $write - ok_i$). The servers are divided into $\mathcal{R}$, the *replica endpoints*, and $\mathcal{D}$, the *directory endpoints*. We assume that $\mathcal{R}$ and $\mathcal{D}$ are finite ($\mathcal{C}$ may be infinite). The interface at a server $i \in \mathcal{D} \cup \mathcal{R}$ consists of $send(m)_{i,j}$ to send message m to endpoint j, $j \in \mathcal{C} \cup \mathcal{D} \cup \mathcal{R}$, and $recv(m)_{j,i}$ to receive m from j.

We assume the crash-fail model, and we model failures by having a $fail_i$ input for every $i \in \mathcal{C} \cup \mathcal{D} \cup \mathcal{R}$. When $fail_i$ occurs, automaton i stops taking any more locally controlled steps.

LDR assumes clients are *well-behaved*. That is, clients do not make consecutive invocations without a receiving a corresponding response in between.

LDR's guarantees are specified by properties of its traces. LDR's liveness guarantee is conditional. Specifically, let $(\mathcal{Q}_R, \mathcal{Q}_W)$ be a *read/write quorum system* over $\mathcal{D}$. That is, $\mathcal{Q}_R, \mathcal{Q}_W \subseteq 2^{\mathcal{D}}$ are collections of subsets of $\mathcal{D}$, with the property that for any sets $Q_1 \in \mathcal{Q}_R$ and $Q_2 \in \mathcal{Q}_W$, $Q_1 \cap Q_2 \neq \emptyset$. Also, let f be any natural number such that $f < |\mathcal{R}|$. Then LDR guarantees the following:

Definition 1. *(Liveness) In any infinite trace of* LDR *in which at most f replicas fail, and some $Q_1 \in \mathcal{Q}_R$ and $Q_2 \in \mathcal{Q}_W$ of directories do not fail, every invocation at a nonfailing client has a subsequent corresponding response at the client.*

LDR's safety guarantee says that client read/write operations appear to execute atomically.

Definition 2. *(Atomicity) Every trace of* LDR, *when projected onto the client invocations and corresponding responses, can be linearized to a trace respecting the semantics of a read/write register with domain V and initial value v_0.*

We refer to [10] for a formal definition of atomicity and linearization.

4   The LDR Algorithm

The clients, replicas and directories have different state variables and run different protocols. The protocols are shown in Figures 1, 2, and 3, resp., and are described below. Figures 4 and 5 show the schematics of the read and write operations, resp. Both the read and write operations involve the client getting an external input, then contacting some directories and replicas to perform the requested action.

4.1   State

A client has the following state variables. Variable *phase* (initially equal to *idle*) keeps track of where a client is in a read/write operation. Variable $utd \in 2^{\mathcal{R}}$ (initially $\emptyset$) stores the set of replicas which the client thinks are most up-to-date. Variable $tag \in \mathbb{N} \times \mathcal{C}$ (initially $t_0{}^3$) is the tag of the latest value of x the client knows. Variable *mid* (initially 0) keeps track of the latest message the client sent; the client ignores responses with $id < mid$.

A replica has one state variable $data \subseteq V \times T \times \{0,1\}$, initially $\emptyset$. For each triple in *data*, the first coordinate is a value of x that the replica is storing. The replica may store multiple values of x; the reason why this is done is explained in Section 7.3. The second coordinate is the tag associated with the value. The third coordinate indicates whether the value is *secured*, as explained in Section 4.3.

A directory has a $utd \subseteq \mathcal{R}$ variable, initially equal to $\mathcal{R}$, which stores the set of replicas that have the latest value of x. It also has a variable $tag \in T$, initially t_0, which is the tag associated with that value of x.

4.2   Client Protocol

When client i does a read, it goes through four phases in order: rdr, rdw, rrr and rok.[4] During rdr, i reads (utd, tag) from a quorum of directories to find the most up-to-date replicas. i sets its own tag and utd to be the (tag, utd) it read with the highest tag. During rdw, i writes (utd, tag) to a write quorum of directories, so that later reads will read i's tag or higher. During rrr, i reads the value of x from a replica in utd. Since each replica may store several values of x, i tells the replica it wants to read the value of x associated with tag. During rok, i returns the x-value it read in rrr.

When i writes a value v, it also goes through four phases in order: wdr, wrw, wdw and wok.[5] During wdr, i reads (utd, tag) from a quorum of directories, then sets its tag to be higher than the largest tag it read. During wrw, i writes (v, tag) to a set acc of replicas, where $|acc| \geq f+1$. Note that the set acc is arbitrary; it does not have to be a quorum. During wdw, i writes (acc, tag) to a quorum of directories, to indicate that acc is the set of most up-to-date replicas, and tag is the highest tag for x. Then i sends each replica a *secure* message to tell them that its write is finished, so that the replicas can garbage-collect older values of x. Then i finishes in phase wok.

---

[3] Here $t_0 < t, \forall t \in T$, where tags are ordered lexicographically, and T denotes the set of all tags.

[4] The phase names describe what happens during the phase. They stand for *read-directories-read, read-directories-write, read-replicas-read,* and *read-ok*, resp.

[5] As for a read, *wdr* stands for *write-directories-read, wrw* for *write-replicas-write, wdw* for *write-directories-write,* and *wok* for *write-ok*.

input **read**$_i$
Effect:
  $mid \leftarrow mid + 1$
  for all $j \in \mathcal{D}$ do $msg[j] \leftarrow \langle read, mid \rangle$
  $phase \leftarrow rdr$

input **write(v)**$_i$
Effect:
  $val \leftarrow v; \ mid \leftarrow mid + 1$
  for all $j \in \mathcal{D}$ do $msg[j] \leftarrow \langle read, mid \rangle$
  $phase \leftarrow wdr$

input **fail**$_i$
Effect:
  stop taking locally-controlled steps

output **read-ok(v)**$_i$
Precondition:
  $(val = v) \wedge (phase = rok)$
Effect:
  $phase \leftarrow idle$

output **write-ok**$_i$
Precondition:
  $phase = wok$
Effect:
  $phase \leftarrow idle$

output **send(m)**$_{i,j}$
Precondition:
  $msg[j] = m$
Effect:
  $msg[j] \leftarrow \perp$

input **recv(m)**$_{j,i}$ where $(m = \langle read\text{-}ok, S, t, id \rangle)$
Effect:
  if $(phase = rdr) \wedge (id = mid)$ then
    $acc \leftarrow acc \cup \{j\}$
    if $(t > tag)$ then
      $tag \leftarrow t; \ utd \leftarrow S$
    if $(\exists Q \in \mathcal{Q}_R : Q \subseteq acc)$ then
      $mid \leftarrow mid + 1$
      for all $j \in \mathcal{D}$ do $msg[j] \leftarrow \langle write, utd, tag, mid \rangle$
      $acc \leftarrow \emptyset; \ phase \leftarrow rdw$

input **recv(m)**$_{j,i}$ where $(m = \langle write\text{-}ok, id \rangle)$
Effect:
  if $(phase = rdw) \wedge (id = mid)$ then
    $acc \leftarrow acc \cup \{j\}$
    if $(\exists Q \in \mathcal{Q}_W : Q \subseteq acc)$ then
      $mid \leftarrow mid + 1$
      for all $j \in utd$ do $msg[j] \leftarrow \langle read, tag, mid \rangle$
      $acc \leftarrow \emptyset; \ phase \leftarrow rrr$

input **recv(m)**$_{j,i}$ where $(m = \langle read\text{-}ok, v, t, id \rangle)$
Effect:
  if $(phase = rrr) \wedge (id = mid)$ then
    $val \leftarrow v; \ tag \leftarrow t; \ phase \leftarrow rok$

input **recv(m)**$_{j,i}$ where $(m = \langle read\text{-}ok, t, id \rangle)$
Effect:
  if $(phase = wdr) \wedge (id = mid)$ then
    $acc \leftarrow acc \cup \{j\}$
    if $(t > tag)$ then
      $tag \leftarrow t$ $//tag = (n, i')$
    if $(\exists Q \in \mathcal{Q}_R : Q \subseteq acc)$ then
      $mid \leftarrow mid + 1; \ tag \leftarrow (n + 1, i)$
      for all $j \in \mathcal{R}$ do $msg[j] \leftarrow \langle write, val, tag, mid \rangle$
      $acc \leftarrow \emptyset; \ phase \leftarrow wrw$

input **recv(m)**$_{j,i}$ where $(m = \langle write\text{-}ok, id \rangle)$
Effect:
  if $(phase = wrw) \wedge (id = mid)$ then
    $acc \leftarrow acc \cup \{j\}$
    if $(|acc| > f)$ then
      $mid \leftarrow mid + 1$
      for all $j \in \mathcal{D}$ do $msg[j] \leftarrow \langle write, acc, tag, mid \rangle$
      $acc \leftarrow \emptyset; \ phase \leftarrow wdw$
    else if $(phase = wdw) \wedge (id = mid)$ then
      $acc \leftarrow acc \cup \{j\}$
    if $(\exists Q \in \mathcal{Q}_W : Q \subseteq acc)$ then
      $mid \leftarrow mid + 1$
      for all $j \in \mathcal{R}$ do $msg[j] \leftarrow \langle secure, tag, mid \rangle$
      $acc \leftarrow \emptyset; \ phase \leftarrow wok$

Fig. 1. Client C_i transitions.

input **recv(m)**$_{j,i}$ where $(m = \langle read, t, mid \rangle)$
Effect:
  if $\exists v : (v, t, *) \in data$ then
    $(v', t') \leftarrow$ choose $\{v \mid (v, t, *) \in data\}$
    $msg[j] \leftarrow \langle read\text{-}ok, v', t', mid \rangle$
  else
    $(v', t') \leftarrow maxst(data)$
    $msg[j] \leftarrow \langle read\text{-}ok, v', t', mid \rangle$

input **recv(m)**$_{j,i}$ where $(m = \langle write, v, t, mid \rangle)$
Effect:
  $data \leftarrow data \cup \{(v, t, 0)\}$
  $msg[j] \leftarrow \langle write\text{-}ok, mid \rangle$

input **recv(m)**$_{j,i}$ where $(m = \langle gossip, v, t \rangle)$
Effect:
  $data \leftarrow data \cup \{(v, t, 1)\} \setminus \{(v, t, 0)\}$
  for all $j \in \mathcal{D}$ do
    $msg[j] \leftarrow \langle write, \{i\}, t \rangle$

input **recv(m)**$_{j,i}$ where $(m = \langle secure, t, mid \rangle)$
Effect:
  if $\exists v : (v, t, 0) \in data$ then
    for all $v : (v, t, 0) \in data$ do
      $data = data \cup (v, t, 1) \setminus \{(v, t, 0)\}$

input **fail**$_i$
Effect:
  stop taking locally-controlled steps

output **send(m)**$_{i,j}$
Precondition:
  $msg[j] = m$
Effect:
  $msg[j] \leftarrow \perp$

internal **gossip**$_i$
Precondition:
  $\exists v, t, : (v, t, 1) \in data$
Effect:
  $(v', t') \leftarrow$ choose $\{(v, t) \mid (v, t, 1) \in data\}$
  for all $j \in \mathcal{R}$ do
    $msg[j] \leftarrow \langle gossip, v', t' \rangle$

internal **gc**$_i$
Precondition:
  $\exists v, t : (v, t, 1) \in data$
Effect:
  $t \leftarrow$ choose $\{t' \mid (v, t', 1) \in data\}$
  for all $v', t' : ((v', t', *) \in data) \wedge (t' < t)$ do
    remove $(v', t', *)$ from $data$

Fig. 2. Replica R_i transitions.

```
input recv(m)_{j,i} where (m = ⟨read, mid⟩)
Effect:
    msg[j] ← ⟨read-ok, utd, tag, mid⟩


input fail_i
Effect:
    stop taking locally-controlled steps


output send(m)_{i,j}
Precondition:
    msg[j] = m
Effect:
    msg[j] ← ⊥


input recv(m)_{j,i} where (m = ⟨write, S, t, mid⟩)
Effect:
    if (t = tag) then
        utd ← utd ∪ S
    else if (t > tag) then
        if |S| ≥ f + 1 then
            utd ← S
        t ← tag
    msg[j] ← ⟨write-ok, mid⟩
```

Fig. 3. Directory D_i transitions.

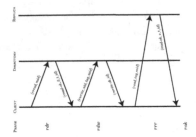

Fig. 4. Client read operation.

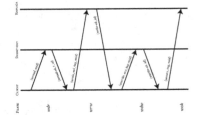

Fig. 5. Client write operation.

4.3   Replica Protocol

The replicas respond to client requests to read and write values of x. Replicas also garbage-collect out of date values of x from *data*, and gossip among themselves the latest value of x. The latter is an optimization to help spread the latest value of x, so that clients can read from a nearby replica.

When replica i receives a message to write value/tag (v, t), i just adds $(v, t, 0)$ to *data*. The 0 in the third coordinate indicates v is not a secured value. When i is asked to read the value associated with tag t, i checks whether it has $(v, t, *)^6$ in *data*. If so, i returns (v, t). Otherwise, i finds the secured triple with the largest tag in *data*, i.e., the $(v', t', 1)$ with the highest tag t' among all triples with third coordinate equal to 1, and returns (v', t'). When i is asked to secure tag t, i checks whether $(*, t, 0)$ exists in *data*, and if so, sets the third coordinate of the triple to 1.

When i garbage-collects out of date values of x, it finds a secured value $(v, t, 1)$ in *data*, and then removes all triples $(v', t', *)$ with $t' < t$ from *data*.

---

6 The $*$ indicates the last coordinate can be a 0 or 1.

When i gossips, it finds a secured value $(v, t, 1)$ in $data$, and sends (v, t) to all the other replicas. When i receives a gossip message for (v, t), it adds $(v, t, 1)$ to $data$.

4.4   Directory Protocol

The directories' only job is to respond to client requests to read and write utd and tag.

When directory i gets a message to read utd and tag, it simply returns (utd, tag). When i is asked to write (S, t) to utd and tag (S is a set of replicas and t is a tag), i first checks that $t \geq tag$. If not, then the write request is out of date, and i sends an acknowledgment but does not perform the write. If $t = tag$, i adds S to utd. If $t > tag$, i checks whether $|S| \geq f + 1$, and if so, sets utd to S.

5   Correctness

In this section, we show that LDR satisfies the liveness and atomicity properties of Defns. 1 and 2, resp. A more detailed proof can be found in the full paper [6].

5.1   Liveness

Consider an execution in which some read and write quorum of directories do not fail, and no more than f replicas fail. Then a client never blocks waiting for a response from a quorum of directories. The client also does not block waiting to read from a set utd of replicas, since we can easily check that $|utd| \geq f + 1$ always. Therefore, every invocation at a nonfailing client always has a response in the execution.

5.2   Atomicity

To prove the atomicity condition, we show that a trace of LDR satisfies Lemma 13.10 of [13]. In [13], it is shown that an algorithm satisfying Lemma 13.10 implements the semantics of an atomic register. The lemma requires us to define a partial order $\prec$ on the operations in a trace of LDR. Let ϕ be a complete operation in a trace, $i.e.$, an invocation and its corresponding response. If ϕ is a read, define $\lambda(\phi)$ to be the tag associated with the value returned by ϕ.[7] If ϕ is a write, define $\lambda(\phi)$ to be the tag of the value written by ϕ. We define $\prec$ as follows:

Definition 3. *Let ϕ and ψ be two complete operations in an execution of* LDR.

1. *If ϕ is a write and ψ is a read, define $\phi \prec \psi$ if $\lambda(\phi) \leq \lambda(\psi)$.*
2. *Otherwise, define $\phi \prec \psi$ if $\lambda(\phi) < \lambda(\psi)$.*

---

[7] Recall that when ϕ reads from a replica in phase rrr, the replica returns $(*, t)$. Then, we set $\lambda(\phi) = t$.

Before proving LDR satisfies Lemma 13.10, we first prove some lemmas. The first lemma says that if a client i asks to read a value with tag t from a replica, then the replica returns a value with tag $\geq t$ to the client.

Lemma 1. *Let ϕ be a complete read operation by client i, and let t be the maximum tag which i read during the rdr phase of ϕ. Then, $\lambda(\phi) \geq t$.*

We briefly argue why this lemma is true. Suppose i read (S, t) from a directory during rdr. Then S is the set of replicas that i asks to read from during rrr. For every replica in S, either $(*, t, *)$ still exists in the replica's *data*, or it was garbage-collected. In the first case, the replica returns $(*, t)$, so $\lambda(\phi) = t$. In the second case, the replica must have secured a value with tag $t' > t$ in *data*. The replica returns $(*, t')$, so $\lambda(\phi) > t$.

The next lemma states that after a read finishes, a write quorum of directories have *tag* at least as high as the tag of the value the read returned.

Lemma 2. *Let ϕ be a complete read operation in an execution of LDR. Then after ϕ finishes, there exists a write quorum of directories with tag $\geq \lambda(\phi)$.*

We argue why the lemma holds. Let t be the largest tag i read during the rdr phase of ϕ. If $\lambda(\phi) = t$, then i writes $(*, t)$ to a write quorum of directories during rdw, before the end of ϕ, and the lemma is true. Otherwise, by the previous lemma, $\lambda(\phi) > t$. This means i tried to read a value with tag t at a replica, but the replica returned a value with a larger tag. Hence, the latter value was secure at the replica, which implies an earlier client had finished its phase wdw while writing that value. That client wrote $\lambda(\phi)$ to a write quorum of directories during its phase wdw, before the end of ϕ, and so the lemma holds.

We can now prove the relation $\prec$ we defined earlier satisfies Lemma 13.10 of [13]. For lack of space, we prove only the most interesting condition in the lemma, the second. The condition is that if an operation ϕ completes before operation ψ begins, then $\psi \not\prec \phi$.

To see this, we consider the four cases where ϕ and ψ are various combinations of reads or writes. If ϕ and ψ are both writes, then ϕ writes $\lambda(\phi)$ to a write quorum of directories before it finishes. Since the read quorum ψ reads from intersects with ϕ's write quorum, ψ will use a larger tag than ϕ, and $\psi \not\prec \phi$. If ϕ is a write and ψ is a read, then by similar reasoning, ψ returns a value with tag at least as large as $\lambda(\phi)$, and the condition again holds. When ϕ is a read and ψ is a write, by Lemma 2, a write quorum of directories have *tag* at least as high as $\lambda(\phi)$ after ϕ finishes, so ψ uses a larger tag than $\lambda(\phi)$, and the condition holds. Lastly, when both ϕ and ψ are reads, then ψ will try to read a value with tag at least as high as $\lambda(\phi)$ from the replicas. By Lemma 1, $\lambda(\psi) \geq \lambda(\phi)$, and so $\psi \not\prec \phi$.

Combining Sections 5.1 and 5.2, we have shown:

Theorem 1. LDR *satisfies the liveness and atomicity properties of Definitions 1 and 2, resp.*

6   Performance Analysis

We analyze the communication and time complexity of *LDR*, and show that these costs are nearly optimal when the size of the data is large compared to the size of the metadata.

We first describe a modification to the client algorithm. Currently, when a client wants to contact a set of directories or replicas, it sends messages to a superset of that set, in case some directories or replicas have failed. However, in practice failures are rare, and so it suffices for the client to send messages to exactly those directories or replicas it wants to contact. This technique greatly improves performance, and in general, does not decrease fault-tolerance. We analyze *LDR* for this optimized implementation.

6.1   Communication Complexity

A basic assumption which *LDR* makes is that the size of the data, *i.e.*, values of x, is much larger than the size of metadata *LDR* uses, such as tags and *utd*'s. Therefore, we also assume it is much more costly to transfer data than metadata. In particular, we assume that the communication cost to transfer one value of x is d, while the cost to transfer one unit of metadata is 1. We assume $d \gg 1$, and also that $d \gg f^2$, where f is the number of replica failures *LDR* tolerates.[8] Lastly, we assume all read and write quorums have size $f + 1$. As an example of our cost measure, it costs $d + 3$ to transfer the message $\langle read - ok, v, t, id \rangle$, where v is a value of x. With this measure, the communication cost of an *LDR* read operation adds up to $d + 2f^2 + 14f + 18$, and the cost of an *LDR* write operation adds up to $(f + 1)d + f^2 + 20f + 19$.

When $d \gg 1$ and $d \gg f^2$, the cost of an *LDR* read is dominated by the d term. However, any replication algorithm must read at least one value of the data during a read. Therefore, the communication complexity of a read for any replication algorithm is $\geq d$ in the worst case. Therefore, for large d, the communication complexity of an *LDR* read is asymptotically optimal. Also, in any replication algorithm tolerating the failure of up to f replicas, the data must be written to at least $f + 1$ replicas. Therefore, the worst case communication complexity of a write for any replication algorithm is $\geq (f + 1)d$.[9] Therefore, *LDR* also has asymptotically optimal write communication complexity.

6.2   Time Complexity

To evaluate the time complexity, we now consider a synchronous communication model. Similar to the communication complexity, we assume that it takes time

---

[8] This assumption is reasonable, since in practice f is quite small, typically < 4.

[9] In fact, it is not necessary to write a complete copy of the data to each server. For example, by encoding the data, one can write smaller chunks of the encoding to each server, decreasing the total amount of communication. However, as any such optimizations can also be applied to *LDR*, they do not change the optimality of *LDR*'s communication complexity.

d to transfer a value of x, and it takes unit time to transfer a piece of metadata. We also assume that when we send messages to multiple destinations, we can send them in parallel, so that the time required to send all the messages equals the time to send the largest message. Then, the time complexity of an LDR read sums to $d + 2f + 18$, and that of a write sums to $d + f + 19$. Any replication algorithm must take at least d time for a read or write, since it has to read or write at least one copy of the data. Thus, for d large, the time complexity of LDR is optimal.

6.3   Comparison to Other Algorithms

We now compare LDR's performance with the performance of the algorithm given in [14]. We choose this comparison because [14] has many attributes in common with LDR, such as not using locks or group communication. Most other replication algorithms rely on these techniques, which makes comparison to them difficult. LDR and [14] are also similar in methodology. In fact, LDR uses a modified form of [14] in its directory protocol. However, the two algorithms differ substantially in their performance. Using the measure for communication cost and latency given above, we compute [14]'s read communication cost as $2(f+1)d$ plus "lower order" (compared to d) terms. For large d, this is a factor of $2(f+1)$ larger than LDR's read communication cost. The write communication cost for [14] is $(f+1)d$ plus lower order terms, which is asymptotically the same as LDR's cost. The latency of a read in [14] is approximately $2d$, which is asymptotically twice that of LDR. The latency of a write is asymptotically the same in [14] and LDR. We note that most replication algorithms have costs similar to that of [14], so that for large d, LDR also performs better than those algorithms.

Lastly, we mention that because LDR does not store data in quorums of replicas, but rather, in arbitrary sets, LDR can take advantage of algorithms which optimize replica placement to further improve performance.

7   Lower Bounds

7.1   Model

We prove our lower bounds in the *atomic servers* model. This computational model is based on the standard client/server model, except that the servers are required to be atomic objects (of arbitrary and possibly different types), which permit concurrent accesses by clients. Each server j's interface consists of $read(-ok)_{i,j}$ and $modify(-ok)_{i,j}$ actions, $\forall i \in C$. $read$ can return any value based on the server's state, but must not change the server's state. $modify$ can change the state of the server arbitrarily, and return any value. The clients have input and output actions corresponding to the outputs and inputs, resp., of the servers. Clients and servers communicate by invoking actions and receiving responses from each other, instead of sending messages.

Let f be a natural number. We say an f-$srca$[10] is an algorithm in the atomic servers model which allows clients to read and write a data object, such that the client operations appear to happen atomically, and such that every client invocation has a response, as long as at most f servers fail.

The atomic servers model is similar to the network-based model we implemented LDR in, and LDR is a network analogue of an f-srca. The lower bounds we prove in the atomic servers model have direct analogues in the network model, which we describe following the proof of each lower bound. The reason we use the atomic servers model is that it simplifies our proofs by removing details, such as message buffering, which are present in the network model; however, it is straightforward to translate the proofs we present to the network model. Therefore, using the atomic servers model does not weaken our lower bounds.

7.2   Write on Read Necessity

Recall that when a client reads in LDR, it writes to the directories during phase rdw. Similarly, in ABD and other replication algorithms, clients also write during reads. Our first lower bound shows that this is inherent: in any f-srca with $f > 0$, clients must write to some servers during a read. More precisely, let ϕ be a complete (read or write) operation by some client i in a trace of an f-srca. We will think of ϕ both as an ordered pair consisting of an invocation and response, and as a subsequence of the trace, beginning at the invocation and ending at the response. We define $\Delta(\phi)$ to be the number of servers j such that $modify(*)_{i,j}$ occurs during (subtrace) ϕ. That is, we count the $modify(*)_{i,*}$ actions occurring during ϕ as writes performed by ϕ. We do this because $modify(*)_{i,j}$ potentially changes the state of server j, and to do so, it must write to j.

The following theorem says that in any f-srca, a read must sometimes write to at least f servers.

Theorem 2. *In any f-srca A, there exists a complete client read operation ϕ in an execution of A such that $|\Delta(\phi)| \geq f$.*

Proof. The intuition for the proof is that during the course of a write operation, the algorithm is sometimes in an ambiguous state, in which another logical read can return either an old value or the new value being written. A reader needs to write to record which value it decided to return, so that later reads can make a consistent decision. Since any server the reader writes to may fail, the reader must write to at least f servers.[11]

Suppose for contradiction there exists an f-srca A, such that for any complete read operation ϕ in any execution of A, $|\Delta(\phi)| < f$. Consider an execution $\alpha = s_0 \pi_1 s_1 \ldots \pi_n s_n$ of A starting from initial state s_0, in which a client w_1 writes a value $v_1 \neq v_0$, where v_0 is the default value of x. Let $\alpha(i) = s_0 \pi_1 s_1 \ldots \pi_i s_i$ be the length $2i+1$ prefix of α ($\alpha(0) = s_0$). Let i^* be the smallest i such that there exists a client read starting from s_i, so that if this read runs in isolation (*i.e.*, we

---

[10] f-srca stands for f-*strongly consistent replica control algorithm.*

[11] We'll see later why the reader writes to f and not $f + 1$ servers.

pause w_1 and only run the read), it may return v_1. Thus, we choose i^* to be the first "ambiguous" point in w_1's write, when a client read can return either v_0 or v_1. Note that all reads starting after $\alpha(i)$, for $i < i^*$, must return v_0. Clearly, $1 \leq i^* \leq n$. Let p_1 be the server, if any, that changed its state from state s_{i^*-1} to s_{i^*}. Note that there can be at most one such server, since only one server can change its state after each action.

Now let α_1 be an execution consisting of $\alpha(i^*)$ appended by a complete logical read operation ϕ_1 returning v_1. Let α_2 be an execution consisting of α_1, appended by another complete logical read operation ϕ_2, such that ϕ_2 does not (physically) read from any server in $\Delta(\phi_1) \cup p_1$. That is, ϕ_2 does not read from any server that ϕ_1 wrote to, nor from p_1. We first argue why ϕ_2 exists. By assumption, $|\Delta(\phi)| < f$, so that $|\Delta(\phi_1) \cup p_1| \leq f$. In ϕ_2, we *delay* processing ϕ_2's read invocations at all the servers in $\Delta(\phi_1) \cup p_1$ indefinitely, so that it looks to ϕ_2 like the servers in $\Delta(\phi_1) \cup p_1$ failed. Since A guarantees liveness when at most f servers fail, ϕ_2 must still terminate, without reading from $\Delta(\phi_1) \cup p_1$. This shows that ϕ_2 exists, and $\alpha(i^*)\phi_1\phi_2$ is a valid execution of A. Note that ϕ_2 returns v_1, since ϕ_2 occurs after ϕ_1, which returns v_1.

We now claim that $\alpha(i^*-1)\phi_2$ is also a valid execution of A. Indeed, only the servers in $\Delta(\phi_1) \cup p_1$ can change their state from the final state of $\alpha(i^*-1)$ to the final state of $\alpha\phi_1$.[12] Since ϕ_2 does not read from any server in $\Delta(\phi_1) \cup p_1$, the final state of $\alpha(i^*-1)$ and $\alpha\phi_1$ look the same to ϕ_2. So, since $\alpha(i^*)\phi_1\phi_2$ is a valid execution of A, $\alpha(i^*-1)\phi_2$ is also a valid execution. However, all logical reads starting after $\alpha(i^*-1)$ return v_0, which is a contradiction because ϕ_2 returns v_1. This shows A does not exist, and all f-srca's must sometimes write to f servers during a read.

To translate this lower bound to the standard network model, we say that for any atomic replication algorithm in the network model tolerating f server faults, there exists a read operation in an execution of the algorithm in which at least f servers change their state.

7.3   Proportional Storage Necessity

Recall that a replica in *LDR* sometimes stores several values of x when there are multiple concurrent client writes. Our second lower bound shows that this behavior is not an artifact of *LDR*, but is inherent in a class of efficient replication algorithms we call *selfish f-srcas*. Intuitively, a selfish f-srca is one in which the clients do not "help" each other (much). Helping is a crucial ingredient in implementing lock-free concurrent objects, as in [11]. But helping has adverse effects on performance, since clients must do work for other operations as well as their own. In a selfish f-srca, we only allow clients to help each other with "cheap" operations. In particular, clients can help each other write metadata, such as tags, but cannot help write data (values of x), since we assume the data is

---

[12] Only p_1 can change its state from s_{i^*-1} to s_{i^*}, and only servers receiving *modify* invocations can change state during ϕ_1.

large and expensive to write. For example, LDR is a selfish f-srca, since a reader never writes data, only metadata, and a writer only writes its own value, and does not help write the values of other writes. On the other hand, ABD is not a selfish f-srca, because a reader writes values of x during its second phase. The comparison in Section 6.3 shows that a selfish f-srca such as LDR can be more efficient than an unselfish one such as ABD. We show that a disadvantage of selfish f-srcas is that they require the servers to use storage that is proportional to the number of concurrently writing clients. In the following, we formalize the notions of selfish f-srcas and the amount of storage that the servers use.

To make our result more general, we want an abstract measure of the storage used by the servers, not tied down to a particular storage format. Let α be an execution of an f-srca, and let $v \in V$. We say v is g-erasable after α if, by failing some set of g servers after α, we ensure that no later client read can return value v. That is, the failure of some g servers after α is enough to "erase" all knowledge of v. We define the multiplicity of v after α, $m(v, \alpha)$, to be the smallest g such that v is g-erasable after α. If $m(v, \alpha) = h$, then intuitively, exactly h servers know about v, and the amount of storage used for v is proportional to h.

We now to formally define selfish f-srcas, trying to capturing the idea that client reads do not write values of x, and client writes only write their own value. Let A be an f-srca. We say an execution of A is server-exclusive if at any point in the execution, there is at most one client accessing any server. In a server-exclusive execution, we can easily "attribute" every action to a particular client. If the action is performed by a client, we attribute the action to that client. If the action is performed by a server, then the server must be responding to some client's invocation; we attribute the action to that client. We now define selfish f-srcas as follows:

Definition 4. Let A be an f-srca. We say that A is selfish if for any server-exclusive execution α of A, the following holds: let π be an action in α attributed to client $i \in C$, let s_π be the state in α before π, and let s'_π be the state in α after π.

1. If the last invocation at C_i is $read_i$, then $\forall v \in V : m(v, s'_\pi) \leq m(v, s_\pi)$.
2. If the last invocation at C_i is $write(v)_i$, then $\forall v' \in V \backslash \{v\} : m(v', s'_\pi) \leq m(v', s_\pi)$.

This definition says that in a server-exclusive execution of a selfish f-srca, client reads do not increase the multiplicity of any value, and clients writes can only increase the multiplicity of their own value.

Definition 5. Let A be an f-srca. Define the storage used by A, $M(A)$, to be the supremum, over all executions α of A, of $\sum_{v \in V} m(v, \alpha)$.

Assuming the storage needed for a value of x is large compared to the storage for metadata that the servers use, $M(A)$ is an abstract measure of the amount of storage used by the servers of A.

Lastly, we define an (f, c)-srca as an f-srca which only guarantees liveness and atomicity when there are $\leq c$ concurrent writers in an execution. We now state the second lower bound.

Theorem 3. *Let A be an (f, c)-srca, where f and c are positive integers.*[13] *Then $M(A) \geq fc$.*

Proof. Suppose for contradiction that $M(A) < fc$. The intuition for the proof is that if we run c client writes concurrently, then because $M(A) < fc$, we can ensure none of the values written have multiplicity greater than f. Then, in later client reads, we can delay responses from f servers at a time to ensure that consecutive reads do not return the same value. But eventually some two non-consecutive reads must return the same value. This violates atomicity, and shows that A does not exist.

Let W be a set of c writer clients, all writing distinct values different from v_0. Construct an execution α starting from an initial state of A using to the following procedure:

1. Repeat steps 2 or 3, as long as no $w \in W$ has finished its write.
2. If any $w \in W$ has an action π enabled, and π is not an invocation at a server, extend α by letting w run π.
3. Otherwise, choose a $w \in W$ with invocation π at server j enabled, such that the following holds: if we extend α to α', by running π and then letting server j run until it outputs a response to π, then $\forall v \in V \backslash \{v_0\} : m(v, \alpha') \leq f$. Set $\alpha \leftarrow \alpha'$.

It is easy to see that α is a server-exclusive execution. Also, every value except possibly v_0 has multiplicity at most f after α. This is because when step 2 of the procedure occurs, only client w changes state, and no servers. Therefore, the multiplicity of any value cannot increase. When step 3 occurs, the server j that runs was chosen so that it does not increase the multiplicity of any value beyond f. Lastly, we claim that some $w \in W$ finishes its write after α. To see this, first observe that in any prefix of α, there must exist a value v_w being written by $w \in W$ that has multiplicity $< f$, since there are c values being written, and the sum of all their multiplicities is at most $M(A) < cf$. Then, the above procedure can run w and any server which w invokes, because doing this increases the multiplicity of v_w by at most 1, and leaves the multiplicity of every other value unchanged (because A is selfish). So, as long as no writer is finished, the procedure can extend α to a longer execution. Thus, since algorithm A guarantees liveness, some writer must eventually take enough steps in α to finish. Let α' be the prefix of α up to when the first writer w finishes.

Now we start a sequence of non-overlapping client reads $\{\phi_i\}_i$ after α'. Let read ϕ_i return value v_i. Since w finished writing v_w, by atomicity, no ϕ_i can return v_0 (x's initial value). For each v_i, let F_i be a set of f servers such that, if we fail F_i, no later client read can return v_i. F_i exists, because no value except possibly v_0 has multiplicity greater than f, and no ϕ_i increases the multiplicity of any value. During ϕ_i, we delay the responses from all servers in F_{i-1} indefinitely, so that it seems to ϕ_i like the servers in F_{i-1} failed. Then, since ϕ_i must tolerate f server failures, ϕ_i must finish without (physically) reading from any server in

---

[13] The theorem does not hold for $f = 0$, as we explain in the full paper [6].

F_{i-1}. Therefore, ϕ_i cannot return v_{i-1}, *i.e.*, two consecutive reads cannot return the same value. Since there are only c values which any client read can return, eventually some $v_i = v_j$, where $j - i > 1$. Choose k such that $i < k < j$. We now have a contradiction because v_k linearizes after v_i, and v_j linearizes after v_k, but $v_i = v_j$. This shows that A does not exist, and $M(A) \geq fc$ for all selfish (f, c)-srcas.

To translate this lower bound to the network model, we say that the servers in any atomic replication algorithm in the network model tolerating f server faults must have storage proportional to the maximum number of concurrently writing clients.

8 Conclusions

In this paper we presented *LDR*, an efficient replication algorithm based on separately replicating data and metadata. Our algorithm is optimal when the size of the data is large compared to the metadata. We also presented two lower bounds. One states that the number of writes necessary within some client read operation equals at least the fault-tolerance of the algorithm. The other states that servers in a selfish replication algorithm need storage proportional to the number of concurrent writers. The separation of data from metadata was the key to *LDR*'s efficiency. We are interested in extending this idea to enhance the performance of other distributed algorithms.

References

1. A. Adya, W. Bolosky, M. Castro, and G. Cermak et al. Farsite: Federated, available, and reliable storage for an incompletely trusted environment. In *Proceedings of the fifth symposium on operating systems design and implementation*, 2002.
2. Y. Amir, D. Dolev, P. Melliar-Smith, and L. Moser. Robust and efficient replication using group communication, 1994.
3. H. Attiya, A. Bar-Noy, and D. Dolev. Sharing memory robustly in message-passing systems. *Journal of the ACM*, 42(1):124–142, January 1995.
4. P. A. Bernstein, V. Hadzilacos, and N. Goodman. *Concurrency control and recovery in database systems*. Addison-Wesley Longman Publishing Co., Inc., 1987.
5. Y. Breitbart and H. F. Korth. Replication and consistency: being lazy helps sometimes. In *Proceedings of the sixteenth ACM SIGACT-SIGMOD-SIGART symposium on Principles of database systems*, pages 173–184. ACM Press, 1997.
6. R. Fan. Efficient replication of large data-objects. Technical Report MIT-LCS-TR-886, Department of Electrical Engineering and Computer Science, MIT, Cambridge, MA 02139, February 2003.
7. David K. Gifford. Weighted voting for replicated data. In *Proceedings of the seventh symposium on Operating systems principles*, pages 150–162, 1979.
8. J. Gray, P. Helland, P. O'Neil, and D. Shasha. The dangers of replication and a solution. In *Proceedings of the 1996 ACM SIGMOD international conference on Management of data*, pages 173–182. ACM Press, 1996.
9. J. Welch H. Attiya. *Distributed Computing*. McGraw Hill International, Ltd., 1998.

10. M. P. Herlihy and J. M. Wing. Axioms for concurrent objects. pages 13–26. ACM Press, 1987.
11. Maurice Herlihy. Wait-free synchronization. *ACM Transactions on Programming Languages and Systems*, 13(1):124–149, January 1991.
12. R. Ladin, B. Liskov, L. Shrira, and S. Ghemawat. Providing high availability using lazy replication. *ACM Transactions on Computer Systems*, 10(4):360–391, 1992.
13. N. Lynch. *Distributed Algorithms*. Morgan Kaufmann Publishers, Inc., San Mateo, CA, March 1996.
14. N. Lynch and A. Shvartsman. Robust emulation of shared memory using dynamic quorum-acknowledged broadcasts. In *Twenty-Seventh Annual International Symposium on Fault-Tolerant Computing (FTCS'97)*, pages 272–281, Seattle, Washington, USA, June 1997. IEEE.
15. E. Pacitti, P. Minet, and E. Simon. Fast algorithms for maintaining replica consistency in lazy master replicated databases. In *VLDB'99, Proceedings of 25th International Conference on Very Large Data Bases, September 7-10, 1999, Edinburgh, Scotland, UK*, pages 126–137. Morgan Kaufmann, 1999.
16. J.-F. Paris. Voting with witnesses:: A consistency scheme for replicated files. In *Proceedings of the 6th International Conference on Distributed Computing Systems (ICDCS)*, pages 606–612, Washington, DC, 1986. IEEE Computer Society.
17. K. Petersen and K. Li. An evaluation of multiprocessor cache coherence based on virtual memory support. In *Proc. of the 8th Int'l Parallel Processing Symp. (IPPS'94)*, pages 158–164, 1994.
18. R. van Renesse and A. S. Tanenbaum. Voting with ghosts. In *Proceedings of the 8th International Conference on Distributed Computing Systems (ICDCS)*, pages 456–462, Washington, DC, 1988. IEEE Computer Society.

On the Locality of Consistency Conditions

Roman Vitenberg[1] and Roy Friedman[2]

[1] Computer Science Department, UCSB, Santa Barbara, CA 93106, USA
romanv@cs.ucsb.edu,
http://www.cs.ucsb.edu/~romanv
[2] Computer Science Department, Technion, Haifa 32000, Israel
roy@cs.technion.ac.il,
http://www.cs.technion.ac.il/~roy

Abstract. *Locality* is a property of consistency conditions indicating that any collection of implementations of a consistency condition C for disjoint subsets of objects is an implementation of C for the entire set of objects. This paper investigates the sources of locality by considering the general model of consistency conditions and capturing their properties. We establish several ways of constructing local conditions as well as new general techniques for analyzing locality of consistency conditions that do not depend on a particular type of shared object. These techniques allow us to formally prove non-locality of a) all conditions stronger than sequential consistency but weaker than or incomparable to linearizability, b) all conditions stronger than or incomparable to coherence but weaker than sequential consistency, and c) a range of conditions that require sequences of operations to execute atomically. These results cover most commonly used consistency conditions as well as many other conditions useful in the context of specific systems.

1 Introduction

Replicating data is a common technique for achieving performance, scalability and availability in distributed systems. It is used in databases, in high-performance cluster-based computing in the form of distributed shared memory, in replicated objects systems, and even in Internet caching. One of the main issues in dealing with replicated data is keeping the various copies consistent, at least to some degree. The definition of the consistency semantics provided by a replicated system is known as a consistency condition. There is a known tradeoff between the performance and scalability of a replicated system, and the strength of the consistency condition it may guarantee, as discussed, e.g., in [6,7]. A weak consistency condition can be implemented more efficiently. On the other hand, a weak condition means that data in replicas may diverge considerably, which may be an annoyance for clients of database systems, complicates the programming model in distributed shared memory systems, and in extreme cases may even be too weak for solving certain problems [5]. Balancing this tradeoff is the motivation behind much of the research dealing with consistency conditions.

F.E. Fich (Ed.): DISC 2003, LNCS 2848, pp. 92–105, 2003.

In recent years, it has become increasingly common to construct complex distributed systems and applications from independently built separate components, each component being responsible for a well defined part of the complex system functionality and tailored for a specific operational environment. While this trend is especially prominent in modern object oriented middlewares like CORBA, .NET and EJB where each component is viewed as a distributed object, it can also be seen in other areas of distributed computing, e.g., in interconnecting shared memory systems [10]. Typically, components in these systems are autonomous and even built without a priori knowledge of each other, which limits the ability to coordinate the operation of different components. This poses the challenge of achieving system wide consistency guarantees when components are replicated. Fortunately, it holds for some consistency conditions that once the condition is preserved independently by each replicated component implementation, it will be preserved by the system as a whole without any component coordination. This highly desired property of consistency conditions, called locality [14],[1] is the focus of this paper. In particular, locality means that the set of objects can change without affecting the implementation of existing objects. Similarly, the implementation of an object can change without requiring alterations to other objects. Not only does locality facilitate software engineering of composite systems but it also greatly simplifies the proof of correctness because it is enough to consider the operation of each individual component separately.

In the past, it was known that linearizability, which is the strongest consistency condition, is local [12,14]. It was also established that sequential consistency [16] and serializability [19] are not local for a particular object type system [14]. However, there was no systematic approach to locality analysis of consistency conditions. In this work, we consider various properties of local conditions. We introduce new techniques, such as the separating sequence construction and logical operations on consistency conditions, for testing locality of a consistency condition by exploiting few basic properties of all existing object type systems. These techniques allow us to formally prove non-locality of a) all conditions stronger than sequential consistency but weaker than or incomparable to linearizability, b) all conditions stronger than or incomparable to coherence but weaker than sequential consistency, and c) a range of conditions that require sequences of operations to execute atomically. The proofs of these results follow the same scheme: we assume by way of contradiction that a given consistency condition is local and then construct a counterexample to the condition's locality by using separating sequences and other methods that we have developed.

In particular, these results imply that most consistency conditions that are known to present a good compromise in the tradeoff between consistency and performance (e.g., PRAM [17], causal consistency [3,4], processor consistency [2], PSO [1,18,15], TSO [1,18,15], and hybrid consistency based on sequential consistency [11]), are non-local. Furthermore, sequential consistency, release consistency [13], and serializability are shown to be non-local for virtually any object type system. However, we do not limit our consideration to standard consistency

---

[1] Sometimes, this property is also called composeability, e.g. in [11].

conditions. The results of this paper are very general as they imply non-locality of other useful conditions whose examples we consider in the context of specific systems.

As a counterbalance to these negative results, we show two distinct groups of local consistency conditions and specify ways of constructing new local conditions. However, only few conditions created this way constitute meaningful guarantees and can be used in systems that exist in practice.

2   System Model

We generally adopt the model and definitions introduced in [14], but slightly adjust them to our needs. A system consists of a finite set of processes named $p_1, p_2, \ldots, p_n$ that communicate through shared objects. Each object has a name and a type. The type defines a set of signatures of primitive operations. These operations provide the only means to manipulate that object; in this work we consider only single object operations. Each operation signature consists of a name and the list of input and output parameter types (including allowed ranges). Without restricting generality, we assume that each operation has exactly one input and one output parameter. For example, the classical Read-Write object type consists of two operations: READ with void input parameter and integer output parameter and WRITE with integer input parameter and void output parameter.

Execution of an operation op has a non-zero duration; this is modeled by an operation invocation event $inv(op)$ and a matching operation response event $resp(op)$. Execution of a system is modeled by a history which is a sequence (finite or infinite) of invocation and response events. For the sake of brevity, we will abuse the notation and use the same term "operation" to refer to operation signature in an object type and operation occurrence in a history (i.e., the matching pair of invocation and response events) whenever it does not lead to a confusion. Let op be an operation on object X performed at process p with input value V^I and output value V^o; X, p, V^I, and V^o will be denoted as $obj(op)$, $pr(op)$, $ival(op)$, and $oval(op)$, respectively. Instead of the full notation $inv(op)$ on X at p and $resp(op)$ on X at p we will use $inv(op)$ and $resp(op)$ wherever the operation's object and process are not relevant.

A history H is complete if for each $inv(op) \in H$, the matching $resp(op)$ also belongs to H. For the sake of presentation simplicity we consider only complete histories in this paper; it can be shown that our results hold for incomplete histories as well but a more scrupulous case analysis would be required.

A history H is sequential if (1) its first event is an invocation and (2) each invocation (response) event is immediately followed (preceded) by the matching response (invocation). A history H is a serialization of a history H' if H is sequential and it consists of the same events as H'.

A process subhistory $H|p$ (H at p) of a history H is the subsequence of all events in H that occurred at p. An object subhistory is defined in a similar way for an object X; it is denoted $H|X$ (H on X). A history H is well-formed if each process subhistory $H|p$ is sequential. In the following we consider only well-formed histories. Such histories model sequential processes accessing concurrent objects. As some operations on the same object may be concurrent, observe that object subhistories of well-formed histories are not necessarily sequential.

A set S of histories is prefix-closed if, whenever H is in S, every prefix of H is also in S. A single-object history is one in which all events are associated with the same object. A sequential specification for an object is a prefix-closed set of single-object sequential histories for that object.[2] A sequential history H is legal if each object subhistory $H|X$ belongs to the sequential specification for X.

A history H induces an irreflexive partial order $<_H$ on operations: $op_1 <_H op_2$ if $resp(op_1)$ precedes $inv(op_2)$ in H. This order captures the notion of "real-time" precedence ordering. If H is sequential, $<_H$ is a total order. Two operations are called non-concurrent if they are ordered by $<_H$ and concurrent otherwise.

2.1 Refining Object Type System

In this section we further elaborate on the object type system to the extent necessary to show the results in the following sections. Recall from Section 2 that a history determines the input and output values of all operation occurrences. Given a history H, a response event $resp(op)$ in H, and an output value V^o that is in the valid range of output values for op, denote $H(oval(op) \leftarrow V^o)$ a history that is obtained from H by substituting the output value of $resp(op)$ with V^o. An output value V^o is legal for a response event $resp(op)$ in a sequential history H if V^o is in the valid range of output values for op and the sequential history $H(oval(op) \leftarrow V^o)$ is legal. An output value V^o is a possible outcome of an operation op with an input value V^I if there is some sequential history H and a response event $resp(op)$ in H such that the matching invocation $inv(op)$ is passed an input value V^I and V^o is legal for $resp(op)$ in H.[3]

We now introduce some assumptions on the object type system and sequential specification. The following list is not intended to be complete in any sense; it just specifies the assumptions under which the results presented in Sections 4 and 5 hold.

Intuitively, sequential specifications are intended to capture the object semantics that is independent of the number of processes in the system (e.g., in a single-process history). For example, sequential specifications define the meaning of the enqueue and dequeue operations in the Enq-Deq type system for FIFO queues [14]. Therefore, the legality of a sequential history does not depend on processes at which history events were executed. Formally,

---

[2] In practice, there are simpler and more succinct ways to define sequential specifications. One common technique is to define the type of an object state, initial object value, set of rules how each operation manipulates the object state, etc.

[3] The definition of a possible operation outcome is a useful shortcut notation when the history and operation occurrence are not relevant.

Assumption 1: If we take a pair of invocation and matching response events which occurred at process p_i in a legal sequential history and change their process name to p_j, the resulting sequential history is also legal.

Next, we define deterministic and history-dependent operations: we will say that an operation op is deterministic if for any sequential history S and any occurrence of op in S with response event $e = resp(op)$, at most one output value can be legal for e. Intuitively, being history-dependent for an operation means that it may return different values for the same input in different executions, or even for different occurrences with the same input in the same execution. Formally, an operation op is history-dependent if there is some input value V^I of op such that there are at least two different output values that are possible outcomes of op with V^I.

Assumption 2: Each object type contains an operation that is both deterministic and history-dependent.

Recall from Section 2 that sequential specifications are typically defined through the notion of object state and the set of rules describing how each operation manipulates it. Such specifications also determine the set of valid output values for each operation, when invoked on a given object state with a given input value. Furthermore, most commonly used object types have a function for which a) at most one output value is legal for any given state and input value and b) different output values are legal for different states even when the input value is fixed. For example, a READ operation in the classical Read-Write type system and a Deq operation in the Enq-Deq type system for FIFO queues [14] maintain these properties. Such operations are deterministic and history-dependent, which explains why Assumption 2 holds in all systems that exist in practice.[4]

2.2   Separating Sequences

We now introduce the concept of a separating sequence, which is the key machinery used in our locality analysis. A separating sequence is a finite single object sequential history Sep containing at least two operations such that Sep is legal but no serialization of Sep in which the last operation of Sep precedes the first operation of Sep is legal. For example, in the case of read-write objects with sequential specifications implying that the initial object value is zero, $\langle W(X,1), R(X) = 1 \rangle$ is a separating sequence; for FIFO queues with an initially empty state, we can take $\langle Enq(X,1), Deq(X) = 1 \rangle$.

Lemma 1. For an object type as defined in Section 2.1, a separating sequence exists.

---

[4] In fact, the determinism assumption can be relaxed by stipulating it only for a small subset of all histories. However, we chose to adopt a less complicated assumption of global determinism that is stronger but still holds in all existing systems.

Proof. Let us take an operation op that is deterministic and history-dependent (such an operation must exist by Assumption 2). Since op is history-dependent, there exists an input value V^I of op such that there are two different output values V_1^o and V_2^o that are possible outcomes of op with V^I. Look at some history H consisting only of an occurrence of op with the input value V^I. Since op is deterministic, at least one of V_1^o and V_2^o is not legal for $\mathrm{resp}(op)$ in H. Assume w.l.o.g. that V_1^o is not legal for $\mathrm{resp}(op)$ in H. Let us look at the shortest legal sequential history Sep which contains an occurrence of op with the input value V^I and output value V_1^o (if there are several histories of the same length, we can take any one of them). If Sep contains just one operation, it is identical to H up to process and object names so that V_1^o cannot be legal for $\mathrm{resp}(op)$ in Sep by Assumption 1. Thus, Sep contains at least two operations. Furthermore, Sep is finite and it ends with $\mathrm{resp}(op)$ because the set of legal histories is prefix closed.

Assume by contradiction that there is a legal serialization S of Sep in which the last operation of Sep precedes the first operation of Sep. Consider the prefix of S up to and including the last operation of Sep. This prefix is a legal sequential history by prefix-closeness and it is shorter than Sep. This contradicts the minimality assumption that Sep is the shortest legal sequential history which contains an occurrence of op with the input value V^I and output value V_1^o. Thus, any serialization of Sep in which the last operation of Sep precedes the first operation of Sep is not legal. Therefore, Sep is a separating sequence.   □

3 Modelling Consistency Conditions

In order to make general conclusions about the locality of consistency conditions, we need to define the universe of consistency conditions over which we perform our analysis:

Definition 1. Consistency condition CC is a boolean predicate over a history H, such that if H satisfies CC, then for every object X, $H|X$ also satisfies CC.

This definition explicitly requires that CC be object projection closed; this trait is central for our locality analysis. It captures an inherent property of all existing consistency conditions. There might be some other requirements from the predicate to represent a reasonable condition but they are not needed for our discussion. The results in this paper hold for such more refined consistency conditions as well.

Note that Definition 1 does not limit the domain of CC to histories of some fixed object type. This reflects the fact that many consistency conditions such as sequential consistency are defined for an arbitrary type system. However, there exist some conditions like PRAM that are meaningful only for specific object types. We consider such conditions only in the context of the type for which they are meaningful.

Strictly speaking, the definition of a consistency condition should explicitly specify all "permissible" object types for a given condition. Then, every property of consistency conditions in Sections 3.1, 4 and 5 should be quantified by "for every permissible object type". However, this would significantly complicate the notation and require several additional definitions. Since all main results in this paper operate with conditions such as linearizability, for which every object type is permissible, we decided to avoid extending the notation in this direction.

It is easy to see that Definition 1 covers the following known conditions: linearizability [14], sequential consistency [16], serializability and strict serializability [19], release consistency [13], entry consistency [8], PRAM [17], causal consistency [3,4], processor consistency [2], PSO [1,18,15], TSO [1,18,15], and hybrid consistency [11]. We omit the definitions of these well-known conditions due to the lack of space.

In addition to these commonly used consistency conditions, Definition 1 covers many other conditions that may be used in specific systems. For example, consider the system that supports sequential consistency for normal updates and queries but allows the client to query the most recently updated copy of the object by providing a strong query that should reflect the results of all preceding updates. Of course, strong query is more expensive compared to a normal query so clients should use it with discretion. Another example is the system that provides sequential consistency for operations performed on most processes but has one master process whose operations are always done on the most recently updated copy. We will denote these two consistency conditions CC_{sq} and CC_{master}, respectively.

3.1   On the Relative Strength of Consistency Conditions

Some of our results in Sections 4 and 5 have the following form: "If a consistency condition CC is stronger than C_1 but weaker than C_2, then it is not local." In order to understand the impact of such results, it is important to consider the relative strength of consistency conditions.

Two consistency conditions C_1 and C_2 are equivalent if a history satisfies the first condition iff it satisfies the second condition. C_1 is stronger than or equivalent to C_2 if a history satisfies C_2 whenever it satisfies C_1; other comparative relations are defined likewise. If there is one history that satisfies C_1 but not C_2 and another history that satisfies C_2 but not C_1, then C_1 and C_2 are incomparable. The fact that consistency conditions can be incomparable substantially complicates locality analysis as we will see below.

The weakest condition by Definition 1 is the one which is satisfied by all histories; The strongest condition is the one which is satisfied by no history. We denote these two conditions CC_{min} and CC_{max} respectively. While they are not useful in practice, we will use them as reference conditions for comparison with others. In addition, we introduce another reference condition $CC_{proclin}$ for read-write objects: denote $H|w$ the subsequence of all events in a history H which are invocations or responses of write operations; $H|p + w$ is the subsequence of all events in H which are either in $H|p$ or in $H|w$. A history H satisfies $CC_{proclin}$ if for each process p, there is a legal serialization of $H|p + w$ that preserves $<_H$.

The relative strength of various consistency conditions is shown in Figure 1. Arrows are drawn from weaker to stronger conditions. General object type condi-

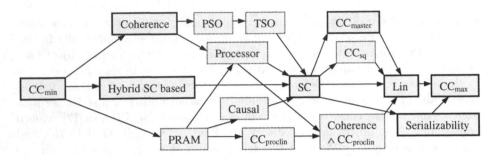

Fig. 1. Relative strength of various consistency conditions.

tions are in bold boxes whereas conditions meaningful for a specific type systems appear in dashed boxes.

It should be noted that there are trivial object types, e.g., with sequential specifications accepting every history as legal. For such object types, many conditions become trivially equivalent so that the hierarchy in Figure 1 partially collapses. This is not important for proving the formal results in Section 4 that explicitly state the assumption that some conditions are not equivalent. However, it should be emphasized for the sake of understanding the implications of these results that for all non-trivial object types that are used in practice, conditions depicted in Figure 1 are not equivalent.

4   Local Consistency Conditions

Locality is typically defined in the following way (see, e.g., [14]): a consistency condition $CC(G)$ is local if a history H satisfies $CC(G)$ iff for each object X, $H|X$ satisfies $CC(G)$. However, the "only if" part holds in all existing consistency conditions as captured by Definition 1. Therefore, only the "if" part is the subject of our study in this paper.

As we explained in Section 1, locality is a desired property of consistency conditions ([11], [12] and [14] also discuss motivation for local consistency conditions). It is easy to see that if a consistency condition partitions a given history H by the object on which operations are performed and requires some condition for each of the objects separately, then it is local. Such conditions can be expressed as a logical conjuction of independent predicates on $H|X$ for each object X. In particular, coherence falls into this category.

Another, less obvious group of local consistency conditions is based on the linearizability requirement that there exists a legal serialization of H that preserves the $<_H$ order. Herlihy and Wing [14] showed that linearizability is a local condition. However, this result can be generalized: in fact, any condition that partitions H into several (possibly overlapping) sets of operations and requires linearizability within each set independently, is local. In particular, condition $CC_{proclin}$ defined in Section 3.1 belongs to this group.

Furthermore, any conjunction or disjunction of two local conditions is local as the following lemma shows. Given a pair of incomparable local conditions, this property provides a way of constructing new conditions that are local. In particular, it implies that the conjunction of coherence and $CC_{proclin}$ is local.

Lemma 2. If two consistency conditions CC_1 and CC_2 are local, then the condition CC defined as their conjunction or disjunction, is local as well.

Proof. The proof follows directly from the definitions of locality and conjunction/disjunction of consistency conditions.   □

Obviously, the above two groups and their conjunctions include infinitely many distinct local conditions that span from the "no consistency" condition CC_{min} to linearizability. However, only few of those are meaningful and can be applied to systems that exist in practice. We now proceed with examining the locality of commonly used conditions.

Theorem 1. If a consistency condition CC is equivalent to or stronger than sequential consistency but weaker than linearizability, then it is not local.

Proof. Assume that such consistency condition CC exists and it is local. Since $CC(G)$ is weaker than linearizability, there is a history H such that $CC(H) =$ true but H is not linearizable, i.e., there is no legal serialization of H that preserves $<_H$. Since H is not linearizable and linearizability is a local condition, there is an object X_0 such that $H|X_0$ is not linearizable. Observe that $H|X_0$ satisfies CC by Definition 1. Therefore, we can assume w.l.o.g. that H is a single object history because we can always take $H = H|X_0$.

Consider the object type of X_0 and a separating sequence Sep for this object type whose existence is guaranteed by Lemma 1. Assume that Sep consists of k operations, i.e., $2 \times k$ events. Recall that n is the number of processes in the system.

We now construct a new history H' by expanding H as follows: we start with $H' = H$. Then, for each response event $\text{resp}(e)$ in H, we introduce a sequence Sep_e of $2 \times k \times n$ events to be specified below; Sep_e is inserted into H' immediately after $\text{resp}(e)$ and before any other event that might follow $\text{resp}(e)$ in H. In other words, H' is obtained from H by substituting each response event in H with $1 + 2 \times k \times n$ events. It is easy to see that since H is a sequence (finite or infinite), the resulting H' is also a sequence of events.

For each $\text{resp}(e)$, Sep_e is constructed as follows: we introduce n new objects $X_{e,1}, X_{e,2}, \ldots, X_{e,n}$, each object being of the same type as X_0. For each object $X_{e,i}$ we take a separating sequence $\text{Sep}_{e,i} = \langle o_1(X_{e,i}), \ldots, o_k(X_{e,i}) \rangle$ that is obtained from Sep by substituting the object name with $X_{e,i}$, the process name of the first operation (event pair) with $pr(e)$, and the process name of the last operation with p_i. Sep_e is formed as all events of $\text{Sep}_{e,1}$ followed by all events of $\text{Sep}_{e,2}$ followed by all events of $\text{Sep}_{e,3}$, etc:

$$\text{Sep}_e = \underbrace{o_1(X_{e,1}) <_{H'} \ldots <_{H'} o_k(X_{e,1})}_{Sep_{e,1}} <_{H'} \underbrace{o_1(X_{e,2}) <_{H'} \ldots <_{H'} o_k(X_{e,2})}_{Sep_{e,2}} <_{H'}$$

$$<_{H^0} \ldots <_{H^0} \underbrace{o_1(X_{e,n}) <_{H^0} \ldots <_{H^0} o_k(X_{e,n})}_{Sep_{e,n}}$$

Observe that for each object X, $CC(H'|X) = $ true: since each $Sep_{e,i} = H'|X_{e,i}$ is legal by itself, it is linearizable, hence it satisfies CC which is weaker than linearizability. Furthermore, $H = H'|X_0$ was chosen as a history which satisfies CC. We are now going to prove that H' does not satisfy sequential consistency. This will imply that H' does not satisfy CC thereby showing a contradiction to the fact that CC is local.

Suppose there is a legal serialization S' of H' that preserves the process order of operations in H'. Note that there is a pair e, f of operations ordered by $<_H$ in H whose order in S' is reversed. Such a pair exists because otherwise $S'|X_0$ would be a legal serialization of H that preserves $<_H$. Assume w.l.o.g. that $pr(f) = p_i$. Let us look at the separating sequence $Sep_{e,i}$ which was inserted into H' as subsequence of Sep_e. Since Sep_e was inserted immediately after $resp(e)$, every operation that follows e in H follows every operation of Sep_e in H'. In particular, $resp(o_k(X_{e,i})) <_{H^0} inv(f)$. Furthermore, $o_k(X_{e,i}))$ and f both occurred at p_i. Similarly, $e <_{H^0} o_1(X_{e,i})$ and they both occurred at $pr(e)$. Since S' preserves the process order of operations in H', the last operation of $Sep_{e,i}$ precedes the first operation of $Sep_{e,i}$ in S':

$$o_k(X_{e,i}) <_{S^0} inv(f) <_{S^0} \ldots <_{S^0} resp(e) <_{S^0} o_1(X_{e,i})$$

Therefore $S'|X_{e,i}$ is not legal by the definition of separating sequence.   □

Note that in order to build a counterexample to locality of CC, the construction in the proof may introduce a large number of new object instances. However, in many systems that exist in practice, locality violation can be observed with just few objects because the shortest non-linearizable history H that satisfies CC is usually very short and because the same object instance can be "reused" for multiple separating sequences.

[14] established that sequential consistency is not local for a particular object type (the Enq-Deq type system for FIFO queues). One important corollary from Theorem 1 is that sequential consistency is not local for any object type system with the assumptions of Section 2.1. However, this theorem is more general: for example, in Section 3 we brought the examples of non-standard CC_{sq} and CC_{master} consistency conditions that lie between sequential consistency and linearizability and that can be useful for specific systems. Theorem 1 establishes that all those conditions are not local.

Yet, Theorem 1 does not cover serializability that is incomparable to linearizability. Serializability is used as the basic correctness condition for concurrent computations by much work on databases. In this model, a transaction is a thread of control that applies a finite sequence of operations to a set of objects shared with other transactions. A history is serializable if it is equivalent to one in which transactions appear to execute atomically, i.e., without interleaving.[5] Stronger types of serializability such as strict serializability have also been defined: a (partial) precedence order is defined on non-overlapping pairs of transactions in the obvious way. A history is strictly serializable if the transactions' order in the sequential history is compatible with their precedence order.

[14] showed that neither serializability nor strict serializability are local for a specific object type system. The following generalization of Theorem 1 extends this result for an arbitrary object type:

Theorem 2. If a consistency condition CC is equivalent to or stronger than sequential consistency but weaker than or incomparable to linearizability, then it is not local.

Proof. Assume that such consistency condition CC exists and it is local. Consider the consistency condition that is defined by logical disjunction of CC and linearizability. This condition is stronger than or equivalent to sequential consistency but weaker than linearizability. Since both CC and linearizability are local, it is also local by Lemma 2. However, it cannot be local by Theorem 1.   □

So far we have only discussed the locality of conditions that are stronger than or equivalent to sequential consistency. Theorem 3 below covers weaker conditions:

Theorem 3. If a consistency condition CC is stronger than or incomparable to coherence but weaker than sequential consistency, then it is not local.

Proof. Assume that such consistency condition CC exists and it is local. Since $CC(G)$ is stronger than or incomparable to coherence, there is a history H such that $CC(H) = $ false but H satisfies coherence. Then, $H|X$ is also coherent for each object X. Therefore, $H|X$ is sequentially consistent for each object X by the definitions of coherence and sequential consistency. Since CC is weaker than sequential consistency, $H|X$ satisfies CC for each object X. Thus, CC is not local.   □

While this result is not so difficult to prove, its covers a significant number of conditions due to the general way in which it is captured. Since coherence and weaker conditions are considered too weak to be useful in practice, this result means that all useful conditions that are weaker than sequential consistency are non-local. In particular, it implies non-locality of many consistency conditions whose strength is discussed in Section 3.1, such as PRAM, causal consistency, processor consistency, TSO, PSO, hybrid consistency based on sequential consistency, and many other conditions that were introduced as performance-effective relaxations of sequential consistency.

---

[5] In practice, serializability is typically provided in conjunction with *failure atomicity*, ensuring that a transaction unable to execute to completion will be automatically rolled back.

However, it should be emphasized that Theorems 2 and 3 together do not imply that any condition that is stronger than or incomparable to coherence but weaker than or incomparable to linearizability is local. There are many local conditions that are stronger than coherence and weaker than linearizability but incomparable to sequential consistency; the conjunction of coherence and $CC_{proclin}$ is an example of such a condition.

5   Locality of Conditions That Imply Atomic Execution

One particular class of commonly used consistency conditions that are not weaker than sequential consistency consists of the conditions requiring that sequences of operations execute atomically without interleaving. Some of those conditions are stronger than sequential consistency such as serializability and strict serializability and therefore they are covered by Theorem 2. However, other conditions such as release consistency are incomparable to sequential consistency. They are the subject of our study in this section.

Recall that for serializability based consistency conditions, for each process p, $H|p$ defines the sequence of operations to execute atomically. However, while serializability stipulates that the serialization of an execution preserve the order of operations within each transaction (i.e., the process order), other conditions pose weaker requirements in this regard. In particular, some conditions only require that for each process p_i, there is a serialization of all transactions that preserves the process order of events that occurred at p_i. Yet, all such conditions imply the atomicity requirement CC_{atom}, i.e., there is a serialization of all transactions in which no operation of a transaction appears between two operations of some other transaction. Formally, the predicate $CC(H)$ of such conditions can be expressed as $CC_0(H) \wedge CC_{atom}(H)$ for some $CC_0(H)$ and

$$CC_{atom}(H) = \exists S, S \text{ is a serialization of } H, \forall p, \forall op_1, op_2 \in H|p,$$
$$(op_1 <_S op_2 \Rightarrow \forall op_3 \notin H|p, op_3 <_S op_1 \vee op_2 <_S op_3) \ .$$

The following theorem states that all conditions lying between CC_{atom} and strict serializability are not local. Since all commonly used conditions that imply atomic execution of transactions fall in this range, the practical consequence of this result is that the requirement of atomic execution rules out locality.

Theorem 4. If a consistency condition CC is stronger than or equivalent to CC_{atom} but weaker than or equivalent to strict serializability, then CC is not local.

Proof sketch: Assume that such a consistency condition CC exists and it is local. Take a separating sequence $Sep = \langle o_1, \ldots, o_n \rangle$. Consider a sequential history H which consists of two copies of the separating sequence on objects X and Y respectively: $\langle o_1$ on X at p, o_1 on Y at q, o_2 on X at p, o_2 on Y at q, $\ldots, o_n$ on X at q, o_n on Y at $p\rangle$. Note that all operations on X except for the last one occur at p and all operations on Y except for the last one occur at q.

It is easy to see that both $H|X$ and $H|Y$ are strictly serializable. However, H does not satisfy CC_{atom}. Thus, CC is not local.   □

There exist some other conditions, such as release consistency and entry consistency, that model atomic sequences in a way that is different from the one which is used in serializability. These conditions introduce special acquire and release operations that serve multiple purposes but in particular denote the start and end points of a sequence to execute atomically.[6] The definition of CC_{atom} and the proof of Theorem 4 can be easily transformed to show that if the acquire operation locks all objects (as it does, e.g., in release consistency), then the consistency condition is not local. However, this negative result does not cover conditions such as entry consistency, in which an acquire operation acquires a lock for a single object.

6   Conclusions

We have developed several techniques for systematically analyzing locality of consistency conditions. Using these techniques, we have been able to prove general negative results about consistency conditions that cannot be local for any object type. As special cases, these results imply that sequential consistency, serializability, strict serializability, release consistency, PRAM, causal consistency, processor consistency, PSO, TSO, hybrid consistency based on sequential consistency, and some other conditions that we have defined are not local. However, there are few known consistency conditions, such as entry consistency and hybrid consistency based on linearizability that have been left uncovered by our analysis. We are looking into ways to further generalize our results in order to cover these conditions as special cases as well.

While we have described two distinct groups that count infinitely many local conditions as well as techniques for constructing other local conditions (such as conjunction and disjunction), we have identified only few local conditions that are deemed meaningful and useful. It is still an open question whether there are local conditions beyond these two groups. One possible extension of this work would be to find the most general form that describes all local conditions.

It has recently been shown in [9] that without the global time axiom, linearizability is no longer a local condition. It is an interesting open problem to check the bounds of locality without the global time assumption.

Acknowledgments. We would like to thank Michel Raynal for many fruitful discussions. We would also like to thank anonymous reviewers for helpful comments and suggestions.

---

[6] In some conditions, the same special operation is used to signify both the end of the previous atomic sequence and the start of the next one. The results of this section hold for such conditions as well.

References

1. SPARC Architecture Manual. Version 8, Jan. 1991.
2. M. Ahamad, R. Bazzi, R. John, P. Kohli, and G. Neiger. The Power of Processor Consistency. In *5th ACM Symposium On Parallel Algorithms and Architectures*, pages 251–260, June 1993.
3. M. Ahamad, P. Hutto, and R. John. Implementing and Programming Causal Distributed Shared Memory. Technical Report TR GIT-CC-90-49, Georgia Institute of Technology, Dec. 1990.
4. M. Ahamad, G. Neiger, P. Kohli, J. Burns, and P. Hutto. Causal Memory: Definitions, Implementation, and Programming. *Distributed Computing*, 9(1), 1993.
5. H. Attiya and R. Friedman. Limitations of Fast Consistency Conditions for Distributed Shared Memories. *Information Processing Letters*, 57(5):243–248, 1995.
6. H. Attiya and R. Friedman. A Correctness Condition for High-Performance Multiprocessors. *SIAM Journal of Computing*, 27(2), Apr. 1998.
7. H. Attiya and J. Welch. Sequential Consistency versus Linearizability. *ACM Transactions on Computer Systems*, 12(2):91–122, May 1994.
8. B. N. Bershad, M. J. Zekauskas, and W. A. Sawdon. The Midway Distributed Shared Memory System. In *Proc. of the 38th IEEE Intl. Computer Conf. (COMPCON)*, pages 528–537, Feb. 1993.
9. B. Charron-Bost and R. Cori. A Note on Linearizability and the Global Time Axiom. *Parallel Processing Letters*, 13(1):19–24, Mar. 2003.
10. A. Fernández, E. Jiménez, and V. Cholvi. On the Interconnection of Causal Memory Systems. In *Proc. of the 19th ACM Symposium on Principles of Distributed Computing*, Apr. 2000.
11. R. Friedman. *Consistency Conditions for Distributed Shared Memories*. PhD thesis, Department of Computer Science, The Technion, 1994.
12. V. K. Garg and M. Raynal. Normality: A Consistency Condition for Concurrent Objects. *Parallel Processing Letters*, 9(1):123–134, 1999.
13. K. Gharachorloo, D. Lenoski, J. Laudon, P. Gibbons, A. Gupta, and J. Hennessy. Memory Consistency and Event Ordering in Scalable Shared-Memory Multiprocessors. In *Proc. of the 17th International Symposium on Computer Architecture*, pages 15–26, May 1990.
14. M. Herlihy and J. Wing. Linearizability: A Correctness Condition for Concurrent Objects. *ACM Trans. on Programming Languages and Systems*, 12(3):463–492, 1990.
15. J. Kawash. *Limitations and Capabilities of Weak Memory Consistency Systems*. PhD thesis, Computer Science Dept., University of Calgary, 2000.
16. L. Lamport. How to Make a Multiprocessor Computer that Correctly Executes Multiprocess Programs. *IEEE Trans. on Computers*, C-28(9):690–691, 1979.
17. R. Lipton and J. Sandberg. PRAM: A Scalable Shared Memory. Technical Report CS-TR-180-88, Computer Science Department, Princeton University, Sept. 1988.
18. V. Luchangco. *Memory Consistency Models for High Performance Distributed Computing*. PhD thesis, MIT Department of Electrical Engineering and Computer Science, 2001.
19. C. Papadimitriou. *The Theory of Concurrency Control*. Computer Science Press, 1986.

Multi-writer Consistency Conditions for Shared Memory Objects

Cheng Shao, Evelyn Pierce, and Jennifer L. Welch

Department of Computer Science
Texas A&M University
College Station, TX 77843-3112, U.S.A
{cshao, pierce, welch}@cs.tamu.edu

Abstract. Regularity is a shared memory consistency condition that has received considerable attention, notably in connection with quorum-based shared memory. Lamport's original definition of regularity assumed a single-writer model, however, and is not well-defined when each shared variable may have multiple writers. In this paper, we address this need by formally extending the notion of regularity to a multi-writer model. We give three possible definitions of regularity in the presence of multiple writers. We then present a quorum-based algorithm to implement each of the three definitions and prove them correct. We study the relationships between these definitions and a number of other well-known consistency conditions, and give a partial order describing the relative strengths of these consistency conditions. Finally, we provide a practical context for our results by studying the correctness of two well-known algorithms for mutual exclusion under each of our proposed consistency conditions.

1 Introduction

1.1 Overview

Distributed computer systems are ubiquitous today, ranging from multiprocessors to local area networks to wide-area networks such as the Internet. Shared memory, the exchange of information between processes by the reading and writing of shared objects, is an important mechanism for interprocess communications in distributed systems. A consistency condition in a shared memory system is a set of constraints on values returned by data accesses when those accesses may be interleaved or overlapping. A shared memory system with a strong consistency condition may be easy to design protocols for, but may require a high-cost implementation. Conversely, a shared memory system with a weak consistency condition may be implemented efficiently, but be difficult for the user to program or reason about. Finding a consistency condition that can be implemented efficiently and that is nonetheless strong enough to solve practical problems is one of the aims of shared memory research.

The preferred consistency condition for shared memory objects is atomicity (or linearizability) ([11]), in which read and write operations behave as though

F.E. Fich (Ed.): DISC 2003, LNCS 2848, pp. 106–120, 2003.

they were executed sequentially, i.e, with no interleaving or overlap, in a sequence that is consistent with the relative order of non-overlapping operations. In many cases, however, this semantics is difficult to implement, particularly in distributed systems where variables are replicated and where the number of processes with access to the variable is not known in advance. For such systems, the related but weaker condition of regularity ([11]) may be easier to implement while retaining some usefulness. For this reason, it has received considerable attention in its own right, notably in connection with quorum-based shared memory ([2], [15], [14] and [13]).

Informally speaking, regularity requires that every read operation return either the value written by the latest preceding write (in real time) or that of some write that overlaps the read. This description is sufficiently clear for the single-writer model[1], in which the order of the writes performed on a given variable in any execution is well-defined; in fact, it was for this model that Lamport gave his formal definition of regularity. In a multi-writer model, however, multiple processes may perform overlapping write operations to the same variable so that the "latest preceding write" for a given read may have no obvious definition.

A common way to circumvent this problem is to rely on a plausible generalization of the informal definition above, e.g. the following, which appears in [15]:

- A read operation that is concurrent with no write operations returns a value written by the last preceding write operation in some serialization of all preceding write operations.
- A read operation that is concurrent with one or more write operations returns either the value written by the last preceding write operation in some serialization of all preceding write operations, or any of the values being written in the concurrent write operations.

Such a definition, however, leaves a good deal of room for interpretation. What is meant by "some serialization" in this context? Is there a single serialization of the writes for which the above is true for all read operations, or does it suffice for there to be some (possibly different) such serialization for each operation? Or should all read operations of the same process perceive writes as occurring in the same order? Such ambiguities can be avoided with a formal definition of multi-writer regularity, but to our knowledge none has yet been proposed.

1.2 Contributions of This Paper

In this paper, we formally extend the notion of regularity to a multi-writer model. Specifically, we give three possible formal definitions of regularity in the presence of multiple writers. We then present a quorum-based algorithm to implement each of these definitions and prove the algorithms correct. The definitions are

---

[1] In the *single-writer* model, only one process can write to a shared object; other processes can only read from it.

strictly increasing in strength, while the implementations are of comparable complexity. While there is no obvious practical advantage to the weaker definitions over the stronger, the first two formalizations serve to point out the ambiguity of the informal notion of regularity, while the third provides stronger guarantees at essentially no additional cost.

We also study the relationships between our definitions of multi-writer regularity and several existing consistency models: linearizability ([8]), sequential consistency ([10]), coherence ([7]), PRAM ([12]) and PCG ([1]). As part of this analysis, we give a partial order describing the relative strengths of these consistency conditions.

Finally, we provide a practical context for our results by studying the correctness of two well-known algorithms for mutual exclusion when the variables are implemented under our three proposed consistency conditions. The algorithms we examine are Peterson's algorithm for 2 processes ([17]) and Dijkstra's algorithm ([18]). We find that Peterson's algorithm is fully correct under all three models. Dijkstra's algorithm satisfies only some of the constraints of the mutual exclusion problem under any of the models.

1.3   Related Work

There is copious literature on consistency conditions for shared memory, both implementations and applications (e.g., [10], [12], [7], [8] and [1]). Our work builds on the the notion of regularity as introduced in [11].

We follow the example of [3] and [1] by using the mutual exclusion problem as an application for our consistency model. In [3], Attiya and Friedman revised Peterson's 2-process algorithm ([17]) to solve the mutual exclusion problem under their hybrid consistency model. In [1], Ahamad et al. examined the correctness of Peterson's algorithm and Lamport's bakery algorithm under the PCG consistency model, showing that Peterson's algorithm solves the mutual exclusion problem under PCG, while Lamport's algorithm fails to do so. In a later study, Higham et al. ([9]) investigated other mutual exclusion algorithms, including Dekker's and Dijkstra's, none of which guarantees mutual exclusion under PCG.

2   Preliminaries

Every shared object is assumed to have a sequential specification that indicates its desired behavior. A sequential specification is a prefix-closed set of sequences of operations, representing the set of behaviors of the object in the absence of concurrency. We define members of this set as legal sequences of operations:

Definition 1. A sequence of operations on a shared object is a legal sequence if it belongs to the sequential specification of the shared object.

In this paper, we consider only read/write objects. For such objects, a sequence of operations is legal if each read returns the value of the most recent preceding write in the sequence. If there is no such write, it returns the initial value.

A consistency condition on a shared memory object specifies a relationship between the sequential specification of the object and the set of executions on the object, where an execution is a sequence of possibly interleaved operation invocations and responses.

We assume a system of n processes labeled $p_0, \ldots, p_{n-1}$. For a given execution σ, we use the symbol $\sigma|i$ to denote the subsequence of σ containing all the invocations and responses performed by process p_i.

Definition 2. An execution σ is admissible if, for each $i, 0 \leq i \leq n - 1$:

- if the number of steps taken by p_i is finite, then the last step by p_i is a response; and
- $\sigma|i$ consists of alternating invocations and matching responses, beginning with an invocation. Thus, at any given point in the execution, each process has at most one operation pending.

Note that this definition allows arbitrary asynchrony of process steps — no constraints are placed on the relative speed with which operations complete or on the time between operation invocations. However, for convenience in analyzing executions, we follow the example of [11] and [6] in employing the useful abstraction of an imaginary global clock. All our references to "real time" in the sequel are with respect to this imaginary clock, which is not available to the processes themselves.

For the remainder of this paper, we will be concerned only with admissible executions.

Given an execution σ, we use the symbol $ops(\sigma)$ to denote the set of all operations whose invocations and responses appear in σ. (Thus $ops(\sigma|i)$ denotes the set of all operations that are performed in σ by process p_i.) Finally, we let $writes(\sigma)$ denote the set of all write operations in execution σ.

A permutation on a subset of $ops(\sigma)$ is σ-consistent if it preserves the partial order of the operations in σ.[2] The formal definition is given below.

Definition 3. Given an execution σ, a permutation π of a subset of $ops(\sigma)$ is σ-consistent if, for any operations o_1 and o_2 in π, o_1 precedes o_2 in π whenever o_1 finishes in σ before o_2 starts.

Note that this definition implies that the per-process order of operations is preserved in a σ-consistent permutation.

3   Multi-writer Regular Variables: Three Specifications

In this section we present three possible definitions of a multi-writer regular variable, in increasing order of strength; we name these MWR1, MWR2 and

---

[2] In most situations of interest, σ represents the order of operation invocations and responses in real time.

M W R 3 respectively. The first two are distinct ways of straightforwardly generalizing Lamport's regularity for single-writer variables, while the third generalizes
a slight strengthening of Lamport's definition.[3]

Definition 4. (MWR1)

An execution σ is mw1-regular (or satisfies MWR1) if, for each read operation $r \in ops(\sigma)$, there exists a permutation π_r of $writes(\sigma) \cup \{r\}$ such that:

- π_r is a legal sequence.
- π_r is σ-consistent.

A shared memory object is mw1-regular if all executions on that object are mw1-
regular.

Informally, an execution σ satisfies MWR1 if each read $r \in ops(\sigma)$ returns
the value of some write w that either overlaps or precedes r in σ, as long as
no other write falls completely between w and r. This definition allows different
reads to behave as though the set of writes occurred in different orders, as long
as all such orderings are consistent with the partial order of the writes in σ.

Figure 1 shows an execution that satisfies MWR1. (In our figures, $W(x, v)$
denotes a write operation that writes value v to variable x, and $R(x, v)$ denotes
a read operation on variable x that returns value v.) For p_2's first read, $W(x, 2)$
is considered to be the latest preceding write, and the read perceives the permutation $W(x, 1), W(x, 2), R(x, 2)$. For the second read, $W(x, 1)$ is considered to
be the latest preceding write; thus the permutation is $W(x, 2), W(x, 1), R(x, 1)$.

```
P0    | W(x,1) |
P1          | W(x,2) |
P2                    | R(x,2) |  | R(x,1) |
```

Fig. 1. Execution that satisfies MWR1

As this example shows, MWR1 is actually a very weak consistency condition,
as it does not require write operations to behave as though they occurred in
any particular order, even from the point of view of a single process. It might,
therefore, be desirable to construct a stronger definition of regularity for the
multi-writer case.

One straightforward approach might be to simply require that all read operations perceive the same ordering of the write operations, i.e, to add to MWR1
the requirement that $\pi_r - \{r\}$ is equal for all r.

However, we contend that such a consistency condition is actually too strong
for distributed multi-writer systems, where message delays may cause a given

---

[3] We justify the continued use of the term "regularity" for this last definition because in the multi-writer model it remains weaker than *atomicity*, the next stronger
consistency condition defined in Lamport's hierarchy.

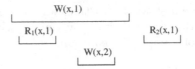

Fig. 2. A problematic execution

write to be "lost" when it is, in essence, overwritten by an overlapping write without being read. Requiring all reads to place this "invisible" write in the same position in their perceived order of writes is unnecessary, and may be difficult.

Consider, for example, the execution in Figure 2. This execution does not satisfy the proposed specification above, but is possible under several variations of the classic quorum-based shared memory protocols described in Section 4.2.

In order to accommodate behavior of this kind, we propose a more sophisticated definition for our second and stronger version of multi-writer regularity, by requiring any pair of reads to agree only on the ordering of writes that are "relevant" to both of them. Toward this end, we use the following additional notation: $writes_{\leftarrow r}(\sigma) = \{w | w \in writes(\sigma)$ and w begins before r ends in $\sigma\}$.

Definition 5. (MWR2) An execution σ is mw2-regular (or satisfies MWR2) if there exists a permutation π of all the operations in $ops(\sigma)$ such that, for any read operation r, the projection π_r of π onto $writes_{\leftarrow r}(\sigma) \cup \{r\}$ satisfies:

− π_r is a legal sequence.
− π_r is σ-consistent.[4]

A shared memory object is mw2-regular if all executions on that object are mw2-regular.

This definition is similar to that of mw1-regularity, except that for any two reads $r1$ and $r2$, the set of writes that do not strictly follow either $r1$ or $r2$ must be perceived by both reads as occurring in the same order. As before, each read returns the value of an overlapping write or the last preceding write in the order.

The execution in Figure 2 satisfies MWR2. Let $\pi = W(x,2), W(x,1),$ $R_1(x,1), R_2(x,1)$. Then the projections for the two reads are $W(x,1), R_1(x,1)$ and
$W(x,2), W(x,1), R_2(x,1)$ respectively. Because the "lost" write follows R_1, it does not appear in the set of ordered writes for that read operation; it can thus be regarded without inconsistency as occurring before $W(x,1)$ from the point of view of R_2. It is easy to verify that these two sequences satisfy the two conditions of MWR2.

---

[4] Note that if there are only a finite number of reads in a given execution, the writes after the last read are not constrained by MWR2 to appear in any particular order. We consider this to be acceptable, as such writes are never observed.

Figure 3 shows another execution that satisfies MWR2. (To see this, consider the permutation $\pi = W(x,1),R_2(x,1),R_3(x,1),W(x,2),R_2(x,2),R_3(x,2)$. It is easy to see that the projections for all four read operations satisfy the two conditions in Definition 5.) By contrast, the execution shown in Figure 1 does not satisfy MWR2, as there is no single way to order the writes that is consistent with the values returned by the reads, given the partial order of the operations in real time.

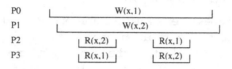

Fig. 3. Execution that satisfies MWR2

A straightforward extension of MWR2 leads to a still stronger consistency condition.

Definition 6. (MWR3) An execution σ is mw3-regular (or satisfies MWR3) if there exists a permutation π of all the operations in $ops(\sigma)$ such that, for any read operation r, the projection π_r of π onto $writes_{\leftarrow r}(\sigma) \cup \{r\}$ satisfies:

- π_r is a legal sequence.
- π_r is σ-consistent.
- If r_1 and r_2 are two read operations of a given p_i, and p_i performs r_1 before r_2, then the writes that appear before r_1 in π_{r_1} appear before r_2 in π_{r_2}.

A shared memory object is mw3-regular if all executions on that object are mw3-regular.

MWR3 is similar to MWR2, but places the following additional constraint on the read operations: any two read operations performed by the same process must appear in π in the order in which they occur at that process.

This is equivalent to the requirement that once a process reads from a given write, it never reads from an "earlier" write in the order of writes perceived by that process, i.e., individual processes read from writes in nondecreasing order. In [14], variables with this property are called monotone variables.

Although the execution in Figure 3 satisfies MWR2, it does not satisfy MWR3. To see this, note that the definition of MWR3 requires that $W(x,1)$ and $W(x,2)$ appear in the same order in the permutation for each of the four read operations. Suppose $W(x,1)$ appears before $W(x,2)$. Then π_{r_1}, the permutation for the first read of p_2, and π_{r_2}, the permutation for the second read of p_2, do not satisfy the last condition of Definition 6. If we reverse the order of the two write operations, however, the same problem occurs with respect to p_3's two read operations. (Note that if the second read of process p_2 were to return 2 instead of 1, then the execution would satisfy MWR3.)

The three consistency conditions that we have defined form a strict hierarchy: MWR3 is strictly stronger than MWR2, which is strictly stronger than MWR1. The reader may verify the implications by examining the definitions; the strictness of the containments has already been shown in the discussion of the figures.

The following lemma emphasizes the relationship between our definitions and the single-writer definition of Lamport.

Lemma 1. For a single-writer shared variable, M W R 1 and M W R 2 are identical and are equivalent to the specification of regularity in [11]. M W R 3 is strictly stronger than Lamport's regularity in the single-writer case, but remains weaker than atomicity. Furthermore, if there is only a single reader, then M W R 3 is equivalent to atomicity.

The proof of this lemma is straightforward, and is omitted for reasons of space.

3.1 A Partial Order of Consistency Conditions

Figure 4 shows the relationship between our three proposed definitions of multi-writer regularity and the following existing consistency models: linearizability ([8]), sequential consistency ([10]), coherence ([7]), PRAM ([12]) and PCG ([1]). Although our three definitions form a strict hierarchy in terms of strength, they are not comparable to any of the more established conditions except linearizability and, in the case of MWR3, coherence. A detailed discussion can be found in [19].

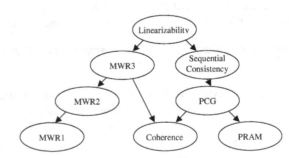

Fig. 4. Relationships among Existing Consistency Conditions

4   Implementations

In this section, we show how to implement a quorum-based shared memory object satisfying each of the definitions of multi-writer regularity proposed in Section 3.

A quorum system $\mathcal{Q}$ over a set S of servers is a set of subsets of the server set, i.e., $\mathcal{Q} \subseteq 2^S$. Each element of a quorum system is called a quorum. In this paper, we assume that the intersection of each pair of quorums is nonempty, i.e., that the quorum system is strict. When we use a quorum system to implement a shared object, each server maintains a local copy of the shared object along with an associated timestamp.

```
Code for p_i, 0 ≤ i ≤ n - 1:

write_i(x, v):
1    for some quorum Q, send(read, x) to each q ∈ Q;
2    wait to receive response (v_q, ts_q) from each q ∈ Q;
3    t := MaxTS({ts_q | q ∈ Q});
4    t_w = IncTS(t);
5    for some quorum Q', send(write, x, v, t_w) to each
     q' ∈ Q';
6    wait to receive ack from each q' ∈ Q';
7    ack_i(x);

read_i(x):
1    for some quorum Q, send(read, x) to each q ∈ Q;
2    wait to receive response (v_q, ts_q) from each q ∈ Q;
3    t := MaxTS({ts_q | q ∈ Q});
4    v := GetValue(t);
5    ret_i(x, v);
```

```
Code for server q:

local:
   v_q   /* local copy of shared variable, initially 0 */
   t_q   /* local copy of timestamp, initially 0 */

When q receives (read, x) from p_i:
1    send(v_q, t_q) to p_i;

When q receives (write, x, v, t) from p_i:
1    if (t_q < t) then
2        v_q = v; t_q = t;
3    endif
4    send(ack) to p_i;
```

Fig. 5. A generic quorum-based algorithm to implement a read/write shared object

A generic algorithm that uses quorums to implement a shared object with read/write semantics is given in Figure 5 . The main idea of the algorithm is as follows. For any operation, a process begins by querying each member of some quorum for its current view of the value and timestamp of the shared object. It then uses the function $MaxTS()$ to obtain the largest timestamp from the resulting set of responses. The operations then continue as follows:

- **read:** The process uses a function $GetValue()$ to find a value associated with the resulting timestamp, and returns that value as the result of the read.
- **write:** The process increments the resulting timestamp using a function $IncTS()$, and writes the new value and the incremented timestamp back to every member of some quorum (which can, but need not, be the same quorum that was queried).

This algorithm is a generalization of several existing quorum-based protocols; the appropriate instantiations of $MaxTS()$ and $GetValue()$ yield, e.g., the algorithms in [15], [5] and [16].

The three algorithms that we present in this section differ in their implementations of the functions used by the generic algorithm. This allows them to use different types of timestamp and different policies by which to select returned values. We will explicitly point out those differences as we introduce each of the algorithms.

4.1   Algorithm *Alg_MW1* for Implementing MWR1

The timestamp used by Alg_MW1 is chosen from the set of natural numbers $\mathcal{N}$. In this case, the $MaxTS()$ function simply returns the largest timestamp in numerical order, while $IncTS(ts)$ increments its argument by 1. Since timestamps are not necessarily unique under this algorithm, several different values may share the same largest timestamp value. In this case, $GetValue()$ simply chooses one arbitrarily and returns that value.

We define the timestamp of a write operation as the timestamp the write operation uses to write to the quorum. Similarly, the timestamp of a read operation is the timestamp value associated with the variable value returned by this operation. For both cases, we use the symbol $ts(op)$ to denote the timestamp of operation op. We say that a read operation r reads from a write operation w if the value-timestamp pair returned by r is equal to the value-timestamp pair of w. If there are several such writes, then we choose some arbitrary write w among them such that r reads from w.

The following lemma states that the timestamp order (numerical order by timestamp) of certain operations extends the partial order of those operations in real time. Its proof, which is omitted due to lack of space, relies on the quorum intersection property.

Lemma 2. For any execution σ of Alg_MW 1, there exist the following relationships between the operations and their timestamps:

- For any read operation r and any write operation w: if w precedes r in σ, then $ts(w) \leq ts(r)$.
- For any two write operations w_1 and w_2: if w_1 precedes w_2 in σ, then $ts(w_1) < ts(w_2)$;

Theorem 1. Algorithm Alg_MW 1 implements MWR1.

Proof. For a read operation r, we construct π_r as follows. We partition the set of writes into two subsets:

- The set of writes that begin before r ends and whose timestamps are at most that of r, i.e., $\{w|w \in writes_{\leftarrow r}(\sigma)$ and $ts(w) \leq ts(r)\}$
- the set of all remaining writes

Each of these two sets is arranged in increasing order of timestamp; writes with identical timestamps are ordered arbitrarily. We insert r into the first sequence immediately after the write that it reads from and then append the second sequence to the first sequence.

The reader can easily verify that the resulting sequence satisfies the two conditions of MWR1.   □

4.2   Algorithm *Alg_MW2* for Implementing MWR2

We implement a shared variable satisfying MWR2 by adding the process id (as in [15]) to the timestamps used by the generic algorithm. In other words, we define the timestamp of an operation as a pair $\langle ts, id \rangle$, where ts is a natural number, and id is a unique process id. Since no individual process chooses the same ts value for two different writes, each write operation is guaranteed a unique timestamp value. This ensures that no matter how many write operations overlap, all read operations that begin after all these write operations finish are able to agree on which is the "last" write. Note that this is a commonly used approach in the implementation of shared variables using quorum systems.

For timestamps of this format, we define $MaxTS()$ as the function that returns the largest timestamp in lexicographic order on the pair $\langle ts, id \rangle$. Because this timestamp is unique, $GetValue()$ simply returns the unique value associated with it. Finally, $IncTS()$ increments the ts field by 1 and places the calling process identifier in the id field.

The proof of correctness of Algorithm Alg_MW2 is based on the following supporting lemma, which in turn relies on Lemma 2:

Lemma 3. The write operations performed using Algorithm Alg_MW2 are totally ordered by timestamp, and this total order is consistent with the partial order of the write operations in real time.

Theorem 2. Algorithm Alg_MW2 implements MWR2.

Proof. We construct the permutation π as follows. We begin by ordering the write operations lexicographically as described above. We then insert each read operation r after the write operation that r reads from and before the next write operation in the total order. Read operations with identical timestamps are ordered arbitrarily. Now we prove that for any r, the projection π_r satisfies the conditions in Definition 5.

The sequence π_r is legal by construction, as r appears immediately after the write it reads from.

Now, consider any two operations op_1 and op_2 in σ such that op_1 finishes before op_2 starts. There are two possible cases:

- op_1 and op_2 are both write operations. Then according to Lemma 3 and our construction method, their order in π_r is consistent with their partial order in real time, i.e., σ-consistent.
- op_1 is a write operation and $op_2 = r$. If r reads from op_1, then op_1 appears immediately before r according to our construction. Otherwise, r reads from a write w whose timestamp is larger than that of op_1. Therefore, they appear in π_r as op_1, w, r, so the order of op_1 and r is again σ-consistent.

There are no other cases, as writes that begin after r completes are not included in $writes_{\leftarrow r}(\sigma)$, and thus do not appear in π_r. □

4.3 Algorithm *Alg_MW3* for Implementing MWR3

Algorithm_MW3 is similar to Algorithm Alg_MW2 except that in Algorithm_MW3, each process keeps a local copy of the value-timestamp pair of the shared variable x. The function $MaxTS()$ and $IncTS()$ are defined in the same way as for Alg_MW2. We change the function $GetValue()$ as follows. If the timestamp returned by $MaxTS()$ is not greater than the timestamp in the local copy, then $GetValue()$ returns the value stored in the local copy.

Theorem 3. Algorithm Alg_MW 3 implements M W R 3.

Proof. We construct π as in the proof of Theorem 2, except that read operations with identical timestamps are ordered consistently with their partial order in real time. Now we prove that π satisfies the conditions in Definition 6.

The first two conditions can be proved using the same arguments as in the proof of Theorem 2.

As for the third condition, consider two read operations r_1 and r_2 of the same process, where r_1 completes before r_2 begins. Because π_{r_1} and π_{r_2} are projected from the same sequence π, it is sufficient to prove that (1) r_1 appears before r_2 in π, and (2) all writes that appear in π_{r_1} also appear in π_{r_2}.

The first claim follows from the fact that, by Alg_MW3, the timestamp of r_2 is at least that of r_1, so our construction method places them in π in the order indicated. The second claim follows from the fact that $writes_{\leftarrow r_1} \subseteq writes_{\leftarrow r_2}$, which is clear by definition of $writes_{\leftarrow r}$ (see Section 3). Thus all writes that appear in π_{r_1} also appear in π_{r_2}.   □

5 Mutual Exclusion Using Regular Shared Variables

In this section, we use the mutual exclusion problem as a practical context to evaluate the strength of our three specifications on multi-writer regular shared variables. Specifically, we study the correctness of two well-known algorithms for mutual exclusion when the variables are implemented according to the three consistency conditions we have proposed. The algorithms we examine are Peterson's algorithm for 2 processes ([17]) and Dijkstra's algorithm for n processes ([18]). The algorithms are shown in Figure 6.[5]

Algorithms for solving mutual exclusion are assumed to have four sections: entry, critical, exit and remainder. The critical section is code that must be protected from concurrent execution. The entry section is the code executed in preparation for entering the critical section. The exit section is executed to release the critical section. The rest of the code is in the remainder section.

An execution of a program (not to be confused with an execution on an object) consists of a partially ordered set of local and shared memory operations performed by the participating processes. The partial order reflects the fact that each process executes the algorithm sequentially in real time. In the case of a mutual exclusion algorithm, each process cycles an infinite number of times through the four sections described above or terminates in the remainder section. In doing so, note that the processes produce admissible executions on each of the shared variables used by the program.

---

[5] Although Lamport's Bakery algorithm and Peterson-Fischer's algorithm are often studied in this context, they are not of interest to us here since these algorithms use only single-writer shared variables.

1. Peterson's Algorithm for 2 Processors
Code for process p_i, $i \in \{0, 1\}$:

shared variables:
  $Flag[0..1]$: integer   /* initially 0 */
  $Turn$: integer   /* initially 0 */

/* entry section */
```
1    repeat
2        Flag[i] := 0;
3        wait until (Flag[1 - i] = 0 or Turn = i);
4        Flag[i] := 1;
5    until (Turn = i or Flag[1 - i] = 0)

6    if (Turn = i) then wait until (Flag[1 - i] = 0);
```

Critical Section

/* exit section */
```
7        Turn := 1 - i;
8        Flag[i] := 0;
```

Remainder Section

2. Dijkstra's Algorithm for n Processors
Code for process p_i, $0 \le i \le n - 1$:

shared variables:
  $Flag[0..n - 1]$: *idle, requesting, in-cs*
  $Turn$: integer

/* entry section */
```
1    repeat
2        Flag[i] := requesting;
3        while (Turn ≠ i) do
4            if (Flag[Turn] = idle) then Turn := i;
5        end while
6        Flag[i] := in-cs;
7    until (∀ j ≠ i, Flag[j] ≠ in-cs)
```

Critical Section

/* exit section */
```
8        Flag[i] := idle;
```

Remainder Section

Fig. 6. Algorithms for Mutual Exclusion

We say that an algorithm A solves mutual exclusion under consistency condition C if, given that the shared variables all satisfy C, all program executions satisfy the following constraints:

- **mutual exclusion (ME):** there is at most one process in the critical section at any point in (real) time.
- **eventual progress (EP):**[6] if there is some process waiting to enter the critical section, then eventually some process enters the critical section.
- **no lockout (NL):** if some process is waiting to enter the critical section, then eventually that process enters the critical section.[7]

We now examine the two mutual exclusion algorithms shown in Figure 6. Table 1 shows which of the conditions of mutual exclusion described above are met by each algorithm when implemented with variables satisfying each of our consistency conditions. As a comparison, we also list the conditions that are guaranteed by these algorithms when the shared variables are linearizable.

We first consider Peterson's algorithm for two processors ([17]).[8] This algorithm uses two single-writer shared variables and one multi-writer shared variable. The proof of the next theorem is very similar to the proof of Theorem 4.10 in [4]. Although [4] assumes that all the variables are atomic, the argument holds unchanged for variables that satisfy MWR1, and therefore MWR2 and MWR3 also.

---

[6] We use this term, rather than the more traditional ND ("no deadlock") in order to avoid ambiguity: the term "deadlock" sometimes includes "livelock" (in which processes continue taking steps but keep one another trapped in a loop due to timing issues) and sometimes does not. The definition of "eventual progress" explicitly precludes either situation.

[7] Although NL implies EP, we include both requirements, partly for historical reasons (e.g., [9]) but primarily because it gives us a finer gauge of the effectiveness of various consistency conditions, *viz.* Dijkstra's algorithm, which solves EP but not NL under MWR2 and MWR3.

[8] We use the presentation of the algorithm from [4].

Table 1. Correctness of mutual exclusion algorithms using MW-regular variables.

	MWR1	MWR2	MWR3	Linearizability
Peterson's Algorithm	ME, EP, NL	ME, EP, NL	ME, EP, NL	ME, EP, NL
Dijkstra's Algorithm	ME	ME, EP	ME, EP	ME, EP

Theorem 4. *Peterson's Algorithm solves mutual exclusion under all the three definitions of regularity.*

Dijkstra's algorithm for n processors uses n single-writer shared variables and one multi-writer shared variable ([18]). Under both MWR2 and MWR3 it behaves the same way as under linearizability: ME and EP are guaranteed, but not NL. Under MWR1, only ME is guaranteed. The proof of the corresponding theorem is omitted for reason of space and can be found in [19].

Theorem 5. *Dijkstra's Algorithm satisfies ME under MWR1 and satisfies ME and EP under both MWR2 and MWR3, but does not satisfy NL under any of the conditions.*

6   Conclusion

If Lamport's consistency conditions continue to be of interest in the area of distributed shared memory, as seems likely, it is essential that these conditions be formally extended into the multi-writer model. While this extension is simple in the case of linearizability, it is more difficult and potentially ambiguous for the weaker condition of regularity.

In this paper we have given three possible formal extensions of Lamport's definition of regularity from a single-writer model ([11]) to a more general multi-writer model. We have analyzed the relationships between these extended consistency conditions and a number of other well-known consistency conditions. We have given quorum-based algorithms to implement each of the extended consistency conditions, and proved their correctness. Finally, we have analyzed the correctness of two well-known algorithms for mutual exclusion under each of our proposed consistency conditions.

The weaker condition of safeness [11] can also be extended to the multi-writer model by means of similar techniques to those we have used here; this is one possible avenue of future work. It might also be worthwhile to expand on the work of [14] by exploring ways to formalize the multi-writer version of the consistency conditions met by the probabilistic quorum systems of [16].

Acknowledgement. This work was supported in part by NSF grant 0098305, Texas Higher Education Coordinating Board grant ARP-00512-0091-2001, and Texas Engineering Experiment Station funds.

References

1. M. Ahamad, R. Bazzi, R. John, P. Kohli, and G. Neiger. The Power of Processor Consistency. *ACM Symposium on Parallel Algorithms and Architectures*, pp.251–260, 1993.
2. H. Attiya, A. Bar-Noy, and D. Dolev. Sharing Memory Robustly in Message Passing Systems. *Journal of the ACM*, Vol.42, No.1, pp.124–142, 1996.
3. H. Attiya and R. Friedman. A Correctness Condition for High Performance Multiprocessors. *Proceedings of the 24th ACM Symposium on Theory of Computing*, pp.679–690, 1992.
4. H. Attiya and J. Welch. *Distributed Computing: Fundamentals, Simulations and Advanced Topics*. McGraw Hill, 1998.
5. R. A. Bazzi. Synchronous Byzantine Quorum Systems. *Distributed Computing*, Vol 13, No.1, pp.45–52, 2000.
6. T. D. Chandra and S. Toueg. Unreliable Failure Detectors for Reliable Distributed Systems. *Journal of the ACM*, Vol.43, No.2, pp.225–267, 1996.
7. J. Goodman. Cache Consistency and Sequential Consistency. Technical Report 61, IEEE Scalable Coherent Interface Working Group, 1989.
8. M. Herlihy and J. Wing. Linearizability: A Correctness Condition for Concurrent Objects. *ACM Transactions on Programming Languages and Systems*, Vol.12, No.3, pp.463–492, 1990.
9. L. Higham and J. Kawash. Bounds for Mutual Exclusion with Only Processor Consistency. *Proceedings of the 14th International Symposium on Distributed Computing*, pp. 44–58, 2000.
10. L. Lamport. How to Make a Multiprocessor Computer That Correctly Executes Multiprocess Programs. *IEEE Transactions on Computers*, Vol. C-28, No.9, pp. 690–691, Sept. 1979.
11. L. Lamport. On Interprocessor Communication. Part I and II. *Distributed Computing*, Vol.1, No.2, pp. 77–101, 1986.
12. R. Lipton and J. Sandberg. PRAM: A Scalable Shared Memory. Technical Report 180–88, Department of Computer Science, Princeton University, 1988.
13. N. Lynch and A. Shvartsman. RAMBO: A Reconfigurable Atomic Memory Service for Dynamic Networks. *Proceedings of the 16th International Symposium on Distributed Computing*, 2002.
14. H. Lee and J. Welch. Applications of Probabilistic Quorums to Iterative Algorithms. *Proceedings of the 21st International Conference on Distributed Computing Systems*, pp.21–30, 2001.
15. D. Malkhi and M. Reiter. Byzantine Quorum Systems. *Distributed Computing*, Vol.11, No.4, pp.203–213, 1998.
16. D. Malkhi, M. Reiter, A. Wool, and R. Wright. Probabilistic Quorum Systems. *Information and Computation*, Vol.170, No.2, pp.184–206, 2001.
17. G. L. Peterson. Myths about the Mutual Exclusion Problem. *Information Processing Letters*, Vol.12, No.3, pp. 115–116, June 1981.
18. M. Raynal. *Algorithms for Mutual Exclusion*. The MIT Press, 1986.
19. C. Shao, E. Pierce, and J. Welch. Multi-Writer Consistency Conditions for Shared Memory Objects. Technical Report 2003–7–1, Department of Computer Science, Texas A&M University, July 2003.

Booting Clock Synchronization in Partially Synchronous Systems

Josef Widder*

Technische Universität Wien, Embedded Computing Systems Group E182/2
Treitlstrasse 3, A-1040 Vienna (Austria), `widder@ecs.tuwien.ac.at`

Abstract. We address the problem of network booting: Distributed processes boot one after the other at unpredictable times in order to start some distributed algorithm; we consider clock synchronization algorithms in systems of $n \geq 3f+1$ processes where at most f exhibit Byzantine behavior. Obviously, assumptions like "there are always at most one third of the running processes Byzantine faulty" do not hold during system startup.

Using a partially synchronous model where upper and lower bounds upon transmission and computation are unknown, we show that a suitable modification of Srikanth & Toueg's non-authenticated clock synchronization algorithm handles network booting and guarantees bounded precision both during normal operation and startup. Accuracy (clocks being within a linear envelope of real-time) is only guaranteed, when sufficiently many correct processes are eventually up and running.

1 Introduction

Synchronized clocks are vital for many applications (see [1] for an overview) and should therefore be provided as early as possible during system operation. Before considering system startup let us first revisit the well-known problem of clock synchronization. Although traditionally studied in systems with known timing behavior where all the processes are equipped with hardware clocks, it can also be solved in partially synchronous systems with software clocks (counters): Every correct process p, which has completed booting and initial synchronization (we call such a process active), maintains an integer-valued clock $C_p(t)$, which can be read at arbitrary real-times t. It must satisfy:

(P) **Precision Requirement.** There is some constant precision $D_{max} > 0$ such that $|C_p(t) - C_q(t)| \leq D_{max}$ for any two active correct processes p and q and any real-time t.

(A) **Accuracy Requirement.** There are some constants $a, b, c, d > 0$ such that $a(t_2 - t_1) - b \leq C_p(t_2) - C_p(t_1) \leq c(t_2 - t_1) + d$ for any active correct process p and any two real-times $t_2 \geq t_1$.

---

* This research is part of the W2F-project, which is supported by the Austrian START programme Y41-MAT. (`http://www.auto.tuwien.ac.at/Projects/W2F/`)

F.E. Fich (Ed.): DISC 2003, LNCS 2848, pp. 121–135, 2003.

According to (P) the difference of any two correct clocks in the system must always be bounded, whereas (A) guarantees some relation between progress of clock-time and progress of real-time. (A) is also called linear envelope requirement. The constants a, b, c, and d determine how fast logical time (measured in ticks representing some logical time unit) progresses with respect to real-time. In case of our solution, a clock ticks whenever its clock synchronization algorithm enters the next round of computation. This usually takes one round-trip time, so logical time progresses at about 1 tick per round-trip time.

It is well known [2] that, without authentication[1], no more than one third of the processes may be Byzantine to ensure (P) and (A). Our goal is to handle system startup without further increasing the number of required processes.

Obviously, the startup problem vanishes if an a priori bound on the period of time required for completing the startup of all correct processes can be guaranteed: A process in a (semi-) synchronous system can simply setup a suitable local timeout before it starts sending its first message. However, many real networks cannot be modeled properly as synchronous systems, and even a single correct process that violates the booting time assumption could cause the initialization to fail. Consequently, a time(r)-free initialization, if available, is preferable.

Let us now take a closer look at the problems evolving in systems of $n \geq 3f+1$ processes where all correct processes are initially down. Let us assume that there is an initialization algorithm $\mathcal{I}$ that handles system startup in presence of up to f Byzantine faulty processes. For liveness, $\mathcal{I}$ must of course also handle the case where Byzantine faulty processes are just down and never send messages. Hence it must reach initial synchrony when at least $n - f$ correct processes are up. Now consider the case where Byzantine faulty processes behave exactly as correct ones during initialization whereas f correct ones have not completed booting yet. It is obvious that $\mathcal{I}$ again initializes the system, but now we have $n_{up} \geq 2f + 1$ running processes with f faulty ones among them. Hence, more than one third of the processes would be faulty here.

A straightforward solution could be based upon determining, at runtime, when sufficiently many (at least $2f + 1$) correct processes are eventually up. A process must wait until it has received messages from $3f + 1$ processes for this purpose. To guarantee liveness also when Byzantine processes do not send any messages, however, the number of required processes must be increased to $4f+1$. The question is: Could this penalty somehow be avoided?

Accomplishments: In this paper we show that the number of processes need not be increased for initial clock synchronization in partially synchronous (and hence also synchronous) systems: By modifying the well-known algorithm by Srikanth and Toueg [3], we provide an algorithm that is completely time- and timer-free and requires only $n \geq 3f + 1$ processes even during system startup. It guarantees precision D_{max} during whole system operation, whereas progress of the clocks (accuracy) can only be guaranteed when sufficiently many correct pro-

---

[1] We do not consider authenticated algorithms since it is never guaranteed that malicious processes cannot break the authentication scheme. Using the algorithm of Srikanth and Toueg [3], our correctness proofs cannot be invalidated by this event.

cesses are up and running. Using our clock synchronization in conjunction with suitable modified higher-level distributed algorithms requiring ε-synchronized clocks may hence lead to solutions which also guarantee higher-level service's safety properties during system startup.

Related Work: Clock synchronization in distributed systems is a very well-researched field, see [2,4,5,6,7,8] for an overview. Still, there are only a few papers [3,8,9,10,11] known to us that deal with initial synchronization, mostly in the context of integrating a new process in an already running system. For initialization it is often assumed that all correct processes are up and listening to the network when the algorithm is started [3,9]. In systems where processes boot at unpredictable times, this assumption is too strong. We will see that it can be dropped.

Some solutions for booting exist for very specific architectures: System startup of TTP—viewed as change from asynchronous to synchronous operation—has been investigated in [11]. Initial clock synchronization for the MAFT architecture [10] has been solved, but under stronger system assumptions: A priori assumptions on message transmission delay and local timers are used there to construct a sufficiently large listen window. Termination is achieved by Byzantine Agreement, which, however, requires $2f + 1$ correct processes to be up and running. This cannot always be guaranteed during startup, however. Our goal is minimizing the number of such a priori assumptions. Still we do not know of any approach that could be compared to ours with respect to partial synchrony in conjunction with initially down correct processes.

Our clock synchronization algorithm has graceful degradation [12] during system booting. This prevents Byzantine processes from corrupting the system state during the startup phase where more than one third of the running processes may be Byzantine. Mahaney and Schneider [12] introduced synchronous approximate agreement algorithms which provide graceful degradation when between 1/3 and 2/3 of the processes are faulty. We reach the same bounds.

If the algorithm would have no graceful degradation, the system could be forced into arbitrary states and the solution for initialization must be self-stabilizing [13]. Most self-stabilizing clock synchronization algorithms [14,15,16] do not stabilize if some processes remain faulty during the whole execution. Exceptions are the algorithms by Dolev and Welch [17], which stabilize even in the presence of Byzantine faults, but they require synchronous systems (enforced by a common pulse) or semi-synchronous systems (processes equipped with physical clocks). This cannot be assumed in partially synchronous models. In fact, self stabilizing algorithms are both unsuitable and an overkill for solving the initial synchronization problem: They cannot guarantee bounded precision during whole system life-time since the transition from illegitimate system states to normal operation cannot always be detected. On the other hand, system startup does not need a stabilizing algorithm's ability to start from arbitrary system state: All processes start from a well-defined state and f must always hold. Self-stabilizing algorithms, however, would be able to recover from a temporal violation of f, at the cost of exponential stabilization times.

Much research has been conducted on partially synchronous systems [18,19, 20,21]. Clock synchronization is an important issue here as well (see [18,22]). Our modifications of Srikanth and Toueg's algorithm [3] are in fact based upon ideas from work conducted on consensus algorithms for partially synchronous systems [18,23]. Still, we do not know of any work that considers system startup. Another system model that is neither completely synchronous nor asynchronous is the Timed Asynchronous Model [24], where processes are equipped with physical clocks. Alternative semi-synchronous models (see e.g. [22]) assume that processes know a priori about the timing bounds of the system. Neither of those requirements is met in our model of partial synchrony.

Our results are related to the crash recovery model [25], where processes crash and recover arbitrarily during the execution of a consensus algorithm. Similar work was conducted in the context of clock synchronization [26]. We, however, consider Byzantine processes and more than $n/2$ "crashed" (actually, "initially dead") processes during startup. This exceeds the bounds used in [25,26].

Organization of the paper: Section 2 contains the model as well as some notation related to the initialization phase. Our algorithm is described in Section 3. Sections 4 and 5 contain the analysis of the algorithm during startup. In Section 6 we shortly discuss our algorithm's accuracy properties during normal operation. Some analysis had to be omitted due to space restriction and can be found in the full version of this paper [27].

2   System Model

We consider a system of n distributed processes denoted as $p, q, \ldots$, which communicate through a reliable, error-free and fully connected point-to-point network. Even under our perfect communication assumption, messages that reach a process that is not booted are lost. We assume that a non-faulty receiver of a message knows the sender. The communication channels between processes need not provide FIFO transmission, and there is no authentication service.

Among the n processes there is a maximum of f faulty ones. No assumption is made on the behavior of faulty processes; they may exhibit Byzantine faults [28]. Since we investigate network startup, correct processes that just have not booted yet are not counted as faulty.

Our model is partially synchronous [18]. Rather than the global stabilization time model, where it is assumed that the system is synchronous from some unknown point in time on, we use a variant of the model where bounds on transmission and computation delays exist but are unknown. Therefore processes have no timing information and can only make decisions based on received messages.

We employ the partially synchronous model of [29], which is based upon the end-to-end computational + transmission delay δ_{pq} between any two correct processes p and q. It assumes that there are both upper and lower bounds $\tau^+ < \infty$ and $\tau^- > 0$ ensuring $\tau^- \leq \delta_{pq} \leq \tau^+$, which are not known a priori and need not be invariant over time. Note that $\tau^- > 0$ must also capture the case $p = q$; $\tau^+ < \infty$ secures that every message is eventually delivered. The resulting timing uncertainty is measured by the transmission delay uncertainty $\varepsilon = \tau^+ - \tau^-$ and the transmission delay ratio $\Theta = \tau^+/\tau^-$.

Note that none of τ^-, τ^+, ε, and Θ shows up in our algorithm's code, but only in the formulas established in the analysis of the achieved precision and accuracy. Moreover, it will turn out that the precision D_{max} of our algorithm depends only upon Θ, not upon τ^+ as in classic clock synchronization research. As argued in [30], this has a number of interesting consequences: Since an assumed bound $\overline{\Theta}$ on Θ may still hold when an assumed bound $\overline{\tau}^+$ on τ^+ is violated during periods of overload etc., our algorithm may still work correctly in situations where synchronous ones fail. Actually, τ^+ and τ^- are the worst case and best case response times, respectively, associated with the distributed real-time scheduling problem underlying the execution of our clock synchronization algorithm. Since clock synchronization is a low-level service, typically using high-priority threads and messages, $\varepsilon = \tau^+ - \tau^-$ is usually much smaller than the application-level delay uncertainty $\varepsilon_A = \tau_A^+ - \tau_A^-$. Typical values for Θ reported in real-time systems research [31,32] are $2\ldots 10$. Note also that Θ can be brought down almost arbitrarily close to 1 by introducing additional delays.

2.1   Model of the Initialization Phase

At the beginning all correct processes are down, i.e. they do not send or receive messages. Every message that arrives at a correct process while it is down is lost. A correct process decides independently when it wishes to participate in the system (or is just switched on). Faulty processes may be Byzantine, we can hence safely assume that faulty processes are always up or at least booted before the first correct one. Correct processes go through the following modes:

1. down: A process is down when it has not been started yet or has not completed booting.
2. up: A process is up if it has completed booting. To get a clean distinction of up and down we assume that a process flushes the input queues of its network interface as first action after booting is completed. Hence it receives messages only if they have arrived when it was up.
   a) passive: Running processes initially perform an initialization algorithm that does not provide the required service to the application. During this phase they are said to be passive.
   b) active: Processes which have completed their initialization in passive mode and provide the required service (in our case clock synchronization) to the application are called active.

Let n_{up} be the number of processes which are up at a given time; n_{up} includes at most f faulty processes.

2.2   Messages

There are only two types of messages sent by our algorithm: (init, k) and (echo, k), where k is the sender's clock value. Since processes that started late could have missed previous messages, we require messages with bounded history: The arrival of (echo, k) implies the arrival of (echo, $k-1$) and (echo, $k-2$) messages (this information is transferred implicitly and therefore requires no additional data). Going back two rounds is—as we will see—sufficient for our algorithm.

3   The Algorithm

The algorithm given in Figure 1 is an extension of the classic non-authenticated clock synchronization algorithm by Srikanth and Toueg [3]. The first three **if** clauses (**line 4** to **line 16**) are in fact identical to their algorithm.

For each correct process
```
1    VAR k : integer := 0;
2    VAR mode : {passive, active} := passive;
3
4    if received (init, k) from at least f + 1 distinct processes
5       → send (echo, k) to all [once];
6    fi
7
8    if received (echo, k) from at least f + 1 distinct processes
9       → send (echo, k) to all [once];
10   fi
11
12   if received (echo, k) from at least n − f distinct processes
13      → if mode = active → C := k + 1; fi /* update clock */
14         k := k + 1;
15         send (init, k) to all [once]; /* start next round */
16   fi
17
18   /* catch-up rule */
19   if received (echo, l) from at least f + 1 distinct processes with l > k + 1
20      → if mode = active → C := l − 1; fi /* update clock */
21         k := l − 1; /* jump to new round */
22         send (echo, k) to all [once];
23   fi

Additional Code for each passive correct process
24   if received (init, x) from at least f + 1 distinct processes
25      → C := max(x − 1, k);
26         k := max(x − 1, k);
27         mode := active;
28         send (echo, k) to all [once];
29   fi
```

Fig. 1. Clock Synchronization Algorithm with Startup

The algorithm basically implements a nearly simultaneous global event in a system of $n \geq 3f + 1$ processes, which is used to simultaneously increment the clocks at all processes: When a local clock has made its kth tick, the process sends an (init, k) message to all. If any correct process receives $f + 1$ (init, k) messages it can be sure that at least one was sent by a correct process and it therefore sends (echo, k). When $f+1$ (echo, k) messages are received at a process it also sends (echo, k). Since correct processes send (init,k) and (echo, k) only if at least one correct clock has made its kth tick (set $C := k$), we summarize them as messages for the kth tick frequently in our discussion. If a process receives $n-f \geq 2f+1$ (echo, k) messages it can be sure that among those are at least $f+1$ messages sent by correct processes. These will be echoed by every other correct process such that, within bounded time, every correct process also receives $n - f$ (echo, k) messages – this property is called relay. This works because $n - f$ is the minimum number of correct running processes in the system. Therefore, every process that has received $n - f$ (echo, k) messages may safely increment its local clock value to $k + 1$ and send (init, $k + 1$).

Srikanth and Toueg showed [3] that the algorithm achieves (P) and (A) for $n \geq 3f+1$ processes if they are initially synchronized. They gave an algorithm for initialization as well, which, however, does not work in our setting: If $n_{up} \geq n - f$ it could be that correct processes make some progress with the "help" of faulty ones. Still, there are not sufficiently many correct processes up to guarantee relay and hence progress at every correct process; (P) and (A) could be violated. A solution for integration of late starters had also been given in [3], which relies on progress which we cannot guarantee for our reduced n_{up}.

We reach our goal of bounded precision (P) during whole system operation based on the following observation: Progress of the clock at any correct process requires always at least $f + 1$ messages from distinct correct processes. Since correct processes always send messages to all, every correct process must get those messages. If a process p receives $f +1$ (echo, l) messages for a future tick l, it can conclude that at least one correct process has the clock value l and process p could update its clock. Therefore we extend Srikanth and Toueg's algorithm by (1) the current clock value k in line 1 (which is not available in the original algorithm [3] since all ticks are observed concurrently) and (2) the catch-up rule in line 19 that triggers if $f + 1$ messages for a future tick are received such that p can update its clock value. Note that a similar construct is used in a clock synchronization algorithm in [18]. In [23] it is used in a phase protocol in a consensus algorithm. Booting is not addressed in those papers, however.

To overcome the problem of lost messages due to initially down processes we add the following protocol (which is not shown in Figure 1): As the first action after getting up, a correct process sends (echo, 0) to all. If a correct process p receives (echo, 0) by a process q it resends the last (echo, k) message it has sent to q. It is easy to see that the first $f + 1$ correct processes are initially synchronized at clock value 0^2, since no correct process can make any progress

---

[2] When hardware clocks (with different values) must be synchronized initially, resetting all clock values to 0 after booting could be regarded as unsatisfactory. We do

before at least $f + 1$ correct processes are up. Before discussing the behavior of correct late starters, we give some useful definitions and lemmas.

Definition 1 (Local Clock Value). $C_p(t)$ denotes the local clock value of a correct process p at real-time t, and σ_p^k is the real-time when process p sets its local clock to $k + 1$, for any $k \geq 0$.

Definition 2 (Maximum Local Clock Value). $C_{max}(t)$ denotes the maximum of all local clock values of correct processes that are up at real-time t. Further $\sigma_{first}^k = \sigma_p^k \leq t$ is the real-time when the first correct process p sets its local clock to $k + 1 = C_{max}(t)$.

The following Lemma 1 shows that progress of $C_{max}(t)$ is only possible via the third **if** (**line 12**), which needs at least $f + 1$ messages by distinct correct processes. This fact will be heavily used in our proofs.

Lemma 1 (3rd if). In a system of $n \geq 3f + 1$ processes, every correct process executing the algorithm given in Figure 1— that sets its clock to $C_{max}(t)$ by time t must do so by the third **if** clause in **line 12**.

Proof. By contradiction. Let a correct process p set its clock to $k = C_{max}(t)$ at instant t by a catch-up rule (**line 19** or **line 24**). At least one correct process must have sent a message for a tick $l > k$ before t. Since correct processes never send messages for ticks greater their local clock value, at least one had a clock value $l > k$ at instant t. Thus $C_{max}(t) > k$, which provides the required contradiction. $\quad\square$

Lemma 2 (Minimal Number of Init Messages). Given an arbitrary point in time t with $l = C_{max}(t)$, let $t' \geq t$ be the instant when C_{max} further increases. For $n \geq 3f + 1$, at least $f + 1$ correct processes set their clocks to $C_{max}(t)$ by the third **if** and therefore send (init, 1) before t'.

Proof. In order for the first correct process to set its clock to $l + 1$, it must have received at least $n - f \geq 2f + 1$ (echo, l) messages sent by distinct processes. At least $f + 1$ of those must originate from correct processes, which must have set their local clock to l by the third **if** (Lemma 1) and sent (init, 1) earlier. $\quad\square$

As we have seen in Lemma 2, $f + 1$ (init, k) messages are sent for every tick k. Correct processes never send (init, k) messages for arbitrarily small ticks compared to C_{max}. These two facts are used for changing from passive to active mode. We have already mentioned that each correct process starts with sending (echo, 0) to all. Then it just executes the algorithm from Figure 1. When a correct passive process p eventually receives $f + 1$ (init, x) messages for a tick x (**line 24**) it can be sure that at least one correct process has sent one. Because x cannot be too far apart from C_{max}, p can conclude that its clock value is within precision and can hence switch to active. We discuss initialization of late starters in Section 5. The precision D_{MCB} of early starters is computed in the following section.

---

not think so, since, in general, initial hardware clock values are meaningless right after booting if considering internal clock synchronization.

4 Degraded Mode

In this section, we will show that the clocks of all correct early starters are always within D_{MCB} of each other. Note that late starters are guaranteed to eventually reach this precision as well. For now we assume that there is a fixed number $n_{up} \leq n$ of processes which are initially up, and all correct ones (at least $n_{up} - f$) have clock value 0. This models exactly our early phase, starting when enough correct processes are up such that progress is possible but not guaranteed. In this section's analysis we assume that there are no late starters (they are incorporated in Section 5). The following Theorem 1 reveals that even a reduced number of processes achieves certain (weak) properties that are sufficient—as we will see in Theorem 2—to guarantee (P) with some precision D_{MCB}. There is no progress guarantee in this phase and hence no guarantee for (A).

Theorem 1 (Weak Synchronization Properties). For $n \geq 3f + 1$ with any n_{up}, where $0 \leq n_{up} \leq n$, the algorithm from Figure 1 achieves:

P1W . Weak Correctness. If at least $f + 1$ correct processes set their clocks to k by time t, then every correct process sets its clock at least to $k - 1$ by time $t + 2\tau^+$.

P2.   Unforgeability. If no correct process sets its clock to k by time t, then no correct process sets its clock to $k + 1$ by time $t + 2\tau^-$ or earlier.

P3W . Weak Relay. If a correct process sets its clock to k at time t, then every correct process sets its clock at least to $k - 2$ by time $t + \varepsilon$.

Proof. Weak Correctness. If $k = C_{max}(t)$ all $f + 1$ correct processes must have set their clocks to k using the third **if** (line 12), and therefore have sent (init, k) by time t (see Lemma 1). These correct processes receive the (init, k) messages by time $t + \tau^+$ and therefore send (echo, k) to all. All correct processes must receive those $f + 1$ (echo, k) messages by time $t + 2\tau^+$ and therefore set their clocks to $k - 1$ by the fourth **if** (line 19), if they have not already done so. If $k < C_{max}(t)$ at least $f + 1$ correct processes have set their clocks to k by time $t' < t$ using the third **if** from line 12 (otherwise no correct process may have set its clock to a value greater than k – see Lemma 1) and therefore all correct processes set their clocks by time $t' + 2\tau^+ < t + 2\tau^+$ (see previous paragraph).

Unforgeability. Setting the clock value can be done via three rules. We derive a contradiction for any of those.
Assume there is a process p that sets its clock to $k + 1$ before instant $t + 2\tau^-$ by the third **if** (line 12). It does so because it has received $n - f \geq 2f + 1$ (echo, k) messages by distinct processes. There are at least $f + 1$ (echo, k) messages sent by correct processes among those, which must have been sent before $t + \tau^-$. Correct processes only send (echo, k) when they have received $f + 1$ (init, k) or (echo, l) messages for some $l \geq k$ from distinct processes. Hence, at least one correct process must have sent a message for tick $l \geq k$ before t. By assumption no tick k messages are sent before t. Since all tick $l > k$ messages are sent after tick k messages by a correct process no such message has been sent by time t, which provides the required contradiction.

Assume that there is a process p that sets its clock to $k+1$ before instant $t+2\tau^-$ using the fourth **if** (**line** 19). Process p does so because it has received $f+1$ (echo, l) messages by distinct processes for some $l > k+1$. That is, at least one (echo, l) message must have been sent by a correct process q before $t+\tau^-$. Process q has sent it, because it has received at least $f+1$ messages for tick $x \geq l$. At least one of these messages must have been sent by a correct process before time t, since messages for tick $x > k$ are sent by a correct process only after tick k messages. But by assumption P2, no tick k message was sent before t, which again provides the required contradiction.

Assume finally that there is a correct process p that sets its clock to $k+1$ before instant $t + 2\tau^-$ using the fifth **if** (**line** 24). Process p does so because it has received at least $f+1$ (init, $k+2$) messages by time $t+2\tau^-$. At least one of these (init, $k+2$) message must have been sent by a correct process q before $t+\tau^-$. Process q has sent it, because it has received at least $n - f \geq 2f+1$ (echo, $k+1$) messages by time $t+\tau^-$, such that at least one (in fact $f+1$) correct process must have sent (echo, $k+1$) before time t. A correct process never sends any $k+1$ messages before it has send a message for tick k. By assumption no tick k message was sent by time t which again provides the contradiction.

Weak Relay. Assume $k = C_{max}(t)$. A correct process must set its clock to k using the third **if** from **line** 12 (recall Lemma 1), when it has received at least $n - f \geq 2f+1$ (echo, $k-1$) messages. Among those are at least $f+1$ messages sent by distinct correct processes. These messages must be received by all correct processes by time $t + \varepsilon$ and therefore they set their clocks to $k-2$ (using the fourth **if**).

If $k < C_{max}(t)$ then at least one correct process has already set its clock to $k' > k$ at time $t' \leq t$ using the third **if** (**line** 12). We have shown in the previous paragraph that all correct processes must set their clocks to $k' - 2$ by time $t' + \varepsilon$ so all correct processes must set their clocks to $k - 2$ by time $t + \varepsilon$. □

Note that P1W and P3W are directed towards past ticks: Progress is not guaranteed because the properties only ensure that processes reach prior clock values. Still, there are time bounds in P1W, P2 and P3W, which are sufficient to satisfy the precision requirement (P), as we will show in Theorem 2. We require some preliminary lemmas for this purpose.

Lemma 3 (Fastest Progress). Let p be the first correct process that sets its clock to k at time t. Then no correct process can reach a larger clock value $k' > k$ before $t + 2\tau^-(k' - k)$.

Proof. By induction on $l = k' - k$. For $l = 1$, Lemma 3 is identical to unforgeability and therefore true. Assume that no correct process has set its clock to $k + l$ before $t + 2\tau^- l$ for some l. Thus no correct process may set its clock to $k+l+1$ before $t+2\tau^- l+2\tau^- = t+2\tau^-(l+1)$ by unforgeability. Hence Lemma 3 is true for $l+1$ as well. □

In our analysis we will frequently require to bound the increase of C_{max} during a given real-time interval $[t_1, t_2]$. Lemma 3 can be applied for this purpose if $t_1 = \sigma_{first}^k$ but not for arbitrary times t_1. As in [33] we will provide a general solution based on the following Definition 3.

Definition 3 (Synchrony). Real-time t is in synchrony with $C_{max}(t)$ if $t = \sigma_{first}^k$ for some arbitrary k, as defined in Definition 2. Let the indicator function of non-synchrony be defined as

$$I_{t \neq \sigma} = I_\sigma(t) = \begin{cases} 0 & \text{if } t \text{ is in synchrony with } C_{max}(t), \\ 1 & \text{otherwise.} \end{cases}$$

Lemma 4 (Maximum Increase of C_{max} within Time Interval). Given any two real-times $t_2 \geq t_1$, $C_{max}(t_2) - C_{max}(t_1) \leq \lfloor \frac{t_2 - t_1}{2\tau^-} \rfloor + I_\sigma(t_1)$.

Proof. Let $k = C_{max}(t_1) - 1$. We have to distinguish the two cases $\sigma_{first}^k = t_1$ and $\sigma_{first}^k < t_1$. The special case $C_{max}(t_1) = 0$, that is $k = -1$, must be handled as the latter: Since correct processes send (echo, 0) when they get up, they are already right in the middle of round 0, thus we must consider $\sigma_{first}^{-1} < t_1$ in this case.

Let $\sigma_{first}^k = t_1$ such that $I_\sigma(t_1) = 0$. From Lemma 3 follows that C_{max} may increase every $2\tau^-$ time-units, hence $\lfloor \frac{t_2 - t_1}{2\tau^-} \rfloor$ times before t_2. Since $I_\sigma(t_1) = 0$, Lemma 4 is true for this case.

Now let $\sigma_{first}^k < t_1$, such that $I_\sigma(t_1) = 1$, and let the real-time $t' = \sigma_{first}^{k+1} > t_1$. We can now apply Lemma 3 starting from time t'. Since $t_2 - t_1 > t_2 - t'$ it follows from Lemma 3 that C_{max} cannot increase more often than $\lfloor \frac{t_2 - t_1}{2\tau^-} \rfloor$ times between t' and t_2. At instant t', C_{max} increases by one such that $C_{max}(t_2) - C_{max}(t_1) \leq \lfloor \frac{t_2 - t_1}{2\tau^-} \rfloor + 1$. Since $I_\sigma(t_1) = 1$ Lemma 4 is true.   □

In the following major Theorem 2 we give a bound for the precision requirement (P). We assume an instant t such that $t = \sigma_p^k$ for a correct process p. From weak relay we can derive a bound for σ_q^{k+2} for any other correct process q, such that $\sigma_q^{k+2} = \sigma_{first}^{k+2}$. Using Lemma 4 we can give a bound for $C_{max}(t)$ and hence bound the achievable precision D_{MCB}.

Theorem 2 (Precision in Degraded Mode). Given a system of $n \geq 3f + 1$ processes with n_{up} processes being up, where $0 \leq n_{up} \leq n$. Let the correct ones among them be initially synchronized to 0. Then the algorithm of Figure 1 satisfies the precision requirement (P) with $D_{MCB} = \lfloor \frac{1}{2}\Theta + \frac{5}{2} \rfloor$.

Proof. If no correct process advances its clock beyond $k = 2$, precision $D_{MCB} \geq 2$ is automatically maintained since all clocks are initially synchronized to $k = 0$.

Assume that a correct process p has local clock value $k \geq 0$ within a still unknown precision D_{MCB} with respect to all other correct processes—and therefore also to $C_{max}(t')$—at real-time t'. We use weak relay, Definition 3 and Lemma 4 to reason about D_{MCB} by calculating $C_{max}(t)$ for some time $t > t'$.

Let process p advance its clock to $k + 1$ such that $\sigma_p^k = t > t'$. Since p has not done so before t, no other correct process has set its clock to $k + 3$ before $t - \varepsilon$, following directly from weak relay (P3W), thus $\sigma_{first}^{k+2} \geq t - \varepsilon$.

From Lemma 4 follows that $C_{max}(t) \le \lfloor \frac{t-(t-\varepsilon)}{2\tau^-} \rfloor + I_\sigma(t-\varepsilon) + C_{max}(t-\varepsilon)$. Let us now take a closer look at the term $I_\sigma(t-\varepsilon) + C_{max}(t-\varepsilon)$: If $\sigma_{first}^{k+2} = t - \varepsilon$ and therefore $t - \varepsilon$ is synchronized with C_{max}, $C_{max}(t-\varepsilon) = k+3$ and $I_\sigma(t-\varepsilon) = 0$ (following Definition 3). If on the other hand $\sigma_{first}^{k+2} > t - \varepsilon$, $C_{max}(t-\varepsilon) = k+2$ and $I_\sigma(t - \varepsilon) = 1$. In both cases $I_\sigma(t - \varepsilon) + C_{max}(t - \varepsilon) = k + 3$ such that $C_{max}(t) \le \lfloor \frac{\varepsilon}{2\tau^-} \rfloor + k + 3$ thus $C_{max}(t) \le \lfloor \frac{1}{2}\Theta + \frac{5}{2} \rfloor + k$.

Process p has clock value $C_p(t') = k$ at time $t' < t$ which is by assumption within precision. Since $C_p(t') < C_p(t)$ and $C_{max}(t') \le C_{max}(t)$, we get a bound for D_{MCB} from the difference $C_{max}(t) - C_p(t') = C_{max}(t) - k \le \lfloor \frac{1}{2}\Theta + \frac{5}{2} \rfloor$.   □

5   Integration

In the previous section, we discussed the behavior of the early starters. We now turn our attention to correct late starters, which get up after there was possibly some progress of C_{max}. The bound for the resulting precision is derived by a worst case analysis in Theorem 3, where it is assumed that a correct process changes to active mode (and hence must satisfy precision) right after booting based on the oldest possible messages. Due to space restrictions, this section just provides a proof sketch. When considering integration, we must of course guarantee that the required clock synchronization conditions (P) and (A) are eventually satisfied when sufficiently many correct processes got up. This is accomplished in Theorem 4.

Theorem 3 (Precision). In a system of $n \ge 3f + 1$ processes, the algorithm given in Figure 1 satisfies precision (P) with $D_{max} = \lfloor 2\Theta + \frac{11}{2} \rfloor$ throughout whole system operation.

Proof Sketch. Since (init) messages are used for the change from passive to active mode, we must first confirm that no (init, k) messages for arbitrarily small k are sent by correct processes, i.e. that $C_{max} - k$ is bounded. This holds true since every correct process requires $n - f$ (echo) messages in order to send (init), such that there must be at least one correct process whose message is used to both increase C_{max} and send (init, k).

For the worst case precision, we must consider a newly started process p that receives $f + 1$ (init, k) messages with k as small as possible compared to C_{max}. Then we give a bound on how much C_{max} can increase before p must change to active at time t, with clock value $k - 1$. After time t, p's clock value becomes and stays better, thus $C_{max}(t) - (k - 1)$ is our bound for precision D_{max}.   □

Theorem 3 shows that (P) is always maintained. In order to show that our algorithm also satisfies (A) when sufficiently many correct processes are up, we give a bound on the maximum time interval it takes to get progress into the system after the $n - f^{th}$ correct processes got up at time t. Since at time t at least one correct process has a clock value of $C_{max}(t)$, (init, $C_{max}(t)$) messages may have been missed by the initializing process. The first tick, for which it is guaranteed that all correct processes receive at least $f + 1$ (init) messages, is $C_{max}(t) + 1$. The following Theorem 4 gives the latest possible instant when those (init, $C_{max}(t) + 1$) messages are received by all correct processes.

Lemma 5. For the algorithm given in Figure 1 for $n \geq 3f + 1$ and $n_{up} \geq n - f$, there are at least $f + 1$ correct processes with local clock values $C_{max}(t)$ or $C_{max}(t) - 1$ at any time t.

Proof. If no correct process advances its clock beyond 1 the lemma is true. Let p be some correct process that sets its clock to $C_{max}(t) > 1$ at instant t such that $C_p(t) = C_{max}(t)$. It does so because it has received at least $n - f \geq 2f + 1$ (echo, $C_p(t) - 1$) messages, i.e. at least $f + 1$ sent by distinct correct processes. Correct processes never send (echo) messages for ticks larger than their local ones. Therefore at least $f + 1$ correct processes must have a clock value of $C_p(t)$ or $C_p(t) - 1$ at time t.   □

Theorem 4 (Initialization Time). Let t be the time the $n - f^{th}$ correct process p gets up. By time $t + \Delta_{init}$, at least $n - f$ correct processes are running in active mode, where $\Delta_{init} = 8\tau^+$.

Proof. Process p sends its first (echo, 0) message at time t. If there is already progress in the system, p will be initialized quickly because it receives the necessary (init) messages τ^+ after they were sent.

If the processes in front are not making progress, the clock value of p at time $t + 2\tau^+$ is $C_p(t + 2\tau^+) \geq C_{max}(t) - 2$ and is reached using the catch-up rule (line 19) as the answers from the $f + 1$ most advanced processes (recall Lemma 5 and the fact that (echo, k) messages have a history, as described in Section 2.2) must be received by then. Process p then sends (echo, $C_{max}(t) - 2$), such that by time $t + 3\tau^+$ every running correct process must have received $n - f$ (echo, $C_{max}(t) - 2$) messages.

Every running correct process now sets its clock to $C_{max}(t) - 1$ (if it has not yet done so) and sends (init, $C_{max}(t) - 1$). Possibly p does not receive $f + 1$ (init, $C_{max}(t) - 1$) messages, because there were too many processes that already had the clock value $C_{max}(t) - 1$. So p does not necessarily switch to active mode.

By time $t + 5\tau^+$, however, all running correct processes set their clocks to $C_{max}(t)$ and by time $t + 7\tau^+$ to $C_{max}(t) + 1$. Therefore p and all other running correct processes receive at least $f + 1$ (init, $C_{max}(t) + 1$) messages by time $t + 8\tau^+$ or earlier. Then, at least $n - f$ correct processes run in active mode.   □

The necessity of $n - f$ messages by distinct processes instead of $2f + 1$ is a drawback that cannot be avoided: Assume a system of $n = 5f + 2$, thus $4f + 2$ correct processes. Assume further that $2f + 1$ correct processes start early and reach some arbitrary clock value. Then there could be $2f + 1$ correct late starters which could learn about the early starters after they reached a smaller common clock value. During this interval, (P) could be violated.

6　Envelope Synchronization

When $n - f$ correct processes are active, we can give stronger properties than the ones following from P1W, P2 and P3W in Theorem 1. The following envelope condition can be derived from these stronger properties, which also guarantee progress.

Theorem 5 (Accuracy). The described system, with $n \geq 3f + 1$, where at least $n - f$ processes are correct and active, satisfies the following envelope condition

$$\tfrac{t_2 - t_1}{2\tau^+} - 4 + \tfrac{1}{\Theta} < C_p(t_2) - C_p(t_1) < \tfrac{t_2 - t_1}{2\tau^-} + D_{max} + 1$$

for every correct active process p and all real-times $t_2 \geq t_1$.

Acknowledgments. I am grateful to Ulrich Schmid, my Ph.D. supervisor, for his support and encouragement.

References

1. Liskov, B.: Practical uses of synchronized clocks in distributed systems. Distributed Computing **6** (1993) 211–219
2. Dolev, D., Halpern, J.Y., Strong, H.R.: On the possibility and impossibility of achieving clock synchronization. Journal of Computer and System Sciences **32** (1986) 230–250
3. Srikanth, T.K., Toueg, S.: Optimal clock synchronization. Journal of the ACM **34** (1987) 626–645
4. Simons, B., Welch, J.L., Lynch, N.: An overview of clock synchronization. In: Fault-Tolerant Distributed Computing. LNCS 448 (1990) 84–96
5. Ramanathan, P., Shin, K.G., Butler, R.W.: Fault-tolerant clock synchronization in distributed systems. IEEE Computer **23** (1990) 33–42
6. Schneider, F.B.: Understanding protocols for byzantine clock synchronization. Technical Report 87–859, Cornell University, Department of Computer Science (1987)
7. Schmid, U., ed.: Special Issue on The Challenge of Global Time in Large-Scale Distributed Real-Time Systems. Real-Time Systems 12(1–3) (1997)
8. Miner, P.S.: Verification of fault-tolerant clock synchronization systems. NASA Technical Paper 3349 (1993)
9. Lundelius-Welch, J., Lynch, N.A.: A new fault-tolerant algorithm for clock synchronization. Information and Computation **77** (1988) 1–36
10. Kieckhafer, R.M., Walter, C.J., Finn, A.M., Thambidurai, P.M.: The MAFT architecture for distributed fault tolerance. IEEE Transactions on Computers **37** (1988) 398–405
11. Steiner, W., Paulitsch, M.: The transition from asynchronous to synchronous system operation: An approach for distributed fault-tolerant systems. Proceedings of the The 22nd International Conference on Distributed Computing Systems (2002)
12. Mahaney, S.R., Schneider, F.B.: Inexact agreement: Accuracy, precision, and graceful degradation. In: Proceedings 4th ACM Symposium on Principles of Distributed Computing, Minaki, Canada (1985) 237–249

13. Dijkstra, E.W.: Self-stabilizing systems in spite of distributed control. Communications of the ACM **17** (1974) 643–644
14. Dolev, S., Welch, J.L.: Wait-free clock synchronization. Algorithmica **18** (1997) 486–511
15. Papatriantafilou, M., Tsigas, P.: On self-stabilizing wait-free clock synchronization. Parallel Processing Letters **7** (1997) 321–328
16. Arora, A., Dolev, S., Gouda, M.G.: Maintaining digital clocks in step. Parallel Processing Letters **1** (1991) 11–18
17. Dolev, S., Welch, J.L.: Self-stabilizing clock synchronization in the presence of byzantine faults. (1995) Preliminary Version.
18. Dwork, C., Lynch, N., Stockmeyer, L.: Consensus in the presence of partial synchrony. Journal of the ACM **35** (1988) 288–323
19. Lynch, N.: Distributed Algorithms. Morgan Kaufman (1996)
20. Attiya, H., Dwork, C., Lynch, N., Stockmeyer, L.: Bounds on the time to reach agreement in the presence of timing uncertainty. Journal of the ACM (JACM) **41** (1994) 122–152
21. Dolev, D., Dwork, C., Stockmeyer, L.: On the minimal synchronism needed for distributed consensus. Journal of the ACM (JACM) **34** (1987) 77–97
22. Ponzio, S., Strong, R.: Semisynchrony and real time. In: Proceedings of the 6th International Workshop on Distributed Algorithms (WDAG'92). (1992) 120–135
23. Attiya, H., Dolev, D., Gil, J.: Asynchronous byzantine consensus. Proceedings of the 3rd ACM Symposium of Distributed Computing (1984) 119–133
24. Cristian, F., Fetzer, C.: The timed asynchronous distributed system model. IEEE Transactions on Parallel and Distributed Systems **10** (1999) 642–657
25. Aguilera, M.K., Chen, W., Toueg, S.: Failure detection and consensus in the crash-recovery model. Distributed Computing **13** (2000) 99–125
26. Barak, B., Halevi, S., Herzberg, A., Naor, D.: Clock synchronization with faults and recoveries (extended abstract). In: Proceedings of the nineteenth annual ACM symposium on Principles of distributed computing, ACM Press (2000) 133–142
27. Widder, J.: Switching On: How to boot clock synchronization in partially synchronous systems. Technical Report 183/1–125, Department of Automation, Technische Universität Wien (2002)
28. Lamport, L., Shostak, R., Pease, M.: The Byzantine generals problem. ACM Transactions on Programming Languages and Systems **4** (1982) 382–401
29. Schmid, U., Fetzer, C.: Randomized asynchronous consensus with imperfect communications. In: 22nd Symposium on Reliable Distributed Systems (SRDS'03). (2003) (to appear).
30. Le Lann, G., Schmid, U.: How to implement a timer-free perfect failure detector in partially synchronous systems. Technical Report 183/1–127, Department of Automation, Technische Universität Wien (2003) (submitted).
31. Ernst, R., Ye, W.: Embedded program timing analysis based on path clustering and architecture classification. In: Digest of Technical Papers of IEEE/ACM International Conference on Computer-Aided Design, IEEE Computer Society (1997) 598–604
32. Gutiérrez, J.P., Garcia, J.G., Harbour, M.G.: Best-case analysis for improving the worst-case schedulability test for distributed hard real-time systems. In: Proceedings of the 10th Euromicro Workshop on Real-Time Systems. (1998) 35–44
33. Schmid, U., Schossmaier, K.: Interval-based clock synchronization. Real-Time Systems **12** (1997) 173–228

Automatic Discovery of Mutual Exclusion Algorithms*

(Preliminary Version)

Yoah Bar-David[1] and Gadi Taubenfeld[2]

[1]P.O.Box 527, Kfar Hes, Israel
yoah@bardavid.com
[2]School of computer science, the Interdisciplinary Center,
P.O.Box 167, Herzliya 46150, Israel
tgadi@idc.ac.il

Abstract. We present a methodology for automatic discovery of synchronization algorithms. We built a tool and used it to automatically discover hundreds of new algorithms for the well-known problem of mutual exclusion. The methodology is rather simple and the fact that it is computationally feasible is surprising. Our brute force approach may require (even for short algorithms) the mechanical verification of hundreds of millions of incorrect algorithms before a correct algorithm is found. Although many new interesting algorithms have been found, we think the main contribution of this work is in demonstrating that the approach suggested for automatic discovery of (correct) synchronization algorithms is feasible.

1 Introduction

1.1 Automatic Discovery of Correct Algorithms

Finding a new algorithmic solution for a given problem is considered as an art. Techniques have been suggested to help with this process, but the core activity relies on human invention and ingenuity. "The process of preparing programs for a digital computer is especially attractive, not only because it can be economically and scientifically rewarding, but also because it can be an aesthetic experience much like composing poetry or music" [Knu73].

We propose a methodology for automatic discovery of synchronization algorithms for finite-state systems, and demonstrate its feasibility by building a tool that is used to automatically find hundreds of new correct algorithms for the well-known problem of mutual exclusion. The methodology is rather simple, the fact that it is computationally feasible is surprising. It works as follows: assume that you want to solve a specific problem P.

1. Write a model-checker M for P. That is, write a program (or use an existing one) that for any proposed algorithm (solution) A, decides whether A solves P.
2. For a given (restricted) programming language, write a program that will produce syntactically all possible (correct and incorrect) algorithms in that language, under certain user-defined parameters, such as: number of lines of code; number of processes; number, type and size of shared variables; etc.
3. For each algorithm A generated in step 2, check if A solves P (using M).

---

* Part of this work was done while the authors were with the Open University of Israel .

F.E. Fich (Ed.): DISC 2003, LNCS 2848, pp. 136–150, 2003.
© Springer-Verlag Berlin Heidelberg 2003

We name this methodology *automatic discovery*. The reason that automatic discovery has not been implemented before for synchronization algorithms is probably due to the fact that (automatic) verification is considered to be a time-consuming process, while our brute force approach may require (even for very short algorithms) to try to verify hundreds of millions of incorrect algorithms before finding a correct one. Although the many new algorithms that the tool has found are rather interesting, we think that the main contribution of this work is in demonstrating that the approach suggested for automatic discovery of (correct) synchronization algorithms is feasible.

An important related area of research, which is discussed in Subsection 1.6, is the synthesis of concurrent systems. We observe that unlike in synthesis, our brute force approach heavily depends on model checking, it lets us specify directly: the number of shared objects their type and size, the number of lines of code in a solution, and the programming language used. It also lets us find all solutions in a given *algorithm space* (i.e., the algorithms generated for a given set of parameters) or prove that no solution exists, which in turn enables to find (what is) the shortest solution possible.

1.2 System Architecture

The architecture of the tool is shown schematically in Figure 1. Via a user-interface, the user can set the problem parameters: (1) number of processes (2) number of lines of code (3) number, size and type of variables (4) type of (*if* and *while* statement) conditions. The parameters are sent to the algorithm generator, which generates all the possible algorithms according to the given parameters. Each algorithm (which passes the optimization checks) is sent to verification. If an algorithm is verified as correct, it is sent back to the user-interface and displayed. Verification results are also returned to the algorithm generator for use in optimizations. A tool based on this system architecture has been implemented in Java and C++, and has around 10,000 lines of code.

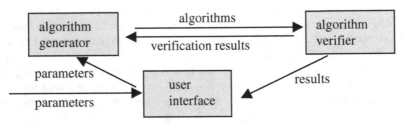

Fig. 1. System architecture for a single computer

1.3 Optimizations and Performance

One of the main challenges in building the tool was to be able to process enough algorithms in a reasonable time, so that interesting results can actually be found. To achieve this, many optimizations were implemented (Section 5). As an example for the importance of optimizations, consider the case of mutual exclusion algorithms for two processes with the following parameters: 3 shared bits, complex conditions[1] are

---

[1] Complex conditions are composed of two simple conditions (terms) related by *and*, *or* or *xor*.

allowed, 4 entry commands and 1 exit command. Even for this setting the *algorithm space* is huge. There are about 10^{21} possible algorithms in the (high-level) generation language[2] (and there are about 10^{48} algorithms in the low-level verification language). Using all optimizations, less than $3 \cdot 10^7$ algorithms were actually generated and tested, requiring about 25 minutes on a Pentium-4/1.6Ghz PC. From all the algorithms in this reduced algorithm space (of size $3 \cdot 10^7$), 105 correct algorithms were found, one of which is the famous Peterson's algorithm (Section 2.6) [Pet81].

While the optimizations reduce the number of algorithms needed to be verified, we apply several other techniques, which dramatically improve the performance. For example, during verification, for each tested algorithm, there is a need to construct a structure called a state transition graph. To improve performance, we do not build such a graph from scratch every time, but rather use a sub-graph of the graph already built for the previously tested algorithm as a basis for building the new graph.

1.4   The Model and the Mutual Exclusion Problem

We make the following assumptions. All processes run the same algorithm[3], but processes have unique integer identifiers. In the case of two processes their ids are 0 and 1. An event is either an atomic read or atomic write of a single shared variable. A shared variable can be read by all processes, and written by a single process or by multiple processes, depending on user-defined parameters (single-writer vs. multi-writer). Initially, all shared variables are set to zero.

The mutual exclusion problem is to design an algorithm that guarantees mutually exclusive access to a critical section among a number of competing processes [Dij65]. It is assumed that each process is executing a sequence of instructions in an infinite loop. The instructions are divided into four continuous sections: the *remainder, entry, critical section* and *exit*. The mutual exclusion problem is to write the entry and the exit code in such a way that the following two basic requirements are satisfied:

1.   *Mutual Exclusion*: no two processes are in their critical section at the same time.
2.   *Deadlock-freedom*: if a process is trying to enter its critical section, then some process, not necessarily the same one, eventually enters its critical section.

We will examine also solutions that satisfy the following stronger requirement:

3.   *Starvation-freedom*: if a process is trying to enter its critical section, then this process must eventually enter its critical section.

The following measures are used when discussing algorithms: (1) number and size of variables, (2) number of commands, (3) whether the *if* and *while* conditions are simple or complex (i.e., one term or two terms), (4) whether starvation-freedom is satisfied or

---

[2] In the high-level generation language, for the given parameters, the number of assignment statements is 53 and the number of conditions (simple, and complex) is 8081. Thus, each of the 5 lines of code is chosen from: 53 assignments, 8081 *if* statements, 8081 *while* statements, and 3 closing (*endif, else, endwhile*).

[3] That is, the algorithm of process *i* can be obtained from that of process *j* by swapping their ids. This assumption helps in reducing the size of the "algorithm space" and does not affect computability.

just deadlock-freedom. These measures are used *only* w.r.t. the specific language we use (as defined in Section 3). In some other language one may be able to write a statement like $a=b$ [c [d]] and count it as a single line of code and 4 variables, where in our model, this line must be written as: $t=c[d]$ followed by $a=b[t]$ which requires 2 lines of code and 5 variables. In the sequel, the terms *entry commands* and *exit commands* mean language instructions used for the entry and exit sections, respectively.

1.5 New Algorithms for Mutual Exclusion

The system was run to find algorithms for *two* processes using 2, 3, 4, 5 or 6 shared bits. A methodical search was conducted to find the shortest solutions: the number of commands was incrementally increased until a solution was found. The lengths of the *shortest* solutions are summarized in the table below. The number of tested algorithms is displayed, along with the number of correct algorithms found. As a result of optimizations, not all generated algorithms were actually tested. The number of tested algorithms counts only those that were actually tested by the algorithm verifier. All correct algorithms that have been found are new (and shorter than previously known solutions), except for Peterson's algorithm. In the starvation-freedom column, "yes" means that *some* of the algorithms satisfy starvation-freedom (and all satisfy deadlock-freedom). All the tests were performed on a Pentium 4/1.6 GHz PC.

User-defined parameters					Results		
Shared bits	Entry comm-ands	Exit comm-ands	Complex conditions	Starvation freedom	Tested algorithms	Correct algorithms	appx. running hours
2	6	1	Yes[4]		7,196,536,269	0	216
2	7	1			846,712,059	66	39
3	4	1	Yes	Yes	25,221,389	105	0.4
3	6	1		Yes	1,838,128,995	10	47
4	4	1	Yes	Yes[5]	129,542,873	480	1
4	5	1			129,190,403	56	1
4	6	1		Yes	*900,000,000	80	12
5	5	1			*22,000,000	106	0.4
6	5	1			*70,000,000	96	1

In Section 2, various conclusions are drawn from these results. Two of them are: (1) when only *simple* conditions are allowed, the shortest algorithm found has 5 entry and 1 exit commands, and it uses 4 bits (with just 5 entry commands, out of which one has to be a *while* command and one *endwhile*, the algorithm can not assign values to too many variables); (2) when *complex* conditions are allowed, Peterson's algorithm (Section 2.6), which has 4 entry and 1 exit command has been rediscovered by the system and proved to be the shortest possible. Many new solutions with the same parameters have also been found. Burns and Lynch had proved that any deadlock-free mutual exclusion algorithm for n processes must use at least n variables

---

[4] Performed in parallel on 5 computers.

[5] In this setting (4 bits, 4 entry, 1 exit, complex), 4 out of the 480 correct algorithms use only single-writer bits. None of these 4 algorithms satisfies starvation-freedom.

* This run was stopped after a few solutions were found. Not all possible algorithms were tested

[BL80,BL93], and hence there is no need to search for solutions for two processes using one variable.

There is a simple method, called tournament, which enables to construct a mutual exclusion algorithm for n processes from any algorithm for two processes [PF77]. Thus any of the new algorithms for two processes corresponds to a new algorithm for many processes. In a tournament algorithm, the processes are divided into two groups, and in each group the processes compete recursively. The two "winners" use the solution for two processes to determine which is the one to enter its critical section.

1.6 Related Work

The mutual exclusion problem was first presented by Dijkstra in [Dij65]. Numerous mutual exclusion algorithms have been published, some are discussed later in the paper. For a survey of some early algorithms for mutual exclusion see [Ray86].

Model checkers have been successfully implemented and used in practice to verify (among other things) communication protocols and circuit designs. For a general introduction on formal methods, which also includes a short survey of existing model checkers and few notable examples of how they have been used in the industry to aid in the verification of newly developed designs, see [CW96]. A comprehensive presentation of the theory and practice of model checking can be found in [CGP00].

An important related area of research is the synthesis of concurrent systems. In system synthesis, a desired specification is transformed into a system that is guaranteed to satisfy the specification. Methods for synthesizing concurrent programs are usually based on extracting a system that meets the specification from a constructive proof that the specification is satisfiable [EC82,MW80,MW84]. A method of synthesizing k similar sequential processes (which, as the authors write, can be automated) is presented in [AE98]. There are two possible approaches for synthesis of concurrent systems: (1) to use a synthesis procedure for a single process, and then decompose the processes [EC82, MW84], and (2) to construct the underlying processes directly [PR90]. We have mentioned only very few of the numerous papers that have been published on this subject. We conclude with a quote from [KV01]: "the real challenge that synthesis algorithms and tools face in the coming years is mostly not that of dealing with computational complexity, but rather of making automatically synthesized systems more practically useful''.

In [PS00], an automatic protocol generation approach, which is similar to our approach, is used to generate security protocols.

2   Tests and Results

The system was run to find mutual exclusion algorithms for two processes using 2, 3, 4, 5 or 6 shared bits. One should keep in mind that: (1) all generated algorithms adhere to the high-level generation language as defined in Section 3. The algorithms may be shorter when expressed in a different language; (2) It is relatively easy to prove that an algorithm discovered by the system is correct, but to formally prove that no other solution exists, requires proving that the entire system is correct. As already mentioned, it is assumed that initially, all shared variables are set to zero.

2.1 Two Shared Bits, Simple Conditions

A known solution, for n processes, is the one-bit algorithm [BL80,BL93,Lam86], which does not satisfy starvation-freedom. When porting it to our high-level language, and trimming it for just two processes, we get a short version (using two bits and simple conditions) with 9 entry commands and 1 exit command. Our system has found a shorter solution. The following table summarizes the results.

Conclusion *The shortest solution found for two bits and simple conditions has 7 entry and 1 exit commands.*

Comment: All the 66 algorithms do not satisfy starvation-freedom. Can it be proved analytically that for this case all correct algorithm satisfy only deadlock-freedom?

Parameters		Results	
Entry comm.	Exit comm.	Tested algorithms	Correct algorithms
4	1	27,372	0
4	2	44,340	0
5	1	925,389	0
5	2	1,235,778	0
6	1	28,522,988	0
7	1	846,712,059	66

Following are 3 sample solutions (for two processes). The identifiers are 0 and 1. Thus, me is in $\{0,1\}$, and next = 1-me.

2 bits, simple conditions, single-writer, deadlock-free		
1 a[me] = 1 2 while a[next] = 1 3 a[me] = next 4 while a[0] = me 5 endwhile 6 a[me] = 1 7 endwhile 8 critical section 9 a[me] = 0	1 a[me] = 1 2 while a[next] = 1 3 while a[0] = me 4 a[me] = 0 5 endwhile 6 a[me] = 1 7 endwhile 8 critical section 9 a[me] = 0	1 a[me] = me 2 while a[0] = me 3 a[me] = 1 4 while a[1] = next 5 a[me] = 0 6 endwhile 7 endwhile 8 critical section 9 a[me] = 0

Notice that in the third solution, process 0 does not initially set its flag bit to 1.

2.2 Three Shared Bits, Simple Conditions

A known solution for this setting is Dekker's starvation-free algorithm [Dij65]. When porting it to our language we get a version with 9 entry and 2 exit commands. Our system has found shorter solutions. The table summarizes the results

Parameters		Results	
Entry comm.	Exit comm.	Tested algorithms	Correct algorithms
4	1	287,579	0
4	2	493,073	0
5	1	24,124,934	0
5	2	36,636,722	0
6	1	1,838,128,995	8 starvation-free 2 deadlock-free

Conclusion *The shortest solution found for three bits and simple conditions has 6 entry and 1 exit commands.*

Comment: Every starvation-free solution contains an "if" statement, while no dead-lock-free solution contains an "if" statement.

3 bits, simple conditions starvation-free	3 bits, simple conditions deadlock-free
1 a[me] = next 2 if b = next 3 b = me 4 while b = a[next] 5 endwhile 6 endif 7 critical section 8 a[me] = me	1 a[me] = 1 2 while b != a[next] 3 while a[b] = me 4 b = a[0] 5 endwhile 6 endwhile 7 critical section 8 a[me] = 0

2.3 Four Shared Bits, Simple Conditions

The table summarizes the results.

Conclusion *The shortest deadlock free solution found for four bits and simple conditions has 5 entry and 1 exit commands.*

Parameters		Results	
Entry comm.	Exit comm.	Tested algorithms	Correct algorithms
4	1	915,350	0
4	2	1,270,897	0
5	1	129,190,403	56 deadlock-free
6	1	*900,000,000	80 starvation-free

Comment: None of the 56 deadlock-free algorithms satisfy starvation-freedom and none of them use only single-writer variables.

Conclusion *The shortest starvation-free solution found for four bits and simple conditions has 6 entry and 1 exit commands.*

Since no solution with 5 entry and 1 exit commands satisfies starvation-freedom, the system was run to check if a starvation-free solution exists when using more lines of code. When looking for solutions with 6 entry commands and 1 exit command, 80 solutions that satisfy starvation-freedom were found, and the execution was stopped before all possible algorithms were tested.

4 bits, simple conditions, deadlock-free	4 bits, simple conditions, starvation-free
1 a[me] = 1 2 b[0] = 0 3 while b[me] != a[next] 4 b[next] = me 5 endwhile 6 critical section 7 a[me] = 0	1 a[me] = 1 2 b[me] = me 3 a[1] = 0 4 a[me] = a[0] 5 while b[next] != a[1] 6 endwhile 7 critical section 8 b[me] = next

---

* This run was stopped after a few solutions were found. Not all algorithms were tested.

2.4 Five and Six Shared Bits, Simple Conditions

Most of the solutions are variants of the solution using four shared bits.

Conclusion *The shortest solution found for 5 and 6 bits and simple conditions has 5 entry and 1 exit commands.*

Conclusion *With simple conditions, having more than 4 bits does not help in finding a shorter algorithm.*

Parameters			Results	
# of bits	Entry comm.	Exit comm.	Tested algorithms	Correct alg.
5	4	1	6,987,284	0
5	4	2	10,729,817	0
5	5	1	*22,000,000	106
6	4	1	6,642,480	0
6	4	2	9,365,248	0
6	5	1	*70,000,000	96

2.5 Two Shared Bits, Complex Conditions

The last run, with 6 entry and 1 exit command, no solution was found. Solutions with 7 entry and 1 exit command using simple conditions are given in Section 2.1

Parameters		Results	
Entry comm.	Exit comm.	Tested algorithms	Correct alg.
4	1	1,264,266	0
5	1	69,400,411	0
6	1	7,196,536,269	0

Conclusion *Using complex conditions does not help in finding a shorter solution when two bits are used.*

2.6 Three Shared Bits, Complex Conditions

For this setting, a known solution is Peterson's algorithm [Pet81], shown on the right. An immediate question is whether it is the shortest possible. The table summarizes the results.

Conclusion Peterson's algorithm is the shortest algorithm found!

Comment: All the 105 algorithms satisfy starvation-freedom and all are variants of Peterson's algorithm. One of them is Peterson's algorithm.

Conclusion *To get a weaker solution that (only) satisfies deadlock freedom but not starvation-freedom, one more bit or one more command is required.*

Peterson's algorithm for 2 processes
1 a[me] = 1
2 turn = next
3 while a[next] = 1 and turn = next
4 endwhile
5 critical section
6 a[me] = 0

Parameters		Results	
Entry comm.	Exit comm.	Tested algorithms	Correct alg.
3	1	75,496	0
3	2	492,707	0
4	1	25,221,389	105 (all s.f.)

---

* This run was stopped after a few solutions were found. Not all algorithms were tested.

Define the contention-free (time) complexity (CFC), as the number times a process has to access shared variables in its entry code when it runs alone [AT96].

Comment: The CFC of each of the 105 starvation-free algorithms found is at least 3.

Comment: There is a deadlock-free solution where the contention-free (time) complexity is 2, which uses two bits, 7 entry and 1 exit commands (see Section 2.1).

Following are 3 examples (out of 105) of additional solutions found:

3 shared bits, complex conditions, starvation-free		

1 a[me] = 1
 2 b = next
 3 while a[1] = a[0] and
       b = next
 4 endwhile
 5 critical section
 6 a[me] = 0
	1 a[me] = 1
	 2 b = me
	 3 while a[next] = me
	      xor b = 0
	 4 endwhile
	 5 critical section
	 6 a[me] = 0
		1 a[me] = 1
		 2 b = next
		 3 while me = 0 xor
		      b != a[b]
		 4 endwhile
		 5 critical section
		 6 a[me] = 0

2.7 Four Shared Bits, Complex Conditions

For this setting there exists a variant of Peterson's algorithm, due to Kessels [Kes82], which uses only single-writer bits. Kessels' algorithm is not symmetric, and it uses "minus" (or negation). Porting the algorithm to our language would result an algorithm with over 15 entry commands. The following table summarizes the results.

Comment: Some of the 480 algorithms satisfy starvation-freedom, but none of these starvation-free algorithms use only single-writer bits.

Comment: 4 of the 480 algorithms use only single-writer bits.

Parameters		Results	
Entry comm.	Exit comm.	Tested algorithms	Correct alg-s
3	1	118,536	0
3	2	1,088,071	0
4	1	129,542,873	480

Conclusion *Using 4 bits instead of just 3 does not help in finding a shorter solution.*

Following are two solutions that were found:

4 shared bits, complex conditions, deadlock-free, single-writer	
1 a[me] = 1 2 while b[me] = me or b[1] != a[next] 3 b[me] = a[0] 4 endwhile 5 critical section 6 a[me] = 0	1 a[me] = 1 2 while b[0] != a[next] or b[me] = next 3 b[me] = a[1] 4 endwhile 5 critical section 6 a[me] = 0

3 Algorithm Generator

3.1 Generating All Possible Algorithms

Initially, an attempt has been made to generate all possible algorithms using the verification assembler-like language (see Section 4). This approach has two main disadvantages: (1) the number of generated algorithms is too large, because there are many ways one can write the same high-level language algorithm in a low-level language, and (2) it takes a long time to manually reverse-engineer an algorithm written in assembler into a high-level language to make it easier to understand. To overcome these problems, a simple high-level language was defined. This language was designed to be simple, so that the number of possible options for each command will be relatively small, but powerful enough so that with just a few lines of code, a solution can be written. The exact language specification is given in the next subsection.

Before running the tool, the following parameters must be specified (by the user):
1. The number of processes and the number of shared variables.
2. The number of entry and exit commands. A command is a single line of code, and the language defines exactly how statements are related to lines of code.
3. The maximal value for each shared variable. The minimum value is zero.
4. Are complex conditions allowed, and if so, with which relations (and, or, xor).
5. Are multi-writer variables allowed (or just single-write variables).

With these parameters set, the system enumerates all possible variables, assignments, conditions, and control structures. A control structure is the assignment of a command type to a line of code (e.g. line 1 is an assignment, line 2 is a while statement). Each algorithm is enumerated by the control-structure number, and for each line, the operand number for that line (which assignment or which condition). Once all language elements are enumerated, the first possible algorithm is generated. After verification, the last line of code is incremented to return the next possible command for this line, and so on. The generator compiles each algorithm into the verification language.

3.2 Language Used to Generate Algorithms

The following table specifies the (high-level) language used. The line breaking within statements must be exactly as below. One of the parameters is the number of lines of code, hence, the language does not allow a single line with multiple statements.

Language elements

Constants	Integers, from zero to the highest allowed value for a variable.
Relative constants	Contain a process number: **me** (my process number, zero for first process), **next** (successor process number), **prev** (predecessor's number).
Simple variables	Integers, can have a value from zero to the highest allowed value for a variable.
Arrays	One-dimensional array of simple variables. The array size is as the number of processes.
Referencable variable	Either a simple variable, or an array variable with an index. The index can be a constant, a relative constant or a simple variable.
Simple conditions	A comparison between 2 variables or a variable and a constant. Comparison operators are = (equals) and != (not equal)
Complex conditions	2 simple conditions, related with **and**, **or** or **xor**

Statements

Assign-ment statement	*referencable-variable = constant* (e.g. v=0 or a[1] = 0) *referencable-variable = referencable-variable* (e.g. v=q or a[1]=b[v])			
if and while statements	**if** *condition* *statement(s)* **endif**	**if** *condition* *statement(s)* **else** *statement(s)* **endif**	**while** *condition* *statement(s)* **endwhile**	**while** *condition* **endwhile**

4 Algorithm Verifier

Model checking is a technique for mechanically verifying finite state concurrent systems. The main challenge in model checking is to deal with the state space explosion problem. We have developed a special very fast verifier which is limited to verify only the correctness of mutual exclusion algorithms.

4.1 Verification Language

To ensure that the verification is according to the model, a verification language was designed. This language is a low-level (assembler like) language, and contains only instructions that can be run atomically. Each instruction is represented by a triplet: an operation code, and 2 optional operands. Each process has 3 local variables that can be read or written only by the single process. These variables are: a program counter, a general purpose register and an index register. For lack of space, the complete instruction set of the verification language is omitted from this version.

4.2 Building the State Transition Graph

A *state* is the snapshot of all information of the system at a single point of time. In our implementation, state information is the contents of all global memory variables, and the contents of all local variables for each process (including program counters).

When a single verification language instruction is executed, the system moves to a new state. To build the entire state transition graph, the system starts with the initial state (i.e., all memory set to zero, and all program counters are before the first instruction) and iteratively adds states that are reachable, until all reachable states are added. Once this procedure is completed, the system has mapped all the reachable states and all possible state transitions, and can run validation checks on them. During the construction, various techniques are applied to reduce the size of the graph.

A key optimization used is the following: when an algorithm is verified, instead of generating the entire graph again, the verifier keeps the sub-graph that was generated for the previous algorithm and is still valid for the new algorithm. This is implemented as follows: comparing the two algorithms, the verifier finds the top-most verification command that was changed, and trims from the state transition graph all states and transitions that may be affected by the algorithm change, but keeps all the states that are not affected.

4.3 Checking If an Algorithm Satisfies the Correctness Properties

To be a valid solution, an algorithm must ensure mutual exclusion and deadlock-freedom. The test for mutual exclusion is done by looking at each reachable state and checking if two processes are in their critical section at that state. If there is a state where two processes are in their critical section, the algorithm is rejected. This test is actually done when adding each new state.

The test for deadlock-freedom is done by looking at all cycles in the state transition graph. A cycle represents an infinite loop. If there is a cycle where all active processes executed at least one instruction, and no process is in its critical section at any state of the cycle, then the algorithm does not satisfy deadlock-freedom, and it is rejected.

The test for starvation-freedom is also done by looking at all cycles in the graph. If there is a cycle where all active processes executed at least one instruction, and some process was not in its critical section during any state of the cycle, then the algorithm does not satisfy starvation-freedom, as the loop can be executed forever, and that process will be starved. If an algorithm satisfies mutual exclusion and deadlock-freedom but not starvation-freedom, it is not rejected. As done in other model checkers, Tarjan's algorithm is used for finding strongly connected components [Tar83].

5 Optimizations

One of the main challenges was to be able to process enough algorithms in a reasonable time, so that interesting results can actually be found. To achieve this, many optimizations were implemented. Following are the main optimizations used.

5.1 Optimizations during Algorithm Generation

1. *Do not generate syntactically incorrect algorithms*: An algorithm is syntactically correct if every open block (*if* or *while*) is properly closed (by *endif* or *endwhile*), and if each *if* command has no more than one *else* section. When the algorithm is not syntactically correct, the entire program structure is rejected, without generating all options for each condition or assignment.

2. *Do not generate equivalent conditions*: Equivalent conditions are generated and tested only once. For example, a=1 is equivalent to 1=a; and a=1 is equivalent to a!=0, when the variable is a single bit.[6]

3. *Do not generate constant conditions*: Some conditions are always true or always false. There is no point in generating them. An example is: (a=0 and a=1).

---

[6] Notice that the following conditions are *not* equivalent: (a=0 and b=0) is not equivalent to (b=0 and a=0). Since only a single read is atomic, the order of reading variables a and b could make a difference.

4. *Heuristics*: *do not allow consecutive assignments to the same variable.* 2 con-
    secutive assignments should not have the same target variable.[7] Example, a=1
    followed by a=0.

5. *Do not generate relative constant "prev" for 2 processes*: For only 2 processes
    relative constant *next* is exactly the same as *prev*, so only one of them is needed.

5.2 Optimizations during Verification

6. *Incremental state graph construction*: Instead of building the graph for each algo-
    rithm from scratch, the largest valid sub-graph of the graph already built for the
    previously tested algorithm is used as a basis for building the new graph.

7. *Stop building state graph on first error*: The standard model-checking approach
    is to build first the entire state transition graph, and then verify all the require-
    ments on this graph. The optimization is that while building the graph, every new
    state is checked if in it 2 processes are in the critical section. If more than one
    process is in the critical section, verification fails immediately, without building
    the rest of the graph. (Also called on-the-fly model checking.)

8. *Minimize number of states*: A new state is generated only if the last executed
    command accessed a (global) variable. If only local variables are accessed
    (change the program-counter or local registers) in the last executed command,
    another command is executed without generating a new state in the graph.

5.3 Interactive Optimizations

The following optimizations use information exchanged between the verifier and the
generator to skip the generation of some algorithms by the algorithm generator.

9. *Sk*i*p generation of alternatives options for statements that are not executed*:
    In some cases, the verifier determines that an algorithm is incorrect without exe-
    cuting all the instructions. For example, the algorithm to the right does not sat-
    isfy mutual exclusion. Since command 3 is never executed, no other assignment
    in line 3 can correct the algorithm. Therefore, there is no need to generate the
    alternative assignments for line 3.

    ```
    1 a = 0
    2 if a = 1
    3   b = a
    4 endif
    5 critical section
    6 a = 0
    ```

---

[7] This restriction should be removed if expressions are added to the language. If the language
is changed to contain operators like "+", then the following code should be made valid: a=1
followed by a=a+b.

10. *Skip generation of alternatives for complex conditions that were not executed*:
     An optimization similar to the previous one applies to partially executed com-
     plex conditions. For example, if the algorithm contains the condition "if (a=1 or
     b=2)" and if during verification, the value of variable a is always evaluated as 1,
     then the right part of the condition (b=2) is never executed, and there is no need
     to generate other alternative conditions for the right part. For an *"and"* relation,
     the same applies when the first condition is always false.

5.4 Optimizations Specific to Mutual Exclusion

11. *Check "solo" runs first*: We first check that, when there is no contention, a sin-
     gle process (when run alone) eventually enters its critical section. This simple
     optimization was found very important in improving the overall performance.

12. *Must have "while" in entry code*: In a correct algorithm a process must wait
     when another process is in its critical section. The only way to busy-wait in our
     model is by using a while loop. Therefore, an algorithm that does not contain a
     while in the entry code is incorrect and does not need to be verified.

13. *Must have an assignment statement in the entry code and in the exit code.*
     At least one assignment in the entry code must assign a value other than zero.

6 Discussion

We have implemented a tool that can automatically discover algorithms for the well-
known problem of mutual exclusion. Using this tool our experiments have successfully discovered many new algorithms (and re-discovered some known ones). Immediate directions for further research are: to add optimizations and heuristics in order to
reduce and search the huge algorithm space; and to apply a similar approach to other
synchronization problems. The results mentioned in Section 2 leave some specific
questions open: Why some sets of parameters have no starvation-free algorithms (or
no single-writer algorithms), while others, not vastly different as defined by the parameters, do? Are there meaningful classes that solutions can be reduced to, which
can help to distinguish between reordering of statements versus a radically different
structure?

References

[AE98]   P. Attie and E. Emerson. Synthesis of concurrent systems with many similar proc-
         esses. *ACM Tran. on Programming Languages and Systems* 20(1):51–115, 1998.

[AT96]   R. Alur and G. Taubenfeld. Contention-free complexity of shared memory algo-
         rithms. *Information and Computation* 126(1):62–73,1996.

[BL80]   J.N. Burns and N.A. Lynch. Mutual exclusion using indivisible reads and writes. In
         18th annual allerton conf. on communication, control and computing, 833–842, 1980.

[BL93]   J.N. Burns and N.A. Lynch. Bounds on shared-memory for mutual exclusion. *Infor-
         mation and Computation,* 107(2):171–184, December 1993.

[CGP00] E.M. Clarke, O. Grumberg and D. Peled. *Model Checking.* The MIT Press, 2000.

[CW96]   E.M. Clarke, J.M. Wing, et al. Formal Methods: State of the art and future directions. *ACM Computing Surveys,* 28(4):626–643, December 1996.

[EC82]   E. Emerson and E.M. Clarke. Using branching time temporal logic to synthesize synchronization skeletons. *Science of Computer Programming* 2:241–266, 1982.

[Dij65]   E.W. Dijkstra. Solutions of a problem in concurrent programming control. *Communications of the ACM,* 8(9):569, 1965.

[Kes82]   J.L.W. Kessels. Arbitration without common modifiable variables. *Acta Informatica,* 17(2):135–141, June 1982.

[Knu73]   D.E. Knuth. *The art of computer programming.* Addison-Wesley, 2nd ed., 1973.

[KV01]   O. Kupferman and M. Vardi. Synthesizing distributed systems. *Proc. of the 16ᵗʰ IEEE Symp. on logic in computer science,* 2001.

[Lam86]   L. Lamport. The mutual exclusion problem: Part II – Statement and Solutions. *Journal of the ACM,* 33:327–348, 1986.

[MW80]   Z. Manna and R. Waldinger. A deductive approach to program synthesis. *ACM Transactions on Programming Languages and Systems* 2(1):90–121, 1980.

[MW84]   Z. Manna and P. Wolper. Synthesis of communicating processes from temporal logic specifications. *ACM Tran. on Programming Lang. and Systems* 6(1):68–93, 1984.

[Pet81]   G.L. Peterson. Myths about the mutual exclusion problem. *Information Processing Letters,* 12(3):115–116, 1981

[PF77]   G.L. Peterson and M.J. Fischer. Economical solutions for the critical section problem in a distributed system. *Proc. 9ᵗʰ ACM Symp. on Theory of Computing,* 91–97, 1977.

[PR90]   A. Pnueli and R. Rosner. Distributed reactive systems are hard to synthesize. *Proc. of the 31ˢᵗ FOCS,* 746–757, 1990.

[PS00]   A. Perrig and D. Song. Looking for diamonds in the desserts: Automatic security protocol generation for three-party authentication and Key distribution. In *Proc. of the 13ᵗʰ IEEE Computer Security Foundation Workshop,* July 2000.

[Ray86]   M. Raynal. *Algorithms for mutual exclusion.* The MIT Press, 1986. Translation of: Algorithmique du parallelisme, 1984.

[Tar83]   R.E. Tarjan, *Data Structures and Network Algorithms.* Society for industrial and Applied Mathematics, 1983.

On the Implementation Complexity of Specifications of Concurrent Programs

Paul C. Attie*

College of Computer Science, Northeastern University, Boston, MA
MIT Laboratory for Computer Science, Cambridge, MA
attie@ccs.neu.edu
http://www.ccs.neu.edu/home/attie/Attie.html

Abstract. We present a decision algorithm for the following problem: given a specification, does there exist a concurrent program which both satisfies the specification and which can be implemented in hardware-available operations in a straightforward manner, i.e, without long correctness proofs, and without introducing excessive blocking and/or centralization? In case our decision algorithm answers "yes," we also present a synthesis method to produce such a program. We consider specifications expressed in branching time temporal logic. Our result gives a way of classifying specifications as either "easy to implement" or "difficult to implement," and can be regarded as the first step towards a notion of "implementation complexity" of specifications.

1   Introduction

One of the major approaches to the construction of correct concurrent programs is successive refinement: start with a high-level specification, and construct a series of programs, each of which "refines" the previous one in some way. In the realm of shared-memory concurrent programs, this refinement usually takes the form of reducing the grain of atomicity of the operations used for inter-process communication and synchronization. For example, a high-level design might assume that the entire global state can be read and updated in a single atomic transition, whilst a low-level implementation would be restricted to the operations typically available in hardware: atomic reads and writes of registers, test-and-set of a single bit, load-linked/store-conditional, compare-and-swap, etc. Each of the successive refinements is considered correct if and only if it conforms to the specification. The notions of conformance to a specification which are widely studied can be roughly categorized into two approaches:

1. The use of an operational specification, e.g., an automaton or a labeled transition system, which is successively refined, via several intermediate levels of abstraction, into an implementation. The implementation is considered correct if and only if each of its externally visible behaviors ("traces") is also a trace of the specification, or if it is "bisimilar" to the specification.

---

* Supported in part by NSF Grant CCR-0204432

F.E. Fich (Ed.): DISC 2003, LNCS 2848, pp. 151–165, 2003.

2. The use of a temporal logic formula as a specification. The program is considered correct iff its "semantic denotation" satisfies the formula. In the branching-time paradigm, the semantic denotation of a program is its global-state transition diagram, which can be viewed as a model-theoretic structure for a suitable branching-time temporal logic. The implementation is correct if and only if the specification is true in each of the initial states of the implementation. In the linear-time paradigm, the semantic denotation of a program is the set of its executions. Each execution can be viewed as a model-theoretic structure for a suitable linear-time temporal logic. The implementation is correct if and only if the specification is true along every execution.

We consider the following question: given a specification, does there exist a concurrent program which both satisfies the specification and which can be easily refined to hardware-available operations in a straightforward and efficient manner, i.e, without long correctness proofs, and without introducing excessive blocking and/or centralization? We use the branching-time temporal logic CTL [9,10] to express specifications. For CTL specifications, we present an algorithm which decides this question in the sense that it detects a condition, temporary stability of action guards, which allows for easy refinement. When this condition holds, we provide a method of mechanically synthesizing a program which satisfies the specification and which can be easily refined.

Related work. Previous synthesis methods [2,8,10,13,14,15,17,18] all produce high-grain concurrent programs. In [10], every process can read and update the global state in a single atomic transition. In [15], the synthesized program consists of a central "synchronizer" process which communicates with satellite processes, who do not communicate amongst each other. The methods of [2,8,13,14, 17,18] all synthesize a single "reactive module," which communicates with the environment. Thus, all these methods produce a centralized system consisting of a single process.

The rest of the paper is as follows. Section 2 presents technical preliminaries: our model of concurrent computation, and the specification language CTL. Section 3 gives some technical background on the CTL decision procedure. Section 4 presents our result: a decision procedure for answering the question posed above, and a synthesis method for the case when the answer is positive. Section 5 applies our result to the mutual exclusion and readers-writers problems. Section 6 discusses further work and concludes.

2 Technical Preliminaries

2.1 Model of Concurrent Computation

We consider concurrent programs of the form $P = P_1 \| \cdots \| P_I$ that consist of a finite number I of fixed sequential processes $P_1, \ldots, P_I$ running in parallel. With every process P_i, $1 \le i \le I$, we associate a single unique index i. Each P_i is a synchronization skeleton [10], that is, a state-machine where each (local) state of P_i represents a region of code intended to perform some sequential computation and where each arc represents a conditional transition (between different regions of sequential code) used to enforce synchronization constraints.

Formally, each P_i is a directed graph where each node is a (local) state of P_i and is labeled by a unique name (s_i), and where each arc is labeled with a guarded command [7] $B_i \rightarrow A_i$ consisting of a guard B_i and corresponding action A_i. With each P_i we associate a set AP_i of atomic propositions, and a mapping V_i from local states of P_i to subsets of AP_i: $V_i(s_i)$ is the set of atomic propositions that are true in s_i. As P_i executes transitions and changes its local state, the atomic propositions in AP_i are updated. Different local states of P_i have different truth assignments: $V_i(s_i) \neq V_i(t_i)$ for $s_i \neq t_i$. Atomic propositions are not shared: $AP_i \cap AP_j = \emptyset$ when $i \neq j$. Other processes can read (via guards) but not update the atomic propositions in AP_i. We define $AP = AP_1 \cup \cdots \cup AP_I$. There is also a set of shared variables $x_1, \ldots, x_m$, which can be read and written by every process. These are updated by the action A.

A global state is a tuple of the form $(s_1, \ldots, s_I, v_1, \ldots, v_m)$ where s_i is the current local state of P_i and $v_1, \ldots, v_m$ is a list giving the current values of $x_1, \ldots, x_m$, respectively. A guard B_i is a predicate on global states, and an action A_i is a parallel assignment statement that updates the shared variables.

We model parallelism as usual by the nondeterministic interleaving of the "atomic" transitions of the individual processes P_i. Hence, at each step of the computation, some process with an "enabled" arc is nondeterministically selected to be executed next. Let $s = (s_1, \ldots, s_i, \ldots, s_I, v_1, \ldots, v_m)$ be the current global state, and let P_i contain an arc from node s_i to s_i' labeled with $B_i \rightarrow A_i$ (we write this arc as the tuple $(s_i, B_i \rightarrow A_i, s_i')$). If B_i holds in s, then a permissible next state is $s' = (s_1, \ldots, s_i', \ldots, s_I, v_1', \ldots, v_m')$ where $v_1', \ldots, v_m'$ are the new values for the shared variables resulting from action A. The transition relation R is the set of all such triples (s, i, s'). The arc from node s_i to s_i' is enabled in state s. A computation path is a sequence of states $s^0, s^1, \ldots, s^k, \ldots$ where $\forall k \geq 0, \exists i \in [1:I] : (s^k, i, s^{k+1}) \in R$,[1] i.e., each successive pair of states is related by R. If $s = (s_1, \ldots, s_i, \ldots, s_I, v_1, \ldots, v_m)$, then we define $s{\restriction}i = s_i$ and $s{\restriction}AP_i = V_i(s{\restriction}i)$.

Definition 1 (Global state transition diagram). Given a concurrent program $P = P_1 \| \cdots \| P_I$ and a set S_0 of initial global states for P, the global state transition diagram generated by P is a structure $M = (S_0, S, R, V)$ given as follows: (1) R is the next-state relation defined above, (2) S is the smallest set of global states satisfying (2.1) $S_0 \subseteq S$ and (2.2) if $\exists s \in S, i \in [1:I] : (s, i, t) \in R$ then $t \in S$, and (3) V is given by $V(s) = V_1(s_1) \cup \cdots \cup V_I(s_I)$, that is, a global state inherits its truth-assignments to atomic propositions from its constituent local states.

---

[1] $[1:I]$ is the set of natural numbers from 1 to I, inclusive.

2.2   The Specification Language CTL

Our specification language is the propositional branching time temporal logic CTL [10]. CTL formulae are built up from the atomic propositions in $\mathcal{AP}$, $\neg$, $\wedge$, and the temporal modalities $\mathsf{EX}_i f$, $\mathsf{A}[f\mathsf{U}g]$, and $\mathsf{E}[f\mathsf{U}g]$ (f, g are sub-formulae).

Formally, we define the semantics of CTL formulae with respect to structures of the same type as global state transition diagrams, i.e., a structure $M = (S_0, S, R, V)$ consisting of a countable set S of global states, a set $S_0 \subseteq S$ of initial states, a relation $R \subseteq S \times [1:I] \times S$, giving the transitions, and a mapping $V : S \mapsto 2^{\mathcal{AP}}$ which labels each state s with a set $V(s) \subseteq \mathcal{AP}$ of atomic propositions true in s. If $s = (s_1, \ldots, s_i, \ldots, s_I, v_1, \ldots, v_m)$, then $V(s) \overset{\mathrm{df}}{=} V_1(s_1) \cup \cdots \cup V_I(s_I)$, where $V_i(s_i) \subseteq \mathcal{AP}_i$ gives the atomic propositions that hold in s_i. We require that R be total, i.e., that $\forall s \in S, \exists i, s' : (s, i, s') \in R$.

A fullpath is an infinite sequence of states $(s^0, s^1, \ldots, s^k, \ldots)$ such that $\forall k \geq 0, \exists i \in [1:I] : (s^j, i, s^{j+1}) \in R$, i.e., an infinite computation path. $M, s \models f$ means that f is true at state s in structure M. We define $\models$ inductively:

$$
\begin{array}{lll}
M, s \models p & \text{iff} & p \in V(s) \\
M, s \models \neg f & \text{iff} & \text{not}(M, s \models f) \\
M, s \models f \wedge g & \text{iff} & M, s \models f \text{ and } M, s \models g \\
M, s \models \mathsf{EX}_i f & \text{iff} & \text{for some state } t, (s, i, t) \in R \text{ and } M, t \models f, \\
M, s \models \mathsf{A}[f\mathsf{U}g] & \text{iff} & \text{for all fullpaths } (s, s^1, s^2, \ldots) \text{ in } M, \\
& & \exists k \geq 0 [M, s^k \models g \wedge (\forall \ell : 0 \leq \ell < k \Rightarrow M, s^\ell \models f)] \\
M, s \models \mathsf{E}[f\mathsf{U}g] & \text{iff} & \text{for some fullpath } (s, s^1, s^2, \ldots) \text{ in } M, \\
& & \exists k \geq 0 [M, s^k \models g \wedge (\forall \ell : 0 \leq \ell < k \Rightarrow M, s^\ell \models f)]
\end{array}
$$

Thus X indicates "nexttime" and U indicates "until": $[f\mathsf{U}g]$ means that g eventually holds, and f holds up to that point. E, A quantify existentially, universally (respectively), over the fullpaths starting from a state. A formula f is satisfiable if and only if there exists a structure M and state s of M such that $M, s \models f$. Such an M is a model of f. $M, U \models f$ abbreviates $\forall s \in U : M, s \models f$, where $U \subseteq S$. We introduce the abbreviations $f \vee g$ for $\neg(\neg f \wedge \neg g)$, $f \Rightarrow g$ for $\neg f \vee g$, $f \equiv g$ for $(f \Rightarrow g) \wedge (g \Rightarrow f)$, $\mathsf{A}[f\mathsf{U}_w g]$ for $\neg\mathsf{E}[\neg g\mathsf{U}(\neg f \wedge \neg g)]$, $\mathsf{AF}f$ for $\mathsf{A}[\mathsf{true}\mathsf{U}f]$, $\mathsf{AG}f$ for $\neg\mathsf{EF}\neg f$, $\mathsf{AX}_i f$ for $\neg\mathsf{EX}_i\neg f$, $\mathsf{EX}f$ for $\mathsf{EX}_1 f \vee \cdots \vee \mathsf{EX}_I f$, and $\mathsf{AX}f$ for $\mathsf{AX}_1 f \wedge \cdots \wedge \mathsf{AX}_I f$.

A formula of the form $\mathsf{A}[f\mathsf{U}g]$ or $\mathsf{E}[f\mathsf{U}g]$ is an eventuality formula. The eventuality $\mathsf{A}[f\mathsf{U}g]$ ($\mathsf{E}[f\mathsf{U}g]$) is fulfilled for s in M provided that for every (respectively, for some) fullpath starting at s, there exists a finite prefix of the fullpath in M whose last state satisfies g and all of whose other states satisfy f.

We annotate transitions in a structure with the index i of the process P_i executing the transition, and the assignment statement A (if any) that P_i executes, e.g., $s \overset{i,A}{\longrightarrow} t$.

2.3   Example Specifications: Mutual Exclusion and Readers-Writers

The CTL specification of the two process mutual exclusion problem is the conjunction of the following ($i, j \in \{1, 2\}, i \neq j$):

$N_1 \wedge N_2$: Both processes are initially in their Noncritical region

$AG(N_i \Rightarrow (AX_iT_i \wedge EX_iT_i))$: Any move P_i makes from its Noncritical region N_i is into its Trying region T_i and such a move is always possible.

$AG(T_i \Rightarrow AX_iC_i)$: Any move P_i makes from its Trying region T_i is into its Critical region C_i.

$AG(C_i \Rightarrow (AX_iN_i \wedge EX_iN_i))$: Any move P_i makes from its Critical region C_i is into its Noncritical region N_i and such a move is always possible.

$AG(N_i \equiv \neg(T_i \vee C_i)) \wedge AG(T_i \equiv \neg(N_i \vee C_i)) \wedge AG(C_i \equiv \neg(N_i \vee T_i))$: P_i is always in one of N_i, T_i, or C_i.

$AG(N_i \Rightarrow AX_jN_i) \wedge AG(T_i \Rightarrow AX_jT_i) \wedge AG(C_i \Rightarrow AX_jC_i)$: A transition by P_i cannot cause a transition by P_j (interleaving model of concurrency).

$AG(T_i \Rightarrow AFC_i)$: P_i does not starve.

$AG(\neg(C_1 \wedge C_2))$: P_1, P_2 do not access their critical regions simultaneously.

$AGEXtrue$: It is always the case that some process can move.

To obtain the specification for readers-writers [6], we replace $AG(T_i \Rightarrow AFC_i)$ by the conjunction of the following, where P_1 is the reader and P_2 is the writer:

$AG(T_1 \Rightarrow AF(C_1 \vee \neg N_2))$: absence of starvation for reader provided writer does not request access

$AG(T_2 \Rightarrow AFC_2)$: absence of starvation for writer

$AG((T_1 \wedge T_2) \Rightarrow A[T_1UC_2])$: priority of writer over reader for access to Critical region

3   Overview of the CTL Decision Procedure

CTL is decidable: given a CTL formula f_0 there exists a decision procedure [10] that determines, in $O(2^{|f_0|})$ deterministic time, whether f_0 is satisfiable or not. The CTL decision procedure first constructs a particular kind of AND/OR graph (a tableau) T_0 for f_0. We use $c, c', \ldots$ to denote AND-nodes, $d, d', \ldots$ to denote OR-nodes, and $e, e', \ldots$ to denote nodes of either type. Each node e is labeled with a set of formulae $L(e)$, each of which is either a subformula of f_0, or a subformula of f_0 preceded by AX or EX. No two AND-nodes (OR-nodes) have the same label.

The CTL decision procedure constructs T_0 by starting with a single "root" OR-node d_0 labeled with $\{f_0\}$, and repeatedly constructing successors of "frontier" nodes until there is no change. The set of AND-node successors Blocks(d) of an OR-node d is determined by expanding d into a tree as follows. A CTL formula is elementary iff it is an atomic proposition, the negation of an atomic proposition, or has either AX_i or EX_i as its main connective. We classify a nonelementary formula as either a conjunctive formula $\alpha \equiv \alpha_1 \wedge \alpha_2$ or a disjunctive formula $\beta \equiv \beta_1 \vee \beta_2$ according to the fixpoint characterization of the main connective, e.g., $AGg \equiv g \wedge AXAGg$, so $\alpha_1 = g$, $\alpha_2 = AXAGg$, and AGg is a α formula, and $AFg \equiv g \vee AXAFg$, so $\beta_1 = g$, $\beta_2 = AXAFg$, and AFg is a β formula. Suppose e is a leaf in the tree constructed so far, and $f \in L(e)$. If $f \equiv \alpha_1 \wedge \alpha_2$, then add a single son to e with label $L(e) - \{f\} \cup \{\alpha_1, \alpha_2\}$. If $f \equiv \beta_1 \vee \beta_2$, then add two sons to e with labels $L(e) - \{f\} \cup \{\beta_1\}$, $L(e) - \{f\} \cup \{\beta_2\}$. This tree construction terminates when all leaves contain only elementary formulae in their labels. This must happen, since each expansion removes one nonelementary formula and replaces it with one or two smaller formulae. Upon termination, let $\mathrm{Blocks}(d)$ contain one AND-node c for each leaf node, whose label $L(c)$ is the union of all node labels along the path from the corresponding leaf back to the root d of the tree. The nodes in $\mathrm{Blocks}(d)$ embody all the different ways in which the (conjunction of the) formulae in $L(d)$ can be satisfied: $L(d)$ is satisfiable iff $L(c)$ is satisfiable for at least one $c \in \mathrm{Blocks}(d)$. In the final tableau, an OR-node must have at least one AND-node successor present.

The set $\mathrm{Tiles}(c)$ of OR-node successors of an AND-node c is $\bigcup_{i \in [1:I]} \mathrm{Tiles}_i(c)$, where $\mathrm{Tiles}_i(c)$ is the set of OR-node successors of c that are associated with P_i. Suppose that c is labeled with n formulae of the form $\mathrm{AX}_i g$, namely $\mathrm{AX}_i g_1, \dots ,$ $\mathrm{AX}_i g_n$, and m formulae of the form $\mathrm{EX}_i h$, namely $\mathrm{EX}_i h_1, \dots , \mathrm{EX}_i h_m$. Then $\mathrm{Tiles}_i(c) \stackrel{\mathrm{df}}{=} \{d_i^1, \dots , d_i^m\}$, where $L(d_i^j) = \{\mathrm{AX}_i g_1, \dots , \mathrm{AX}_i g_n\} \cup \{\mathrm{EX}_i h_j\}$, for $j \in [1:m]$. Finally, the edge from c to every node in $\mathrm{Tiles}_i(c)$ is labeled with the process index i, to indicate that this successor is associated with P_i. $\mathrm{Tiles}(c)$ is exactly the set of successors required to satisfy all of the nexttime formulae in the label of c: $L(c)$ is satisfiable iff $L(d)$ is satisfiable for all $d \in \mathrm{Tiles}(c)$, and $LP(c)$ is satisfiable, where $LP(c) = \{f \in L(c) \mid f \text{ is a proposition or its negation}\}$.

We continue generating successors of frontier nodes ("expanding" a node) until there are no more frontier nodes, i.e., every node in T_0 has at least one successor. If a node is ever created which has the same label as an already present node of the same type (i.e., AND or OR), then we merge the two nodes. Since the number of possible labels is finite ($O(2^{|f_0|})$), this process terminates.

The next step is to apply the deletion rules given in Figure 1 to T_0. Roughly speaking, these rules remove all nodes e whose label is propositionally inconsistent, or who do not have enough successors, or who are labeled with an eventuality formula which is not fulfilled. The presence of a suitable full subdag (path) rooted at e serves to certify the fulfillment of an eventuality $\mathrm{A}[g\mathrm{U}h]$ ($\mathrm{E}[g\mathrm{U}h]$) in $L(e)$. A full subdag D rooted at node e in T_0 is a directed acyclic subgraph of T_0 such that: (1) e is the unique node from which all other nodes in D are reachable, (2) for every AND-node c in D, if c has any sons in D, then every successor of c in T_0 is a son of c in D, and (3) for every OR-node d in D, there exists precisely one AND-node c in T_0 such that c is a son of d in D. We repeatedly apply the deletion rules until there is no change. Since each application removes one node, and T_0 is finite, this procedure must terminate. Upon termination, if the root of T_0 is has been removed, then f_0 is unsatisfiable. Otherwise f_0 is satisfiable, in which case let T^* be the tableau induced by the remaining nodes.

For each eventuality $\mathrm{A}[g\mathrm{U}h] \in L(c)$, let $\mathrm{DAG}[c, \mathrm{A}[g\mathrm{U}h]]$ be the directed acyclic graph that results from removing all the OR-nodes in a full subdag D rooted at c that fulfills $\mathrm{A}[g\mathrm{U}h]$, and for each eventuality $\mathrm{E}[g\mathrm{U}h] \in L(c)$, let $\mathrm{DAG}[c, \mathrm{E}[g\mathrm{U}h]]$ be the path that results from removing all the OR-nodes in a path starting from c that fulfills $\mathrm{E}[g\mathrm{U}h]$. In both cases we connect up the AND-nodes so that $c' \to c''$ in $\mathrm{DAG}[c, g]$ only if $c' \to d \to c''$ for some removed OR-node d. These DAG's exist by virtue of Figure 1.

For each AND-node c in T^*, we construct a "fragment" FRAG[c] by connecting up copies of the DAG's for the eventualities in $L(c)$, so that for $\mathsf{A}[g\mathsf{U}h] \in L(c)$, every infinite path from c encounters DAG[c, $\mathsf{A}[g\mathsf{U}h]$], and for $\mathsf{E}[g\mathsf{U}h] \in L(c)$, some infinite path from c has DAG[c, $\mathsf{E}[g\mathsf{U}h]$] as a prefix. Thus, all eventualities in $L(c)$ are fulfilled in FRAG[c]. We construct a model M for f_0 by connecting up copies of all the FRAG's so that every state (AND-node) c has at least one successor. This is done by identifying the root of one FRAG with a frontier node of another FRAG if they have the same label. The truth assignment V is given by $V(c) = L(c) \cap \mathcal{AP}$, where $\mathcal{AP}$ is the set of atomic propositions in spec. In M, every state satisfies all the formulae in its label. From M, a correct concurrent program can be produced by projecting onto the individual processes, as given in Definition 2 below.

DeleteP Delete any propositionally inconsistent node.

DeleteOR Delete any OR-node all of whose successors are already deleted.

DeleteAND Delete any AND-node one of whose successors is already deleted.

DeleteAU Delete any node e such that $\mathsf{A}[g\mathsf{U}h] \in L(e)$ and there does not exist a full subdag rooted at e where $h \in L(c')$ for every frontier node c' and $g \in L(c'')$ for every interior AND-node c''.

DeleteEU Delete any node e such that $\mathsf{E}[g\mathsf{U}h] \in L(e)$ and there does not exist an AND-node c' reachable from e via a path π such that $h \in L(c')$ and for all AND-nodes c'' along π up to but not necessarily including c', $g \in L(c'')$.

Fig. 1. The deletion rules for the CTL decision procedure.

4   Refinability of Specifications

4.1   Implementing the Guards: Temporary Stability

Suppose that in a program $P = P_1 \| \cdots \| P_I$, a guard B_i of an arc $a_i = (s_i, B_i \to A_i, t_i)$ of process P_i is temporarily stable, [12], that is, once B_i holds, it continues to hold until P_i executes some transition, not necessarily a transition corresponding to the execution of a_i. In this case, P_i can test for the truth of B_i by repeatedly reading the individual variables referenced in B_i. More formally, let $(s_i, B_i \to A_i, t_i)$ be an arc of P_i, and let $M = (S_0, S, R, V)$ be the global state transition diagram of P given by Definition 1. We require

$$M, S_0 \models \mathsf{AG}(\ (\{s_i\} \land B_i) \Rightarrow \mathsf{A}[B_i \ \mathsf{U_w} \ \neg\{s_i\}]\ ).\qquad \text{(GSTAB)}$$

where $\{s_i\} = "(\bigwedge_{Q \in AP_i \cap V_i(s_i)} Q)\ \land\ (\bigwedge_{Q \in AP_i - V_i(s_i)} \neg Q)"$. $\{s_i\}$ characterizes s_i in that $s_i \models \{s_i\}$, and $s_i' \not\models \{s_i\}$ for all local states s_i' such that $s_i' \neq s_i$, i.e., it converts a local state into a propositional formula. GSTAB requires that once P_i is in state s_i and guard B_i holds, then B_i continues to hold until P_i

leaves s_i, if ever. Note the use of the weak until $\mathsf{U_w}$: $[B_i \, \mathsf{U_w} \, \neg\{s_i\}]$ means that B_i holds until $\neg\{s_i\}$ becomes true (i.e., P_i leaves s_i), or, B_i holds forever if $\neg\{s_i\}$ never becomes true. Thus, P_i can check B_i by reading the atomic propositions and shared variables in B_i sequentially, i.e., in a non-atomic manner. If P_i ever observes that B_i holds, then P_i can subsequently execute a_i.

We say that "M satisfies GSTAB" if and only if GSTAB holds for every arc $(s_i, B_i \rightarrow A_i, t_i)$ of every process P_i of P.

Given a CTL formula spec, we wish to answer the following question: does there exist a program P which both satisfies spec and whose guards are temporarily stable? More technically, does there exist a program P with global state transition diagram $M = (S_0, S, R, V)$ such that $M, S_0 \models$ spec, and M satisfies GSTAB? Since the tableau T^* for spec that is generated by the CTL decision procedure encodes every possible model of spec, we can answer this question by analyzing T^*. Figure 2 presents an algorithm which performs this analysis.

To explain the operation of the algorithm, we first discuss how we extract a program from a structure M that conforms to the interleaving model, i.e., only transitions by P_i change atomic propositions in $\mathcal{AP}_i$. A P_i-family [3] F in $M = (S_0, S, R, V)$ is a maximal subset of R such that (1) all members of F are P_i-transitions, and have the same label $\xrightarrow{i,A}$, and (2) for any pair $s \xrightarrow{i,A} t, s' \xrightarrow{i,A} t'$ of members of F: $s\lceil i = s'\lceil i$ and $t\lceil i = t'\lceil i$. If $s \xrightarrow{i,A} t \in F$, then let $F.start$, $F.finish$, $F.assig$, $F.label$ denote $s\lceil i$, $t\lceil i$, A, and $\xrightarrow{i,A}$ respectively. Given that $T.begin$ denotes the source state of transition T, i.e., $T.begin = s$ for transition $T = s \xrightarrow{i,A} t$, let $F.guard$ denote $\bigvee_{T \in F}\{(T.begin)\lfloor i\}$, where $s\lfloor i$ is s with its P_i-component removed, and $\{s\lfloor i\} = $ "$(\bigwedge_{Q \in (AP-AP_i) \cap V(s)} Q) \wedge (\bigwedge_{Q \in (AP-AP_i)-V(s)} \neg Q) \wedge (\bigwedge_x x = s(x))$", where x ranges over the shared variables. $\{s\lfloor i\}$ converts global state s into an "equivalent" propositional formula, with the omission of the component $s\lceil i$.

Definition 2 (Program Extraction). Let $M = (S_0, S, R, V)$ be a structure that conforms to the interleaving model. Then the program $P = P_1 \| \cdots \| P_I$ extracted from M is as follows. Process P_i contains arc $(s_i, B_i \rightarrow A_i, t_i)$ if and only if:

there exists a P_i-family F in M such that
$$F.start = s_i, \; F.finish = t_i, \; F.assig = A_i, \; F.guard = B_i.$$
The truth assignment V_i is given by $V_i(s_i) = V(s) \cap AP_i$ where $s \in S$ is such that $s\lceil i = s_i$.

The key idea is this: for the guard B_i to be temporarily stable, we need that, once a global state s is entered which has an outgoing transition belonging to F, i.e., $s\lceil i = s_i$ and $\exists t : s \xrightarrow{i,A} t \wedge t\lceil i = t_i$, then every transition by some process other than P_i must lead to a state which also has an outgoing transition belonging to F, i.e., to a state u such that $u\lceil i = s_i$ and $\exists v : u \xrightarrow{i,A} v \wedge v\lceil i = t_i$.

Consider AND-node c which has an outgoing AND-OR transition $t = c \xrightarrow{i} d$. If c is present as a state in the final extracted model M, then there will be an outgoing transition from c (in M) corresponding to the AND-OR transition t. This transition is a member of a family F. To check that M satisfies the above condition, we check that T^*, from which M is extracted, satisfies an analogous condition, applied to the AND-nodes of T^*, which become states in M. The algorithm of Figure 2 performs this check as follows. First invoke the CTL decision procedure on spec, halting if spec is unsatisfiable. If not, then analyze the tableau T^* as follows. For every AND-node in T^*, compute the set C of all AND-nodes reachable from c by paths not labeled with index i, i.e., corresponding to executions by processes other than P_i. Then, check every AND-node c' in C to ensure that it has an outgoing AND-OR transition $c' \xrightarrow{i} d'$ in T^* such that $d'\lceil AP_i = d\lceil AP_i$, i.e., an AND-OR transition that will generate, in the extracted model M, a transition in family F. If not, then c' causes a violation of GSTAB, and must be made unreachable from c by deleting all of the OR-AND transitions from OR-nodes in C to c'. If all such necessary deletions can be made without causing the root node to be deleted, according to the deletion rules of Figure 1, then a model M can be extracted from the resulting tableau, using the same method as in the CTL decision procedure, and M will satisfy GSTAB.

---

1. Apply the CTL decision procedure to spec. If the root of T_0 is deleted, then output "there exists no program satisfying spec" and halt.
   Otherwise, let T^* be the resulting tableau.
2. **for** every process index i, and every AND-OR transition $t = c \xrightarrow{i} d$ in T^*:
   $C := \{e \mid e$ is reachable from c by a path not containing process index $i\}$;
   forall AND-nodes $c' \in C$ in increasing distance from c **do**

   > **if** there exists an AND-OR transition $c' \xrightarrow{i} d'$ in T^* such that
   > $d'\lceil AP_i = d\lceil AP_i$ **then**
   > > mark c' as "satisfying with respect to t"
   >
   > **else**
   > > delete all the OR-AND transitions from OR-nodes in C to c';
   > > recompute C to account for the deletion of the OR-AND transitions
   >
   > **endif**

   endfor;
   /* call the resulting tableau T_s */
3. Apply the deletion rules of Figure 1 to T_s;
4. **if** the root node of T_s is undeleted **then**   /* positive decision */
   > let T be the subgraph of T_s induced by the remaining undeleted nodes;
   > extract M from T using the same method as in the CTL decision procedure

   else   /* negative decision */
   > output "there exists no program satisfying the specification whose guards
   > > are temporarily stable"

   endif

Fig. 2. The Test for Specifications that allow Temporarily Stable guards

Shared Variables. The algorithm of Figure 2 does not take shared variables into account. We introduce shared variables to distinguish between global states which have different labels, but which assign the same values to all atomic propositions [10]. This is necessary, since only atomic propositions are implemented in the synthesized program, whereas the labels which distinguish different states in the tableau consist of not only atomic propositions, but CTL formulae in general. Thus, if propositionally identical but globally different states are not distinguished, the effect would be to "merge" such states, which could lead to violation of liveness, e.g., if the $[T_1\ T_2]$ states c_6 and c_7 in Figure 3 are merged in this way, then the liveness specification $\mathsf{AG}(T_i \Rightarrow \mathsf{AF}C_i)$, $i \in \{1, 2\}$, is violated. So, in Figure 3, we introduce a shared variable x which has value 1 in c_6 and value 2 in c_7. This requires adding an assignment $x := 1$ to all transitions entering c_6, and an assignment $x := 2$ to all transitions entering c_7. Whilst x will appear in the guards of the synthesized program, the temporary stability of these guards is dependent solely on the existence of the appropriate AND-OR transitions $c' \xrightarrow{i} d'$ as determined by the algorithm of Figure 2. The subsequent introduction of a shared variable does not change this, provided however, that the assignment to the shared variable is performed along all transitions of P_i which belong to the same transition family.

Theorem 1. Let spec be a CTL formula, and suppose that the algorithm of Figure 2 produces a model M when applied to spec. Then, M satisfies G STAB.

4.2   Implementing the Multiple Assignments: Lock-Free Multi-object Operations

Execution of an arc $(s_i, B_i \rightarrow A_i, t_i)$ involves both changing the atomic propositions in $\mathcal{AP}_i$ which are true from those in $V_i(s_i)$ to those in $V_i(t_i)$ (all other atomic propositions remaining unchanged) and updating the shared variables according to the parallel assignment A_i, which has the form $x, y, \ldots := v, w, \ldots$ where $x, y, \ldots$ is a list of shared variables, and $v, w, \ldots$ is a list of constants.

We implement this as follows. First, we consolidate all the atomic propositions of each P_i into a single variable L_i, whose value in local state s_i is $V_i(s_i)$: $s_i(L_i) = V_i(s_i)$, i.e., L_i is the set of atomic propositions in $\mathcal{AP}_i$ that are true in s_i. In practice, L_i could be encoded efficiently as a bit string. Thus, in executing the arc $(s_i, B_i \rightarrow A_i, t_i)$, we update the value of L_i from $V_i(s_i)$ to $V_i(t_i)$. We now have a multiple assignment of the form $L_i, x, y, \ldots := V_i(t_i), v, w, \ldots$ To implement this multiple assignment, we use any lock-free method for implementing multiple-object operations atomically [1,11,16,19]. We do not need the more expensive wait-free implementations, because we only need to correctly implement the transitions in the model M, and, a lock-free implementation suffices for this. Liveness properties are still satisfied, since M satisfies liveness properties under nondeterm inistic scheduling, i.e., no matter which transition is next selected for execution. In particular, no form of fairness is needed.

4.3   Implementation in Hardware-Available Primitives

Let M be a model for spec resulting from the algorithm of Figure 2, and let P be a program extracted from M according to Definition 2. Let $M_P = (S_0, S, R, V)$ be the global state transition diagram of P given by Definition 1. Then, $M_P, S_0 \models$ spec by the soundness of the CTL decision procedure [10]. Also, M_P satisfies GSTAB, since we can show that M_P and M are strongly bisimilar [5]. Let $(s_i, B_i \rightarrow A_i, t_i)$ be an arc of P_i in program P, where A_i is $x, y, \ldots := v, w, \ldots$. We implement this arc as follows:

1. **while** the guard B_i is not observed to be true
     read sequentially all the atomic propositions and shared variables in B_i;
     evaluate B_i
   endwhile;
2. Invoke a lock-free multiple object operation to implement the multiple assignment $L_i, x, y, \ldots := V_i(t_i), v, w, \ldots$.

We show that this implementation of P is correct by establishing a stuttering bisimulation [5] between M_P and the global-state transition diagram M_{imp} of the implementation, which is formally defined along the lines of Definition 1. See [4] for examples of such definitions for low-atomicity implementations. A state s of M and a state u of M_{imp} are related by stuttering bisimulation iff they assign the same values to all atomic propositions and shared variables. Since states related by stuttering bisimulation satisfy the same formulae of CTL $-$ X (CTL without the EX_i, AX_i modalities) this is sufficient to establish typical safety and liveness properties. Also, if a conjunct of spec has the forms $\mathsf{AG}(p_i \Rightarrow \mathsf{AX}_i q_i)$, $\mathsf{AG}(p_i \Rightarrow \mathsf{EX}_i q_i)$, then $\mathsf{AG}(p_i \Rightarrow \mathsf{AX}_i(p_i \vee q_i))$, $\mathsf{AG}(p_i \Rightarrow \mathsf{EX}_i(p_i \vee q_i))$, respectively, is satisfied by the implementation, where p_i, q_i specify local states of P_i. We defer details of this to the full paper.

Theorem 2. Let spec be a CTL formula, and suppose that the algorithm of Figure 2 produces a model M of spec. Let P be the program extracted from M by Definition 2, let M_{imp} be the global state transition diagram of the implementation of P given above, and let S^0_{imp} be the set of initial states of M_{imp}. Let f be a conjunct of spec which contains no EX_i or AX_i modality. Then $M_{imp}, S^0_{imp} \models f$.

5   Examples: Mutual Exclusion and Readers-Writers

We now apply the above test to the mtual exclusion and readers-writers specifications. Figure 3 shows the tableau produced by the CTL decision procedure for the mutual exclusion specification given in Section 2.3. The OR-nodes are named d_k, and the AND-nodes are named c_k. These names are not part of the decision procedure, and are provided only to facilitate the discussion. The initial OR-node is d_0. Upon applying the algorithm of Figure 2 to the tableau of Figure 3, we find that the tableau passes the test. Consider, for exampe, the transition $t = c_1 \xrightarrow{1} d_5$, in which P_1 moves from T_1 to C_1, and the application of the test to t. The set of nodes reachable from c_1 by a path not containing process index 1 is $\{d_6, c_6, c_7, d_{11}, c_{10}, d_1, c_2\}$. AND-node c_6 is marked as "satisfying w.r.t. t", since c_6 has an OR-node successor d_{10} which reflects the same transition by P_1, namely from T_1 to C_1. AND-node c_7, on the other hand, fails the test, since it does not have a suitable OR-node successor. Hence, the OR-AND transition from d_6 to c_7 is deleted. This causes the remaining nodes to become unreachable

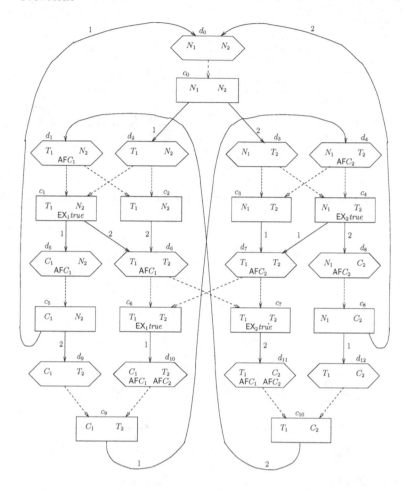

Fig. 3. Tableau for the mutual exclusion specification

from c_1 by paths not containing process index 1, and so we are done. The tableau as a whole remains viable, since d_6 still has a single successor, c_6. For reasons of symmetry, d_7 will be left with sole successor c_7 when the test is applied to transition $c_4 \xrightarrow{2} d_8$. Thus, the root is not deleted, and the synchronization skeletons shown in Figure 4 can be extracted from the tableau.

Figure 5 shows the tableau produced by the CTL decision procedure for the readers-writers specification given in Section 2.3. The initial OR-node is d_0. Consider the transition $t = c_1 \xrightarrow{1} d_5$, in which P_1 moves from T_1 to C_1, and the application of the test to t. The set of nodes reachable from c_1 by a path not containing process index 1 is $\{d_6, c_7, d_{11}, c_{10}, d_1, c_2\}$. The AND-node c_7 fails the test, since it does not have a suitable OR-node successor. Hence, the OR-AND transition from d_6 to c_7 is deleted. This now leaves d_6 without a successor. Hence, when the deletion rules of Figure 1 are applied, d_6 is deleted. This, in

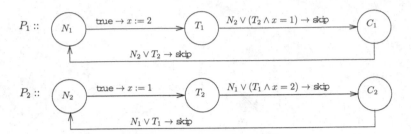

Fig. 4. Synchronization skeleton program for the mutual exclusion specification

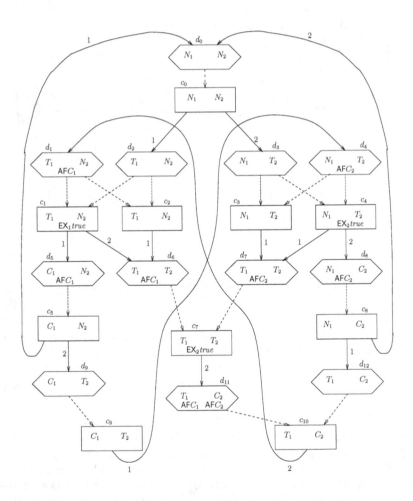

Fig. 5. Tableau for the readers-writers specification

turn results in the deletion of c_1 and c_2, since they are AND-nodes, and so require all successors to be undeleted. This results in the deletion of d_1 and d_2 since they are left without successors. The deletion of d_2 causes the deletion of AND-node c_0, and this causes the deletion of the root node d_0, since c_0 is the only successor of d_0. Thus the tableau is not viable, and we conclude that there exists no concurrent program which satisfies the readers-writers specification and which has temporarily-stable guards.

Intuitively, we see that the readers-writers specification imposes a "flickering" guard on the reader, since it allows the writer to always preempt the reader's ability to enter the critical section: when the writer is in N_2 and the reader in T_1, the reader is enabled to enter C_1, but the writer can autonomously preempt this enablement by entering T_2. This is inherent in the writer priority requirement of the specification.

6   Conclusions and Further Work

We presented a method for deciding whether a specification can be implemented by a concurrent program which has the property of being "easily" refined to a low-grain atomicity program that uses primitives available in hardware. The refinement process is automatic, and the final program does not resort to inefficient strategies such as using a central module which controls everything. In practice, our method can be used iteratively. If the procedure of Figure 2 outputs "no" for a given specification spec, then every program which satisfies spec must contain "flickering" guards, which can transit from true to false before the arc that they label is executed. Detecting the truth of such guards is difficult: it requires high atomicity operations, or inefficient strategies such as blocking or centralization. In this case, the best course of action may be to modify the specification and reapply the method. Extending the method to give advice on modifying the specification so that it passes the test of Figure 2 is a topic of future work.

Our test can be viewed as a design rule: specifications which fail it are in some sense bad specifications, as they necessitate inefficient programs. Our result therefore contributes to software engineering, as it provides a criterion for judging the quality of a specification. More generally, our work suggests a notion of implementation complexity for specifications: can we define a complexity measure on specifications which indicates the "difficulty" of implementing a concurrent program P that satisfies the specification. This "difficulty" may take several attributes into account: the amount of blocking and centralization in P, the length of the proof that P satisfies the specification, etc. We will examine this issue further in future work.

References

1. James H. Anderson and Mark Moir. Universal constructions for multi-object operations. In *Symposium on Principles of Distributed Computing*, 1995.

2. A. Anuchitanukul and Z. Manna. Realizability and synthesis of reactive modules. In *Proceedings of the 6th International Conference on Computer Aided Verification*, volume 818 of *Lecture Notes in Computer Science*, pages 156–169, Berlin, 1994. Springer-Verlag.

3. P. C. Attie and E. A. Emerson. Synthesis of concurrent systems for an atomic read/atomic write model of computation (extended abstract). In *Fifteenth Annual ACM Symposium on Principles of Distributed Computing*, pages 111–120, Philadelphia, Pennsylvania, May 1996. ACM Press.

4. P. C. Attie and E. A. Emerson. Synthesis of concurrent systems for an atomic read/write model of computation. *ACM Trans. Program. Lang. Syst.*, 23(2):187–242, Mar. 2001. Extended abstract appears in ACM Symposium on Principles of Distributed Computing (PODC) 1996.

5. M.C. Browne, E. M. Clarke, and O. Grumberg. Characterizing finite kripke structures in propositional temporal logic. *Theoretical Computer Science*, 59:115–131, 1988.

6. P.J. Courtois, H. Heymans, and D.L. Parnas. Concurrent control with readers and writers. *Communications of the ACM*, 14(10):667–668, 1971.

7. E. W. Dijkstra. *A Discipline of Programming*. Prentice-Hall Inc., Englewood Cliffs, N.J., 1976.

8. D.L. Dill and H. Wong-Toi. Synthesizing processes and schedulers from temporal specifications. In *International Conference on Computer-Aided Verification*, number 531 in LNCS, pages 272–281. Springer-Verlag, 1990.

9. E. A. Emerson. Temporal and modal logic. In J. Van Leeuwen, editor, *Handbook of Theoretical Computer Science*, volume B, *Formal Models and Semantics*. The MIT Press/Elsevier, Cambridge, Mass., 1990.

10. E. A. Emerson and E. M. Clarke. Using branching time temporal logic to synthesize synchronization skeletons. *Sci. Comput. Program.*, 2:241–266, 1982.

11. Timothy L Harris, Keir Fraser, and Ian Pratt. A practical multi-word compare-and-swap operation. In *IEEE Symposium on Distributed Computing*, 2002.

12. S. Katz. Temporary stability in parallel programs. Tech. Rep., Computer Science Dept., Technion, Haifa, Israel, 1986.

13. O. Kupferman, P. Madhusudan, P.S. Thiagarajan, and M.Y. Vardi. Open systems in reactive environments: Control and synthesis. In *Proc. 11th Int. Conf. on Concurrency Theory (CONCUR)*, Springer LNCS volume 1877, pages 92–107.

14. O. Kupferman and M.Y. Vardi. Synthesis with incomplete information. In *2nd International Conference on Temporal Logic*, pages 91–106, Manchester, July 1997. Kluwer Academic Publishers.

15. Z. Manna and P. Wolper. Synthesis of communicating processes from temporal logic specifications. *ACM Trans. Program. Lang. Syst.*, 6(1):68–93, Jan. 1984. Also appears in Proceedings of the Workshop on Logics of Programs, Yorktown-Heights, N.Y., Springer-Verlag Lecture Notes in Computer Science (1981).

16. M. Moir. Transparent support for wait-free transactions. In *Workshop on Distributed Algorithms*, 1997.

17. A. Pnueli and R. Rosner. On the synthesis of a reactive module. In *Proceedings of the 16th ACM Symposium on Principles of Programming Languages*, pages 179–190, New York, 1989. ACM.

18. A. Pnueli and R. Rosner. On the synthesis of asynchronous reactive modules. In *Proceedings of the 16th ICALP*, volume 372 of *Lecture Notes in Computer Science*, pages 652–671, Berlin, 1989. Springer-Verlag.

19. N. Shavit and D. Touitou. Software transactional memory. In *ACM Symposium on Principles of Distributed Computing*, Ontario, Canada, 1995.

Competitive Management of Non-preemptive Queues with Multiple Values

Nir Andelman and Yishay Mansour

School of Computer Science, Tel-Aviv University, Tel-Aviv, Israel

Abstract. We consider the online problem of active queue management. In our model, the input is a sequence of packets with values $v \in [1, \alpha]$ that arrive to a queue that can hold up to B packets. Specifically, we consider a FIFO non-preemptive queue, where any packet that is accepted into the queue must be sent, and packets are sent by the order of arrival. The benefit of a scheduling policy, on a given input, is the sum of values of the scheduled packets. Our aim is to find an online policy that maximizes its benefit compared to the optimal offline solution.
Previous work proved that no constant competitive ratio exists for this problem, showing a lower bound of $\ln(\alpha) + 1$ for any online policy. An upper bound of $e\lceil \ln(\alpha) \rceil$ was proved for a few online policies. In this paper we suggest and analyze a RED-like online policy with a competitive ratio that matches the lower bound up to an additive constant proving an upper bound of $\ln(\alpha) + 2 + O(\ln^2(\alpha)/B)$. For large values of α, we prove that no policy whose decisions are based only on the number of packets in the queue and the value of the arriving packet, has a competitive ratio lower than $\ln(\alpha) + 2 - \epsilon$, for any constant $\epsilon > 0$.

1 Introduction

One of the main bottlenecks in the traffic flow inside communication networks is the management of queues in the connection points, such as switches and routers. If incoming traffic from several sources is directed towards the same destination, it may be impossible to immediately direct all the traffic towards the outgoing link, since the bandwidth of the outgoing link is limited, and packet loss is therefore unavoidable.

The traffic in communication networks tends to arrive in bursts, which is the motivation of buffering the packets in queues, located either at the incoming links, or the outgoing links, or both. The packets arriving in a burst are stored in queues, and are later sent in a speed determined by the bandwidth of both outgoing links and the backbone of the connection device. If the traffic is not too heavy, the queues will drain before more bursts arrive, avoiding packet loss. This best effort approach relies on statistical characteristics of communication traffic, assuming that the capacity of the links is not always fully used.

The best effort approach is not sufficient for service providers who wish to guarantee Quality of Service (QoS) to their users. QoS can be considered as a contract between the communication service provider and the network user. As

F.E. Fich (Ed.): DISC 2003, LNCS 2848, pp. 166–180, 2003.
© Springer-Verlag Berlin Heidelberg 2003

long as the user's traffic does not exceed certain quotas agreed in the contract, the service provider guarantees specific characteristics of the network service, such as minimal bandwidth, maximal delay time, jitter, packet loss, etc. The demand for QoS results in a couple of problems that the service provider must solve. One problem is to determine what the service provider can guarantee to a user. The other is what to do with the user's traffic when it does not fulfill the terms of the contract.

One solution to the problem of QoS is Premium Service [14], in which the traffic is shaped upon the entry to the network. The service provider guarantees that customers who payed for QoS will have a certain portion of the bandwidth allocated for their use. Packets that are not part of the Premium Service are treated by best effort mechanism, and might be dropped due to congestion. From the point of view of the user, the shared network is almost indistinguishable from a private link. From the point of view of the service provider, this is a solution with high utilization that allows dedicating private links, since the dedicated bandwidth may be used for general traffic when the traffic from paying customers is idle.

Assured Service [6] is a different approach that relies on statistical multiplexing, which takes into account the fact that usually worst case scenarios, where all users use the same network resources at once, do not occur. This assumption allows the service provider to apply an 'overbooking' policy, which relaxes the constraints on the users' usage of the communication network, risking a potential buffer overflow, when congestion occurs. Assured Service supplies a relative guarantee to the user, which is a vague promise that certain traffic will be treated with higher priority at times of network congestion, achieving better throughput relative to the rest of the traffic. The concept that some packets are worth more than others is the basis of Differentiated Services. Packets that have QoS guarantee are distinguished from normal packets. Furthermore, the service provider may decide to treat differently packets of different paying customers (in a 'pay more - get more' fashion).

We use the following abstraction to analyze the performance of a single queue: The system is a queue that can hold up to B packets. The input packets that arrive to the queue have values of $v \in [1, \alpha]$. A packet's value represents the priority given to the packet by the service provider. The queue management is an online policy that decides for each packet, when it arrives, whether to place it in the queue or to reject it. Preemption is not allowed, meaning that any accepted packet is eventually transmitted and cannot be rejected later. At arbitrary times a packet is sent from the queue (if not empty), at FIFO order, i.e. at the order of arrival. We assume that packet values are accumulative, so the benefit on the policy over a given input is the sum of values of accepted packets. We use competitive analysis [5] to analyze online policies, meaning that we derive bounds on the ratio between the benefit of the optimal offline scheduling, to the benefit of the online policy, over the worst case input.

Online packet scheduling with a non-preemptive queue was first analyzed in [1] for two packet values only, 1 and $\alpha > 1$. A general lower bound of $2 - 1/\alpha$

was derived, and several online policies were analyzed, deriving upper and lower bounds for each policy. An optimal online policy for the two value case with a competitive ratio of $2-1/\alpha$ was analyzed in [2]. The continuous case, were packet values may vary along the range $[1, \alpha]$ was also considered in [2]. A general lower bound of $\ln(\alpha) + 1$ was derived for any online policy, and an upper bound of $e\lceil \ln(\alpha) \rceil$ was proved for two policies.

Our results. In this paper we analyze a RED-like [7] online policy for continuous values, with a provable upper bound of $\ln(\alpha) + 2 + O(\ln^2(\alpha)/B)$, which nearly matches the lower bound. Similarly to Random Early Detection, we suggest a policy that detects the possibility of congestion before the queue is full, and drops packets in advance. While RED uses probabilities to decide whether to drop a packet, we use the packet's value for this decision. Our analysis measures the exact influence of the queue size on the competitive ratio. For large values of α, we prove that $\ln(\alpha) + 2$ is a lower bound for a large family of policies, which in addition to the value of the arriving packet, consider only the number of packets in the queue. For a low value of α, we analyze an alternative policy, which is an extension of the optimal online policy for the case of two packet values, and prove that its competitive ratio in this case is strictly lower than $\ln(\alpha) + 2$, for any low value of α.

Related work. A preemptive FIFO queue allows preempting packets, which were already accepted, from the queue. Online algorithms in the preemptive FIFO model were analyzed in [2,9,10,13,15]. Since the optimal offline is non-preemptive, preemptive policies have better competitive ratios than non preemptive ones. For inputs with two values, the currently known best lower and upper bounds are approximately 1.28 [15] and 1.30 [13], respectively. For unlimited values, the lower and upper bounds are $\sqrt{2}$ and 2, respectively [2,9]. Recently, Kesselman et al. [12] have designed a policy that beats the 2-competitive ratio of the greedy policy, and is $2 - \epsilon$, for some constant $\epsilon > 0$.

Generalized versions of managing FIFO queues include managing a bulk of FIFO queues [3], where the policy has also to decide from which queue to send a packet, and shared memory switches [8,11], where the queues are not fixed in size, but their total size is fixed. Another extension is the delay bounded queue [2,9], where packets may be sent in arbitrary order, but each packet arrives with a expiration time. Packets that are not sent by this deadline expire and are lost.

Paper organization. Section 2 defines the non-preemptive queue model. Section 3 defines the Selective Barrier Policy, which is analyzed in Section 4. We improve the policy for low values of α in Section 5. In Section 6 we prove a lower bound of $\ln(\alpha) + 2$ for a family of policies. Our concluding remarks appear in Section 7.

2   Model and Notations

2.1   Packets

A packet is a basic unit that describes the input of the system. Each packet is identified by its value v, which is the benefit that the system gains by sending the packet. Packet values may vary from 1 to α, where $\alpha \geq 1$ is an arbitrary value, known in advance. For simplicity, v refers both to the packet itself and to its value.

2.2   Input Streams

The input to the system is a finite stream of events, occurring at discrete times $t = 1, 2, ..., n$. There are two types of events, `arrive(v)`, which is the arrival of a packet with value v to the system and `send()`, which allows the system to send one of the packets that arrived earlier.

2.3   FIFO Queues

The system uses a queue for buffering the arriving packets. B denotes the maximal number of packets that can be held in the queue. In our analysis we assume that $B \geq \ln(\alpha) + 2$. This is a reasonable assumption since usually buffers are fairly large. In addition, if $B = o(\ln(\alpha))$, no online policy has a logarithmic order competitive ratio. Each `arrive(v)` event invokes a response from the system, which is either to accept the packet and place it inside the queue, or the reject it. The decision whether to accept or to reject a packet depends on the specific policy used to manage the queue. No more than B packets can be stored in the queue at the same time, and preemption is not allowed. During a `send()` event the system extracts the most recent packet in the queue and sends it, if the queue is not empty.

2.4   Online Policies

A policy is an algorithm that given an input stream decides which packets to accept and which packets to reject. Given an input stream and a policy A, let $h_A(t)$ denote the number of packets in the queue at time t. Let $V_A(t)$ denote the total value of packets accepted until time t. Notice that since we restrict ourselves to non-preemptive queues, each accepted packet is eventually sent, so $V_A(t)$ can be regarded as the total benefit assured by policy A until time t over the input stream.

A policy is considered an online policy if the decision to accept or reject a packet determines only on the previous and current events. We use competitive ratio [5] to analyze the performance of online policies. An online policy is c-competitive if for any input sequence $c \cdot V_{ON} \geq V_{OPT}$, where V_{ON} is the benefit of the online policy and V_{OPT} is the benefit of an optimal offline policy.

3   Smooth Selective Barrier Policy

We define a policy that is analogous to the mechanism of Random Early Detection (RED) [7] gateways for congestion avoidance in packet switched networks. The RED gateway measures the number of packets in the FIFO queue, and marks or drops packets with a certain probability, if this number exceeds a certain threshold. The probability of marking/droping a packet depends on the number of packets in the queue. RED gateways are designed to accompany a congestion control protocol such as TCP. By marking or dropping packets, the gateway hails the connections to reduce their windows, and thus keeps the number of packets in the queue low.

The `Selective Barrier Policy` is an online policy intuitively designed as a derandomized variation of RED. Like RED, the policy becomes more restrictive as the queue size increases. Unlike RED (which is ignorant to packet values), the decision to drop a packet is deterministically based on the packet's value, and the number of packets in the queue.

Formally, we define $\mathcal{F}(v) : [1, \alpha] \to [1, B]$ to be a monotone function that bounds the maximal number of packets that can be in the queue if a packet of value v was just accepted. If an $\texttt{arrive}(v)$ event occurs at time t then the packet is accepted if $\mathcal{F}(v) \geq h_{ON}(t) + 1$ and is rejected otherwise. Intuitively, $\mathcal{F}^{-1}(h)$ is the lowest value of a packet that will be accepted by the policy when the queue already holds $h - 1$ packets.

The competitive ratio of the Selective Barrier Policy depends on the exact mapping of $\mathcal{F}(\cdot)$. In [2] an upper bound of $e \cdot \lceil \ln(\alpha) \rceil$ was derived, where $\mathcal{F}(v) = \frac{i}{\lceil \ln(\alpha) \rceil} B$ for each $v \in [e^{i-1}, e^i)$. This mapping divides the queue equally into $\lceil \ln(\alpha) \rceil$ sub-queues, and increments the threshold for accepting packets in exponential steps. Due to the division to sub-queues, the policy might accept only a $1/\lceil \ln(\alpha) \rceil$ fraction of the packets in a certain range. The e factor in the competitive ratio is mainly due to the fact that packet values in $[e^{i-1}, e^i)$ may differ by a factor of e in their value, but the policy treats them identically.

The main contribution of this work is defining a finer $\mathcal{F}(\cdot)$, and even more importantly, being able to prove a tight bound on its competitive ratio. Specifically, we consider the mapping $\mathcal{F}(v) = \mathcal{F}(1) + \frac{\ln(v)}{\ln(\alpha)} S$, where $\mathcal{F}(1) = \lceil \frac{B}{\ln(\alpha)+2} \rceil$ and $S = B - \mathcal{F}(1)$. We name this variant of the Selective Barrier Policy as the `Smooth Selective Barrier Policy`. Intuitively, the first $\mathcal{F}(1)$ slots in the queue are unrestricted, meaning that the policy accepts any packet into these slots, regardless of the packet value. In the remaining slots we accept packets if their value is larger than a threshold that increases in an exponential rate, yet it is smooth, as can be observed by the following lemma:

Lemma 1. For any $h \in [\mathcal{F}(1), B - 1]$, we have $\mathcal{F}^{-1}(h + 1) = \mathcal{F}^{-1}(h)\alpha^{1/S}$

Proof. Let v be the value such that $\mathcal{F}(v) = h$. Since the mapping of $\mathcal{F}(\cdot)$ is monotone increasing, then v is unique and $\mathcal{F}^{-1}(\mathcal{F}(v)) = v$. By the definition of $\mathcal{F}(\cdot)$, we have the following:

$$\mathcal{F}(v) + 1 = \mathcal{F}(1) + \frac{\ln(v)}{\ln(\alpha)} S + 1 = \mathcal{F}(1) + \frac{\ln(v) + \frac{\ln(\alpha)}{S}}{\ln(\alpha)} S$$

$$= \mathcal{F}(1) + \frac{\ln(v) + \ln(\alpha^{1/S})}{\ln(\alpha)} S = \mathcal{F}(1) + \frac{\ln(v\alpha^{1/S})}{\ln(\alpha)} S = \mathcal{F}(v\alpha^{1/S})$$

Therefore, we have

$$\mathcal{F}^{-1}(h+1) = \mathcal{F}^{-1}(\mathcal{F}(v)+1) = \mathcal{F}^{-1}(\mathcal{F}(v\alpha^{1/S})) = v\alpha^{1/S} = \mathcal{F}^{-1}(h)\alpha^{1/S}$$

which completes the proof. □

4   Analysis

We prove an upper bound for the Smooth Selective Barrier Policy with the function $\mathcal{F}(\cdot)$ defined as in Section 3 by comparing it to an optimal offline policy over an arbitrary input. Our proof is constructed from two stages: First, we simplify the input by modifying the values of the packets in a conservative way such that the competitive ratio cannot decrease due to the modification. In the second stage we define a potential function that bounds the possible additional benefit that the offline can gain, without any gain to the benefit of the online. We use this potential function to prove inductively that given a modified input, the ratio between the benefit of the online and the benefit of the offline plus its potential is always bounded.

In our proof we use ON to denote the Smooth Selective Barrier Policy while OPT denotes the optimal offline. We perform a simple relaxation on the input stream, defined as follows: If the online accepts a packet v at time t, then we may reduce the value of v to $v' = \mathcal{F}^{-1}(h_{ON}(t))$, i.e. the value of v' is the lowest value that the online policy still accepts. We derive the following claims for relaxed inputs:

Lemma 2. The Competitive ratio of a relaxed input is at least the same as the competitive ratio of the original input.

Proof. We analyze the competitive ratio after each change of a packet value v to v', and notice that it does not reduce the competitive ratio. After changing the value of a single packet, the decisions of the Smooth Selective Barrier Policy remain unchanged, since the policy does not consider the values of previously accepted packets, only their amount, and therefore loses a benefit of exactly $v - v'$. The optimal offline is unaffected if it rejected v in the original schedule, and loses at most benefit $v - v'$ if it did accept the packet. Since the competitive ratio is at least 1, it cannot decrease over the relaxed input. □

In the following lemma we prove an upper bound on the values of the packets that the offline accepts, which depends on the state of the online queue.

Lemma 3. In a relaxed input, if the offline accepts v at time t, then

$$\mathcal{F}^{-1}(h_{ON}(t)) \geq v$$

Proof. If the online policy also accepts the packet v, then by the relaxation we have $\mathcal{F}^{-1}(h_{ON}(t)) = v$. Otherwise, the packet was rejected, which means that $\mathcal{F}^{-1}(h_{ON}(t)) > v$. □

We define a potential function $\phi(t)$. Intuitively, $\phi(t)$ measures the extra benefit that the offline can gain without changing the online. The potential $\phi(t)$ is defined as follows:

$$\phi(t) = \begin{cases} \max\left(0, \frac{h_{\mathrm{ON}}(t)}{\mathcal{F}(1)}B - h_{\mathrm{OPT}}(t)\right) & : \quad h_{\mathrm{ON}}(t) < \mathcal{F}(1) \\ (B - h_{\mathrm{OPT}}(t))\mathcal{F}^{-1}(h_{\mathrm{ON}}(t)) + \sum_{i=\mathcal{F}(1)}^{h_{\mathrm{ON}}(t)-1} \mathcal{F}^{-1}(i) & : \quad h_{\mathrm{ON}}(t) \geq \mathcal{F}(1) \end{cases}$$

Notice that both functions used in the definition of $\phi(t)$ are equal at $h_{\mathrm{ON}}(t) = \mathcal{F}(1)$. When $h_{\mathrm{ON}}(t) \geq \mathcal{F}(1)$, $\phi(t)$ measures the maximal possible gain in the benefit of the offline, without increasing the benefit of the online. The offline can fill its queue with $B - h_{\mathrm{OPT}}(t)$ packets, which will be rejected by the online if their values are less than $\mathcal{F}^{-1}(h_{\mathrm{ON}}(t))$. Then, the offline can send packets in order to accept more packets, but the online sends packets too, so the new packets must have decreasing values, otherwise the online will accept them. When $h_{\mathrm{ON}}(t) < \mathcal{F}(1)$, $\phi(t)$ increments in linear steps, measuring how near the online queue is to $\mathcal{F}(1)$, which is the threshold for accepting packets with value 1. Using the potential $\phi(t)$ we prove the following invariant:

Theorem 1. For any relaxed input sequence and for any time t,

$$C \cdot V_{\mathrm{ON}}(t) \geq V_{\mathrm{OPT}}(t) + \phi(t),$$

where $C = \max\left\{\ln(\alpha) + 2, B\alpha^{1/S} - B + 1\right\}$.

Proof. The proof is by induction. For $t = 0$ we have $V_{\mathrm{ON}}(0) = 0 = V_{\mathrm{OPT}}(0)$. Since $h_{\mathrm{ON}}(0) = 0$ we also have $\phi(0) = 0$ and the claim holds. Assuming the claim holds for $t = t_0$, we will prove it holds for time $t + 1$.

If at time t_0 both queues are empty and the input has ended, then the inequality holds trivially for any $t \geq t_0$. Otherwise, the event at time $t + 1$ is either `arrive(v)` or `send()`. We analyze each case separately.

If the next event is `arrive(v)`, we analyze its effect in two stages: First, the online policy decides whether to accept v or to reject it, then the offline decides. This separation obviously has no effect on the behavior of both policies, so it is sufficient to prove that the claim holds after each stage. Using this technique, at each state either $V_{\mathrm{ON}}()$ or $V_{\mathrm{OPT}}()$ remains unchanged. If at any stage the active policy rejects the packet, then the inequality remains unchanged and therefore the claim obviously holds. If the packet is accepted we analyze the inequality separately for each policy and for each status of $h_{\mathrm{ON}}(t)$.

If the online policy accepts v and $h_{\mathrm{ON}}(t) < \mathcal{F}(1)$: Since the online accepts any packet when $h_{\mathrm{ON}}(t) < \mathcal{F}(1)$, its value in the relaxed input must be 1. Since $V_{\mathrm{ON}}(t+1) - V_{\mathrm{ON}}(t) = v = 1$, the left side of the inequality increases by C. As for the right size of the inequality, it remains unchanged if $\frac{h_{\mathrm{ON}}(t+1)}{F^{-1}(1)}B \leq h_{\mathrm{OPT}}(t)$, since the potential remains 0. Otherwise the increase of the potential is bounded by:

$$\frac{h_{\mathrm{ON}}(t+1)}{\mathcal{F}(1)}B - h_{\mathrm{OPT}}(t) - \frac{h_{\mathrm{ON}}(t)}{\mathcal{F}(1)}B + h_{\mathrm{OPT}}(t) = \frac{h_{\mathrm{ON}}(t+1) - h_{\mathrm{ON}}(t)}{\mathcal{F}(1)}B$$

$$= \frac{B}{\mathcal{F}(1)} = \frac{B}{\left\lceil \frac{B}{\ln(\alpha)+2} \right\rceil} \leq \frac{B}{\frac{B}{\ln(\alpha)+2}} = \ln(\alpha) + 2$$

The claim holds for $C \geq \ln(\alpha) + 2$.

If the offline policy accepts v and $h_{ON}(t+1) < \mathcal{F}(1)$: By Lemma 3 we must have $v = 1$. The left side of the inequality remains unchanged while the right side changes as follows:

$$v + \frac{h_{ON}(t+1)}{\mathcal{F}(1)} B - h_{OPT}(t+1) - \frac{h_{ON}(t+1)}{\mathcal{F}(1)} B + h_{OPT}(t)$$
$$= v - [h_{OPT}(t) + 1] + h_{OPT}(t) = 1 - h_{OPT}(t) - 1 + h_{OPT}(t) = 0,$$

and the claim holds.

If the online policy accepts v and $h_{ON}(t) \geq \mathcal{F}(1)$: Due to the relaxation of the input, we have $v = \mathcal{F}^{-1}(h_{ON}(t))$. The benefit of the online increases by v, therefore the left side of the equation increases by vC. The change in the potential is:

$$(B - h_{OPT}(t)) \mathcal{F}^{-1}(h_{ON}(t+1)) + \sum_{i=\mathcal{F}(1)}^{h_{ON}(t+1)-1} \mathcal{F}^{-1}(i)$$

$$- (B - h_{OPT}(t)) \mathcal{F}^{-1}(h_{ON}(t)) - \sum_{i=\mathcal{F}(1)}^{h_{ON}(t)-1} \mathcal{F}^{-1}(i)$$

$$= (B - h_{OPT}(t)) \left[\mathcal{F}^{-1}(h_{ON}(t) + 1) - \mathcal{F}^{-1}(h_{ON}(t)) \right] + \mathcal{F}^{-1}(h_{ON}(t) + 1 - 1)$$

$$= (B - h_{OPT}(t)) \left(v\alpha^{1/S} - v \right) + v = v \left[(B - h_{OPT}(t)) \left(\alpha^{1/S} - 1 \right) + 1 \right]$$

$$\leq v \left[B \left(\alpha^{1/S} - 1 \right) + 1 \right]$$

Where the second identity is by Lemma 1. The inductive claim holds for $C \geq B\alpha^{1/S} - B + 1$.

If the offline policy accepts v and $h_{ON}(t) \geq \mathcal{F}(1)$: By Lemma 3, we have $v \leq \mathcal{F}^{-1}(h_{ON}(t+1))$. The left side of the inequality remains unchanged, which the change to the right side is as follows:

$$V_{OPT}(t+1) - V_{OPT}(t) + (B - h_{OPT}(t+1)) \mathcal{F}^{-1}(h_{ON}(t+1))$$

$$- (B - h_{OPT}(t)) \mathcal{F}^{-1}(h_{ON}(t+1)) + \sum_{i=\mathcal{F}(1)}^{h_{ON}(t+1)-1} \mathcal{F}^{-1}(i) - \sum_{i=\mathcal{F}(1)}^{h_{ON}(t+1)-1} \mathcal{F}^{-1}(i)$$

$$= v + (h_{OPT}(t) - h_{OPT}(t+1)) \mathcal{F}^{-1}(h_{ON}(t+1)) + 0$$

$$= v - \mathcal{F}^{-1}(h_{ON}(t+1)) \leq 0$$

This implies that the right side of the inequality cannot increase, and therefore the inductive claim remains true.

In the case of a **send()** event, the benefit of both policies remains unchanged. It is sufficient to prove that the potential does not increase due to a **send()** event.

If the queue of the Smooth Selective Barrier Policy is already empty when the send() event occurs, then the potential is 0, and remains unchanged. If the queue of the optimal policy is empty when the send() event occurs, then the queue of the online must be empty as well, otherwise the offline has rejected at least one packet falsely, and can be improved. Therefore, it is sufficient to analyze the case where both queues drain one packet.

If $h_{ON}(t) < \mathcal{F}(1)$ then the potential is either 0 or $\frac{h_{ON}(t)}{\mathcal{F}(1)}B - h_{OPT}(t)$. If after a packet is sent the potential is 0 then trivially the potential did not increase. Otherwise, the change in the potential is at most:

$$\phi(t+1) - \phi(t)$$
$$= \frac{h_{ON}(t+1)}{\mathcal{F}(1)}B - h_{OPT}(t+1) - \frac{h_{ON}(t)}{\mathcal{F}(1)}B + h_{OPT}(t)$$
$$= \frac{h_{ON}(t)-1-h_{ON}(t)}{\mathcal{F}(1)}B - h_{OPT}(t) + 1 + h_{OPT}(t) = 1 - \frac{B}{\mathcal{F}(1)}$$

Since $\mathcal{F}(1) \leq B$ the potential can only decrease, and therefore the inductive claim holds.

If $h_{ON}(t) \geq \mathcal{F}(1)$ the change in the potential is:

$$\phi(t+1) - \phi(t)$$
$$= (B - h_{OPT}(t+1))\mathcal{F}^{-1}(h_{ON}(t+1)) + \sum_{i=\mathcal{F}(1)}^{h_{ON}(t+1)-1} \mathcal{F}^{-1}(i)$$
$$- (B - h_{OPT}(t))\mathcal{F}^{-1}(h_{ON}(t)) - \sum_{i=\mathcal{F}(1)}^{h_{ON}(t)-1} \mathcal{F}^{-1}(i)$$
$$= (B - h_{OPT}(t) + 1)\mathcal{F}^{-1}(h_{ON}(t) - 1) + \sum_{i=\mathcal{F}(1)}^{h_{ON}(t)-2} \mathcal{F}^{-1}(i)$$
$$- (B - h_{OPT}(t))\mathcal{F}^{-1}(h_{ON}(t)) - \sum_{i=\mathcal{F}(1)}^{h_{ON}(t)-1} \mathcal{F}^{-1}(i)$$
$$= (B - h_{OPT}(t))\left[\mathcal{F}^{-1}(h_{ON}(t) - 1) - \mathcal{F}^{-1}(h_{ON}(t))\right] \leq 0$$

As the potential does not increase, the claim holds.

Since the claim is not violated after any step of the induction, it holds for any appropriate value of C. The constraints on C are dictated by the values of B and α, and are set to:

$$C \geq \max\left(\ln(\alpha) + 2, B\alpha^{1/S} - B + 1\right)$$

□

Theorem 1 proves the existence of a competitive ratio C, for the Smooth Selective Barrier Policy with the suggested function $\mathcal{F}(\cdot)$. Assuming $B \geq \ln(\alpha) + 2$, we derive the following bound on C.

Theorem 2. For $B \geq \ln(\alpha) + 2$ The competitive ratio of the Smooth Selective Barrier Policy is at most $C \leq \max\left\{8.155, \ln(\alpha) + 2 + \frac{9\ln^2(\alpha)}{B} + \frac{3\ln(\alpha)}{B}\right\}$

Proof. We first prove the bound for $\alpha \geq e$. We prove the claim separately for each part of the maximum expression derived in Theorem 1. For $C \geq \ln(\alpha) + 2$ The claim trivially holds. We notice that for $\alpha \geq e$ we have $\ln(\alpha) \geq 1$ and analyze $B\alpha^{1/S} - B + 1$.

$$B\alpha^{1/S} - B + 1 = B\alpha^{\frac{1}{B - B/(\ln(\alpha)+2)0}} - B + 1 = Be^{\frac{\ln(\alpha)}{B - B/(\ln(\alpha)+2) - 1}} - B + 1$$

Given the inequality $e^x \leq 1 + x + x^2$, which holds for any $0 \leq x \leq 1$, we substitute x with $\ln(\alpha)/[B - B/(\ln(\alpha)+2) - 1]$. Note that $B - \lceil B/(\ln(\alpha)+2)\rceil \geq \ln(\alpha)$ since we assume $B \geq \ln(\alpha) + 2$.

$$B\left(1 + \frac{\ln(\alpha)}{B - B/(\ln(\alpha)+2) - 1} + \left(\frac{\ln(\alpha)}{B - B/(\ln(\alpha)+2) - 1}\right)^2\right) - B + 1$$

$$= \frac{B\ln(\alpha)}{B - B/(\ln(\alpha)+2) - 1} + \frac{B\ln^2(\alpha)}{(B - B/(\ln(\alpha)+2) - 1)^2} + 1$$

$$= 1 + \frac{\ln(\alpha)}{1 - 1/(\ln(\alpha)+2) - 1/B} + \frac{\ln^2(\alpha)}{B[1 - 1/(\ln(\alpha)+2) - 1/B]^2}$$

Since $\alpha \geq e$ and $B \geq \ln(\alpha) + 2$, we have $\ln(\alpha) \geq 1$ and $B \geq 3$. Therefore, the last part of the expression is bounded by:

$$\frac{\ln^2(\alpha)}{B[1 - 1/(\ln(\alpha)+2) - 1/B]} \leq \frac{\ln^2(\alpha)}{B[1 - 1/3 - 1/3]^2} = \frac{9\ln^2(\alpha)}{B}$$

The rest of the expression is bounded as follows:

$$1 + \frac{\ln(\alpha)}{1 - 1/(\ln(\alpha)+2) - 1/B} = \ln(\alpha) + 1 + \frac{\frac{\ln(\alpha)}{\ln(\alpha)+2} + \frac{\ln(\alpha)}{B}}{1 - 1/(\ln(\alpha)+2) - 1/B}$$

$$= \ln(\alpha) + 1 + \frac{1 - \frac{2}{\ln(\alpha)+2} + \frac{\ln(\alpha)}{B}}{1 - 1/(\ln(\alpha)+2) - 1/B} = \ln(\alpha) + 2 + \frac{\frac{\ln(\alpha)}{B} - \frac{1}{\ln(\alpha)+2} + \frac{1}{B}}{1 - 1/(\ln(\alpha)+2) - 1/B}$$

$$\leq \ln(\alpha) + 2 + \frac{3\ln(\alpha)}{B}$$

The last inequality holds since $B \geq \ln(\alpha) + 2$ and $\alpha \geq e$. Adding the parts of the analysis together, we have

$$B\alpha^{1/S} - B + 1 \leq \ln(\alpha) + 2 + \frac{9\ln^2(\alpha)}{B} + \frac{3\ln(\alpha)}{B} = \ln(\alpha) + 2 + O\left(\frac{\ln^2(\alpha)}{B}\right)$$

This completes the proof for $\alpha \geq e$ and $B \geq \ln(\alpha) + 2$. For $1 \leq \alpha \leq e$ we use a different analysis. We rely on the following lemma from [1], relating to a greedy policy, which accepts packets as long as the queue is not full, but might use a smaller queue:

Lemma 4. [1] A greedy policy with a queue of size xB, for some $0 < x \leq 1$ accepts at least a x fraction of the number of packets that any other policy with a queue of size B accepts.

The Smooth Selective Barrier Policy accepts packets greedily until the number of packets in the queue reaches the threshold of $B/\mathcal{F}(1)$. Inductively, its queue always holds more packets than a greedy policy with a queue of size $B/\mathcal{F}(1)$, and therefore, by Lemma 4 the competitive ratio of accepted packets (ignoring packet values) is at least:

$$\frac{B}{\mathcal{F}(1)} = \frac{B}{\left\lceil \frac{B}{\ln(\alpha)+2} \right\rceil} \leq \ln(\alpha) + 2$$

At a worst case scenario, the Smooth Selective Barrier Policy accepts only packets of value 1, while the offline accepts only packet of value α. Therefore, the competitive ratio (considering packet values) is at most the ratio of the number of accepted packets times the ratio between the largest and smallest packet values, meaning that for $\alpha \leq e$,

$$\alpha(\ln(\alpha) + 2) \leq e(\ln(e) + 2) = 3e \approx 8.155,$$

which completes the proof. $\square$

5   Improved Bounds for Low α

For a sufficiently large B such that $B = \omega(\ln^2 \alpha)$ factor of $\ln^2(\alpha)/B$ is negligible. The main bottleneck in Theorem 2 is when $1 \leq \alpha \leq e$, and causes the competitive ratio to be 8.155 rather than approximately 3. If α is sufficiently small, setting $\mathcal{F}(v) = B$ for any $v \in [1, \alpha]$ may be better. This policy is is equivalent to a greedy policy which accepts any packet, and its competitive ratio, as shown is [1], is as follows.

Theorem 3. [1] The competitive ratio of the greedy policy is α

Since $\alpha \leq \ln(\alpha) + 2$ for $1 \leq \alpha \leq e$ we have the following corollary:

Corollary 1. A combined policy that runs the Smooth Selective Barrier Policy for $\alpha \geq e$ and the Greedy Policy for $1 \leq \alpha < e$ has a competitive ratio of at most $\ln(\alpha) + 2 + O(\frac{\ln^2(\alpha)}{B})$

Solving numerically, a competitive ratio of α is better than $\ln(\alpha) + 2$ for any $1 \leq \alpha \leq 3.146$. However, better bounds exist for low values of α. We define the Rounded Ratio Partition Policy, which has the following competitive ratio:

Theorem 4. The competitive ratio of the Rounded Ratio Partition Policy is at most $2\sqrt{\alpha} - 1 + O(\sqrt{\alpha}/B)$

The definition of the policy and the proof of Theorem 4 appear in the full version of this paper. If B is large enough such that $O\left(\frac{\sqrt{\alpha}}{B}\right)$ is negligible, and assuming that α is small, the Rounded Ratio Policy is preferable over the greedy policy and the Smooth Selective Barrier Policy. Combining policies, we derive the following corollary:

Corollary 2. A combined policy that based on the value of α, runs either the Smooth Selective Barrier Policy or the Rounded Ratio Partition Policy, has a competitive ratio of

$$\min\left\{2\sqrt{\alpha} - 1, \ln(\alpha) + 2\right\} + O\left(\frac{\ln^2(\alpha)}{B}\right)$$

Solving numerically, the competitive ratio is improved for $1 \le \alpha \le 5.558$, since in that range $2\sqrt{\alpha} - 1 \le \ln(\alpha) + 2$.

6   Lower Bound

By changing the function $\mathcal{F}(\cdot)$ used by the Smooth Selective Barrier Policy we can define any online policy that takes into account only the value of the arriving packet and the number of packets in the queue in order to decide whether to accept or reject a packet, ignoring the values of the packets in the queue, or the history of the input sequence. We refer to such policies as Static Threshold Policies. In this section we prove a lower bound of asymptotically $\ln(\alpha) + 2$ for the competitive ratio of Static Threshold policies. Specifically, we prove the following theorem:

Theorem 5. For any value $\epsilon > 0$, there exists a value β such that for any $\alpha \ge \beta$, no Static Threshold policy has a competitive ratio of less than $\ln(\alpha) + 2 - \epsilon$.

To prove Theorem 5, we observe the performance of an arbitrary Static Threshold policy on two sets of $n+1$ different inputs each, where n will be determined later. We denote the first set as $Up(i)$, and the second set as $UpDown(i)$, where $i \in [0, n]$. First, we prove several properties that are common to all online policies, using the Up series. We then define the $UpDown$ series as extensions to Up series, and observe how these extensions can increase the competitive ratio for Static Threshold policies. The proofs are omitted and appear in the full version of this paper. Before defining the input series, we introduce the notations that will be used in our analysis:

Definition 1. Let V_i and $\widehat{V}_i$ denote the benefits of an arbitrary Static Threshold policy on inputs $Up(i)$ and $UpDown(i)$, respectively. Let U_i and $\widehat{U}_i$ denote the benefits of the optimal offline on inputs $Up(i)$ and $UpDown(i)$, respectively. Let $\rho_i = U_i/V_i$ and $\widehat{\rho}_i = \widehat{U}_i/\widehat{V}_i$.

$Up(0)$ is defined as a burst of B packets with value 1 that arrive at $t = 0$. $Up(i)$ is defined as the same packets from $Up(i-1)$ followed by B packets with value $\alpha^{i/n}$. The optimal offline response to $Up(i)$ is to accept only the last B packets, gaining a benefit of $U_i = B\alpha^{i/n}$. The online will accept $x_0 = \lfloor \mathcal{F}(1) \rfloor$ packets with value 1, $x_1 = \max\{0, \lfloor \mathcal{F}(\alpha^{1/n}) \rfloor - x_0\}$ packets with value $\alpha^{1/n}$, etc. gaining a total benefit of $V_i = \sum_{0 \le j \le i} x_j \alpha^{j/n}$. The competitive ratio of the online over the i-th input is $\rho_i = U_i/V_i$.

The Up series was used in [2] to prove a general lower bound of $\ln(\alpha) + 1$, for the competitive ratio of any online policy. Without loss of generality, we assume that $\sum_{0 \le i \le n} x_i = B$, otherwise we can increase x_0 appropriately and lower all the ρ_i. The following convenient convexity property holds for the sequence:

Lemma 5. Assume $\sum_{0 \le i \le n} x_i = B$. If we increase x_j, then ρ_j decreases, but for some other $k \ne j$, ρ_k increases.

The main conclusion from Lemma 5 is that given a series of constraints $\rho_i \le a_i$, we can search for a feasible solution $x_0, x_1, ..., x_n$ in a greedy manner: Select x_0 such that $\rho_0 = a_0$, then select x_1 such that $\rho_1 = a_1$, etc. If at the end of the process we have $\sum_i x_i \le B$ then we have a feasible solution. Otherwise, if $\sum_i x_i > B$ then by Lemma 5 no feasible solution exists, since any change in the x_i that will decrease one of the ρ_i, will necessarily increase another.

We now define the $UpDown$ series. $UpDown(0)$ is identical to $Up(0)$. The beginning of $UpDown(i)$ is similar to $Up(i)$, however the sequence continues after $t = 0$, with i bursts of packets. At time $t = x_i$, x_i packets of value $\alpha^{(i-1)/n}$ arrive. At time $t = x_i + x_{i-1}$, x_{i-1} packet of value $\alpha^{(i-2)/n}$ arrive. The sequence continues with packets of decreasing value, until at time $x_1 + x_2 + ... + x_i$, the last burst containing x_1 packets with value 1 arrives. Since the number of packets in each burst equals the number of time units that passed since the last burst, there has to be enough space in the queue to accept all the packets in the burst, regardless of the policy. However, for a Static Threshold policy, when a burst arrives, the number of packets in the queue is equal to the threshold for which the policy rejects packets with this value. Therefore, we have the following observation:

Observation 6 The benefit of a Static Threshold policy for input $UpDown(i)$ is V_i, the same as the benefit for input $Up(i)$. The benefit of the optimal policy for input $UpDown(i)$ is $\widehat{U_i} = U_i + \sum_{1 \le j \le i} x_j \alpha^{j/n}$.

Unfortunately, the convexity property from Lemma 5 does not hold for $UpDown$ series. For example, for large n and small α, increasing x_0 and decreasing x_1 appropriately, may lower all the ρ_i. Therefore, we cannot search for feasible solutions in a greedy manner. Instead, we measure how bad is the $Down$ part in the $UpDown$ series by comparing $\widehat{\rho_i}$ to ρ_i.

The following lemma lower bounds the gain to the competitive ratio derived by $UpDown$ inputs, compared to the competitive ratio over Up inputs:

Lemma 6. $\widehat{\rho_i} \ge \max\left\{\rho_i, \rho_i + \alpha^{-1/n} - \rho_i \alpha^{-(i+1)/n}\right\}$

Proof of Theorem 5: Obviously, if $\rho_i \geq \ln(\alpha) + 2$, then also $\widehat{\rho_i} \geq \ln(\alpha) + 2$. Otherwise, we have from Lemma 6 that $\widehat{\rho_i} \geq \rho_i + \alpha^{-1/n} - \frac{\ln(\alpha)+2}{\alpha^{(i+1)/n}}$. Due to the general lower bound of $\ln(\alpha) + 1$ (from [2]), for sufficiently large n there exists an index i such that $\rho_i \geq \ln(\alpha) + 1 - \frac{1}{2}\epsilon$, where $\epsilon > 0$ is arbitrary small. If $\rho_i < \ln(\alpha) + 2$ we have to prove that $\widehat{\rho_i} \geq \rho_i + 1 - \frac{1}{2}\epsilon \geq \ln(\alpha) + 2 - \epsilon$. For $n \geq \frac{4}{\epsilon}\ln(\alpha) \geq -\ln(\alpha)/\ln(1 - \frac{1}{4}\epsilon)$, we have $\alpha^{-1/n} \geq 1 - \frac{1}{4}\epsilon$. To complete our proof we have to show that $(\ln(\alpha) + 2)\alpha^{-(i+1)/n} \leq \frac{1}{4}\epsilon$ holds for sufficiently large α. However, this holds only if $i \geq cn - 1$, for some constant $c > 0$. For $i < cn - 1$ we can only conclude that $\widehat{\rho_i} \geq \rho_i$.

The following lemma proves that for any integer m, even if we allow ρ_0, ρ_1, ...,$\rho_{n/m}$ to be slightly larger than $\ln(\alpha) + 1$ (but less than $\ln(\alpha) + 2$), the competitive ratio for the remaining inputs cannot be much lower than $\ln(\alpha) + 1$.

Lemma 7. Assume $\alpha > e^2$. Let $m \geq 4$, let $\delta = \frac{2}{m} + \frac{1}{\ln(\alpha)} < 1$ and let $n > m\ln(\alpha)(\ln(\alpha) + 1)$, such that $n = km$ for some integer k. There is no feasible solution for $x_0, x_1, ..., x_n$ such that $\rho_i < \ln(\alpha) + 2 - \delta$ for $0 \leq i \leq n/m$ and $\rho_i < \ln(\alpha) + 1 - \delta$ for $n/m + 1 \leq i \leq n$.

For any $0 < \epsilon < 1$ we choose $m = \frac{5}{\epsilon}$ and $\beta = m^{3m}$. This ensures that for any $\alpha \geq \beta$ we have $\frac{\epsilon}{2} > \delta = \frac{2}{m} + \frac{1}{\ln(\alpha)}$ and $\frac{\epsilon}{4} > (\ln(\alpha) + 2)\alpha^{-1/m}$. For any fixed α we set $n > m\ln(\alpha)(\ln(\alpha) + 1)$, which ensures that $\alpha^{-1/n} > 1 - \frac{\epsilon}{4}$.

If there exists an i such that $\rho_i > \ln(\alpha) + 2 - \epsilon$, we are done. Otherwise, by Lemma 7, there exists an $i > \frac{n}{m}$ such that $\rho_i > \ln(\alpha) + 1 - \frac{\epsilon}{2}$, and by Lemma 6, we have $\widehat{\rho_i} > \rho_i + 1 - \frac{\epsilon}{4} - \frac{\epsilon}{4} \geq \ln(\alpha) + 2 - \epsilon$, which completes our proof. $\square$

7   Conclusion

We have presented a nearly optimal online policy for non-preemptive queue management with continuous values. The policy is suboptimal due to the static threshold for the value of the next accepted packets. We note that the same threshold used when the queue was filled is still used as the queue drains. Potentially, the online policy may lose packets with accumulating value of almost the queue's contents as the queue drains, which explains the difference between the lower bound of $\ln(\alpha) + 1$ to the asymptotic upper bound $\ln(\alpha) + 2$. It might be the case that a policy with dynamic thresholds, that considers the entire history of the sequence, i.e. arrival times and values of both the packets in the queue and the packets that were already sent or rejected, will have a competitive ratio that beats the asymptotic $\ln(\alpha) + 2$ bound.

References

1. Aiello, W., Mansour, Y., Rajagopolan, S. and Rosen, A. Competitive Queue Policies for Differentiated Services. In *Proc. of IEEE INFOCOM*, 2000.

2. Andelman, N., Mansour, Y. and Zhu, A. Competitive Queueing Policies for QoS Switches. In *Proc. of 14th ACM-SIAM Symposium on Discrete Algorithms (SODA)*, 2003.
3. Azar, Y. and Richter, Y. Management of Multi-Queue Switches In QoS Networks In *Proc. of 35th ACM Symposium on Theory of Computing (STOC)*, 2003.
4. Black, D, Blake, S., Carlson, M., Davis, E., Wang Z. and Weiss, W. An Architecture for Differentiated Services. *Internet RFC 2475*, 1998.
5. Borodin A. and El-Yaniv, R. *Online Computation and Competitive Analysis.* Cambridge University Press, 1998.
6. Clark D. and Wroklawski, J. An Approach to Service Allocation in the Internet. Internet draft, 1997. Available from `diffserv.lcs.mit.edu`.
7. Floyd, S. and Jacobson, V. Random Early Detection Gateways for Congestion Avoidance. In *IEEE/ACM Trans. on Networking*, Vol. 1(4), 1993.
8. Hahne, E. L., Kesselman, A. and Mansour, Y. Competitive Buffer Management for Shared Memory Switches. In *Proc. of 13th ACM Symposium on Parallel Algorithms and Architectures (SPAA)*, 2001.
9. Kesselman, A., Lotker, Z., Mansour, Y., Patt-Shamir, B., Schieber, B. and Sviridenko, M. Buffer Overflow Management in QoS Switches. In *Proc. of 33rd ACM Symposium on Theory of Computing (STOC)*, 2001.
10. Kesselman, A. and Mansour, Y. Loss-Bounded Analysis for Differentiated Services. In *Proc. 12th ACM-SIAM Symposium on Discrete Algorithms (SODA)*, 2001.
11. Kesselman, A. and Mansour, Y. Harmonic Buffer Management Policy for Shared Memory Switches. In *Proc. of IEEE INFOCOM*, 2002.
12. Kesselman, A., Mansour, Y. and van Stee, R. Improved Competitive Guarantees for Qos Buffering. To appear in *Proc. of 11th European symposium on Algorithms (ESA)*, 2003.
13. Lotker, Z. and Patt-Shamir, B. Nearly Optimal FIFO Buffer Management for DiffServ. In *Proc. of 21st ACM Symposium on Principles of Distributed Computing (PODC)*, 2002.
14. Nichols, K., Jacobson, V. and Zhang, L. A Two-bit Differentiated Services Architecture for the Internet, *Internet draft*, 1997.
15. Sviridenko, M. A Lower Bound for On-Line Algorithms in the FIFO Model. Unpulished Manuscript, 2001.

Constructing Disjoint Paths for Secure Communication

Amitabha Bagchi, Amitabh Chaudhary, Michael T. Goodrich, and
Shouhuai Xu

Dept. of Information & Computer Science,
University of California,
Irvine, CA 92697-3425, USA
{bagchi,amic,goodrich,shxu}@ics.uci.edu

Abstract. We propose a bandwidth-efficient algorithmic solution for
perfectly-secure communication in the absence of secure infrastructure.
Our solution involves connecting vertex pairs by a set of k edge-disjoint
paths (a structure we call a k-*system*) where k is a parameter determined
by the connectivity of the network. This structure is resilient to adversaries with bounded eavesdropping capability. To ensure that bandwidth
is efficiently used we consider connection requests as inputs to the k-
Edge Disjoint Path Coloring Problem (k-EDPCOL), a generalization of
the Path Coloring Problem, in which each vertex pair is connected by a
k-system, and each k-system is assigned a color such that two overlapping k-systems do not have the same color. The objective is to minimize
the number of colors. We give a distributed and competitive online algorithm for k-EDPCOL. Additionally, since security applications are our
focus we prove that a malicious adversary which attacks the algorithm
during the process of construction of a k-system cannot learn anything
more than if it had attacked the k-system once it was built.

1 Introduction

Secure communication over a public network is one of the most important issues in deploying distributed computing. Various solutions have been proposed to
this problem, yet those solutions typically assume the existence of a trusted third
party or a public key infrastructure. For large-scale applications or Internet-wide
distributed computing this assumption about the existence of either a trusted
third party or a public key infrastructure often lead to both technical and non-
technical complications. Therefore alternatives that facilitate secure communications without relying on such assumptions could potentially be extremely useful.
In this paper, we explore one such alternative and show that network properties
can be used to provide infrastructureless secure communications.

In a pioneering work, Dolev et. al. [14] showed how high connectivity can be
used for perfectly secure transmission in the presence of bounded adversaries.
In that work the authors used the notion of wires disjoint paths connecting
sender to receiver. The simple expedient of breaking up data into several shares

F.E. Fich (Ed.): DISC 2003, LNCS 2848, pp. 181–195, 2003.
© Springer-Verlag Berlin Heidelberg 2003

and sending them along these disjoint paths makes it difficult for an adversary with bounded eavesdropping capability to intercept a transmission or tamper with it. They established bounds on the number of wires required for the kind of security they wished to provide, and described protocols using those wires. They did not, however, make any attempt to actually construct these wires. The main contribution of our paper is in formalizing the algorithmic setting for this construction.

We define a k-system: a set of k edge disjoint paths joining a vertex pair. In realizing the wires of [14] we give an algorithm for constructing k-systems between requesting pairs.

We use the theoretical abstraction of a uniform capacity optical network. Each edge has uniform capacity divided into a number of wavelengths, also known as colors in routing terminology. A path from source to sink is routed using the same wavelength on all the edges it traverses. See [29] for an elaboration of this setting. For simplicity of analysis we require that all the k paths of a given k-system use the same wavelength.

To ensure that each connection gets enough bandwidth we ensure that the total number of wavelengths sharing the edges' capacity is minimized.   We define a generalization of the Minimum Path Coloring Problem (MPCP) [29] called k-EDPCOL (in Section 4) for this purpose and build k-systems to provide a competitive and distributed solution to this problem.

We ensure that the communication complexity of constructing these k-systems is as low as possible. Given that the applications we propose for our k-systems are in the realm of security, we show that a disruptive adversary operating during the running of our algorithm will not be able to learn more than if it had attacked a correctly constructed k-system.

The second contribution of this paper is to show the applications of k-systems to secure communications. Our k-systems can be used to realize the wires required in [14] so that perfectly secure communications can be achieved. In [14], in fact, the wires refer to vertex disjoint paths, to allow processor as well as edge faults. Our k-systems, however, work when the faults are limited to edges.[1]

As another application to allow computationally secure communications, we introduce the notion, and construction, of Identity Based Key Distribution (IBKD). An IBKD scheme allows a pair of parties to conduct secure communications without relying on any trusted third party or public key infrastructure.

Organization of the paper. In the next section we formally define paths systems and our adversarial models. In Section 3 we discuss how the k-systems produced by our algorithm can be used for secure key distribution and secure transmission. In Section 4 we provide some terminology and definitions and provide a context for our work. In Section 5 we outline the algorithm and analyze it. Finally we conclude in Section 6 with a discussion of the issues raised by our work and the open problems remaining.

---

[1] Note that finding vertex disjoint paths in graphs is considered to be a significantly harder problem than finding edge disjoint paths. See [22] and [23] for details.

2   Paths Systems and Adversaries

Since the connectivity of the underlying network is a foundational aspect of our work we begin this section by defining it formally:

Definition 1. An edge cut of a graph G is a set $S \subseteq E(G)$ such that $G' = (V, E \setminus S)$ is not connected. A graph G is k-connected if every edge cut has at least k edges. The connectivity of G is the maximum k such that G is k-connected.

Path Systems and k-systems. For a given sender s and receiver t, a path system is a set $\mathcal{P}$ of paths between s and t in the underlying communication network. A k-path system is a path system with $|\mathcal{P}| = k$. If all the paths in $\mathcal{P}$ are edge disjoint, we call it an edge disjoint path system. A k-edge disjoint path system is an edge disjoint path system with $|\mathcal{P}| = k$. In the following we refer to a k-edge disjoint path system simply as a k-system. Our focus in this paper is on algorithms for construction of k-systems.

Adversaries and Compromised paths. An α-passive adversary, also called a listening or eavesdropping adversary, is one that listens to messages on a fixed set L of edges in the communication network with $|L| \leq \alpha$. The objective of a passive adversary is to learn the confidential communication between s and t.[2]

An (α, β)-active adversary, also called a malicious adversary, is one that listens to messages on a fixed set L of edges, and in addition, disrupts, alters, and generates messages on a fixed set $D \subseteq L$ of edges in the communication network, with $|L| \leq \alpha$ and $|D| \leq \beta$. An active adversary may behave arbitrarily in both phases: the establishment of a k-system, and the future communication over it. The objective of an active adversary is, in addition to learning any confidential communication, to prevent t from correctly receiving confidential communication from s.

A compromised edge is an edge on which an active or passive adversary is operating. We assume that, in general, an edge is used for two way communication and an adversary can compromise communication in both directions. A compromised path is a path in which at least one edge has been compromised.

3   Security Applications of Edge Disjoint Paths

In this section we investigate some interesting security applications of k-systems. In general, we are interested in protocols for secure communication over k-systems in the presence of active and passive adversaries. Here, we present two applications, one each from the two categories: (1) those that require perfect security (see Section 3.1), and (2) those that require just computational security (see Section 3.2).

---

[2] Informally, "to learn" means that the adversary improves its ability to guess what the messages are. See [14] for a formal definition.

3.1   As a Building Block for Perfectly Secure Message Transmission

Perfectly secure message transmission is a fundamental problem in distributed computing. It is known that every function of n inputs can be efficiently and securely computed by a complete network of n participants even in the presence of $t < \frac{n}{3}$ Byzantine faults [6,12]. In general communication networks, researchers have been striving to pursue alternatives for perfectly secure message transmission. The classic result, which simultaneously achieves perfect secrecy, perfect resilience, and worst-case time linear in the diameter of the network, is due to [14]. Specifically, using the protocol of [14] for perfectly secure message transmissions, the completeness theorem can be naturally extended to general networks of necessary connectivity $2t+1$. This has recently been extended (for instance) to accommodate more powerful communication capability [17] and non-threshold adversary capability [25]. Note that these schemes typically require multiple rounds of communications.

In [14], it is assumed that a set of wires (e.g., vertex-disjoint paths or edge-disjoint paths) are given as input to their algorithms. As a consequence, the k-system produced by our algorithms presented in Section 5, can be directly used as the input to their algorithms. Of course, security is naturally translated into the context of tolerating an adversary that is only able to corrupt up to certain number of edges.

3.2   Applications to Identity-Based Key Distribution

Identity-based cryptography is a notion introduced by Shamir [31]. Such schemes have the advantages (over traditional schemes such as those based on public key infrastructures) that secure communications can be established as long as a sender knows the identity of a receiver; this is a perfect analogy of the real-world mail system. There have been secure identity-based signature schemes [16] and secure public key cryptosystems [9]. Although it has never been explicitly stated, identity-based symmetric key cryptography (with the same functionality similar to Shamir's) has also been intensively investigated (see [7,8,26] and their follow-ons). However, all of the above mentioned (public key and symmetric key) schemes assume the existence of a trusted third party that predistributes certain secrets to the participants, and the existence of a set of system-wide cryptographic parameters. As we shall see, our k-systems facilitate identity-based key distribution (IBKD) without relying on any trusted third party or the existence of system-wide cryptographic parameters. In the sequence, we first present a definition for IBKD and then suggest some practical constructions.

Definition 2. (Identity-Based Key Distribution, IBKD) An IBKD scheme consists of three probabilistic polynomial-time algorithms: **Init**, **Send**, and **Receive**. Let S denote a sender and $\mathcal{R}$ denote a receiver.

Init. This process may include the following steps.
1. S chooses a security parameter κ and generates a fresh secret K and a cryptographic setting $\mathbb{E}$ (e.g., algorithm identification).

2. S chooses an appropriate secret sharing scheme to split K into a set of shares $(K_1, K_2, \cdots, K_k)$ and possibly some accompanying information T.

3. The sender runs the algorithm presented in Section 5 to produce a k-system $P = \{p_1, \dots, p_k\}$.

Send. For a given $P = \{p_1, \dots, p_k\}$, S sends $(\mathbb{E}, K_i, T)$ to the receiver via path p_i, where $1 \leq i \leq k$.

Receive. After receiving $\{(\mathbb{E}_i, K_i, T_i)\}_{1 \leq i \leq k}$, $\mathcal{R}$ executes according to the $\mathbb{E}_i$'s and T_i's to reconstruct the secret K.

Definition 3. We call an IBKD scheme (α, β)-secure, if an (α, β)-adversary is (1) unable to learn any information about the secret K, and (2) unable to prevent the receiver $\mathcal{R}$ from reconstructing the secret K.

Concrete Constructions. For concreteness, we outline two IBKD schemes that are secure against a computationally-bound adversary (this is an adversary we confront in the real-world). The first instantiation is based exactly on Shamir's secret sharing [30]. When Alice intends to conduct secure communication with Bob, she simply executes according to the specification with $T = \emptyset$. Note that the original Shamir secret sharing scheme is at best $(\frac{k-1}{3}, \frac{k-1}{3})$-secure [27], where secrecy is in an information-theoretical sense[3]. The second instantiation is an extension to Shamir's secret sharing. It is an $(\frac{k-1}{2}, \frac{k-1}{2})$-secure IBKD scheme. The trick is that we can let T be certain checksum so that the receiver $\mathcal{R}$ can differentiate invalid incoming messages from valid ones. As a simple implementation (see, e.g., [19]), one could let $T = (f(K_1), \cdots, f(K_1))$ where f is an appropriate one-way function.

4   Path Coloring and Bandwidth Maximization

The network setting we assume is a uniform capacity network provisioned with optical fibre links and optical switches. Each link can provide bandwidth B on C different wavelengths i.e. each link can accomodate at most C different paths through it at a maximum rate of B bits per second for each path. Since we assume that every request entering the system has to be serviced, it is likely that the number of wavelengths required is more than C. In this case it might be be necessary to use time division multiplexing to share a given edge between several k-systems, thereby reducing the effective bandwidth available to each. In general, therefore, it is desirable to keep the number of different wavelengths down to the minimum possible.

Formally speaking the problem we wish to solve is stated as follows: Given an undirected graph $G = (V, E)$ and a (multi) set of request pairs $T = \{(s_i, t_i) | s_i \neq t_i, s_i, t_i \in V\}$. For each demand pair (s_i, t_i), find k edge disjoint paths (called

---

[3] Perfect secrecy here is achieved at the price of a single round of communication. However, the secret itself will be used for communication that is secure in a computational sense.

a k-system) that connect s_i and t_i. Assign a color to each k-system such that no two k-systems which share an edge have the same color. The objective is to minimize the number of colors used. We call this the k-Edge Disjoint Path Coloring problem (k-EDPCOL).

Note that the requirement that each of the k paths in a k-system be colored the same color is inessential to the basic project of constructing k-systems. We impose this requirement to simplify the competitive analysis of the algorithm. In a real-world setting it might be advisable to remove this constraint.

k-EDPCOL is a generalization of the well known Minimum Path Coloring Problem (MPCP) [28] and was first defined in [4]. There is a rich and interesting literature on the MPCP. Due to space constraints we omit a discussion of it here, referring the reader to the full version of this paper [3].

4.1   Flow Number

We begin by reintroducing the Flow Number, a network measure introduced in [24], which allows for more precise bounds for MPCP. One important property of this parameter which we would like to mention at the outset is that the Flow Number can be computed exactly in polynomial time which gives it a major advantage over other routing parameters like the expansion and the Routing Number.

Before we introduce the flow number, we need some notation. In a concurrent multicommodity flow problem there are k commodities, each with two terminal nodes s_i and t_i and a demand d_i. A feasible solution is a set of flow paths for the commodities that obey capacity constraints but need not meet the specified demands. An important difference between this problem and the unsplittable flow problem is that the commodity between s_i and t_i can be routed along multiple paths. The (relative) flow value of a feasible solution is the maximum f such that at least $f \cdot d_i$ units of commodity i are simultaneously routed for each i. The max-flow for a concurrent multicommodity flow problem is defined as the maximum flow value over all feasible solutions. For a path p in a solution, the flow value of p is the amount of flow routed along it. A special class of concurrent multicommodity flow problems is the product multicommodity flow problem (PMFP). In a PMFP, a nonnegative weight $\pi(u)$ is associated with each node $u \in V$. There is a commodity associated with every pair of nodes (u, v) whose demand is equal to $\pi(u) \cdot \pi(v)$.

Suppose we have a network $G = (V, E)$ with arbitrary non-negative edge capacities. For every node v, let the capacity of v be defined as

$$c(v) = \sum_{w:\{v,w\}\in E} c(v, w)$$

and the capacity of G be defined as $\Gamma = \sum_v c(v)$. Given a concurrent multi-commodity flow problem with feasible solution $\mathcal{S}$, let the dilation $D(\mathcal{S})$ of $\mathcal{S}$ be defined as the length of the longest flow path in $\mathcal{S}$ and the congestion $C(\mathcal{S})$ of $\mathcal{S}$ be defined as the inverse of its flow value (i.e., the congestion tells us how many times the edge capacities would have to be increased in order to fully satisfy all the original demands, along the paths of S). Let I_0 be a multicommodity flow problem in which each pair of nodes (v, w) has a commodity with demand $c(v) \cdot c(w)/\Gamma$. The flow number $F(G)$ of a network G is the minimum of $\max\{C(S), D(S)\}$ over all feasible solutions S of I_0. When there is no risk of confusion, we simply write F instead of $F(G)$. Note that the flow number of a network is invariant to scaling of capacities.

The smaller the flow number, the better are the communication properties of the network. For example, $F(\text{line}) = \Theta(n)$, $F(\text{mesh}) = \Theta(\sqrt{n})$, $F(\text{hypercube}) = \Theta(\log n)$, $F(\text{butterfly}) = \Theta(\log n)$, and, $F(\text{expander}) = \Theta(\log n)$.

5   The Algorithm

In this section we describe our algorithm to construct k-systems for secure communication in optical networks, optimizing the bandwidth usage. The framework under which our algorithm is designed has the following features:

Requests come online. When a request, in the form of a sender-receiver node pair (s, t) that has to be connected by a k-system, comes it has to be satisfied before the next request comes [4]. Note that we do not assume any probability model for the requests.

Distributed computation. There is no central authority that accepts requests and constructs k-systems. Each request comes at the corresponding sender node s. The onus is on s to construct the k-system to connect with the receiver t. Initially the nodes do not have any global information about the network topology; they do, however, know who their immediate neighbors are. Thus s needs to send messages, first to its neighbors, and then through them to other nodes to learn the topology and construct the k-system. We assume that the protocol for constructing the k-systems is followed by all nodes, and that some information can be stored on links that facilitates this protocol.

Presence of an active adversary. The k-systems, after construction, are used for secure communication. In addition, we assume that an adversary is present even during the construction phase, and attempts to disrupt proper construction of k-systems.

Correspondingly, we describe our algorithm in three steps: Section 5.1 describes a centralized algorithm that has a bounded competitive ratio for any online request sequence; Section 5.2 details a distributed implementation of this algorithm; and finally, Section 5.3 tackles the question of resilience to an adversary attacking the algorithm while it runs.

5.1   The Online Algorithm and Its Competitive Ratio

We run a Bounded Greedy Algorithm for k-EDPCOL.[5] A high level description of **BoundedGreedy** would be:

---

[4] This is the standard model for *online algorithms*. See [10] for a general introduction.
[5] The usage of bounded greedy algorithms for path routing problems was pioneered by Kleinberg in [22].

For a given pair (s, t) find the lowest color class c such that a k-system with no more than $L = 24k^2F$ edges can be established between s and t that does not share an edge with any other k-system colored c — where F is the flow number of the communication network.

The algorithm works by looking for a non-intersecting k-system of bounded length in one color class after the next, establishing a new color class if it fails to do so. The value for L specified is necessary for the analysis of the competitive ratio.

The analysis of **BoundedGreedy** is a simple extension of the analysis of the bounded greedy algorithm for solving the k Edge Disjoint Paths problem (k-EDP) introduced in [5].[6] k-EDP is the admission control version of k-EDPCOL. Formally speaking: In the k-EDP we are given an undirected graph $G = (V, E)$ and a set of terminal pairs (or requests) T. The problem is to find a maximum subset of the pairs in T such that each chosen pair can be connected by k disjoint paths (k-systems) and, moreover, the paths for different pairs are mutually disjoint.

In [5] a bounded greedy algorithm was given for k-EDP and a competitive ratio of $O(k^3F)$ was proved which was subsequently improved to $O(k^2F)$ [4]. Our own **BoundedGreedy** is an iterated version of that algorithm.

We state the result here, omitting the proof.

Theorem 1. BoundedGreedy run on set T with parameter $L = 24k^2 \cdot F$ is a $O(k^2F \cdot \log |T|)$ competitive algorithm for k-EDPCOL.

Note that the algorithm requires knowledge of the flow number F of the communication network. This value can be pre-computed and stored at all nodes, and updated as an when the network topology changes significantly.

5.2   Distributed Implementation

The essential computation in **BoundedGreedy** is constructing the minimum sized k-system between s and t that can be colored c. To begin with, remove all edges that already have a k-system colored c. The rest of the problem can be easily formulated as a min cost flow problem, and any min cost flow algorithm can be used to solve it (see, e.g., [1]). We use an algorithm, based on Galil and Yu's work [18].[7]

In the distributed implementation of **BoundedGreedy** each sender node s finds a k-system to receiver t of size L, in the lowest color class possible. To prevent conflicts on edges, each edge e stores a list $colors(e)$ of the colors of all exisiting k-systems that use e. Initially, s does not know the topology of

---

[6] A similar connection has been observed independently by Aumann and Rabani [2] in the case of the path colouring problem and the edge disjoint paths problem.

[7] We refer the reader to Galil and Yu's paper for a discussion of the relationship of their algorithm to the previous work done in similar settings by Jewell [21], Iri [20], and Busaker and Gowen [11]; and by Tomizava [32], and Edmonds and Karp [15].

the network, except for its neighbors. It learns the topology by sending explicit messages to the nodes it knows at any given point of time. We take care to ensure that these messages are kept to a minimum and that we consider only that part of the network which is absolutely essential for our needs.

Before delving into the internal workings of the algorithm we need some definitions.

Definition 4. Let $H = \langle V, E \rangle$ be a directed network with edge capacity function $g : E \mapsto \Re^+$ and edge cost function $\lambda : E \mapsto \Re$.

- The cost function is said to be skew symmetric if $\forall (i,j) \in E : \lambda_{ij} = -\lambda_{ji}$.
- A k-flow from node s to t is a function $f : E \mapsto \Re^+$, such that, $\forall (i,j) \in E :$
  $0 \leq f_{ij} \leq g_{ij}$, and $\forall i \in V, i \neq s, t, \sum_{(i,j) \in E} f_{ij} = \sum_{(j,i) \in E} f_{ji}; \sum_{(s,j) \in E} f_{sj} = \sum_{(j,s) \in E} f_{js} + k; \sum_{(i,t) \in E} f_{it} = \sum_{(t,i) \in E} f_{ti} + k$. The cost of this flow is $cost(f) = \sum_{(i,j) \in E} \lambda_{ij} \cdot f_{ij}$. A minimum cost k-flow is one that minimizes $cost(f)$.
- Given flow f, the residual capacity function r is defined as $r_{ij} = g_{ij} + f_{ji} - f_{ij}$. The residual network $H(f)$ induced by f is one consisting only of edges with positive residual capacities, with capacity function r and the same cost function λ.

An unweighted undirected graph G can be transformed into a directed network H with edge capacities and a skew symmetric cost function by replacing each edge $(i,j) \in V(G)$ with a directed subgraph $\langle V_{i,j}, E_{i,j} \rangle$, where $V_{i,j} = \{i, j, l_{ij}, l_{ji}\}$ and $E_{i,j}$ consists of four pairs of opposite edges between i and l_{ij}, l_{ij} and j, j and l_{ji}, l_{ji} and i. Edges in directed cycle i, l_{ij}, j, l_{ji} have capacity 1 and cost 1, and edges in directed cycle i, l_{ji}, j, l_{ij} have capacity 0 and cost -1.

We also define the following node potential function which will help us bound the time complexity of our min cost flow algorithm.

Definition 5. A node potential is a function $\pi : V \mapsto \Re$. The reduced cost function λ^π is defined as $\lambda_{ij}^\pi = \lambda_{ij} + \pi(i) - \pi(j)$.

BoundedGreedy is described in Figure 1. The communication network is represented by G. To find a min cost k flow in G we construct a shortest path tree τ in the residual network $H(f)$ using λ^π as edge length. Finding a shortest path requires significant knowledge of the network. Since the sender's knowledge is only local to begin with, and augmenting this knowledge incurs a communication cost, we compute the tree using a lazy version of the classic Dijkstra's algorithm. **LazyDijkstra** is described in Figure 2 (we have omitted some bookkeeping details for a simpler presentation). During its execution our knowledge about the graph may increase. On these occasions, computing the value of the potential π for the new nodes is easy, since it is easy to prove the following claim that allows us to update π using distances from a previous iteration.

BoundedGreedy (t, L)

/* **Initialize the graph with the local information available at** s. */

1:    $G \leftarrow \langle \{s\} \cup \{u | u \text{ is a neighbor of } s\}, \{(s, u) | u \text{ is a neighbor of } s\}\rangle$.

2:    $c \leftarrow 0$.

3:    $connected \leftarrow$ **false**.

/* **Find a** k-**system that can be colored** c. */

4:    While($connected =$ **false**)

5:        $G_{\overline{c}} \leftarrow G \setminus \{\text{edges that are part of an existing } k\text{-system colored } c\}$.

/* **Transform the graph into a form suitable for our min cost flow algorithm.** */

6:        $H \leftarrow G_{\overline{c}}$

7:        $\forall e(i, j) \in E(H) : f_{ij} \leftarrow 0$.

8:        $\forall u \in V(H) : \pi(u) = 0$.

9:        $b \leftarrow 0$.

/* **Finding a min cost** k **flow from** s **to** t. */

10:        While($b < k$)

/* **Find a min cost augmenting path in the residual network. First construct shortest path tree using LazyDijkstra; this can potentially increase the information about** G **available at** s. */

11:            $\tau \leftarrow$ **LazyDijkstra**$(H(f), \lambda^{\pi}, t, b, c)$.

12:            $\forall u \in V(H) :$ let $d(u) \leftarrow$ distance of u from s in τ.

13:            If($d(t) = \infty$) restart outer while loop with $c \leftarrow c + 1$.

14:            Else /* **Pass a unit flow through the augmenting path.***/

15:                Let $p'(b)$ be a shortest path in τ from s to t.

16:                $f \leftarrow f+$ unit flow in $p'(b)$ from s to t.

17:                $\forall u \in V(H) : \pi(u) \leftarrow \pi(u) + d(u)$.

18:                $b \leftarrow b + 1$.

19:        $\{p_1, \ldots, p_k\} \leftarrow$ edge disjoint paths formed by decomposing the flow in $\bigcup_b p'(b)$.

20:        If($|\bigcup_b p(b)| \leq L$)

21:            $\forall (u, v) \in \bigcup_b p(b)$: Send message COLOR_EDGE to u and v requesting adding c to $colors(u, v)$.

22:            If($\forall (u, v) \in \bigcup_b p(b)$: Coloring request granted) $connected \leftarrow$ **true**.

23:        Else $c \leftarrow c + 1$.

/* **If** k-**system cannot be used, or request denied, restart with next color.** */

Fig. 1. The **BoundedGreedy** algorithm: Constructs a k-system, of size at most L, from sender node s to receiver node t in the minimum color class possible. The computation is performed at s.

C l a i m . In **BoundedGreedy**, the potential $\pi(u)$ of any node u in the beginning of iteration b is equal to its shortest distance from s in the residual network at the beginning of iteration $b - 1$, using λ^{π} as the edge length.

Once a node has been visited, its information is stored at s. This is so even if the node is not useful in the current iteration because of color conflicts. It is

---

LazyDijkstra$(H(f), \lambda^\pi, t, b, c)$

1:   $S \leftarrow s$.
     /* Initialize the set S that contains vertices currently in τ. */
2:   $Q \leftarrow V(H(f)) \setminus \{s\}$.

3:   While($Q \neq \emptyset$)
     /* Find shortest paths to as many nodes as possible. */
4:      $u \leftarrow$ node in Q with minimum λ^π distance from s (using edges only in and from S).
5:      If(u has not been visited before)
6:         If($t \in S$) **return**.
7:         Send message LIST_NEIGHBORS to u requesting the set $L = \{(w, colors(u, w)) | w$ is a neighbor of $u\}$.
8:         $\forall w$, w is a neighbor of u, and there is no visited node v such that w is a neighbor of v:
           /* Update graph G (and thereby H), set Q, and potential function π with the newly learned vertices. */
9:            $G \leftarrow \langle V(G) \cup \{w\}, E(G) \cup \{(u, w)\} \rangle$.
10:           If($c \notin colors(u, w)$):
11:              $Q \leftarrow Q \cup \{w\}$.
12:              $\pi(w) \leftarrow$ shortest distance of w from s, using λ as edge length, in the residual network at the start of the previous iteration, i.e., the network $H(\sum_{q=0}^{b-2}$ flow in $p'(q))$.
13:        Mark u as visited.
14:        $S \leftarrow S \cup \{u\}$.
           /* Include u in S and update shortest distance estimates. */
15:        $\forall w$, w is a neighbor of u :
16:           If(distance$(s, w) >$ distance$(s, u) + \lambda\pi(u, w)$)
17:              distance$(s, w) \leftarrow$ distance$(s, u) + \lambda^\pi(u, w)$.

Fig. 2. The **LazyDijkstra** subroutine: $H(f)$ is the residual network of the graph currently known at s. The reduced cost function λ^π is used as edge length in $H(f)$. A shortest path tree τ is constructed from s to as many vertices in $H(f)$ as is possible without sending messages on the network. If, however, τ does not include receiver t, messages are sent to learn the graph necessary to include t in τ. b is the iteration index in **BoundedGreedy**. c is the color being considered.

easy to see that a node is visited only when it is essential for the computation of the shortest path to t.

Time and Communication Complexity. In [18], Galil and Yu show that Dial's implementation [13] of Dijkstra's algorithm finds a k-flow in $O(km)$ time, where m is the number of edges in G. If we ignore time for communication, this is true in our case too. So, barring communication time, **BoundedGreedy** runs in time $O(c \cdot km)$, where c is the number of colors used, and m is the number of edges in the network examined. Note that the size of the network examined is dependent on the edges that have been taken by the existing k-systems, and so cannot be characterized easily. Luckily, we can give a better bound on this value if we introduce a simple addition, described next.

A slightly improved algorithm. Let $\mathcal{P} = \{p_1, \ldots, p_k\}$ be the k-system obtained by decomposing the k-flow. Suppose we maintain $\mathcal{P}$ through all the k iterations. At any point, if the number of edges in $\mathcal{P}$ exceeds L, we know that we need to go to the next color class. If we add this check, only nodes that are within a distance of L from s will ever be considered. Denote the subgraph of these nodes by $N_s(L)$. The time bound is now $O(c \cdot k \cdot |E(N_s(L)|)$.

The above check also gives a bound on the communication complexity, defined as the sum of the number of hops made by all the messages sent. Messages are sent only to nodes in $N_s(L)$. Each such node is at distance at most L. So the complexity is bounded by $O(L \cdot |N_s(L)|)$.

5.3   Resilience to a Active Adversary

The **BoundedGreedy** algorithm, as described, is resilient to a passive listening adversary, but not to an active disrupting adversary. A disrupting adversary controlling only a few edges may succeed in deceiving the sender s in constructing an incorrect k-system, or prevent it from constructing a k-system in color class c when it is possible. This is because, even though a k-system is itself used to provide communication through k edge disjoint paths, the algorithm does not specify the paths used by the messages like LIST_NEIGHBORS and COLOR_EDGE it sends. All these messages may pass through a small number of edges that may all be under the control of the adversary.

It is not necessary that, to be usable, the k-path system constructed should necessarily consist of k edge disjoint paths. In particular, we can say:

Theorem 2. Every protocol for secure communication over a k-system in the presence of an (α, β)-active adversary, can be used for secure communication over a k-path system $\mathcal{P}$ in the presence of an (α, β)-active adversary, if $\mathcal{P}' \subseteq \mathcal{P}$ of at least $k - \beta$ paths are edge disjoint and the adversary is limited to listening on at most $\alpha - \beta$ edges in the paths in $\mathcal{P}'$.

We omit the proof due to lack of space. Now, if detection of an unusable k-system is the only issue, it can be easily done by a slight modification to the last part of the algorithm. When a message is sent to nodes u and v to color edge $(u, v) \in p(b)$, we specify that it takes the specific path $p(b)$. We also ensure that the replies are sent back along this very path. If any node reports an error, we discard the k-system as unusable. We claim that if the adversary can compromise at most β edges, at least $k - \beta$ paths in the k-system are edge disjoint and not compromised.

The above idea can be extended to ensure that the algorithm finds a usable k-system in color class c if one exists. Following an idea introduced earlier, let $\mathcal{P} = \{p_1, \ldots, p_k\}$ be the k-system obtained by decomposing the k-flow. Modify the algorithm to maintain the current $\mathcal{P}$ at every stage. Further, in LazyDijkstra, we abandon the notion of a visited node. To every node u extracted from Q we send a LIST_NEIGHBORS message. Care is taken that this message goes along the path p in $\mathcal{P}$ that u would be a part of, and that the reply comes back along the same path. Lastly, if at any stage, the paths in $\mathcal{P}$ change such that the path to a node u in $\mathcal{P}$ is different from what was used by the LIST_NEIGHBORS message sent to it, we confirm our information about u by sending the message (and receiving a reply) again through the new path. Call this the ModifiedLazyDijkstra algorithm.

Claim. A k-path system found by **BoundedGreedy** using ModifiedLazyDijkstra, in the presence of an (α, β)-adversary has at least $k - \beta$ paths that are edge disjoint and the adversary is limited to listening on at most $\alpha - \beta$ edges on these paths. Further, such a k-system can always be found as long as a $(k + \beta)$-system exists.

Proof Sketch. Let the k-system found be $\mathcal{P}$. Each path $p \in \mathcal{P}$ is edge disjoint with every other path in $\mathcal{P}$. Further, all information about p is obtained by using only edges in p. This implies that with a single edge the disrupting adversary can deceive with respect to at most a single path in $\mathcal{P}$. Thus, with β edges, it can deceive with respect to at most β paths. Further, it can listen on at most $\alpha - \beta$ edges on the remaining $k - \beta$ paths.

Similarly, if a $(k + \beta)$-system exists, the adversary can deceive with respect to at most β paths in it. The rest of the paths form a k-system, which will be discovered by the "unhindered" algorithm.   □

6   Conclusions and Open Problems

Our primary concern here is to develop an efficient algorithm for a security problem. However, by using already extant network resources for our purpose we propose a new kind of resource efficiency and backward compatibility.

Our work also has important implications for network design. It can provide input as to what kind of parameters need to be tuned when networks are provisioned. For example, building a network with a low Flow Number might be very useful since the average latency and the competitive ratio of our algorithm are directly related to this quantity.

A number of areas for future investigation are thrown up by our work. It would be interesting to see what kind of algorithmic solutions can be obtained for constructing vertex disjoint path systems. We feel that security applications can give a new lease of life to research in this area. A useful investigation would be to see if we can adjust the algorithm to produce customized k-systems. For example, Alice may want $k = 11$ and Bob may only need $k = 5$. Such capability will enable the users to achieve security that is proper to their applications at a reasonable cost.

Acknowledgements. The authors thank Moti Yung for helping clarify the relationship between this work and [14], Petr Kolman and Ankur Bhargava for helpful discussions on k-EDPCOL, and Tanu Malik for proof reading and suggestions.

References

1. R.K. Ahuja, T.L. Magnanti, and J.B. Orlin. Network Flows. Prentice Hall, New Jersey, 1993.
2. Y. Aumann and Y. Rabani. Improved bounds for all-optical routing. In *Proc. of the 6th ACM-SIAM Symposium on Discrete Algorithms*, pages 567–576, 1995.
3. A. Bagchi, A. Chaudhary, M.T. Goodrich, and S. Xu. Constructing disjoint paths for secure communication (full version). Available online at http://www.ics.uci.edu/~bagchi/pub.html.
4. A. Bagchi, A. Chaudhary, and P. Kolman. Short length Menger's theorem and reliable optical routing. In *Proc. of the 15th Annual Symp. on Parallel Algorithms and Architectures*, pages 246–247, 2003.
5. A. Bagchi, A. Chaudhary, P. Kolman, and C. Scheideler. Algorithms for fault-tolerant routing in circuit-switched networks. In *Proc. 14th ACM Symp. on Parallel Algorithms and Architectures*, pages 265–274, 2002.
6. M. Ben-Or, S. Goldwasser, and A. Wigderson. Completeness theorems for non-cryptographic fault-tolerant distributed computing (extended abstract). In *Proc. of 20th Annual Symposium on the Theory of Computing*, pages 1–10, 1988.
7. R. Blom. An optimal class of symmetric key generation systems. In *Proc. of EUROCRYPT '84*, pages 335–338, 1984.
8. C. Blundo, A. D. Santis, A. Herzberg, S. Kutten, U. Vaccaro, and M. Yung. Perfectly-secure key distribution for dynamic conferences. In *CRYPTO'92*, pages 471–486, 1992.
9. D. Boneh and M. Franklin. Identity-based encryption from weil pairing. In *Proc. of CRYPTO 2001*, pages 213–229, 2001.
10. A. Borodin and R. El-Yaniv. *Online Computation and Competitive Analysis*. Cambridge University Press, 1998.
11. R.G. Busaker and P.J. Gowen. A procedure for determining minimal-cost flows by doubling scaling. Technical Report ORO Technical Report 15, Operational Research Office, Johns Hopkins University, Baltimore, MD, 1961.
12. D. Chaum, C. Crepeau, and I. Damgard. Multiparty unconditionally secure protocols. In *Proc. of 20th Annual Symposium on the Theory of Computing*, pages 11–19, 1988.
13. R. Dial. Algorithm 360: Shortest path forest with topological ordering. *Comm. ACM*, pages 632–633, 1969.
14. D. Dolev, C. Dwork, O. Waarts, and M. Yung. Perfectly secure message transmission. *JACM*, 40(1):17–47, 1993.
15. J. Edmonds and R.M. Karp. Theoretical improvements in algorithmic efficiency for network .ow problems. *J. ACM*, 19:248–264, 1972.
16. A. Fiat and A. Shamir. How to prove yourself: Practical solutions to identification and signature problems. In *Proc. of CRYPTO'86*, pages 186–194, 1986.
17. M. Franklin and R. Wright. Secure communication in minimal connectivity models. In *Proc. of EUROCRYPT'98*, pages 346–360, 1998.
18. Z. Galil and X. Yu. Short length versions of Menger's theorem. In *Proc. of the 27th Annual ACM Symposium on Theory of Computing*, pages 499–508, 1995.
19. L. Gong. Increasing availability and security of an authentication service. *IEEE J. Selected Areas in Communications*, 11(5):657–662, 1993.
20. M. Iri. A new method for solving transportation-network problems. *Journal of the Operations Research Society of Japan*, 3:27–87, 1960.

21. W.S. Jewell. Optimal flow through networks. Technical Report Interim Technical Report 8, Operation Research Center, MIT, Cambridge, MA, 1958.
22. J. Kleinberg. *Approximation Algorithms for Disjoint Paths Problems*. PhD thesis, Department of Electrical Engineering and Computer Science, Massachusetts Institute of Technology, 1996.
23. S.G. Kolliopoulos and C. Stein. Approximating disjoint-path problems using greedy algorithms and packing integer programs. In *Proc. of the 6th International Integer Programming and Combinatorial Optimization Conference (IPCO)*, pages 153–168, 1998.
24. P. Kolman and C. Scheideler. Improved bounds for the unsplittable flow problem. In *Proc. of the 13th ACM-SIAM Symposium on Discrete Algorithms*, pages 184–193, 2002.
25. M. Kumar, P. Goundan, K. Srinathan, and C. Pandu Rangan. On perfectly secure communication over arbitrary networks. In *Proc. of 21st Annual ACM Symposium on the Principles of Distributed Computing*, pages 193–202, 2002.
26. T. Leighton and S. Micali. Secret-key agreement without public-key cryptography (extended abstract). In *Proc. of CRYPTO '93*, pages 456–479, 1993.
27. R. McEliece and D. Sarwate. On sharing secrets and Reed-Solomon codes. *Comm. ACM*, 24(9):583–584, 1981.
28. Y. Rabani. Path coloring on the mesh. In *Proc. of the 37th Annual IEEE Symposium on Foundations of Computer Science*, pages 400–409, 1996.
29. P. Raghavan and E. Upfal. Efficient routing in all-optical networks. In *Proc. of the 26th Annual Symposium on the Theory of Computing*, pages 133–143, 1994.
30. A. Shamir. How to share a secret. Comm. ACM, 22(11): 612–613, 1979.
31. A. Shamir. Identity-based cryptosystems and signature schemes. In *Proc. of CRYPTO '84*, pages 47–53, 1984.
32. N. Tomizava. On some techniques useful for solution of transportation network problems. *Networka*, 1:173–194, 1972.

Compact Routing for Flat Networks

Kazuo Iwama and Masaki Okita

School of Informatics, Kyoto University, Kyoto 606-8501, Japan
{iwama, okita}@kuis.kyoto-u.ac.jp

Abstract. Cowen presented a universal compact routing algorithm with a stretch factor of three and a table-size of $O(n^{2/3} \log^{4/3} n)$, based on a simple and practical model [1]. (The table-size is later improved to $O(\sqrt{n} \log^3 n)$ [2].) This stretch factor of three matches a general lower bound given in [3] and also matches a much tighter lower bound if we restrict the model to the Cowen's [4]. Thus it seems quite hard to improve the stretch factor. However, her analysis is of course for the worst case; the situation might differ if we assume some desirable property that average-case networks often possess. As such a property, we consider the notion of flatness in this paper and it is shown that the stretch factor can be significantly improved if the given network is almost flat. Our new algorithm achieves a stretch factor of $s < 3$ and a table size of $O(\sqrt{n \log n})$.

1   Introduction

Compact routing has a long history of research, whose goal is to reduce the size of a routing table being stored in each processor. The size of the routing table usually has a trade-off against the stretch factor, i.e., the ratio of the length of the path computed by the algorithm over the length of the shortest path. To assure the shortest-path routing between any two nodes in any graph, each node needs the routing table of size $O(n \log n)$, where n is the number of nodes in the graph. However, in [1], Cowen presented a universal compact-routing algorithm with a stretch factor of three and a table-size of $O(n^{2/3} \log^{4/3} n)$, based on a simple and practical model. The table-size is later improved by Thorup and Zwick to $O(\sqrt{n} \log^3 n)$ [2]. However the stretch factor of three is tight due to [3], namely, Gavoille and Gengler showed that in order to guarantee a stretch factor of less than three, any compact-routing algorithm (under a general setting) needs a total table-size of at least $\Omega(n^2)$. In addition, if we focus ourselves on the Cowen's model, the table-size of each node should be $(1 - o(1))n \log n$ for the stretch factor of less than three [4].

Thus it seems impossible to improve the stretch factor while keeping the table-size significantly less than $n \log n$. Recall, however, that those results are obtained for general graphs; if we impose some restriction to networks, the situation can of course differ. As such a restriction, it has been constantly popular to consider well known subclasses of graphs, such as rings, trees and planar networks, for which we can often obtain interesting results from a theoretical point of view. Unfortunately, however, those results are sometimes not too important for actual communication networks like Internet.

F.E. Fich (Ed.): DISC 2003, LNCS 2848, pp. 196–210, 2003.
© Springer-Verlag Berlin Heidelberg 2003

1.1   Our Contribution

In this paper, we introduce the notion of flatness as the property that average-case networks appear to possess. If a given network has this property, we can achieve a smaller stretch factor than three by a relatively straightforward extension of the Cowen's algorithm. However, it is also true in general that real networks include several exceptions violating a rather mathematical property. Our main contribution is to show that we can nevertheless achieve a small stretch factor if the number of such exceptional nodes is limited. Such networks, satisfying the relaxed condition and called almost-flat networks, are much more realistic and many existing networks appear to be in this category.

Intuitively, flat networks are those networks which have a "natural" distribution in the distance between their nodes. For example, suppose that a network G includes t nodes within a distance of r from a node v. Then if G includes (roughly) $4t$ nodes within a distance of $2r$ from v, i.e., the number of nodes is roughly proportional to the area, then we consider that G satisfies the condition of flatness (its exact definition is a little different, see Section 3). G is almost flat if G becomes flat if we remove a certain number of nodes which violate the flatness condition.

For such networks, we can achieve a stretch factor of s ($1 < s < 3$) and a table-size of $O((n^{1-\alpha} \log n + \beta n^{\alpha}) \log n)$, where α and β are parameters depending on the degree of flatness. The table-size can be reduced to $O(\sqrt{n \log n})$ if β is constant. We give an example of almost flat networks for which a detailed analysis of the table-size and the stretch factor will be made. Another example, given in Section 6, might be also interesting, since our algorithm is optimal for this class of networks. A brief observation on how the randomized approach [2] works against this example is given as well.

1.2   Previous Research

The flatness condition is quite natural and may have appeared in the literature for different purposes. One very recent example is [5], where Karger and Ruhl showed that the complexity of finding nearest neighbors can be greatly reduced by preparing a sample set which has a low expansion-rate property. Although this condition is a little stronger than our flatness, it obviously has the same flavor. Also, the underlying idea is similar in "growth-bounded networks" in [6].

The notion of compact routing already appears in the literature in the 70's [7]. After that, studies are mainly focused on for restricted networks such as rings and trees [8], complete networks and grids [9,10] and separable graphs [11, 12]. For general networks, Peleg and Upfal give the first nontrivial lower bound, i.e., a total table-size of $\Omega(n^{1+1/(2s+4)})$ to realize a stretch factor of s [13]. For networks whose maximum degree is d, a total table-size of $\Omega(n^2 \log d)$ is needed in order to guarantee shortest-path routing [14]. For upper bounds, Awerbuch, Bar-Noy, Linial and Peleg give a compact-routing algorithm which achieves a stretch factor of at most three and a total table-size of $O(n^{3/2} \log n)$ [15] (but a table-size of a single node can only be bounded by $O(n \log n)$). Eilam, Gavoille and Peleg give an algorithm with a stretch factor of at most five and a table-size (in each node) of $O(\sqrt{n} \log^{3/2} n)$ [16]. As mentioned before, Cowen first achieves a stretch factor of three with a sub-liner table-size, and the table-size is improved later by Thorup and Zwick.

Compact routing for restricted networks has also been popular. Recently, for example, Narayanan and Opatrny have presented a shortest-path routing algorithm for a chordal ring of degree four, i.e., an n-nodes ring such that there are edges from ith node to $((i+c) \mod n)$th node. Their algorithm can achieve a table-size of $O(\log n)$ in each node and the time complexity of $O(1)$ for calculating each path [17]. Gavoille and Hanusse have shown that if the network is planar then we can achieve the shortest-path routing with a table-size of $8n + o(n)$ [18]. Also, Buhrman, Hoepman and Vitányi have shown that a table-size of $3n + o(n)$ is enough with high probability to guarantee $s = 1$ for random graphs whose diameter is very small [19]. More recently, Fraigniaud and Gavoille have shown, for an arbitrary tree, the shortest-path scheme with each node's (tight) table-size of $O(\log^2 n / \log \log n)$ [20].

2   Models and Notations

Let $G = (V, E)$, $|V| = n$, be an undirected and connected graph, or a network, where each edge $e \in E$ has a positive cost which satisfies the triangular inequality. For a node $v \in V$, the set of its closest n^{α} neighbors is called the n^{α}-ball of v and is denoted by $B_v(n^{\alpha})$. The algorithm in [1] is summarized as follows, whose basic structure does not change in our new algorithm.

We first need some preparations: (i) The value α is optimized at the end, but it actually takes approximately $1/3$. (ii) We first compute $B_v(n^{\alpha})$ for all $v \in V$. (iii) Then compute a hitting set C for $B_v(n^{\alpha})$'s, i.e., a set C such that $C \cap B_v(n^{\alpha}) \neq \emptyset$ for all $v \in V$. (We can obtain such a C whose size is $O(n^{1-\alpha} \log n)$ in polynomial time[15].) (iv) Let D be the set of vertices v such that v belongs to at least $n^{\frac{1+\alpha}{2}}$ n^{α}-balls of other nodes, and let $L = C \cup D$. (v) For each $v \in V$, let ℓ_v, called the landmark of v, be the node which is in L and is closest from v. Now the algorithm consists of three parts, i.e., Labeling, Table-Construction and Routing rules. (The following description is slightly different from [1], but it similarly works).

Labeling: Each node $v \in V$ has its own label which is used as a header of a packet to be sent to v: If $v \neq \ell_v$, then its label is $(v, \ell_v, e_{\ell_v}(v))$ where $e_u(v)$, for $u, v \in V$, denotes the port number of node u to be used for sending the packet along the shortest path from u to v. If $v = \ell_v$, then its label is $(v, v, *)$, where $*$ means null.

Table-Construction: The routing table at node u has the following entries: If $u \in L$, then the table includes entries $(\ell, e_u(\ell))$ for all $\ell \in L$. If $u \notin L$, then it includes the same entries $(\ell, e_u(\ell))$ as above and furthermore includes $(v, e_u(v))$ for all $v \in V$ such that $u \in B_v(n^{\alpha})$ and u is closer to v than l_v is.

Routing rules: The routing rules at node u for packet $P = (v, w, p)$ are as follows: (i) If $u = v$, then P is sent to a special port connected to the host processor, (ii) Otherwise, if the table at u includes (v, q_1) then P is sent to port q_1, (iii) Otherwise, if the table includes (w, q_2) then P is sent to port q_2, (iv) Otherwise, P is sent to port p which is given as the third element of the label. Recall that v is the destination and w is v's landmark. Roughly speaking, P, starting from a node u outside $B_v(n^\alpha)$, first heads for its landmark ℓ_v (see Table-Construction above). Once P arrives at ℓ_v, then it heads for v along the shortest path inside $B_v(n^\alpha)$ where the table includes the entry for v. A problem might occur only when P leaves ℓ_v since ℓ_v can belong to many $B_w(n^\alpha)$'s (see (iv)) and its table cannot include the port information for v. Here we can use the third element of the label. Note that once P has left ℓ_v, P never meets another landmark until it gets to final destination v (see (v)).

It is proved in [1] that the algorithm guarantees a stretch factor of at most three and a table-size of $O(n^{2/3} \log^{4/3} n)$. As far as we use the same model, this bound is very tight, i.e., the upper and lower bound of the table-size increases to $(1 - o(1))n \log n$ (almost equal to the trivial upper bound) to achieve a stretch factor of less than three [4].

3   Flat and Almost Flat Networks

[4] gives a worst-case example of networks for the Cowen's scheme (see Fig. 1). As one can see, the network in this example is "concentrated", or the (shortest) distance between a pair of nodes is mostly one or two. This seems unusual in real networks; we can expect more natural distribution in the distances between nodes. Here comes the notion of flatness:

For a network $G = (V, E)$, $|V| = n$, let s and m be two parameters such that $1 < s < 3$ and $0 < m < n$. Define r_v, called a radius of $B_v(m)$, as $r_v = \max_{u \in B_v(m)} d(u, v)$, where $d(u, v)$ denotes the distance between u and v. Then a key parameter β_v is defined as the value such that the size of $U = \{u | u \in V$ and $d(u, v) \le \frac{4s}{s-1} r_v\}$ is $\beta_v \cdot m$, in other words, such that U can be written as $B_v(\beta_v m)$ (see Fig. 2). Now G is called (s, m, β)-flat if $\beta_v \le \beta$ for all $v \in V$. From now on, we always set $m = n^\alpha$ for a constant $0 < \alpha < 1$.

Suppose for instance that $\alpha = \frac{1}{3}$ and $s = 2$. Then β_v is the ratio of the number of nodes which are located within the distance of $8 \cdot r_v$ from v over the size of v's $n^{1/3}$-ball (whose radius is r_v). If we assume that the number of nodes is proportional to the area of the circle (see Fig. 2), then β_v would be roughly 64. If, for example, $\beta_v \le 80$ for all $v \in V$ actually, then the network is $(2, n^{1/3}, 80)$-flat. (The n^α-ball is not involved in the definition of the low expansion-rate property in [5], i.e., for any r, if the number of nodes within radius r is k, the number of nodes within radius $c_1 r$ must be at most $c_2 k$.) We also need another parameter γ_v similar to β_v: Namely the number of nodes u such that $d(u, v) \le \frac{2s}{s-1} r_v$ is $\gamma_v \cdot n^\alpha$. One can easily see that $\beta_v \ge \gamma_v \ge 1$. Also, note that those parameters are not uniquely determined for a particular (flat) network. For example, there

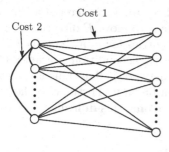

Cost 1

Cost 2

Fig. 1. Worst-case example

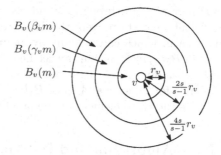

$B_v(\beta_v m)$

$B_v(\gamma_v m)$

$B_v(m)$

r_v

$\frac{2s}{s-1}r_v$

$\frac{4s}{s-1}r_v$

Fig. 2. Closest neighbor sets

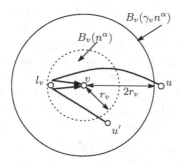

$B_v(\gamma_v n^\alpha)$

$B_v(n^\alpha)$

l_v

v

u

r_v $2r_v$

u'

Fig. 3. Route of packets

is some freedom to choose $1 < s < 3$ and $0 < \alpha < 1$, but β is determined by those values and the network.

Real-world networks are sometimes hierarchical and include "upper-level" nodes which have high-speed links to many nodes. One can see easily that the existence of upper-level nodes tends to violate the condition of flat networks. A lmost flat networks do allow such nodes under a certain condition: A network $G = (V, E)$, $|V| = n$, is called $(s, n^\alpha, \beta, \gamma)$-almost-flat if there exists a set $A \subseteq V$ which satisfies the following three conditions: (i) For any $v \in V$, $\gamma_v \leq \gamma$. (ii) For any $v \in V$, $|B_v(\gamma_v n^\alpha) \cap A| \leq 1$. (iii) If all nodes in A are removed, then the resulting graph G' is still connected and is (s, n^α, β)-flat. (Note that G' has less nodes than G, but uses the original value for n.) Thus the nodes in A can act as the upper-level nodes. The second condition is important, i.e., each $\gamma_v n^\alpha$-ball can contain at most one node in A.

Here is the basic idea why flat networks are desirable for a small stretch factor. See Fig. 3. Suppose that $s = 2$ and a packet P has a destination v. If P starts from a node u which is outside $B_v(\gamma_v n^\alpha)$, then, as the figure shows, its stretch factor is obviously less than two even though P moves through the (worst-case) landmark ℓ_v. However, if P starts from u' which is inside $B_v(\gamma_v n^\alpha)$, then P may also go through ℓ_v and its stretch factor can increase as large as three. What we do to prevent this inconvenience is to move P directly along the shortest path, which can be done by including entries for v in the table of each node u' in $B_v(\gamma_v n^\alpha)$. As one can see later, the flatness condition guarantees that the table-size does not become too large if the network is flat. This is obviously not possible for nodes $a \in A$ since $B_a(\gamma_a n^\alpha)$ can be large. Fortunately, however, we can use the third element of the label to overcome this difficulty.

4   New Algorithm and Its Analysis

Our new algorithm for an $(s, n^\alpha, \beta, \gamma)$-almost-flat network uses the same model as the Cowen's. A label for each node is given as $v(v, w, p)$ as before, where v and w are nodes and p is a port number. Our routing rules are also exactly the same as before: Suppose that a packet $P = (v, w, p)$ is now in node u. Then we look up the routing table at u to find an entry for v and w in this order. If no table entry exists either for v or w, then we choose the third element p as the port P is sent to. In the following we describe how to give a label to each node and how to construct a table at each node. Recall that our network is denoted by G, the four parameters by α, β, γ and s, the set of "upper-level" nodes by A, and the distance between two nodes u and v by $d(u, v)$.

Labeling: (i) We first compute $B_v(n^\alpha)$ for all $v \in V$.
(ii) Compute a hitting set C for $B_v(n^\alpha)$'s exactly as before and define a landmark set L as $L = A \cup C$.
(iii) Then select a landmark $\ell_v \in L$ for each node $v \in V$ as before, i.e., ℓ_v is the node in L which is closest from v. See Fig. 4. $d(\ell_v, v)$ is denoted by R_v. Let $L(\ell)$ be the set of nodes v such that the landmark of v is ℓ, i.e, if u and v are in $L(\ell)$ then $\ell_u = \ell_v = \ell$. We also need another notation $LL(\ell)$, which is the set of nodes u such that there is a node $v \in L(\ell)$ such that $d(u, v) < \frac{2}{s-1} R_v$. Equivalently,

$$LL(\ell) = \cup_{v \in L(\ell)} \left\{ u \in V \mid d(u, v) < \frac{2}{s-1} R_v \right\}.$$

(iv) Now we are ready to compute the label of v. There are several cases (see Lemma 1 for the uniqueness of this labeling).

(Case 1: $\ell_v \in C$, and $LL(\ell_v)$ includes a node $a \in A$ such that $d(a, v) < \frac{2}{s-1} R_v$, see Fig. 5) The label of v is $(v, \ell_v, e_a(v))$. This rule is referred to by $(\mathbf{L} - \mathbf{1})$ later.

(Case 2: $\ell_v \in C$ and $LL(\ell_v)$ includes a node $a \in A$, but for any such a, $d(a, v) \geq \frac{2}{s-1} R_v$, see Fig. 6) The label of v is $(v, \ell_v, e_a(\ell_v))$. $(\mathbf{L} - \mathbf{2})$.

(Case 3: $\ell_v \in C$ and $LL(\ell_v) \cap A = \emptyset$, see Fig. 7) The label is $(v, \ell_v, e_{\ell_v}(v))$. $(\mathbf{L} - \mathbf{3})$.

(Case 4: $\ell_v \in A$) The label is $(v, \ell_v, e_{\ell_v}(v))$. $(\mathbf{L} - \mathbf{4})$.

Table-Construction: When constructing a routing table at a node u, an entry $(v, e_u(v))$ is put into the table if the node v is a landmark of some node or v is relatively close to u. However, we need to be careful if u is in A or C, since the

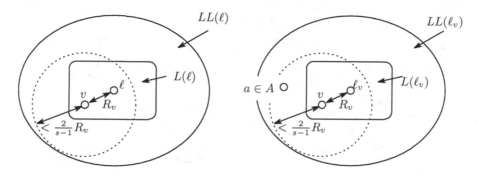

Fig. 4. The sets around landmarks   **Fig. 5.** Case 1 of labeling

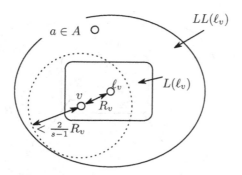

Fig. 6. Case 2 of labeling

routing at u may be determined not by the table there but by the third element of the packet header. For example, look at Fig. 5 again. Since the label of v is $(v, \ell_v, e_a(v))$ by (L − 1), it is intended that the routing for v at node a should be done by the third element of the label. Therefore entry $(v, e_a(v))$ does not need to be in the table at a. On the other hand, the table at ℓ_v should include the entry $(v, e_{\ell_v}(v))$ since the third element in the label can be used only at one node (at a in this case). This is an important difference between our algorithm and the Cowen's. In the latter, each landmark ℓ never includes an entry $(v, e_\ell(v))$ unless v is (another) landmark. Now here is how to construct the routing table for a node u:

(Case 1: $u \in A$) In this case, we consider entries only for landmarks. For each $\ell \in L - \{u\}$, we put $(\ell, e_u(\ell))$ into the table unless there exists a node v such that it's label is $(v, \ell, e_u(v))$ or $(v, \ell, e_u(\ell))$. This rule is referred to by **(T − 1)**. (Suppose that v's label is $(v, \ell, e_u(v))$. Then it is intended that for the packet $P = (v, \ell, e_u(v))$, we should use the third element when P is in the node u. If there would be the entry $(\ell, e_\ell(\ell))$ in the table, however, this could not happen since the second element in the label has a priority.)

(Case 2: $u \notin A$) In this case, we also consider entries for nearby nodes: (a) For each $\ell \in L - \{u\}$, we put $(\ell, e_u(\ell))$ in the table. Referred to by **(T − 2)**. (b)

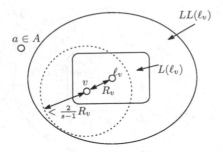

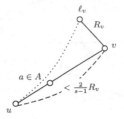

Fig. 8. Special case of routing

Fig. 7. Case 3 of labeling

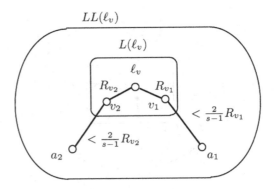

Fig. 9. Correctness of labeling

For each $v \in V - L$ such that $d(u,v) < \frac{2}{s-1}R_v$, we put $(v, e_u(v))$ into the table unless v's label is $(v, u, e_u(v))$. Referred to by **(T − 3)**. (Since $u \notin A$, this can only happen for the case that the third element is $e_u(v)$.) We do NOT put $(v, e_u(v))$ into the label, either, if there is a node $a \in A$ on the shortest path from u to v and $e_u(v) = e_u(\ell_v)$. Referred to by **(T − 4)**. (See Fig. 8. This is important in terms of the size of routing tables, since there can be too many nearby nodes v if there is such node a. Note that the packet still moves on the shortest path to v since the table contains $(\ell_v, e_u(\ell_v))$ and the port for v is the same as the port for ℓ_v. Also note that if $e_u(v) \neq e_u(\ell_v)$ then $(v, e_u(v))$ does exist in the table, see Lemma 3 for the size of the table in this case.)

Now we shall prove that our algorithm is correct and satisfies the bound of stretch factor and table-size.

Lemma 1. Our labeling algorithm gives a unique label to each node $v \in V$.

Proof. Recall (L − 1) and (L − 2). One can easily see that for this lemma, it is enough to prove that there is at most one node $a \in A$ in each $LL(\ell)$. Suppose for contradiction that there are $a_1 \in A$ and $a_2 \in A$ ($a_1 \neq a_2$) in $LL(\ell)$. Then by definition there must be v_1 and v_2 in $L(\ell)$ such that (see Fig. 9):

$$\ell_{v_1} = \ell_{v_2} = \ell$$

$$d(a_1, v_1) < \frac{2}{s-1} R_{v_1} \quad \text{and} \quad d(a_2, v_2) < \frac{2}{s-1} R_{v_2}$$

Now we can claim: (i) Since $d(a_2, v_2) < \frac{2}{s-1} R_{v_2} \leq \frac{2s}{s-1} R_{v_2} \leq \frac{2s}{s-1} r_{v_2}$ (recall that r_{v_2} is the radius of the n^α-ball for v_2 and so $r_{v_2} \leq R_{v_2}$), a_2 is in $B_{v_2}(\gamma_{v_2} n^\alpha)$. (ii) Now we assume that $R_{v_1} \leq R_{v_2}$. By the triangular inequality, $d(a_1, v_2) \leq d(a_1, v_1) + d(v_1, \ell) + d(\ell, v_2) \leq \frac{2}{s-1} R_{v_1} + R_{v_1} + R_{v_2} \leq \frac{2s}{s-1} R_{v_2} \leq \frac{2s}{s-1} r_{v_2}$, which means a_1 is also in $B_{v_2}(\gamma_{v_2} n^\alpha)$. These (i) and (ii) contradict the definition of $(s, n^\alpha, \beta, \gamma)$-almost-flat networks since $B_{v_2}(\gamma_{v_2} n^\alpha)$ contains two different nodes in A. $\square$

Lemma 2. If a packet $P = (v, \ell_v, p)$ is now at a node $u \in V$ such that $d(u, v) < \frac{2}{s-1} R_v$, then P moves to the final destination v on the shortest path from u to v.

Proof. First of all one can see that $v \notin L$, since otherwise, v must be equal to ℓ_v and $R_v = 0$. Let us consider two cases as with the table construction.

(Case 1: $u \in A$) See Fig. 5 again. One can regard that our current u is the node a in the figure. In this case p must be $e_u(v)$ by (L − 1). Also, by (T − 1), there is no table entry for v (since v is not a landmark) or for ℓ_v (due to the "unless-part"). Hence we have to use the third element of the label and P is sent to the port $e_u(v)$.

(Case 2: $u \notin A$) If $P = (v, u, e_u(v))$, then we have no table entry for v or u by (T − 3). Otherwise, we have table entry $(v, e_u(v))$ by (T − 3). Note that there is no such $(v, e_u(v))$ if there is a node $a \in A$ on the shortest path by (T − 4), but the packet still goes on the shortest path as mentioned previously.

Thus the packet is sent on the shortest path in any case. Formally speaking, we need to use mathematical induction with the distance to the destination, but the above argument would be enough to claim the lemma. $\square$

Theorem 1. A packet $P = (v, \ell_v, p)$ is correctly routed by our algorithm.

Proof. Once P gets to a node u such that $d(u, v) < \frac{2}{s-1} R_v$, then, after that, P stays on the shortest path to its destination by Lemma 2. So, to claim the theorem, it is enough to show that if P is at node u such that $d(u, v) \geq \frac{2}{s-1} R_v$, then P is on the shortest path to its landmark ℓ_v. (If P actually gets to ℓ_v, then P moves on the shortest path to v since $d(\ell_v, v) = R_v < \frac{2}{s-1} R_v$. P might get to $u' \neq \ell_v$ such that $d(u', v) < \frac{2}{s-1} R_v$ before it arrives at ℓ_v, but this obviously does not cause any problem, either.)

So suppose that $P = (v, \ell_v, p)$ is now at u such that $d(u, v) \geq \frac{2}{s-1}R_v$. Then there is no table entry for v by the table construction. However, there is the entry for ℓ_v by (T − 1) and (T − 2). Only one exception appeared in the unless part of (T − 1). In this case, we have no table entry for ℓ_v but we can use the third entry of the label as mentioned there. Thus P is sent to the port which is on the shortest path to ℓ_v. □

We next examine the stretch factor.

Theorem 2. The stretch factor of our algorithm is at most s.

Proof. By Lemma 2, we only have to consider the case that a packet $P = (v, \ell_v, p)$ starts from a node u such that $d(u, v) \geq \frac{2}{s-1}R_v$. Then P first goes to ℓ_v and then goes to v both on the shortest path as described in the proof of Theorem 1. (P might enter the shortest path to v before it arrives at ℓ_v, but this is even better for the stretch factor.) Now let $A = d(u, v)$, $B = d(u, \ell_v)$ and $C = d(\ell_v, v)$. Then $A \geq \frac{2}{s-1}C$ by the assumption. By the triangular inequality, $B \leq A + C$. Consequently, the stretch factor is at most $(B + C)/A \leq (A + 2C)/A = 1 + 2C/A \leq 1 + 2/\frac{2}{s-1} = s$. □

Now we discuss the table-size. Recall that each table contains entries for (almost) all nodes in L and for some nearby nodes. Let G' denote the graph which is obtained from G by removing all nodes in A and associated edges.

Lemma 3. The number of entries for vertices not in L is bounded by βn^α in each node.

Proof. Recall the table construction. Roughly speaking, the entry $(v, e_u(v))$ for node $v \notin L$ exists in the table at node u only if $d(u, v) < \frac{2}{s-1}R_v$. It should be noted that this distance between u and v is the distance in the original network G. The distance does not differ in G' if there is no vertex in A on the shortest path from u to v. If a node $a \in A$ does exist on the shortest path, then the distance can change in G'. See Fig. 8 again. By the triangle inequality, $d(u, \ell_v) \leq d(u, v) + d(v, \ell_v)$. Suppose that $(v, l_v(v))$ exists in the table at u. Then the shortest path to v and the shortest path to ℓ_v have different ports in u by (T − 4), and hence there is no node in A on the shortest path from u to ℓ_v or ℓ_v to v because there must be at most one node in A in this area. Therefore the distance between u and v in G', denoted by $d'(u, v)$, can be bounded as

$$\begin{aligned} d'(u, v) &\leq d(u, \ell_v) + d(\ell_v, v) \\ &\leq d(u, v) + 2d(v, \ell_v) \\ &\leq \frac{2s}{s-1}R_v \end{aligned}$$

Thus we can conclude that if $(v, e_u(v))$ is in the table at u, then $d'(u, v) \leq \frac{2s}{s-1}R_v$. (Note that this also covers the case that there is no vertex in A between u and v since $s > 1$.) Recall that r_v is the radius of the n^α-ball for node v in G and let r'_u be the radius of the n^α-ball for v in G'. Then $r'_v \geq r_v$ for the following reason: If we remove vertices in A from G, then some vertices in the n^α-ball for v are also removed. Since the number of vertices in the n^α-ball is the same in G and G', we need to add some new vertices (whose distance from v is larger or equal to that of removed vertices) to construct the n^α-ball in G', which means the radius increases . As a result, it follows that

$$d'(u,v) \leq \frac{2s}{s-1}R_v \leq \frac{2s}{s-1}r_v \leq \frac{2s}{s-1}r'_v$$

This means that the node u is in $B_v(\gamma_v n^\alpha)$ in G'. Namely, the number of entries we want to obtain is bounded by the size of $X_u = \{v|u \in B_v(\gamma_v n^\alpha)\}$. Let $v_0 \in X_u$ be the node such that $d(u,v_0) \geq d(u,v)$ for any other node $v \in X_u$. Then for any $v \in X_u$,

$$\begin{aligned} d(v_0,v) &\leq d(v_0,u) + d(u,v) \\ &\leq 2d(v_0,u) \leq 2 \cdot \tfrac{2s}{s-1}r_{v_0} = \tfrac{4s}{s-1}r_{v_0} \end{aligned}$$

Thus any $v \in X_u$ belongs to $B_{v_0}(\beta_{v_0} n^\alpha)$, namely, $|X_u| \leq |B_{v_0}(\beta_{v_0} n^\alpha)| \leq \beta n^\alpha$ because of the flatness condition. $\square$

Theorem 3. For any node v, the size of v's table, $|T_v|$, is,

$$O\left((n^{1-\alpha}\log n + \beta n^\alpha)\log n\right).$$

Proof. If $v \in A$, then v has only entries for landmarks and so $|T_v|$ is obviously small. Otherwise, $|T_v|$ includes, at most, entries for $A \cup C \cup \{$the nodes discussed in Lemma 3$\}$. $|C| = O(n^{1-\alpha}\log n)$ as mentioned before. $|A| = O(n^{1-\alpha})$ because $B_v(\gamma_v n^\alpha)$ includes at most one node in A and $|B_v(\gamma_v n^\alpha)| \geq n^\alpha$. Thus the number of entries in T_v is bounded by $O(n^{1-\alpha}\log n) + \beta n^\alpha)$ by Lemma 3. The theorem now follows since each entry needs $O(\log n)$ bits. $\square$

Note that if we set $\alpha = \frac{1}{2} + \frac{\log \beta^{-1} + \log \log n}{2\log n}$ and β is constant, then $O\left((n^{1-\alpha}\log n + \beta n^\alpha)\log n\right) = O(\sqrt{n}\log n)$. To make this possible, however, the network G must be $(s, n^{1/2+(\log\beta^{-1}+\log\log n)/2\log n}, \beta, \gamma)$-almost-flat for some constants β and γ. Note that it is not always possible to set $\alpha \simeq \frac{1}{2}$. For example, there is a simple example of a network G which is flat for, $\alpha = 1/3$, but not for $\alpha = 1/3 + \varepsilon$. See Fig. 10. G consists of G_1 through $G_{n^{2/3}}$, each of which is an $n^{1/3}$-nodes clique such that all the links have weight one. Another kind of links exist between any pair of G_i's and G_j's nodes whose weight is sufficiently larger than one. Then this network is $(1+\epsilon, n^{1/3}, 1.0)$-flat since each $n^{1/3}$-ball of v in G_i stays within G_i. However, the radius of $(n^{1/3}+1)$-ball of v in G_i becomes almost the same as the diameter of the whole network and therefore it cannot be $(s, n^{1/3}+1, \beta)$-flat for any $s \leq 3 - \epsilon$ and $\beta < n^{2/3}$. (Since $\beta(n^{1/3}+1) \leq n$, $\beta \leq n^{2/3}$ apparently.)

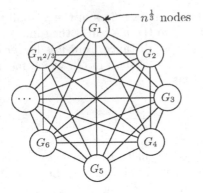

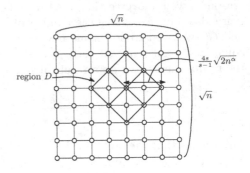

Fig. 11. Mesh network

Fig. 10. Flat network for $\alpha = 1/3$

5   Examples of Flat Networks

The mesh is a typical example of flat networks, where the network has $\sqrt{n}$ rows and $\sqrt{n}$ columns. n processors are located at their intersections and each processor (excepting the boundary ones) has four unit-cost links to its neighbors (see Fig.11). Since its structure is very regular, the flatness condition can be achieved for the wide range of parameter values, which in turn makes it convenient to analyze the relation between the table-size and the stretch factor. It should be noted that if we use a regular numbering for each processor, for example, (i, j) for the processor at the i-th column and the j-th row, then the trivial shortest-path routing is possible just by comparing the destination-node number and the number of the current processor. In this section we assume that no information about the position of processors can be obtained from node numbers as we did in the previous sections.

Also, the regularity allows us to add the A-vertices efficiently. Fig. 11 shows one simple way of doing this; we divide the whole mesh into areas of diamond-shape (whose diameter is $\frac{4s}{s-1}\sqrt{2n^\alpha}$ as shown in the figure). Suppose that we have M diamonds and introduce k A-vertices. Then links are provided from each A-vertex to the center vertices of roughly M/k diamonds. Here these M/k diamonds are chosen as evenly as possible from the whole network. Although details are omitted (a bit messy around the border of the mesh), we can show that when we add k A-vertices, the degree of each A-vertex (the degree of other vertices are still at most five) and the diameter of the network are,

$$O\left(\frac{(s-1)^2}{s^2}\frac{n^{1-\alpha}}{k}\right) \quad \text{and} \quad O\left(\frac{sk}{s-1}\sqrt{n^\alpha}\right),$$

respectively. By the condition of almost flat networks, k must be at most $\frac{(s-1)^2}{4s^2}n^{1-\alpha}$. So if we set $\alpha \simeq \frac{1}{2}$ and $k \simeq n^{\frac{1}{8}}$, then both of the above values become $O(n^{\frac{3}{8}})$.

Also note that the above upper bound on the number of A-vertices shows that the size of A is relatively small for $1 < s < 3$. Hence the size of each routing table does not increase too much even though we add the entries for all those A-vertices into the table. So suppose for simplicity that we neglect the extra size for those A-vertices. Then the table-size is determined by the number of landmarks. Again, the regularity of the mesh allows us to place landmarks more efficiently than the general case, namely, one in the center of each diamond in Fig. 11. Now straightforward calculation shows that the table-size at each node is at most

$$\left(2\sqrt{\left(\frac{4s}{s-1} + \frac{1}{2} \right)^2 + \frac{1}{2}} \right) \sqrt{n}.$$

Some specific values are given in Table 1 to see the tradeoff between the table-size and the stretch factor. It should be noted that there is a gap between $s = 3$ and $s = 3 - \epsilon$. This is due to the existence of A-vertices. If $s = 3$, then $\frac{2}{s-1} R_v = R_v$, which means $LL(\ell)$ does not contain any node in A (otherwise, such a node in A would be a landmark). Hence, only (L – 3) and (L – 4) apply in the labeling algorithm. Also one can see that (T – 4) doesn't happen because there is no node included in A. And so we do not need to worry about the situation illustrated in Fig. 8. Hence the u's table has to hold only entries for v such that $d(u, v) \leq \frac{2}{s-1} R_v$, instead of $\frac{2s}{s-1} R_v$, which is the main reason for the gap. If we use no A-vertices or the whole network is flat, then such a gap does not exist of course.

Table 1. Tradeoff between the table-size and the stretch factor

s	3	$3 - \epsilon$	2	1.5	1.1
table-size	$2\sqrt{n}$	$7.14\sqrt{n}$	$5.20\sqrt{n}$	$14.1\sqrt{n}$	$45.0\sqrt{n}$

6   Randomized Landmark Selection

Thorup and Zwick [2] showed that the table-size in [1] can be improved by using the randomized, greedy approach for the selection of landmarks without changing the routing scheme: (i) Select p nodes at random as landmarks. (ii) Remove all the nodes u such that the number of node v for which u has to include as an entry in its table (i.e., $d(v, u) < d(v, l_v)$ since we now assume the stretch factor of three) is at most $\frac{4n}{p}$. Then go back to (i) and repeat (i) and (ii) until the graph includes only landmarks. They proved that the number of repetition is at most $2 \log n$ and if we set $p = \sqrt{n/\log n}$, then the table size is bounded by $O(\sqrt{n \log n})$. Namely it is guaranteed that a good number of u's are removed in each repetition in the case that our target stretch factor is three.

This approach also works for a smaller stretch factor by changing the condition for removing u such as $d(u, v) < \delta d(v, l_v)$ for some $\delta > 1$ and by adjusting the value $4n/p$. However, one can see that this change of the condition makes it harder to remove u. See, for example, the graph G in Fig. 10 again. Suppose we know that G is $(1+\epsilon, n^{1/3}, 1.0)$-flat and $n^{2/3}$ landmarks (one in each G_i) are enough for the stretch factor of $1+\epsilon$. (Actually the latter fact can be found true if we construct all $n^{1/3}$-balls. Also one can see that this number of landmarks is optimal.) Then a reasonable setting of the value for p is at most $n^{2/3}$. So suppose that we select $n^{2/3}$ landmarks at random. Then a constant fraction of G_i's remain without landmarks with high probability, which means we cannot remove any single u to achieve the stretch factor $1+\epsilon$ and a table-size of $n^{2/3}$ which balances with the number of landmarks. By straightforward probability calculation, we need to choose $\Omega(n^{2/3} \log n)$ landmarks until the number of such landmark-less G_i's because $n^{1/3}$ with high probability. (If it becomes $n^{1/3}$, then the number of all those node is $n^{2/3}$ and hence all the non-landmark nodes are removed.) Thus the random sampling method selects significantly more landmarks than what is optimal. Of course our method obtains an optimal solution through the construction of all the $n^{1/3}$-balls.

7   Concluding Remarks

Throughout this paper, we assume that an (almost) flat network is given explicitly with the set of A-vertices and the parameter values. In some situations, we have to find those parameter values against a given graph and how to do it is obviously an important future work. Also in this paper, we consider flat networks only in the framework of the Cowen's routing model. However, flat networks apparently make things easy for other routing models. For example, interval routing[10] and related ones where we can make use of node numbering should be interesting, since this approach is very powerful in the mesh and flat networks have a somewhat similar flavor as the mesh.

Another future work is to consider more examples of flat networks and relations to existing networks. The mesh discussed in Section 5 is obviously too artificial. For example, some kind of random graphs where nodes are located in the two-dimensional Euclidean space and links are provided between relatively close nodes, might be interesting.

References

1. Cowen, L.J.: Compact routing with minimum stretch. In: Proceedings of the 10th Annual ACM Symposium on Discrete Algorithms (SODA), ACM/SIAM (1999) 255–260
2. Thorup, M., Zwick, U.: Compact routing schemes. In: Proceedings of the 13th Annual ACM Symposium on Parallel Algorithms and Architectures (SPAA). (2001) 1–10
3. Gavoille, C., Gengler, M.: Space-efficiency of routing schemes of stretch factor three. In Krizanc, D., Widmayer, P., eds.: Proceedings of the 4th International Colloquium on Structual Information & Communication Complexity (SIROCCO), Carleton Scientific (1997) 162–175

4. Iwama, K., Kawachi, A.: Compact routing with stretch factor of less than three. In: Proceedings of the 19th Annual ACM Symposium on Principles of Distributed Computing (PODC), ACM PRESS (2000) 337 (A longer version in 21th IASTED PDCS. (2000) 223–228)

5. Karger, D.R., Ruhl, M.: Finding nearest neighbors in growth-restricted metrics. In: Proceedings of the 34th Annual ACM Symposium on Theory of Computing (STOC). (2002) 741–750

6. Plaxton, C.G., Rajaraman, R., Richa, A.W.: Accessing nearby copies of replicated objects in a distributed environment. In: Proceedings of the 9th Annual ACM Symposium on Parallel Algorithms and Architectures (SPAA). (1997) 311–320

7. Kleinrock, L., Kamoun, F.: Hierarchical routing for large networks; performance evaluation and optimization. Computer Networks **1** (1977) 155–174

8. Santoro, N., Khatib, R.: Labelling and implicit routing in networks. The Computer Journal **28** (1985) 5–8

9. van Leeuwen, J., Tan, R.B.: Routing with compact routing tables. The Book of L (1986) 259–273

10. van Leeuwen, J., Tan, R.B.: Interval routing. The Computer Journal **30** (1987) 259–273

11. Frederickson, G.N., Janardan, R.: Space-efficient message routing in c-decomposable networks. SIAM Journal on Computing **19** (1990) 164–181

12. Frederickson, G.N., Janardan, R.: Designing networks with compact routing tables. Algorithmica (1988) 171–190

13. Peleg, D., Upfal, E.: A tradeoff between space and efficiency for routing tables. In: Proceedings of the 20th Annual ACM Symposium on Theory of Computing (STOC), Carleton Scientific (1988) 43–52

14. Gavoille, C., Pérennès, S.: Memory requirement for routing in distributed networks. In: Proceedings of the 15th Annual ACM Symposium on Principles of Distributed Computing (PODC). Volume 1644 of Lecture Notes in Computer Science., ACM PRESS (1996) 125–133

15. Awerbuch, B., Bar-Noy, A., Linial, N., Peleg, D.: Compact distributed data structures for adaptive routing. In: Proccedings of the 21st Annual ACM Symposium on Theory of Computing (STOC). (1989) 479–489

16. Eilam, T., Gavoille, C., Peleg, D.: Compact routing schemes with low stretch factor. In: Proceedings of the 17th Annual ACM Symposium on Principles of Distributed Computing (PODC). (1998) 11–20

17. Narayanan, L., Opatrny, J.: Compact routing on chordal rings of degree four. In: Proceedings of the 4th International Colloquium on Structual Information & Communication Complexity (SIROCCO), Carleton Scientific (1997) 125–137

18. Gavoille, C., Hanusse, N.: Compact routing tables for graphs of bounded genus. In Wiedermann, J., van Emde Boas, P., Nielsen, M., eds.: Proceedings of the 26th International Colloquium on Automata, Languages and Programming (ICALP). Volume 1644 of Lecture Notes in Computer Science., Springer (1999) 351–360

19. Buhrman, H., Hoepman, J.H., Vitányi, P.: Space-efficient routing tables for almost all netowrks and the incompressibility method. SIAM Journal on Computing **28** (1999) 1414–1432

20. Fraigniaud, P., Gavoille, C.: A space lower bound for routing in trees. In: Proceedings of the 19th International Symposium on Theoretical Aspects of Computer Science (STACS), Springer (2002)

Lower Bounds for Oblivious Single-Packet End-to-End Communication

Pierre Fraigniaud[1] and Cyril Gavoille[2]

[1] CNRS, Laboratoire de Recherche en Informatique, Univ. Paris-Sud, France[* * *]
[2] Laboratoire Bordelais de Recherche en Informatique, Univ. Bordeaux I, France[†]

Abstract. The end-to-end communication problem is a protocol design problem, for sending a packet from a specified source-node s to a specified target-node t, through an unreliable asynchronous communication network G. The protocol must insure reception and termination. In this paper, we measure the complexity of the protocol in term of header size, i.e., the quantity of information that must be attached to the packets to insure their delivery. We show that headers of $\Omega(\log \log \tau)$ bits are required in every network, where τ denotes the tree-width of the network. In planar networks, $\Omega(\log \tau)$ bits are required. In particular, this latter lower bound closes the open problem by Adler and Fich in PODC '99 about the optimality of the *hop-count* protocol in square meshes.

Keywords: End-to-End, Sequence Transmission, Tree-Width.

1 Introduction

The end-to-end communication problem is the problem of sending a (sequence of) packet(s) from a specified source-node s to a specified target-node t, through an unreliable communication network G (see, e.g., [13,29]). The sequence transmission [38] problem and the reliable communication [24] problem are other names for the end-to-end communication problem (cf. the survey [25]). By an unreliable network, it is generally meant that links can lose, reorder, and duplicate packets. Moreover, networks are assumed to be asynchronous, i.e., the time for a packet to traverse a link is finite but otherwise unbounded. In particular, a processor cannot distinguish between an inoperational link and an operational link which is just very slow. Hence, an instance of the end-to-end communication problem is described by an (unreliable and asynchronous) network, modeled by an undirected graph G, and two nodes s and t of G. Solving the problem consists in designing a distributed protocol which (1) allows s to send a packet, or a sequence of packets, to t through the network G, and (2) generates a finite amount of traffic for each packet. In other words, the end-to-end protocol must satisfy

---

[* * *] Supported by the Action Spécifique Dynamo of CNRS. pierre@lri.fr, http://www.lri.fr/~pierre

[†] gavoille@labri.fr, http://dept-info.labri.fr/~gavoille

F.E. Fich (Ed.): DISC 2003, LNCS 2848, pp. 211–223, 2003.

the two following requirements: (1) reception, i.e., the target must eventually receive at least one copy of each packet sent by the source; (2) termination, i.e., after a finite time, no copy of the packet(s) remains in the network.

1.1 The Oblivious Single-Packet End-to-End Communication Problem

For the sake of simplicity, this paper will consider a static model, that is we assume that each link is either operational or not. If there exists at least one operational path from s to t in G, it is the role of the protocol to find such a non-faulty path, which is of course a priori unknown. Note that the case of dynamic faults, that is when links can alternate between being operational and inoperational, can be treated similarly by assuming, as in [1,14,28], infinitely frequent path stability, i.e., infinitely often there is a path P from s to t such that a packet sent from s along P will arrive at t (see also [3]).

Performance of end-to-end communication protocols is commonly measured in terms of (1) the amount of communication performed over the links of the network, and (2) the amount of storage space used by intermediate nodes in the networks. Oblivious protocols, a.k.a. memoryless protocols, take their routing decision at every node x (i.e., on which link(s) x has to forward a packet) based solely on the content of the header of the packet. In particular, a node does not store any knowledge about the traffic that previously passed through it. It can however forward several copies of the received packet, and it can modify the header of this packet. As mentioned in [1], the practical advantage of oblivious protocols is their high tolerance to processor crashes. Indeed, as soon as a node recovers from a crash, the protocol is ready to proceed with no risk of corruption due to an altered writable memory (RAM). Moreover, the extremal behavior of oblivious protocols (in the sense that they consume no local memory at all) allows concentrating the analysis of end-to-end communication protocols on the amount of information transmitted over the links of the network. More specifically, this paper focuses on minimizing the packet-header size, i.e., the quantity of additional information that must be attached to every packet to insure its correct delivery.

The header content has two distinct functions: (1) to control the order in which packets arrive at the destination; (2) to find a route from the source s to the destination t (reception), and to insure that residual packets are eventually removed from the network (termination). In this paper, we are interested by the routing part of the problem, that is, by the problem of finding the non faulty route from the source to the destination, while insuring termination. We will therefore concentrate our analysis on the process of sending a single packet from s to t. In other words, we consider the single packet end-to-end communication problem, as opposed to the stream-of-packets end-to-end communication problem, the latter problem requiring the transmission of a sequence of packets from the source to the destination [22]. Hence, let us summarize our problem.

Our problem . We are given an unreliable and asynchronous network G, and two nodes s and t of G. We consider the design of an oblivious distributed protocol which allows the transmission of a packet from s to t (if there is a fault-free path between s and t in G), and which eventually lets the network empty of packets. Such a protocol is required to use packet-headers of small size. The quality of the protocol is indeed measured by the maximum size of the headers involved during its execution.

Previous work. In the context of static link failures (i.e., every link is operational or not but its status does not change during the execution of the routing protocol), the hop-count protocol [32] uses headers of size $O(\log n)$ in n-node networks. It proceeds by flooding the network as follows. The source sends a copy of the original packet to all its neighbors, with header 1. A node receiving a packet whose header contains the hop count $i < n - 1$ updates the header by replacing i by $i + 1$, and forwards a copy of the packet to each of its neighbors. A node receiving a packet whose header contains the hop count $n - 1$ removes the packet from the network. If s and t are connected despite the faulty links, then a path of length at most $n - 1$ exists between s and t, and therefore at least one copy of the packet sent by s eventually arrives in t. Moreover, the remaining copies of the packet are removed from the network after a finite time since no packet can traverse n or more links.

In [1], Adler and Fich showed that if a network G contains H as a minor, i.e., if H can be obtained from G by edge contraction, node and edge deletion, then the oblivious single-packet end-to-end communication problem in G requires headers of size at least as large as for H. Hence the problem is closed under taking minors. They also showed that the complete graph of n nodes requires headers of size $\Omega(\log n)$. Therefore, an n-node network G which contains the complete graph of k nodes as a minor requires headers of size $\Omega(\log k)$. Adler and Fich also gave upper bounds on the header size based on the notion of feedback vertex sets. A feedback vertex set is a subset of nodes S such that every cycle in the network contains at least a node in S. They showed that if there exists a feedback vertex set of size f, then there exists an oblivious protocol using headers with size $O(\log f)$. They also pointed out that any minimum feedback vertex set of an $\sqrt{n} \times \sqrt{n}$ mesh is of size $\Omega(n)$, and thus the feedback vertex set protocol does not offer significant improvement in the mesh, compared to the hop-count protocol. Since the mesh is planar, it does not contain K_5 as minor, and thus it lets a big gap between the best known upper and lower bounds for mesh networks. Adler, Fich, Goldberg, and Paterson [2] recently closed this gap for "narrow" meshes, i.e., $p \times q$ meshes with $p = O(1)$. They have shown that there exists a protocol for n-node meshes using headers of size $O(p(\log p + \log \log n))$, and that any $p \times q$ mesh requires headers of size $\Omega(\log \log n)$ for $3 \leqslant p \leqslant q$. A constant size header protocol exists if $p \leqslant 2$.

1.2   Outline of Our Results

In this paper, we provide lower bounds of the header-size of oblivious end-to-end protocols as a function of the tree-width of the input graph. The notion of tree-width is a very rich concept with many algorithmic implications. Many NP-complete problems are polynomial for graphs of bounded tree-width [10,16]. In addition, the notion of tree-width is in the kernel of the graph minor theory [20]. Recall that tree-width can be seen as a measure of "how far" a graph is from a tree. More precisely, let $G = (V, E)$ be a graph of n nodes, a tree-decomposition of G is a pair $(\S, T)$ where $\S$ is a collection $\{S_i \mid i \in I\}$ of subsets of nodes and $T = (I, F)$ is a tree, such that the three following conditions are satisfied:

1. $\bigcup_{i \in I} S_i = V$;
2. For every edge $e = \{u, v\}$ of G, there exists $i \in I$ such that both u and v belong to S_i;
3. For every $u \in V$, the subgraph of T induced by the set of nodes $\{i \in I \mid u \in S_i\}$ is a tree.

For any graph G, there exists at least one tree-decomposition of G by choosing $\S = \{V\}$, i.e., T is reduced to a single node. The width of a tree-decomposition $(\S, T)$ is defined as $\max_{i \in I} |S_i| - 1$. The tree-width $tw(G)$ of G is then defined as the minimum of the width of any tree-decomposition of G. Roughly speaking, $tw(G)$ denotes the minimum size c such that G has a recursive separator of at most c nodes. A c-decomposable graph has tree-width $O(c)$, a tree has tree-width 1, a cycle has tree-width 2, a square mesh has tree-width $\sqrt{n}$, and a complete graph has tree-width $n - 1$. Determining the tree-width of a graph is NP-hard [11]. However, Bodlaender [17] gave a linear time algorithm for recognizing graphs of bounded tree-width. There are also $O(\log n)$-approximation algorithms for computing the tree-width of an arbitrary graph [18,33], and even $O(\log \tau)$-approximation algorithms where τ is the tree-width [9,19].

Theorem 1. Any protocol designed for the instance (G, s, t) of the oblivious single-packet end-to-end communication problem uses headers of size at least $\Omega(\log \log \tau)$ bits where τ is the tree-width of the graph $G_{s,t}$ obtained from $G, s,$ and t by deleting every edge e not on a simple path from s to t.

As we will see in more details in Section 3, the bound of Theorem 1 derives from an optimal bound for square meshes, and from an upper bound of the "excluding grid" theorem of Robertson and Seymour [35]. This latter bound is likely far from best possible and, as mentioned in [21], Robertson, Seymour and Thomas [36] think that the upper bound might be exponentially improved so that the lower bound of Theorem 1 would be $\Omega(\log \tau)$.

Actually, for planar graphs, we derive a larger lower bound:

Theorem 2. Any protocol designed for the instance (G, s, t) of the oblivious single-packet end-to-end communication problem, G planar, uses headers of size at least $\Omega(\log \tau)$ bits where τ is the tree-width of the graph $G_{s,t}$.

In particular Theorem 2 solves the conjecture mentioned in [1] stating that headers of $\Omega(\log n)$ bits are required to insure packet-delivery in the two dimensional square mesh. All these results establish (as also suggested in [1]) connections between, on one hand, the number of header bits needed to send a single packet through an unreliable network G, and, on the other hand, graph-theoretic properties of G's topology.

Finally, notice that our lower bounds obviously apply to the stream-of-packets problem too.

1.3   Related Work

The case of links with fixed or bounded traversal time has been considered in [8, 41]. Probabilistic faults and delivery times have been considered in [27,30,31]. In the deterministic setting, i.e., the context of this paper, solutions for the stream-of-packets end-to-end problem differ according to the type of faults. Wang and Zuck [40] have shown that any protocol tolerating both packet reordering and duplication requires unbounded headers. Afek et al. [6] have shown that packet reordering and loss create the same effect, that is either unbounded headers or non termination (i.e., the same packet can be received an unbounded number of times). Fekete and Lynch [23] have shown that just packet loss implies that some header information must be attached to the packets for the stream of packets to be treated correctly. These three latter results hold even if G consists of a single edge $\{s,t\}$. Despite these impossibility results, efficient protocols have nevertheless been successfully designed. We refer to [12,37,39] if links are subject to packet duplication, reordering and lose, to [15,30] if links are subject to packet duplication and loss (but no reordering), and to [5,7,29] in case of static link-failures. In [1], it is noticed that the latter protocols can be adapted to the case where links can loose packets — but otherwise transmit them in order and without duplication, by using the techniques in [4]. Although some of these protocols use very short headers, none of them is oblivious, i.e., they all require the local storage of information at intermediate nodes during the execution of the protocol. The stream-of-packet protocol of Dolev and Welch [22] is oblivious (i.e., intermediate processors do not change state) and apply to the static link failure (i.e., the model of this paper). It uses headers of $O(\log p)$ bits where p is the number of distinct simple paths between s and t in G. Although p can be quite large in general (e.g., $\Theta(n!)$ in K_n), this protocol was proved optimal for many topologies, including complete graphs, meshes, and series-parallel graphs (see [1]). Fich and Jakoby [26] considered the same model for directed acyclic graphs. They proved that a single bit header suffices in DAGs, which contrasts with the case of arbitrary graphs.

Several oblivious protocols have been proposed in the literature to solve the single-packet end-to-end problem. We already presented the hop-count protocol described by Postel [32], using headers of $O(\log n)$ bits in n-node graphs. We also mentioned the protocol of Dolev and Welch [22] which applies to the single-packet problem as well. Adler and Fich [1] derived lower and upper bounds for the header size in specific networks (e.g. meshes, hypercubes, butterflies, de Bruijn, etc.). Adler, Fich, Goldberg, and Paterson [2] addressed the problem in $p \times q$ meshes, $p = O(1)$. They proved the somewhat surprising result stating that headers of size $\Theta(\log \log n)$ bits are necessary and sufficient in $3 \times n/3$ meshes (whereas headers of constant size are sufficient in $2 \times n/2$ meshes).

For a more detailed descriptions of the end-to-end protocols mentioned above, we refer to [25], and the references therein.

2 Preliminary Results

We start by proving the following lemma which is an extension to arbitrary networks of a result by Adler and Fich [1] valid for complete graphs only. Then, in Theorem 3, we show how to apply this result to meshes.

Lemma 1. Let $e_i = \{x_i, y_i\}$, $i = 1, \ldots, k$, be k distinct edges of G. Let $\Pi \subseteq \Sigma_k$ be a subset of permutations of k symbols such that, for any $\pi \in \Pi$, there is a simple path P_π in G from s to t, traversing the e_i's from the x_i's to the y_i's, in the order $e_{\pi(1)}, e_{\pi(2)}, \ldots, e_{\pi(k)}$. Then any oblivious end-to-end communication protocol from s to t requires headers of at least $(\log_2 |\Pi|)/k$ bits.

Proof. Let us given an oblivious end-to-end communication protocol A from s to t. Let h be the total number of distinct headers involved in protocol A. We use the same terminology as in [1]. The transcript of a simple path P_π is defined as the word w_π of length k on the alphabet $\{0, \ldots, h-1\}$ obtained by concatenating the headers of the packets transmitted through the e_i's, from the x_i's to the y_i's, when only the edges of P_π are operational. More precisely, let us consider a packet b_π going from s to t along P_π. This packet generates a word w_π whose ith letter is the value of the header h_i of b_i when traversing the edge e_i from x_i to y_i. This word is the transcript of P_π. (Obviously, the transcript may depend on the choice of the packet b_π. This packet is chosen arbitrarily.) There are at most h^k transcripts, and therefore, if $h^k < |\Pi|$, then at least two paths have the same transcript. Thus assume, for the purpose of contradiction, that $h^k < |\Pi|$, and let P_π and $P_{\pi'}$ be two paths with the same transcript $h_1 h_2 \ldots h_k$. Since $\pi \neq \pi'$, there is a pair (i, j), $i \neq j$, such that e_i is traversed before e_j in P_π, and e_i is traversed after e_j in $P_{\pi'}$.

Assume now that both paths P_π and $P_{\pi'}$ are operational. Since the protocol has no way to distinguish an operational link from a link that is just very slow, and since the protocol is oblivious, the headers of packets b_π and $b_{\pi'}$, respectively following P_π and $P_{\pi'}$, will be the same as those used to traverse these two paths when only one of them is operational. In particular, when y_i receives a packet from x_i with header h_i, it cannot know whether P_π, or $P_{\pi'}$, or both paths, are operational. Therefore, y_i forwards the packet through both paths. The same holds for y_j.

As a consequence, the following situation occurs. A packet traverses e_i with header h_i, eventually reaches x_j along P_π, traverses e_j with header h_j, eventually reaches x_i along $P_{\pi'}$, traverses e_i again, still with header h_i, and so on. This creates an infinite loop, in contradiction with the termination requirement. Therefore $h^k < |\Pi|$ cannot hold, and thus $h \geqslant |\Pi|^{1/k}$.   □

The main theorem is the following:

Theorem 3. Any oblivious end-to-end communication protocol in the $p \times q$ mesh requires headers of at least $\Omega(\log \min\{p, q\})$ bits.

Proof. Let $M_{p,q}$ be the $p \times q$ mesh. Assume, w.l.o.g., that $p \leqslant q$ (otherwise exchange the role of p and q). We see the mesh $M_{p,q}$ as with p rows and q columns. Rows are labeled from 0 to $p-1$, and columns from 0 to $q-1$. One can draw the mesh so that $(0,0)$ is the top-left corner, and $(p-1,q-1)$ is the bottom-right corner. Let s and t be the source node and the target node, respectively. The $p \times q$ mesh contains three node-disjoint $(p-2) \times \lfloor \frac{q-2}{3} \rfloor$ sub-meshes. At least one of these sub-meshes does not contain s nor t. Let M be this sub-mesh. One can construct two disjoint paths P_s and P_t in $M_{p,q} \setminus M$, respectively leading from s to the "top-left" corner of M, and from t to the "top-right" corner of M. Any oblivious end-to-end protocol must perform successfully even if all links in $M_{p,q} \setminus (M \cup P_s \cup P_t)$ are faulty. Hence one can assume, w.l.o.g., that s is node $(0,0)$ and t is node $(0,q-1)$.

Let $k = \lfloor \min\{ \frac{p-1}{4}, \sqrt{\frac{q}{12}} \} \rfloor$. Hence $p \geqslant 4k+1$ and $q \geqslant 12k^2 \geqslant 4k^2 + 6k + 2$. Let us consider the edges $e_i = \{x_i, y_i\}$, $i = 1, \dots, k$, where $x_i = (2k, i(4k+2) - 1)$ and $y_i = (2k, i(4k+2))$. Fig. 1 illustrates the idea of the construction: 8 edges are displayed on row $2k$ (the horizontal and vertical scales are different). From the setting of k, there are exactly $2k$ rows above row $2k$ (which contains all the e_i's), and at least $2k$ rows bellow row $2k$. Also, there are exactly $4k$ columns separating column 0 from e_1, $4k$ columns separating two consecutive e_i's, and at least $4k$ columns separating column $q-1$ from e_k.

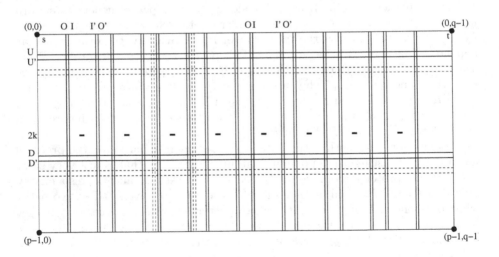

Fig. 1. Associated rows and columns.

Let $\pi \in \Sigma_k$ be any permutation of k symbols. Let us show that there is a simple path from s to t, passing through e_i from x_i to y_i for every i, in the order $e_{\pi(1)}, e_{\pi(2)}, \dots, e_{\pi(k)}$. To each $e_{\pi(i)}$ are associated 4 rows and $4k$ columns. The rows associated to $e_{\pi(i)}$ are rows

$$U_i = 2i - 2, \quad U_i' = 2i - 1, \quad D_i = 2k + 2i - 2, \quad \text{and} \quad D_i' = 2k + 2i - 1.$$

Fig. 1 shows the 4 rows associated to some $e_{\pi(i)}$. U stands for "up", and D for "down". The dashed rows are examples of rows associated to some $e_{\pi(j)}$, $j > i$. Note that, since $p \geqslant 4k + 1$, row $p - 1$ is not associated to any $e_{\pi(i)}$. Let $c_i = i(4k + 2) - 1$ be the column coordinate of x_i, $i = 1, \ldots, k$. The columns associated to $e_{\pi(i)}$ are columns

$$I_{i,j} = c_j - 2i + 1, \ O_{i,j} = c_j - 2i, \ I'_{i,j} = c_j + 2i - 1, \text{ and } O'_{i,j} = c_j + 2i, \ j = 1, \ldots, k.$$

Fig. 1 shows the $4k$ columns associated to some $e_{\pi(i)}$. I stands for "inside", and O for "outside". The dashed columns are examples of columns associated to some $e_{\pi(j)}$, $j > i$. There is no overlapping between associated columns. Moreover, columns $0, \ldots, 2k$ and $4k^2 + 4k, \ldots, q - 1$ are not associated columns.

Now, for $i = 1, \ldots, k$, we define the path P_i as follows. (The construction is illustrated on Fig. 2 where the integer displayed above an edge indicates the order of the edge in the permutation π.)

P_1 starts from node $s = (0, 0)$ following the row U_1 until it reaches column $I_{1,j}$ where $j = \pi(1)$. Then P_1 follows $I_{1,j}$ downward until row $2k$. At this point P_1 follows row $2k$ rightward until it traverses edge $e_{\pi(1)}$. At node y_j, P_1 turns down to reach row $2k + 1$, and follows this row leftward until column $O_{1,j}$. Then it goes upward on $O_{1,j}$ until row U'_1, and finally follows this row until node $(1, 0)$ where it ends.

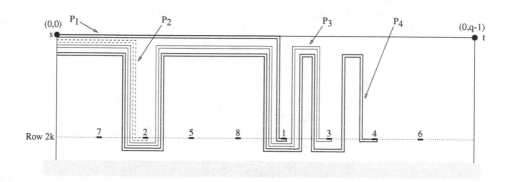

Fig. 2. The path P_i's.

P_i starts from node $(2(i - 1), 0)$. Let $l_1, l_2, \ldots, l_h$ be the indices $l < i$ such that $e_{\pi(l)}$ is on the left of $e_{\pi(i)}$. For instance, on Fig. 2, this sequence is 2, 1, 3, for $e_{\pi(4)}$. Up to relabeling, one can assume, w.l.o.g., that $e_{\pi(l_a)}$ is on the left of $e_{\pi(l_{a+1})}$. Let $j = \pi(i)$. P_i goes rightward from node $(2(i - 1), 0)$ along row U_i until it reaches column I_{i,l_1}. Then it goes downward until it reaches row D_i, and turns right. P_i follows D_i until column I'_{i,l_1}, and then goes upward along that column, until it reaches row U_i. This "detour" around the edges $e_{\pi(l_a)}$'s is repeated for each $1 \leqslant a \leqslant h$. (See for instance the path P_4 on Fig. 2.) More precisely, let $a \in \{1, \ldots, h\}$. P_i remains on U_i until it reaches column I_{i,l_a}. Then it goes downward until it reaches row D_i, and turns right. P_i follows D_i until column I'_{i,l_a}, and then goes upward along that column, until it reaches row U_i again.

After the last detour around $e_{\pi(l_h)}$, P_i goes rightward on U_i until it reaches $I_{i,j}$. Then it goes downward on $I_{i,j}$ until it reaches row $2k$, and turn rightward along that row. P_i follows row $2k$ until it traverses $e_j = e_{\pi(i)}$. At node y_j, P_i turns down to reach row $2k+1$, and follows this row leftward until column $O_{i,j}$. Then it goes upward on $O_{i,j}$ until row U'_i. At this point, P_i starts its journey leftward on U'_i, back to column 0.

More precisely, P_i follows the same shape of path as when it went rightward from column 0 (see Fig. 2). That is, it proceeds along U'_i but during so detours around edges $e_{\pi(l_a)}$'s. Let $a \in \{1, \ldots, h\}$. A detour around $e_{\pi(l_a)}$ consists in leaving U'_i to go downward along O'_{i,l_a} until row D'_i is reached. Then P_i follows D'_i leftward until column O_{i,l_a}, and follows this column upward until it reaches again U'_i. After the last detour (i.e., the detour around $e_{\pi(l_1)}$), P_i follows row U'_i until node $(2i-1, 0)$ where it ends.

The following two properties are satisfied:

P1. For every $1 \leqslant i \leqslant k$, P_i is a simple path.

P2. For every $i \neq j$, P_i and P_j have no node in common. More precisely, the paths fit one into another as displayed on Fig. 3. In this figure, $a < b < i < j$. P_a goes straight above e because there is no need of a detour as P_b is not set yet. P_b traverses e. Both P_i and P_j must go around e. By construction, since $i < j$, they follow different associated rows and columns and therefore do not intersect.

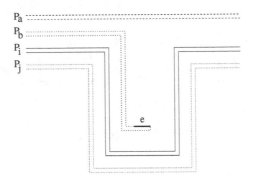

Fig. 3. Two paths P_i and P_j do not intersect.

Now, let P be the following path from s to t:

$$P = P_1, f_1, P_2, f_2, \ldots, P_{k-1}, f_{k-1}, P_k, Q$$

where f_i is the edge between nodes $(2i-1, 0)$ and $(2i, 0)$, and Q is the simple path from node $(2k-1, 0)$ to t following column 0, then row $p-1$, and finally column $q - 1$. From properties $\mathcal{P}1$ and $\mathcal{P}2$, P is a simple path from s to t which traverse edges e_i's in the order $e_{\pi(1)}, e_{\pi(2)}, \ldots, e_{\pi(k)}$.

The construction applies for any permutation $\pi \in \Sigma_k$. Therefore, thanks to Lemma 1, any oblivious end-to-end communication protocol in the $p \times q$ mesh requires headers of at least $\Omega(\log(k!)/k) = \Omega(\log k)$ bits. Since $k = \lfloor \min\{\frac{p-1}{4}, \sqrt{\frac{q}{12}}\} \rfloor$, $\log k = \Omega(\log \min\{p, q\})$ which completes the proof.   □

3   Proofs of Theorems 1 and 2

3.1   Proof of Theorem 1

We use the "excluding grid" theorem of Robertson and Seymour, whose short proofs can be found in [20,21]:

Theorem 4 (Robertson & Seymour [35]). For every integer r there is an integer k such that every graph of tree-width at least k has an $r \times r$ mesh as minor.

So, let us define $f(r)$ as the smallest integer k satisfying Theorem 4. The constructive proof of the excluding grid theorem, given in [21] shows that $f(r) \leqslant 2^{5r^5 \log_2 r}$. Let τ be the tree-width of $G_{s,t}$, i.e., the graph obtained from G by deleting every edge not on a simple path from s to t. Let $r = \lfloor (\frac{1}{5} \log_2 \tau)^{1/6} \rfloor$. By the excluding grid theorem, $G_{s,t}$ contains an $r \times r$ mesh as minor since $\tau \geqslant f(r)$.

Now, any oblivious end-to-end protocol on $G_{s,t}$ requires headers of size as least as large as those required for the $r \times r$ mesh (recall that the end-to-end problem is closed under minor taking, as shown by Alder and Fich [1]). By Theorem 3, the headers for $r \times r$ meshes are of size at least $\Omega(\log r) = \Omega(\log \log \tau)$, which completes the proof of Theorem 1.

Remark. Any polynomial upper bound on $f(r)$ in r would prove a lower bound of $\Omega(\log \tau)$ on the header size. So far, the best known upper bound on $f(r)$ is $f(r) \leqslant 2^{9r^5}$ (cf. [36]). It is conjectured that the correct order of magnitude for $f(r)$ is $O(r^2 \log r)$.

3.2   Proof of Theorem 2

For $r \geqslant 0$, and $c > 0$, two integers, the $r \times c$ cylinder is the graph composed of r radial lines and c circles as shown on Fig. 4.

Theorem 5 (Robertson & Seymour [34], p. 62). If G is planar and has no $r \times r$ cylinder as minor, then G has tree-width at most $\frac{3}{2}(r^2 + 2r) - 2$.

It is clear that an $r \times r$ cylinder contains an $r \times r$ mesh as minor. Let $\tau = \text{tw}(G_{s,t})$, and let $r = \lfloor \sqrt{\tau/5} \rfloor$ so that $\tau > \frac{3}{2}(r^2 + 2r) - 2$. Thus, by Theorem 5, $G_{s,t}$ contains the $r \times r$ mesh as minor. Therefore the header size for end-to-end communication in $G_{s,t}$ is at least the header size for end-to-end communication in the $r \times r$ mesh, that is at least $\Omega(\log r) = \Omega(\log \tau)$ by Theorem 3. This completes the proof of Theorem 2.

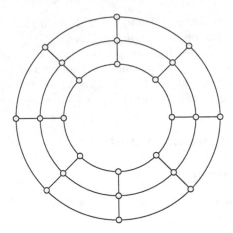

Fig. 4. An 8×3 cylinder.

4   Conclusion

This paper provides lower bounds on the header-size for arbitrary and planar graphs. The design of matching upper bounds remains open. Note that the tree-width of a graph G can be alternatively defined as the minimum k for which G is a partial k-tree, i.e., a subtree of a k-tree, where k-trees are inductively defined as follows: A clique with $k+1$ nodes is a k-tree; given a k-tree T with n nodes, a k-tree with $n+1$ nodes is constructed by adding a new node x to T, x being adjacent to every node of a k-clique of T, and non adjacent to any of the $n-k$ other nodes of T. This definition connects the tree-width of a graph with its triangulation. Recall that a graph is triangulated if it contains no chordless cycle of length greater than three. A triangulation of a graph G is then a triangulated graph H with the same set of nodes and such that G is a subgraph of H. The tree-width of a graph G is then the maximum size (minus one) of a clique in a minimal triangulation of G, i.e., a triangulation of G with the minimum number of edges. Solving the end-to-end communication problem in k-trees may be the good way to solve the problem for arbitrary graphs, although it looks like a challenging task.

References

1. M. Adler and F. Fich. The Complexity of End-to-End Communication in Memory-less Networks. In 18th ACM Symposium on Principles of Distributed Computing (PODC), pages 239–248, 1999.
2. M. Adler, F. Fich, L. Goldberg, and M. Paterson. Tight Size Bounds for Packet Headers in Narrow Meshes. In 27th Int. Colloquium on Automata, Languages and Programming (ICALP), Springer, LNCS 1853, pages 756–767, 2000.
3. Y. Afek, B. Awerbuch, and E. Gafni. Applying Static Network Protocols to Dynamic Networks. In 28th IEEE Annual Symposium on Foundations of Computer Science (FOCS), pages 358–370, 1987.

4. Y. Afek, and E. Gafni. End-to-End Communication in Unreliable Networks. In 7th ACM Symposium on Principles of Distributed Computing (PODC), pages 131–148, 1988.

5. Y. Afek, and E. Gafni. Bootstrap Network Resynchonization. In 10th ACM Symposium on Principles of Distributed Computing (PODC), pages 295–307, 1991.

6. Y. Afek, H. Attiya, A. Fekete, M. Fischer, N. Lynch, Y. Mansour, D.-W. Wang, and L. Zuck. Reliable Communication Over Unreliable Channels. Journal of the ACM 41(6):1267–1297 (1994).

7. Y. Afek, B. Awerbuch, E. Gafni, Y. Mansour, A. Rosén, and N. Shavit. Slide–The Key to Polynomial End-to-End Communication. Journal of Algorithms 22(1):158–186 (1997).

8. A. Aho, J. Ullman, A. Wyler, and M. Yannakakis. Bounds on the Size and Transmission Rate of Communication Protocols. Computers and Math with Applications 8(3):205–214 (1982).

9. E. Amir. Efficient approximation for triangulation of minimum treewidth. In 17th Conference on Uncertainty in Artificial Intelligence (UAI), 2001.

10. S. Arnborg. Efficient Algorithms for Combinatorial Problems on Graphs with Bounded Decomposability–A Survey. BIT 25:2–23 (1985).

11. S. Arnborg, D. Corneil, and A. Proskurowski. Complexity of Finding Embeddings in a k-Tree. SIAM J. Alg. Disc. Meth. 8:277–284 (1987).

12. B. Awerbuch and S. Even. Reliable Broadcast Protocols in Unreliable Networks. Networks 16:381–396 (1986).

13. B. Awerbuch, Y. Mansour, and N. Shavit. Polynomial End-to-End Communication. In 30th IEEE Annual Symposium on Foundations of Computer Science (FOCS), pages 358–363, 1989.

14. B. Awerbuch, O. Goldreich, and A. Herzberg. A Quantitative Approach to Dynamic Networks. In 9th ACM Symposium on Principles of Distributed Computing (PODC), pages 189–203, 1990.

15. K. Bartlett, R. Scantleburg, and P. Wilkinson. A Note on Reliable, Full-Duplex Transmission over Half-Duplex Links. Communication of the ACM 12:260–261 (1969).

16. H. Bodlaender. A Tourist Guide through Treewidth. Acta Cybernetica 11:1–21 (1993).

17. H. Bodlaender. A Linear-Time Algorithm for Finding Tree-Decompositions of Small Treewidth. SIAM Journal on Computing, 25:1305–1317, 1996.

18. H. Bodlaender, J. Gilbert, H. Hafsteinsson, and T. Kloks. Approximating Treewidth, Pathwidth, Frontsize, and Shortest Elimination Tree. Journal of Algorithms 18:238–255 (1995).

19. V. Bouchitté, D. Kratsch, H. Müller, and I. Todinca. On treewidth approximations. In 1st Cologne-Twente Workshop on Graphs and Combinatorial Optimization (CTW), 2001.

20. R. Diestel. Graph Theory (2nd edition). Springer-Verlag, New York, 2000.

21. R. Diestel, T.R. Jensen, K.Y. Gorbunov, and C. Thomassen. Highly connected sets and the excluded grid theorem. Journal of Combin. Theory B 75:61–73 (1999).

22. S. Dolev and J. Welch. Crash Resilient Communication in Dynamic Networks. IEEE Transactions on Computers 46(1):14–26 (1997).

23. A. Fekete, and N. Lynch. The Need for Headers: An Impossibility Result for Communication over Unreliable Channels. In 1st Int. Conf. on Theories of Concurrency: Unification and Extension (CONCUR), Springer, LNCS 458, pages 199–215, 1990.

24. A. Fekete, N. Lynch, Y. Mansour, and J. Spinelli. The Impossibility of Implementing Reliable Communication in the Face of Crashes. Journal of the ACM 40(3):1087–1107 (1993).
25. F. Fich. End-to-End Communication Protocols. In 2nd Int. Conference on Principles of Distributed Systems (OPODIS), Hermes, pages 37–43, 1998.
26. F. Fich and A. Jakoby. Short Headers Suffice for Communication in a DAG with Link Failures. In 14th International Symposium on Distributed Computing (DISC), Springer, LNCS, pages 360–373, 2000.
27. O. Goldreich, A. Herzberg, and Y. Mansour. Source to Destination Communication in the Presence of Faults. In 8th ACM Symposium on Principles of Distributed Computing (PODC), pages 85–101, 1989.
28. A. Herzberg. Connection-Based Communication in Dynamic Networks. In 11th ACM Symposium on Principles of Distributed Computing (PODC), pages 13–24, 1992.
29. E. Kushilevitz, R. Ostrovsky, and A. Rosén. Log-Space Polynomial End-to-End Communication. In 28th ACM Symposium on Theory of Computing (STOC), pages 559–568, 1995.
30. R. Ladner, A. LaMarca, and E. Tempero. Counting Protocol for Reliable End-to-End Transmission. Journal of Computer and System Sciences 56:96–111 (1998).
31. Y. Mansour and B. Schieber. The Intractability of bounded Protocols for On-Line Sequence Transmission over Non-FIFO Channels. Journal of the ACM 39(4):783–799 (1992).
32. J. Postel. Internet Protocol. Internet Engineering Task Force Request For Comments 791, 1981.
33. B. Reed. Finding Approximate Separators and Computing Treewidth Quickly. In 24th ACM Symposium on Theory of Computing (STOC), pages 221–228 (1992).
34. N. Robertson, and P.D. Seymour. Graph Minors. III. Planar Tree-Width. Journal of Combin. Theory B 36:49–64 (1984).
35. N. Robertson, and P.D. Seymour. Graph Minors. V. Excluding a planar graph. Journal of Combin. Theory B 41:92–114 (1986).
36. N. Robertson, P.D. Seymour, and R. Thomas. Quickly excluding a planar graph. Journal of Combin. Theory B 62:323–348 (1994).
37. N. Stenning. A Data Transfer Protocol. Computer Networks 1(2):99–110 (1976).
38. E. Tempero, and R. Ladner. Recoverable Sequence Transmission Protocols. Journal of the ACM 42(5):1059–1090 (1995).
39. U. Vishkin. A Distributed Orientation Algorithm. IEEE Transaction on Information Theory 29, 624–629 (1983).
40. D.-W. Wang, and L. Zuck. Tight Bounds for the Sequence Transmission Problem. In 8th ACM Symposium on Principles of Distributed Computing (PODC), pages 73–83, 1989.
41. D.-W. Wang, and L. Zuck. Real-Time Sequence Transmission Problem. In 10th ACM Symposium on Principles of Distributed Computing (PODC), pages 111–124, 1991.

Efficient Gossip and Robust Distributed Computation*

Chryssis Georgiou[1], Dariusz R. Kowalski[1,2], and Alex A. Shvartsman[1,3]

[1] Department of Computer Science and Engineering,
University of Connecticut, Storrs, CT 06269, USA
[2] Instytut Informatyki, Uniwersytet Warszawski, Warsaw, Poland
[3] Computer Science and Artificial Intelligence Laboratory,
Massachusetts Institute of Technology, Cambridge, MA 02139, USA
{cg2,kowalski,aas}@cse.uconn.edu

Abstract. This paper presents an efficient deterministic gossip algorithm for p synchronous, crash-prone, message-passing processors. The algorithm has time complexity $T = O(\log^2 p)$ and message complexity $M = O(p^{1+\varepsilon})$, for any $\varepsilon > 0$. This substantially improves the message complexity of the previous best algorithm that has $M = O(p^{1.77})$, while maintaining the same time complexity. The strength of the new algorithm is demonstrated by constructing a deterministic algorithm for performing n tasks in this distributed setting. Previous solutions used coordinator or check-pointing approaches, immediately incurring a work penalty $\Omega(n + f \cdot p)$ for f crashes, or relied on strong communication primitives, such as reliable broadcast, or had work too close to the trivial $\Theta(p \cdot n)$ bound of oblivious algorithms. The new algorithm uses p crash-prone processors to perform n similar and idempotent tasks so long as one processor remains active. The work of the algorithm is $W = O(n + p \cdot \min\{f + 1, \log^3 p\})$ and its message complexity is $M = O(fp^\varepsilon + p \min\{f + 1, \log p\})$, for any $\varepsilon > 0$. This substantially improves the work complexity of previous solutions using simple point-to-point messaging, while "meeting or beating" the corresponding message complexity bounds. The new algorithms use communication graphs and permutations with certain combinatorial properties that are shown to exist. The algorithms are correct for any permutations, and in particular, the same expected bounds can be achieved using random permutations.

1 Introduction

The effectiveness of distributed solutions for specific problems depends on our ability to exploit parallelism in multiprocessor systems. Gathering and disseminating information in distributed settings is a key element in obtaining efficient solutions for many computation problems. The *gossip* problem is an abstraction of information propagation activity: given a set of processors where each processor initially has some piece of information, called *rumor*, the goal is to have every processor learn each rumor.

In systems of larger scale the set of processors available to a computation may dynamically change due to failures, due to processors being reassigned to other tasks, or

---

* This research was supported by the NSF Grants 9988304, 0121277, and 0311368. The work of the second author was supported by the NSF-NATO Award 0209588. The work of the third author was supported by the NSF CAREER Award 9984778.

becoming unavailable for other reasons. Thus it is necessary to design algorithms that combine efficient parallelism with the ability to tolerate perturbations in the computing medium. We consider the case where synchronous processors are subject to crashes, i.e., a processor stops and does not perform any further actions. This models both the common failure assumption and the situation where processors are reassigned to a new computation. In this setting, it may not be always possible to collect the rumor of a processor that crashes, even if some other processors learned the rumor before it crashed, since these processors may crash as well. Hence, we consider the gossip problem solved if (a) each non-faulty processor learns the rumors of all other non-faulty processors, and (b) for each crashed processor, all non-faulty processors either learn its rumor or learn that the processor crashed.

In this paper we first consider the gossip problem with p processors in a synchronous message passing system and under an adaptive adversary that can cause up to $f < p$ processor crashes. We present a new algorithm solving the gossip problem that obtains a substantially better message complexity then the previous best known solution. We demonstrate the advantage of the new algorithm by showing how to solve a standard problem of performing work in a distributed setting. Specifically, our new gossip algorithm allows us to derive a more efficient solution for the *Do-All* problem of Dwork, Halpern and Waarts [7]: given p processors, perform n tasks in the presence of up to $f < p$ processor crashes. The *Do-All* problem is considered solved, when all tasks are performed and at least one non-faulty processor knows about this.

Background and prior results. The efficiency of algorithmic solutions to the gossip problem in synchronous message-passing models is measured in terms of time and the number of point-to-point messages. The best deterministic solution for the gossip problem under adaptive adversaries that cause processor crashes is due to Chlebus and Kowalski [5]. Other work on the gossip problem in failure-prone settings dealt with link failures or processor failures under oblivious adversaries, or considered random failures – see the survey by Pelc [13]. A trivial solution to the gossip problem is to have every processor send its rumor to all other processors. This requires $O(1)$ time and $O(p^2)$ messages. To achieve better message complexity, Chlebus and Kowalski [5] trade computation steps for messages. Their algorithm runs in $O(\log^2 p)$ time, sends $O(p^{1.77})$ point-to-point messages, and tolerates up to $p - 1$ crashes. They also presented a lower bound for the gossip problem that states that the time has to be at least $\Omega(\log p / \log \log p)$ in order for the message complexity to be $O(p \, \text{polylog} \, p)$. They also showed how to use their gossip algorithm to obtain an efficient synchronous algorithm for the *consensus* problem (processors must agree on a common value).

Algorithms for the *Do-All* problem in the message-passing models are evaluated according to the number of computation steps taken in performing the tasks (i.e., the *available processor steps* [11]), and according to their communication efficiency. Trivial solutions to *Do-All* are obtained by having each processor obliviously perform each of the n tasks. Such solutions have work $\Theta(n \cdot p)$ and require no communication. To achieve better work efficiency we trade messages for computation steps.

Algorithms solving *Do-All* have been provided by Dwork, Halpern and Waarts [7], by De Prisco, Mayer and Yung [6], and by Galil, Mayer and Yung [8]. (The analysis in [7] uses task-oriented work that allows processors to idle.) The algorithm by Galil *et al.* [8]

has work $O(n + fp)$ and message complexity $O(fp^\varepsilon + p \min\{f + 1, \log p\})$ These deterministic algorithms rely on single coordinators or checkpointing. Such strategies are subject to the lower bound of $\Omega(n + (f+1)p)$ on work [6]. The solution of Chlebus *et al.* [3,9] beats this lower bound by using multiple coordinators. It has work $O(\log f(n + p \log p / \log(p/f)))$ and message complexity $O(n + p \log p / \log(p/f) + pf)$ when $f \leq p / \log p$, and work $O(\log f(n + p \log p / \log \log p))$ and message complexity $O(n + p \log p / \log \log p + pf)$ when $f > p / \log p$, however it uses *reliable broadcast*.

We seek solutions that obtain better work and message efficiency and that use the conventional point-to-point messaging. We see the key to such solutions in the ability to share knowledge among processors by means that are less authoritarian than the use of coordinators. Chlebus *et al.* [4] pursued such an approach and developed an algorithm with the combined work and message complexity of $O(n + p^{1.77})$, however the work bound is still close to the quadratic bound obtained by oblivious algorithms.

An important aspect of *Do-All* algorithms is the sequencing of tasks. The algorithms of Anderson and Woll [2] for the shared-memory model and of Malewicz *et al.* [12] for partitionable networks use approaches that provide processors with sequences of tasks based on permutations with certain combinatorial properties.

Contributions. Our objectives are to improve the efficiency of solutions for the gossip problem with p processors and to demonstrate the utility of the new solution. The first objective is achieved by providing a new solution for the gossip problem with the help of communication over expander graphs and by using permutations with specific combinatorial properties. The second objective is met by using the gossip algorithm to solve the p-processor, n-task *Do-All* problem using an algorithmic paradigm that does not rely on coordinators, checkpointing, or reliable broadcast. Instead we use an approach where processors share information using our gossip algorithm, where the point-to-point messaging is constrained by means of a communication graph that represents a certain subset of the edges in a complete communication network. Our approach also equips processors with schedules of tasks based on permutations that we show to exist. Thus the two major contributions presented in this paper are as follows:

1. We present a new algorithm for the *gossip* problem that for p processors has time complexity $O(\log^2 p)$ and message complexity $O(p^{1+\varepsilon})$, for any $\varepsilon > 0$.

Our gossip algorithm substantially improves on the message complexity $M = O(p^{1.77})$ of the previously best known algorithm of Chlebus and Kowalski [5], that has the same asymptotic time complexity.

2. We demonstrate the strength of our gossip result by presenting a new algorithm for p processors that solves the *Do-All* problem with n tasks in the presence of any pattern of f crashes $(f < p)$ with work complexity $W = O(n + p \cdot \min\{f + 1, \log^3 p\})$ and message complexity $M = O(fp^\varepsilon + p \min\{f + 1, \log p\})$, for any $\varepsilon > 0$. The algorithm uses our new gossip algorithm as a building block to implement information sharing.

This result improves the work complexity $W = O(n + fp)$ of the algorithm of Galil *et al.* cited earlier [8], while obtaining the same message complexity. We also improve on the result of Chlebus *et al.* [4] that has $W = O(n + p^{1.77})$ and $M = O(p^{1.77})$. Unlike the algorithm of Chlebus *et al.* [3] that has comparable work complexity but relies on reliable broadcast, our algorithm uses simple point-to-point messaging.

The complexity analysis of our algorithms relies on permutations that we show to exist. The required permutations can be identified through exhaustive search, and it is an open problem how to construct such permutations efficiently. We show that the algorithms are correct when using arbitrary permutations, however in that case the efficiency cannot be guaranteed. When using random permutations, then the time, work and message bounds become expected bounds. Note that when using random permutations our algorithms compare favorably to the previous randomized solutions for adaptive adversaries [5,4].

Document structure. We define the model of computation, the problems, and complexity measures in Section 2. In Section 3 we develop combinatorial tools used in the analysis of algorithms. The new gossip algorithm and its analysis is in Section 4. In Section 5 we give the new *Do-All* algorithm and its analysis. Finally, in Section 6 we discuss future work. Complete proofs appear in the full version of the paper [10].

2   Models and Definitions

Here we define the models, the problems we consider, and the complexity measures.

Distributed setting. We consider a system consisting of p synchronous message-passing processors; each processor has a unique identifier (pid) from the set $[p] = \{1, 2, \dots, p\}$. We assume that p is fixed and is known to all processors. Processor activities are structured in terms of synchronous *steps*, each taking constant time.

Model of failures. A processor may crash at any moment and once crashed it does not restart. We let an omniscient *adversary* impose failures, and we use the term *failure pattern* to denote the set of crashes. A *failure model* $\mathcal{F}$ is the set of all failure patterns. For a failure pattern F, we define its *size* $|F|$ to be the number of crashes. We let f denote the maximum number of crashes that the adversary can cause. To guarantee progress, we assume that $f < p$. Formally, $|F| \leq f < p$, for any $F \in \mathcal{F}$. The processors have no knowledge of F, $|F|$, or f (in particular, we require that algorithms must be correct for any F as long as $|F| < p$).

Communication. We assume a known upper bound on message delays. Specifically, each processor can send a message to any subset of processors in one step and the message is delivered to each (non-faulty) recipient in the next step. Messages are not corrupted and are not lost in transit. We do not assume reliable multicast: if a processor crashes during its multicast then an arbitrary subset of the recipients gets the message.

The *Gossip* problem. We define the *Gossip* problem as follows:

Given a set of p processors, where initially each processor has a distinct piece of information, called a rumor, the goal is for each processor to learn all the rumors in the presence of any pattern of crashes. The following conditions must be satisfied:

(1) Correctness: (a) All non-faulty processors learn the rumors of all non-faulty processors, (b) For every failed processor v, non-faulty processor w either knows that v has failed, or w knows v's rumor.

(2) Termination: Every non-faulty processor eventually terminates its protocol.

We let $Gossip(p, f)$ stand for the *Gossip* problem for p processors (and p rumors) and any pattern of crashes $F \in \mathcal{F}$ such that $|F| \leq f < p$.

Tasks. We define a *task* to be a computation that can be performed by any processor in at most one time step; its execution does not dependent on any other task. The tasks are also *idempotent*, i.e., executing a task many times and/or concurrently has the same effect as executing the task once. Tasks are uniquely identified by their task identifiers (tid) from the set $\mathcal{T} = [n]$. We assume that n is fixed and is known to all processors.

The *Do-All* problem. We define the *Do-All* problem as follows:

> Given a set $\mathcal{T}$ of n tasks, perform all tasks using p processors, in the presence of any pattern of crashes. The following conditions must be satisfied:
> (1) Correctness: All n tasks are completed and at least one processor knows this.
> (2) Termination: Every non-faulty processor eventually terminates its protocol.

We let $Do\text{-}All(n, p, f)$ stand for *Do-All* for n tasks, p processors, and any pattern of crashes with $|F| \leq f < p$. We consider $Do\text{-}All(n, p, f)$ as **solved** when all tasks are done and at least one processor knows about it.

Measuring efficiency. We define the measures of efficiency used in studying the complexity of the *Gossip* and the *Do-All* problems. For the *Gossip* problem we consider *time complexity* and *message complexity*. Time complexity is measured as the number of parallel steps taken by the processors by the *termination time*, where the termination time is defined to be the first step when the correctness condition is satisfied and at least one (non-faulty) processor terminates its protocol.[1]

Definition 1. *If a p-processor algorithm solves a problem in the presence of a failure pattern F in the model $\mathcal{F}$ by time $\tau(p, F)$, then its time complexity T is defined as* $T(p, f) = \max_{F \in \mathcal{F}, |F| \leq f} \{\tau(p, F)\}$.

Message complexity is measured as the total number of point-to-point messages sent by the processors by termination time. When a processor communicates using a multicast, its cost is the total number of point-to-point messages. For a p-processor computation subject to a failure pattern $F \in \mathcal{F}$, denote by $M_i(p, F)$ the number of point-to-point messages sent by the processors in step i of the computation.

Definition 2. *If a p-processor algorithm solves a problem in the presence of a failure pattern F in the model $\mathcal{F}$ by time $\tau(p, F)$, then its message complexity M is defined as* $M(p, f) = \max_{F \in \mathcal{F}, |F| \leq f} \{\sum_{i \leq \tau(p, F)} M_i(p, F)\}$.

Where message complexity M depends on the size of the problem n, we similarly define it as $M(n, p, f)$.

In measuring work complexity, we assume that a processor performs a unit of work per unit of time. Note that the idling processors consume a unit of work per step. For a p-processor, n-task computation subject to a failure pattern $F \in \mathcal{F}$, denote by $P_i(n, p, F)$ the number of processors surviving step i of the computation.

---

[1] The complexity results in this paper, except for the results in Section 5.3, also hold for a stronger definition of the termination time that requires that each non-faulty processor terminates its protocol.

Definition 3. *If a p-processor algorithm solves a problem of size n in the the presence of a failure pattern F in the model $\mathcal{F}$ by time $\tau(n, p, F)$, then its work W is defined as $W(n, p, f) = \max_{F \in \mathcal{F}, |F| \leq f} \{\sum_{i \leq \tau(n, p, F)} P_i(n, p, F)\}$.*

3   Combinatorial Tools

We now develop tools used to control the message complexity of our gossip algorithm.

Communication Graphs. We now describe communication graphs—conceptual data structures that constrain communication patterns. Here processor v can send a message to any processor w that v considers to be non-faulty and that is a neighbor of v according to the communication graph. We use the following terminology and notation. Let $G = (V, E)$ be a (undirected) graph, with V the set of nodes (representing processors, $|V| = p$) and E the set of edges. For a subgraph G_Q of G induced by Q ($Q \subseteq V$), we define $N_G(Q)$ to be the subset of V consisting of all the nodes in Q and their neighbors in G. The maximum node degree of graph G is denoted by Δ.

Let f denote a positive integer with the property that even if f nodes are removed from V, the graph induced by the remaining nodes will guarantee "progress in communication". Let G_{V_i} be the subgraph of G induced by the sets V_i of nodes (corresponding to processors that haven't failed by step i). We assume that sets V_i have the following two properties: $V_{i+1} \subseteq V_i$ and $|V_i| \geq p - f$.

Intuitively "progress in communication" according to graph G is achieved if there is at least one "good" connected component G_{Q_i} of G_{V_i}, which evolves suitably with time and satisfies the following properties: (i) the component contains "sufficiently many" nodes so that collectively that have learned "suitably many" rumors; (ii) it has "sufficiently small" diameter so that information can be shared among the nodes of the component without "undue delay"; and (iii) $Q_{i+1} \subseteq Q_i$ to guarantee consistency of computation. We formalize the above intuitive definition of G_{Q_i} as follows:

Definition 4. *Graph $G = (V, E)$ has the* Compact Chain Property CCP (p, f, ε), *if:*
I. *The maximum degree of G is at most $\left(\frac{p}{p-f}\right)^{1+\varepsilon}$,*
II. *For a given sequence $V_1 \supseteq \ldots \supseteq V_k$ ($V = V_1$), where $|V_k| \geq p - f$, there is a sequence $Q_1 \supseteq \ldots \supseteq Q_k$ such that for every $i = 1, \ldots, k$:*
(a) $Q_i \subseteq V_i$, **(b)** $|Q_i| \geq |V_i|/7$, *and* **(c)** *the diameter of G_{Q_i} is at most $31 \log p$.*

We prove existence of graphs satisfying CCP for some parameters.

Lemma 1. *For $p > 2$, every $f < p$ and constant $\varepsilon > 0$, there is a graph G of $O(p)$ nodes satisfying* CCP (p, f, ε).

Sets of Permutations and their Properties. We deal with sets of permutations that satisfy certain properties. These permutations are used by the processors in the gossip algorithm to decide the subset of processors they will communicate their information with at a given point of the computation. Consider the group S_t of all permutations on set $\{1, \ldots, t\}$, with the composition operation $\circ$, and identity e_t. For permutation $\pi = \langle \pi(1), \ldots, \pi(t) \rangle$ in S_t, we say that $\pi(i)$ is a d-left-to-right maximum (d-lrm in short), if there are less than d previous elements in π of value greater than $\pi(i)$, i.e., $|\{j < i : \pi(j) > \pi(i)\}| < d$.

Let Υ and Ψ, $\Upsilon \subseteq \Psi$, be two sets containing permutations from S_t. For every σ in S_t, let $\sigma \circ \Upsilon$ denote the set of permutation $\{\sigma \circ \pi : \pi \in \Upsilon\}$. For given permutation π, let (d)-LRM(π) denote the number of d-left-to-right maxima in π. Now we define the notion of *surfeit*[2]. For a given Υ and permutation $\sigma \in S_t$, let $(d, |\Upsilon|)$-Surf(Υ, σ) be equal to $\sum_{\pi \in \Upsilon}(d)$-LRM$(\sigma^{-1} \circ \pi)$. We then define the (d, q)-surfeit on set Ψ as (d, q)-Surf$(\Psi) = \max\{(d, |\Upsilon|)$-Surf$(\Upsilon, \sigma) : \Upsilon \subseteq \Psi, |\Upsilon| = q, \sigma \in S_t\}$.

We obtain the following results for (d, q)-surfeit.

Theorem 1. *For a random set of p permutations Ψ from S_t, the event "for every positive integers d and $q \le p$, (d, q)-Surf$(\Psi) > t \ln t + 10qd \ln(t + p)$" holds with probability at most $e^{-t \ln t \cdot \ln(9/e^2)}$.*

Using the probabilistic method [1] we obtain the following result.

Corollary 1. *There is a set of p permutations Ψ from S_t such that, for every positive integers d and $q \le p$, (d, q)-Surf$(\Psi) \le t \ln t + 10qd \ln(t + p)$.*

The efficiency of our gossip algorithm relies on the existence of the permutations in the thesis of the corollary (however the algorithm is correct for any permutations).

4   The Gossip Algorithm

Our new gossiping algorithm, called GOSSIP$_\varepsilon$, improves on the algorithm in [5]. The improvement are obtained by using the better properties of communication graphs described in Lemma 1, and by using many phases instead of the two phases in [5]. The challenges motivating our techniques are: (i) how to assure low communication during every phase, and (ii) how to switch between phases without a "huge complexity hit".

4.1   Description of Algorithm GOSSIP$_\varepsilon$

Suppose constant $0 < \varepsilon < 1/3$ is given. The algorithm proceeds in a loop that is repeated until each non-faulty processor v learns either the rumor of every processor w or that w has failed. A single iteration of the loop is called an *epoch*. The algorithm terminates after $\lceil 1/\varepsilon \rceil - 1$ epochs. Each of the first $\lceil 1/\varepsilon \rceil - 2$ epochs consists of $\alpha \log^2 p$ *phases*, where α is such that $\alpha \log^2 p$ is the smallest integer that is larger than $341 \log^2 p$. Each phase is divided into two *stages*, the *update* stage, and the *communication* stage. In the update stage processors update their local knowledge regarding other processors' rumor (known/unknown) and condition (failed/operational) and in the communication stage processors exchange their local knowledge (more momentarily). We say that processor v *heard about processor w* if either v knows the rumor of w or it knows that w has failed. Epoch $\lceil 1/\varepsilon \rceil - 1$ is the terminating epoch where each processor sends a message to all the processors that it haven't heard about, requesting their rumor.

---

[2] We will show that *surfeit* relates to the redundant activity in our algorithms i.e., "overdone" activity, or literally "surfeit".

Iterating epochs	Terminating epoch ($\lceil 1/\varepsilon \rceil - 1$)
for $\ell = 1$ **to** $\lceil 1/\varepsilon \rceil - 2$ **do**	update stage;
if BUSY is empty **then**	**if** $status = $ collector **then**
set $status$ to idle;	**send** $\langle$ACTIVE, BUSY, RUMORS, call$\rangle$ to
NEIGHB$= \{v : v \in$ ACTIVE $\wedge\ v \in N_{G_\ell}\}$;	each processor in WAITING;
repeat $\alpha \log^2 p$ times	**receive** messages;
update stage;	**send** $\langle$ ACTIVE, BUSY, RUMORS, reply$\rangle$ to
communication stage;	each processor in ANSWER;
	receive messages;
	update RUMORS;

Fig. 1. Algorithm GOSSIP$_\varepsilon$. Code for processor v.

The pseudocode of the algorithm is given in Figure 1 (we assume, where needed, that every **if-then** has an implicit **else** clause containing the necessary number of no-ops to match the length of the code in the **then** clause). The correctness of the algorithm is shown in the full paper [10].

Local knowledge and Messages. Initially each processor v has its $rumor_v$ and permutation π_v from a set Ψ of permutations on $[p]$, such that Ψ satisfies the thesis of Corollary 1. Moreover, each processor v is associated with the variable $status_v$. Initially $status_v = $ collector (and we say that v is a collector), meaning that v has not heard from all processors yet. Once v hears from all other processors, then $status_v$ is set to informer (and we say that v is an informer), meaning that now v will inform the other processors of its status and knowledge. When processor v learns that all non-faulty processors w also have $status_w = $ informer then at the beginning of the next epoch, $status_v$ becomes idle (and we say that v idles), meaning that v idles until termination, but it might send responses to messages (see call-messages below).

Each processor maintains several lists and sets. We now describe the lists maintained by processor v. List ACTIVE$_v$ contains the pids of the processors that v considers to be non-faulty. Initially, list ACTIVE$_v$ contains all p pids. List BUSY$_v$ contains the pids of the processors that v consider as collectors. Initially list BUSY$_v$ contains all pids except from v, *permuted according to* π_v. List WAITING$_v$ contains the pids of the processors that v did not hear from. Initially list WAITING$_v$ contains all pids except from v, *permuted according to* π_v. List RUMORS$_v$ contains pairs of the form $(w, rumor_w)$ or $(w, \perp)$. The pair $(w, rumor_w)$ denotes the fact that processor v knows processor w's rumor and the pair $(w, \perp)$ means that v does not know w's rumor, but it knows that w has failed. Initially list RUMORS$_v$ contains the pair $(v, rumor_v)$.

A processor can send a message to any other processor, but to lower the message complexity, in some cases (see communication stage) we require processors to communicate according to a conceptual communication graph G_ℓ, $\ell \leq \lceil 1/\varepsilon \rceil - 2$, that satisfies property $CCP(p, p - p^{1-\ell\varepsilon}, \varepsilon)$ (see Definition 4). When processor v sends a message m to another processor w, m contains lists ACTIVE$_v$, BUSY$_v$ RUMORS$_v$, and the variable $type$. When $type = $ call, processor v requires an answer from processor w and we refer to such message as a *call-message*. When $type = $ reply, no answer is required—this message is sent as a response to a call-message.

We now present the sets maintained by processor v. Set ANSWER_v contains the pids of the processors that v received a call-message. Initially set ANSWER_v is empty. Set CALLING_v contains the pids of the processors that v will send a call-message. Initially CALLING_v is empty. Set NEIGHB_v contains the pids of the processors that are in ACTIVE_v and that according to the communication graph G_ℓ, for a given epoch ℓ, are neighbors of v ($\text{NEIGHB}_v = \{w : w \in \text{ACTIVE}_v \wedge w \in N_{G_\ell}(v)\}$). Initially, NEIGHB_v contains all neighbors of v (all nodes in $N_{G_1}(v)$).

Communication stage. In this stage the processors communicate in an attempt to obtain information from other processors. This stage contains 4 *sub-stages*. In the first sub-stage, every processor v that is either a collector or an informer (i.e., $status_v \neq \texttt{idle}$) sends message $\langle \text{ACTIVE}_v, \text{BUSY}_v, \text{RUMORS}_v, \texttt{call} \rangle$ to every processor in CALLING_v. The idle processors do not send any messages in this sub-stage. In the second sub-stage, all processors (collectors, informers and idling) collect the information sent to by the other processors in the previous sub-stage. Specifically, processor v collects lists ACTIVE_w, BUSY_w and RUMORS_w of every processor w that received a call-message from and v inserts w in set ANSWER_v. In the third sub-stage, every processor (regardless of its status) responds to each processor that received a call-message from. Specifically, processor v sends message $\langle \text{ACTIVE}_v, \text{BUSY}_v, \text{RUMORS}_v, \texttt{reply} \rangle$ to the processors in ANSWER_v and empties ANSWER_v. In the fourth and final sub-stage, the processors receive the responses to their call-messages.

Update stage. In this stage each processor v updates its local knowledge based on the messages it received in the *last communication stage*. If $status_v = \texttt{idle}$, then v idles. We now present the six **update rules** and their processing. Note that the rules are not disjoint, but we apply them in the order from (r1) to (r6):

(r1) Updating BUSY_v or RUMORS_v: For every processor w in CALLING_v (i) if v is an informer, it removes w from BUSY_v, (ii) if v is a collector and RUMORS_w was included in one of the messages that v received, then v adds the pair $(w, rumor_w)$ in RUMORS_v and, (iii) if v is a collector but RUMORS_w was not included in one of the messages that v received, then v adds the pair $(w, \perp)$ in RUMORS_v.

(r2) Updating RUMORS_v and WAITING_v: For every processor w in $[p]$, (i) if $(w, rumor_w)$ is not in RUMORS_v and v learns the rumor of w from some other processor that received a message from, then v adds $(w, rumor_w)$ in RUMORS_v, (ii) if both $(w, rumor_w)$ and $(w, \perp)$ are in RUMORS_v, then v removes $(w, \perp)$ from RUMORS_v, and (iii) if either of $(w, rumor_w)$ or $(w, \perp)$ is in RUMORS_v and w is in WAITING_v, then v removes w from WAITING_v.

(r3) Updating BUSY_v: For every processor w in BUSY_v, if v receives a message from processor v' so that w is not in $\text{BUSY}_{v'}$, then v removes w from BUSY_v.

(r4) Updating ACTIVE_v and NEIGHB_v: For every processor w in ACTIVE_v (i) if w is not in NEIGHB_v and v received a message from processor v' so that w is not in $\text{ACTIVE}_{v'}$, then v removes w from ACTIVE_v, (ii) if w is in NEIGHB_v and v did not receive a message from w, then v removes w from ACTIVE_v and NEIGHB_v, and (iii) if w is in CALLING_v and v did not receive a message from w, then v removes w from ACTIVE_v.

(r5) Changing status: If the size of RUMORS_v is equal to p and v is a collector, then v becomes an informer.

(r6) Updating CALLING$_v$: Processor v empties CALLING$_v$ and (i) if v is a collector then it updates set CALLING$_v$ to contain the first $p^{(\ell+1)\varepsilon}$ pids of list WAITING$_v$ (or all pids of WAITING$_v$ if $sizeof(\text{WAITING}_v) < p^{(\ell+1)\varepsilon}$) and all pids of set NEIGHB$_v$, and (ii) if v is an informer then it updates set CALLING$_v$ to contain the first $p^{(\ell+1)\varepsilon}$ pids of list BUSY$_v$ (or all pids of BUSY$_v$ if $sizeof(\text{BUSY}_v) < p^{(\ell+1)\varepsilon}$) and all pids of set NEIGHB$_v$.

Terminating epoch. Epoch $\lceil 1/\varepsilon \rceil - 1$ is the last epoch of the algorithm. In this epoch, each processor v updates its local information based on the messages it received in the last communication stage of epoch $\lceil 1/\varepsilon \rceil - 2$. If after this update processor v is still a collector, then it sends a call-message to every processor that is in WAITING$_v$ (containing pids of the processors whose rumor v does not know or processors that failed). Then every processor receives the call-messages sent by the other processors. Next, every processor that received a call-message sends its local knowledge to the sender. Finally each processor v updates RUMORS$_v$ based on any received information.

4.2   Analysis of Algorithm GOSSIP$_\varepsilon$

For simplicity we assume that $\lceil 1/\varepsilon \rceil = 1/\varepsilon$. Consider some set Q_ℓ, $|Q_\ell| \geq p^{1-\ell\varepsilon}$, of processors that are not idle at the beginning of epoch ℓ and survive epoch ℓ. Let $Q'_\ell \subseteq Q_\ell$ be such that $|Q'_\ell| \geq |Q_\ell|/7$ and the diameter of the subgraph induced by Q'_ℓ is at most $31 \log p$. Q'_ℓ exists because of Lemma 1 applied to graph G_ℓ and set Q_ℓ (chains have size 2). We let $d = (31 \log p + 1)p^{(\ell+1)\varepsilon}$. For any processor v, let CALL$_v$ = CALLING$_v \setminus$ NEIGHB$_v$. We will be referring to the call-messages sent to the processors whose pids are in CALL as *progress-messages*.

Lemma 2. *The total number of progress-messages sent by processors in Q'_ℓ from the beginning of epoch ℓ until the first processor in Q'_ℓ will have its list WAITING (or list BUSY) empty, is at most $(d, |Q'_\ell|)$-Surf(Ψ).*

We now define an invariant, that we call I_ℓ, for $\ell = 1, \dots, 1/\varepsilon - 2$:

I_ℓ: There are at most $p^{1-\ell\varepsilon}$ non-faulty processors having status collector or informer in any step after the end of epoch ℓ.

Using Lemma 2 and Corollary 1 we show the following:

Lemma 3. *In any execution of algorithm GOSSIP$_\varepsilon$, the invariant I_ℓ holds for any epoch $\ell = 1, \dots, 1/\varepsilon - 2$.*

Theorem 2. *Algorithm GOSSIP$_\varepsilon$ solves the Gossip(p, f) problem with time complexity $T = O(\log^2 p)$ and message complexity $M = O(p^{1+3\varepsilon})$.*

Proof. First we show the bound on time. Observe that each update and communication stage takes $O(1)$ time. Therefore each of the first $1/\varepsilon - 2$ epochs takes $O(\log^2 p)$ time. The last epoch takes $O(1)$ time. From this and the fact that ε is a constant, we have that the time complexity of the algorithm is in the worse case $O(\log^2 p)$. We now show the bound on messages. From Lemma 3 we have that for every $1 \leq \ell < 1/\varepsilon - 2$, during epoch $\ell + 1$ there are at most $p^{1-\ell\varepsilon}$ processors sending at most $2p^{(\ell+2)\varepsilon}$ messages in every communication stage. The remaining processors are either faulty (hence they do not send any messages) or have status idle – these processors only respond to call-messages and their total impact on the message complexity in epoch $\ell + 1$ is at most as large as the others. Consequently the message complexity during epoch $\ell + 1$ is at most $4(\alpha \log^2 p) \cdot (p^{1-\ell\varepsilon} p^{(\ell+2)\varepsilon}) \leq 4\alpha p^{1+2\varepsilon} \log^2 p \leq 4\alpha p^{1+3\varepsilon}$. After epoch $1/\varepsilon - 2$ there are, per $I_{1/\varepsilon-2}$, at most $p^{2\varepsilon}$ processors having list WAITING not empty. In epoch $1/\varepsilon - 1$ each of these processors sends a message to at most p processors twice, hence the message complexity in this epoch is bounded by $2p \cdot p^{2\varepsilon}$. From the above and the fact that ε is a constant, we have that the message complexity of the algorithm is $O(p^{1+3\varepsilon})$.

5   The Do-All Algorithm

We now put the gossip algorithm to use by constructing a new *Do-All* algorithm.

5.1   Description of Algorithm DOALL$_\varepsilon$

The algorithm proceeds in a loop that is repeated until all the tasks are executed and all non-faulty processors are aware of this. A single iteration of the loop is called an *epoch*. Each epoch consists of $\beta \log p + 1$ *phases*, where $\beta > 0$ is a constant integer. We show that the algorithm is correct for any integer $\beta > 0$, but the complexity analysis of the algorithm depends on specific values of β that we show to exist. Each phase is divided into two *stages*, the *work* stage and the *gossip* stage. In the work stage processors perform tasks, and in the gossip stage processors execute an instance of the GOSSIP$_\varepsilon$ algorithm to exchange information regarding completed tasks and non-faulty processors (more details momentarily). Computation starts with epoch 1. We note that (unlike in algorithm GOSSIP$_\varepsilon$) the non-faulty processors may stop executing at different steps. Hence we need to argue about the termination decision that the processors must take. This is done in the paragraph "Termination decision".

The pseudocode for a phase of epoch ℓ of the algorithm is given in Figure 2 (again we assume that every **if-then** has an implicit **else** containing no-ops as needed). The correctness of the algorithm is shown in the full paper [10].

Work stage
```
repeat Tℓ times
    if TASK not empty then
        perform task whose id is first in TASK;
        remove task's id from TASK;
    elseif TASK empty and done = false
        then set done to true;
    if TASK empty and done = false then
        set done to true;
```

Gossip stage
```
run GOSSIPε/3 with rumor = (TEMP, PROC, done);
if done = true and donew = true for all w
received rumor from then
    TERMINATE;
else
    update TASK and PROC;
```

Fig. 2. A phase of epoch ℓ of algorithm DOALL$_\varepsilon$. Code for processor v.

Local knowledge. Each processor v maintains a list of tasks TASK_v it believes not to be done, and a list of processors PROC_v it believes to be non-faulty. Initially $\text{TASK}_v = \langle 1, \ldots, n \rangle$ and $\text{PROC}_v = \langle 1, \ldots, p \rangle$. The processor also has a boolean variable $done_v$, that describes the knowledge of v regarding the completion of the tasks. Initially $done_v$ is set to false, and when processor v is assured that all tasks are completed $done_v$ is set to true.

Task allocation. Each processor v is equipped with a permutation π_v from a set Ψ of permutations on $[n]$.[3] We show that the algorithm is correct for any set of permutations on $[n]$, but its complexity analysis depends on specific set of permutations Ψ that we show to exist.

Initially TASK_v is permuted according to π_v and then processor v performs tasks according to the ordering of the tids in TASK_v. In the course of the computation, when processor v learns that task z is performed (either by performing the task itself or by obtaining this information from some other processor), it removes z from TASK_v while preserving the permutation order.

Work stage. For epoch ℓ, each work stage consists of $T_\ell = \left\lceil \frac{n + p \log^3 p}{\frac{p}{2^l} \log p} \right\rceil$ work *substages*. In each sub-stage, each processor v performs a task according to TASK_v. Hence, in each work stage of a phase of epoch ℓ, processor v must perform the first T_ℓ tasks of TASK_v. However, if TASK_v becomes empty at a sub-stage prior to the T_ℓ^{th} sub-stage, then v performs no-ops in the remaining sub-stages (each no-op operation takes the same time as performing a task). Once TASK_v becomes empty, $done_v$ is set to true.

Gossip stage. Here processors execute algorithm $\text{GOSSIP}_{\varepsilon/3}$ using their local knowledge as the rumor, i.e., for processor v, $rumor_v = (\text{TASK}_v, \text{PROC}_v, done_v)$. At the end of the stage, each processor v updates its local knowledge based on the rumors it received. The **update rule** is as follows: (a) If v does not receive the rumor of processor w, then v learns that w has failed (guaranteed by the correctness of $\text{GOSSIP}_{\varepsilon/3}$). In this case v removes w from PROC_v. (b) If v receives the rumor of processor w, then it compare TASK_v and PROC_v with TASK_w and PROC_w respectively and updates its lists accordingly—it removes the tasks that w knows are already completed and the processors that w knows that have crashed. Note that if TASK_v becomes empty after this update, variable $done_v$ *does not* change to true. It will change in the next work stage (we do this for technical reasons).

Termination decision. We would like all non-faulty processors to learn that the tasks are done. Hence, it would not be sufficient for a processor to terminate once the value of its $done$ variable is turned to true. It has to be assured that all other non-faulty processors' $done$ variables are set to true as well, and then terminate. This is achieved as follows: If processor v starts the gossip stage of a phase of epoch ℓ with $done_v = \text{true}$, and all rumors it receives suggest that all other non-faulty processors know that all tasks are done (their $done$ variables are set to true), then processor v terminates. If at least one processor's $done$ variable is set to false, then v continues to the next phase of epoch ℓ (or to the first phase of epoch $\ell + 1$ if the previous phase was the last of epoch ℓ).

---

[3] This is distinct from the set of permutation on $[p]$ required by the gossip algorithm.

Remark 1. In the complexity analysis of the algorithm we first assume that $n \leq p^2$ and then we show how to extend the analysis for the case $n > p^2$. In order to do so, we assume that when $n > p^2$, before the start of algorithm DOALL$_\varepsilon$, the tasks are partitioned into $n' = p^2$ chunks, where each chunk contains at most $\lceil n/p^2 \rceil$ tasks. In this case it is understood that in the above description of the algorithm, n is actually n' and when we refer to a task we really mean a chunk of tasks.

5.2   Analysis of Algorithm DOALL$_\varepsilon$

We now derive the work and message complexities for algorithm DOALL$_\varepsilon$. Our analysis is based on the following terminology. Consider phase i in epoch ℓ. For a given failure pattern F, let $V_i(F)$ denote the set of processors that are non-faulty at the beginning of phase i. Let $p_i(F) = |V_i(F)|$. Let $U_i(F)$ denote the set of tasks z such that z is in some list TASK$_v$, for some $v \in V_i(F)$, at the beginning of phase i. Let $u_i(F) = |U_i(F)|$.

Now we classify the possibilities for phase i as follows. If at the beginning of phase i, $p_i(F) > p/2^{\ell-1}$, we say that phase i is a *majority* phase. Otherwise, phase i is a *minority* phase. If phase i is a minority phase and at the end of i the number of surviving processors is less than $p_i(F)/2$, i.e., $p_{i+1}(F) < p_i(F)/2$, we say that i is an *unreliable* minority phase. If $p_{i+1}(F) \geq p_i(F)/2$, we say that i is a *reliable* minority phase. If phase i is a reliable minority phase and $u_{i+1}(F) \leq u_i(F) - \frac{1}{4}p_{i+1}(F)T_\ell$, then we say that i is an *optimal* reliable minority phase (the task allocation is optimal – the same task is performed only by a constant number of processors on average). If $u_{i+1}(F) \leq \frac{3}{4}u_i(F)$, then i is a *fractional* reliable minority phase (a fraction of the undone tasks is performed). Otherwise we say that i is an *unproductive* reliable minority phase (not much progress is obtained). The classification possibilities for phase i of epoch ℓ are depicted in Figure 3.

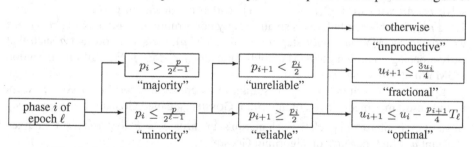

Fig. 3. Classification of a phase i of epoch ℓ; the failure pattern F is implied.

Our goal is to choose a set Ψ of permutations such that for any failure pattern there will be no unproductive and no majority phases. To do this we analyze sets of random permutations, prove certain properties of our algorithm for such sets (in Lemmas 4 and 5), and finally use the probabilistic method to obtain an existential deterministic solution.

Lemma 4. *Let Q be a fixed nonempty subset of processors. Then the probability of event "for every failure pattern F such that $V_{i+1}(F) \supseteq Q$ and $u_i(F) > 0$, the following inequality holds $u_i(F) - u_{i+1}(F) \geq \min\{u_i(F), |Q|T_\ell\}/4$," is at least $1 - 1/e^{\Omega(|Q|T_\ell)}$.*

Lemma 5. *Assume $n \leq p^2$. There exists a constant integer $\beta > 0$ such that for every phase i of epoch ℓ, for any epoch ℓ, if there is a task unperformed by the beginning of phase i then (a) the probability that phase i is a majority phase under some failure pattern F is at most $e^{-\Omega(p \log p)}$, and (b) the probability that phase i is a minority reliable unproductive phase under some failure pattern F is at most $e^{-\Omega(T_\ell)}$.*

Theorem 3. *There is a set of permutations Ψ and a constant integer $\beta > 0$ such that algorithm DOALL_ε, using permutations from Ψ, solves the Do-All(n, p, f) problem with work $W = O(n + p \log^3 p)$ and message complexity $M = O(p^{1+2\varepsilon})$.*

Proof. (Sketch.) We first consider the case $n \leq p^2$ and then we show the result for the case $n > p^2$. The idea of the proof is as follows: using Lemmas 4 and 5 we reason about the probability of a phase i of an epoch ℓ belonging to one of the classes illustrated in Figure 3, and about the work that phase i contributes to the total work, depending on its classification. We then reason that a set of permutations Ψ and a constant integer $\beta > 0$ exist so that the complexity bounds are as desired. See the full paper [10] for details.

5.3 Sensitivity Training and Failure-Sensitive Analysis

We note that the complexity bounds we obtained in the previous section do not show how the bounds depend on f, the maximum number of crashes. In fact it is possible to subject the algorithm to "failure-sensitivity-training" and obtain better results. To do so we slightly modify algorithm $\text{DOALL}_{\varepsilon/2}$. We add two new epochs, called epoch -1 and epoch 0. We call the new algorithm, algorithm $\text{DOALL}'_\varepsilon$.

Epoch -1 of algorithm $\text{DOALL}'_\varepsilon$ is based on the check-pointing algorithm from [6], where the check-pointing and the synchronization procedures are taken from [8]. We refer to this algorithm as DGMY. The goal of using this algorithm in epoch -1 is to solve *Do-All* with work $O(n + p(f + 1))$ and communication $O(fp^\varepsilon + p \min\{f + 1, \log p\})$ if number of failures is small, mainly concerning the case $f \leq \log^3 p$. Hence we execute DGMY only until step $a \cdot (n/p + \log^3 p)$, for some constant a such that early-stopping condition of DGMY holds for every $f \leq \log^3 p$. We call this execution $\text{DGMY}(a \cdot (n/p + \log^3 p))$.

Epoch 0 of algorithm $\text{DOALL}'_\varepsilon$ is similar to an epoch of algorithm DOALL_ε, except that we use a modified version of algorithm $\text{GOSSIP}_{\varepsilon/3}$, called $\text{GOSSIP}'_{\varepsilon/3}$ in each gossip stage of every phase of epoch 0. Each gossip stage lasts $g_0 = a' \log^2 p$ steps, for a fixed constant a' which depends on algorithm $\text{GOSSIP}'_{\varepsilon/3}$.

Algorithm $\text{GOSSIP}'_{\varepsilon/3}$ is obtained by adding a new epoch in $\text{GOSSIP}_{\varepsilon/3}$ and by slightly modifying the remaining epochs of $\text{GOSSIP}_{\varepsilon/3}$. We show that $\text{GOSSIP}'_{\varepsilon/3}$ solves the *Gossip(p, f)* problem with time complexity $T = O(\log^2 p)$ and message complexity $M = O(p)$ when $f \leq \frac{p}{\log^2 p}$, and with $T = O(\log^2 p)$ and $M = O(p^{1+3\varepsilon/4})$ otherwise. Details can be found in the full version of the paper [10].

Finally we show the following result for algorithm $\text{DOALL}'_\varepsilon$, using Theorem 3, the analysis of epochs -1 and 0, and the complexity of algorithm $\text{GOSSIP}'_{\varepsilon/3}$.

Theorem 4. *There exists a set of permutations Ψ and a constant integer $\beta > 0$ such that algorithm $\text{DOALL}'_\varepsilon$ solves the Do-All(n, p, f) problem with work $W = O(n + p \cdot \min\{f + 1, \log^3 p\})$ and message complexity $M = O(fp^\varepsilon + p \min\{f + 1, \log p\})$.*

6   Discussion and Future Work

In this paper we presented two contributions. We improved the previously best known algorithm that solves the gossip problem for synchronous, message-passing, crash-prone processors. Using our new gossip algorithm we developed a new algorithm for the *Do-All* problem. Our algorithm achieves better work and message complexity than any previous *Do-All* algorithms in the same model, for the full range of crashes ($f < p$). Our techniques involve the use of conceptual communication graphs and sets of permutations with specific combinatorial properties. A future direction is to investigate how to efficiently construct permutations with the required combinatorial properties. Another direction is to extend the techniques developed in this paper to other models, for example, for synchronous restartable fail-stop processors. It is also interesting to consider other distributed computing problems where the use of our efficient gossip algorithm can lead to better results.

References

1. N. Alon and J.H. Spencer. The Probabilistic Method. J. Wiley and Sons, Inc., second edition (2000)
2. R.J. Anderson and H. Woll. Algorithms for the certified Write-All problem. SIAM Journal of Computing, Vol. 26 5 (1997) 1277–1283
3. B. Chlebus, R. De Prisco and A.A. Shvartsman. Performing tasks on restartable message-passing processors. Distributed Computing, Vol. 14 1 (2001) 49–64
4. B.S. Chlebus, L. Gasieniec, D.R. Kowalski and A.A. Shvartsman. Bounding work and communication in robust cooperative computation. 16th International Symposium on Distributed Computing (2002) 295–310
5. B.S. Chlebus and D.R. Kowalski. Gossiping to reach consensus. 14th Symposium on Parallel Algorithms and Architectures (2002) 220–229
6. R. De Prisco, A. Mayer and M. Yung. Time-optimal message-efficient work performance in the presence of faults. 13th Symposium on Principles of Distributed Computing (1994) 161–172
7. C. Dwork, J. Halpern and O. Waarts. Performing work efficiently in the presence of faults. SIAM Journal on Computing, Vol. 27 5 (1998) 1457–1491
8. Z. Galil, A. Mayer and M. Yung. Resolving message complexity of byzantine agreement and beyond. 36th Symp. on Foundations of Comp. Sc. (1995) 724–733
9. Ch. Georgiou, A. Russell and A.A. Shvartsman. The complexity of synchronous iterative Do-All with crashes. 15th Int-l Symposium on Distributed Computing (2001) 151–165
10. Ch. Georgiou, D. Kowalski and A.A. Shvartsman. Efficient gossip and robust distributed computation. http://www.engr.uconn.edu/~aas/GKS-2003.ps
11. P.C. Kanellakis and A.A. Shvartsman. Efficient parallel algorithms can be made robust. Distributed Computing, Vol. 5 4 (1992) 201–217
12. G. Malewicz, A. Russell and A.A. Shvartsman. Distributed cooperation during the absence of communication. 14th Int-l Symp. on Distr. Computing (2000) 119–133
13. A. Pelc. Fault-tolerant broadcasting and gossiping in communication networks. Networks, Vol. 28 (1996) 143–156

Condition-Based Consensus in Synchronous Systems

Yoav Zibin

Technion—Israel Institute of Technology
zyoav@cs.technion.ac.il

Abstract. The *condition-based* approach for solving problems in distributed systems consists of identifying sets of input vectors, called *conditions*, for which it is possible to design more efficient protocols. Recent work suggested using the condition based approach in *asynchronous systems* suffering from crashes, for solving various agreement problems [5, 9, 1, 4, 6]. This paper designs a fast condition-based consensus protocol for *synchronous systems*.

1 Introduction

The consensus problem stands in the heart of distributed systems prone to failures [2]. In this problem each process proposes a value and all correct processes must agree on one of the proposed values. It is well known that consensus cannot be solved in *asynchronous systems* even in the presence of a single possible crash. Many ways have been suggested to circumvent this impossibility result, such as considering a weaker problem (approximate agreement, set agreement, and randomized algorithms) or a stronger environment (failure detectors, and partially asynchronous environment).

The *condition-based* approach, which is the focus of this paper, consists of identifying sets of input vectors, called *conditions*, for which a problem is solvable. Recent work used the condition based approach in asynchronous systems suffering from crashes, for solving consensus [5], set-agreement [9, 1], and interactive-consistency [6]. These problems were also studied in the presence of Byzantine errors [6, 4]. A correlation with error correcting codes was recently found [4], where crashes correspond to erasures, and Byzantine faults to corruption errors.

Consider, for example, the condition C_d^{max} which includes only input vectors in which the largest value appears at least d times. It is easy to solve consensus if the input always belongs to C_{f+1}^{max}, where f is the number of processes that can crash. The difficulty is in designing a *strict consensus protocol*, i.e., a protocol which also handles inputs that do not belong to the condition. Mostefaoui et al. [5] presented a strict consensus protocol which always guarantee safety (i.e., agreement and validity), however the protocol may not terminate if the input does not belong to C_{f+1}^{max}. More generally, Mostefaoui et al. defined the class of d-legal conditions and presented a generic protocol for any $f + 1$-legal condition. A more efficient consensus protocol for stronger conditions was presented later [8, 7].

In *synchronous systems* it is well known that solving consensus requires at least $f+1$ rounds. This paper uses the condition-based approach in order to design a consensus protocol which requires a smaller number of rounds. Specifically, for d-legal conditions, $1 \le d \le f+1$, we present a protocol which solves consensus in $(f+1)-(d-1)$

F.E. Fich (Ed.): DISC 2003, LNCS 2848, pp. 239–248, 2003.

rounds if the input always belongs to the condition. We also present a strict consensus protocol which adds an additional validation round to ensure all processes reached agreement (we assume that $2f < n$). More precisely, if the input belongs to the condition then consensus is solved in $(f + 1) - (d - 1) + 1$ rounds, otherwise it is solved in $f + 1$ rounds.

Outline Sec. 2 presents our notation and defines the strict and non-strict variants of the condition-based approach. Sec. 3 defines the consensus problem and describes the well-known flood-set protocol for solving it. The non-strict consensus protocol for any d-legal condition is presented in Sec. 4, and its strict variant in Sec. 5. Finally, open problems and direction for future research are discussed in Sec. 6.

2 Notation

This paper assumes a standard *synchronous message passing* model. The number of processes is denoted by n, and f is a bound on the number of processes that can *crash* (without ever recovering). A process that did not crashed is called *correct*.

Definition 1 (Immediate crash). *A process which crashes in the first round is said to* immediately crash. *(Note that this process can still send messages in the first round to a subset of the other processes.) Similarly, an* immediate crash *is a crash that occurred in the first round.*

The finite set of input values is denoted by $\mathcal{V}$. We assume a default value $\bot$ not in $\mathcal{V}$. Let $\mathcal{V}^n$ be the set of all possible vectors (of size n) with entries from $\mathcal{V}$, and let $\mathcal{V}_f^n$ be the set of all possible vectors with entries from $\mathcal{V} \cup \bot$, with at most f entries equal to $\bot$. We typically denote by I a vector in $\mathcal{V}^n$ and by J a vector in $\mathcal{V}_f^n$.

Definition 2 (Partial view). *For vectors $J_1, J_2 \in \mathcal{V}_f^n$, we say that J_1 is a partial view of J_2, denoted $J_1 \leq J_2$, if for $k = 1, \ldots, n$, $J_1[k] \neq \bot \Rightarrow J_1[k] = J_2[k]$, i.e., J_1 can be* extended *into J_2 by changing some of its $\bot$ entries.*

Definition 3 (Union of partial views). *When $J_1, J_2 \in \mathcal{V}_f^n$ are partial views of the same vector I, i.e., $J_1, J_2 \leq I$, we define their union $J = J_1 \cup J_2$, such that for $k = 1, \ldots, n$,*

$$J[k] = a \neq \bot \Leftrightarrow J_1[k] = a \text{ or } J_2[k] = a.$$

Observe that $J_i \leq J \leq I$ for $i = 1, 2$.

We define two functions:

- $\#_x(J) = |\{i \mid J[i] = x\}|$, i.e., the number of entries of J whose value is x.
- $\text{dist}(J_1, J_2) = |\{i \mid J_1[i] \neq J_2[i]\}|$, i.e., the Hamming distance between J_1 and J_2.

We assume that there is some linear ordering of $\mathcal{V}$ and we can define the function $\max : \wp(\mathcal{V}) \mapsto \mathcal{V}$. Next, we assume that $\bot$ is the smallest value, and extend $\max$ to handle also $\bot$ values. We will sometimes treat a vector $J \in \mathcal{V}_f^n$ as a set and write $\max(J)$; Note that $\bot$ will never be picked by $\max$ unless $J = \{\bot\}^n$. By defining a lexicographic ordering over $\mathcal{V}^n$, we can extend this function to handle vectors, i.e., $\max : \wp(\mathcal{V}^n) \mapsto \mathcal{V}^n$. (No confusion will occur due to this overloading of the $\max$ function.)

Definition 4 (Conditions). *A condition $C \subseteq \mathcal{V}^n$ is a set of input vectors.*

A protocol which solves *non-strict* consensus [4] for a given condition C need to consider only input vectors in C, i.e., if the input vector does not belong to C then no guarantees are made on the output. In contrast the *strict* variant must consider every possible input vector in $\mathcal{V}^n$. In an *asynchronous* environment [5, 8, 9, 7, 4], a strict protocol must always guarantee safety (i.e., agreement and validity), even for input vectors that do not belong to C, but it may not terminate. (The consequences of making other properties more strict can be found in [5, 4], e.g., a correct process must always terminate but it may sometimes decide on $\perp$.) In a *synchronous* environment the protocol must always terminate, and it must terminate faster for input vectors in C.

Definition 5 (d-legal conditions). *A condition C is called d-legal if there exists a mapping $h : C \mapsto \mathcal{V}$ with the following properties:*

1. *$\forall I \in C : \#_{h(I)}(I) \geq d$,*
2. *$\forall I_1, I_2 \in C : h(I_1) \neq h(I_2) \Rightarrow \mathrm{dist}(I_1, I_2) \geq d$.*

It was shown [5, 4] that $(f + 1)$-legal conditions are necessary and sufficient for solving both strict and non-strict consensus in asynchronous systems.

An example of a d-legal condition is C_d^{max},

$$C_d^{\mathrm{max}} = \{I \in \mathcal{V}^n \mid \#_{\mathrm{max}(I)}(I) \geq d\}, \text{i.e., } d \text{ occurrences of the maximum value.}$$

The mapping h associated with C_d^{max} returns the maximal value in the vector. It is straight forward to verify the two properties h must have according to Def. 5.

3   Consensus Problem

In the *consensus* problem each process has to *decide* on a value (the output value), such that the following properties holds:

Agreement: No two different values are decided by *correct* processes.
Termination: A correct process must decide.
Validity: The decided value is one of the proposed values.

In all the protocols in this paper, whenever a process decides it also halts. Therefore every process that decides (whether correct or *faulty*) chooses the same value; this property is called *uniform agreement*, and our protocols in fact solve *uniform consensus*. (If processes are allowed to halt after they decided then solving consensus requires at least $t + 1$ rounds, whereas solving uniform consensus requires at least $t + 2$ rounds [3], where $t < f - 1$ is the number of processes that actually crashed.)

Protocol 1 describes the well-known *flood-set protocol* (see e.g., [2]) in which sets of input values are iteratively flooded during d rounds. Each process p_i represents its set as a partial view $J_i \leq I$ which is extended during d rounds. It is well known that after $f + 1$ rounds all the partial views are equal and thus FloodSet$_{f+1}$ solves consensus.

In order to prove our results in the next sections, we will need the following lemmas.

Protocol 1 FloodSet$_d$
___

Input: a value $x_i \in \mathcal{V}$.
Output: a decided value $y_i \in \mathcal{V}$, and a partial view $J_i \in \mathcal{V}_f^n$.
Code for process p_i:

1: $J_i \leftarrow \{\bot\}^n$
2: $J_i[i] \leftarrow x_i$ // *we always maintain the invariant that $J_i \leq I$*
3: **For** $r = 1, \ldots, d$ **do** // *run for d rounds*
4:     **Send** J_i to all processes (including yourself)
5:     $V \leftarrow \emptyset$ // *the set of partial views received*
6:     **Upon receiving** J_j from p_j **do** $V \leftarrow V \cup \{J_j\}$
         // *update our partial view*
7:     $J_i \leftarrow \bigcup_{J_j \in V} J_j$
8: **end For**
9: $y_i \leftarrow \max(J_i)$
10: **return** $\langle y_i, J_i \rangle$

___

Lemma 1. *For every correct process p_i, $J_i \leq I$.*

Proof. Observe that J_i is updated only in lines 1,2 and 7. By induction, each $J_j \in V$ satisfies $J_j \leq I$, and therefore their union also satisfies $\bigcup_{J_j \in V} J_j \leq I$.

Lemma 2. *Let p_i be a correct process. If p_j did not immediately crash then $J_i[j] = I[j]$, and if $J_i[j] = \bot$ then p_j must have immediately crashed.*

Proof. If p_j did not immediately crash then it must have sent its input to p_i, i.e., $J_i[j] = I[j] \neq \bot$.

Lemma 3. *Let $J_i, J_j \leq I$ be two resulting partial views from running FloodSet$_d$. Then, if there exist I_i', I_j', such that $J_i \leq I_i'$, $J_j \leq I_j'$, and $\mathrm{dist}(I_i', I_j') \geq k$, then there were at least k immediate crashes.*

Proof. Assume by contradiction that there were less than k immediate crashes. Let $S \subseteq [1,n]$, $|S| \geq k$, be the set of indices where I_i' and I_j' differ, i.e., for every $m \in S$, $I_i'[m] \neq I_j'[m]$. Then, there is some $m \in S$ such that p_m did not immediately crashed. From Lemma 2, if either $J_i[m] = \bot$ or $J_j[m] = \bot$ then p_m immediately crashed. Therefore, both $J_i[m] \neq \bot$ and $J_j[m] \neq \bot$. Since $J_i, J_j \leq I$, we have that $J_i[m] = J_j[m]$. Since $J_i \leq I_i'$ and $J_j \leq I_j'$, then $I_i'[m] = I_j'[m]$; contradiction.

Lemma 4. *If d immediate crashes occurred then after running FloodSet$_{(f+1)-(d-1)}$ all the partial views are equal.*

Proof. Since in the first round there were at least d immediate crashes, there could be at most $(f - d)$ crashes in the remaining $(f - d) + 1$ rounds. Therefore, there must be a round in which no crashes occurred, after which all the partial views become equal.

In order to gain some intuition on the consensus protocols of the next sections, we first show how to solve non-strict consensus for the specific condition $C_d^{\max}$.

Lemma 5. *Running* $\mathsf{FloodSet}_{(f+1)-(d-1)}$ *solves non-strict consensus for the condition* $C_d^{\max}$.

Proof. It is straightforward to prove **Validity** and **Termination** in $(f+1) - (d-1)$ rounds. Next we prove **Agreement**. Let $I \in C_d^{\max}$ be the input vector. Then, there are at least d processes whose input is $\max(I)$. On the one hand, suppose that one of those d processes did not *immediately crash*. Then according to Lemma 2, for every correct process p_i, we have $\max(I) \in J_i$, and thus p_i decides on $\max(I)$. On the other hand, if those d processes did *immediately crash*, then according to Lemma 4, all the partial views are equal, i.e., $J_i = J_j$, and every correct process decides on the same $\max(J_i)$.

Lemma 6. *It is not possible to solve non-strict consensus for* $C_d^{\max}$ *in less than* $(f+1) - (d-1)$ *rounds.*

Proof. Observe that, when $d = 1$, $C_1^{\max} = \mathcal{V}^n$, i.e., we need to solve the problem for any possible input and therefore the known lower bound of $f + 1$ rounds holds. When $d > 1$, by causing $d - 1$ of the processes with the maximal input to crash even before they start, we returned to the general form of the problem. Specifically, afterwards we need to solve consensus with up to $f - (d-1)$ crashes for *any possible input*, which cannot be done in less than $(f - (d - 1)) + 1$ rounds.

4   Non-strict Consensus Protocol

Given a d-legal condition C, and its associated mapping $h : C \mapsto \mathcal{V}$ (see Def. 5), the protocol for solving *non-strict consensus* is presented in Protocol 2. Remember that when the input does not belong to C we make no guarantees on the protocol.

Protocol 2 Non-strict consensus protocol for a d-legal condition C with the mapping $h : C \mapsto \mathcal{V}$

Input: a value $x_i \in \mathcal{V}$.
Output: a decided value $y_i \in \mathcal{V}$, and a partial view $J_i \in \mathcal{V}_f^n$.
Code for process p_i:
```
1: J_i ← FloodSet_{(f+1)-(d-1)}(x_i) // Run the protocol for (f+1) - (d-1) rounds
2: E_i ← {I' ∈ C | h(I') ∈ J_i and J_i ≤ I'} // Determining the set of candidate vectors
3: If E_i = ∅ then
       // It must be that #⊥(J_i) ≥ d, and thus J_i = J_j for all correct processes p_i, p_j.
4:    y_i ← max(J_i)
5: else
6:    I'_i ← max(E_i)
7:    y_i ← h(I'_i)
8: return ⟨y_i, J_i⟩
```

In line 1 process i calculates its partial view J_i by running $\mathsf{FloodSet}_{(f+1)-(d-1)}$. The essence of the protocol is that J_i is either "close enough" to the input vector or that all the partial are equal. Lines 2–7 are a deterministic procedure to select the agreed value y_i. In line 2 we determine a set of candidate vectors from C. Each candidate I' must satisfy two requirements: (i) I' is an extension of J_i, $J_i \leq I'$, and (ii) $h(I') \in J_i$. The second requirement ensures the validity of our protocol, however because of it, the input vector I might not be a candidate. If the set of candidates is empty we will prove that all the partial views are equal and the processes can agree on $\max(J_i)$ (lines 3–4). Otherwise, we can deterministically select any candidate vector and agree on $h(I_i')$ (lines 6–7). We note that the use of the max function in lines 4 and 6 is arbitrary; Any other deterministic decision procedure will maintain the correctness of the protocol.

Consider, for example, the condition $C_2^{\max}$, where the maximal value must appear at least twice, and h returns the maximal value in a vector. Assume that $f = 3, n = 5$, and $V = \{1, 2, 3, 4\}$. Suppose that we run the protocol with the input $I = \langle 1, 4, 4, 3, 2 \rangle$, and process i finishes with the partial view $J_i = \langle \bot, \bot, \bot, 3, 2 \rangle$. There are many extensions of J_i which belong to C, e.g.,

$$I = \langle 1, 4, 4, 3, 2 \rangle$$
$$I' = \langle 1, 3, 3, 3, 2 \rangle$$

The set $\mathcal{E}_i$ includes I' since $J_i \leq I'$ and $h(I') = 3 \in J_i$, but

$$I \notin \mathcal{E}_i,$$

since $h(I) = 4 \notin J_i$.

In general, the fact that $I \notin \mathcal{E}_i$ is not surprising. Recall that we demanded that for every $I \in C$, $\#_{h(I)}(I) \geq d$. It might be the case that all those d processes crashed, and you cannot choose $h(I)$ because you have not seen $h(I)$, i.e., $h(I) \notin J_i$. However, we will prove that in such a case all the partial views J_i are equal, and thus you can safely choose $\max(J_i)$.

Theorem 1. *Protocol 2 solves non-strict consensus for any d-legal condition C, i.e., for any input vector $I \in C$ it satisfies:*

Agreement *No two different values are decided.*
Termination *A correct process decides in $(f + 1) - (d - 1)$ rounds.*
Validity *The decided value is one of the proposed values, i.e., $y_i \in I$.*

Proof. It is straightforward to see that every correct process decides after exactly $(f + 1) - (d - 1)$ rounds.

Next we prove **Validity**, i.e., $y_i \in I$. From Lemma 1, we have that $J_i \leq I$. On the one hand, if $\mathcal{E}_i = \emptyset$ then $y_i \in J_i$, and since $y_i \neq \bot$ we have that $y_i \in I$. On the other hand, every $I' \in \mathcal{E}_i$ satisfies $h(I') \in J_i$, and again since $y_i = h(I') \neq \bot$ we have that $y_i \in I$. (Note that validity holds even when $I \notin C$.)

Finally we prove **Agreement**. Assume by contradiction that two processes p_i and p_j decided on different values $y_i \neq y_j$. Note that lines 2–8 are deterministic, i.e., if $J_i = J_j$ then $y_i = y_j$ (which will be a contradiction). We wish to show that d processes *immediately* crashed, since by applying Lemma 4, after running $\mathsf{FloodSet}_{(f+1)-(d-1)}$, we will have the contradiction that $J_i = J_j$.

Suppose that one of p_i or p_j reached line 4. W.l.o.g., assume it is p_i, i.e., $\mathcal{E}_i = \emptyset$. Since $J_i \leq I$ and $I \notin \mathcal{E}_i$ we have that $h(I) \notin J_i$. From the first property of h (see

Def. 5), $\#_{h(I)}(I) \geq d$. Thus those d entries must be $\perp$ in J_i, and we have d processes which *immediately crashed*.

Now suppose that both p_i and p_j reached line 6, i.e., $y_i = h(I'_i)$ and $y_j = h(I'_j)$. Since the condition is d-legal we have that

$$h(I'_i) \neq h(I'_j) \Rightarrow \text{dist}(I'_i, I'_j) \geq d.$$

Since $J_i, J_j \leq I$, $J_i \leq I'_i$, $J_j \leq I'_j$, and $\text{dist}(I'_i, I'_j) \geq d$, from Lemma 3 we know that d processes *immediately crashed*.   □

5   Strict Consensus Protocol

It was proven [5, Theorem 7.1] that in order to solve strict consensus (for a non-trivial condition) in an *asynchronous* system, you must assume that $2f < n$. Although this is not mandatory in *synchronous* systems, we also assumed that $2f < n$ in our strict consensus protocol which is presented in Protocol 3.

This protocol amends the non-strict consensus protocol of the previous section by adding an additional validation round. If the processes reached an agreement then the protocol stops after running for only $(f+1) - (d-1) + 1$ rounds. Otherwise the input does not belong to the condition, and the protocol runs for $f + 1$ rounds.

The idea is to check if we reached consensus using Protocol 2, and in parallel to continue running the basic flood-set protocol. If we reached consensus after running Protocol 2 in line 1, then all the suggestions y_i will be equal, and all processes will reach line 19 and terminate. However, it is possible that consensus have not been reached and still one process will terminate in line 19 and return the value y, and another process p_j will not.

If we removed our assumption that $2f < n$ then it is possible that p_j will decide on a different value in line 19. But if $2f < n$, we can be sure that y is the majority value among the suggestions p_j received, and p_j will reach line 21 and eventually decide on y.

Another problematic scenario is the possibility that one process p_i decides on a majority value m_i in line 26, and another process p_j decides on the maximal value in J_j in line 28. To avoid this possibility, the majority value m_i is flooded to all other processes using the Majority message. Since we ran for $f + 1$ rounds there must be a round in which no crashes occurred. Therefore, either (i) consensus was reached in line 1 or (ii) a Majority message will reach p_j. In both cases p_j will not decide in line 28.

Theorem 2. *When $2f < n$, Protocol 3 solves strict consensus for any d-legal condition C, i.e., it satisfies:*

Agreement *No two different values are decided.*
Termination *A correct process decides in at most $f + 1$ rounds.*
Improved_Termination *When the input belongs to the condition, a correct process decides in $(f + 1) - (d - 1) + 1$ rounds.*
Validity *The decided value is one of the proposed values.*

Protocol 3 Strict consensus protocol, when $2f < n$, for a d-legal condition C

Input: a value $x_i \in \mathcal{V}$.
Output: a value in $\mathcal{V}$.
Code for process p_i:

1: $\langle J_i, y_i \rangle \leftarrow$ run Protocol 2 on x_i // *Runs for* $(f+1) - (d-1)$ *rounds*
    // y_i *is the* suggestion *of process i*
2: $m_i \leftarrow \perp$ // *The majority value among the suggestions*
3: **For** $r = 1, \ldots, d-1$ **do** // *run for $d-1$ more rounds*
4:      **If** $m_i = \perp$ **then**
5:          **Send** $\langle$Suggestion, $J_i, y_i \rangle$ **to** all processes (including yourself)
6:      **else**
7:          **Send** $\langle$Majority, $m_i \rangle$ **to** all other processes
8:      $V \leftarrow \emptyset$ // *the set of partial views received*
9:      $S \leftarrow \{\perp\}^n$ // *the vector of suggestions received*
10:     **Upon receiving** msg_j **from** p_j **do**
11:         **If** $\langle$Majority, $m_j \rangle = \text{msg}_j$ **then**
12:             $m_i \leftarrow m_j$
13:         **else**
14:             Let $\langle$Suggestion, $J_j, y_j \rangle = \text{msg}_j$
15:             $V \leftarrow V \cup \{J_j\}$ // *Collect the partial views*
16:             $S[j] = y_j$ // *Collect the suggestions*

17:     **If** $m_i = \perp$ **then**
18:         **If** $\exists y$ such that: $\#_y(S) = n - \#_\perp(S)$ **then** // *all the values in S are equal to y*
19:             **return** y
20:         **else if** $\exists y$ such that: $\#_y(S) > \frac{n}{2}$ **then** // *y is the majority value*
21:             $m_i \leftarrow y$
22:         **else**
23:             $J_i \leftarrow \bigcup_{J_j \in V} J_j$ // *update our partial view*
24: **end For**

25: **If** $m_i \neq \perp$ **then**
26:     **return** m_i
27: **else**
28:     **return** $\max(J_i)$

Proof. **Termination** in $f+1$ rounds is straight forward: we run Protocol 2 for $(f + 1) - (d - 1)$ and then we run for $d - 1$ more rounds. **Improved_Termination** is also easy: when the input belongs to the condition, all the values y_i returned from Protocol 2 are equal, and in the next round all processes will reach line 19 and terminate.

Next we prove **Validity**. Note that the validity proof of the non-strict version (see Thm 1) did not use the fact that the input belongs to the condition, i.e., $I \in C$. Therefore, after line 1, we have that $y_i \in J_i \leq I$. Since we decide either on some suggestion y_i or on $\max(J_i)$, the decided value is one of the proposed values.

Finally we prove **Agreement**. Assume by contradiction that two processes p_i and p_j decided on different values. It cannot be that both p_i and p_j decided in line 19 or 26, because it cannot be that two different suggestions are in majority. Therefore, at least one of p_i or p_j decided in line 28, w.l.o.g., assume it is p_i. Note that $m_i = \bot$, i.e., no Majority message reached p_i.

Suppose that some process decided in line 19 on the value y, i.e., p_j only saw suggestions for the value y. Then, in the same round it must be that all the other processes saw at least $\lceil \frac{n}{2} \rceil$ suggestions for y. Otherwise, the number of correct processes is less than $\lceil \frac{n}{2} \rceil$. But that cannot be for p_i, since p_i decided in line 28 and $m_i = \bot$.

Therefore p_j decided in line 26 or 28. Since both p_i and p_j ran for $f + 1$ rounds, and there are at most f crashes, there must be a round r in which no crashes occurred. If $r \leq f - d + 2$, then after running Protocol 2 in line 1 all processes would reach consensus and terminate in line 19. Therefore, $r \geq f - d + 3$. In round r, all processes will have the same set V, and therefore starting from that round we always have that $J_i = J_j$. Process p_j cannot decided in line 28 since $J_i = J_j \Rightarrow \max(J_i) = \max(J_j)$. Thus, p_j decided in line 26.

It must be that p_j received its Majority message exactly in *the last round*, since otherwise p_j would send a Majority message to p_i the next round (but p_i decided in line 28 so it did not receive any Majority message). Note that a process p_k can reach line 21 only in round $f - d + 3$ because the number of suggestions with the majority value can only decrease in time due to crashes. By examining Protocol 3 we can see that there must be a series of Majority messages starting from a process p_k that reached line 21 in round $f - d + 3$ and ending with process p_j in the last round (without ever reaching p_i). But this is a contradiction since in some round $r \geq f - d + 3$ there were no crashes. $\qquad\square$

6 Open Problems

This paper presented both a strict and a non-strict consensus protocol for any d-legal condition in synchronous systems. When the input belongs to the condition, the non-strict protocol saves $d - 1$ rounds, and the strict protocol saves $d - 2$ rounds. It is easy to modify the protocols described here to solve the interactive-consistency problem in which the processes need to agree on an equal vector (see the author website[1]).

We could neither prove the optimality of our algorithms nor the necessity of assuming $2f < n$ in the strict variant.

The most important problem this paper leaves open is finding classes of conditions for which k-set agreement can be solved more efficiently. Even in asynchronous systems, except for the wait-free case [1], no necessary conditions were found. Finally, generalizing the results for other kinds of crashes, e.g., Byzantine faults, also seems like a worthwhile task.

---

[1] http://www.cs.technion.ac.il/~zyoav

References

1. H. Attiya and Z. Avidor. Wait-free n-set consensus when inputs are restricted. In *Proceedings of the 16th International Symposium on DIStributed Computing (DISC 2002)*, pages 118–132. Springer LNCS 2508, 2002.
2. H. Attiya and J. Welch. *Distributed Computing: Fundamentals, Simulations, and Advanced Topics*. McGraw-Hill, 1998.
3. B. Charron-Bost and A. Schiper. Uniform consensus harder than consensus. Technical Report DSC/2000/028, École Polytechnique Fédérale de Lausanne, Switzerland, May 2000.
4. R. Friedman, A. Mostefaoui, S. Rajsbaum, and M. Raynal. Distributed agreement and its relation with error-correcting codes. In *Proceedings of the 16th International Symposium on DIStributed Computing (DISC 2002)*, pages 63–87. Springer LNCS 2508, 2002.
5. A. Mostefaoui, S. Rajsbaum, and M. Raynal. Conditions on input vectors for consensus solvability in asynchronous distributed systems. In *Proceedings of the 33rd annual ACM symposium on Theory of computing*, pages 153–162. ACM Press, 2001.
6. A. Mostefaoui, S. Rajsbaum, and M. Raynal. Asynchronous interactive consistency and its relation with error-correcting codes. In *Proceedings of the 21st annual symposium on Principles of distributed computing*, pages 253–253. ACM Press, 2002.
7. A. Mostefaoui, S. Rajsbaum, M. Raynal, and M. Roy. Efficient condition-based consensus. In *Proceedings of the 8th International Colloquium on Structural Information and Communication Complexity (SIROCCO'01)*, pages 275–291. Carleton Univ. Press, 2001.
8. A. Mostefaoui, S. Rajsbaum, M. Raynal, and M. Roy. A hierarchy of conditions for consensus solvability. In *Proceedings of the 20th annual ACM symposium on Principles of distributed computing*, pages 151–160. ACM Press, 2001.
9. A. Mostefaoui, S. Rajsbaum, M. Raynal, and M. Roy. Condition-based protocols for set agreement problems. In *Proceedings of the 16th International Symposium on DIStributed Computing (DISC 2002)*, pages 48–62. Springer LNCS 2508, 2002.

Using Conditions to Expedite Consensus in Synchronous Distributed Systems

Achour Mostefaoui[1], Sergio Rajsbaum[2], and Michel Raynal[1]

[1] IRISA, Campus de Beaulieu, 35042 Rennes Cedex, France
{achour,raynal}@irisa.fr
[2] Instituto de Matemáticas, UNAM, D. F. 04510, Mexico
rajsbaum@math.unam.mx

Abstract. The condition-based approach to solve consensus has initially been developed in the context of asynchronous systems. It identifies a class of *acceptable* conditions on the set of input vectors that, when satisfied by the actual input vector, are exactly the conditions that allow to solve consensus despite up to t faulty processes. This paper investigates the use of conditions to solve consensus in synchronous systems prone to process crash failures. It first shows that for any acceptable condition there is a condition-based protocol solving uniform consensus that enjoys the following property: when the input vector belongs to the condition, it terminates in a single round if no process crashes, and in two rounds otherwise. When the input vector does not belong to the condition, the actual number of rounds is upper bounded by $t + 1$ (it actually depends on both the crash pattern and the input vector). The paper then extends the previous protocol to combine early decision with the condition-based approach. It presents a general protocol that enjoys the previous properties (decision in one or two rounds) when the input vector belongs to the condition and terminates in at most $\min(t + 1, f + 2)$ rounds when the input vector does not belong to the condition (where f is the actual number of faulty processes). Finally, the paper presents corresponding matching lower bounds. It shows that acceptable conditions are the only ones for which a consensus protocol can enjoy the previous properties.

1 Introduction

Context of the paper. The consensus problem can be informally stated as follows: each process proposes an input value and the non-faulty processes have to decide (termination) on the same output value (agreement) that has to be one of the proposed values (validity). Two versions of the consensus problem are usually distinguished. They differ in the statement of the agreement property. In the uniform consensus version, no two processes, faulty or not, can decide differently. In the non-uniform version, called consensus in the following, agreement is required only on the non-faulty processes.

In a synchronous system, let t be the maximal number of processes that can crash. Both consensus and uniform consensus can be solved in $t + 1$ rounds,

F.E. Fich (Ed.): DISC 2003, LNCS 2848, pp. 249–263, 2003.
© Springer-Verlag Berlin Heidelberg 2003

and this is known to be a lower bound [6,17]. Then, researchers turned to early decision and showed that in cases where the actual number of crashes in an execution is f $(0 \leq f \leq t)$, consensus can be solved in only $f + 1$ rounds, while uniform consensus can be solved in $\min(f + 2, t + 1)$ rounds, and these bounds are tight [4,5,14,18,17].

The case $f = 0$ is of special importance, since in practice it is often the case that there are no failures. The previous results show that in such cases uniform consensus can be solved in two rounds. In this paper we show that actually there are many other situations where uniform consensus can be solved in two rounds. Moreover, we show that a uniform consensus protocol can be tuned to terminate in two rounds on certain combinations of input values that may be common in practice.

In this paper we address uniform consensus because it is harder than consensus, and because this case implies corresponding lower bounds for partial synchrony models (e.g., [10,15]). However, we show that it is easy to extend our results to consensus.

M otivation and content of the paper. In [20] we introduced the condition-based approach to characterize the set of input vectors for which consensus can be solved in an asynchronous system with crash failures. An input vector contains an entry per process, each entry containing the value proposed by the corresponding process. This approach is practically relevant when the input vectors are likely to satisfy some condition (e.g., in some applications, more than a majority of processes nearly always do propose the same value).

This paper investigates the use of the condition-based approach to solve uniform consensus in the context of a synchronous system with crash failures. The goal of the paper is to identify the conditions (i.e., sets of input vectors) on which a decision can be made very fast, even when processes crash at every round. That is, as mentioned earlier, it is known that for every uniform consensus protocol there is an input vector, and an execution starting from it, that takes at least $f + 2$ rounds to decide. But it was not known how many rounds are needed to terminate in other input vectors. We are interested in uniform consensus protocols that terminate in less than $f + 2$ rounds in as many input vectors as possible, even in executions with f failures. In particular, in this paper we look for protocols that terminate in at most two rounds in as many input vectors as possible. Roughly speaking, it turns out that we can identify all conditions that allow for this early deciding, and there is a gap result: there is a protocol that terminates in at most two rounds for input vectors in such a condition independently of the actual number of faults f; for all other input vectors $f + 2$ rounds are needed to decide in at least one execution.

Here are our results in more detail. We start by defining a class of conditions, called acceptable conditions. We then show that, for any acceptable condition C, uniform consensus can be solved in one round when the input vector is in the condition and there is no crash, and requires only one additional round when the input vector is in the condition and there are crashes. In the other cases, it requires at most $t+1$ rounds (the number of rounds depends on both the actual pattern failure and input vector).

The paper then extends the protocol to get a protocol whose number of rounds to decide depends on f instead of t. The uniform consensus protocol merges optimally early decision and the condition-based approach to benefit from the best of both worlds: it never requires more than $\min(t+1, f+2)$ for the processes to decide (which is the known lower bound [4,14])[1], and decides in one (resp., two) round(s) when the input vector belongs to the condition and there is no crash (resp., there are crashes).

It was not a priori clear that the combination of conditions and early deciding could keep the advantages of both approaches optimally. The incremental construction of the general protocol from the basic condition-based synchronous protocol was not obvious as it required to enrich the early deciding part in order to be able to terminate in two rounds when there are no failures (and the input vector is not in the condition). The difficulty to be addressed comes from the fact that the value decided from the vector of proposed values by the early deciding mechanism and the value possibly decided from the condition may not be the same. Solving this conflict without adding rounds actually requires "subtleties" in the introduction of appropriate statements.

Finally, the paper focuses on proving matching lower bounds. It shows that if C is the set of input vectors on which a uniform consensus protocol decides in one (resp. two) round(s) when $f = 0$ (resp. $f > 0$), then C must be acceptable.

It is remarkable that acceptable conditions are actually the same set of conditions that allow to solve consensus in asynchronous systems (i.e., correspond to the acceptable conditions of [20]). In this sense, the paper not only presents new, more efficient consensus protocols for synchronous systems, but also contributes to the effort of works such as [9,13] of providing a better understanding of the relation between synchronous and asynchronous fault-tolerant computation.

Related work. All other work on the condition based approach was done for asynchronous systems, identifying sets of input vectors (called conditions) for which it is possible to solve (or solve faster) a given problem, without additional timing or failure detection assumptions[2]. Most work has been on the consensus problem (e.g., [20,22]). The basic condition based approach has been generalized in two directions in [8]: one to cope with Byzantine process behavior, the other to solve the more constrained problem of interactive consistency. The less constrained problem of set agreement was studied in [1,23].

The use of fast failure detectors in synchronous distributed systems is investigated in [2]. As conditions, fast failure detectors are not necessary to solve consensus or related problems in synchronous systems. They are used to expedite the consensus decision. See [25] for a survey on synchronous consensus including other failure models like omission and Byzantine failures.

---

[1] Let us notice that the protocol terminates in only three rounds whatever the number $f > 0$ of crashes, when those crashes occur before the protocol execution.

[2] In contrast to protocols that are based on failure detectors or leader oracles (e.g. [3, 11,12,16,24]).

Roadmap. The paper is made up of five sections. Section 2 presents the computation model and consensus. Section 3 introduces the condition-based approach. Then, Section 4 presents an optimal condition-based synchronous consensus protocol. For ease of exposition this presentation is done in an incremental way: Section 4.1 presents first a simple condition-based synchronous consensus protocol, and then Section 4.2 combines it with early decision. Section 5 is dedicated to lower bounds. Due to page limitations missing proofs can be found in [21].

2   Computation Model and the Consensus Problem

The system consists of a finite set of processes, $\Pi = \{p_1, \ldots, p_n\}$, that communicate by sending and receiving messages through channels. Every pair of processes p_i and p_j is connected by a channel.

Round-Based Synchronous System. The executions consist of a sequence of rounds identified by the successive integers $1, 2$, etc. For the processes, the current round number appears as a global variable r that they can read, and whose progress is managed by the underlying system. A round is made up of three consecutive phases: A send phase in which each process sends messages; A receive phase in which each process receives messages sent in the same round; A computation phase during which each process processes the messages it received during that round and executes local computation.

Failure Model. The underlying communication system is assumed to be failure-free: there is no creation, alteration, loss or duplication of message. A process is faulty during an execution if it prematurely stops its execution (crash). After it has crashed, a process does nothing. If a process crashes in the middle of a sending phase, only the subset of the messages it sent before it crashed will actually be sent. A correct process is a process that is not faulty. At most t processes may be faulty in an execution, and f is the actual number of faulty processes during an execution ($0 \leq f \leq t$ and $1 \leq t < n$).

The Consensus Problem. Each process p_i proposes a value v_i and all correct processes have to decide on a value v, such that the following three properties are satisfied:
- Termination: Every correct process eventually decides.
- Validity: If a process decides v, then v was proposed by some process.
- Agreement: No two correct processes decide different values.

   Notice that the agreement property allows a correct process to decide differently from a faulty process. Uniform Consensus is defined by the previous Termination and Validity properties plus the following Agreement property:
- Uniform Agreement: No two (correct or not) processes decide different values.

In the following $\mathcal{V}$ denotes the set of values that can be proposed by the processes.

3   The Condition-Based Approach

The condition-based approach has been introduced in the context of asynchronous systems prone to process crashes in [20], where conditions C that make the consensus problem solvable despite up to t faulty processes were studied. In a synchronous model consensus is solvable for any condition, since it is solvable for all input vectors. But if the condition allows all input vectors, $t + 1$ rounds are necessary to solve consensus. We are interested in conditions that allow to solve consensus in two rounds.

3.1   Principles and Notation

An input vector is a size n vector, whose i-th entry contains the value proposed by p_i, or $\bot$ if p_i did not take any step in the execution ($\bot$ denotes a default value such that $\bot \notin \mathcal{V}$). We usually denote with I an input vector with all entries in $\mathcal{V}$, and with J an input vector that may have some entries equal to $\bot$. As (by assumption) at most t processes can crash, we consider only input vectors J with at most t entries equal to $\bot$, called views. Let $\mathcal{V}^n$ be the set of all possible input vectors with all entries in $\mathcal{V}$, and $\mathcal{V}^n_t$ be the set of all possible input vectors with all entries in $\mathcal{V} \cup \{\bot\}$ and at most t entries equal to $\bot$. Thus, when we consider the consensus problem in a system where up to t processes can crash, every vector $J \in \mathcal{V}^n_t$ is a possible input vector. For $I \in \mathcal{V}^n$, let $\mathcal{I}_t$ be the set of possible views, i.e., the set of all input vectors J such that J is equal to I except for at most t entries that are equal to $\bot$. We call a set C, $C \subseteq \mathcal{V}^n$, a condition. Let $\mathcal{C}_t$ be the union of the $\mathcal{I}_t$'s over all $I \in C$. Every vector in $\mathcal{C}_t$ is a possible input vector of the condition. For vectors $J1, J2 \in \mathcal{V}^n_t$, $J1 \leq J2$ if $\forall k : J1[k] \neq \bot \Rightarrow J1[k] = J2[k]$, and we say that $J2$ contains $J1$, or $J1$ can be extended to $J2$. Finally, $\#_a(J)$ denotes the number of occurrences of a value a in the vector J, with $a \in \mathcal{V} \cup \{\bot\}$.

3.2   Acceptable Conditions

The conditions that allow to solve consensus in an asynchronous system[3] are identified in [20], and called acceptable. For the purposes of designing a consensus protocol it was convenient to define an acceptable condition in terms of three properties that should be satisfied by a predicate P and a deterministic function S. A consensus protocol is instantiated with P and S. Intuitively, the predicate P allows a process p_i to test if the input vector can belong to the condition; thus, P returns true at least for all those input vectors J such that $J \in \mathcal{I}_t$ for $I \in C$ (property $\mathrm{T}_{C \to P}$). The second property ($\mathrm{V}_{P \to S}$) is related to validity: a decided value has been proposed. The third property ($\mathrm{A}_{P \to S}$) concerns agreement: if two processes p_i and p_j get views $J1$ and $J2$, one an extension of the other, and both in the condition, these processes can decide the same value, which should be in both $J1$ and $J2$. More precisely,

---

[3] Not all conditions have this property; there is no solution for $C = \mathcal{V}^n$, due to the FLP impossibility result of [7].

- Property $T_{C \to P}$:
    $I \in C \Rightarrow \forall J \in \mathcal{I}_t : P(J)$. (Or equivalently, $\forall J \in \mathcal{C}_t : P(J)$.)
- Property $V_{P \to S}$:
    $\forall I \in \mathcal{V}^n : \forall J \in \mathcal{I}_t : P(J) \Rightarrow S(J) =$ a non-$\perp$ value of J (determ. chosen).
- Property $A_{P \to S}$:
    $\forall I \in \mathcal{V}^n : \forall J1, J2 \in \mathcal{I}_t : P(J1) \wedge P(J2) \wedge (J1 \leq J2) \Rightarrow S(J1) = S(J2)$.

Definition 1. [20] A condition C is t-acceptable if there exist a predicate P and a function S satisfying the properties $T_{C \to P}$, $A_{P \to S}$ and $V_{P \to S}$.

Theorem 1. [20] A condition C allows to solve consensus in an asynchronous system prone to up to t process crashes if and only if it is t-acceptable.

3.3   Example of a Condition

Two natural conditions have been introduced in [20]. A general method to define linear conditions is described in [22]. By way of example, we present here the condition $C1$. Let $\max(I)$ denote the greatest non-$\perp$ value of an input vector I, and $\#_a(I)$ be the number of times a occurs in I.

$$(I \in C1) \quad \overset{def}{=} \quad [\, a = \max(I) \Rightarrow \#_a(I) > t \,].$$

It is shown in [20] that $C1$ is t-acceptable with the following predicate P and function S: $P1(J) \equiv a = \max(J) \Rightarrow \#_a(J) > t - \#_\perp(J)$, and $S1(J) = \max(J)$. So, [20] shows that when at least $t + 1$ entries of every input vector are equal to its greatest entry, then consensus can be solved despite up to t process crashes in an asynchronous system.

4   Condition-Based Consensus in Synchronous Systems

In the following, we consider a predicate P and function S associated with some t-acceptable condition C, as in Definition 1. We present two synchronous protocols that solve uniform consensus, and in addition terminate in at most two rounds for inputs in C. Both terminate in at most $t + 1$ rounds. The second is an early-deciding extension of the first. For each t-acceptable C, the protocols are instantiated with corresponding P and S. Some of the proofs are omitted for lack of space, and appear in [21].

4.1   A Condition-Based Protocol for Synchronous Systems

The protocol. Figure 1 presents a uniform consensus protocol for C that terminates in at most $t + 1$ rounds. Each process p_i maintains an array V_i keeping its view of the proposed input vector, a variable w_i to store the value decided from the condition (if any), and a boolean $flagC_i$ indicating if the decided value has to be the one determined from the condition. The other local variables of

p_i (new_i, $rec\_from_i[j]$ and W_i) are auxiliary variables related to the content of messages sent and received during each round.

During each round r ($1 \leq r \leq t+1$, lines 102-116), p_i first sends to every process all the proposed values it has learnt during the previous round, plus the current value of w_i (line 104). It is important that, during a sending phase, each p_i sends first to p_1, then to p_2, then to p_3, etc. This guarantees that, at any round, if neither p_k nor p_ℓ have crashed, the views V_k and V_ℓ are such that $k \leq \ell \Rightarrow V_\ell \leq V_k$ (see Lemma 1)[4].

The protocol relies on the following principle: as soon as a process p_i sees a value $w_i = v$ obtained from the condition, either directly at the first round (line 112) or indirectly from another process at a later round (line 113), it sets its flag $flagC_i$ (line 115) in order to decide at the next round (line 105). So, if p_i decides at line 105, it has previously sent $w_i(= v)$ to all processes (line 104), thereby guaranteeing the propagation of the value v (to get uniform agreement).

If p_i does not decide at line 105 (notice that this is always the case at the first round), it first increases its knowledge of the input vector by updating its view V_i according to the proposed values it learns during that round (lines 108-111). Then, the behavior of p_i depends on the round number:
- If $r = 1$ (line 112), p_i tests if its view can be obtained from a vector of the condition (i.e., "does V_i belong to C_t?") by evaluating $P(V_i)$. If this is the case, it sets w_i to the decision value determined from the condition, i.e., $S(V_i)$. Moreover, p_i also tests if its view V_i is full (i.e., all its entries contain non-$\perp$ values). If this is the case, p_i early decides as it then knows that the view V_j obtained by any other process p_j (be that view V_j be full or not) is such that $P(V_j)$ is true. It follows that the processes decide in one round when the input vector belongs to the condition and there are no failures
- If $r > 1 \wedge w_i = \perp$, then, if p_i has heard from another process that there is a decision value v determined from the condition, then it adopts it (line 113).

It is relatively easy to see that the protocol terminates in two rounds when the input vector I belongs to the condition C, whatever the actual number f of failures. When $I \notin C$, the number of rounds depends on the failure pattern and the fact that some processes p_i get a view V_i such that $P(V_i)$ is satisfied. As soon as a process p_i gets such a view, it computes $v = S(V_i)$ and if a correct process p_j gets v during a round r, p_j terminates at $r+1$, and no process terminates after $r+2$. If no process gets such a view, then all correct processes terminate at round $t+1$. In that case a process p_i decides $\min(V_i)$ ($\perp$ is assumed to be greater than any proposed value).

The reader can notice that if we suppress from the protocol all the parts concerned by the condition, i.e., we suppress $flagC_i$, the value w_i in the messages that are sent, lines 107-105 and 112-115, and keep only the statement $return$ $\min(V_i)$ at line 117, we get the well-known flood set protocol [18].

A remark is now in order: while a process p_i could test $P(V_i)$ at every round (provided that $w_i = \perp$), it does it only during the first round. This is because the view of a process can only increase as the round number progresses, so if

---

[4] This containment property is obtained in asynchronous systems using snapshots [20].

$P(V_k)$ is not true during the first round, it would not become true in a later round.

Function $CB\_Consensus(v_i)$

(101) $V_i \leftarrow [\bot, \dots, \bot]$; $new_i \leftarrow \{(v_i, i)\}$; $w_i \leftarrow \bot$; $flagC_i \leftarrow false$;
(102) **when** $r = 1, 2, \dots, t+1$ **do**
(103) **begin_round**
(104)   **send** (new_i, w_i) **to** $p_1, \dots, p_n$ **in that order;**
(105)   **if** $flagC_i$ **then** return (w_i) **end_if;**
(106)   **let** $rec\_from_i[j] = new_j$ set received from p_j (if any), otherwise $\emptyset$;
(107)   **let** $W_i =$ set of w_j values received; % $W_i = \{v\}$ or $\{\bot\}$ or $\{v, \bot\}$ %
(108) $new_i \leftarrow \emptyset$;
(109)   **for_each** j **do for_each** $(x, k) \in rec\_from_i[j]$ **do**
(110)   **if** $(V_i[k] = \bot)$ **then** $V_i[k] \leftarrow x$; $new_i \leftarrow new_i \cup \{(x, k)\}$ **end_if**
(111)   **end_do end_do;**
(112)   **case** $(r = 1)$ **:** **if** $P(V_i)$ **then** $w_i \leftarrow S(V_i)$;
                                         if $(\bot \notin V_i)$ **then** return (w_i) **end_if**
                           end_if
(113) $(r > 1)$ **:** **if** $\big(w_i = \bot \wedge (v \neq \bot \in W_i)\big)$ **then** $w_i \leftarrow v$ **end_if**
(114)   **end_case;**
(115)   **if** $(w_i \neq \bot)$ **then** $flagC_i \leftarrow true$ **end_if**
(116) **end_round;**
(117) **if** $flagC_i$ **then** return (w_i) **else** return $(min(V_i))$ **end_if**

Fig. 1. A Synchronous Condition-Based Uniform Consensus Protocol

If we are interested only in the consensus problem (instead of uniform consensus), the protocol can easily be modified to save one round (when we consider the round $r > 1$ during which a process decides): p_i can decide as soon as it sets its flag $flagC_i$ (line 115), and terminates one round later when it sees its flag is up (line 105).

Proof of the Protocol. The proof assumes that the considered condition C is t-acceptable and that there are no more than t process crashes. The following notation is used: UP^r denotes the set of processes that have not crashed by the end of r, V_i^r denotes the value of V_i at the end of r, and w_i^r denotes value of w_i at the end of r.

Lemma 1. (Containment) $\forall r \geq 1$: $\forall p_i, p_j \in UP^r$: $i < j \Rightarrow V_j^r \leq V_i^r$.

Proof Let us first observe that an entry k of any array V_i is initially equal to $\bot$, and then it can only be equal to v_k (the value proposed by p_k). This comes from lines 109-111 and the fact that, as far as the update of an array V_i is concerned, messages carry pairs made up of a proposed value and the identity of the process that proposed it.

Let p_i and p_j be two processes that have not crashed by the end of round r, such that $i < j$. Let $V_j^r[k] = v \neq \perp$. We have to show that $V_i^r[k] = v$. Due to the initialization of the V arrays (line 101), $V_j^r[k] = v \neq \perp$ implies that p_j has received (during a round $1 \leq r' \leq r$) from some process p_ℓ a message carrying the pair (v, k). During r', before p_ℓ sent such a message to p_j, it previously sent the same message to p_i because, due to $i < j$, a message is first sent to p_i and only then to p_j. As messages are not lost, p_i received that message by the end of the round r', and consequently $V_i^r[k] = v$. $\square_{Lemma\ 1}$

Lemma 2. $\forall p_i, p_j \in \mathrm{UP}^1:$ $P(V_i^1) \wedge P(V_j^1) \Rightarrow S(V_i^1) = S(V_j^1).$

Proof Let us first observe that, as the condition C is t-acceptable, the property $A_{P \rightarrow S}$ is satisfied, i.e., we have $\forall I \in \mathcal{V}^n : \forall J1, J2 \in \mathcal{I}_t\colon P(J1) \wedge P(J2) \wedge (J1 \leq J2) \Rightarrow S(J1) = S(J2)$. Moreover, due to Lemma 1, we have $V_j^1 \leq V_i^1$, assuming w.l.o.g. $i < j$. We immediately conclude $S(V_i^1) = S(V_j^1)$ from $A_{P \rightarrow S}$. $\square_{Lemma\ 2}$

Theorem 2. The protocol in Figure 1 solves the uniform consensus problem .

Proof The proof of the Termination and Validity properties can be found in [21]. We focus here on the Uniform agreement property. Let p_i and p_j two processes that decide. Each decides by executing either $return\ (w_i)$ at line 105, 112 or 117, or $return\ (\min(V_i))$ at line 117. We consider three cases.

- Case 1: p_i and p_j execute $return\ (w_i)$ and $return\ (w_j)$, respectively. In that case, as we have previously seen in the proof of the validity property, there are p_k and p_ℓ such that $P(V_k^1)$ and $P(V_\ell^1)$ were satisfied and $w_i = S(V_k^1)$ and $w_j = S(V_\ell^1)$. It then follows from Lemma 2 that $S(V_k^1) = S(V_\ell^1)$, from which we conclude $w_i = w_j$.

- Case 2: p_i and p_j execute $return\ (w_i)$ and $return\ (\min(V_j))$, respectively. We show that this case cannot occur. Let r be the first round during which a process p_i executes $return\ (w_i)$. We consider the following four subcases:

  - $r = 1$ and p_i decides at line 112 by executing $return\ (w_i)$. In that case, V_i^1 is exactly the input vector (without $\perp$ entries), and it belongs to the condition C. It follows that, due to the $T_{C \rightarrow P}$ property, the view V_j^1 of any other process is such that $V_j^1 \leq V_i^1$ and (since V_i^1 belongs to the condition) $P(V_j^1)$ is satisfied. Moreover, due to the $A_{P \rightarrow S}$ property, we have $S(V_j^1) = S(V_i^1)$. Lastly, if p_j does not decide at line 112, it sets $flagC_j$ to true, and consequently will not decide by executing $return\ (\min(V_j))$ at line 117.

  - $r < t + 1$: In that case, p_i decides at line 105, and before deciding it sets $flagC_i$ to true during $r - 1$ (let us notice that, due to the initial value of w_i and line 115 we can conclude that such a round $r - 1$ does exist). This means that during the sending phase of round r, p_i has sent $w_i \neq \perp$ to all processes. It follows that the processes p_j that have not crashed by the end of r have $w_j \neq \perp$. So, they set their flag $flagC_j$ during r, and consequently cannot decide $\min(V_j)$. (From then on they can only decide by executing $return\ (w_i)$, and then Case 1 applies.)

- $r = t + 1$ and p_i decides at line 105. This case is similar to the previous one (p_i sets $flagC_i$ to true during $r - 1$ and disseminates w_i to all processes at the beginning of r).
- $r = t + 1$ and p_i executes $return(w_i)$ at line 117. In that case, p_i updated w_i from $\bot$ to some value $v \neq \bot$ at round $t + 1$. That value v has been computed by some process p_ℓ during the first round. We have: $w_i^1 = \bot$ and $w_\ell^1 = v$, from which we can conclude that $V_i^1 \neq V_\ell^1$. Because p_i and p_ℓ did not get the same view during the first round we can conclude that at least one process (say p_k) crashed during the first round.

  As p_i receives v only during the round $t + 1$, it follows that from p_ℓ included (that computed v during the first round) to p_i excluded, the value v has been forwarded by t distinct processes. When we consider (1) the set made up of those t processes plus p_k, and (2) the fact that at most t processes can be faulty, it follows that one of the t processes that forwarded v is correct (actually that process is the last one of the chain of the forwarding processes). Hence, that process sent v to all processes. It follows that if a process p_j has not decided before $t + 1$, it has its $flagC_j$ set to true at $t + 1$, and consequently cannot execute $return(\min(V_j))$.

- Case 3: p_i executes $return(\min(V_i))$. In that case, due to the Case 2 impossibility, it follows that no process p_k executes $return(w_k)$. It also follows that all the processes that decide do it at the end of round $t + 1$. In that case, the behavior of the protocol is the same as the one of the classic flood set protocol where all processes p_i that decide do it at round $t + 1$ and have then the same array V_i at that round. (A proof of the flood set protocol can be found in [18].)

$$\square_{Theorem\ 2}$$

Theorem 3. Consider the protocol described in Figure 1 for condition C, and let I be an input vector. (1) If $I \in C$ decision is reached in one round if there is no failure, and in at most two rounds otherwise. (2) If $I \notin C$ and a process p_i has a view in C_t and does not crash by the end of the second round, p_i decides during the second round and any other process p_j decides at the latest during the third round (whatever the failure pattern). (3) A process always executes at most $t + 1$ rounds.

4.2   Combining Early Decision and Conditions

The previous consensus protocol has a "very early decision" flavor in the sense that a process p_i that, during the first round, gets a view belonging to C_t, can decide by the end of the second round (and during the first round if additionally V_i^1 does not contain $\bot$). But, except for the first round, the design of this protocol does not consider the fact that the number f of actual crashes can be less than t. It is known that the round complexity of early deciding uniform consensus is $\min(f + 2, t + 1)$ [4]. Here we extend the previous protocol to get a protocol that benefits from the best of both worlds: a protocol that decides as early as possible (1) when the input vector belongs to the condition, or (2) when few processes crash.

The protocol. A protocol combining condition and early decision is presented in Figure 2. It is built from the protocol described in Figure 1, by the addition of a few statements. To make those new statements visible at a glance, they have been put inside boxes in the figure. Basically, these statements manage at each process p_i a new flag ($flagED_i$) and a set variable ($R_i[r]$) that represents the set of processes from which p_i has received messages during the round r.

The $flagED_i$ local variable is set to true as soon as there are two consecutive rounds (after the first round) during which p_i has received messages from the same set of processes (line 215), i.e., when $R_i[r-1] = R_i[r]$ [17]. The setting of $flagED_i$ to true is motivated by the following observation. Assuming $r > 1$, let us notice that $R_i[r-1] \supseteq \mathrm{UP}^{r-1} \supseteq R_i[r]$ (let us remind that UP^{r-1} denotes the set of processes that are not crashed at the end of the round $r-1$, or equivalently not crashed at the beginning of r). So, $R_i[r-1] = R_i[r]$ means that $R_i[r-1] = \mathrm{UP}^{r-1} = R_i[r]$, from which p_i can conclude that it has received a message from all the processes that were not crashed at the beginning of r. Consequently, $R_i[r-1] = R_i[r]$ allows p_i to conclude that it knows "all" that was known at the beginning of r: it cannot learn more on the values proposed by the processes or the value v that could be decided from the condition.

As we can see at lines 205, 215 and 217, the protocol gives priority to $flagC_i$ with respect to $flagED_i$; both in the order these flags are set, and in the order they are read to decide. More precisely, a process p_i checks first $flagC_i$ to decide, and only then $flagED_i$ (see lines 205 and 217). In that sense, the protocol gives priority to the early decision due to the condition with respect to the early decision due to the pattern failure. More generally, when we consider a protocol merging condition and early decision due to the failure pattern, each process p_i has two inputs:

- The first one is the value it proposes, namely v_i. That value is implicitly defined at round 0.
- The second one is the value w_i. That value is explicitly computed during the first round.

So, for each process, the pair made up of both of those inputs is not determined before the end of the first round. This means that, only from $r = 2$, p_i can conclude from $R_i[r-1] = R_i[r]$ that it knows not only all the proposed values that can be known, but also the value decided from the condition (if any). This motivates the test $r > 1$ in the "else" part of the statement of line 215.

A crucial issue of an early deciding protocol is to allow the processes to decide in $\min(t+1, f+2)$ rounds in the worst case (e.g., in two rounds when there is no failure)[5]. But, in our case, this has not to be done in contradiction with the value possibly decided from the condition. Preventing such a conflict, while maintaining the $\min(t+1, f+2)$ lower bound, is done at line 205. First the priority is given to the value decided from the condition if any (test of $flagC_i$). Then, if both $flagC_i$ and $flagED_i$ are false, a process checks if it has

---

[5] Considering the protocol without the condition $R_i[r] \geq n - r + 2$ at line 205 gives a protocol terminating in at most $\min(t+1, f+3)$ when $I \notin C$.

Function $ED\_CB\_Consensus(v_i)$

(201) $V_i \leftarrow [\perp, \ldots, \perp]$; $new_i \leftarrow \{(v_i, i)\}$; $w_i \leftarrow \perp$; $flagC_i \leftarrow false$;
$\boxed{flagED_i \leftarrow false;}$
(202) **when** $r = 1, 2, \ldots, t + 1$ **do**
(203) **begin_round**
(204)   **send** (new_i, w_i) **to** $p_1, \ldots, p_n$ **in that order**;
          let $R_i[r]$ = set of processes from which p_i received messages during r;
(205)   **if** $flagC_i$ **then** return (w_i) **else**
              $\boxed{\textbf{if } \big(flagED_i \vee \underline{|R_i[r]| \geq n - r + 2}\big) \textbf{ then } return (min(V_i)) \textbf{ end\_if}}$
          end_if;
(206)   **let** $rec\_from_i[j]$ = new_j set received from p_j (if any), otherwise $\emptyset$;
(207)   **let** W_i = set of w_j values received; % $W_i = \{v\}$ or $\{\perp\}$ or $\{v, \perp\}$ %
(208) $new_i \leftarrow \emptyset$;
(209)   **for_each** j **do for_each** $(x, k) \in rec\_from_i[j]$ **do**
(210)   **if** $(V_i[k] = \perp)$ **then** $V_i[k] \leftarrow x$; $new_i \leftarrow new_i \cup \{(x, k)\}$ **end_if**
(211)   **end_do end_do**;
(212)   **case** $(r = 1)$: **if** $P(V_i)$ **then** $w_i \leftarrow S(V_i)$;
                                  if $(\perp \notin V_i)$ **then** return (w_i) **end_if**
                  end_if
(213) $(r > 1)$: **if** $\big(w_i = \perp \wedge (v \neq \perp \in W_i)\big)$ **then** $w_i \leftarrow v$ **end_if**
(214)   **end_case**;
(215)   **if** $(w_i \neq \perp)$ **then** $flagC_i \leftarrow true$ **else**
              $\boxed{\textbf{if } \big((r > 1) \wedge (R_i[r - 1] = R_i[r])\big) \textbf{ then } flagED_i \leftarrow true \textbf{ end\_if}}$
          end_if
(216) **end_round**;
(217) **if** $flagC_i$ **then** return (w_i) **else** return $(min(V_i))$ **end_if**

Fig. 2. A Synchronous Early Deciding Condition-Based Uniform Consensus Protocol

received messages from at least $n - r + 2$ processes (this test is underlined in the box of line 205). If this is the case, p_i decides from the early deciding point of view by executing $return$ $(min(V_i))$. The intuition behind the underlined test is the following. If there are exactly f crashes (notice those can span f different rounds), we do have $|R_i[r]| \geq n - f$ at any round r and for any p_i (not crashed at r), from which we can conclude that, at the latest at $r = f + 2$, we have $R_i[r] \geq n - r + 2$. Using this test to direct a process to decide ensures that no process will decide after the round $f + 2$. Interestingly, as shown by the proof of the protocol, the way the tests are sequenced at line 205 enjoys the nice property not to entail a conflict between the value possibly decided from the condition by a process p_i (because $flagC_i$ is true) and the value decided from the early decision mechanism by another process p_j (because $flagED_j \vee R_j[r] \geq n - r + 2$ is true): at any round r, if both the conditions $flagC_i$ and $(flagED_j \vee R_j[r] \geq n - r + 2)$ are simultaneously true, then $flagC_j$ is also true.

Theorem 4. The protocol in Figure 2 solves the uniform consensus problem.

Theorem 5. Consider the protocol described in Figure 2 for condition C, and let I be an input vector. (1) If $I \in C$ decision is reached in one round if $f = 0$, and in at most two rounds otherwise. (2) If $I \notin C$ and a process p_i has a view in C_t and does not crash by the end of the second round, p_i decides during the second round and any other process p_j decides at the latest during the third round (whatever the failure pattern). (3) A process always executes at most $\min(t + 1, f + 2)$ rounds.

Remark. Concerning the $\min(t + 1, f + 2)$ lower bound a remark is now in order. Only the underlined test (namely, $|R_i[r]| \geq n - r + 2$) is actually used to prove that the protocol meets the lower bound. The $flagED_i$ is not necessary to establish it. So, an interesting question is "Why to use the $flagED_i$ local variables?" The answer is simple: the $flagED_i$ variable allows p_i to decide "as early as possible", while the underlined test allows it not to bypass the lower bound. To be more explicit, let us consider the case where $f \geq 1$ processes crash before the protocol execution (and no process crashes later during the execution). In that case, using only the $|R_i[r]| \geq n - r + 2$ test would delay the processes to decide at round $f + 2$. The use of the $flagED_i$ boolean allows a process p_i to decide by the end of the third round.

5   Lower Bound

Considering any given uniform consensus protocol, this section proves a lower bound theorem corresponding to Theorem 5. The proof technique is similar to the one used in [14] (which is based on [19]), but extended to t failures (as opposed to one failure).

Theorem 6. (1) Let C be a set of input vectors for which a protocol always decides in one round when there are no failures. Then, C is $(t - 1)$-acceptable. (2) Let C be a set of input vectors for which a protocol decides in at most two rounds when there are failures. Then, C is $(t - 1)$-acceptable.

Proof We prove part (1) by defining P and S satisfying the acceptability definition. Part (2) is similar and deferred to the full version. First, P is defined to be true for $\forall J \in C_t$. For an input vector $I \in C$, let $S(I)$ be the value decided in one round by the processes when there are no failures. From the Validity property it follows that $S(I)$ is a non-$\perp$ value from I, and Property $V_{P \rightarrow S}$ holds. Consider an input vector J, $J \leq I$, with $\#_\perp(J) \leq t - 1$, i.e., $J \in \mathcal{I}_{t-1}$. Let Q be the set of processes with $\perp$ entries in J. Let p_i be the process outside of Q with smallest index i. Consider an execution starting in I where the processes of Q fail in the first round and send a message only to p_i (in addition to perhaps processes of Q), p_i fails in the second round (which is possible since $|Q| < t$), and does not send any messages in that round, and these are the only failures.

Thus, p_i is the only one (outside of Q) that knows the input values of processes in Q, and fails before being able to announce them to other processes. Since p_i receives messages from all processes in the first round, it still decides $S(I)$ at the end of the first round. Each correct process must eventually decide (Termination requirement), and the correct processes must decide $S(I)$ (Uniform Agreement). But these processes do not hear from processes in Q so they would behave the same in an execution starting from J where p_i fails at the beginning of the second round. That is, they decide $S(I)$ which must be in J from the Validity property. Thus, we can define $S(J)$ to be equal to $S(I)$ and satisfy both Property $V_{P \rightarrow S}$ and Property $A_{P \rightarrow S}$. $\square_{Theorem\ 6}$

It follows that the set of t-acceptable conditions is the largest set of conditions that allow a protocol to terminate in one (two) round(s) when the input vector belongs to the condition and $f = 0$ ($f > 0$).

References

1. Attiya H., and Avidor Z., Wait-Free n-Set Consensus When Inputs Are Restricted. *Proc. 16th Int. Symposium on DIStributed Computing (DISC'02)*, Springer Verlag LNCS #2508, pp. 326–338, Toulouse, October 2002.
2. Aguilera M.K., Le Lann G. and Toueg S., On the Impact of Fast Failure Detectors on Real-Time Fault-Tolerant Systems. *Proc. 16th Int. Symposium on Distributed Computing (DISC'02)*, Springer-Verlag LNCS #2508, pp. 354–370, 2002.
3. Chandra T.K. and Toueg S., Unreliable Failure Detectors for Reliable Distributed Systems. *Journal of the ACM*, 43(2):225–267, March 1996.
4. Charron-Bost B. and Schiper A., Uniform Consensus is Harder than Consensus. *Technical Report DSC/2000/028*, EPFL, Lausanne, May 2000.
5. Dolev D., Reischuk R. and Strong R., Early Stopping in Byzantine Agreement. *Journal of the ACM*, 37(4):720–741, April 1990.
6. Fischer M.J. and Lynch N., A Lower Bound for the Time to Assure Interactive Consistency. *Information Processing Letters*, 71:183–186, 1982.
7. Fischer M.J., Lynch N.A. and Paterson M.S., Impossibility of Distributed Consensus with One Faulty Process. *Journal of the ACM*, 32(2):374–382, 1985.
8. Friedman R., Mostefaoui A., Rajsbaum S. and Raynal M., Asynchronous Distributed Agreement and its Relation with Error Correcting Codes. *Proc. 16th Int. Symposium on DIStributed Computing (DISC'02)*, Springer Verlag LNCS #2508, pp. 63–87, Toulouse (F), 2002.
9. Gafni E., Round-by-Round Fault Detectors: Unifying Synchrony and Asynchrony. *Proc. 17th ACM Symposium on Principles of Distributed Computing (PODC'98)*, ACM Press, pp. 133–143–152, New York, 1998.
10. Guerraoui, R., Indulgent Algorithms. *Proc. 19th ACM Symposium on Principles of Distributed Computing (PODC'00)*, ACM Press, pp. 289–297, New York, 2000.
11. Guerraoui R. and Raynal M., A Generic Framework for Indulgent Consensus. *Proc. 23rd Int. IEEE Conference on Distributed Computing Systems (ICDCS'03)*, pp. 88–97, Providence (RI), May 2003.
12. Hurfin M., Mostefaoui A. and Raynal M., A Versatile Family of Consensus Protocols Based on Chandra-Toueg's Unreliable Failure Detectors. *IEEE Transactions on Computers*, 51(4):395–408, 2002.

13. Herlihy M.P., Rajsbaum S. and Tuttle M.R., Unifying Synchronous and Asynchronous Message-Passing Models. *Proc. 17th ACM Symposium on Principles of Distributed Computing (PODC'98)*, ACM Press, pp. 133–142, New York, 1998.

14. Keidar I. and Rajsbaum S., A Simple Proof of the Uniform Consensus Synchronous Lower Bound. *Information Processing Letters*, 85:47–52, 2003.

15. Keidar I. and Rajsbaum S., On the Cost of Fault-tolerant Consensus When There Are No Faults. Technical Report MIT-LCS-TR-821, MIT Lab. for CS, May 2001.

16. Lamport L., The Part-Time Parliament. *ACM TOCS*, 16(2):133–169, 1998.

17. Lamport L. and Fischer M., Byzantine Generals and Transaction Commit Protocols. *Unpublished manuscript*, 16 pages, April 1982.

18. Lynch N.A., Distributed Algorithms. *Morgan Kaufmann Pub.*, 872 pages, 1996.

19. Moses, Y. and Rajsbaum, S. A Layered Analysis of Consensus, *SIAM Journal of Computing* 31(4):989–1021, 2002.

20. Mostefaoui A., Rajsbaum S. and Raynal M., Conditions on Input Vectors for Consensus Solvability in Asynchronous Distributed Systems. *Proc. 33rd ACM Symposium on Theory of Computing (STOC'01)*, ACM Press, pp. 153–162, 2001.

21. Mostefaoui A., Rajsbaum S. and Raynal M., Using Conditions to Expedite Consensus in Synchronous Distributed Systems. *IRISA Research Report #1510*, (http://www.irisa.fr/bibli/publi/pi/2003/1510/1510.html), Rennes (F), 2003.

22. Mostefaoui A., Rajsbaum S., Raynal M. and Roy M., Efficient Condition-Based Consensus. *8th Int. Colloquium on Structural Information and Communication Complexity (SIROCCO'01)*, Carleton Univ. Press, pp. 275–293, 2001.

23. Mostefaoui A., Rajsbaum S., Raynal M. and Roy M., Condition-Based Protocols for Set Agreement Problems. *Proc. 16th Int. Symposium on Distributed Computing (DISC'02)*, Springer Verlag LNCS #2508, pp. 48–62, Toulouse, October 2002.

24. Mostefaoui A. and Raynal M., Leader-Based Consensus. *Parallel Processing Letters*, 11(1):95–107, 2001.

25. Raynal M., Consensus in Synchronous Systems: a Concise Guided Tour. *Proc. 9th IEEE Pacific Rim Int. Symposium on Dependable Computing (PRDC'02)*, Tsukuba (Japan), IEEE Computer Press, pp. 221–228, Dec. 2002.

Tight Bounds on Early Local Decisions in Uniform Consensus

(Extended Abstract)*

Partha Dutta, Rachid Guerraoui, and Bastian Pochon

Distributed Programming Laboratory, EPFL

Abstract. When devising a uniform consensus algorithm, it is common to minimize the time complexity of *global* decisions, which is typically measured as the number of communication rounds needed for *all* correct processes to decide. In practice, what we might want to minimize is the time complexity of *local* decisions, which we define as the number of communication rounds needed for *at least one* correct process to decide. We investigate tight bounds on uniform consensus local decisions in crash-stop message-passing models where at most t processes may fail in any given run.

In the synchronous model, we show that any uniform consensus algorithm has (1) a run in which at most $f \leq t - 1$ processes crash such that *no correct process* decides before round $f + 1$ in that run, and (2) a run in which at most $f \leq t - 3$ processes crash such that *at most one correct process* decides before round $f + 2$ in that run. We show that the above lower bounds are tight by pointing out a simple uniform consensus algorithm.

In the eventually synchronous model, we show that any uniform consensus algorithm has a *synchronous run* in which at most $f \leq t - 3$ processes crash such that *no correct process* decides before round $f + 2$ in that run. We present a new uniform consensus algorithm that globally decides in $f + 2$ rounds in every synchronous run in which at most f processes crash. Thus the local and the global decision tight bounds are the same for synchronous runs of the eventually synchronous model.

1 Introduction

Motivation. Determining how long it takes to reach uniform consensus [11, 16] among a set of processes is an important question in distributed computing. For instance, the performance of a replicated system is impacted by the performance of the underlying uniform consensus service used to ensure that the replica processes agree on the same order to deliver client requests [15]. Traditionally, lower bounds on the time complexity of uniform consensus have been stated in terms of the number of communication rounds (also called communication steps) needed

---

* This work is partially supported by the Swiss National Science Foundation (project number 510-207).

F.E. Fich (Ed.): DISC 2003, LNCS 2848, pp. 264–278, 2003.

for all correct processes to decide [8, 3, 13] (i.e., global decision), or even halt [4], possibly as a function of the number of failures f that actually occur, out of the total number t of failures that are tolerated.

From a practical perspective, what we might sometimes want to measure and optimize, is the number of rounds needed for at least one correct process to decide, i.e., for a local decision. Indeed, a replicated service can respond to its clients as soon as a single replica decides on a reply and knows that other replicas will reach the same decision (even if they did not decide yet).

Background. We consider two message-passing crash-stop models where communication among a set of n processes proceed by exchanging messages in a round by round manner: (1) the well-known synchronous model [14] and (2) an eventually synchronous model. In any run, at most t processes might fail, and they can only do so by crashing. In a given run, if a process crashes in that run, it is called faulty; otherwise, it is correct.

In the synchronous model, the $f+2$ round global decision lower bound states the following: for every $f \leq t-2$, any uniform consensus algorithm has a run in which at most f processes crash such that some correct process decides in round $f+2$ or in a higher round in that run [3, 13]. In other words, for all correct processes to decide, we need at least $f+2$ rounds. However, a global decision lower bound does not say whether some correct process can decide before round $f+2$ in every run with f crashes, and if yes, how many processes may actually do so.[1]

In the eventually synchronous model, we know from [9] that for every $f \leq t$, any uniform consensus algorithm has a run in which at most f processes crash such that processes decide after arbitrarily large number of rounds in that run (because the run may remain "asynchronous" for an arbitrary number of rounds). However, if we focus on the synchronous runs of any algorithm (i.e., the runs which are "synchronous" from the very beginning) we can bound the number of rounds required for processes to decide. In fact it is easy to see that the $f+2$ round global decision lower bound in synchronous model immediately extends to synchronous runs of the algorithms in the eventually synchronous model. However, unlike the synchronous model, devising an algorithm that matches the $f+2$ round global decision lower bound has been an open problem [5, 12].

Contributions. This paper first shows that, in the synchronous model, the local decision tight bound is $f+1$. In other words, for every $f \leq t-1$, (1) any uniform consensus algorithm has a run in which at most f processes crash such that no correct process decides in a round lower than $f+1$ in that run, and (2) there is a uniform consensus algorithm such that in every run in which at most f processes crash, some correct process decides by round $f+1$.

Furthermore, we show that, for $f \leq t-3$, any uniform consensus algorithm has a run in which at most f processes crash such that either none or exactly one process decides before round $f+2$ in that run; this gives a bound on the

---

[1] We assume that processes may take steps after their decision events.

number of correct processes which can decide before the global decision lower bound (i.e., $f+2$) in every run with at most f failures. This result generalizes the global decision lower bound of [3, 13] which states that any uniform consensus algorithm has a run in which at most f processes crash such that at least one correct process decides in round $f+2$ or in a higher round in that run: our result implies that there is a run in which at most f processes crash such that at least $n - f - 1$ correct processes decide in round $f + 2$ or in a higher round in that run (because there are at least $n - f$ correct processes in a run in which at most f processes crash, and at most one of them can decide before round $f + 2$).

In the eventually synchronous model, we show that, for $f \leq t-3$, any uniform consensus algorithm has a synchronous run in which at most f processes crash such that no process decides before round $f + 2$ in that run. We give a matching algorithm which globally decides (and hence, locally decides) by round $f + 2$ in every synchronous run in which at most f processes crash, for every $0 \leq f \leq t$. Thus the local decision tight bound is the same as the global decision tight bound.

Roadmap. Section 2 presents the two distributed system models we consider. Section 3 recalls the uniform consensus problem and its time complexity metrics. Section 4 presents a key lemma for our proofs, which is a variant of a lemma of [13]. Section 5 presents our lower bound proofs in the synchronous model and Section 6 presents the lower bound proof in the eventually synchronous model. Finally, Section 7 exhibits a matching algorithm for the eventually synchronous model.

2   Models

We assume a distributed system composed of $n \geq 3$ processes, $\Pi = \{p_1, p_2, \ldots, p_n\}$. The processes communicate by message-passing and every pair of processes is connected by a bi-directional communication channel. Channels do not alter or duplicate messages. The processes may fail by crashing and do not recover from a crash. Any process that does not crash in a run is said to be correct in that run; otherwise the process is faulty. In any given run, at most $t < n$ processes may crash. We consider two round-based models: the well-known synchronous model [14], which we denote by SCS, and an eventually synchronous model, which we denote by ES. Computation proceeds in rounds of message exchanges with increasing round numbers starting from 1. Each round consists of a two phases: (a) in the send phase, processes are supposed to send messages to all processes; (b) in the receive phase, processes receive some messages sent in the send phase, update local states, and (possibly) decide. We say that a message m sent from p_i to p_j is lost, if p_j never receives m in that run. We now describe the guarantees of the two models we consider:

- In SCS, if a process p_i crashes in the send phase of some round k, then any subset of the messages sent by p_i in that round may be lost, but the remaining round k messages sent by p_i are received in round k. If p_i does not crash in the send phase of round k, then no process completes round k without receiving the round k message from p_i.

— In ES, the runs may be "asynchronous" for an arbitrary yet finite number of rounds but eventually become "synchronous." A message sent in the "asynchronous period" may be delayed for a finite number of rounds; i.e., received in a round higher than in which it was sent. More precisely, for every run in ES, the following properties hold: (1) (t-resilience) Every process which completes any round k, receives the round k messages from at least $n - t$ processes, (2) (reliable channels) any message sent by a correct process to a correct process is never lost but may be delayed for an arbitrary yet finite number of rounds, (3) (eventual synchrony) there is an unknown but finite round number K such that, in every round $k \geq K$, if p_i crashes in round k then any subset the messages sent by p_i in that round may be lost, but the remaining round k messages sent by p_i are received in round k, and if p_i does not crash in round k, then no process completes round k without receiving the round k message from p_i.

We say that a run in ES is synchronous if $K = 1$ in that run. Obviously, for every run $r1$ in SCS there is a synchronous run $r2$ in ES such that no process can distinguish $r1$ from $r2$.

3   Time Complexity of Uniform Consensus

We define the uniform consensus problem using two primitives: propose($*$) and decide($*$). Every process is supposed to propose a value through the procedure propose($*$), and a process decides a value by invoking decide($*$). Uniform consensus ensures the following properties: (1) (validity) if a process decides v then some process has proposed v, (2) (uniform agreement) no two processes decide differently, and (3) (termination) every correct process eventually decides. Binary uniform consensus is a variant of uniform consensus in which proposal values are restricted to 0 and 1. We only consider deterministic uniform consensus algorithms.

Consider any uniform consensus algorithm in SCS or ES. We say that a process decides in round $k \geq 1$ if it decides in the receive phase of round k. A run of an algorithm globally decides in round k if all correct processes decide in round k or in a lower round, and some correct process decides in round k. A run of an algorithm locally decides in round k if all correct processes decide in round k or in a higher round and some correct process decides in round k.

In SCS (resp. ES), for every $0 \leq f \leq t$, we define the global decision tight bound as the round number k such that: (1) every uniform consensus algorithm has a run (resp. synchronous run) in which at most f processes crash and which globally decides in round k or in a higher round, and (2) there is a uniform consensus algorithm, which globally decides by round k in every run (resp. synchronous run) in which at most f processes crash. For every $0 \leq f \leq t$, we define the local decision tight bound as the round number k such that: (1) every uniform consensus algorithm has a run (resp. synchronous run) in which at most f processes crash and which locally decides in round k or in a higher round, and (2) there is a uniform consensus algorithm, which locally decides by round k in every run (resp. synchronous run) in which at most f processes crash.

4   Proof Preliminaries

Our lower bound proofs are devised following the layering technique of [17], also used in [13]. Since every uniform consensus algorithm also solves the binary version of the problem, for lower bound proofs, we consider binary uniform consensus algorithms only.

Consider any algorithm A that solves binary uniform consensus in SCS. A round k configuration ($k \geq 1$) in a run of A consists of the states of all processes at the end of round k. (Since in SCS, no message is received in a round different from the one in which it was sent, we do not need to consider the states of the communication channels at the end of a round.) The state of a process which has crashed in a configuration is a special symbol denoting that the process has crashed. We say that a process p_i is alive in a given configuration if p_i has not crashed in that configuration. An initial configuration (or round 0 configuration) in a run consists of initial states of all processes in that run. For any configuration C at round k, we define $r(C)$ as the run in which (1) round k configuration is C, and (2) no processes crashes after round k. We denote by $val(C)$ the decision value of the correct processes in $r(C)$. Note that a process p_i is alive in C iff p_i is correct in $r(C)$.

Two configurations C and D at the same round are similar, denoted $C \sim D$, if they are identical or there exists a process p_j such that (1) C and D are identical except at p_j, and (2) there exists a process $p_i \neq p_j$ that is alive in both C and D. A set of configurations SC is similarity connected if, for every $C, D \in SC$ there are configurations $C = C_0, \ldots, C_m = D$ such that $C_i \sim C_{i+1}$ for all $0 \leq i < m$.

Let $scs1(A)$ be the runs of A in SCS in which the following holds: (1) at most one process crashes in every round, and (2) in any round k, if some process p_i crashes then: if some process p_j does not receive the round k message from p_i then every process p_l such that $l < j$ does not receive the round k message from p_i. (In other words, messages from the crashed process are lost by only a prefix of Π.) Let $Init$ be the set of initial configurations of all the runs in $scs1(A)$.

For the runs in $scs1(A)$, [13] shows the following two lemmas. Lemma 2.1 of [13] states that, if $n > 1$, then $Init$ is similarity connected. Lemma 2.3 of [13] states that: for $k \leq t$, if $Init$ is similarity connected, then the set of round k configurations of all runs in $scs1(A)$ is a similarity connected set of configurations in which no more than k processes have crashed in each configuration. Using these lemmas, we now sketch the proof of the following lemma. (We present a detailed proof in the full-version of the paper [6].)

Lemma 1. For any k such that $0 \le k \le t$, there are two runs of A in SCS such that their round k configurations, y and y', satisfy the following: (1) at most k processes have crashed in each configuration, (2) the configurations differ at exactly one process, and (3) $val(y) = 0$, whereas $val(y') = 1$.

Proof. (Sketch) Since every run in $scs1(A)$ is a run of A in SCS, it is sufficient to show that there are two round k configurations of the runs in $scs1(A)$ with the above properties.

Consider a run $r0$ of A in which every process proposes 0 and no process crashes. From the definition of $scs1(A)$, $r0$ is in $scs1(A)$. Consider the round k configuration, say y, of $r0$. From uniform consensus validity, $val(y) = 0$. Similarly, consider a run $r1$ in which every process proposes 1 and no process crashes. Clearly, $r1$ is in $scs1(A)$. Consider the round k configuration, say y' of $r1$. From uniform consensus validity, $val(y') = 1$.

Since we assume $n \ge 3$ and $k \le t$, Lemma 2.3 of [13] implies that, the set of round k configurations of all runs in $scs1(A)$ is a similarity connected set of configurations in which no more k processes have crashed in each configuration. From the definition of similarity connected, it follows that there are some round k configurations in $scs1(A)$, $y = y_0, y_1, \ldots, y_m = y'$, such that $y_j \sim y_{j+1}$ for all $0 \le j < m$. Clearly, there is some $y_i \in \{y_0, \ldots, y_{m-1}\}$ such that, $val(y_0) = \ldots = val(y_i) \ne val(y_{i+1})$. (Otherwise, $val(y) = val(y_0) = val(y_1) = \ldots = val(y_m) = val(y')$, a contradiction.)

Thus, $val(y_i) = 0$ and $val(y_{i+1}) = 1$. As $y_i \sim y_{i+1}$, the two configurations are either identical or differ at exactly one processes. Since, $val(y_i) \ne val(y_{i+1})$, the configurations cannot be identical.

5   Lower Bounds in Synchronous Model

Proposition 1. Let $1 \le t \le n - 1$. For every f such that $0 \le f \le t - 1$, any uniform consensus algorithm has a run in which at most f processes crash such that no correct process decides before round $f + 1$ in that run.

Proof. Suppose by contradiction that there is an algorithm A that solves uniform consensus in SCS, a round number f such that $0 \le f \le t - 1$, and in every in which at most f processes crash, some correct process decides before round $f+1$.

From Lemma 1 we know that there are two runs of A in SCS such that their round f configurations, y and y', satisfy the following: (1) at most f processes have crashed in each configuration, (2) the configurations differ at exactly one process, say p_i, and (3) $val(y) = 0$ and $val(y') = 1$.

From our initial assumption, it follows that in y there is an alive process q_1 which has already decided. (Otherwise, since every correct process in $r(y)$ is an alive process in y, $r(y)$ is a run with f crashes in which no correct process decides before round $f + 1$.) Furthermore, q_1 has decided $val(y) = 0$ in y because q_1 is a correct process in $r(y)$. Similarly, in y', there is an alive process q_2 which has decided $val(y') = 1$. There are two cases to consider.

(1) $q_1 \neq p_i$: As y and y' are identical at all processes different from p_i, in y', q_1 is alive and has decided 0. Thus in $r(y')$, q_1 is a correct process and decides 0. However, in $r(y')$ every correct process decides $val(y') = 1$; a contradiction.

(2) $q_1 = p_i$: We distinguish two subcases:

- $q_2 = p_i$: Thus $p_i = q_1 = q_2$, and hence, p_i is alive in y and y'. Consider a run $r1$ which extends y and in which p_i crashes before sending any message in round $f + 1$. (Recall that $f \leq t - 1$.) As p_i has decided 0 in y, from uniform agreement, it follows that every correct process decides 0 in $r1$. Since $t < n$, there is at least one correct process, say p_l in $r1$. Now consider a run $r2$ which extends y' and in which p_i crashes before sending any message in round $f+1$. Notice that no correct process can distinguish $r1$ from $r2$: at the end of round f no alive process which is distinct from p_i can distinguish y from y', and p_i crashes before sending any message in round $f + 1$. Thus every correct process decides the same value in $r1$ and $r2$, in particular p_l decides 0 in $r2$. However, $p_i = q_2$ decides 1 in $r2$; a contradiction with uniform agreement.
- $q_2 \neq p_i$: Then, q_2 has the same state in y and y'. Thus in y, q_2 is alive and has decided 1. In any run which extends y, $p_i = q_1$ has decided 0 and q_2 has decided 1; a contradiction with uniform agreement.   □

It is easy to design an algorithm that matches Proposition 1. We give a brief sketch of one such algorithm. Every process maintains a variable est which is initialized to the proposal value of the process. In each round i, such that $1 \leq i \leq t + 1$, process p_i sends its est to all processes, and if any process p_j receives the round i message from p_i, p_j updates its own est to the est received from p_i. At the end of round $i \leq t$, p_i decides on its own est value, and at the end of round $t + 1$, every alive process which has not yet decided, decides on its own est value. Validity and termination properties of the algorithm are easy to see. To see why the agreement property holds, consider the first process p_i which decides. If $i \leq t$, then p_i completed the send phase of round i, and hence, every process which completes round i adopts the est value of p_i. Thus, no value distinct from the est sent by p_i in round i can be decided in a higher round. If $i = t + 1$, then every process in $\{p_1, \ldots, p_t\}$ are faulty, and hence, p_{t+1} is correct. Thus, every process receives the est of p_{t+1} in round $t + 1$, and decides on that value. To see the early local decision property of the algorithm, notice that in a run in which at most f processes crash, at least one of the the processes in $\{p_1, \ldots, p_{f+1}\}$ is correct, and it decides by the end of round $f + 1$. In the full-version of the paper [6], we further optimize the algorithm for early global decision and discuss the special case for $f = t$.

From the above tight bound on local decision, we know that, in runs in which at most f processes crash, the decision of any correct process requires $f + 1$ rounds. On the other hand, the global decision lower bound states that, in runs in which at most f processes crash, decision of all correct processes requires $f + 2$ rounds. It is natural to ask whether we can devise a uniform consensus algorithm in which more than one correct process can decide in round $f + 1$, in every run in which at most f processes crash. In the following proposition we show that the answer is negative.

Proposition 2. Let $3 \leq t \leq n - 1$. For every f such that $0 \leq f \leq t - 3$, any uniform consensus algorithm has a run in which at most f processes crash such that at most one correct process decides before round $f + 2$ in that run.

Proof. Suppose by contradiction that there is an algorithm A that solves uniform consensus in SCS, a round number $f + 1$ such that $0 \leq f \leq t - 3$, and in every run of A in which at most f processes crash, there are two correct processes which decide before round $f + 2$.

From Lemma 1 we know that there are two runs of A in SCS such that their round f configurations, y and y', satisfy the following: (1) at most f processes have crashed in each configuration, (2) the configurations differ at exactly one process, say p_i, and (3) $val(y) = 0$ and $val(y') = 1$. Let z and z' denote the configurations at the end of round $f + 1$ of $r(y)$ and $r(y')$, respectively.

From our initial assumption, it follows that in z, there are two alive processes q_1 and q_2 which have decided $val(y) = 0$. Similarly, in z', there are two alive processes q_3 and q_4 which have decided $val(y') = 1$. Since q_1 and q_2 are distinct, at least one of them is distinct from p_i, say q_1. Similarly, without loss of generality we may assume that q_3 is distinct from p_i.

Thus we have (1) an $f + 1$ round configuration z in which at most f processes have crashed such that z has an alive process q_1 which has decided 0, (2) an $f + 1$ round configuration z' in which at most f processes have crashed such that z' has alive process q_3 which has decided 1, and (3) process p_i is distinct from both q_1 and q_3. (Processes q_1 and q_3 may or may not be distinct.) There are two cases to consider.

Case 1. Process p_i is alive in y and y'. Consider the following two runs of A in SCS:

R1 is a run such that (1) the round f configuration is y, (2) p_i crashes in the send phase of round $f + 1$ such that only q_1 receives the message from p_i, (3) q_1 and q_3 crash before sending any message in round $f + 2$, and (4) no process distinct from p_i, q_1, and q_3 crashes after round f. Notice that q_1 cannot distinguish the round $f + 1$ configuration of R1 from z, and therefore, decides 0 at the end of round $f + 1$ in R1. By uniform agreement, every correct process decides 0. Since $t \leq n - 1$, there is at least one correct process in R1, say p_l.

R2 is a run such that (1) the round f configuration is y', (2) p_i crashes in the send phase of round $f + 1$ such that only q_3 receives the message from p_i, (3) q_1 and q_3 crash before sending any message in round $f + 2$, and (4) no process distinct from p_i, q_1, and q_3 crashes after round f. Notice that q_3 cannot distinguish the round $f + 1$ configuration of R2 from z', and therefore, decides 1 at the end of round $f + 1$ in R2. However, p_l cannot distinguish R1 from R2: at the end of round $f + 1$, the two runs are different only at p_i, q_1, and q_3, and none of the three processes sends messages after round $f + 1$ in both runs. Thus (as in R1) p_l decides 0 in R2; a contradiction with uniform agreement.

C ase 2. Process p_i has crashed in either y or y'. (Process p_i is not crashed in both y and y' because p_i has different states in y and y'.) Without loss of generality, we can assume that p_i has crashed in y, and hence, p_i is alive in y'. (Recall that the state of p_i in y is distinct from that in y'.) Consider the following two runs of A in SCS:

R12 is a run such that (1) the round f configuration is y (and hence, p_i has crashed before round $f + 1$), (2) no process crashes in round $f + 1$, (3) q_1 and q_3 crash before sending any message in round $f+2$, and (4) no process distinct from p_i, q_1 and q_3 crashes after round f. Observe that the round $f + 1$ configuration of $R12$ is z, and hence, q_1 decides 0 at the end of round $f + 1$ in $R12$. Due to uniform agreement, every correct process decides 0 in $R12$. Since $t \leq n - 1$, there is at least one correct process in $R12$, say p_l.

R21 is a run such that (1) the round f configuration is y', (2) p_i crashes in the send phase of round $f + 1$ such that only q_3 receives the message from p_i, (3) q_1 and q_3 crash before sending any message in round $f + 2$, and (4) no process distinct from p_i, q_1 and q_3 crashes after round f. Notice that q_3 cannot distinguish the round $f + 1$ configuration of $R21$ from z' because it receives the message from p_i in both runs. Thus (as in z') q_3 decides 1 at the end of round $f + 1$ in $R21$. However, p_l cannot distinguish $R12$ from $R21$: at the end of round $f + 1$, the two runs are different only at p_i, q_1 and q_3, and none of them sends messages after round $f + 1$ in both runs. Thus (as in $R12$), p_l decides 0 in $R21$; a contradiction with uniform agreement.   □

6   Lower Bound in Eventually Synchronous Model

In synchronous runs of any uniform consensus algorithm in ES we show that there is a run in which at most f processes crash, such that no correct process decides before round $f + 2$ in that run; i.e., the local decision lower bound is $f + 2$. This one round difference between local decisions in SCS and that of synchronous runs in ES, can be seen as a price paid by algorithms in ES to tolerate a weaker model.

In ES, a round k configuration ($k \geq 1$) consists of the states of all processes at the end of round k and the set of delayed messages in each communication channel at the end of round k. (Since messages may be delayed, to completely describe the state of the system at the end of a round, we need to take into account the delayed messages in every channel.) An initial configuration (or round 0 configuration) in a run consists of initial states of all processes in that run and empty communication channels. A synchronous configuration is a configuration of some synchronous run. As there are no delayed messages in a synchronous run, all communication channels are empty in any synchronous configuration. For any synchronous configuration C at round k, we define $R(C)$ as a synchronous run in which (1) round k configuration is C, and (2) no processes crashes after round k. We denote by $Val(C)$ the decision value of the correct processes in $R(C)$.

Consider any algorithm A that solves uniform consensus in ES. As no process can distinguish a run of A in SCS from some synchronous run of A in ES, and the communication channels are empty in every synchronous configuration, it follows from Lemma 1 that,

Claim ES1. For any k such that $0 \leq k \leq t$, there are two distinct synchronous runs of A in ES such that their round k synchronous configurations, y and y', satisfy the following: (1) at most k processes have crashed in each configuration, (2) the configurations differ at exactly one process, and (3) $Val(y) = 0$, whereas $Val(y') = 1$.

Proposition 3. Let $1 \leq t \leq n-1$. For every f such that $0 \leq f \leq t-3$, any uniform consensus algorithm has a synchronous run in which at most f processes crash such that no correct process decides before round $f + 2$ in that run.

Proof. Suppose by contradiction that there is an algorithm A that solves uniform consensus in ES, a round number f such that $0 \leq f \leq t-3$, and in every synchronous run of A in which at most f processes crash, some correct process decides by round $f + 1$. From Claim ES1, we know that there are two round f synchronous configurations of A, y and y', such that: (1) at most f processes have crashed in each configuration, (2) the configurations differ at exactly one process, say p_i, and (3) $Val(y) = 0$ and $Val(y') = 1$. Let z and z' denote the round $f+1$ configurations in the synchronous runs $R(y)$ and $R(y')$, respectively.

From our initial assumption on A, in z, there is at least one alive process, say q_1, which has decided 0. Similarly, in z', there is at least one alive process, say q_3, which has decided 1. There are three cases to consider.

Case 1. $p_i \notin \{q_1, q_3\}$. This case is exactly similar to the case in the proof of Proposition 2. We can derive a contradiction by constructing the same runs R1, R2, R12, and R21. (We can ignore the states of the communication channels in any synchronous configuration because the channels are empty in such a configuration.)

Case 2. $p_i \in \{q_1, q_3\}$ and p_i is alive in both y and y'. Notice that if $p_i = q_1$ then $R1$ (in the proof of Proposition 2) is not a run of A ES: p_i cannot crash in the send phase of round $f + 1$, and decide at the end of round $f + 1$. (Similarly, if $p_i = q_3$ then $R2$ is not a run in ES.) Hence we construct non-synchronous runs of A to show the contradiction. Without loss of generality we can assume that $p_i = q_1$. (Note that the proof holds even if $p_i = q_1 = q_3$.) Consider the following synchronous run $R3$ and two non-synchronous runs, $R4$ and $R5$.

R3 is a run such that (1) the round f configuration is y, (2) p_i crashes in round $f + 1$ before sending any message, (3) if $q_3 \neq p_i$ then q_3 crashes before sending any message in round $f + 2$ and every message sent by q_3 in round $f + 1$ is received in round $f + 1$, and (4) no process distinct from p_i and q_3 crashes after round f. Since $t \leq n - 1$, there is at least one correct process in $R3$, say p_l. Suppose p_l decides $v \in \{0, 1\}$ in some round $K1 \geq f + 1.$[2]

---

[2] To see that p_l cannot decide before round $f+1$ in $R3$, notice that the state of p_l at the end of round f is the same in runs $R(y)$, $R(y')$ and $R3$. If p_l decides v before round $f + 1$ in $R3$ then it also decides v in $R(y)$ and $R(y')$. However, $Val(y) \neq Val(y')$.

R4 is a run such that (1) the round f configuration is y, (2) in round $f+1$, p_i and q_3 receive the round $f+1$ message from p_i, and the round $f+1$ message from p_i to other processes are delayed until round $K1+1$, (3) p_i and q_3 crashes in round $f+2$ before sending any message in that round, and (4) no process distinct from p_i and q_3 crashes after round f. Notice that p_i cannot distinguish the configuration at the end of round $f+1$ in $R4$ from z, and thus, p_i decides 0 at the end of round $f+1$ in $R4$. However, p_l cannot distinguish the round $K1$ configuration of $R4$ from that of $R3$ because (1) at the end of round f, the two runs are different only at p_i, and all round $f+1$ messages from p_i to processes distinct from p_i and q_3 are delayed until round $K1+1$, and (2) p_i and q_3 do not send messages after round $f+1$. Thus (as in $R3$) p_l decides v at the end of round $K1$.

R5 is a run such that (1) the round f configuration is y', (2) in round $f+1$, p_i and q_3 receive the round $f+1$ message from p_i, and the round $f+1$ message from p_i to other processes are delayed until round $K1+1$, (3) p_i and q_3 crashes in round $f+2$ before sending any message in that round, and (4) no process distinct from p_i and q_3 crashes after round f. Notice that q_3 cannot distinguish the configuration at the end of round $f+1$ in $R5$ from z' (because q_3 receives the message from p_i in round $f+1$ of $R5$), and thus, q_3 decides 1 at the end of round $f+1$ in $R5$. However, p_l cannot distinguish the round $K1$ configuration of $R5$ from that of $R3$ because, (1) at the end of round f the two runs are different only at p_i, and all round $f+1$ messages from p_i to processes distinct from p_i and q_3 are delayed until round $K1+1$, and (2) p_i and q_3 do not send messages after round $f+1$. Thus (as in $R3$) p_l decides v at the end of round $K1$.

Clearly, either $R4$ or $R5$ violates uniform agreement: p_l decides v in both runs, however, p_i decides 0 in $R4$ and q_3 decides 1 in $R5$.

Case 3. $p_i \in \{q_1, q_3\}$ and p_i has crashed in either y or y'. (Process p_i is not crashed in both y and y' because p_i has different states in y and y'.) Notice that the case $p_i = q_1 = q_3$ is not possible because, in that case, p_i is alive in z and z', and hence in y and y'. We show the contradiction for the case when $p_i = q_1 \neq q_3$. (The contradiction for $p_i = q_3 \neq q_1$ is symmetric.)

Since, $p_i = q_1$, p_i is alive in z, and hence, alive in y. Thus p_i has crashed in y'. Consider the following non-synchronous run.

R6 is a run such that (1) the round f configuration is y, (2) in round $f+1$, only p_i receives the round $f+1$ message from itself, and the round $f+1$ message from p_i to other processes are delayed until round $f+2$, (3) p_i crashes in round $f+2$ before sending any message in that round, and (4) no process distinct from p_i crashes after round f. At the end of round $f+1$ in $R6$, $p_i = q_1$ cannot distinguish the configuration from z, and therefore, decides 0. However, q_3 does not receive the round $f+1$ message from p_i in $R6$ (the message is delayed until round $f+2$), and hence, q_3 cannot distinguish the configuration at the end of round $f+1$ in $R6$ from z'. (In z', q_3 does not receive the round $f+1$ message from p_i because p_i has crashed in y'.) Consequently, q_3 decides 1 in $R6$; a contradiction with uniform agreement.   □

A closer look at the proof of Proposition 3 reveals that the non-synchronous runs we construct (R4, R5, and R6) satisfy the following "weak synchrony" property: for any round k and any process p_i, if a round k message from p_i is delayed, then p_i crashes before sending any message in round $k + 1$. It is easy to see that such runs can also be constructed in the synchronous send-omission model [10] as well as in an asynchronous round-by-round model enriched with a Perfect failure detector [2]. Thus the $f + 2$ local decision lower bound in synchronous runs also extend to these two models.

7   A Matching Algorithm

Figure 1 presents a uniform consensus algorithm A_{f+2} in ES which matches the $f + 2$ round global decision lower bound (and hence, matches the local decision bound) in synchronous runs. Namely, the algorithm satisfies the following property: (Fast Early Decision) For $0 \le t < n/2$,[3] in every synchronous run of A_{f+2} in which at most f processes crash ($0 \le f \le t$), every process which decides, decides by round $f + 2$.

For simplicity of presentation, A_{f+2} assumes an independent uniform consensus algorithm C,[4] accessed through procedure propose$_C(*)$. The fast decision property is achieved by A_{f+2} regardless of the time complexity of C. More precisely, our algorithm assumes: (1) the model ES with $0 \le t < n/2$, (2) messages sent by a process to itself are received in the same round in which they are sent, (3) an independent uniform consensus algorithm C in ES, and (4) the set of proposal values in a run is a totally ordered set, e.g., every process p_i can tag its proposal value with its index i and then the values can be ordered based on this tag.

The processes invoke propose($*$) with their respective proposal values, and the procedure progresses in rounds. Every process p_i maintains three primary variables:

- STATE$_i$ is updated at the end of a round as follows. If p_i considers (a) the run to be non-synchronous then p_i sets STATE$_i$ to NSYNC, (b) the run to be synchronous but p_i cannot decide at the next round then p_i sets STATE$_i$ to SYNC1, (c) the run to be synchronous with a possibility of deciding at the next round then p_i sets STATE$_i$ to SYNC2.
- est_i is the estimate of the possible decision value, and roughly speaking, the minimum value seen by p_i.
- $Halt_i$ is a set of processes. At the end of a round, $Halt_i$ contains p_j if any of the following holds in the current round or in a lower round: (1) p_i did not receive a message from p_j, (2) p_i receives a messages from p_j with STATE $=$ NSYNC, or (3) p_i receives a messages from p_j containing $Halt_j$ such that $p_i \in Halt_j$.

---

[3] Uniform consensus is impossible to solve in ES when $t \ge n/2$ [2].

[4] This algorithm can be any $\Diamond P$-based or $\Diamond S$-based uniform consensus algorithm (e.g., the one based on $\Diamond S$ in [2]) transposed to ES.

at process p_i

```
 1: procedure propose(v_i)
 2:    start Task1; start Task 2

 3:    Task 1
 4:    STATE_i ← SYNC1 ; est_i ← v_i; Halt_i ← ∅
 5:    for 1 ≤ k_i ≤ t + 2
 6:       send(k_i, est_i, STATE_i, Halt_i) to all
 7:       wait until received messages of round k_i
 8:       if received any (k_i, est', DECIDE, *) then
 9:          decide(est'); send(k_i + 1, est', DECIDE, ∅) to Π\p_i; return      {decision}
10:       if STATE_i ∈ {SYNC1, SYNC2} then
11:          Halt_i ← Halt_i∪ {p_j | (p_i received(k_i, *, NSYNC, *) from p_j) or
             (p_i received(k_i, *, *, Halt_j) from p_j s.t. p_i ∈ Halt_j) or (p_i did not receive any round k_i
             message from p_j)}
12:          msgSet_i ← { m | m is a round k_i message received from p_j ∉ Halt_i}
13:          est_i ← Min{est | (k_i, est, *, *) ∈ msgSet_i}
14:          if (STATE_i = SYNC2) and (|Halt_i| ≤ t) and (STATE = SYNC2 for every message in msgSet_i)
             then
15:             decide(est_i); send(k_i + 1, est_i, DECIDE, ∅) to Π\p_i; return      {decision}
16:          if |Halt_i| ≤ k_i − 1 then
17:             STATE_i ← SYNC2
18:          if k_i ≤ |Halt_i| ≤ t then
19:             STATE_i ← SYNC1
20:          if |Halt_i| > t then
21:             STATE_i ← NSYNC
22:       if (STATE = NSYNC) and (received any (k_i, est', SYNC2, *)) then
23:          est_i ← est'
24:    propose_C(est_i); return      {decision}

25:    Task 2
26:    upon receiving (k', est', DECIDE, *) and (k_i ≥ k' + 1) do
27:       stop propose_C(*); decide(est'); send(k_i, est', DECIDE, ∅) to Π\p_i; return      {decision}
```

Fig. 1. A Consensus algorithm A_{f+2} in ES

In the first $t + 2$ rounds, the processes exchange these three variables and then update their variables depending on the messages received. At the end of round $t + 2$, if a process p_i has not yet decided, then p_i invokes the underlying uniform consensus algorithm C with the latest value of est_i as the proposal value. From the termination property of C, we know that if p_i does not crash then it eventually decided in C. The algorithm ensures the following elimination property: if a process completes some round $k < t + 2$ with STATE $=$ SYNC2 and $est = est'$ and no process decides in round k or in a lower round, then every process which completes round k with STATE $=$ SYNC1 has $est \geq est'$, and every process which completes round k with STATE $=$ SYNC2 has $est = est'$. (Processes which complete round k with STATE $=$ NSYNC might have $est < est'$.)

We give a proof of the elimination property and that of the correctness of A_{f+2} in the full-version of the paper [6]. We now briefly discuss how the uniform agreement property of A_{f+2} follows from the elimination property. If every process which decides, decides at a round higher than $t + 2$ then uniform agreement follows from the corresponding property of algorithm C. Consider the lowest round $k' \leq t + 2$ in which some process p_i decides, say d. From line 14, at least $n - t$ processes (a majority) send round k' messages with STATE $=$ SYNC2, and hence, every process which completes round k' receives at least one round

k' message with STATE $=$ SYNC2. From line 11, every process with STATE $=$ SYNC1 or STATE $=$ SYNC2, only considers messages with STATE $=$ SYNC1 or STATE $=$ SYNC2 while updating its est (i.e., ignores messages with STATE $=$ NSYNC). From the elimination property we know that, every round k' message with STATE $=$ SYNC1 has $est \geq d$, and every round k' message with STATE $=$ SYNC2 has $est = d$. Since every process receives a message with STATE $=$ SYNC2, processes with STATE $=$ SYNC1 or STATE $=$ SYNC2 adopts d as their est. Furthermore, every process which completes round k' with STATE $=$ NSYNC receives at least one message with STATE $=$ SYNC2 and $est = d$ and updates its est to d (line 22). Consequently, every process which completes round k', does so with $est = d$, and no value distinct from d can be decided at round k' or at a higher round.

References

1. Aguilera M. K. and Toueg S., A Simple Bivalency Proof that t-Resilient Consensus Requires $t + 1$ Rounds. *Information Processing Letters (IPL)*, 71(3–4):155–158, 1999.
2. Chandra T. D. and Toueg S., Unreliable Failure Detectors for Reliable Distributed Systems. *Journal of the ACM (JACM)*, 43(2):225–267, 1996.
3. Charron-Bost B. and Schiper A., Uniform Consensus Harder than Consensus. *Technical Report ID: DSC/2000/028*, Swiss Federal Institute of Technology in Lausanne (EPFL), 2000.
4. Dolev D., Reischuk R. and Strong R., Early stopping in byzantine agreement. *Journal of the ACM (JACM)*, 37(4):720–741, 1990.
5. Dutta P. and Guerraoui R., The Inherent Price of Indulgence. *Proc. 21st ACM Symposium on Principles of Distributed Computing, (PODC'02)*, ACM Press, pp. 88–97, Monterey (CA), 2002.
6. Dutta P., Guerraoui R. and Pochon B., Early Local Decisions in Distributed Agreement. *Technical Report ID: 200324*, School of Computer and Communication Sciences, Swiss Federal Institute of Technology in Lausanne (EPFL). Available at: `http://ic2.epfl.ch/publications/documents/IC_TECH_REPORT_200324.pdf`.
7. Dwork C., Lynch N. and Stockmeyer L., Consensus in the Presence of Partial Synchrony. *Journal of the ACM (JACM)*, 35(2):288–323, 1988.
8. Fischer M., Lynch N., A Lower Bound for the Time to Assure Interactive Consistency. *Information Processing Letters (IPL)*, 14(4):183–186, 1982.
9. Fischer M.J., Lynch N. and Paterson M.S., Impossibility of Distributed Consensus with One Faulty Process. *Journal of the ACM (JACM)*, 32(2):374–382, 1985.
10. Hadzilacos V., Byzantine Agreement Under Restricted Types of Failures (Not Telling the Truth is Different from Telling Lies.) *Technical Report ID: TR-19-83*, Aiken Computation Laboratory, Harvard University.
11. Hadzilacos V., On the relationship between the Atomic Commitment and Consensus problems. *Proc. 9th International Workshop on Fault-Tolerant Computing*, Springer Verlag (LNCS 448), pp. 201–208, 1987.
12. Keidar I. and Rajsbaum S., Open Questions on Consensus Performance in Well-Behaved Runs. *Future Directions in Distributed Computing (FuDiCo)*, Springer Verlag (LNCS 2584).

13. Keidar I. and Rajsbaum S., A Simple Proof of the Uniform Consensus Synchronous Lower Bound. *Information Processing Letters (IPL)*, 85(1):47–52, 2003.
14. Lynch N., Distributed Algorithms. *Morgan Kaufmann Pub.*, San Francisco (CA), 872 pages, 1996.
15. Lamport L., The Part-Time Parliament. *ACM Transactions on Computer Systems (TOCS)*, 16(2):133–169, 1998.
16. Lamport L., Shostak R. and Pease M., The Byzantine Generals Problem. *ACM Transactions on Programming Languages and Systems (TOPLAS)*, 4(3):382–401, 1982.
17. Moses Y. and Rajsbaum S., A Layered Analysis of Consensus. *SIAM Journal on Computing*, 31(4):989–1021, 2002.

Tight Bounds for k-Set Agreement with Limited-Scope Failure Detectors

Maurice Herlihy* and Lucia Draque Penso

Computer Science Department
Box 1910, Brown University
Providence, RI 02912

Abstract. A system with *limited-scope* failure detectors ensures that there are q subsets X_i of x_i processes, $0 \leq i \leq q - 1$, such that some correct process in X_i is never suspected by any process in X_i. Let x be the sum of x_i and X be the union of X_i. The failure detector class $S_{x,q}$ satisfies this property all the time, while $\diamond S_{x,q}$ satisfies it eventually.

This paper gives the first tight bounds for the k-set agreement task in asynchronous message-passing models augmented with failure detectors from either the $S_{x,q}$ or $\diamond S_{x,q}$ classes.

For $S_{x,q}$, we show that any k-set agreement protocol that tolerates f failures must satisfy $f < k + x - q$. This result establishes for the first time that the protocol of Mostéfaoui and Raynal for the $S_x = S_{x,1}$ failure detector is optimal.

For $\diamond S_{x,q}$, our lower bound is $f < min(\frac{n+1}{2}, k+x-q)$. We give a novel protocol that matches our lower bound, disproving a conjecture of Mostéfaoui and Raynal for the $\diamond S_x = \diamond S_{x,1}$ failure detector.

Our lower bounds exploit techniques borrowed from Combinatorial Topology, demonstrating for the first time that this approach is applicable to models that encompass failure detectors.

1 Introduction

In the k-set agreement problem [5], each process in a group starts with a private input value, communicates with the others, and then halts after choosing a private output value. Each process is required to choose some process's input, and at most k distinct values may be chosen.

We consider this problem in an asynchronous message-passing system of $n + 1$ processes, of which at most f may fail by halting. Each process is equipped with a failure detector [3,4], an unreliable oracle that informs each process when it suspects other processes to have failed. A failure detector is a mathematical abstraction that models time-out and related techniques used by real systems to detect failures.

In this paper, we are concerned with *limited-scope* failure detectors [13,17], which formally capture the idea that a process can typically detect some failures more easily than others. For example, timeouts may reliably detect failures on the same local area network, but less reliably over a wide-area network.

* Research supported by NSF 9912401.

To capture this distinction, Mostéfaoui and Raynal [13] consider *limited-scope* failure detectors. These detectors ensure there is a cluster X of x processes, containing at least one correct process, whose local detectors do not erroneously suspect one of them to be faulty.

One can easily extend the notion of *limited-scope* failure detectors to admit multiple sets of processes $X_0, \ldots, X_{q-1}$, where $|X_i| = x_i$, X is the union of X_i and x is the sum of x_i, $0 \leq i \leq q - 1$. Each process in X_i has a correct process that is never suspected by any process in X_i, either from the very beginning or at some point, depending whether the failure detector is perpetual or eventual. Such a model might correspond to a network with q local area networks.

A failure detector class is characterized by a *completeness* property and an *accuracy* property. The limited-scope failure detectors considered here satisfy

– **Strong Completeness:** Eventually, every process that crashes is permanently suspected by every correct process.

We consider two alternative accuracy properties.

In each, there are multiple sets of processes $X_0, \ldots, X_{q-1}$ (where $|X_i| = x_i$ and $0 \leq i \leq q - 1$) such that

– **Perpetual Weak (x, q)-Accuracy:** some correct process in X_i is never suspected by any process in X_i.
– **Eventual Weak (x, q)-Accuracy:** there is a time after which some correct process in X_i is never suspected by any process in X_i.

We focus on two failure detector classes in this paper:

– $S_{x,q}$ satisfies strong completeness and perpetual weak (x, q)-accuracy.
– $\diamond S_{x,q}$ satisfies strong completeness and eventual weak (x, q)-accuracy.

In a system of $n+1$ processes, the well-known failure detector S introduced by Chandra and Toueg [4] is just $S_{n+1,1}$, and $\diamond S$ is $\diamond S_{n+1,1}$. Also, the *limited-scope* failure detectors considered by Mostéfaoui and Raynal [13], S_x and $\diamond S_x$ are just $S_{x,1}$ and $\diamond S_{x,1}$. Note that both $S_{x,q}$ and $\diamond S$ are at least as strong as $\diamond S_{x,q}$.
This paper makes the following contributions.

– *Lower bounds*: We give the first lower bounds for k-set agreement protocols employing failure detector classes $S_{x,q}$ and $\diamond S_{x,q}$. For $S_{x,q}$, we show that any k-set agreement protocol must satisfy $f < k+x-q$, while for $\diamond S_{x,q}$, $f < min(\frac{n+1}{2}, k+x-q)$. Our proof employs mechanisms from Combinatorial Topology [9,11]. These methods have been successful in other models, but this is the first time such methods have been applied to failure detectors.
– *Upper bounds*: For $S_{x,q}$, our lower bound implies that the elegant *TWA-based* protocol of Mostéfaoui and Raynal [13] is optimal for S_x, as they had conjectured, and that it can suffer a minor modification so that it becomes also optimal for $S_{x,q}$. The modification consists of changing the number of processes in the *TWA* protocol from $m = min(n+1, k+x-1)$ to $m = min(n+1, k+x-q)$. For $\diamond S_{x,q}$, we give a novel protocol that matches our lower bound. This protocol has an unexpectedly simple

structure: it alternates the TWA-based protocol with a novel *convergence detection* protocol that halts when it detects that an earlier iteration of TWA has succeeded. Our protocol disproves a conjecture of Mostéfaoui and Raynal, who suggested that a weaker protocol may be optimal.

2 Related Work

As noted, we address and extend problems first raised by Mostéfaoui and Raynal [13]. Our lower bound arguments show their TWA-based protocol for S_x to be optimal, while we improve their protocol for $\diamond S_x$ from[1]

$$ f < max(k, max_{1 \leq \alpha \leq k}(min(n + 1 - \alpha \left\lfloor \frac{n+1}{\alpha+1} \right\rfloor, \alpha + x - 1))) $$

to an optimal

$$ f < min(\frac{n+1}{2}, k + x - 1). $$

Moreover, our lower bound arguments also show a slightly modified version of their protocol to be optimal for $S_{x,q}$, while our protocol is actually optimal for $\diamond S_{x,q}$. As remarked before, one should just change the number of processes in the TWA protocol from $m = min(n + 1, k + x - 1)$ to $m = min(n + 1, k + x - q)$ for a $S_{x,q}$ protocol.

Anceaume et al. [?] give a communication-efficient k-set agreement protocol for $\diamond S_{x,1}$ that tolerates $f < \frac{n+k-1}{2}$ failures when $x > f$.

Borowsky and Gafni [2], Herlihy and Shavit [11], and Saks and Zaharoglou [15] showed there is no wait-free protocol for k-set agreement in asynchronous message-passing or read/write memory models. Chaudhuri, Herlihy, Lynch, and Tuttle [6], Herlihy, Rajsbaum, and Tuttle [9,10] derive lower bounds on round complexity for the synchronous fail-stop message-passing mode. Many of these proofs rely, directly or indirectly on mechanisms and techniques adapted from Combinatorial Topology.

Failure detectors [3,4] have received an enormous amount of attention, most of which has focused on solving the consensus problem. Yang, Neiger, and Gafni [17], and Mostéfaoui and Raynal [13] have proposed k-set agreement protocols for models that encompass limited-scope failure detectors, but we are unaware of any prior lower bounds for these models.

Gafni [7] introduces the notion of *round-by-round* failure detectors to give a number of novel reductions between models.

Attiya and Avidor [1] and A. Mostéfaoui et al. [12] have investigated the related problem of solving k-set agreement when inputs are restricted.

Our new algorithm for eventual weak accuracy failure detectors has a style similar to the *k-converge algorithm* of Yang, Neiger, and Gafni [17]: it alternates an eventually-successful agreement protocol with an eventually-successful termination-detection protocol. The protocols and underlying models, however, are quite different.

---

[1] When comparing our formulas to those of Moustéfaoui and Raynal, be aware that they assume n processes in the system, while we assume $n + 1$, which simplifies topological calculations.

3   Topological Model

In our model, a set of $n + 1$ *processes* communicate by message-passing. An initial or final state of a process is modeled as a vertex, $v = \langle t, v \rangle$, a pair consisting of a process id t and a value v (either input or output).

Definition 1. *A d-dimensional simplex (or d − simplex) $S^d = (s_0, \ldots, s_d)$ is a set of $d + 1$ vertexes that model mutually compatible initial or final process states. We say that $s_0, \ldots, s_d$ span S^d. Simplex T is a (proper) face of S^d if the vertexes of T form a (proper) subset of the vertexes of S^d.*

A key idea is the concept of a *pseudosphere* [9], a simple combinatorial structure in which each process from a set of processes is independently assigned a value from a set of values. Pseudospheres have a number of nice combinatorial properties (for example, they are closed under intersection), but their principal interest lies in the observation that the behavior of the protocols we consider can be characterized as simple compositions of pseudospheres.

Definition 2. *Let $S^m = (s_0, \ldots, s_m)$ be a simplex and $U_0, \ldots, U_m$ be a sequence of finite sets. The pseudosphere $\psi(S^m; U_0, \ldots, U_m)$ is the following complex. Each vertex is a pair $\langle s_i, u_i \rangle$, where s_i is a vertex of S^m and $u_i \in U_i$. Vertexes $\langle s_{i_0}, u_{i_0} \rangle, \ldots, \langle s_{i_\ell}, u_{i_\ell} \rangle$ span a simplex of $\psi(S^m; U_0, \ldots, U_m)$ if and only if the s_i are distinct. A pseudosphere in which all U_i are equal to U is simply written $\psi(S^m; U)$.*

Definition 3. *A* simplicial complex *(or complex) is a set of simplexes closed under containment and intersection. The* dimension *of a complex is the highest dimension of any of its simplexes. $\mathcal{L}$ is a* subcomplex *of $\mathcal{K}$ if every simplex of $\mathcal{L}$ is a simplex of $\mathcal{K}$.*

We sometimes indicate the dimension of a simplex or complex as a superscript.

Definition 4. *A* protocol *is a program in which each process starts with a private input value, communicates with the other processes via message-passing, and eventually halts with a private output value. Processes may crash, halting in the middle of the protocol, and messages in transit may be delayed for arbitrary finite durations. Processes may use failure detectors to decide when to stop waiting for messages. Without loss of generality, we restrict attention to* full-information *protocols in which each process sends its entire state in each message.*

Definition 5. *Any protocol has an associated* protocol complex *$\mathcal{P}$, defined as follows. Each vertex is labeled with a process id and a possible local state for that process. A set of vertexes $\langle P_0, v_0 \rangle, \ldots, \langle P_d, v_d \rangle$ spans a simplex of $\mathcal{P}$ if and only if there is some protocol execution in which $P_0, \ldots, P_d$ finish the protocol with respective local states $v_0, \ldots, v_d$. Each simplex thus corresponds to an equivalence class of executions that "look the same" to the processes at its vertexes. The protocol complex $\mathcal{P}$ depends both on the protocol and on the timing and failure characteristics of the model.*

It is convenient to treat a protocol complex as an *operator* carrying input simplexes or complexes to protocol complexes.

Informally, a complex is k-connected if it has no holes in dimensions k or less. More precisely:

Definition 6. *A complex $\mathcal{K}$ is k-connected if every continuous map of the ℓ-sphere to $\mathcal{K}$ can be extended to a continuous map of the $(\ell + 1)$-disk [16, p. 51], for all $0 \leq \ell \leq k$. By convention, a complex is (-1)-connected if it is nonempty.*

This definition of k-connectivity may appear difficult to use, but fortunately we can do all our reasoning in a combinatorial way, using the following elementary consequence of the Mayer-Vietoris sequence [14, p. 142].

Theorem 1. *If $\mathcal{K}$ and $\mathcal{L}$ are complexes such that $\mathcal{K}$ and $\mathcal{L}$ are k-connected, and $\mathcal{K} \cap \mathcal{L}$ is $(k - 1)$-connected, then $\mathcal{K} \cup \mathcal{L}$ is k-connected.*

As a base case for all such inductions, any simplex S^n is n-connected.

Theorem 2 ([9]). *If $U_0, \ldots, U_m$ are all nonempty, then $\psi(S^m; U_0, \ldots, U_m)$ is $(m-1)$-connected.*

Finally, the notion of k-connectivity lies at the heart of all known lower bounds for k-set agreement. We now give a general theorem linking $(k - 1)$-connectivity with impossibility of k-set agreement, originally stated in [8]. Note that this theorem is model-independent in the sense that it depends on the connectivity properties of protocol complexes, not on explicit timing or failure properties of the model.

Theorem 3. *Let I^m be an input simplex of dimension m. If, for all input simplexes I^m, where $n - f \leq m \leq n$, $\mathcal{P}(I^m)$ is $(m - (n - k) - 1)$-connected, then $\mathcal{P}$ cannot solve k-set agreement in the presence of f failures.*

4   Models of Computation

Without loss of generality, we assume that processes execute in *asynchronous rounds*: at round r, a process broadcasts a message containing its state to all of the others, and then waits until it receives round-r messages from all unsuspected processes (including itself). Messages are *full-information*, containing each process's complete state, including a history of all messages sent and received up to that point. Failure detectors satisfy *strong completeness*: if after some point Q never sends a message to P, then P will eventually suspect Q and stop waiting for that message.

The *basic* model of computation guarantees only that each non-faulty process at round r will eventually receive round-r messages from at least $n - f + 1$ unsuspected processes. (The type of failure detector may influence which messages will be received.)

A message-passing model satisfies *causality* if it satisfies the following condition. Suppose

1. process P sends a message p to all processes,
2. Q receives p and later sends q to all processes, and
3. R receives q at round r.

Then R receives p at a round less than or equal to r.

We claim that causality adds nothing to the computational power of a model. Informally, because messages are full-information, any process can simulate receiving any missing messages when it receives a later one. It follows that if there is no k-consensus protocol in the basic model, then there is no such protocol in the basic model with causality.

A message-passing model satisfies *eventual delivery* if every message is eventually delivered to every non-faulty process. The *standard model* is the basic model with causality and eventual delivery.

We claim that if there is no k-consensus protocol in the basic model with causality, then there is no such protocol in the standard model.

Suppose we have a protocol $\mathcal{P}$ that always terminates in the standard model, but has an infinite execution in the basic model with causality (caused by undelivered messages). Define a *lost* message to be one that is never delivered to some non-faulty process. Let L be the set of processes that send a lost message, M the set of those that don't, and F the set of those that fail. (L and M are disjoint, but may overlap F.)

Once a process P in L sends a lost message, it can never send another message to any process in M, because the later message would be forwarded to every non-faulty process, and causality would force delivery of the earlier "lost" message to every non-faulty process. Once P falls silent to M, it will eventually be suspected by every process in M.

We claim that $|L \cup F| \leq f$. Wait until every process in L has sent a lost message and fallen silent to M, and every process in F has failed and fallen silent to M. Messages from at least $n - f + 1$ processes continue to be delivered to each process in M, so the missing processes can only come from $L \cup F$.

The infinite execution of $\mathcal{P}$ in the basic model with causality is thus indistinguishable, to the processes in M, from an infinite execution in the standard model where processes in L fail as soon as they send a lost message.

It is convenient to prove our lower bounds in the basic model. We have just seen, however, that these lower bounds extend to the standard model.

5   Perpetual Weak (x, q)-Accuracy

Without loss of generality, assume that each process's input value is an integer from the set $V = \{0, \dots, K\}$, and that process P_i is the process trusted by the set of processes X_i, where $P_i \in X_i$, $|X_i| = x_i$, X is the union of X_i and x is the sum of x_i, $0 \leq i \leq q-1$. Let S^n be the n-simplex whose vertexes are labeled with process ids $P_0, \dots, P_n$. Let $\mathcal{I}^n$ be the input complex in which each process is independently given an input value from V. This complex is a pseudosphere: $\mathcal{I}^n = \psi(S^n; V)$.

Let $\mathcal{D}$ be the operator that corresponds to a one-round execution in the basic model in which all failure detectors satisfy only strong completeness. For any n-simplex I^n of $\mathcal{I}^n$, the one-round operator is a pseudosphere:

$$\mathcal{D}(I^n) = \psi(I^n; U_{n-f}),$$

where U_{n-f} is the set of faces of I^n of dimension at least $n - f$, corresponding to the $n - f + 1$ or more messages received. (For simplicity, we assume a process may or may not receive a message from itself.) It follows that $\mathcal{D}(I^n)$ is $(f - 1)$-connected.

Let $\mathcal{D}^r(I^n)$ denote the r-round protocol complex on input simplex I^n. Recall that S^n is an n-simplex where vertex i is labeled with process id i, $\psi(S^n; \{u_0\}, \dots, \{u_n\})$ is a simplex where vertex i is labeled with process id i and value u_i.

Theorem 4. *If $\mathcal{D}^r(\psi(S^n; \{u_0\}, \ldots, \{u_n\})$ is $(f-1)$-connected, so is $\mathcal{D}^r(\psi(S^n; U_0, \ldots, U_n))$ for sets $U_0, \ldots, U_n$.*

Proof. We proceed by induction on f. For the base case, let $f = 0$. $\mathcal{D}^r(\psi(S^n; U_0, \ldots, U_n))$ is non-empty, hence $(f-1)$-connected.

Define the following partial order on sequences of sets: $(U_0, \ldots, U_m) \prec (V_0, \ldots, V_m)$ if each $U_i \subseteq V_i$, and for at least one set, the inclusion is strict.

We argue by induction on the partially ordered sequence. For the base case, let I^n be the simplex $\psi(S^n, \{v_0\}, \ldots, \{v_n\})$. $\mathcal{D}^r(I^n)$ is $(f-1)$-connected by hypothesis.

For the induction step for the set sequences, assume the claim for every sequence less than $U_0, \ldots, U_m$. There must be some index i such that $U_i = V_i \cup \{v\}$, where V_i is nonempty. The pseudosphere is the union of

$$\mathcal{K} = \mathcal{D}^r(\psi(S^m; U_0, \ldots, V_i, \ldots, U_m))$$

and

$$\mathcal{L} = \mathcal{D}^r(\psi(S^m; U_0, \ldots, \{v\}, \ldots, U_m)).$$

By the induction hypothesis for the sets, both $\mathcal{K}$ and $\mathcal{L}$ are $(f-1)$-connected.

A vertex is in $\mathcal{K}$ and $\mathcal{L}$ if and only if P_i does not appear in any vertex label. We can view the complex $\mathcal{K} \cap \mathcal{L}$ as the complex of r-round executions of an n-process protocol (omitting P_i) with $f-1$ failures. By the induction hypothesis on f, $\mathcal{K} \cap \mathcal{L}$ is $(f-2)$-connected, and by Theorem 1, $\mathcal{K} \cup \mathcal{L}$ is $(f-1)$-connected.

Theorem 5. *$\mathcal{D}^r(I^n)$ is $(f-1)$-connected.*

Proof. We argue by induction on r. For the base case, $r = 1$, and $\mathcal{D}(I^n)$ is a pseudosphere, and therefore $(n-1)$-connected and also $(f-1)$-connected.

For the induction step, assume $\mathcal{D}^{r-1}(I^n)$ is $(f-1)$-connected. By Theorem 4, $\mathcal{D}^{r-1}$ applied to any pseudosphere over I^n is also $(f-1)$-connected. In particular, $\mathcal{D}(I^n)$ is a pseudosphere, so $\mathcal{D}^{r-1}(\mathcal{D}(I^n)) = \mathcal{D}^r(I^n)$ is $(f-1)$-connected.

Now let $\mathcal{D}^r_{X,Q}$ be the operator that corresponds to an r-round execution in which all failure detectors also satisfy perpetual weak (x, q)-accuracy. As before, X is the union of the q X_i sets, $0 \leq i \leq q-1$. Let Q be the set containing the indexes of the q correct processes (one for each X_i).

Theorem 6. *If $\mathcal{D}^r_{X,Q}(\psi(S^n; \{u_0\}, \ldots, \{u_n\})$ is $(f-x+q-1)$-connected, so is $\mathcal{D}^r_{X,Q}(\psi(S^n; U_0, \ldots, U_n))$ for sets $U_0, \ldots, U_n$.*

Proof. We proceed by induction on f and q. For the base case, let $f = x-1$ and $q = 1$. $\mathcal{D}^r_{X,Q}(\psi(S^n; U_0, \ldots, U_n))$ is non-empty, hence $(f-x+q-1)$-connected.

Define the usual following partial order on sequences of sets. We argue by induction on the partially ordered sequence. For the base case, let I^n be the simplex $\psi(S^n, \{v_0\}, \ldots, \{v_n\})$. $\mathcal{D}^r_{X,Q}(I^n)$ is $(f-x+q-1)$-connected by hypothesis.

For the induction step for the set sequences, assume the claim for every sequence less than $U_0, \ldots, U_m$. There must be some index i such that $U_i = V_i \cup \{v\}$, where V_i is nonempty. The pseudosphere is the union of

$$\mathcal{K} = \mathcal{D}^r_{X,Q}(\psi(S^m; U_0, \dots, V_i, \dots, U_m))$$

and

$$\mathcal{L} = \mathcal{D}^r_{X,Q}(\psi(S^m; U_0, \dots, \{v\}, \dots, U_m)).$$

By the induction hypothesis for the sets, both $\mathcal{K}$ and $\mathcal{L}$ are $(f - x + q - 1)$-connected.

A vertex is in $\mathcal{K}$ and $\mathcal{L}$ if and only if P_i does not appear in any vertex label. Conversely, any vertex whose label does not contain P_i is in both $\mathcal{K}$ and $\mathcal{L}$.

There are two cases to consider. Suppose $i \in Q$. Every process in X receives a message from $P_{i \in Q}$, so no vertex with a label in X_i appears in $\mathcal{K} \cap \mathcal{L}$. We can view the complex $\mathcal{K} \cap \mathcal{L}$ as an application of $\mathcal{D}^r_X(\cdot)$ to an input simplex with $(n + 1) - (x_i) - (\sum_{j \neq i} x_i) + (q - 1)$ processes and $f - x + q - 1$ failures. By Theorem 5 and the induction hypothesis, $\mathcal{K} \cap \mathcal{L}$ is $(f - x + q - 2)$-connected, and so by Theorem 1, $\mathcal{K} \cup \mathcal{L}$ is $(f - x + q - 1)$-connected.

Suppose $i \notin Q$. Because every vertex labeled with $P_{i \notin Q}$ appears in $\mathcal{K} \cap \mathcal{L}$, but no vertex labeled with $P_{j \in Q}$, we can view the complex $\mathcal{K} \cap \mathcal{L}$ as an application of $\mathcal{D}^r_X(\cdot)$ to an input simplex with n processes ($P_{i \notin Q}$ is missing) and $f - 1$ failures. By the induction hypothesis, $\mathcal{K} \cap \mathcal{L}$ is $(f - x + q - 2)$-connected, and so by Theorem 1, $\mathcal{K} \cup \mathcal{L}$ is $(f - x + q - 1)$-connected.

Theorem 7. $\mathcal{D}^r_{X,Q}(I^n)$ *is* $(f - x + q - 1)$-*connected.*

Proof. We argue by induction on r. For the base case, $r = 1$, and $\mathcal{D}_{X,Q}(I^n)$ is a pseudosphere, and therefore $(n - 1)$-connected and also $(f - x + q - 1)$-connected.

For the induction step, assume $\mathcal{D}^{r-1}_{X,Q}(I^n)$ is $(f - x + q - 1)$-connected. By Theorem 6, $\mathcal{D}^{r-1}_{X,Q}$ applied to any pseudosphere over I^n is also $(f - x + q - 1)$-connected. In particular, $\mathcal{D}_{X,Q}(I^n)$ is a pseudosphere, so $\mathcal{D}^{r-1}_X(\mathcal{D}_{X,Q}(I^n)) = \mathcal{D}^r_{X,Q}(I^n)$ is $(f - x + q - 1)$-connected.

Theorem 8. $\mathcal{D}^r_{X,Q}(\mathcal{I}^n)$ *is* $(f - x + q - 1)$-*connected.*

Proof. By Theorem 7, $\mathcal{D}^r_{X,Q}$ applied to any pseudosphere over S^n is also $(f - x + q - 1)$-connected. In particular, $\mathcal{I}^n$ is a pseudosphere over S^n, so $\mathcal{D}^r_{X,Q}(\mathcal{I}^n) = \mathcal{D}^r_{X,Q}(\psi(S^n; V))$ is $(f - x + q - 1)$-connected.

Theorem 9. *There exist protocols solving k-set agreement for $n + 1$ processes with failure detectors of type $S_{x,q}$ if and only if $f < k + x - q$.*

Proof. By Theorems 3 and 8, a protocol exists only if $f < k + x - q$. The matching protocol is the same as the $S_{x,1}$ protocol of Mostéfaoui and Raynal [13], but with $m = k + x - q$ instead of $m = k + x - 1$, where m is the number of processes given to the TWA protocol. This slight modification is necessary to generalize it to the case when there are q sets X_i forming X, $0 \leq i \leq q - 1$, each one having its own correct process. From Mostéfaoui and Raynal [13], it is straightforward to see that this slightly modified protocol solves k-set agreement in asynchronous distributed systems equipped with failure detectors from class $S_{x,q}$.

Theorem 10. *There exist protocols solving k-set agreement for $n + 1$ processes with failure detectors of type $\diamond S_{x,q}$ if and only if $f < \min(\frac{n+1}{2}, k + x - q)$.*

Proof. Both $S_{x,q}$ and $\diamond S$ are at least as strong as $\diamond S_{x,q}$, and Chandra and Toueg [4] show that $f < \frac{n+1}{2}$ for $\diamond S$. Moreover, by Theorem 9, $f < k + x - q$ for $S_{x,q}$. It follows that $f < \min(\frac{n+1}{2}, k + x - q)$ for $\diamond S_{x,q}$. The matching protocol is given in the next section.

6   Eventual Weak (x, q)-Accuracy

In this section, we present a novel protocol that matches our lower bound for failure detectors in the class $\Diamond S_{x,q}$. We start with a slightly modified version of the *Terminating Weak Agreement* (TWA) protocol of Mostéfaoui and Raynal, illustrated by Java pseudocode in Figure 1. This protocol takes a set of m participating processes, an initial value for each participating process, a round number, and the ID of the calling process. It guarantees that if the set of participating processes includes q sets X_i of x_i processes such that some correct process in X_i is not suspected by any process in X_i, then at most $m - x + q$ values are decided.

```
int TWA(int id, Set particip, int estimate, int round) {
    int m = min(n+1, k + x - q);
    for (int c = 0; c < m; c++) {
        if (particip.get(c) == id) {   // I am coordinator
            Message.broadcast(new TWAMessage(round, estimate));
        } else {                       // I am not coordinator
        try {
            Message message = Message.receive(round);
            estimate = message.estimate; // take other's estimate
        } catch (suspectedException e) {
            // skip if process suspected
        }
        }
    }
    return estimate;
}
```

Fig. 1. The TWA Protocol

It is straightforward to extend the TWA protocol to solve k-set agreement for the $S_{x,q}$ failure detector: simply run TWA for each subset of $m = \min(n + 1, k + x - q)$ processes (Figure 2). Each process has an *estimate*, originally its input value. Each iteration introduces no new estimates. Each process chooses a new estimate at the end of each round, and retains the estimate it decided in the previous iteration. At some point, the m processes will encompass the processes in X, and the m processes will henceforth agree on at most $k = m - x + q$ distinct estimates. Every process not participating in that round's TWA protocol waits for a message from a participant (which will arrive reducing the maximum number of distinct estimates from $n + 1$ to $k = m - x + q$). See Mostéfaoui and Raynal [13] for a more complete discussion.

For our new $\Diamond S_{x,q}$ protocol, we repeatedly run the TWA-based protocol. Eventually, when all failure detectors have achieved weak (x, q)-accuracy, each subsequent iteration

```
int SxqAgree(int id, int estimate) {
  int m = min(n+1, k + x - q);
  // try all sets of size m
  for (round = 0; round < C(n+1, m); round++) {
    // next subset of m processes
    Set particip = ProcessSet.subset(round);
    if (particip.contains(id)) {   // I'm in the group
      estimate = TWA(id, particip, estimate, round);
      Message.broadcast(new Message(round, estimate));
    } else {
      Message message = Message.receive(round);
      // take other's value
      estimate = message.estimate;
    }
  }
  return estimate;
}
```

Fig. 2. k-Set agreement protocol for $S_{x,q}$

of the TWA-based algorithm will yield k or fewer values. The challenge is to detect when the TWA-based algorithm has converged.

We cycle through all permutations of the $n + 1$ processes. A *low-order* process in a permutation is one with rank less than or equal to $\lfloor \frac{n+1}{2} \rfloor + 1$, and the rest are *high-order* processes. Each process broadcasts its estimate, waits to receive $\lfloor \frac{n+1}{2} \rfloor + 1$ messages, and changes its estimate to the estimate from the least-ranked process in the current permutation. Because $f < \frac{n+1}{2}$, each high-order process will receive a message from a low-order process, so at the end of the round, every process will have switched to an estimate from a low-order process. If we can determine that the low-order processes had at most k distinct estimates at the start of the round, then all processes will have at most k estimates at the end of the round.

Each process includes in its message a history of its estimates at the start of all earlier rounds. Suppose, in round r, a process P receives messages from a set S of $\lfloor \frac{n+1}{2} \rfloor + 1$ processes. Let $s \leq r$ be the most recent round, if any, for which S was the set of low-order processes for the permutation at round s. P checks the histories received to determine whether the processes in S had at most k distinct values at round s. If so, the protocol has converged, and P can halt. The protocol is illustrated in Figure 3.

It is worth emphasizing that the DiamondAgree protocol does not actually depend on the TWA-based protocol, or even on $S_{x,q}$. It requires only (1) that the embedded protocol does not increase the set of original estimates, (2) it eventually solves k-set agreement, and (3) that there are fewer than $(n + 1)/2$ failures.

```
public int DiamondAgree(int id, int estim) {
  for (int r = 0; ; r++) {   // run until accuracy achieved
    estim = SxqAgree(id, estim);
    // cycle through permutations
    for (int p = 0; p < (n+1)!; p++) {
      Perm perm = new Perm(p); // construct permutation
      Message.broadcast(new Message(r, p, id, estim, hist));

      // wait for ((n+1)/2)+1 messages
      MessageSet mSet = Message.receive(r, p, ((n+1)/2)+1);

      // take estimate from low-order process
      estim = mSet.getLowOrderEstimate();

      // when were these processes all low-order?
      ProcessSet pSet = mSet.getProcesses();
      int lowOrderRound = Perm.firstLowOrder(pSet);
      if (lowOrderRound <= round) {  // has it happened yet?
        // get low-order estimates from that round
        EstimateSet eSet = mSet.getEstimates(lowOrderRound);
        if (eSet.size() <= k)
          Message.broadcast(new SuccessMessage());
          return estim;
      }
    }
  }
}
```

Fig. 3. k-Set agreement protocol for $\diamond S_{x,q}$

Theorem 11. *Let* $f < min(\frac{n+1}{2}, k+x-q)$. *The protocol illustrated in Figure 3 solves* k-*set agreement in asynchronous distributed systems equipped with failure detectors from class* $\diamond S_{x,q}$.

Proof. The proof has three parts. Note that $m = min(n+1, k+x-q)$, as in the code.

Validity follows from validity of the $S_{x,q}$ protocol, and because every estimate is always set to another process's estimate.

Termination. Because $f < m = min(n+1, k+x-q)$, each TWA instance terminates and at least one process from the participating set broadcasts an estimate. Moreover, no process waits forever for $\lfloor \frac{n+1}{2} \rfloor + 1$ messages.

The eventual (x, q)-accuracy property ensures that at some point there are q sets X_i of x_i processes such that some correct process in X_i is not suspected by any process in X_i. Consider the first round for which this property holds. The first subsequent execution of the $S_{x,q}$ agreement protocol will reduce the number of distinct estimates to no more than k. After the $S_{x,q}$ protocol execution, the processes run through the permutations.

At some round, some non-faulty process must receive messages from the processes that were the low-order processes for some permutation that occurred after the $S_{x,q}$ protocol execution, but before the current permutation. Checking the histories, that process will detect that the low-order processes had k or fewer distinct estimates, and the protocol will terminate when that process broadcasts an announcement.

Agreement. The protocol terminates if and only if there is a correct process that identifies an earlier permutation such that there were at most k distinct estimates among the low-order processes. Because every process sets its estimate to an estimate from a low-order process, there can be at most k distinct estimates among all processes.

7   Conclusion

It would be interesting to know if the round and message complexity of these protocols can be substantially reduced.

References

1. Hagit Attiya and Zvi Avidor. Wait-free n-set consensus when inputs are restricted. In Dahlia Malkhi, editor, *Distributed Computing, 16th International Conference, DISC 2002, Toulouse, France, October 28-30, 2002 Proceedings*, volume 2508 of *Lecture Notes in Computer Science*, pages 326–338. Springer, 2002.
2. E. Borowsky and E. Gafni. Generalized flp impossibility result for t-resilient asynchronous computations. In *Proceedings of the 1993 ACM Symposium on Theory of Computing*, May 1993.
3. Tushar Deepak Chandra, Vassos Hadzilacos, and Sam Toueg. The weakest failure detector for solving consensus. *Journal of the ACM (JACM)*, 43(4):685–722, 1996.
4. Tushar Deepak Chandra and Sam Toueg. Unreliable failure detectors for reliable distributed systems. *Journal of the ACM (JACM)*, 43(2):225–267, 1996.
5. S. Chaudhuri. Agreement is harder than consensus: set consensus problems in totally asynchronous systems. In *Proceedings of the Ninth Annual ACM Symosium on Principles of Distributed Computing*, pages 311–234, August 1990.
6. Soma Chaudhuri, Maurice Herlihy, Nancy A. Lynch, and Mark R. Tuttle. Tight bounds for k-set agreement. *Journal of the ACM (JACM)*, 47(5):912–943, 2000.
7. Eli Gafni. Round-by-round fault detectors (extended abstract): unifying synchrony and asynchrony. In *Proceedings of the seventeenth annual ACM symposium on Principles of distributed computing*, pages 143–152. ACM Press, 1998.
8. Maurice Herlihy and Sergio Rajsbaum. Algebraic spans. *Mathematical Structures in Computer Science*, 10(4):549–573, August 2000. Special Issue: Geometry and Concurrency.
9. Maurice Herlihy, Sergio Rajsbaum, and Mark R. Tuttle. Unifying synchronous and asynchronous message-passing models. In *Proceedings of the seventeenth annual ACM symposium on Principles of distributed computing*, pages 133–142. ACM Press, 1998.
10. Maurice Herlihy, Sergio Rajsbaum, and Mark R. Tuttle. A new synchronous lower bound for set agreement. In *Proceedings of DISC 2001*, pages 136–150, 2001.
11. Maurice Herlihy and Nir Shavit. The topological structure of asynchronous computability. *Journal of the ACM (JACM)*, 46(6):858–923, 1999.
12. A. Mostéfaoui, S. Rajsbaum, M. Raynal, and M. Roy. Condition-based protocols for set agreement problems. In Dahlia Malkhi, editor, *Distributed Computing, 16th International Conference, DISC 2002, Toulouse, France, October 28-30, 2002 Proceedings*, volume 2508 of *Lecture Notes in Computer Science*, pages 48–62. Springer, 2002.

13. Achour Mostéfaoui and Michel Raynal. k-set agreement with limited accuracy failure detectors. In *Proceedings of the nineteenth annual ACM symposium on Principles of distributed computing*, pages 143–152. ACM Press, 2000.
14. J.R. Munkres. *Elements Of Algebraic Topology*. Addison Wesley, Reading MA, 1984. ISBN 0-201-04586-9.
15. Michael Saks and Fotios Zaharoglou. Wait-free k-set agreement is impossible: The topology of public knowledge. *SIAM Journal on Computing*, 29(5):1449–1483, 2000.
16. E.H. Spanier. *Algebraic Topology*. Springer-Verlag, New York, 1966.
17. Jiong Yang, Gil Neiger, and Eli Gafni. Structured derivations of consensus algorithms for failure detectors. In *Proceedings of the seventeenth annual ACM symposium on Principles of distributed computing*, pages 297–306. ACM Press, 1998.

On Failure Detectors and Type Boosters
(Extended Abstract)[*]

Rachid Guerraoui and Petr Kouznetsov

Distributed Programming Laboratory, EPFL

Abstract. The power of a set S of object types can be measured as the maximum number n of processes that can solve consensus using only types in S and registers. This number, denoted by $h_m^r(S)$, is called the *consensus power* of S. The use of failure detectors can however "boost" the consensus power of types.

This paper addresses the *weakest failure detector type booster* question, which consists in determining the weakest failure detector D such that, for any set S of types with $h_m^r(S) = n$, $h_m^r(S; D) = n + 1$.

We consider the failure detector Ω_n (introduced in [18]) which outputs, at each process, a set of at most n processes so that, eventually, all correct processes detect the same set that includes at least one correct process. We prove that Ω_n is the weakest failure detector type booster for *deterministic one-shot* types.

As an interesting corollary of our result, we show that Ω_t is the weakest failure detector to boost the resilience level of $(t - 1)$-resilient objects solving consensus.

1 Introduction

Background. Key agreement problems, such as consensus, are not solvable in an asynchronous system where processes communicate solely through registers (i.e., read-write shared memory), as long as one of these processes can fail by crashing [7,17]. Circumventing this impossibility has sparked off two research trends:

(1) Augmenting the system model with synchrony assumptions about relative process speeds and communication delays [6]. Such assumptions could be encapsulated within a failure detector abstraction defined with axiomatic properties [5]. In short, a failure detector uses the underlying synchrony assumptions to provide each process with (possibly unreliable) information about the failure pattern, i.e., about the crashes of other processes. This trend led to the identification of the weakest failure detector to solve consensus [4,15]. This failure detector, denoted by Ω, outputs one process at every process so that, eventually, all correct processes detect the same correct process. The very fact that Ω is the weakest to solve consensus means

---

[*] This work is partially supported by the Swiss National Science Foundation (project number 2100-066768).

F.E. Fich (Ed.): DISC 2003, LNCS 2848, pp. 292–305, 2003.

that any failure detector that solves consensus can emulate the output of Ω. In a sense, Ω encapsulates the minimum amount of synchrony needed to solve consensus among any number of processes communicating through registers.

(2) Augmenting the system model with more powerful communication primitives, typically defined as shared object types with sequential specifications [10,17]. It has been shown, for instance, that consensus can be solved among any number of processes if objects of the compare&swap type can be used [10]. This trend led to define the power of a set of types S, denoted by $h^r_m(S)$ (we follow the standard notations of [14]), as the maximum number n of processes that can solve consensus using only objects of types in S and registers. For instance, the power of the register type is simply 1 whereas the compare&swap type has power ∞. An interesting fact here is the existence of types with intermediate power, like test-and-set or FIFO queue, which have power 2 [10,17].

Motivation. At first glance, the two trends appear to be fundamentally different. Failure detectors encapsulate synchrony assumptions and provide information about failure patterns, but cannot however be used to communicate information between processes. On the other hand, conventional object types with sequential specifications can be used for inter-process communication, but they do not provide any information about failures. It is intriguing to figure out whether these trends can be effectively combined [18]. Indeed, in both cases, the goal is to augment the system model with abstractions that are powerful enough to solve consensus, and it is appealing to determine whether abstractions from different trends add up. For instance, we can question ourselves whether the weakest failure detector to solve consensus using registers and queues is strictly weaker than Ω.

A way to effectively combine the two trends is to determine a failure detector hierarchy, $\mathcal{D}_k$, $k \in \mathbb{N}$, such that $\mathcal{D}_k$ would be the weakest failure detector to solve consensus among $k+1$ processes using any set of types S, such that $h^r_m(S) = k$. $\mathcal{D}_k$ would thus be the weakest failure detector (in the sense of [4]) to boost (in the sense of [11]) the power of S to higher levels of the consensus hierarchy.

A reasonable candidate for such a failure detector hierarchy was introduced in [18]. This hierarchy is made of weaker variants of Ω, denoted by Ω_k, $k \in \mathbb{N}$, where Ω_k is a failure detector that outputs, at each process, a set of processes so that all correct processes eventually detect the same set of at most k processes that includes at least one correct process. Clearly, Ω_1 is Ω. It was shown in [18] that Ω_n is sufficient to solve $(n+1)$-process consensus using any set of types S, such that $h^r_m(S) = n$. It was also conjectured in [18] that Ω_n is the weakest failure detector to boost the power of S to the level $n+1$ of the consensus hierarchy. As pointed out in [18], the proof of this conjecture appears to be challenging. The motivation of this work was to take up that challenge.

Contribution. In this paper, we consider deterministic one-shot types [11]. Although these restrict every process to invoke at most one operation on each object, (a) they exhibit complex behavior with respect to the weakest failure detector type booster question (in the parlance of the robustness problem [11, 14,16,2]) and, as we will explain below, (b) they allow a precise answer to the the weakest failure detector resilience booster question (in the parlance of the resilience vs. wait-freedom question [3,1]).

Our result can be viewed as a generalization of the fundamental result of [4], and more precisely its extension to the shared memory model [15]. Indeed, we prove that Ω_n is the weakest failure detector that boosts the power of a collection of deterministic one-shot types from consensus number n to $n + 1$.

Proving our result comes down to showing that any algorithm that solves $(n+1)$-process consensus, using any failure detector and any set of deterministic one-shot types $\mathcal{S}$, such that $h_m^r(\mathcal{S}) \leq n$, can be used to emulate the output of Ω_n. A major difficulty in our case, with respect to the proofs of [4,15], is that the consensus algorithm uses not only registers but also other objects. We cannot rely on any information about the operations through which these objects can be accessed. The only information that we can rely on is that these objects instantiate deterministic one-shot types that collectively have consensus power at most n.

As an interesting corollary of our result, we show that Ω_t is actually the weakest failure detector to boost the resilience of a set of objects solving consensus from level $t - 1$ to level t. We show that, for all $1 \leq t < n$, any algorithm that solves t-resilient n-process consensus using a failure detector, registers and any set of $(t - 1)$-resilient objects of any (not necessarily one-shot deterministic) type, can be used to emulate the output of Ω_t. On the other hand, there is an algorithm that implements t-resilient consensus out of registers and $(t-1)$-resilient objects using Ω_t. Thus, Ω_t encapsulates the exact amount of synchrony needed to circumvent the resilience boosting impossibility of [3,1].

The full version of the paper is available as a technical report [8].

Roadmap. Section 2 presents the system model. Section 3 presents the technical details necessary for our result. Section 4 states our main result. Section 5 applies our result to boost the resilience of a set of objects.

2   Model

Our model of processes communicating through shared objects is based on that of [13,14] and our notion of failure detectors follows from [4,15]. Below we recall what is substantial to show our result.

We consider a system Π of $n + 1$ asynchronous processes $p_0, \ldots, p_n$ ($n \geq 1$) that communicate using shared objects. The processes might fail by crashing, i.e. stop executing their steps.

Objects and types. Let $\mathbb{N}$ denote the set of natural numbers and, for every $k \in \mathbb{N}$, $\mathbb{N}_k = \{0, \ldots, k - 1\}$. An object is a data structure that can be accessed concurrently by the processes. Every object is an instance of a type which is defined by a tuple (Q, O, n_p, R, δ). Here Q is a set of states, O is a set of operations, n_p is a positive integer denoting the number of ports (used as an interface between processes and objects), R is a set of responses, and δ is a relation known as the sequential specification of the type that carries each state, operation and port number to a set of response and state pairs. We assume that objects are deterministic: the sequential specification is a function $\delta : Q \times O \times \mathbb{N}_{n_p} \rightarrow Q \times R$. A type is said to be k-ported if $n_p = k$.

We consider here linearizable [12] objects: operations on the objects must appear in one-at-a-time order consistent with their real time order. Unless otherwise stated, we assume that the objects are wait-free [10]: any process completes any operation in a finite number of steps, regardless of delays or failures of other processes.

A process accesses objects by invoking operations on the ports of the objects. A process can use only one port of each object. Each port of a one-shot type can be used only once by a unique process. The binding scheme that defines how a process determines the port to access is not important for our result.

Consensus. The (binary) k-process consensus problem [7] consists for k processes to decide on some final values (0 or 1) based on their initial proposed values in such a way that: (agreement) no two processes decide on different values,[1] (validity) every decided value is a proposed value, and (termination) every correct process eventually decides.

To prove our result, we also use a restricted form of consensus, k-process team consensus [19]. This variant of consensus ensures agreement among k processes only if the input values satisfy certain conditions. More precisely, assume that there exists a (known a priori) partition of k processes into two non-empty sets (teams). A k-process team consensus algorithm guarantees agreement if all processes on the same team have the same input value. Obviously, k-process team consensus can be solved whenever k-process consensus can be solved. Surprisingly, the converse is also true [19] (the proof can also be found in the full version of the paper [8]):

Lemma 1. Let S be any set of types. If S solves k-process team consensus, then S also solves k-process consensus.

The consensus power [10,14] of a set of types S, denoted by $h_m^r(S)$, is the largest k, such that k-process consensus can be solved using objects of types in $S \cup \{\text{register}\}$, or ∞ if no such largest k exists.

Failure detectors. To simplify the presentation of our model, we assume the existence of a discrete global clock. This is a fictional device: the processes have no direct access to it. We take the range $\mathbb{T}$ of the clock's ticks to be the set of natural numbers and 0 ($\mathbb{T} = \{0\} \cup \mathbb{N}$). A failure pattern F is a function from the global time range $\mathbb{T}$ to 2^{Π}, where $F(\tau)$ denotes the set of processes that have crashed by time $\tau \in \mathbb{T}$. Processes do not recover after the crash: $\forall \tau \in \mathbb{T} : F(\tau) \subseteq F(\tau + 1)$. We define $\text{correct}(F) = \Pi - \cup_{\tau \in \mathbb{T}} F(\tau)$ to be the set of correct (in F) processes. A process that is not correct is said to be faulty.

A failure detector $\mathcal{D}$ is defined as a map of each failure pattern F (i.e., which processes crash at what times) to a set of failure detector histories $\mathcal{D}(F)$ (i.e.,

---

[1] In fact, our weakest failure detection result holds even for the *non-uniform* variant of consensus, where we require only that no two *correct* processes decide differently [9].

what each process knows about failures at what time). Any failure detector $\mathcal{D}$ has a range $\mathcal{R}_{\mathcal{D}}$ so that, for any F, any history $H \in \mathcal{D}(F)$ is a function from $\Pi \times \mathbb{T}$ to $\mathcal{R}_{\mathcal{D}}$ ($H(p_i, \tau)$ is the output of the failure detector module of p_i at time τ). Note that the output of a failure detector depends only on the failure pattern: it cannot give any information on the state of processes or shared objects.

If an asynchronous system with registers is augmented with the failure detector Ω, which eventually permanently outputs the identifier of the same correct process at all correct processes, then consensus is solvable for any number of processes [15]. Moreover, it was shown that the output of Ω can be emulated by any consensus algorithm using a failure detector and registers [15]. In a sense we recall below, Ω is said to be the weakest failure detector to solve consensus with registers.

Algorithms. An algorithm A using a failure detector $\mathcal{D}$ is a collection of $n + 1$ deterministic automata, one for each process in the system. Computation proceeds in atomic steps of A. In each step, a process (1) invokes an operation on a shared object and receives a response,[2] or queries its failure detector module of $\mathcal{D}$, and (2) updates its local state according to the current state, the response from the shared object or the value output by the failure detector. A step s is defined by the triple (p_i, o, v) where p_i is the identity of the process that takes the step, o is either an operation (on a register or an object of a one-shot deterministic type) invoked by p_i during the step or $query$, and v is the response of the invoked operation or, if $o = query$, the failure detector value seen by p_i during the step. If o is an operation on a shared object X, we say that the step s accesses X. Otherwise, if $o = query$, we say that the steps s is a query step.

A configuration defines the current state of each process and each object in the system. A step $s = (p_i, o, v)$ of an algorithm A is applicable to a configuration C if and only if o is the next operation of p_i defined by A for C. An execution e of an algorithm A is a (finite or infinite) sequence of steps of A. ($e_\perp$ denotes an empty execution.) An execution $e = s_1, s_2, \ldots$ is applicable to a configuration C if and only if (a) $e = e_\perp$, or (b) s_1 is applicable to C, s_2 is applicable to $s_1(C)$, etc. Given an execution e applicable to a configuration C, $e(C)$ denotes the configuration resulting from applying e to C.

Reducibility. We say that a failure detector $\mathcal{D}$ is weaker than a failure detector $\mathcal{D}'$, we write also $\mathcal{D} \preceq \mathcal{D}'$, if there exists an algorithm $T_{\mathcal{D}' \to \mathcal{D}}$ (it is called a reduction algorithm) that, for any failure pattern, can emulate the output of $\mathcal{D}$ using only $\mathcal{D}'$ and registers. We say that $\mathcal{D}$ is strictly weaker than $\mathcal{D}'$, we write also $\mathcal{D} \prec \mathcal{D}'$, if $\mathcal{D} \preceq \mathcal{D}'$, but $\mathcal{D}' \npreceq \mathcal{D}$.

Hierarchy of Ω_k. In this paper, we focus on the hierarchy of failure detectors Ω_k introduced in [18]. For any $k \in \mathbb{N}$, the output of Ω_k is a set of at most k processes so that, eventually, the same set is output at all correct processes and this set includes at least one correct process. One can easily see that Ω_1 is Ω [4]. It was

---

[2] Our objects are linearizable [12], so any execution can be viewed as a sequence of atomic invocation-response pairs.

furthermore shown in [18] that, for any $1 \leq k \leq n$, (a) $\Omega_{k+1} \prec \Omega_k$ and, (b) for any set of types $\mathcal{S}$, such that $h_m^r(\mathcal{S}) = k$, $\mathcal{S}$ and Ω_k (shared by n processes) can solve n-process consensus.

3   The Proof Technique

In this section, we introduce some necessary technical details of our proof that Ω_n is necessary to boost the power of any set $\mathcal{S}$ of deterministic one-shot types from level n to level $n + 1$. In particular, we recall and generalize the notions of DAG, decision gadget and deciding process [4,15].

An outline of the proof. Let $\mathsf{Cons}_{\mathcal{D}}$ be any consensus algorithm that solves $(n+1)$-process consensus using registers, a failure detector $\mathcal{D}$, and objects of types in $\mathcal{S}$, for any set $\mathcal{S}$ of deterministic one-shot types, such that $h_m^r(\mathcal{S}) \leq n$. Our goal is to define a reduction algorithm $T_{\mathcal{D} \to \Omega_n}$ that emulates the output of Ω_n out of $\mathcal{D}$. $T_{\mathcal{D} \to \Omega_n}$ should have all correct processes agree eventually on the same set of at most n processes that includes at least one correct process.

The principle of the reduction algorithm $T_{\mathcal{D} \to \Omega_n}$ is the following. Processes periodically query their failure detector modules of $\mathcal{D}$ and exchange the values returned using registers. As a result, each process p_i maintains an ever growing directed acyclic graph (DAG), denoted by G_i, that captures a sample of the failure detector history output by $\mathcal{D}$. This information allows p_i to simulate locally, for any initial configuration I, a number of finite executions of the $\mathsf{Cons}_{\mathcal{D}}$ algorithm and build an ever growing simulation tree, denoted by Υ_i^I. Since registers provide reliable (though asynchronous) communication, all such Υ_i^I converge to the same infinite simulation tree Υ^I. It turns out, that, for some initial configuration I, Υ^I has a finite subtree γ, called a decision gadget, that provides sufficient information to detect a set of at most n processes, called the deciding set of γ, that includes at least one correct process. Thus, eventually, the correct processes detect the gadget and agree on its deciding set which is sufficient to emulate Ω_n.

DAGs. Let F be any failure pattern, H be any failure detector history in $\mathcal{D}(F)$ and I be any initial configuration of $\mathsf{Cons}_{\mathcal{D}}$. Let G be an infinite directed acyclic graph (DAG) defined by the set of vertexes $\mathcal{V}(G)$ and a set of directed edges $\mathcal{E}(G)$ of the form $v \to v'$, where $v \in \mathcal{V}(G)$ and $v' \in \mathcal{V}(G)$, with the following properties:

(1) The vertexes of G are of the form $[p_i, d, k]$ where $p_i \in \Pi$, $d \in \mathcal{R}_{\mathcal{D}}$ and $k \in \mathbb{N}$. There is a mapping $f : \mathcal{V}(G) \to \mathbb{T}$ that associates a time with each vertex of G, such that:
   (a) For any $v = [p_i, d, k] \in \mathcal{V}(G)$, $p_i \notin F(f(v))$ and $d = H(p_i, f(v))$.
   (b) For any edge $v \to v' \in \mathcal{E}(G)$, $f(v) < f(v')$.
(2) If $[p_i, d, k] \in \mathcal{V}(G)$, $[p_i, d', k'] \in \mathcal{V}(G)$ and $k < k'$ then $[p_i, d, k] \to [p_i, d', k'] \in \mathcal{E}(G)$.
(3) G is transitively closed.

(4) Let $U \subseteq \mathcal{V}(G)$ be a finite set of vertexes and p_i be any correct process in F. There is $d \in \mathcal{R}_D$ and $k \in \mathbb{N}$, such that for every vertex $v \in \mathcal{V}(G)$, $v \to [p_i, d, k]$ is an edge of G.

Informally, G stores a sample of $\mathcal{D}$'s output at different processes and some temporal relationships between them: an edge $[p_i, d, k] \to [p_j, d', k'] \in \mathcal{E}(G)$ can be interpreted as "p_i saw failure detector value d (in its k-th query) before p_j saw failure detector value d' (in its k'-th query)".

Simulation trees. A path $g = [q_1, d_1, k_1], [q_2, d_2, k_2], \dots$ in G and an initial configuration I of Cons_D induce a unique execution $e = (q_1, o_1, u_1), (q_2, o_2, u_2), \dots$ of Cons_D applicable to I, such that $u_i = d_i$ whenever $o_i = query$. The set of all executions of Cons_D induced by G and I implies a tree Υ^I, called the simulation tree induced by G and I, defined as follows. The set of vertexes of Υ^I is the set of finite executions e that are induced by G and I. The root of Υ^I is an empty execution $e_\perp$. There is an edge from a vertex e to a vertex e' if and only if $e' = e \cdot s$ for a step s. Thus, for each (finite or infinite) path of Υ^I, there is a unique execution $e = s_1, s_2, \dots$.

Any path in the tree in which every correct process takes an infinite number of steps is a run of Cons_D. Thus, eventually every correct process decides in the path. As a result, every vertex of Υ^I has a descendant in the tree in which every correct process decides (Lemma 6.2.6 of [4]). We assign a set of tags to each vertex of Υ^I. Vertex C of Υ^I gets tag u if and only if it has a descendant C' such that some correct process has decided u in $C'(I)$. according to the decisions taken by their descendants. If the only decision taken by descendants of a vertex is $u \in \{0, 1\}$, the vertex is called u-valent. A 0-valent or 1-valent vertex is called univalent. A vertex is called bivalent if it has both tags.

A tree Υ^I is called u-valent (bivalent) if $e_\perp$ is u-valent (bivalent) in Υ^I. For a univalent vertex C of Υ^I, $val(C)$ denotes the valence of C.

Decision gadgets. From now on, we assume that processes communicate using shared objects of types in $\{\mathsf{register}\} \cup \mathcal{S}$ where $\mathcal{S}$ contains only deterministic one-shot types and $h_m^r(\mathcal{S}) \leq n$. Following [4], we introduce the notion of a decision gadget[3] A decision gadget γ is a finite subtree of Υ^I rooted at $e_\perp$ that includes a vertex C (called the pivot of the gadget), such that one of the following conditions is satisfied:

(**fork**) There are two steps s_i and s_i' of a process p_i, such that $s_i(C)$ and $s_i'(C)$ are two leaves of γ of opposite valence.
(**hook**) There is a step s_i of a process p_i and step s_j of a process p_j ($i \neq j$), such that $s_i(s_j(C))$ and $s_i(C)$ are two leaves of γ of opposite valence, and s_i and s_j do not access the same object of a type in $\mathcal{S}$.
(**rake**) There is a set $U \subseteq \Pi$, $|U| \geq 2$, an object X of a type in $\mathcal{S}$, such that, for any $p_i \in U$, any step s_i of p_i applicable to C (w.r.t. Cons_D) accesses X (U is called the participating set of γ). Let E be the set of all sequences of

---

[3] We slightly modify here the definition of a hook given in [4] and introduce a new notion of a rake.

steps in $\{s_i | p_i \in U\}$ in which every process in U takes atmost one step, such that $\forall e \in E$, $e(C) \in \Upsilon^I$ and, for any e and e' in E, e is not a prefix of e' (E is called the execution set of γ). Then γ, E, C and U satisfy the following conditions:

(i) C' is a leaf of γ if and only if $\exists e \in E$: $C' = e(C)$.

(ii) No process $p_j \in \Pi - U$ ever accesses X in any descendant of C in Υ^I.

(iii) If E includes all sequences of steps in $\{s_i | p_i \in U\}$ in which every process takes exactly one step, then every leaf of γ is univalent, and γ has at least one 0-valent leaf and at least one 1-valent leaf.

Let γ be a rake. If the condition of item (iii) above is satisfied, we say that γ is complete. Otherwise, γ is said to be incomplete.

Examples of decision gadgets are depicted in Figure 1.

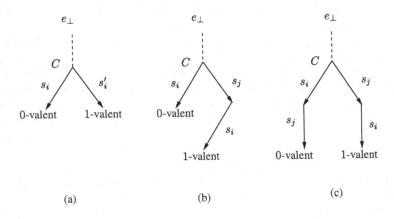

Fig. 1. Examples of decision gadgets: (a) a fork with $s_i = (p_i, query, d)$ and $s_i' = (p_i, query, d')$, (b) a hook where s_i and s_j do not access the same object of a type in $\mathcal{S}$, (c) a complete rake with the participating set $U = \{p_i, p_j\}$ and the execution set $E = \{s_i \cdot s_j, s_j \cdot s_i\}$, where s_i and s_j access the same object X of a type in $\mathcal{S}$.

The following lemma is the key result of our proof. Note that the lemma uses our assumption that types in $\mathcal{S}$ are deterministic.

Lemma 2. Let γ be a complete rake with a pivot C, a participating set U and an execution set E, such that $|U| = n + 1$ and, for any executions e and e' in E that begin with the same step s_j, $val(e(C)) = val(e'(C))$. There exist a process p_j and two executions e_0 and e_1 in E, such that (a) $val(e_0(C)) \neq val(e_1(C))$, and (b) p_j has the same state in $e_0(C)$ and $e_1(C)$.

Proof. For each execution $e \in E$, we associate the configuration $e(C)$ with a vertex of a graph, denoted by $\mathcal{K}$. Two vertexes of $\mathcal{K}$ corresponding to the configurations $e(C)$ and $e'(C)$ are connected with an edge if and only if at least one process p_j has the same state in $e(C)$ and $e'(C)$.

Claim 1: $\mathcal{K}$ is connected.

Proof of Claim 1: By contradiction, assume that $\mathcal{K}$ is not connected, i.e., consists of two or more disconnected components.

Let $e(C)$ and $e'(C)$ be any two vertexes of $\mathcal{K}$, such that the corresponding executions e and e' begin with the step s_i of the same process p_i. Since p_i takes exactly one step in both e and e' and all types considered are deterministic, p_i has the same state in $e(C)$ and $e'(C)$. Thus, the two vertexes belong to the same component of $\mathcal{K}$.

Let $\mathcal{K}_1$ be one of the components of $\mathcal{K}$. We divide the system into two teams Π_1 and Π_2. Team Π_1 consists of all processes p_i, such that any execution that begins with the step s_i of p_i is in $\mathcal{K}_1$. Team Π_2 consists of all other processes. Since $\mathcal{K}$ consists of at least two disconnected components, Π_1 and Π_2 are non-empty. We show now that $\mathcal{S}$ and two registers can solve $(n+1)$-process team consensus for teams Π_1 and Π_2.

Let X be the object of a type in $\mathcal{S}$ accesses by each step in $\{s_j | p_j \in U\}$. We initialize X to its state in $C.$[4] Every process p_i writes its input value into its team's register and then executes the step s_i of Cons_D defined for C. By construction of $\mathcal{K}$, the resulting state of p_i can belong to a vertex of exactly one component of $\mathcal{K}$. If the state of p_i corresponds to a vertex in $\mathcal{K}_1$, then p_i outputs the value of Π_1's register, otherwise, p_i outputs the value of Π_2's register. As a result, processes agree on the component to which the resulting state of the system belongs.

Clearly, every correct process eventually decides on some proposed value. Assume now that all processes on the same team (Π_1 or Π_2) propose the same value. Since the processes always agree on the component in $\mathcal{K}$, and no two different values are ever written into the teams' registers, no two processes decide on different values.

Thus, $\mathcal{S} \cup \{\text{register}\}$ solve $(n+1)$-process team consensus. By Lemma 1, $\mathcal{S} \cup \{\text{register}\}$ solve $(n+1)$-process consensus - a contradiction with the assumption that $h_m^r(\mathcal{S}) \leq n$. Thus, $\mathcal{K}$ is connected. (End of proof of Claim 1)

Now we color each vertex $e(C)$ of $\mathcal{K}$ with $val(e(C))$. Since γ is complete, there are two executions e and e' in E of opposite valence, and for every e in E, $e(C)$ is univalent. That is, each vertex of $\mathcal{K}$ has exactly one color (0 or 1) and, for each $u \in \{0, 1\}$, there is at least vertex in $\mathcal{K}$ colored by u. Since $\mathcal{K}$ is connected, $\mathcal{K}$ includes at least two vertexes of different colors, $e_0(C)$ and $e_1(C)$, connected with an edge. By construction, there is a process p_j that has the same state in $e_0(C)$ and $e_1(C)$ and $val(e_0(C)) \neq val(e_1(C))$.   □

The following result is a generalization of Lemma 6.4.1 of [4] (the proof is given in the full paper [8]):

Lemma 3. Any bivalent simulation tree Υ^I has a decision gadget.

Deciding sets. Instead of the notion of a deciding process given in [4], we introduce the notion of a deciding set $V \subset \Pi$. The deciding set V of a decision gadget γ is computed as follows:

---

[4] The possibility to initialize objects cannot increase their consensus power [2].

(1) Let γ be a fork defined by steps s_i and s'_i. Then $V = \{p_i\}$.
(2) Let γ be a hook defined by steps s_i and s_j. Since, by definition, s_i and s_j do not access the same object of a type in $\mathcal{S}$, there are the following cases to consider:

   (2a) s_j is a query step or s_j reads a register. Then $V = \{p_j\}$.
   (2b) s_j writes into a register, or s_j accesses an object X of a type in $\mathcal{S}$ and s_i does not access X. Then $V = \Pi - \{p_j\}$.

(3) Let γ be a rake defined by a pivot C, a participating set U and an executions set E and a pivot C. The following cases are possible:

   (3a) γ is incomplete, i.e., there is an execution $e \in E$ and a process $p_j \in U$, such that p_j takes no steps in e. Then $V = \Pi - \{p_j\}$.
   (3b) γ is complete and $|U| \leq n$. Then $V = U$.
   (3c) γ is complete, $|U| = n + 1$, and there is a process $p_j \in U$ such that, for some e and e' in E that begin with s_j, $e(C)$ and $e'(C)$ have different valences. Then $V = \Pi - \{p_j\}$.
   (3d) γ is complete, $|U| = n + 1$, and for any e and e' in E that begin with the same step s_j, $e(C)$ and $e'(C)$ have the same valence. Lemma 2 guarantees that some process p_j "mixes" two configurations of opposite valence, i.e., there exist two executions e and e' in E, such that p_j has the same state in $e(C)$ and $e'(C)$, and $val(e(C)) \neq val(e'(C))$. Then $V = \Pi - \{p_j\}$.

By construction, in each case, V is a set of at most n processes.

Lemma 4. The deciding set of a decision gadget contains at least one correct process.

(The proof of Lemma 4 [8] uses the assumption that $\mathcal{S}$ consists of one-shot types.)

4   The Main Result

In this section, we present our reduction algorithm $T_{\mathcal{D} \to \Omega_n}$ (Figure 2). As in [4, 15], each process p_i maintains a shared variable G_i that contains a finite ever growing DAG representing a sample of failure detector output values at different processes as well as causal relationships between them. Let $G_i(\tau)$ denote the value of G_i at the end of the last step of p_i before time $\tau \in \mathbb{T}$. There is an infinite DAG G (defined in Section 3) such that, for any correct process p_i, $\cup_{\tau \in \mathbb{T}} G_i(\tau) = G$ (Lemma 6.6.1.2 and Lemma 6.6.1.4 of [4]).

Every process p_i periodically scans the registers G_j $(j = 1, .., n)$ and adds the new vertexes and edges from each G_j $(j = 1, .., m)$ to G_i. Then p_i queries its failure detector module, adds a new vertex corresponding to the output value to G_i and an edge to the vertex from each old vertex of G_i.

Let I^j $(j = 0, .., n + 1)$ denote an initial configuration of $\mathsf{Cons}_{\mathcal{D}}$ in which processes $p_0, .., p_{j-1}$ propose 1 and processes $p_j, .., p_n$ propose 0. Process p_i constructs then a simulation forest — the set of simulation trees $\{\Upsilon_i^j\}_{j=1,...,n+1}$, where Υ_i^j denotes the simulation tree induced by G_i and I^j. Let $\Upsilon_i^j(\tau)$ $(\tau \in \mathbb{T})$ denote the simulation tree induced by $G_i(\tau)$ and I^j. Similarly, $\cup_{\tau \in \infty} \Upsilon_i^j(\tau) = \Upsilon^j$, where Υ^j is induced by G and I^j.

```
1: output_i ← {p_i}
2: G_i ← ∅
3: k ← 1
4: while true do
5:     for all j ∈ {0,...,n}, i ≠ j do
6:         G_i ← G_i ∪ G_j
7:     d ← D_i
8:     k ← k + 1
9:     G_i ← G_i ∪ G_j
10:    add [p_i, d, k] to G_i and edges from all other vertexes of G_i to [p_i, d, k]
11:    for all j ∈ {0,...,n+1} do
12:        Υ_i^j ← simulation tree induced by G_i and I^j
13:    if there is no critical Υ_i^k in {Υ_i^j}_{j=0,...,n+1} then
14:        output_i ← {p_i}
15:    else
16:        if every Υ_i^j is univalent then
17:            k ← the smallest j, such that Υ_i^j is 1-valent
18:            output_i ← {p_k}
19:        else
20:            output_i ← the deciding set of the smallest decision gadget in
                {Υ_i^j}_{j=0,...,n+1}
```

Fig. 2. Reduction algorithm $T_{\mathcal{D}\to\Omega_n}$ for process p_i.

Process p_i tags each vertex $C \in \Upsilon_i^j$ according to the decision taken in C's descendants. We say that Υ_i^j is critical if and only if Υ_i^{j-1} is 0-valent and Υ_i^j is 1-valent or bivalent. A finite tree Υ_i^j might have no tags though, hence there might be no critical simulation tree in $\{\Upsilon_i^j\}_{j=0,...n+1}$.

As a result of the reduction algorithm, every process p_i maintains a variable $output_i$, the value of which is returned each time the failure detector module of Ω_n at p_i is queried.

Theorem 1. Let S be any set of one-shot deterministic types, such that $h_m^r(S) \leq n$. If a failure detector $\mathcal{D}$ implements $(n+1)$-process consensus in a system of processes, using only registers and objects of types in S, then $\Omega_n \preceq \mathcal{D}$.

Proof. (Sketch) By the validity property of consensus, Υ^0 is 0-valent and Υ^{n+1} is 1-valent. Hence, there exists a critical tree in $\{\Upsilon^j\}_{j=0,...n+1}$.

In the algorithm of Figure 2, every correct process eventually identifies the critical tree Υ^k. The following cases are possible:

(1) Υ^k is univalent. In this case, every correct process p_i eventually permanently outputs p_k. By Lemma 6.5.1 of [4], p_k is correct.
(2) Υ^k is bivalent. By Lemma 3, there exists a decision gadget in Υ^k. In this case, eventually, every correct process p_i eventually permanently outputs the deciding set V of the smallest decision gadget of Υ^k. By Lemma 4, the

deciding set (of size at most n) of any decision gadget includes at least one correct process.

In both cases, the output of Ω_n is emulated.   □

Theorem 1 and [18] imply the following result:

Theorem 2. Let S be any set of one-shot deterministic types, such that $h^r_m(S) = n$. Ω_n is the weakest failure detector D, such that $h^r_m(S; D) = n + 1$.

5   Boosting Resilience with Ω_t

So far we considered systems in which processes communicate through wait-free linearizable implementations of shared objects. Every process can complete every operation on a wait-free object in a finite number of its own steps, regardless of the behavior of other processes.

In contrast, in this section we consider t-resilient implementations. They guarantee that a process completes its operation, as long as no more than t process crash, where t is a specified parameter. If more than t processes crash, no operation on a t-resilient implementation is obliged to return.

Assume that k processes communicate through registers and t-resilient linearizable implementations of shared object [3]. We will simply call these t-resilient objects (these are called t-resilient services in [1]).

The classical results on (a) consensus universality [10] and (b) t-resiliency [3] imply the following impossibility result:

Theorem 3. Let k and t be any integers, such that $k > t \geq 1$. There is no t-resilient implementation of k-process consensus from registers and $(t-1)$-resilient objects.

(The proof of Theorem 3 based on the results of [10,3] is given in the full version of the paper [8]. An alternative self-contained proof for message passing systems is given in [1].)

Thus, it is not possible to obtain a more fault-tolerant system solving consensus by combining less fault-tolerant components. Not surprisingly, this impossibility can be circumvented by augmenting the system with a failure detector abstraction. Interestingly, our result on boosting the power of deterministic one-shot types implies the following theorem (the proof is given in the full paper [8]):

Theorem 4. Let k and t be any integers, such that $t > f \geq 1$. Let S be any set of types (not necessarily deterministic one-shot), such that registers and $(t-1)$-resilient objects of types in S implement $(t-1)$-resilient k-process consensus. Ω_t is the weakest failure detector to implement t-resilient k-process consensus using registers and $(t-1)$-resilient objects of types in S.

References

1. P. Attie, N. Lynch, and S. Rajsbaum. Boosting fault-tolerance in asynchronous message passing systems is impossible. Technical report, MIT Laboratory for Computer Science, MIT-LCS-TR-877, 2002.
2. E. Borowsky, E. Gafni, and Y. Afek. Consensus power makes (some) sense! In *Proceedings of the 13th ACM Symposium on Principles of Distributed Computing (PODC)*, pages 363–372, August 1994.
3. T. Chandra, V. Hadzilacos, P. Jayanti, and S. Toueg. Wait-freedom vs. t-resiliency and the robustness of wait-free hierarchies. In *Proceedings of the 13th ACM Symposium on Principles of Distributed Computing (PODC)*, pages 334–343. ACM Press, 1994.
4. T. D. Chandra, V. Hadzilacos, and S. Toueg. The weakest failure detector for solving consensus. *Journal of the ACM (JACM)*, 43(4):685–722, July 1996.
5. T. D. Chandra and S. Toueg. Unreliable failure detectors for reliable distributed systems. *Journal of the ACM (JACM)*, 43(2):225–267, March 1996.
6. C. Dwork, N. Lynch, and L. Stockmeyer. Consensus in the presence of partial synchrony. *Journal of the ACM (JACM)*, 35(2):288–323, 1988.
7. M. J. Fischer, N. A. Lynch, and M. S. Paterson. Impossibility of distributed consensus with one faulty process. *Journal of the ACM (JACM)*, 32(3):374–382, April 1985.
8. R. Guerraoui and P. Kouznetsov. On failure detectors and type boosters. Technical report, IC, EPFL, ID:IC/2003/48, 2003. Available at http://icwww.epfl.ch/publications/.
9. V. Hadzilacos. On the relationship between the atomic commitment and consensus problems. In *Proceedings of the Workshop on Fault-Tolerant Distributed Computing*, volume 448 of *LNCS*, pages 201–208. Springer-Verlag, 1986.
10. M. Herlihy. Wait-free synchronization. *ACM Transactions on Programming Languages and Systems (TOPLAS)*, 13(1):124–149, January 1991.
11. M. Herlihy and E. Ruppert. On the existence of booster types. In *Proceedings of the 41st IEEE Symposium on Foundations of Computer Science (FOCS)*, pages 653–663, 2000.
12. M. Herlihy and J. M. Wing. Linearizability: a correctness condition for concurrent objects. *ACM Transactions on Programming Languages and Systems (TOPLAS)*, 12(3):463–492, June 1990.
13. P. Jayanti. Wait-free computing. In *Proceedings of the 9th International Workshop on Distributed Algorithms (WDAG)*, volume 972 of *LNCS*, pages 19–50. Springer Verlag, 1995.
14. P. Jayanti. Robust wait-free hierarchies. *Journal of the ACM (JACM)*, 44(4):592–614, 1997.
15. W.-K. Lo and V. Hadzilacos. Using failure detectors to solve consensus in asynchronous shared-memory systems. In *Proceedings of the 8th International Workshop on Distributed Algorithms (WDAG)*, volume 857 of *LNCS*, pages 280–295. Springer Verlag, 1994.
16. W.-K. Lo and V. Hadzilacos. All of us are smarter than any of us: Nondeterministic wait-free hierarchies are not robust. *SIAM Journal of Computing*, 30(3):689–728, 2000.
17. M. C. Loui and H. H. Abu-Amara. Memory requirements for agreement among unreliable asynchronous processes. *Advances in Computing Research*, pages 163–183, 1987.

18. G. Neiger. Failure detectors and the wait-free hierarchy. In *Proceedings of the 14th ACM Symposium on Principles of Distributed Computing (PODC)*, pages 100–109, August 1995.

19. E. Ruppert. Determining consensus numbers. *SIAM Journal of Computing*, 30(4):1156–1168, 2000.

GeoQuorums: Implementing Atomic Memory in Mobile *Ad Hoc* Networks

(Extended Abstract)

Shlomi Dolev[1], Seth Gilbert[2], Nancy A. Lynch[2],
Alex A. Shvartsman[3,2], and Jennifer L. Welch[4]

[1] Department of Computer Science, Ben-Gurion University, dolev@cs.bgu.ac.il
[2] MIT CSAIL, {sethg,lynch}@theory.lcs.mit.edu
[3] Department of Computer Science and Engineering, University of Connecticut,
alex@theory.lcs.mit.edu
[4] Department of Computer Science, Texas A&M University, welch@cs.tamu.edu

Abstract. We present a new approach, the GeoQuorums approach, for implementing atomic read/write shared memory in *ad hoc* networks. Our approach is based on abstract nodes associated with certain geographic locations. We assume the existence of *focal points*, geographic areas that are normally "populated" by mobile hosts. For example, a focal point may be a road junction, a scenic observation point, or a water resource in the desert. Mobile hosts that happen to populate a focal point participate in implementing shared atomic put/get objects, using a replicated state machine approach. These objects are then used to implement atomic read/write operations. The GeoQuorums algorithm defines certain intersecting sets of focal points, known as quorums. The quorum systems are used to maintain the consistency of the shared memory. We present a mechanism for changing quorum systems on the fly, thus improving efficiency. Overall, the new GeoQuorums algorithm efficiently implements read and write operations in a highly dynamic, mobile network.

1 Introduction

In this paper, we introduce a new approach to designing algorithms for mobile ad hoc networks. An ad hoc network uses no pre-existing infrastructure, unlike cellular networks that depend on fixed, wired base stations. Instead, the network

---

[*] This work is supported in part by NSF grant CCR-0098305 and NSF ITR Grant 0121277. Part of the work of the first author has been done during visits to MIT and Texas A&M. The first author is partially supported by an IBM faculty award, the Israeli ministry of defense, NSF, and the Israeli Ministry of Trade and Industry. The second and third authors are partially supported by AFOSR Contract #F49620-00-1-0097, DARPA Contract #F33615-01-C-1896, NSF Grant 64961-CS, NTT Grant MIT9904-12. The fourth author is partially supported by the NSF Grant 9988304, 0311368 and by the NSF CAREER Award 9984774. The fifth author is partially supported by NSF Grant 0098305 and Texas Advanced Research Program 000512-0091-2001.

F.E. Fich (Ed.): DISC 2003, LNCS 2848, pp. 306–320, 2003.

is formed by the mobile nodes themselves, which cooperate to route communication from sources to destinations.

Ad hoc communication networks are, by nature, highly dynamic. Mobile hosts are often small devices with limited energy that spontaneously join and leave the network. As a mobile host moves, the set of neighbors with which it can directly communicate may change completely. The nature of ad hoc networks makes it challenging to solve the standard problems encountered in mobile computing, such as location management (e.g., [1]), using classical tools. The difficulties arise from the lack of a fixed infrastructure to serve as the backbone of the network. In this paper, we begin to develop a new approach that allows existing distributed algorithms to be adapted for highly dynamic ad hoc environments.

Providing atomic [2] (or linearizable [3]) read/write shared memory in ad hoc networks is a fundamental problem in distributed computing. Atomic memory is a basic service that facilitates the implementation of many higher-level algorithms. For example, one might construct a location service by requiring each mobile host to periodically write its current location to the memory. Alternatively, a shared memory could be used to collect real-time statistics, for example, recording the number of people in a building. We present here a new algorithm for atomic multi-writer/multi-reader memory in mobile, ad hoc networks.

The GeoQuorums Approach.   We divide the problem of implementing atomic read/write memory into two parts. First, we define a static, abstract system model that associates abstract nodes with certain fixed geographic locales. The mobile hosts implement this model using a replicated state machine approach. In this way, the dynamic nature of the ad hoc network is masked by a static model. Second, we present an algorithm to implement atomic memory using the static network model.

The geographic model specifies a set of physical regions, known as focal points. The mobile hosts within a focal point cooperate to simulate a single virtual process. Each focal point is required to support a local broadcast service, which provides reliable, totally ordered broadcast. This service allows each node in the focal point to communicate reliably with every other node in the focal point. The local broadcast service is used to implement a type of replicated state machine, one that tolerates joins and leaves of mobile hosts. If every mobile host leaves the focal point, the abstract node fails.

The atomic memory algorithm is implemented on top of the geographic abstraction. Nodes implementing the atomic memory algorithm use a GeoCast service (as in [4,5]) to communicate with the virtual processes, that is, with the focal point nodes. In order to achieve fault tolerance and availability, the algorithm replicates the read/write shared memory at a number of focal points. In order to maintain consistency, accessing the shared memory requires updating certain sets of focal points, known as quorums [6,7,8,9,10]. (Note that the members of our quorums are focal points, not mobile hosts.) The algorithm uses two sets of quorums: (i) get-quorums, and (ii) put-quorums, with the property that every get-quorum intersects every put-quorum.[1] The use of quorums allows the algorithm to tolerate the failure of a limited number of focal points.

Our atomic memory algorithm uses a Global Position System (GPS) time service, allowing it to process writes using a single phase; prior single-phase write algorithms made other strong assumptions, for example, relying either on synchrony [8] or single writers [9]. Our algorithm also allows for some reads to be processed using a single phase: the atomic memory algorithm flags the completion of a previous read or write to avoid using additional phases, and propagates this information to various focal points. As far as we know, this is an improvement on previous quorum-based algorithms.

For performance reasons, at different times it may be desirable to use different sets of get-quorums and put-quorums. For example, during periods of time when there are many more read operations than write operations, it may be preferable to use smaller, more geographically distributed, get-quorums that are fast to communicate with, and larger put-quorums that are slower to access. If the operational statistics change, it may be useful to reverse the situation. The algorithm presented here includes a limited reconfiguration capability: it can switch between a finite number of predetermined configurations. As a result of the static underlying model, in which focal points neither join nor leave, this is not a severe limitation. The resulting reconfiguration algorithm, however, is quite efficient compared to prior reconfigurable atomic memory algorithms [11, 12]. Reconfiguration does not significantly delay read or write operations, and, as no consensus service is required, reconfiguration terminates rapidly.

This paper contains three primary contributions. First, we introduce the geographic abstraction model, which allows simple, static algorithms to be adapted for highly dynamic environments. Second, we provide an implementation of the abstract model using mobile hosts. Third, we implement a reconfigurable, atomic read/write shared memory, using the static model.

Other Approaches.   Quorum systems are widely used to implement atomic memory in static distributed systems [6,7,8,9,13,14]. More recent research has pursued application of similar techniques to highly dynamic environments, like ad hoc networks. Many algorithms depend on reconfiguring the quorum systems in order to tolerate frequent joins and leaves and changes in network topology. Some of these [15,16,14,10] require the new configurations to be related to the old configurations, limiting their utility in ad hoc networks. Englert and Shvartsman [17] showed that using any two quorum systems concurrently preserves atomicity during more general reconfiguration. Recently, Lynch and Shvartsman introduced RAMBO [11] (extended in [12]), an algorithm designed to support distributed shared memory in a highly dynamic environment. The RAMBO algorithms allow arbitrary reconfiguration, supporting a changing set of (potentially mobile) participants. The GeoQuorums approach handles the dynamic aspects of the network by creating a geographic abstraction, thus simplifying the atomic

---

[1] These are often referred to as read-quorums and write-quorums; the put/get terminology more accurately describes the operations performed on the focal points in the quorums, since read operations may use both types of quorums.

memory algorithm. While prior algorithms use reconfiguration to provide fault tolerance in a highly dynamic setting, the GeoQuorums approach depends on reconfiguration primarily for performance optimization. This allows a simpler, and therefore more efficient, reconfiguration mechanism.

Haas and Liang [18] also address the problem of implementing quorum systems in a mobile network. Instead of considering reconfiguration, they focus on the problem of constructing and maintaining quorum systems for storing location information. Special participants are designed to perform administrative functions. Thus, the backbone is formed by unreliable, ad hoc nodes that serve as members of quorum groups. Stojmenovic and Pena [19] choose nodes to update using a geographically aware approach. They propose a heuristic that sends location updates to a north-south column of nodes, while a location search proceeds along an east-west row of nodes. Note that the north-south nodes may move during the update, so it is possible that the location search may fail. Karumanchi et al. [20] focus on the problem of efficiently utilizing quorum systems in a highly dynamic environment. The nodes are partitioned into fixed quorums, and every operation updates a randomly selected group, thus balancing the load.

Document Structure.   The rest of the paper is organized as follows. The system model appears in Section 2. The algorithms for emulating a focal point and implementing GeoQuorums appear in Section 3. The atomicity proof for the implementations appear in Section 4. Section 5 contains a discussion of the performance of the algorithm. Finally, in Section 6, we conclude and present some areas for future research. The complete code for the algorithms and selected proofs are given in the full technical report [21].

2   System Model

In this section, we describe the underlying theoretical model, and discuss the practical justifications.

Theoretical Model.   Our world model consists of a bounded region of a two-dimensional plane, populated by mobile hosts. The mobile hosts may join and leave the system, and may fail at any time. (We treat leaves as failures.) The mobile hosts can move on any continuous path in the plane, with bounded speed. The computation at each mobile host is modeled by an asynchronous automaton, augmented with a geosensor. The geosensor is a device with access to a real-time clock and the current, exact location of the mobile host in the plane. It provides the mobile host with continuous access to this information.

While we make no assumption about the motion of the mobile hosts, we do assume that there are certain regions that are usually "populated" by mobile hosts. We assume that there is a collection of some n uniquely identified, non-intersecting regions in the plane, called focal points, such that (i) at most f focal points fail (for some $f < n$), in the sense that there is a period of time during which no mobile host is in the focal point region, and (ii) the mobile hosts in each focal point are able to implement a reliable, atomic broadcast service. Condition (i) is used to ensure that sufficiently many focal points remain available. Once a focal point becomes unavailable due to "depopulation", we do not allow it to recover if it is repopulated. (The algorithm we present in this paper can be modified to allow a "failed" focal point to recover, however, we do not discuss this modification here.) Condition (ii) ensures that all mobile hosts within a focal point can communicate reliably with each other, and that messages are totally ordered. We assume that each mobile host has a list of all the focal point identifiers.

Each mobile host also has a finite list of configurations. A configuration, c, consists of a unique identifier and two sets of quorums: get-quorum $s(c)$ and put-quorum $s(c)$. Each quorum consists of a set of focal points identifiers, and they have the following intersection properties: if $G \in$ get-quorum $s(c)$ and $P \in$ put-quorum $s(c)$, then $G \cap P \neq \emptyset$. Additionally, for a given c, we assume that for any set of f focal points, F, there exist $G \in$ get-quorum $s(c)$ and $P \in$ put-quorum $s(c)$ such that $F \cap G = \emptyset$ and $F \cap P = \emptyset$. This allows an algorithm based on the quorums to tolerate f focal points failing. Fur the purposes of this presentation, we assume there are only two configurations, c_1 and c_2.

Mobile hosts depend on two broadcast services: (i) LBCast, a local, atomic broadcast service, and (ii) GeoCast, a global delivery service. The LBCast service allows nodes within a focal point to communicate reliably. Each focal point is assumed to support a separate LBCast service: if we refer to focal point h, its broadcast service is referred to as lbcast$_h$. The LBCast service takes one parameter, a message, and delivers it to every node in the focal point region. If mobile host i is in focal point h, and broadcasts a message m using lbcast$_h$ at time t, and if j is also in focal point h at time t, and remains in h, then j receives message m. Additionally, the service guarantees that all mobile hosts receive all messages in the same order. That is, if host i_1 receives message m_1 before message m_2, then if host i_2 receives messages m_1 and m_2 it will receive message m_1 before message m_2.

The GeoCast service delivers a message to a specified destination in the plane, and optionally delivers it to a specified node at that location. The GeoCast service takes three parameters: (i) message, (ii) destination location, (iii) ID of a destination node (optional). If no destination ID is specified, then the destination location must be inside some focal point, h. In this case, if message m is GeoCast at time t, then there exists some time $t' > t$ such that if mobile host i is in focal point h at time t', and remains in h, then i receives message m. If a destination-ID is specified, and if the destination node remains near the destination location until the message is delivered, and the destination node does not fail until the message is delivered, then the service will eventually deliver the message to the node with the correct destination-ID.

Practical Aspects.   This theoretical model represents a wide class of real mobile systems. First, there are a number of ways to provide location and time services, as represented by the geosensor. GPS is perhaps the most common means, but others, like Cricket [22], are being developed to remedy the weaknesses in GPS, such as the inability to operate indoors. Our algorithms can tolerate small errors in the time or location, though we do not discuss this.

Second, the broadcast services specified here are reasonable. If a focal point is small enough, it should be easy to ensure that a single broadcast, with appropriate error correction, reaches every mobile node at the focal point. If the broadcast service uses a time-division/multiple-access (TDMA) protocol, which allocates each node a time slot in which to broadcast, then it is easy to determine a total ordering of the messages. A node joining the focal point might use a separate reservation channel to compete for a time slot on the main TDMA communication channel This would eliminate collisions on the main channel, while slightly prolonging the process of joining a focal point.

The GeoCast service is also a common primitive in mobile networks: a number of algorithms have been developed to solve this problem, originally for the internet protocol [4] and later for ad hoc networks (e.g., [23,5]).

We propose one set of configurations that may be particularly useful in practical implementations. We take advantage of the fact that accessing nearby focal points is usually faster than accessing distant focal points. The focal points can be grouped into clusters, using some geographic technique [24]. Figure 1 illustrates the relationship among mobile hosts, focal points, and clusters. For configuration c_1, the get-quorums are defined to be the clusters. The put-quorums consist of every set containing one focal point from each cluster. Configuration c_2 is defined in the opposite manner. Assume, for example, that read operations are more common than write operations (and most read operations only require one phase). Then, if the clusters are relatively small and are well distributed (so that every mobile host is near to every focal point in some cluster), then configuration c_1 is quite efficient. On the other hand, if write operations are more common than read operations, configuration c_2 is quite efficient. Our algorithm allows the system to switch safely between two such configurations.

Another difficulty in implementation might be agreeing on the focal points and ensuring that every mobile host has an accurate list of all the focal points and configurations. Some strategies have been proposed to choose focal points: for example, the mobile hosts might send a token on a random walk, to collect information on geographic density [25]. The simplest way to ensure that a mobile host has access to a list of focal points and configurations is to depend on a centralized server, through transmissions from a satellite or a cell-phone tower. Alternatively, the GeoCast service itself might facilitate finding other mobile hosts, at which point the definitive list can be discovered.

3   Focal Point Emulator and Operation Manager

The GeoQuorums algorithm consists of two components: the Focal Point Emulator (FPE) and the Operation Manager (OM). Figure 2 describes the relationships among the different components of the algorithm.

For example, a client at some node i may request a read (the "read" arrow from the Client to the OM). The OM notes the mobile host's current location, using the Geosensor (right "geo-update" arrow). The OM then sends GeoCast messages to focal points ("geoc-send" arrow), including its current location. The GeoCast message is received by the FPE at some other node, j, ("geoc-rcv"

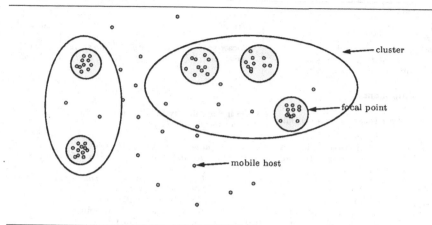

Fig. 1. Clusters

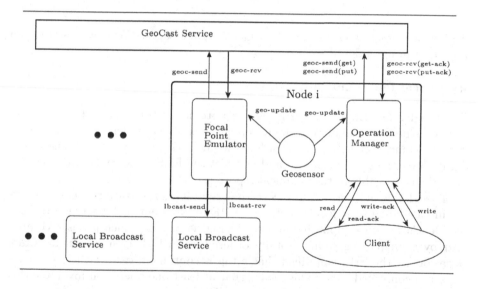

Fig. 2. System Architecture

arrow). The FPE at j first sends a local broadcast of the request ("lbcast-send" arrow), and then sends a response to i ("geoc-send" arrow), using the position of the client received in the GeoCast message. The OM at i uses the responses received ("geoc-rcv" arrow) from the FPEs to compute the response to the read operation, which it sends to the Client ("read-ack" arrow).

A FPE determines that the mobile host is in a focal point region using information from the Geosensor (left "geo-update" arrow). Then the FPE uses the LBCast service to perform the join protocol ("lbcast-send", "lbcast-rcv"),

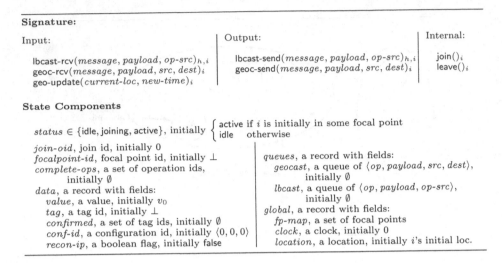

Signature:

Input:

lbcast-rcv$(message, payload, op\text{-}src)_{h,i}$
geoc-rcv$(message, payload, src, dest)_i$
geo-update$(current\text{-}loc, new\text{-}time)_i$

Output:

lbcast-send$(message, payload, op\text{-}src)_{h,i}$
geoc-send$(message, payload, src, dest)_i$

Internal:

join$()_i$
leave$()_i$

State Components

$status \in \{\mathsf{idle}, \mathsf{joining}, \mathsf{active}\}$, initially $\begin{cases} \mathsf{active} & \text{if } i \text{ is initially in some focal point} \\ \mathsf{idle} & \text{otherwise} \end{cases}$

join-oid, join id, initially 0
focalpoint-id, focal point id, initially $\perp$
complete-ops, a set of operation ids,
  initially $\emptyset$
data, a record with fields:
  value, a value, initially v_0
  tag, a tag id, initially $\perp$
  confirmed, a set of tag ids, initially $\emptyset$
  conf-id, a configuration id, initially $\langle 0, 0, 0 \rangle$
  recon-ip, a boolean flag, initially false

queues, a record with fields:
  geocast, a queue of $\langle op, payload, src, dest \rangle$,
    initially $\emptyset$
  lbcast, a queue of $\langle op, payload, op\text{-}src \rangle$,
    initially $\emptyset$
global, a record with fields:
  fp-map, a set of focal points
  clock, a clock, initially 0
  location, a location, initially i's initial loc.

Fig. 3. Focal Point Emulator FPE_i Signature and State

after which point it can respond to GeoCast messages. We now describe the algorithm in more detail.

3.1 Focal Point Emulator

The Focal Point Emulator (FPE) is the automaton that allows the members of a focal point to simulate a single replica. The FPE implements a replicated state machine, using the totally ordered local broadcast to ensure consistency. Figure 3 contains the signature and state of the FPE. The remaining code for the FPE is available in the technical report [21].

The FPE maintains a data record that represents the state replicated at every mobile host in the focal point. The FPE receives put and get requests from the GeoCast service, updating and retrieving data.value. Each put is accompanied by a unique tag from a totally ordered set, which is stored in data.tag. Occasionally the FPE is notified that a tag is confirmed; data.confirmed tracks the set of confirmed tags. (This means that at least one operation involving this tag has fully completed.) Requests to the FPE contain the id of a configuration; data.conf-id stores the largest known configuration id. data.recon-ip is a flag that indicates whether a reconfiguration is in progress.

The FPE receives various messages from the GeoCast service, sent by mobile hosts. Each incoming message is immediately rebroadcast, using the LBCast service. The FPE takes no other action in response to GeoCast messages.

The FPE also receives messages from the LBCast service. Each FPE automaton can be idle, joining, or active. If a node is not idle (even if it is in the process of joining), then it will process incoming messages and update its local state, in order to maintain consistency. If the node is active (and joining is completed), then the FPE enqueues a response, if required. Finally, if any node notices that a new configuration is being used, it sets a flag to remember that a reconfiguration is in progress.

The LBCast service delivers four types of messages: (i) If FPE_i (the FPE at node i) receives a get message and no other node has responded, then FPE_i sends a response via the GeoCast service, containing its current data.tag, data.value, and data.confirmed. (ii) If FPE_i receives a put message, then it updates its data.tag, data.value and data.confirmed using the data in the message. If no other node has responded, then FPE_i sends a response using the GeoCast service, indicating that the update is complete. (iii) If FPE_i receives a confirm message, then it updates its local copy of the confirmed flag. (iv) If node i receives a recon-done message, then it sets its local recon-ip flag to false to indicate that the reconfiguration is completed.

The final piece of the FPE is the join protocol, which enables a mobile host to join a focal point. Recall that the Geosensor service periodically notifies the mobile host of its new location. When the host has entered a focal point, it begins the join protocol by sending a join-request message using the LBCast service; this message contains a unique identifier for the join request consisting of the requester's node identifier and the current time. When node i receives the join-request message, if no other node has responded, then node i sends a response using the LBCast; this response includes data.tag, data.value, and data.confirmed. As soon as the initiator of the join protocol receives any response, it updates its current data.value, data.tag, and data.confirmed with the information in the response message, and then becomes active.

3.2   Operation Manager

The Operation Manager (OM) maintains the state described in Figure 4. The OM uses the GeoCast service to communicate with FPEs (see Figure 5), sending get, put, and confirm messages, and receiving appropriate responses. The OM

Signature:

Input:	Output:	Internal:
read()$_i$	read-ack($value$)$_i$	read-2()$_i$
write($value$)$_i$,	write-ack()$_i$	recon-2()
recon($config$-$name$)$_i$	recon-ack()$_i$	confirm()$_i$
geoc-rcv($op, payload, src, dest$)$_i$	geoc-send($op, payload, src, dest$)$_i$	

State Components

confirmed, a set of tag ids, initially $\emptyset$
conf-id, a configuration id, initially $\langle 0, 0, 0 \rangle$
recon-ip, a boolean flag, initially false
G_1, P_2, G_2, P_2, the sets of get-quorums and put-quorums for configurations 1 and 2
global, a record with fields:
  location, a location, initially $\perp$
  clock, a time, initially 0
  fp-map, a set of focal point definitions

op, a record with fields:
  type $\in$ {read, write, recon}
  phase $\in$ {idle, get, put}, initially idle
  tag, a tag id, initially $\perp$
  value, a value, initially $\perp$
  recon-ip, a boolean flag, initially false
  oid, an operation id, initially 0
  acc, a set of process ids, initially $\emptyset$
  loc, a location, initially $\perp$

Fig. 4. Operation Manager OM_i Signature and State

Input geoc-rcv(op-ack, *oid, tag, val,*
           conf, cid, rec-ip, src, dest)$_i$
Effect:
  if *op.oid = oid* then
    if op-ack = get-ack and *tag > op.tag* then
      op.tag ← tag
      op.val ← val
      acc ← acc ∪ {*lookup*(*src.loc, global.fp-map*)}
    if *cid > conf-id* then
      conf-id ← cid
      op.recon-ip ← true
      recon-ip ← true
      if *op.type =* recon then
        op.phase = idle
    else if *cid = conf-id* then
      if *rec-ip =* false then *recon-ip ←* false
    if *conf =* true then
      confirmed ← confirmed ∪ {*tag*}

Output geoc-send(*message, payload, src, dest*)$_i$
Precondition:
  if (*op.phase* ≠ idle) then
    message = op.phase ∨
             message ∈ {confirm, recon-done}
  else
    message ∈ {confirm, recon-done}
  payload contains operation specific
    information (i.e., *data.tag,*
    data.value, etc.)
  src = ⟨*i, global.location*⟩
  fp-name ∈ *FP*
  dest = ⟨focal-point, *fp-name*⟩
Effect:
  None

Fig. 5. Operation Manager OM_i GeoCast Send/Receive

uses the FPEs as replicas, guaranteeing both atomicity and fault tolerance. For each phase of each operation, the OM receives messages from a quorum of FPEs.

Read/Write Operations.   The code for read/write operations is presented in Figure 6. When OM $_i$ receives a write request, it examines its clock to choose a tag for the operation. OM $_i$ uses the GeoCast service to send the new tag and new value to a number of focal points. Let c be the value of conf-id$_i$ when the operation begins. If all responses indicate that c is the most recent configuration (i.e., no reconfiguration is in progress), then the operation terminates when OM $_i$ receives at least one response from each focal point in some P ∈ put-quorum s(c). If any response indicates that a reconfiguration is in progress, then OM $_i$ waits until it also receives responses from each focal point in some P' ∈ put-quorum s(c'), where c' is the other configuration. (We have assumed there are only two configurations – if there are more than two configurations, OM $_i$ would need to hear from all of them.) After the operation is complete, OM $_i$ can optionally notify focal points that the specified tag has been confirmed, indicating that the operation is complete.

When OM $_i$ receives a read request, it sends out messages to a number of focal points. Let c be the value of conf-id$_i$ when the operation begins. As for write operations, if all responses indicate that c is the most recent configuration, then the first phase terminates when OM $_i$ receives a response from each focal point in some G ∈ get-quorum s(c). Otherwise, the phase completes when OM $_i$ also receives a response from each focal point in some G' ∈ get-quorum s(c'), where c' is the other configuration. At this point, OM $_i$ chooses the value associated with the largest tag from any of the responses. If the chosen tag has been confirmed, then the operation is complete. Otherwise, OM $_i$ begins a second phase that is identical to the protocol of the write operation.

Notice that the knowledge of the confirmed tags is used to short-circuit the second phase of certain read operations. The second phase is only required in the case where a prior operation with the same tag has not yet completed. By

Input read()$_i$
Effect:
    $op \leftarrow \langle read, get, \bot, \bot, recon\text{-}ip,$
        $\langle global.clock, i\rangle, \emptyset, global.location\rangle$
	Input write(v)$_i$
	Effect:
	    $op \leftarrow \langle write, put, \langle global.clock, i\rangle, v, recon\text{-}ip,$
	        $\langle global.clock, i\rangle, \emptyset, global.location\rangle$

Input read()$_i$
Effect:
    $op \leftarrow \langle read, get, \bot, \bot, recon\text{-}ip,$
        $\langle global.clock, i\rangle, \emptyset, global.location\rangle$

Output read-ack(v)$_i$
Precondition:
    $conf\text{-}id = \langle c, p, n\rangle$
    if $op.recon\text{-}ip$ then
        $\exists p_0 \in P_0, p_1 \in P_1$ such that $acc \supseteq p_0 \cup p_1$
    else
        $\exists p_n \in P_n$ such that $acc \supseteq p_n$
    $op.phase = \text{put}$
    $op.type = \text{read}$
    $v = op.value$
Effect:
    $op.phase \leftarrow \text{idle}$
    $confirmed \leftarrow confirmed \cup \{op.tag\}$

Output read-ack(v)$_i$
Precondition:
    $conf\text{-}id = \langle c, p, n\rangle$
    if $op.recon\text{-}ip$ then
        $\exists g_0 \in G_0, g_1 \in G_1$ such that $acc \supseteq g_0 \cup g_1$
    else $\exists g_n \in G_n$ such that $acc \supseteq g_n$
    $op.phase = \text{get}$
    $op.type = \text{read}$
    $op.tag \in confirmed$
    $v = op.value$
Effect:
    $op.phase \leftarrow \text{idle}$

Input write(v)$_i$
Effect:
    $op \leftarrow \langle write, put, \langle global.clock, i\rangle, v, recon\text{-}ip,$
        $\langle global.clock, i\rangle, \emptyset, global.location\rangle$

Internal read-2()$_i$
Precondition:
    $conf\text{-}id = \langle c, p, n\rangle$
    if $op.recon\text{-}ip$ then
        $\exists g_0 \in G_0, g_1 \in G_1$ s.t. $op.acc \supseteq g_0 \cup g_1$
    else
        $\exists g_n \in G_n$ such that $acc \supseteq g_n$
    $op.phase = \text{get}$
    $op.type = \text{read}$
    $op.tag \notin confirmed.$
Effect:
    $op.phase \leftarrow \text{put}$
    $op.recon\text{-}ip \leftarrow \text{false}$
    $op.oid \leftarrow \langle global.clock, i\rangle$
    $op.acc \leftarrow \emptyset$
    $op.loc \leftarrow my\text{-}location$

Output write-ack()$_i$
Precondition:
    $conf\text{-}id = \langle c, p, n\rangle$
    if $op.recon\text{-}ip$ then
        $\exists p_0 \in P_0, p_1 \in P_1$ such that $acc \supseteq p_0 \cup p_1$
    else
        $\exists p_n \in P_n$ such that $acc \supseteq p_n$
    $op.phase = \text{put}$
    $op.type = \text{write}$
Effect:
    $op.phase \leftarrow \text{idle}$
    $confirmed \leftarrow confirmed \cup \{op.tag\}$

Fig. 6. Operation Manager OM_i Read/Write Transitions

notifying focal points when the tag has been confirmed, the algorithm allows later operations to discover that a second phase is unnecessary.

Reconfiguration.   The code for the reconfiguration algorithm is presented in Figure 7. The reconfiguration algorithm is a variant of the reconfiguration mechanism presented in the RAMBO II algorithm [12]: the presented algorithm is a special case of the general algorithm, in which there are only a small, finite number of legal configurations. This simplification obviates the need for a consensus service, and therefore significantly improves efficiency. A reconfiguration operation is similar to a read or write operation, in that it requires contacting appropriate quorums of focal points from the two different configurations, c_1 and c_2. First, OM $_i$ determines a new, unique, configuration identifier, by examining the local clock, its node id, and the name of the desired configuration. Then OM $_i$ sets a flag, indicating that a reconfiguration is in progress. At this point, the first phase of the reconfiguration begins: OM $_i$ sends messages to a number of focal points. The first phase terminates when OM $_i$ receives a response from every node in four different quorums: (i) a get-quorum of c_1, (ii) a get-quorum of c_2, (iii) a put-quorum of c_1, and a (iv) put-quorum of c_2. Then the second phase begins, again sending out messages to focal points. It terminates when OM $_i$ re-

---

Input recon($conf\text{-}name$)$_i$
Effect:
   $conf\text{-}id = \langle global.clock, i, conf\text{-}name \rangle$
   $recon\text{-}ip = $ true
   if $op.type = $ recon then
      $op.phase = $ idle

Internal recon-upgrade-2(cid)$_i$
Precondition:
   $\exists g_0 \in G_0, g_1 \in G_1, p_0 \in P_0, p_1 \in P_1$
      such that: $acc \supseteq g_0 \cup g_1 \cup p_0 \cup p_1$
   $op.type = $ recon
   $op.phase = $ get
   $cid = conf\text{-}id$

Effect:
   $op.phase \leftarrow $ put
   $op.oid \leftarrow \langle global.clock, i \rangle$
   $op.acc \leftarrow \emptyset$
   $op.loc \leftarrow global.location$

Internal recon-upgrade(cid)$_i$
Precondition:
   $recon\text{-}ip = $ true
   $op.phase = $ idle
   $cid = conf\text{-}id$
Effect:
   $op \leftarrow \langle$recon, get, $\perp, \perp,$ true, $\langle global.clock, i \rangle,$
      $\emptyset, global.location\rangle$

Output recon-ack(cid)$_i$
Precondition:
   $conf\text{-}id = \langle c, p, n \rangle$
   $\exists p_n \in P_n$ such that $acc \supseteq p_n$
   $op.type = $ recon
   $op.phase = $ put
   $cid = conf\text{-}id$
Effect:
   $recon\text{-}ip = $ false
   $op.phase \leftarrow $ idle

Fig. 7. Operation Manager OM_i Reconfiguration Transitions

ceives responses from every node in some put-quorum of the new configuration. OM_i may then broadcast a message to various focal-points, notifying them that the new configuration is established and that the reconfiguration is done.

4 Atomic Consistency

In this section, we discuss the proof that the GeoQuorums algorithm guarantees atomic consistency. For the complete proof, see the technical report [21]. The proof is divided into two parts. First, we show that each FPE acts like an atomic object with respect to put, get, confirm, and recon-done operations. Then we show that the OM guarantees atomic consistency.

Focal Point Emulator. The FPE uses the totally ordered LBCast service to implement a replicated state machine, which guarantees that the FPE implements an atomic object. If no new node joins a particular focal point after the beginning of the execution, it is easy to show that the FPE implements an atomic object: each request to the FPE is rebroadcast using the LBCast service; therefore every FPE receives requests in the same order. If the response for one operation precedes the request for a second operation, then clearly the request for the second comes after the request for the first in the LBCast total ordering. Therefore the second request will be processed after the first request.

The same conclusion holds when nodes join the focal point after the beginning of the execution. A joining node is sent a summary of all requests that occur prior to its beginning the join protocol, and receives from the LBCast service all requests for operations that occur after it begins the join protocol. Therefore, when the join protocol completes, the FPE has processed every request ordered by the LBCast service prior to the completion of the join protocol. We conclude that the FPE implements an atomic object.

Operation Manager.   The proof that the OM guarantees atomic consistency relies on establishing a partial order on read and write operations, based on the tag associated with each value. First, assume that all read operations complete in two phases (rather than being short-circuited by the confirmed flag). If no reconfiguration occurs, then it is easy to see that atomic consistency is guaranteed: assume operation π_1 completes before operation π_2 begins. First, assume that both use configuration c. Then π_1 accesses a put-quorum of c in its second phase, and π_2 accesses a get-quorum of c in its first phase. By the quorum intersection property, there is some focal point, h, that is in both quorums. Then focal point h first receives a message containing the request for π_1, and then sends a message in response to the request for π_2.

Next, assume that a reconfiguration occurs such that either π_1 or π_2 has the data.recon-ip flag set. The operation that has the flag set accesses quorums in both configurations c_1 and c_2 (or all configurations, if there are more than two), and therefore, as in the previous case, is guaranteed to contact a focal point, h, that is part of the quorum contacted by the other operation. Finally, assume that π_1 uses one configuration, say, c_1, and π_2 uses the other configuration, say, c_2, and that neither has set the data.recon-ip flag. Then at least one reconfiguration operation must begin during or after π_1 and complete before π_2, and we can show that this reconfiguration operation learns about π_1 in its first phase, and propagates information to π_2 in its second phase. (If there are more than two configurations, then the tag is conveyed from π_1 to π_2 because reconfiguration involves all existing configurations.)

Now we consider one-phase read operation. If a read operation terminates after one phase, then it has received a message that the associated tag has been confirmed. However, a tag is only confirmed when a prior operation has already completed the propagation of the tag.

Putting these pieces together, we obtain the following, which leads (by Lemma 13.16 in [26]) to the conclusion that atomic consistency is guaranteed:

Theorem 1. If π_1 and π_2 are read/write operations, and π_1 completes before π_2 begins, then $tag(\pi_1) \leq tag(\pi_2)$. If π_2 is a write operation, then $tag(\pi_1) < tag(\pi_2)$.

5   Performance Discussion

The performance of the GeoQuorums algorithm is directly dependent on the performance of the two communication services. Assume that every GeoCast message is delivered within time d_G, and every LBCast message is delivered within time d_{LB}; let $d = d_G + d_{LB}$. Then every read and write operation terminates within $8d$: each phase takes at most two round-trip messages. (An extra round of communication may be caused by the discovery during the first round that a reconfiguration is in progress.) The algorithm as specified also allows the implementation to trade-off message complexity and latency. In each phase, the node initiating the operation must contact a quorum of focal points. It can accomplish this by sending one message to every focal point, thereby ensuring the fastest result, at the expense of a high message complexity. Alternatively, the node can send a message only to focal points in a single quorum. If not all responses are received (due, perhaps, to quorum members failing), the node can try another quorum, and continue until it receives a response from every member of some quorum. This leads to lower message complexity, but may take longer.

6   Conclusions and Future Work

We have presented a new approach, the GeoQuorums approach, to implementing algorithms in mobile, ad hoc networks. We have presented a geographic abstraction model, and an algorithm, the Focal Point Emulator, that implements it using mobile hosts. We have presented the Operation Manager, which uses the static model to implement an efficient, reconfigurable atomic read/write memory.

The GeoQuorums approach transforms a highly dynamic, ad hoc environment into a static setting. This approach should facilitate the adaptation of classical distributed algorithms to ad hoc networks. Unfortunately, the two components presented are tightly coupled: the implementation of the FPE is specific to the semantics of a reconfigurable atomic memory. We plan to further separate the two levels of the algorithm. This separation will allow the GeoQuorums approach to be applied to other challenging problems in mobile computing.

We also believe that our approach will be useful in studying hybrid networks, consisting of both mobile nodes and fixed infrastructure. In areas where there are non-mobile, fixed participants, simpler and more efficient versions of the FPE can be used. When nodes enter areas with no infrastructure, the more dynamic algorithm can seamlessly take over.

There are many open questions relating to the geographic abstraction. We have assumed a static definition of focal points and configurations, but it remains an open question to construct these in a distributed fashion, and to modify them dynamically. There are also questions related to the practical implementation of the model; we mention some ideas in Section 2, but open questions remain.

References

1. Dolev, S., Pradhan, D.K., Welch, J.L.: Modified tree structure for location management in mobile environments. Computer Communications: Special Issue on Mobile Computing **19** (1996) 335–345
2. Lamport, L.: On interprocess communication – parts I and II. Distributed Computing **1** (1986) 77–101
3. Herlihy, M.P., Wing, J.M.: Linearizability: A correctness condition for concurrent objects. ACM Trans. on Programming Languages and Systems **12** (1990) 463–492
4. Navas, J.C., Imielinski, T.: Geocast – geographic addressing and routing. In: ACM/IEEE Intl. Conference on Mobile Computing and Networking. (1997) 66–76
5. Camp, T., Liu, Y.: An adaptive mesh-based protocol for geocast routing. Journal of Parallel and Distributed Computing: Special Issue on Mobile Ad-hoc Networking and Computing (2002) 196–213

6. Gifford, D.K.: Weighted voting for replicated data. In: Proceedings of the seventh symposium on operating systems principles. (1979) 150–162
7. Thomas, R.H.: A majority consensus approach to concurrency control for multiple copy databases. Transactions on Database Systems **4** (1979) 180–209
8. Upfal, E., Wigderson, A.: How to share memory in a distributed system. Journal of the ACM **34** (1987) 116–127
9. Attiya, H., Bar-Noy, A., Dolev, D.: Sharing memory robustly in message-passing systems. Journal of the ACM **42** (1995) 124–142
10. Prisco, R.D., Fekete, A., Lynch, N.A., Shvartsman, A.A.: A dynamic primary configuration group communication service. In: Proceedings of the 13th International Symposium on Distributed Computing. (1999) 64–78
11. Lynch, N., Shvartsman., A.: RAMBO: A reconfigurable atomic memory service for dynamic networks. In: Proc. of the 16th Intl. Symp. on Distributed Computing. (2002) 173–190
12. Gilbert, S., Lynch, N., Shvartsman, A.: RAMBO II:: Rapidly reconfigurable atomic memory for dynamic networks. In: Proc. of the Intl. Conference on Dependable Systems and Networks. (2003) 259–269
13. Garcia-Molina, H., Barbara, D.: How to assign votes in a distributed system. Journal of the ACM **32** (1985) 841–860
14. Herlihy, M.: Dynamic quorum adjustment for partitioned data. Trans. on DB Systems **12** (1987) 170–194
15. El Abbadi, A., Skeen, D., Cristian, F.: An efficient fault-tolerant protocol for replicated data management. In: Proc. of the 4th Symp. on Principles of Databases, ACM Press (1985) 215–228
16. Dolev, D., Keidar, I., Lotem, E.Y.: Dynamic voting for consistent primary components. In: Proc. of the Sixteenth Annual ACM Symp. on Principles of Distributed Computing, ACM Press (1997) 63–71
17. Englert, B., Shvartsman, A.: Graceful quorum reconfiguration in a robust emulation of shared memory. In: Proc. of the International Conference on Distributed Computer Systems (ICDCS'2000). (2000) 454–463
18. Haas, Z.J., Liang, B.: Ad hoc mobile management with uniform quorum systems. IEEE/ACM Transactions on Networking **7** (1999) 228–240
19. Stojmenovic, I., Pena, P.E.V.: A scalable quorum based location update scheme for routing in ad hoc wireless networks. Technical Report TR-99-11, Computer Science, SITE, University of Ottawa (1999)
20. Karumanchi, G., Muralidharan, S., Prakash, R.: Information dissemination in partitionable mobile ad hoc networks. In: Proceedings of IEEE Symposium on Reliable Distributed Systems. (1999) 4–13
21. Dolev, S., Gilbert, S., Lynch, N.A., Shvartsman, A.A., Welch, J.L.: Geoquorums: Implementing atomic memory in ad hoc networks. Technical Report LCS-TR-900, MIT (2003)
22. Priyantha, N.B., Chakraborty, A., Balakrishnan, H.: The cricket location-support system. In: Proc. of the 6th ACM MOBICOM. (2000) 32–43
23. Ko, Y.B., Vaidya, N.: Geotora: A protocol for geocasting in mobile ad hoc networks. In: Proc. of the IEEE Intl. Conference on Network Protocols. (2000) 240–249
24. de Berg, M., van Kreveld, M., Overmars, M., Schwarzkopf, O.: Computational Geometry: Algorithms and Applications. 2nd edn. Springer-Verlag (2000)
25. Dolev, S., Schiller, E., Welch, J.: Random walk for self-stabilizing group communication in ad-hoc networks. In: Proceedings of the 21st IEEE Symposium on Reliable Distributed Systems. (2002) 70–79
26. Lynch, N.: Distributed Algorithms. Morgan Kaufman (1996)

Asymptotically Efficient Approaches to Fault-Tolerance in Peer-to-Peer Networks

Kirsten Hildrum and John Kubiatowicz

University of California, Berkeley
{hildrum,kubitron}@cs.berkeley.edu

Abstract. In this paper, we show that two peer-to-peer systems, Pastry [13] and Tapestry [17] can be made tolerant to certain classes of failures and a limited class of attacks. These systems are said to operate properly if they can find the closest node matching a requested ID. The system must also be able to dynamically construct the necessary routing information when new nodes enter or the network changes. We show that with an additional factor of $O(\log n)$ storage overhead and $O(\log^2 n)$ communication overhead, they can continue to achieve both of these goals in the presence of a constant fraction nodes that do not obey the protocol. Our techniques are similar in spirit to those of Saia *et al.* [14] and Naor and Wieder [10]. Some simple simulations show that these techniques are useful even with constant overhead.

1 Introduction

In peer-to-peer systems, all nodes are roughly equal. This equality brings with it the potential for great power: such systems lack a central point of failure and thus could, in principle, be less vulnerable to faults and directed attacks. Unfortunately, achieving this advantage is difficult because peer-to-peer algorithms propagate information widely—greatly expanding the damage wrought by faulty or malicious nodes. In this paper, we take a step forward by showing how two peer-to-peer systems, Pastry [13] and Tapestry [17], can be made tolerant to a limited class of failures and attacks.

Peer-to-peer networks such as Tapestry and Pastry are comprised of many overlay nodes, each with a unique random identifier.[1] One of the most important tasks in a peer-to-peer network is routing, the ability to pass a message from a source node to a destination node whose ID most closely matches a requested destination. It is this task that we wish to accomplish in the presence of failures.

To accomplish this task, each overlay node maintains a table of connections to a few (normally $O(\log n)$ or sometimes $O(1)$) of the other peer-to-peer nodes, called neighbors. These connections are chosen such that routing decisions require only information about the destination ID while keeping the number of hops in overlay path short. In Tapestry and Pastry (and some other systems), an

---

[1] The name space is chosen large enough that the probability that two randomly assigned names are the same is negligible.

F.E. Fich (Ed.): DISC 2003, LNCS 2848, pp. 321–336, 2003.
© Springer-Verlag Berlin Heidelberg 2003

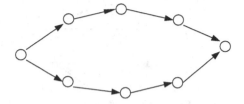
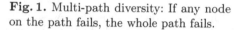
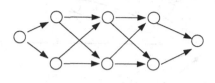

Fig. 1. Multi-path diversity: If any node on the path fails, the whole path fails.

Fig. 2. Wide-path diversity: Two nodes must fail at same level to break path.

additional consideration is keeping the network distance short by choosing short links over long ones when possible.

These systems operate properly if they successfully route messages. Moreover, they must be able to dynamically construct their routing information. We show that an additional factor of $O(\log n)$ space overhead (ie, the normal table size is $O(\log n)$, and for the fault tolerant algorithms, it needs to be $O(\log^2 n)$) they can continue to achieve both of these goals in the presence of a constant fraction nodes that do not obey the protocol. This paper considers a model in which nodes may be faulty at the overlay level, but cannot modify messages on the wire. Also, the faulty nodes have no control over their IDs or location. While this model is weaker than one might like, it does address the very common cases of bad code and flaky hardware, and even adversaries of limited power.

The key idea of this paper is to exploit redundancy to tolerate faults, both in building the neighbor table and in routing. There are two basic approaches to routing illustrated in Figures 1 and 2. The first idea (in Figure 1) is to use multiple paths. As long as one path is failure-free, the message will make it from the source to the destination. However, notice that if one node fails in a path, the whole path is useless.

Figure 2 shows a different technique. Instead of two separate paths, this diagram show a single path that is two nodes wide. This means that all the nodes in a given step send to all the nodes in the next step. If any node in one step gets the message, then all the nodes in the next step will also get the message. For the routing to be blocked, at some step, both the top and the bottom nodes must simultaneously fail. This provides much greater fault-tolerance per redundant overlay node than multiple paths (even normalizing for bandwidth consumed). We will exploit this technique later.

There is another, orthogonal, routing design decision. The routing outlined above is recursive. In recursive routing, the intermediate nodes forward the query on to the next intermediate node. In contrast, some routing algorithms (including the ones described in this paper) are iterative. In iterative routing, at each step, the initiating node contacts some other node (or a set of nodes) to get the next hop. The difference is illustrated in Figure 3. Iterative routing is less efficient, but gives the originating node more control, which can be important in a faulty network.

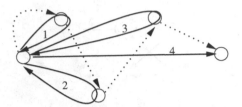

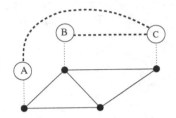

Fig. 3. Iterative vs Recursive routing: The source is on the left, the destination is on the right. The solid arrows, labeled by number, represent the iterative path, and the dotted arrows represent the corresponding recursive path.

Fig. 4. Overlay nodes (hollow circles) with neighbor links (dashed lines) above physical nodes (solid circles) and network links (solid lines). B cannot interfere with messages from A to C, but C can interfere with messages from A to B.

1.1 Related Work

The research community has described a diverse set of peer-to-peer systems [5, 8,9,12,13,14,16,17]. Some of the techniques of this paper may apply to other systems.

In a recent paper, Sit and Morris [15] identify some basic categories of attacks on peer-to-peer networks and some general responses to them. Their suggested responses are general enough to apply to most peer-to-peer networks, so they are in some cases not completely specified. Thus, they do not formally prove that their approaches succeed. Two of their concerns are the two problems addressed in this paper—attacks on dynamically building of the routing tables and routing itself. They also suggest that iterative routing may be better in faulty networks.

Douceur in [3] describes the Sybil attack, in which a faulty node generates many IDs and then pretends to be many nodes. He shows that it is practically impossible to prevent this attack without a centralized authority which either explicitly or implicitly distributes IDs. (An IP address is an example of an implicit identifier.)

Castro et al. [2] address many the same issues as the Sit and Morris, but as they relate to Pastry in particular. For example, to route securely, Castro et al. first route normally, and then perform a routing failure test to determine whether the routing has gone wrong. If their test detects that routing may not have been correct, they retry routing with a secure routing protocol.

Their secure routing protocol uses a different data structure that, unlike the normal routing table, does not take into account network distance. With the assumption that nodes cannot choose their location in the network, and an algorithm to build the normal table correctly with high probability, [2] this backup table may be less important.

---

[2] With high probability means the probability of failure to be less than $1/n^c$ for $k = c' \log n$, for some c' that depends on c.

Their secure routing technique is essentially that of Figure 1. That is, they send a message from r different starting points. But this technique requires r to be polynomial in n to get a failure probability (over all paths) to be less than a constant. This paper introduces a different technique, using the "wide" paths of Figure 2, that can gives a failure probability of $1/n^c$ when r is only $O(\log n)$ (or $O(\log^2 n)$ in an stronger fault model).

Saia et al. [14] and Naor and Wieder[10] also made use of the wide paths depicted in Figure 2. In both cases, they group together nodes into groups of size $O(\log n)$ and use those groups as a single virtual node in the overlay. The network routes correctly as long as one node in each unit follows the protocol. Their routing algorithms are recursive, rather than iterative.

Fiat and Saia [4] construct a butterfly network of virtual nodes where each virtual node is made up of $O(\log n)$ real nodes. (In [14] they make this construction dynamic.) By having more than one starting point, even when the failures are picked to be the worst possible, their system still performs well for almost all objects and almost all searchers. In their system, nodes have degree $O(\log^2 n)$. Naor and Wieder take a different approach. They build a constant-degree DHT (detailed in [9]), and then force each node to act for $O(\log n)$ others. Since the original degree was constant, the final degree is still a reasonable $O(\log n)$.

Section 4 gives similar techniques that can be used to "retrofit" Pastry and Tapestry with fault tolerance. These techniques may be useful even with constant overhead, and in Section 5 shows some simple experiments that suggests this.

1.2   The Main Idea

We address two problems. The first is how to build the data structures necessary for routing in the presence of faulty nodes. The second, is how to route securely. As mentioned above, we discuss Pastry [13] and Tapestry [17]. Both of these are closely related to the static object location system described by Plaxton, Rajaraman, and Richa in [11]. In these systems, routing is prefix routing based on the nodes IDs. This means that a node must store, for every prefix of its ID, a node with every one-digit extension of that prefix.

A destination defines a tree on the network (with the root at the destination), and this routing process involves traveling from the leaf to the root. (A different destination gives a different tree on the network.) At each routing step, the message travels to some node that is closer to the root in the ID space (that is, the a node with a longer ID match). Generally, there are many such nodes, and the systems choose the node that is closest in terms of network distance. This gives a short path, not just in terms of overlay hops, but also in terms of network distance. However, if the path uses one bad node, the message may never reach the root, or it may reach the wrong root. Since there are $O(\log n)$ hops, the probability that at least one of them is faulty is quite large.

The solution in both cases is avoid relying on a single source and to use measurements of network distance to decide what information is valid.

Section 3 looks at the difficulty of building a correct table when nodes send incorrect information. In systems like Chord, neighbors are fixed based on their

Table 1. Summary of paper results: All algorithms assume that $c^2 < b$, and that l is $\Omega(\log n)$ and chosen sufficiently large that with high probability, one node in l is good.

Scheme	Redundancy	Extra Work fail-stop	bad-data	additional assumption?
Neighbor Table (Section 3)	l	$O(l^2)$	$O(l^2)$	—
Routing I (Section 4.1)	l	$O(l)$	$O(l^2)$	fraction bad nodes $< 1/c^2$
Routing II (Section 4.2)	l	$O(l^2)$	$O(l^2)$	—

ID, while in Pastry and Tapestry, nodes are given freedom to choose from among a set of choices. This flexibility gives better performance. However, both [15] and [2] argue that this flexibility is harmful because it means that a node has a difficult time determining what information can be trusted.

We show that the tables used by Tapestry and Pastry can be built correctly even in the presence of faulty nodes by using a factor of $O(\log n)$ additional storage, where n is the number of nodes in the network. (This gives a total storage of $O(\log^2 n)$.) The key idea is to gather a list of candidates for a given slot from enough sources that the probability all are faulty is low. Then we can use the network distance to determine which candidate is the best.

Section 4 presents two routing techniques presented in this paper are similar in spirit to that of [14,10] in that they route to a set of nodes at each level instead of just one. However, in this paper, these sets are not determined based on IDs, but on network distance. At each step, the algorithm queries the nodes in the current set to get the next set. If one node in the current set is good, the hope is that at least one node in the next step is also good. There is a subtlety here. If the the nodes in the current set return do not return the same set of nodes for the next step, the next set could be larger than the current set. This growth in the set size means that this technique could amount to flooding the network, which would be very inefficient.

However, if the algorithm eliminate some next set possibilities, there is a danger it will eliminate the only good possibilities. (And if failed nodes tend to return other failed nodes, the percentage of failed nodes may be higher than the percentage of failed nodes in the network as a whole.) The algorithm must ensure that it always keeps at least one good possibility for the next step. Our idea is to use the network distance from the query originator to determine which nodes are in the next set, since in our model, the adversary cannot manipulate ht network distance. For a small enough fraction of failing nodes, this succeeds with high probability when the sets are of size about $O(\log n)$. Section 4 presents two algorithms implementing this general idea. Both results rely on a restricted-growth assumption about the network, but these techniques may still perform well in other situations.

Table 1 summarizes our results.

1.3   Model

Defining an appropriate failure mode is a difficult task. A weak model may not be realistic enough, and a model that is too strong is impossible to make claims about. Our goal is to present a model that is strong enough to deal with at least some real problems, but that still allows analysis.

To explain our model, it helps to view the network as made up of two layers. The underlying layer can be trusted to deliver messages. The upper layer, or overlay layer, consists of the peer-to-peer nodes and the connections they maintain with each other (using the underlying layer for routing). This overlay is not trusted. These nodes can misbehave, but they cannot destroy or modify message on the wire, only messages that make go to the overlay layer. Figure 4 shows this distinction. Furthermore, this paper makes the following assumption about overlay nodes:

- Node IDs are assigned securely.
- Nodes fail, or become corrupted, independent of their location.
- The network must form a restricted-growth metric space. This essentially means that the number of nodes within distance r is polynomial in r.
- Part of the trusted component is the ability to measure network distance(i.e., by pinging).
- For one of the secure routing algorithms (Section 4.1, we assume the fraction of bad nodes is small compared to the growth rate of the graph.

All our results apply to the fail-stop model, where nodes that fail simply cease responding to messages, but do not misbehave. However, they also apply in a worse case, in which "failed" nodes send messages with bad data.

The major difference between our model and that of Castro et al. [2] is focused around our assumptions on the network topology. This paper requires a secure way of measuring network distance, supplemented with the assumption that nodes fail independently of their distance. While these requirements may seem limiting, note that changing distance measurements, particularly making them shorter, is actually quite difficult without interrupting the flow of messages at the lowest level—a capability for denial of service that is outside the scope of this paper (and of the Castro et al. solution).

Second, relaxation of the location independence requirement can lead to routing failure in regions with high local concentrations of bad nodes; in this circumstance, our techniques could be supplemented with any non-local technique (for example [2,10,14]).

2   Preliminaries

This section briefly describes the Tapestry neighbor table and routing algorithm (for the object location algorithm, see [7]). Note that the data structure presented here is almost identical to Pastry (and very similar to [11]), though the two systems differ markedly in how they handle object location. Discussing this difference is outside the scope of this paper.

A peer or node in Tapestry is assigned a random ID (all the IDs are the same length) with digits in some base b. The name space is chosen large enough so no two IDs will be the same. A message is routed toward a destination using prefix routing. That is, if the destination is 1234, the first routing hop goes to a node with an ID beginning with 1, the second hop goes to a node with an ID beginning with 12, and so on. To do this, for each prefix α of a node's ID, the node must keep a pointer to one node with each possible extension of that prefix. For example, for $\alpha = 12$, the node 1234 must keep a pointer to a node beginning with 120, 121, 122, etc.

When there is more than one node meeting a condition, the closest such node is chosen. As a result, links belonging to shorter prefixes in the neighbor tables tend to be shorter in network distance than the ones on higher levels, because there are more nodes meeting shorter prefixes. In the class of networks considered in this paper, these link lengths are geometrically increasing, so the distance traveled is proportional to the distance between the source and the destination, and is independent of the number of hops. Let $\mathcal{B}_r(A)$ be the ball of radius r around A, or all the points within r of A. Then the condition needed is

$$|\mathcal{B}_{2r}(A)| \le c\,|\mathcal{B}_r(A)|, \tag{1}$$

where c the expansion constant of the network.

In words, this means that for a given node A, the number of nodes within $2r$ of A is no more than a constant times the number of nodes within r of A. Graphs that can be modeled as grids for some dimension d meet this condition with $c = 2^d$. This condition probably does not hold on the Internet; however, this may still be a useful model in practice.

At some point in the routing, there may be no node matching a given ID, and the two systems differ in how they handle this case. Pastry keeps a list nodes with nearby IDs, called the leaf set. (In most cases, this list contains the nodes in the highest levels of the tree. It is useful in ways not discussed here, see [13].) When a hole is encountered in the routing table, routing proceeds using these nodes. Tapestry defines a substitute or surrogate node for the missing node and routes towards that node.

For the purposes of this paper, it is convenient to notice that each destination is the root of a tree containing all nodes in the network. Then, a route is a path from a leaf to the root of the tree. Relative to the root, each node has a level, where the level of a node is the length of the longest matching prefix with the root.[3] For simplicity, imagine that a level-i node is also a level-$(i-1)$ node, a level-$(i-2)$ node, and so on. The longer the matching prefix, the higher up in the tree a node is, and a level-0 node is a leaf. Then every level-i node takes as its parent the closest level-$(i+1)$ node, where closest refers to network distance (i.e. ping time). Sometimes nodes will have multiple parents. The k parents of a level-i node are the k closest level-$(i+1)$ nodes to be its parents.

---

[3] In Pastry, using the leaf sets bypasses some of these levels, however, in almost all cases, the number of levels bypassed this way is small.

A path through the network is then a path from a leaf in this tree to the root. For example, the ID 1234, the root of the tree is the node with ID 1234, its children are the nodes with IDs beginning with 123, and their children are the nodes beginning with ID 12, and so on. Each node in the network then participates in n trees, but in only needs to store b parents at each level in the tree (see [11,13,7]). This means that its total storage is $b \log_b n$. For simplicity and ease of exposition, the rest of this paper imagines that there is only one tree.

A recent paper [7] shows how to build these neighbor tables in a distributed way. Here, we improve on that algorithm by making it more tolerant to faults. First, let us state a lemma from that paper. Suppose a ball around A of radius r contains k nodes at level-i. The lemma bounds the probability that a larger ball around A (of size $3r$) contains k level-i nodes that also satisfy predicate $p(X)$ where nodes satisfy $p(X)$ independently with probability f. The following lemma is proved, though not in exactly this form, in [7].

Lemma 1. Suppose the inner ball of radius r contains $k = O(\log n)$ level-i nodes. Then so long as $f c^2 < 1$, the ball of radius $3r$ contains no more than k level-i nodes satisfying p (where c is the expansion constant of the network.)

The special case when $p(X)$ is the probability that X is a level-$(i+1)$ node will turn out to be particularly useful, so we formally state it in Corollary 1. This lemma and the remainder of the paper require that $c^2 < b$.

Corollary 1 Suppose the inner ball of radius r contains $k = O(\log n)$ level-i nodes. Then so long as $c^2/b < 1$, the ball of radius $3r$ contains no more than k level-$(i+1)$ nodes.

3   Building the Neighbor Table in the Presence of Faults

Recall that for a $O(b \log_b n)$ of different prefixes, a node must store the closest, in terms of network distance, node with that prefix. (It is beyond the scope of this paper to motivate this choice.) When nodes are inserted, they must also be able to find the closest node with the given prefix. The algorithm of the section gives a way to do this.

Viewing the algorithm as a black box would require running it once for every prefix. In fact, it can also be used more cleverly. By choosing the appropriate starting point, in one pass it finds one entry at every level. Further, [7] showed that by choosing parameters carefully, we can use this technique to fill the entire table.

3.1   The Fragile Algorithm

Recall that nodes are divided into levels of geometrically decreasing size, such that the ith level contains roughly n/b^i nodes. Further, recall that a level-i node chooses as its parent (or parents) the closest level-$(i+1)$ node. (This arrangement was motivated by [1,11,18] which used that to get paths through the network

method FINDNEARESTNEIGHBOR (*QueryNode*,**RootSet**)
1   *maxLevel* ← LEVEL(**RootSet**)
2   **list** ← **RootSet**
3   **for** *i* = *maxlevel* - 1 **to** 0
4   **list** ← GETNEXTLIST(**list**, *i*, *QueryNode*)
    end FINDNEARESTNEIGHBOR

method GETNEXTLIST (**neighborlist**, *level*, *QueryNode*)
1   **nextList** ← ∅
2   **for** *n* ∈ **neighborlist**
3   **temp** ← GETCHILDREN(*n*, *level*))
4   **nextList** ← KEEPCLOSESTK(**temp** ∪ **nextList**)
5   **return** **nextList**
    end GETNEXTLIST

Fig. 5. Finding the Nearest Neighbor: This algorithm operates with respect to the tree defined by the **RootSet**. For more detail, see text.

---

that not only had few hops, but also short network distance.) Figure 5 shows the algorithm of [7]. Section 3.2 will explain how a slight modification in the data structures used by this algorithm makes the algorithm much more robust.

The algorithm starts with a list of the k closest nodes at m axLevel We call this list the **RootSet**, since in the fragile version of the algorithm, this set contains only the root. Assume that these are all the nodes at m axLevelor the closest k such nodes. Then, to go from the level-$(i + 1)$ list to the level-i list, query each node on the level-$(i + 1)$ list for all the level-i nodes they know, or, in other words, their children. The algorithm trims this list, keeping only the closest k nodes. The proof that the k nodes kept at each step are actually the closest nodes at that level is deferred to the next section.

3.2   The Robust Algorithm

The existence of one failed node can cause the algorithm to return a wrong answer. In particular, if the nearest neighbor is B, and the parent of B does not respond or does not report the existence of B, then the querying node never finds out about a B. This fragility is clearly undesirable.

This problem is solved without changing the algorithm, by changing the definition of "parent". Each level-i node B, (where level-i is defined with respect to a particular tree), now finds the closest l level-$(i + 1)$ nodes and treats them as its parents, and it, in turn, is a child of all those l nodes. Notice that if any parent reports B, the querying node will be able to find B.

With l parents, and a failure probability of f, the probability that all the parents fail is f^l (here, failure means the node should return B but either does not reply, or returns a list without B). If $l = O(\log n)$ and f is constant, then the probability of a failure is an inverse polynomial in n. (Unless the root is assumed to be good, the **RootSet** must also be of size l. If this is not given to the algorithm, we can use the fault tolerant routing described in Section 4 to find a set of nodes at the right level.)

In order for this argument to hold, the algorithm must query all of B's parents, so clearly k must be large enough that the algorithm will query all of B's parents. The following argument shows that this can be done with k still $O(\log n)$ (so long as $l = O(\log n)$). The idea is that any nearby node has its parents nearby as well, for the correct definitions of nearby.

Lemma 2. For $k > bl$, with $l = \Omega(\log n)$, with high probability, the k closest level-$(i + 1)$ nodes contain all the parents of the closest k level-i nodes.

Pick $k > bl$. Then the expected number of level-$(i + 1)$ nodes in a set of k level-i nodes is at least l, and if $k = O(\log n)$, we can say that the number of level-$(i+1)$ nodes is at least l with high probability. Now let r_i be the radius of the ball containing k level-i nodes. We just argued that this ball also contains l level-$(i + 1)$ nodes. But now apply the Circle Lemma (Lemma 3) to say that if B is within the radius of the closest l level-$(i + 1)$ nodes, then it is also with r_i. That means its parents are within $3r_i$, and by Lemma 1, $3r_i < r_{i+1}$. So with high probability, the k closest level-$(i + 1)$ nodes contain all the parents of any level-i node within distance r_i.   □

Since this is a high probability result, we can use the union bound to argue that over even $\log n$ levels, with high probability, there is no failure at any level.

4   Routing in a Faulty Network

In [2], the authors present a routing technique for dealing with hostile networks. Their idea is to use r different paths to the root, and then they argue that if a fraction f of the nodes are corrupted, then the probability a message reaches the destination along a particular path is $(1 - f)^{1+\log_b n}$. The probability that all r of the paths fail is $((1 - f)^{1+\log_b n})^r$. Asymptotically, this is a rather low probability of success. In fact, using their formulation, the probability of failure is more than $(1 - (1 - f)^{1+\log_b n})^r$, which is approximately $\exp(-rn^{\frac{\ln(1-f)}{\ln b}})$. If the desired failure probability is constant, then r must be a polynomial in n.

We give two techniques for more fault tolerant routing. Both use iterative routing. Recall that in iterative routing, the initiating node controls the process. Given a list of ith hop nodes, the node wanting to route contacts one of them asks for possible $i + 1$st hops.

If an ith hop node returns nodes that look like good $(i + 1)$st hops but are not, then the initiating node does not know which of the nodes are good. Consider the case where the nodes are malicious but of limited power and want to pass messages on to a particular subnet (perhaps their own, because they control it, or perhaps another to get rid of traffic). Picking from among the returned nodes at random may also be a problem, since the misconfigured nodes may be more likely to return other misconfigured nodes, while the correct nodes may return misconfigured nodes with probability proportional to the fraction of misconfigured nodes. Both of the techniques of this section attempt to deal with this case by using network distance information to pick from this set of returned nodes ones that are reasonably likely to be good.

Assume that the fraction of faulty nodes is f. Both of our techniques require each node to store not one neighbor in each entry in the routing table, but $l = O(\log n)$. In the tree terminology, this means each node stores not one parent, but l parents, so the structure is no longer a tree, but the parent and child terminology still applies.

The first technique is simpler and more practical algorithm, but the analysis is more complicated and holds only holds when f is small.

4.1   Routing Technique I

The technique is in some sense a sort of reverse of the nearest neighbor algorithm described in the previous section. The algorithm works as follows.

- The query node starts with a list of l level-i nodes. It then contacts each of these nodes and asks for the their l closest level-$(i+1)$ nodes.
- The query node then gets a list of nodes, eliminates duplicates, and measures the distance to all of them. It then chooses the closest l, and goes back to the first step.

At some point, there will be no nodes at the next level, and the algorithm has found the root. To prove this works, we need to show is that at each step, there is at least one good node among the l.

Let the query node be Q. We start by proving the following lemma relating distance to a node to the distance to its parent.

Lemma 3 (Circle Lemma). Let r be a radius such that $\mathcal{B}_r(Q)$ (the ball of radius r around Q) contains at least l level-$(i+1)$ nodes. Then for any level-i node within r of Q, all its parents are within distance $3r$ of Q.

Proof. See Figure 6. Suppose B is a level-i node within distance r of Q. Note that B has l potential parents within r of Q. By the triangle inequality, all these nodes are within $2r$ of B. If B chooses different parents than the nodes within the smaller ball, it could only be because they were closer, so all of B's parents are within $2r$ of B. But this means they are within $3r$ of Q.   □

Now, let r_i be the radius of the smallest ball around Q containing l level-i nodes (r_{i+1} is defined similarly). By Lemma 1, $3r_i < r_{i+1}$ with high probability. Combining that with the Circle Lemma, gives

Corollary 2 Consider a set of l level-i nodes within r_{i+1} of Q. Suppose $fc^2 < 1$ (that is, the fraction of bad nodes is sufficiently low) and that there is at least one good node among the l nodes. Then with high probability, we will be able to find l level-$(i+1)$ nodes within r_{i+2} such that at least one of them is good.

Proof. Consider the ball of r_{i+1} around Q. We know that there is at least one good level-i node inside r_{i+1}. Call this node B. By the Circle Lemma, B's parents

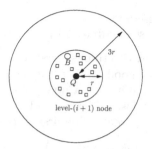

Fig. 6. The parents of B lie within the big circle. The squares represent some of the level-$(i+1)$ nodes that B could choose as parents.

---

are all with $3r_{i+1}$, and by Lemma 1, $3r_{i+1} < r_{i+2}$. Then B's most distant parent gives us a bound on the distance to the furthest node in the next level list.

Using Lemma 1, the number of bad level-$(i+1)$ nodes within $3r_{i+1}$ is less than $c^2 fl$ with high probability for $l = O(\log n)$. So if $fc^2 < 1$, there are not enough bad nodes within the bound given by B's parent, so of the l level-$(i+1)$ nodes, at least one of them is good.   □

Note that this is a pessimistic proof. Even if there are l bad nodes close enough to the query node, it is not immediately clear how bad nodes could take advantage of that fact without a great deal of coordination.

This algorithm does l^2 extra work in the worst case, since each of these l nodes could return l different parents, giving a total of l^2 answers, each of which must be contacted. In the fail-stop case, where nodes do not return bad data but simply stop working, most of these l^2 nodes will be the same, so the algorithm need only ping $O(l)$. To see this, consider the level-i list. All those nodes are within r_{i+1}, and all their parents will be within r_{i+2}. By the Equation 1, the number of $i+1$ nodes within r_{i+2} is expected to be $c^2 l$.

4.2   Routing Technique II

This algorithm gives a tighter bound in the proof and works for any value of f (by picking l large enough), independent of the network, but this would not be as convenient to implement in practice.

At every step, this algorithm ensures that it knows the closest l level-i nodes. In Section 4.1, the algorithm did not guarantee that it had the "closest" l nodes. Knowing that they are the closest means they are determined by the structure of the network and not by the misbehavior of the bad nodes, so the probability of failures is independent (given our network assumptions) among these l nodes. The algorithm works as follows:

1. From the level-i nodes, pick all the level-$(i+2)$ nodes. In Lemma 4, we show that $l = O(\log n)$ is big enough such that with high probability, at least one of the level-i nodes is good level-$(i+2)$ node.

2. Get the children of these nodes.
3. Pick the closest l of these children to be the set of level-$(i + 1)$ nodes.

To prove this works, we show two things. First, that the first step succeeds; that is, that there is at least one good level-$(i + 2)$ node among the l level-i nodes. Second, we show that if there is such a node, it will be able to return all good children. This is true if the closest l level-$(i + 1)$ nodes all have the level-$(i + 2)$ nodes from the first step as parents. The first step is shown next.

Lemma 4. For $l \geq \log(1/\epsilon)\frac{b^2}{1-f}$, the probability than none of the level-i nodes are good level-$(i + 2)$ nodes is less than ϵ.

Proof. Given a level-i node chosen uniformly at random, the probability it is a level-$(i+2)$ node is $1/b^2$. Since failures are independent of node ID and location, the l closest level-i nodes are independent trials. The probability a node is good is $(1 - f)$, so the probability is it a level-$(i+2)$ node and not faulty is $\frac{(1-f)}{b^2}$. Given l level-i nodes, the probability that none of them are good level-$(i + 2)$ nodes is $(1 - \frac{(1-f)}{b^2})^l \leq \exp(-\frac{l(1-f)}{b^2})$, and picking $l = \log(1/\epsilon)\frac{b^2}{1-f}$, the probability the list does not contain a suitable level-$(i + 2)$ node is less than ϵ. □

Setting $\epsilon = 1/n^c$, the bound is a high probability bound. Next, we show the second part, that the level-$(i + 2)$ nodes chosen have as children the closest l level-$(i + 1)$ nodes.

Lemma 5. Suppose A is a level-$(i + 2)$ node and is among the closest l level-i nodes to B. Then for $l = O(\log n)$, with high probability, the closest l level-$(i+1)$ nodes to B point to A.

Proof. We prove this using Corollary 1. As usual, let r_{i+1} be the smallest radius such that the ball of radius r_{i+1} around B contains l level-$(i + 1)$ nodes.

Consider a level-$(i + 1)$ node, call it C, within r_{i+1}. Notice that C has a potential parent, A, within distance $r_{i+1} + r_i \leq 2r_{i+1}$. If it does not have A as a parent, then it is the case that there are more than l level-$(i + 2)$ nodes within $2r_{i+1}$ of C. But since $d(B, C) \leq r_{i+1}$, this implies that there are at most l level-$(i + 2)$ nodes within $3r_{i+1}$ of B. Now apply Corollary 1 to say that this is unlikely when $c^2 < b$ and l is chosen large enough. □

5 Experiments

We implemented the nearest neighbor (Section 3) algorithm and the routing algorithm of Section 4.1. The simulation used 50,000 nodes, using a base of 10 (this means the number of steps to the root was five or six.) The underlying topology used was a grid, where the overlay points were chosen at random.

The failed nodes in both cases only return information about other failed nodes. This is worse that the fail-stop model, since here nodes are actually getting bad data, but is not the worst that bad nodes could do.

For varying fractions of bad nodes, we ran the nearest neighbor algorithm, and calculated the number of times that algorithm gave the incorrect answer

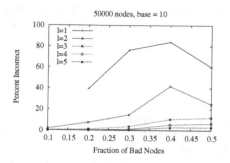

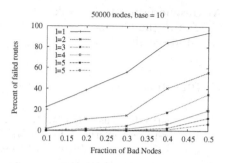

Fig. 7. Percentage of incorrect entries over 5,000 trials in a network of 50,000 nodes. Even a small amount of redundancy (shown here as l) significantly reduces the number of incorrect entries.

Fig. 8. Percentage of routes that fail to reach the root when the algorithm of Section 4.1 is used. Notice that a small amount of redundancy (shown here as l) helps tremendously.

because of the failed nodes.[4] See Figure 7. Notice that when half the nodes are failed, the number of incorrect (i.e., not closest) nodes actually decreases; this is because return only other failed nodes does not cause problems if the the end answer is also a failed node.

There was large variance; if nodes near the root had failed, the number of incorrect nodes returned was quite high. The situation was particularly bad for one parent is used, so no data point was included on the graph.

Figure 8 shows that chance of reaching the root improves a great deal with only a little additional overhead. Note that Tapestry already stores two backups for every entry, so $l = 3$ requires no additional overhead. (And the nearest neighbor algorithm uses these backups.)

6   Conclusion

Tolerating misbehaving components is a requirement for any large-scale system. In this paper, we took a step toward achieving this goal for peer-to-peer overlay networks—by harvesting redundancy. We showed how to build routing tables that take advantage of locality in the network even in the presence of faulty nodes. We also presented a technique for fault-tolerant routing that gives a high probability of success with small overhead. Although we applied these techniques to the specific instances of Tapestry and Pastry, these techniques appear to be generally applicable and could enhance other systems.

---

[4] The algorithm implemented here is an improved version of the algorithm described in [7] that follows the same general outline but changes k during the course of the algorithm. For details, see [6].

Acknowledgments. Thanks are due to Satish Rao, Sean Rhea, Jeremy Stribling, and the OceanStore group for their comments on this paper and many helpful discussions.

References

1. M. Castro, P. Druschel, Y. C. Hu, and A. Rowstron. Exploiting network proximity in peer-to-peer overlay networks. In *Proceedings of the International Workshop on Future Directions in Distributed Computing*, 2002.
2. Miguel Castro, Peter Druschel, Ayalvadi Ganesh, Antony Rowstron, and Dan S. Wallach. Secure routing for structured peer-to-peer overlay networks. In *Proceedings of the 5th Symposium on Operating Systems Desgin and Implementation*, pages 299–314, 2002.
3. John Douceur. The Sybil attack. In *Proceedings of IPTPS*, pages 251–260, 2002.
4. Amos Fiat and Jared Saia. Censorship resistant peer-to-peer content addressable networks. In *Proceedings of Symposium on Discrete Algorithms*, 2002.
5. Nicholas J.A. Harvey, Marvin Theimer Michael B. Jones, Stefan Sarouiu, and Alec Wolman. Skipnet: A peer-to-peer overlay network. In *Proceedings of the fourth USENIX Symposium on Internet Technologies and Systems*, 2003.
6. Kirsten Hildrum, John Kubiatowicz, and Satish Rao. Improved bounds on finding nearest neighbors in growth-restricted metrics.
   http://www.cs.berkeley.edu/~hildrum/nn.ps.
7. Kirsten Hildrum, John D. Kubiatowicz, Satish Rao, and Ben Y. Zhao. Distributed object location in a dynamic network. In *Proceedings of the Fourteenth ACM Symposium on Parallel Algorithms and Architectures*, 2002.
8. Dahlia Malkhi, Moni Naor, and David Ratajczak. Viceroy: a scalable and dynamic emulation of the butterfly. In *Proceedings of the twenty-first annual symposium on Principles of distributed computing*, pages 183–192, 2002.
9. Moni Naor and Udi Wieder. Novel architectures for p2p applications: the continuous-discrete approach. In *Proceedings of the fifteenth annual ACM symposium on Parallel algorithms and architectures*, pages 50–59, 2003.
10. Moni Naor and Udi Wieder. A simple fault tolerant distributed hash table. In *Second International Workshop on Peer-to-Peer Systems*, 2003.
11. C. Greg Plaxton, Rajmohan Rajaraman, and Andrea W. Richa. Accessing nearby copies of replicated objects in a distributed environment. In *Proc. of the 9th Annual Symp. on Parallel Algorithms and Architectures*, pages 311–320, 1997.
12. Sylvia Ratnasamy, Paul Francis, Mark Handley, Richard Karp, and Scott Schenker. A scalable content-addressable network. In *Proc. of SIGCOMM*, pages 161–172, 2001.
13. Antony Rowstron and Peter Druschel. Pastry: Scalable, distributed object location and routing for large-scale peer-to-peer systems. In *Proceedings of IFIP/ACM Middleware*, 2001.
14. Jared Saia, Amos Fiat, Steve Gribble, Anna R. Karlin, and Stefan Saroiu. Dynamically fault-tolerant content addressable networks. In *First International Workshop on Peer-to-Peer Systems*, 2002.
15. Emil Sit and Robert Morris. Security considerations for peer-to-peer distributed hash tables. In *Proceedings of the first International Workshop on Peer-to-Peer Systems*, Cambridge, MA, 2002.

16. Ion Stoica, Robert Morris, David Karger, M. Frans Kaashoek, and Hari Balakr-ishnan. Chord: A scalable peer-to-peer lookup service for internet applications. In *Proc. of SIGCOMM*, pages 149–160, 2001.
17. Ben Y. Zhao, Ling Huang, Sean C. Rhea, Jeremy Stribling, Anthony D Joseph, and John D. Kubiatowicz. Tapestry: A global-scale overlay for rapid service deploy-ment. *IEEE Journal on Selected Areas in Communications*, 2003. Special Issue on Service Overlay Networks, to appear.
18. Ben Y. Zhao, Anthony Joseph, and John Kubiatowicz. Locality-aware mechanisms for large-scale networks. In *Proc. of Workshop on Future Directions in Distributed Comp.*, 2002.

Maximizing Remote Work in Flooding-Based Peer-to-Peer Systems*

Qixiang Sun, Neil Daswani, and Hector Garcia-Molina

Computer Science Department
Stanford University, Stanford, CA 94305, USA
{qsun,daswani,hector}@cs.stanford.edu

Abstract. In peer-to-peer (P2P) systems where individual peers must cooperate to process each other's requests, a useful metric for evaluating the system is how many remote requests are serviced by each peer. In this paper we apply this remote work metric to flooding-based P2P search networks such as Gnutella. We study how to maximize the remote work in the entire network by controlling the rate of query injection at each node. In particular, we provide a simple procedure for finding the optimal rate of query injection and prove its optimality. We also show that a simple prefer-high-TTL protocol in which each peer processes only queries with the highest time-to-live (TTL) is optimal.

1 Introduction

Flooding-based peer-to-peer systems like Gnutella [4] have been deployed and used by millions of users worldwide to share and exchange files. As of April 2003, Gnutella has over one million users (with at least one hundred thousand concurrent users [5]) and ten tera-byte of shared data. Also according to [3], there are over 10 vendors actively developing Gnutella-style clients for their applications.

While there is significant research interest in distributed hash tables [8] [9] [11] [14], Gnutella-style systems are used in practice for four reasons: 1) simple to implement, 2) easy to deploy, 3) extremely robust in handling frequent peer arrivals and departures, and 4) supports wild-card searches. Moreover, in ad-hoc wireless environments where unicast is just as expensive as broadcast, a flooding-based mechanism is more desirable.

Although a flooding-based search mechanism can be inefficient as a search query is forwarded to all nodes within a certain number of hops (e.g., 7 hops), Gnutella-style networks have, nevertheless, scaled to millions of users by using a super-node architecture where high speed (CPU and bandwidth) nodes act as proxies for regular (slower) nodes. Figure 1 shows a sample super-node network with 3 super-nodes and 16 regular nodes. Each super-node indexes the content of its attached regular nodes and performs the flooding-based search on

---

* This work is supported in part by NSF Graduate Fellowship and NSF Grants EIA 0085896, IIS-9817799, and CCR-0208683.

F.E. Fich (Ed.): DISC 2003, LNCS 2848, pp. 337–351, 2003.

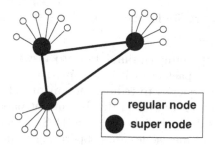

Fig. 1. A sample super-node network.

behalf of the regular nodes. In this architecture, a network with millions of users can be reduced to one with tens of thousands of super-nodes, where a flooding mechanism is adequate.

Even with this architecture, super-node networks are still susceptible to overloading when too many search queries are generated by users. In the extreme case, if every super-node uses all of its processing capacity to inject new search queries instead of answering and propagating existing queries, no "useful" work is done because queries are not answered by anyone. We define "useful" or *remote work* as a super-node processing a query that is not inject by itself or by its attached regular node. At the other extreme, if super-nodes inject too few new queries, they will have available capacity to process remote queries, but there will not be enough queries to keep the super-nodes busy. Thus, our goal is to pick a query-injection rate between these two extremes that maximizes the remote work performed.

We chose *remote work* as our objective metric because it succinctly captures the goal of users. The more remote super-nodes that process a given user query, the more potential answers the user will receive. From among the answers, the user can then select those he wants, and the larger the selection, the better. For instance, if the user searches for compositions by "Bach," he can then select titles that sound appealing, or files that have a good recording quality.

One approach to maximizing the remote work is to change the search protocol itself, e.g., using random walkers [7] or iterative deepening [13]. In this paper we attack the problem from a different angle: we control the rate of query injection at individual super-nodes. We address the following questions:

- How do we model query injection, processing, and propagation in a Gnutella-style system?
- What is the optimal number of new queries that each super-node should inject each round as to maximize the remote work done in a network?
- What is the impact of using different protocols to select which queries to process and propagate? Is there an optimal protocol?
- Should we enforce a fair policy where every super-node injects the same number of new queries into the network? Or should highly-connected super-nodes in the "critical" part of the network inject more queries (or less)?
- What is the penalty in terms of reduced remote work for using a fair policy?

– What are some heuristics for more complex systems that are outside of our simple model?

Daswani et al. in [1] conducted simulations to answer some of the above questions focusing on the impact of malicious super-nodes who purposely generate large number of bogus queries to reduce the amount of "useful" work done in a flooding-based peer-to-peer system. In the current paper, we do not consider malicious super-nodes doing denial-of-service (DoS) attacks using bogus queries. Instead, we assume all super-nodes are cooperating to maximize useful work in the network. The results in this paper provide a firm theoretical foundation for studying the effects of DoS attacks and establish a baseline of comparison. These results can be easily incorporated into [1] to further extend their results.

Knowing the theoretical optimal rate of query injection and the maximum remote work possible can improve the construction of the overlay network. For example, a super-node can use the optimal query-injection rate to dynamically decide whether it should accept more clients or disconnect existing ones. We can also use remote work as metric to evaluate different types of overlay topologies.

Although our work is specific to Gnutella-like systems, we do address an issue that we believe will be of growing importance in distributed systems, that of getting autonomous components to provide services for each other. Whether the system is a publish-subscribe one, or a sensor net, or an ad-hoc wireless network, nodes must balance their local needs (e.g., disseminate events or messages originating locally) with the services they provide to others (e.g., packet forwarding, resource discovery). As far as we know, this "distributed resource coordination" problem has not been studied in detail. Our paper is a first study of such coordination for autonomous systems.

2   Assumptions and a Model

We use a very simple model of Gnutella to capture key performance characteristics that are relevant to our goal of maximizing remote work. Given that regular nodes always access the network via a super-node, we only need to capture the activities of the super-nodes. Specifically, we model the super-node network as a graph $G = (V, E)$ where edges represent connections between super-nodes. For brevity, when we say "node" in the remainder of this paper, we mean super-node unless stated otherwise explicitly.

We model the P2P system as operating in rounds, where search queries are injected and processed during the round and forwarded to neighboring peers between rounds. Although the system does not have to be sychronous, we will assume sychrony for analysis purposes. Note that queries "injected" by a super-node are typically initiated by the regular nodes attached to it.

We assume each query has a time-to-live (TTL) field that is decremented by one each time when forwarded to other peers. When the TTL becomes negative, the query is removed from the network. For our purpose of maximizing remote work, we only model the propagation of search queries and ignore other communication such as search replies, ping-pong messages, and actual file transfers.

We also assume the bottleneck of the system is the processing capacity of the super-nodes rather than the network bandwidth. Furthermore, we assume receiving queries from the network has negligible processing cost as compared to the actual processing of a query. There are three reasons for these assumptions: (1) super-nodes have excellent network connectivities, e.g., 10 megabits or better; (2) backbone bandwidth is grossly over-provisioned; and (3) wild-card search queries are expensive to evaluate because simple hashing techniques do not work well.

We assign each super-node a processing capacity of C queries per round. A super-node may use its capacity in two ways: (1) accept and process a new search query from an attached regular node, or (2) process a remote query forwarded to it by a neighboring super-node. We refer to case 1 as a super-node *injecting new queries*, and refer to case 2 as *processing remote queries*. For clarification, processing a remote query involves two steps: one, match the query against the shared data indexed by this super-node; and two, forward this query to neighboring nodes. Obviously in a single round, the number of new queries injected plus the number of remote queries processed is at most C.

In most of our analysis in this paper, we assume all nodes have the same processing capacity to make the analysis tractable. Although Sariou et. al. [10] observed large variations among Gnutella clients, variations among super-nodes are much smaller. We will briefly outline the difficulties in handling super-nodes with different capacities as an open problem in Section 9.2.

Although each node can only process up to C queries per round, its neighboring nodes may send it more than C remote queries. Because we assumed that network bandwidth is not the limiting factor and that the cost of receiving data from the network is negligible, we allow each node to receive all the incoming remote queries even if it does not have the capacity to process them all. A node must then decide which remote queries to process this round and drop the remaining queries. We do not allow a node to "temporarily" buffer excess *remote* queries for processing at a later round because we are interested in the long-term system behavior where nodes are constantly overloaded.

The long-term behavior of a peer-to-peer system certainly depends heavily on how each node decides which queries to process and drop. For brevity, we use the term *protocol* to refer to a node's decision mechanism. As an example, a node is said to be using a random protocol if it picks which queries to process uniformly at random.

One important parameter of a protocol is how a node divides its capacity between injecting new queries and processing remote queries. We use a fraction ρ between 0 and 1 to denote this parameter. For example, $\rho = \frac{1}{3}$ implies one third of a node's capacity is allocated for injecting new queries while the other two third is used for processing remote queries. We assume that a super-node injects its full quota of ρC new queries each round, i.e., there is always an abundance of queries that regular nodes want to submit. This assumption is reasonable because our goal is to study the maximum amount of remote work possible which can only occur if nodes are generating sufficient number of new queries to keep the system busy. In practice, a super-node can inject new *local* queries at a fixed rate by buffering and delaying new search queries from its attached regular nodes.

Rather than trying to build an accurate model that can predict the actual performance of the peer-to-peer system, we have made many simplifying assumptions to make our study of the fundamental system behavior feasible. This simplified model retains all the important aspects of a flooding-based peer-to-peer protocol and does not restrict design decisions.

3   Notation and Problem Definition

- ρ_v denotes the fraction of processing capacity node v allocates for injecting new queries per round.
- $\bar{\rho} = \{\rho_v \mid v \in V\}$ denotes the set of ρ_v used by all nodes in network G.
- $\delta(u, v)$ denotes the minimum hop distance between nodes u and v in network G.
- $D(v, \tau)$ denotes the set of nodes u, excluding v, in G such that $\delta(u, v) \leq \tau$.
- $\hat{D}(v, \tau)$ denotes $D(v, \tau) \cup \{v\}$.
- $W_t^{\mathcal{P}}(v, \bar{\rho})$ denotes the set of queries processed by node v, using protocol $\mathcal{P}$ with settings $\bar{\rho}$ for the nodes, during round t. The set $W_t^{\mathcal{P}}(v, \bar{\rho})$ includes both new queries injected by v and processed remote queries. We drop the superscript $\mathcal{P}$ when the context is clear.
- $R_t^{\mathcal{P}}(v, \bar{\rho}) \subset W_t^{\mathcal{P}}(v, \bar{\rho})$ denotes the set of remote queries processed by node v at time t.
- $RW_t^{\mathcal{P}}(\bar{\rho}) = \sum_{v \in V} |R_t^{\mathcal{P}}(v, \bar{\rho})|$ denotes the number of remote queries processed by all nodes in network G at time t.

With the notation above, maximizing the remote work of a network G using protocol $\mathcal{P}$ can be stated formally as:

Problem: Given a graph $G = (V, E)$, maximum TTL τ, processing capacity C, and a protocol $\mathcal{P}$, find the optimal rate of injecting new queries $\bar{\rho} = \{\rho_v \mid v \in V\}$ such that $\sum_t RW_t^{\mathcal{P}}(\bar{\rho})$ is maximized.

The maximization problem is stated above as the cumulative number of remote queries processed over all nodes and all time. We chose to sum over all time to take into account of protocols with nondeterministic or irregular behaviors. However, as we will see, the protocols studied here all have some form of "steady-state" behavior.

4   Protocols

Before describing the protocols, we first need to discuss how to tag each query with an ID to avoid processing duplicate queries and to remove queries when their TTL expires. For a query q, we use a triplet (src, ttl, mid) where src is the

---

Deterministic Prefer-High-TTL Protocol $\mathcal{H}^{\mathcal{D}}$

During every round, each node $v \in V$ performs the following tasks in the order shown below:

1. Inject $\rho_v \cdot C$ new queries with the triplet identifiers $\{v, \tau, 1\}$, $\{v, \tau, 2\}$, $\ldots, \{v, \tau, \rho_v C\}$. Denote this set of local queries L_v. (For clarity in the presentation, we assume $\rho_v C$ is an integer. We can take the floor if it is not an integer.)
2. Sort all incoming queries from adjacent super-nodes in decreasing order of TTL, break ties in a deterministic manner that is independent of the current time, and remove queries that are duplicates or have already been processed at some previous time step. Denote this sorted list of new incoming queries I_v.
3. Take the first $(1 - \rho_v)C$ queries in I_v. Denote this set of remote queries R_v.
4. Service queries in L_v and R_v against local index.
5. Decrement the TTL of queries in L_v and R_v by 1.
6. Forward all queries in L_v and R_v that have $TTL \geq 0$ to all neighbors.

Fig. 2. An informal description of the deterministic prefer-high-TTL protocol.

---

node that injected the query, *ttl* is the current time-to-live of q as q moves around the network, and *mid* is an internal sequence number where $1 \leq mid \leq C$. We enforce three invariants about the IDs: (1) for any two queries injected by the same node in the same round, their *mids* are different; (2) $0 \leq ttl \leq \tau$ where τ is the maximum TTL; and (3) a query with ID (src, ttl, mid) at time t is injected at time $t - \tau + ttl$.

Note that when the query travels around the network, its ID changes as the *ttl* is decremented. To determine whether two query IDs q_1 and q_2 at times t_1 and t_2, respectively, refer to the same query, we check whether these two IDs have the same *src* node, the same *mid*, and were injected into the network at the same time. For example, assuming all queries initially have a TTL τ when injected, then a query with ID $q_1 = (u, 5, 2)$ at time step 8 is the same query as a query with ID $q_2 = (u, 3, 2)$ at time step 10 because both queries are injected by node u at time $8 + 5 - \tau = 10 + 3 - \tau = 13 - \tau$ with sequence number 2.

Using these IDs, we describe the operations of the deterministic prefer-high-TTL protocol $\mathcal{H}^{\mathcal{D}}$ in Figure 2. Essentially, after each node injects its new queries for the round, it then processes remote queries in decreasing TTL order until the processing capacity has been exhausted. If two queries have the same TTL, the tie is broken deterministically, e.g., lexicographically by source node ID and then the sequence number.

Similarly, the randomized prefer-high-TTL protocol $\mathcal{H}^{\mathcal{R}}$ performs the same steps as $\mathcal{H}^{\mathcal{D}}$ except ties are broken randomly. Though $\mathcal{H}^{\mathcal{R}}$ and $\mathcal{H}^{\mathcal{D}}$ are very similar, they exhibit different steady-state behavior as we will see in the next section. This distinction has significant impact on how efficiently we can simulate the protocols for experimental studies. A third protocol that we will use for illustrative purposes is the prefer-low-TTL protocol $\mathcal{L}$. Instead of sorting all the incoming queries in the set I_v in decreasing order of TTL during step 2 (of Figure 2), protocol $\mathcal{L}$ sorts the queries in increasing order of TTL.

5   Steady State

Regardless of the transient behavior at the beginning of time, a protocol that processes the most remote queries in the steady state will process the most remote work in the long run. Therefore, if two protocols have steady states, then we can simply compare their per-round performance in the steady state. It turns out that not all protocols have some form of steady state. In the technical report [12] , we trace out the execution of the prefer-low-TTL protocol $\mathcal{L}$ on a chain of five nodes where the per-round remote work oscillates with periodicity 2.

There are two flavors of steady state that are of particular interest because they distinguish between protocols $\mathcal{H}^{\mathcal{D}}$ and $\mathcal{H}^{\mathcal{R}}$. The first kind is a *strong* steady state where we can determine exactly which queries will be processed by every node. Formally,

Definition 1. *(Strong steady state) A protocol $\mathcal{P}$ has a* strong steady state *if given any $\bar{\rho}$, there exists t_0 such that for every node v and all $t > t_0$, $R_t^{\mathcal{P}}(v, \bar{\rho}) = R_{t_0}^{\mathcal{P}}(v, \bar{\rho})$.*

In other words, *strong steady state* guarantees that after time t_0, each node will process remote queries with the same triplet ID as the previous time step. For example, if node v processed a query with ID $(u, 5, 2)$ at time t_0, then v will process a query of the same ID from then on. Thus having a strong steady state makes simulation studies easier. Note that the same triple ID at two different times does not mean the same query because the two queries are created at different times.

An alternative is to relax the constraint of processing queries with the same triplet IDs.

Definition 2. *(Weak steady state) A protocol $\mathcal{P}$ has a* weak steady state *if given any $\bar{\rho}$, there exists t_0 such that for every node v and all $t > t_0$, $|R_t^{\mathcal{P}}(v, \bar{\rho})| = |R_{t_0}^{\mathcal{P}}(v, \bar{\rho})|$.*

A weak steady state only requires the number of remote queries processed to be the same rather than the query IDs to be the same. Since our objective is to maximize the total number of remote queries processed, having a weak steady state is sufficient for our analysis. Clearly, strong steady state implies weak steady state.

With these two notions of steady state, we now show protocol $\mathcal{H}^{\mathcal{D}}$ has a strong steady state. In particular, we show $\mathcal{H}^{\mathcal{D}}$ has a monotonicity property.

Proposition 1. *(Monotonicity) In protocol $\mathcal{H}^{\mathcal{D}}$, given $\bar{\rho}$, for any node v and a query ID $q = (src, ttl, mid)$,*

1. if $q \in W_{\tau - ttl_q}(v, \bar{\rho})$, then $q \in W_t(v, \bar{\rho})$ for all $t \geq \tau - ttl_q$.
2. if $q \in W_t(v, \bar{\rho})$ for some $t > \tau - ttl_q$, then $q \in W_{\tau - ttl_q}(v, \bar{\rho})$.

Monotonicity states that once a query ID q is in $W_{t_1}(v, \bar{\rho})$ for any node v and time t_1, the ID q can never disappear from $W_{t_2}(v, \bar{\rho})$ for all $t_2 > t_1$. It also guarantees the first appearance of q is at time $\tau - ttl_q$. The monotonicity is the result of breaking ties among queries of the same TTL in a deterministic fashion. Using this monotonicity, one can show that protocol $\mathcal{H}^{\mathcal{D}}$ has a strong steady state.

Theorem 1. *Protocol $\mathcal{H}^{\mathcal{D}}$ reaches a strong steady state in τ time steps.*

Our proofs of Proposition 1 and Theorem 1 are given in the technical report [12].

Unlike protocol $\mathcal{H}^{\mathcal{D}}$, the randomized version $\mathcal{H}^{\mathcal{R}}$ only has a weak steady state. Clearly $\mathcal{H}^{\mathcal{R}}$ does not have a strong steady state because the random selections do not guarantee a node will consistently choose remote queries with the same IDs. The fact that $\mathcal{H}^{\mathcal{R}}$ has a weak steady state is a directly corollary of a theorem in the next section that states both protocols $\mathcal{H}^{\mathcal{D}}$ and $\mathcal{H}^{\mathcal{R}}$ are "optimal" in the number of remote queries processed. Since $\mathcal{H}^{\mathcal{D}}$ and $\mathcal{H}^{\mathcal{R}}$ processes the same number of remote queries and $\mathcal{H}^{\mathcal{D}}$ reaches a strong steady state in τ time steps, then $\mathcal{H}^{\mathcal{R}}$ must reach a weak steady state in τ time steps.

6   Optimality of Protocol $\mathcal{H}^{\mathcal{R}}$

We now show that for any settings of $\bar{\rho}$, the two prefer-high-TTL protocols, $\mathcal{H}^{\mathcal{D}}$ and $\mathcal{H}^{\mathcal{R}}$, processes as much remote work as any other protocols using the same $\bar{\rho}$ settings, and hence are optimal. Since protocol $\mathcal{H}^{\mathcal{D}}$ is a special case of protocol $\mathcal{H}^{\mathcal{R}}$, we only show the optimality of protocol $\mathcal{H}^{\mathcal{R}}$. We prove this claim by first establishing an upper bound on the amount of remote work any protocol can process, and then showing protocol $\mathcal{H}^{\mathcal{R}}$ achieves this upper bound.

For the upper bound, notice that regardless of which protocol we use, the number of remote queries a node v can process, $|R_t(v, \bar{\rho})|$, is limited by two factors: (1) node v's processing capacity, and (2) how many queries are injected by nodes within τ hops of v. At maximum capacity, a node v can process $(1 - \rho_v)C$ queries per round. We call such a node *saturated*.

When a node v is not saturated, it can receive up to $K_v = C \cdot \sum_{u \in D(v, \tau)} \rho_u$ queries from nodes within τ hops. For protocols without steady state, the actual number of queries processed by node v may vary between rounds, (e.g., process no queries during one round, but a large amount the next round); however, the average number of queries processed per round, over time, is bounded by K_v.

We get our upper bound by combining the two limiting factors and taking the minimum number of remote queries processed in case 1 and case 2 (along with a special case when $t < \tau$).

Proposition 2. *For any protocol* $\mathcal{P}$, *any node* v, *and any setting* $\bar{\rho}$,

$$\sum_t |R_t(v, \bar{\rho})| \leq C \cdot \sum_t \min \left(1 - \rho_v, \sum_{w \in D(v, \min(\tau, t))} \rho_w \right)$$

We now show in two steps that protocol $\mathcal{H}^{\mathcal{R}}$ achieves this upper bound. In the first step, we claim that if a node v's "neighbors" cannot inject enough queries to continuously saturate v, then node v will process every query injected by these "neighbors." Stated formally,

Lemma 1. *Consider protocol* $\mathcal{H}^{\mathcal{R}}$ *and any node* v. *Suppose for some hop count* $h \leq \tau$, $\sum_{w \in D(v,h)} \rho_w \leq 1 - \rho_v$. *Then for all nodes* $w \in D(v, h)$ *and all* i *such that* $1 \leq i \leq \rho_w C$, *the query with triplet ID* $(w, \tau - \delta(w, v), i) \in R_t(v, \bar{\rho})$ *for all time* $t \geq \delta(w, v)$.

In the second step, we claim that if node v's "neighbors" are continuously injecting more queries than v can process, then node v processes exactly $(1 - \rho_v)C$ queries each round. Formally,

Lemma 2. *In protocol* $\mathcal{H}^{\mathcal{R}}$, *for any node* v *and hop count* h, *if* $\sum_{w \in D(v,h)} \rho_w > 1 - \rho_v$, *then node* v *is saturated after time* h, *i.e.,* $|R_t(v, \bar{\rho})| = (1 - \rho_v)C$ *for all* $t \geq h$.

This claim is not immediately obvious because the random selections in protocol $\mathcal{H}^{\mathcal{R}}$ may result in many duplicate queries arriving at a node v and reduce the number of remote queries processed. Fortunately, the prefer-high-TTL mechanism ensures "enough" non-duplicate queries arrive at v to saturate its processing capacity. The detailed proofs of these lemmas are given in the technical report [12].

Combining Lemmas 1 and 2 with $h = \tau$, we get that if node v's neighbors within τ hops do not inject enough queries to saturate v's processing capacity, then node v processes every query injected by them. On the other hand, if there is more than enough queries, then node v processes at maximum capacity $(1 - \rho_v)C$. Consequently,

Theorem 2. *In protocol* $\mathcal{H}^{\mathcal{R}}$, *for any node* v *and any setting* $\bar{\rho}$,

$$|R_t(v, \bar{\rho})| = C \cdot \min \left(1 - \rho_v, \sum_{u \in D(v, \min(\tau, t))} \rho_u \right)$$

Applying Theorem 2, we immediately obtain that $\sum_t |R_t(v, \bar{\rho})|$ is equal to the upper bound established in Proposition 2. Hence,

Corollary 1. *No protocols can achieve more remote work than protocol* $\mathcal{H}^{\mathcal{R}}$.

Find_Optimal_Single_ρ:

1. order the vertex set $V = \{v_1, v_2, \ldots, v_n\}$ such that $|\hat{D}(v_i, \tau)| \leq |\hat{D}(v_{i+1}, \tau)|$.
2. construct the sequence of non-increasing real numbers $\{d_1, d_2, \ldots d_n\}$ where $d_i = \frac{1}{|\hat{D}(v_i, \tau)|}$.
3. find the smallest k such that $\sum_{i=1}^{k} |\hat{D}(v_i, \tau)| \geq n$.
4. return d_i.

Fig. 3. Procedure for finding the optimal $\hat{\rho}$ when all nodes have the same ρ.

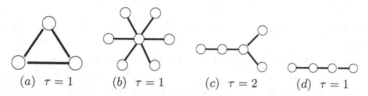

(a) $\tau = 1$ (b) $\tau = 1$ (c) $\tau = 2$ (d) $\tau = 1$

Fig. 4. Four example topologies.

Another important consequence of Theorem 2 is that in computing remote work, we do not have to worry about which queries were duplicates or which path a query traveled on. Therefore, we can treat all queries as indistinguishable from each other and rewrite our optimization problem into a simple linear program (LP). The LP is given in the technical report [12]. However, solving the LP gives us little insight into the problem's structure. The next section builds such insights for a special case of the problem where each node has the same ρ setting, i.e., $\rho_v = \rho$ for all v.

7   Identical ρ for All Nodes

The instance of every node having the same ρ is of particular interest because it captures fairness in the super-node network. In other words, every super-node injects the same number of new queries into the network. This instance also arises when the software clients have a hard-coded and pre-determined capacity allocation. Clearly, finding the optimal $\hat{\rho}$ setting that maximizes the total remote work is dependent on the network topology. In addition to presenting a procedure for selecting the optimal $\hat{\rho}$, we also show that imposing this "fair" criterion of identical ρ for all nodes does not significantly reduce the maximum amount of remote work.

Figure 3 shows our procedure for selecting $\hat{\rho}$. To illustrate, consider examples (a), (b), and (c) in Figure 4. We first write out $|\hat{D}(v_i, \tau)|$ for all nodes v_i in a non-decreasing sequence, and then add the numbers in sequence from the beginning until the sum exceeds the number of nodes. When we stopped adding at node i, the optimal $\hat{\rho}$ is the corresponding $d_i = \frac{1}{|\hat{D}(v_i, \tau)|}$. In example (a), we get the sequence of $|\hat{D}(v_i, \tau)|$ as $\{3, 3, 3\}$. Because 3 is the number nodes in this network, we stop immediately at $i = 1$ and get the optimal $\hat{\rho} = \frac{1}{3}$, as expected. Moving to the more complicated examples, we see example (b) generates the sequence $\{2, 2, 2, 2, 2, 2, 7\}$. After adding the first four 2s, we get $8 > 7$, thus the optimal $\hat{\rho} = d_4 = \frac{1}{|\hat{D}(v_4, \tau)|} = \frac{1}{2}$. In example (c), we get the sequence $\{3, 4, 4, 5, 5\}$ which yields the optimal $\hat{\rho} = \frac{1}{4}$ when $3 + 4 > 5$.

The correctness of the *Find_Optimal_Single_ρ* procedure is the result of the following theorem.

Theorem 3. *In protocol $\mathcal{H}^{\mathcal{R}}$ with the same ρ, the optimal $\hat{\rho} = d_k$ where k is the smallest integer such that $\sum_{i \leq k} |\hat{D}(v_i, \tau)| \geq n$.*

The formal proof is given in the technical report [12]. Here we outline the general idea behind the theorem. Note that given any ρ, we can divide the nodes into two categories: the set of saturated nodes S and the set of unsaturated nodes U. Now consider using $\rho' = \rho + \epsilon$ for some $\epsilon > 0$. For all nodes $v \in S$, v's remote work is reduced by ϵ, i.e., we lose a total of $R^- = \epsilon |S|$. However, for all nodes $w \in U$, w's remote work has increased by $\epsilon |\hat{D}(w, \tau)|$, or we gain $R^+ = \epsilon \sum_{w \in U} |\hat{D}(w, \tau)|$. Thus intuitively, when $R^- = R^+$, we have found a candidate for the optimal $\hat{\rho}$. Fortunately, there is only one such candidate, which corresponds precisely to Theorem 3.

There is a special case for Theorem 3 when $\sum_{i \leq k} |\hat{D}(v_i, \tau)| = n$. In this situation, there are multiple optimal $\hat{\rho}$ for a single round in the steady state. Specifically,

Corollary 2. *If $\sum_{i \leq k} |\hat{D}(v_i, \tau)| = n$ for some k, then for all ρ where $d_k \geq \rho \geq d_{k+1}$, $RW(\rho)$ is optimal.*

Example (d) in Figure 4 illustrates this occurrence of multiple optimal $\hat{\rho}$. The sequence of $\{|\hat{D}(v_i, \tau)|\}_i$ in this case is $\{2, 2, 3, 3\}$. Notice that $|\hat{D}(v_1, \tau)| + |\hat{D}(v_2, \tau)| = 2 + 2 = 4$ which is the number of nodes. By Corollary 2, we can conclude for example (d), any ρ where $\frac{1}{3} \leq \rho \leq \frac{1}{2}$ yields the optimal amount of remote work in a single round of the steady state.

Now that we know how to find the optimal for this special case of identical ρ for each node, a natural question is how much remote work did we sacrifice in restricting to the special case instead of using arbitrary $\bar{\rho}$? To bound this amount of lost remote work, we use the following the theorem.

Theorem 4. *For any connected network $G = (V, E)$ where $|V| = n \geq \tau + 1$, compute the optimal $\hat{\rho}$ using the* Find_Optimal_Single_ρ *procedure. Then in steady state, $RW_t(\hat{\rho}) \geq \frac{\tau}{\tau+1} nC$.*

The proof follows from a lemma used in proving Theorem 3 and is given in the technical report [12]. The immediate consequence of Theorem 4 is that even with the restriction of identical ρ's, nodes in the network are processing at $\frac{\tau}{\tau+1}$ of the maximum capacity. Hence, the fraction of loss due to the restriction is at most $\frac{1}{\tau+1}$. A secondary consequence is that regardless of what kind of network G we use, we can always process remote work at $\frac{\tau}{\tau+1}$ of the capacity.

8   Different ρ for Each Node

If we have all nodes inject the same number of queries into the network, some nodes will not operate at their maximum capacities. Thus it is possible to achieve more remote work by allowing nodes to inject different amounts of work, i.e., use a different ρ for each node. To illustrate the difference in the amount of remote work, we reuse the examples in Figure 4. In (b), by setting the ρ for the center of the star to 1 and 0 for the other nodes, we can saturate every node and get a total remote work of $6C$. In contrast, the identical-ρ case only yields total remote work of $\frac{7}{2}C$. Similarly, we get $4C$ and $2C$ for examples (c) and (d) respectively by setting the ρ of the nodes with the highest degrees to 1 and 0 for the other nodes. Using identical ρ, we get $\frac{7}{2}C$ and $2C$ respectively for examples (c) and (d).

In this general case where nodes can have different ρ values, there are many possible optimal solutions. In particular, there is one subset of the optimal solutions that corresponds to the *minimum fractional dominating-set* (MFDS) of distance τ for the network topology graph $G = (V, E)$. In MFDS, each node v is assigned a weight w_v where $0 \le w_v \le 1$. The dominating set condition is that for every node v, the sum of the weights from nodes within τ hops of v is at least 1. The goal is to come up with a set of weights w_v that satisfies the dominating condition while minimizing the sum of the weights. The MFDS is a well understood problem. Reducing our problem to the MFDS exposes some underlying structure in finding the optimal ρ_v's and allows us to leverage many existing techniques for solving it. Fortunately, there is a simple mapping from an optimal solution of MFDS to our problem. Specifically,

Theorem 5. *For any optimal solution $\{w_v\}$ to the minimum fractional dominating set of G with distance τ, the solution $\bar{\rho}$ where $\rho_v = w_v$ maximizes the total remote work in the network G.*

To prove the above claim, we observe that when all nodes are saturated, maximizing remote work is equivalent to minimizing new-query injection (i.e., MFDS). Therefore we simply need to show that there exists an optimal $\hat{\rho}$ where all nodes are saturated. Intuitively, for any optimal $\hat{\rho}$ where some node v is not saturated, we can "boost" ρ_v until v is saturated without changing the amount of remote work. The details of this "boosting" step and the proof of Theorem 5 are given in the technical report [12] .

Although using different ρ's leads to more remote work, note that we are setting ρ to 0 for a large number of nodes, which means these nodes cannot inject any queries. In practice, a node that cannot inject any queries is not useful. Therefore a combination of using a small fixed ρ (e.g., using d_n from the previous section) to guarantee some fairness while allocating the remaining capacity through the dominating set is more practical.

Distributed ρC Estimation

For every 2τ rounds (say at time t), each node $v \in V$ does the following:

1. If $|W_t(v, \rho_v)| < C$ (i.e., not enough remote work),
2.   broadcast an $inc(1 - \frac{|W_t(v,\rho_v)|}{C})$ message with TTL τ.
3. If $|W_t(v, \rho_v)| > C$ (i.e., too much remote work),
4.   for every node w such that $\exists (w, ttl, mid) \in W_t(v, \rho_v)$
5.   send a $dec(\frac{|W_t(v,\rho_v)|}{C} - 1)$ message to node w.

Upon receiving an $inc(p)$ or $dec(p)$ message, each node adjusts its ρC by 1 with probability p.

Fig. 5. An informal description of a distributed ρC estimation heuristic.

9 Open Problems

We now outline two open problems that are practical variations of the maximizing remote work problem we studied in this paper.

9.1 Distributed Algorithm

In Sections 7 and 8, we described centralized solutions for finding the optimal ρ for each node that maximizes the total remote work in the network. Our solutions require knowing the entire network topology in advance. However in a P2P environment, with nodes constantly joining and leaving, it is impractical for any node to gather the entire network topology information. Even if we could efficiently gather such information, the rapidly changing topology will quickly render a solution based on the current topology obsolete and sub-optimal. Nevertheless, the results about the centralized solutions are important because they form the basis of comparison for distributed solutions.

For the instance of using a different ρ for each node, distributed solutions are possible by adapting fractional dominating set algorithms [2], [6]. However, these algorithms have long running times for our problem, cannot handle different capacities at each node, and must be re-run each time as the network topology changes. Here, we propose a simple heuristic for estimating how many new queries each node should inject (i.e., the value of $\rho_v C$ for each node v) in a distributed fashion. Figure 5 outlines the steps in our distributed approach. Every node only makes local decisions. When a node does not have enough queries to saturate its processing capacity, it tells all of its neighbors to inject one more local query per round. If a node has too much remote work, it tells all the nodes that have sent remote work to it to inject one less local query per round. We have performed some initial simulations to compare our heuristic against the optimal solution. The heuristic performs very well when the capacity C, in number of queries, is large compared to the number of nodes within τ hops.

The randomization for $inc(p)$ and $dec(p)$ is necessary to avoid oscillation and to stabilize the system. However, the resulting stable setting may not be optimal.

Hence, a better solution is needed. However, note that the proposed heuristic is estimating the number of new queries ρC rather than the fraction of capacity ρ as in the fraction dominating set approach. Thus this heuristic does not assume all the nodes have the same capacity C.

9.2   Nodes with Different Capacities

In reality, super-nodes may have different processing capacities. The results from the previous sections no longer hold because we cannot determine, independent of the network topology, when a node is saturated. Recall that if nodes have the same capacity, then Lemma 2 guarantees that a node v is saturated when v's neighbors are injecting more queries than v's capacity. However, when nodes have different capacities, there is a simple counterexample.

Consider nodes u, x, and v connected in a line in that order. Now assign capacity $2C$ to nodes u and v and capacity C to x. Since all the work from u must travel through x to reach v, the amount of remote work at v is limited by the capacity at x. Even if node u is injecting $2C$ queries, at most C of them will reach v each round, which invalidates Lemma 2 for the case of different capacities. In this particular example, the extra capacities at nodes u and v are irrelevant.

Even for the simple case where only one node x has more capacity than the rest, the solution is non-obvious and topology dependent. For example, if x is in an area of the network where nodes are under-saturated, then it should use its extra capacity to inject more queries. On the other hand, if x is in an area where nodes are already saturated, then the extra capacity should only be used to increase the amount of remote work at node x.

Our current approach is an incremental heuristic that combines multiple optimal solutions. The basic idea is as follows: Suppose nodes have one of two possible capacities C_1 and C_2 where $C_1 < C_2$. Then our heuristic is to find the optimal $\bar{\rho}$ setting for the entire network assuming all the nodes have capacity C_1. We then create a subgraph of the original network that includes only nodes with capacity C_2. Note that the subgraph may be disconnected. We then compute another optimal $\bar{\rho}'$ setting on the subgraph assuming all the nodes have the capacity $C_2 - C_1$. For nodes with capacity C_1, their corresponding ρ' value is 0. To get the final solution, we let each node inject $\rho_v C_1 + \rho_v'(C_2 - C_1)$ queries.

10   Concluding Remarks

This paper uses a simple model to study remote work in a flooding-based peer-to-peer network. In particular, we showed

1. For any setting $\bar{\rho}$, protocol $\mathcal{H}^{\mathcal{R}}$ processes the most remote work.
2. Under protocol $\mathcal{H}^{\mathcal{R}}$ with all nodes using the same ρ, if we order the nodes $\{v_1, \ldots, v_k\}$ where $|\hat{D}(v_i, \tau)| \le |\hat{D}(v_{i+1}, \tau)|$, then the optimal $\hat{\rho} = \frac{1}{|\hat{D}(v_k, \tau)|}$ where k is the smallest integer such that $\sum_{i=1}^{k} |\hat{D}(v_i, \tau)| \ge n$.

3. When nodes use different ρ, any optimal solution to the minimum fractional dominating-set of the network graph G is an optimal $\hat{\rho}$ solution.

We believe that our results can serve as a benchmark for more complex systems. For example, the proposed heuristic load management scheme of Section 9.1 can be compared against a system where $\bar{\rho}$ is selected using our optimal and centralized solutions. In addition, our solutions can form the basis for heuristics, as illustrated in Section 9.2.

Acknowledgment. We thank Kamesh Munagala for valuable discussions on approximation algorithms for fractional bin-packing.

References

1. N. Daswani and H. Garcia-Molina. Query-flood DoS attacks in Gnutella. In *ACM Conference on Computer and Communications Security*, Washington, DC, November 2002.
2. N. Garg and J. Könemann. Faster and simpler algorithms for multicommodity flow and other fractional packing problems. In 39th *Annual Symposium on Foundations of Computer Science*, pages 300–309, Palo Alto, California, November 1998.
3. The Gnutella Developer Forum (GDF). Database of vendor codes. http://groups.yahoo.com/group/the_gdf/.
4. Gnutella. Website http://gnutella.wego.com.
5. Concurrent Gnutella Hosts. http://www.limewire.com/.
6. Fabian Kuhn and Roger Wattenhofer. Constant-time distributed dominating set approximation. In 22nd *ACM Symposium on Principles of Distributed Computing*, Boston, MA, July 2003.
7. Q. Lv, P. Cao, E. Cohen, K. Li, and S. Shenker. Search and replication in unstructured peer-to-peer networks. In *Proceedings of the 16th annual ACM International Conference on Supercomputing (ICS)*, 2002.
8. S. Ratnasamy, P. Francis, M. Handley, R. Karp, and S. Shenker. A scalable content-addressable network. In *Proceedings of ACM SIGCOMM*, pages 149–160, San Diego, August 2001.
9. A. Rowstron and P. Druschel. Storage management and caching in past, a large-scale, persistent peer-to-peer storage utility. In *Proceedings of SOSP '01*, 2001.
10. S. Sariou, P. K. Gummadi, and S. D. Gribble. Measuring and analyzing the characteristics of Napster and Gnutella hosts. In *Multimedia Computing and Networking (MMCN)*, San Jose, CA, January 2002.
11. I. Stoica, R. Morris, D. Karger, M. F. Kaashoek, and H. Balakrishnan. Chord: A scalable peer-to-peer lookup service for internet applications. In *Proceedings of ACM SIGCOMM*, pages 160–177, San Diego, August 2001.
12. Q. Sun, N. Daswani, and H. Garcia-Molina. Maximizing remote work in flooding-based peer-to-peer systems. Technical report, Stanford University, 2003. http://dbpubs.stanford.edu:8090/pub/2003-05.
13. B. Yang and H. Garcia-Molina. Efficient search in peer-to-peer networks. In *Proceedings of the 22nd IEEE International Conference on Distributred Computing Systems (ICDCS)*, Vienna, Austria, July 2002.
14. B. Y. Zhao, J. Kubiatowicz, and A. Joseph. An infrastructure for fault-tolerant wide-area location and routing. Technical Report UCB/CSD-01-1141, University of California at Berkeley, 2001.

Overcoming the Majority Barrier in Large-Scale Systems

Haifeng Yu*

Computer Science Department, Duke University, Durham, NC 27708
yhf@cs.duke.edu

Abstract. In asynchronous environments, the *majority barrier* prevents us from achieving consensus when more than half of the nodes fail. We argue that the majority barrier significantly limits the availability of practical systems such as peer-to-peer systems. To overcome the barrier realistically, this paper proposes a *witness model* that probabilistically strengthens the traditional asynchronous model for large-scale systems. The model is motivated by the prevalence of fuzzy partitions in today's Internet, namely, reachability is far from transitive. Our assumptions in the model are strictly weaker than those in previous approaches. To show that the model is realistic, we carefully use real Internet measurements to validate our strengthening assumptions. On the other hand, we design three consensus protocols under the witness model that can tolerate $n-1$ failures, showing that the model is strong enough to overcome the majority barrier.

1 Introduction

Distributed consensus [21], which allows nodes to reach a common decision, has long been a key problem in distributed systems. This paper is motivated by the application of distributed consensus in a large-scale *dynamic replication system* such as a peer-to-peer system [25]. Upon replica failure, a dynamic replication system is able to shift to a new configuration. To ensure consistency/atomicity, the new configuration should be agreed upon by all the old replicas.

We focus on consensus among n *players* in the presence of fail-stop failures. In asynchronous environments such as the Internet, it has been well known that consensus is impossible even with a single player failure (the FLP theorem) [15]. Much research has been done to overcome such fundamental limitation. The resulting techniques, such as randomization[7], sacrificing liveness [19], and assuming partial synchrony [13], can solve consensus satisfactorily in most practical contexts (e.g., in Petal [20]). However, most of the techniques are still limited by a further impossibility result [8], namely, they cannot tolerate more than $n/2$ player failures. The fundamental reason is that when majority players fail, the other players cannot be sure whether those players have failed, or there is a partition (or the mixture of both). Yet they still need to decide within finite time. We call such limitation as the *majority barrier*.

For practical systems, we argue that overcoming the majority barrier is crucial for improving system availability. Availability has recently become a key design goal for

---

* This research is supported in part by the National Science Foundation (EIA-99772879, ITR-0082912), Hewlett Packard, IBM, and Intel.

F.E. Fich (Ed.): DISC 2003, LNCS 2848, pp. 352–366, 2003.

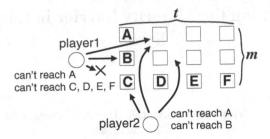

Fig. 1. Two players and 3×4 witnesses. The two players reach the same witness for the first key. There is a *witness mismatch* for the second key, since the two players reach different witnesses. The first player cannot reach the last key.

many distributed systems in the Internet, and is in fact, the utility bottleneck of many Internet services [18] such as E-commerce systems. The majority barrier forces a system to block whenever a majority of players fail. If each replica in a replication system fails independently with probability of 0.1, then always requiring a majority of four replicas yields 95% availability. On the other hand, if the system can tolerate three failures, four replicas can achieve 99.99% availability, which would entail 13 replicas if we required a majority. Such difference increases as we approach 100% availability. The majority barrier also has serious impacts on the availability of consensus-related problems such as atomic commit and group membership.

Unfortunately, most traditional consensus research has been focusing on the FLP impossibility and falls short of addressing the majority barrier. For the few techniques [5, 10,13] that do break the barrier, the assumptions are rather strong and it is unclear how realistic they are.

To overcome the majority barrier, this paper proposes a *witness model* that probabilistically strengthens the scheduler in the standard asynchronous model. The main challenge is, of course, to design the model weak enough to be realistic, while strong enough to break the barrier. Our model is motivated by the prevalence of fuzzy partitions in today's Internet, namely, reachability in the network is far from transitive [1,29,32]. Our assumptions in the model are strictly weaker than those in previous approaches [5, 10,13]. Also different from the previous approaches, the consensus protocols under our model have tunable small probabilities of violating safety.

1.1   Overview of Results

The witness model is designed for large-scale distributed systems (e.g., peer-to-peer systems) with N nodes ($N \gg n$), from which we choose $m \times t$ nodes as *witnesses* to help the n players. A player may also be a witness, and there is no restriction on the value of m and t with respect to n. However, for now, it is convenient to imagine that players and witnesses are disjoint. Witnesses may fail at any time. We do *not* assume that majority players, or majority witnesses, or majority players and witnesses, are non-faulty.

The witnesses are organized into an $m \times t$ matrix and provide a functionality similar to quorum intersection to the players. Each player communicates with only m witnesses from the matrix. Specifically, each row of the matrix is called a *key*, and a player uses the first witness from left to right that it can *reach* for each key (Fig. 1). A player *reaches* a witness if the player sends a request to the witness and a reply is received within a timeout. A key is *non-faulty* if at least one witness in the corresponding row is non-faulty. A *witness mismatch* happens when using the same non-faulty key, two players do not reach the same witness. The main assumption of the witness model is that for players without near-player network congestion or failures, witness mismatches (with probability P_{mis}) are independent for different keys. The immediate guarantee from such an assumption is that if two such players both use the same s non-faulty keys, then they observe at least one witness in common (*collide*) with probability of $1 - P_{mis}^s$. This common witness will help the two players to achieve consensus. Safety (same decision value for all players) can then be guaranteed when all pairs of players collide.

In the witness model, the system can be available (consensus protocol can terminate) as long as i) one out of n players is non-faulty; ii) one out of mt witnesses is non-faulty; and iii) the non-faulty player can reach the non-faulty witness. Notice that we do *not* require more than one non-faulty key. However, we will still be able to prove that when t is above some easy-to-satisfy threshold, we have $P_{nc} \leq mP_{mis}^m$, where P_{nc} is the probability of two players not colliding. Furthermore, the expected message complexity to contact m keys is $O(m)$, independent of t. As a result, availability can be improved using a larger t without negatively affecting safety or complexity. Load balancing among the witnesses is not an explicit goal of our approach, and the left-most witnesses are the most loaded. We can, however, combine the witness model with quorum systems to achieve load balancing.

It is now clear why we conceptually separate players and witnesses. Different from players, not all mt witnesses participate in the protocol. On average only $O(m)$ witnesses are active during an execution and mt can be much larger than n. The second difference is that to ensure safety, players need to collide, but not witnesses. As a result, safety can always be improved by increasing m.

The witness model overcomes the majority barrier by ensuring that two partitioned players collide with high probability. The experimental motivation behind the model is that in today's Internet, most network failures result in fuzzy partitions and reachability in the network is far from transitive [1,29,32]. As long as two nodes do not have near-player network failures, it is possible to route around most network failures via a third node as in RON [1] and Detour [29]. In our terminology, this is to say that two players can both reach the same witness.

To validate the witness model, we use real Internet measurement traces [1,32] to study the correlation coefficients among witness mismatches for different keys, and the average is below 4% in all our experiments. We also observe that P_{nc} decreases exponentially with the number of non-faulty keys. The model is further studied analytically and compared against systems requiring majority. Finally, practicality is a key goal of the witness model and implementing it requires zero effort in peer-to-peer systems.

The second part of this paper designs several consensus protocols that can tolerate $n - 1$ player and $mt - 1$ witness failures under the witness model. All our protocols are conceptually simple. The first protocol is based on randomized shared-memory consensus protocols. Specifically, we define and implement a probabilistic register in the witness model, which is then used in a shared-memory consensus protocol [28]. The resulting protocol has expected $O(n^2)$ time complexity, $O(n^3 m)$ message complexity and $16n^2 P_{nc}$ unsafety (probability of violating safety). Next, we design two deterministic protocols based on a strong "initially dead" assumption. Both protocols have $\binom{n}{2} P_{nc}$ unsafety, with $O(m)$ and $O(1)$ time complexity, respectively. Finally, we prove a lower bound of $\binom{n}{2} P_{nc}$ on unsafety.

The next section discusses related work and Section 3 presents the formal witness model. In Section 4, we validate the model experimentally and Section 5 studies its property analytically. Then we design three $(n-1)$-resilient consensus protocols under the witness model in Section 6. Finally, Section 7 draws the conclusions.

2 Related Work

Despite extensive research on consensus, very few approaches [5,10,13] overcome the majority barrier. We do not consider Disk Paxos [16] as breaking the barrier, since it assumes majority non-faulty disks. We believe that the scarcity of such solutions is because: i) traditionally the majority barrier does not receive much theoretical attention; and ii) timing assumptions, which are hard to validate without real measurements, are necessary to overcome the barrier.

Among the few approaches that do overcome the barrier, the deterministic protocol in [5,13] requires synchronous communication and eventually synchronous players. Our model provides a practical way to (probabilistically) achieve synchronous communication. On the other hand, we allow fully asynchronous players but our randomized protocol does not terminate deterministically. It is trivial to extend our randomized protocol with the failure detector of $\Diamond W$ [10]. The resulting protocol will terminate deterministically when the assumptions in [5,13] are met, yet still terminate probabilistically in other cases.

The second approach to achieve consensus without majority is to use a strongly complete, weakly accurate failure detector of S [10]. Such failure detector requires one non-faulty player that is *never* suspected by any other non-faulty player. When $t = 1$, the witness model can be viewed as a *pair-wise* failure detector, where for any two non-faulty players, there exists a non-faulty player not suspected by either of them. Obviously, such failure detector is strictly weaker than S. Pair-wise failure detectors are also related to limited scope failure detector S_k [24], which can be used to achieve consensus with less than k failures. In order to tolerate $n - 1$ failures, however, k must be equal to n and S_k actually becomes S.

Consensus has also been extensively studied in shared-memory environments. Shared-memory consensus is still impossible [11], but there is no majority barrier. Our approach of implementing probabilistic registers is similar to [4]. However, previous emulations [4,14,22] of shared-memory all require a majority (or a quorum) of non-faulty nodes. By using the witness model, we are able to emulate shared-memory without requiring a majority, which in turn help to overcome the majority barrier in message-passing systems.

Our strengthening assumptions in the witness model are made for the scheduler of the system. Similar approaches are used in [8] to solve consensus with less than half failures and in [17] for leader election. These approaches typically assume that false time-outs are independent. For example, Gupta et al. [17] assume that node failures and excess message latencies are all independent. These assumptions necessarily imply independent witness mismatches and are thus strictly stronger. There are two fundamental differences between our work and these previous approaches: i) we assume independence only for different *keys*, and not for all players and messages; and ii) witness mismatches can be much less likely than false time-outs.

The witness model achieves similar functionality as a quorum system [6], namely, ensuring player collision. In particular, our model appears similar to probabilistic quorums [23]. However, we choose not to present the model as a quorum system because it cannot be fully captured under the quorum framework. One critical aspect of the model is that the players must contact the witnesses according to a particular policy. In other words, they try to find a live quorum according to a specific order to maintain the model's property. In some cases, even a single witness can be a quorum, but the high possibility of collision is preserved because the player is required to try and fail to find other quorums before using this small quorum. Neither strict quorums nor probabilistic quorums capture such notion of "ordered search for live quorums". In some sense, the witness model is orthogonal to quorums: The witness model specifies how to find a live quorum, while quorum techniques specify which quorum to start from.

In terms of availability, our witness model achieves strictly better availability than majority quorums. Some quorum systems [6] do not require a majority, but it has been proven [26] that the simple majority quorum achieves the best availability when node failure probability is below 0.5. Probabilistic quorums also achieve better availability than majority quorums by using smaller quorums and enforcing an *access strategy* on how quorums are chosen. The strategy does not, however, specify how to find a live quorum. Because of this, implementing a particular access strategy in a failure-prone asynchronous system can be challenging. The difficulty is that the scheduler of the system is able to bias the achieved access strategy by simply delaying some messages and forcing players to use certain quorums. Our witness model addresses such issue by enforcing a strict order on how quorums should be tried, and by making additional assumptions on witness mismatches.

Quorum systems do achieve much better load balancing than our approach. Similar load balancing in the witness model can be achieved by combining with quorums. A quorum system with t nodes will be simulated using a single $m \times t$ witness matrix, such that each node in the quorum system corresponds to a witness column. When contacting a particular node in the quorum system, we still perform an ordered search from left to right, starting from the corresponding column (and with potential wrapping over at the end of the matrix). Obviously, when the witness model is available, all nodes in the quorum system are available. If the quorum system imposes load equally on each node, then the load on the witnesses are also balanced.

3   System Model and Witness Model

We consider a standard asynchronous system [21] with unbounded message propagation delay and processor speed. Nodes may experience fail-stop failures, and message delivery can be unreliable. A message sent indefinitely often is ultimately received, given that

```
% Let wit[1..m][1..t] be the matrix of witness nodes
object witness(int k, object request) {
    for (i = 1; i ≤ t; i++) {
        send request to wit[k][i] and wait until timeout;
        if (reply received within timeout) return reply;
    }
    return cannot_reach_key;
}
```

Fig. 2. The **witness**() primitive.

the receiver does not fail. Unreliable messages will not make consensus much harder in our case because of the strengthening assumptions in the witness model. In an execution, a node is *correct* or *non-faulty* if it does not crash. Otherwise it is *faulty*. We do not consider Byzantine failures. The system contains N nodes and we study how to achieve consensus among a subset of n nodes where $N \gg n$. To avoid confusion, we call the n nodes as *players*. Each player tries to decide on some *decision* value, which must be the *input* value of some player. *Safety* is preserved if all players reach the same decision.

3.1   Witness Model

To enable consensus with up to $n-1$ player failures, we randomly choose $m \times t$ *witness nodes* (or simply *witnesses*) from the system to help the players. A player may also be a witness. The mt witnesses are organized into an $m \times t$ matrix (Fig. 1). Each row of the matrix corresponds to a *witness key* or simply a *key*, which can be mapped to any of the t witnesses in the row. In an execution, a key is *non-faulty* if at least one of the t witnesses is correct. To map a key to a witness, a player conceptually scans the row corresponding to the key from left to right, and chooses the first witness that it can *reach*. A player *reaches* a witness if it sends a request to the witness and a reply is received within some timeout[1]. If no such witness exists in that row, we say that the player cannot *reach* the key. Not being able to reach a witness can result from message lost, network failure, witness failure or overload. The primitive "reply **witness**(key, request)" allows a player to send request to the witness currently corresponding to key, and then obtain the reply (Fig. 2).

A witness has state that does not survive crash. Even though the processing of request is assumed to be atomic, the primitive **witness**() may not. It is possible that the witness processes the request without the player receiving the reply. It also follows that multiple witnesses may process the same request.

Before we make the major assumption in the model, we define *strongly correct players*:

---

[1] We do assume that each player has a local clock. But clock drift, or even clock *rate* drift, may not be bounded. The only requirement for the clocks is embedded in Assumption 2. Namely, at least on one player, the timeout should not expire too early so that the player can reach enough keys and become strongly correct.

Definition 1. Strongly correct player. In a given execution and for a given integer $h > 0$, a correct player is *strongly correct* if there exists a set of h keys, such that for any key, key, in the set: i) the player uses key at least once; and ii) the player can reach key in any **witness**() invocation using key.

The above definition can be viewed as a filtering step to exclude players with near-player network congestion or failures. Those players are unlikely to be strongly correct because they will not be able to reach h keys. In practice, as will be shown in Section 4.1, h can be a small constant such as 1 or 2.

The same key may be mapped to different witnesses when i) witnesses fail in the middle of the protocol; or ii) a correct player cannot reach a correct witness:

Definition 2. Witness mismatch. Suppose that strongly correct players p and q each invoke **witness**() once using the same non-faulty key, key. Define $Mis(key)$ (*witness mismatch*) as the event that i) p cannot reach key; or ii) q cannot reach key; or iii) p and q can both reach key, but key is mapped to different witnesses in the two invocations. Otherwise we call the event *witness match*.

See Fig. 1 for an example of witness mismatch. The witness model strengthens the standard asynchronous model by assuming that witness mismatches are independent for different keys:

Assumption 1 Independent witness mismatches. Let p and q be any pair of strongly correct players and $S = \{key_1, key_2, \ldots, key_{|S|}\}$ be any set of non-faulty keys. The witness model assumes:

1. There exists $\varepsilon > 0$, such that for $1 \leq i \leq |S|$, $P_{mis} = P[Mis(key_i)] \leq 1 - \varepsilon$.
2. The events $Mis(key_1), Mis(key_2), \ldots, Mis(key_{|S|})$ are mutually independent.

The intuition behind this assumption is that for strongly correct players, witness mismatches are mostly caused by near-witness problems. These problems may be witness crash / overload, or network congestion / failure around the witness. If witnesses are randomly distributed across the Internet, these problems are most likely independent. Notice that Assumption 1 implies independent witness failures. It is important that the independence assumption is only made for different keys. Independence for different **witness**() invocations is much less likely to be valid because past mismatches may indicate higher probabilities of future mismatches.

Different from some previous approaches [5,10,13], our assumption in the model is made probabilistically instead of deterministically (e.g., simply assuming no witness mismatches). We argue that such modeling is important because it exposes the value of ε, so that we can analyze how the error is potentially amplified in different protocols.

To utilize Assumption 1, we need to ensure:

Assumption 2 Existence of strongly correct player. The witness model assumes that each execution has at least one strongly correct player.

Notice that it is rather reasonable to assume the existence of a player without near-player network failures, since to provide useful service to end users, some player should have good network connection. So the real assumption is requiring h correct keys.

An execution is called *non-trivial* if it satisfies Assumption 2, otherwise it is *trivial*. Our consensus protocols block in trivial executions, whose probability is defined as *unavailability*.

Only strongly correct players actively "participate" in our consensus protocols, while other players passively wait to learn of the decision value. Thus we only rely on independent witness mismatches for strongly correct players. When two strongly correct players p and q invoke **witness**() using the same set S of non-faulty keys, they *collide* if they have a witness match on at least one key. It is easy to see that the possibility of p and q not colliding (P_{nc}) is $P_{mis}^{|S|}$. Our consensus protocols ensure safety if all pairs of strongly correct players collide. We define *unsafety* as the probability of executions with multiple decision values over all non-trivial executions.

Practicality is a key goal of the witness model and implementing the model requires zero effort in recent systems [25] with peer-to-peer routing functionality [27,30]. A player does *not* need to maintain the $m \times t$ witness matrix, rather it uses m random numerical values as keys. These random keys are generate from the same seed known by all players, so that all players agree on the m keys. To reach a key, a player simply sends the request using peer-to-peer routing, which automatically routes the request to the node corresponding to the key. The same key may not be routed to the same node, and such behavior is already abstracted in the witness model: This is exactly why we may have mismatches. It is also possible that multiple keys are mapped to the same node, thus affecting the independence assumption. However, such effects tend to be negligible when we use random keys in a large-scale system. Time out mechanism and the tunable value t are already part of peer-to-peer routing.

4   Witness Model Validation

4.1   Experimental Validation

In this section, we use three real Internet measurement traces [1,32] to validate Assumption 1 and 2 in our witness model. Due to space limitations, we only give an overview of the validation results; see [31] for full details. We use two players throughout this section because Assumption 1 is made for pairs of players. While for Assumption 2, using two players only makes our results look worse.

To verify the independence of witness mismatches, we first compute witness mismatch correlation coefficients between each pair of keys. See [31] for why we choose not to perform a statistical hypothesis test, and why studying correlation coefficients (rather than stochastic independence) is sufficient for our purpose. Fig. 3 presents the correlation coefficients between all pairs of witness keys for six keys in one trace based on one mapping from the nodes in the trace to the players and witnesses in our model. In Fig. 4, we also present the average correlation coefficient between all pairs of keys for all mappings as a function of h. We argue that the near-zero correlation coefficients in both Fig. 3 and Fig. 4 are good indications of non-correlated witness mismatches. The trend in Fig. 4 also demonstrates the effectiveness of the h threshold to exclude those players with near-player failures, and thus decrease the correlation among witness mismatches.

Our second analysis studies the effects of witness mismatches on P_{nc}. Fig. 5 plots P_{nc} as a function of m under one trace with log-scale y-axis. See [31] for similar results

–	-0.05	-0.02	0.06	0.04	-0.03
-0.05	–	-0.07	0.05	0.06	-0.001
-0.02	-0.07	–	0.02	0.002	-0.02
0.06	0.05	0.02	–	0.18	0.10
0.04	0.06	0.002	0.18	–	0.11
-0.03	-0.001	-0.02	0.10	0.11	–

Fig. 3. Correlation coefficient matrix for six keys based on one mapping under the TACT trace with $m = 6$, $t = 1$ and $h = 1$.

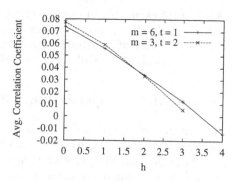

Fig. 4. Average witness mismatch correlation coefficients for all pairs of witness keys under the TACT trace.

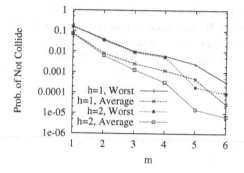

Fig. 5. P_{nc} under the TACT trace for $t = 1$. The average is average across all possible mappings.

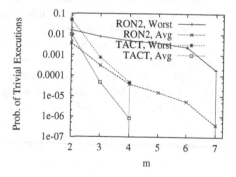

Fig. 6. Unavailability for $h = 2$ and $t = 1$. The average is average across all possible mappings.

under all other traces, which show that P_{nc} decreases roughly exponentially with m. Finally, Fig. 6 presents the probability of trivial executions under two traces. The figure shows that unavailability decreases exponentially with m before reaching zero.

4.2 When Witness Mismatches Are NOT Independent

As explained earlier, the witness model is motivated by the prevalence of fuzzy partitions. In the rare cases of clean partitions, the assumption on independent witness mismatches can be violated. Interestingly, it has been proven [12] that with the power-law distribution of node degrees and the hierarchical structure of the Internet, the largest partition tends to be much larger than the rest of the Internet. Namely, there will be one huge *primary* partition, with many tiny *secondary* partitions around it. When players are randomly distributed, with high probability some players will be in the primary partition. For those players, our assumptions still hold and they will achieve consensus. For players in secondary partitions, when h is not too small, they are unlikely to reach enough keys to become strongly correct. To know whether a player is in a secondary partition under small h values, the player can also check whether all witnesses reached are in its local domain, since clean partitions mostly occur at domain boundaries. Thus, clean partitions probably will not affect unsafety much, but may increase unavailability because players in secondary partitions will not be strongly correct.

5   Analytical Properties and Comparison

This section uses analytical methods to study the model's unavailability, unsafety and message complexity, and then compares the model to majority quorums.

We assume that there is at least one correct player without near-player network failures, so that we can focus on the witness "part" of the model. Based on Assumption 1 (which was validated in the last section), we use a fixed probability (P_{mis}) for independent witness mismatches on each key. Remember that Assumption 1 necessarily implies independent witness failures, and we use P_{fail} for such probability. To study unavailability, we need to make an additional assumption in this section. We assume that the correct player (we assumed earlier) cannot reach a correct witness with probability P_{time} due to network failures or overload. We further assume that such events are independent for different witnesses, since the player has no near-player network failures. Such assumption on P_{time} is based on the same intuition behind Assumption 1.

In the witness model, the correct player cannot reach a key with probability of $(P_{fail} + P_{time})^t$. With a worst case analysis, the system blocks when the player cannot reach h keys, whose probability is:

$$unavail_{wit} = \sum_{i=m-h+1}^{m} \binom{m}{i} (P_{fail} + P_{time})^{t \times i} (1 - (P_{fail} + P_{time})^t)^{m-i} . \quad (1)$$

All our consensus protocols have an unsafety of $O(n^2 P_{nc})$, where P_{nc} is:

$$P_{nc} = \sum_{i=h}^{m} \binom{m}{i} (1 - P_{fail}^t)^i P_{fail}^{t(m-i)} P_{mis}^i . \quad (2)$$

Larger h results in lower unsafety but higher unavailability. However, the following theorem shows that P_{nc} can be rather independent of h. The reason is that the probability of a faulty key (P_{fail}^t) can easily be much smaller than P_{mis}, and thus unsafety is mostly incurred when all m keys are non-faulty.

Theorem 1. [2] *If $P_{fail}^t \leq P_{mis}/m$, then $P_{nc} \leq m P_{mis}^m$.*

Notice that the condition of $P_{fail}^t \leq P_{mis}/m$ can be easily met. Since P_{nc} is largely determined by m, it is beneficial to use the smallest h possible. The h value still needs be large enough to exclude players with near-player failures, but as shown in Section 4.1, $h = 1$ or 2 is enough. We summarize the result on unsafety, unavailability and message complexity in the following theorem:

Theorem 2. *When $P_{fail}^t \leq P_{mis}/m$ and $h = 1$, P_{nc} is at most $m P_{mis}^m$ and unavailability is at most $(P_{fail} + P_{time})^{mt}$. The expected message complexity to use **witness**() once on all m keys is at most $m/(1 - P_{fail} - P_{time})$.*

---

[2] The proof of all theorems in this paper can be found in [31].

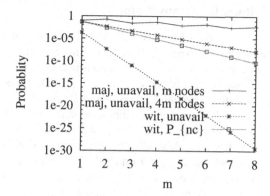

Fig. 7. Unavailability and P_{nc} of the witness (wit) model and majority (maj) quorum for $t = 4$, $h = 1$, $P_{fail} = 0.1$, $P_{time} = 0.02$ and $P_{mis} = 0.05$. The value of P_{time} is based on the failure rate of an average Internet path [9].

One immediate result from the above theorem is that unavailability can be decreased using a larger t without negatively affecting complexity or unsafety.

Next, we compare the witness model against a simple majority quorum system. We will allow the quorum system to access all the witnesses used in our model. A majority quorum system with mt nodes incurs $O(mt)$ rather than $O(m)$ messages per access. For completeness, we thus compare our model against two majority quorum systems with m nodes and mt nodes each. Trivially, a majority quorum system with k nodes blocks with probability:

$$unavail_{maj} = \sum_{i=k/2}^{k} \binom{k}{i} P_{fail}^i (1 - P_{fail})^{k-i} > \binom{k}{k/2} (P_{fail} - P_{fail}^2)^{k/2}$$

$$> (2P_{fail} - 2P_{fail}^2)^{k/2} \geq (P_{fail})^{k/2}, \quad \text{when } P_{fail} \leq 0.5 . \tag{3}$$

The previous pessimistic analysis shows that as long as $P_{time} < \sqrt{P_{fail}} - P_{fail}$, the witness model will have lower unavailability than even the majority quorum system with mt nodes. Further notice that the condition is sufficient but not necessary. Of course, the improved availability comes at the cost of a small unsafety, which decreases quickly with increasing m. Fig. 7 plots the unavailability and P_{nc} of three systems under some specific parameters.

6   Consensus Protocols under the Witness Model

In this section, we design three consensus protocols for the witness model that can tolerate $n - 1$ player failures. We then give a lower bound on unsafety and discuss deterministic termination. Since the focus of this paper is the witness model and its validation, we defer the details of our protocols to [31] and this section gives an overview.

6.1   Randomized Witness Consensus Protocol

The witness model ensures (probabilistic) collision of any two players even without a majority of correct witnesses. This enables us to emulate shared-memory without majority, which in turn transforms wait-free shared-memory consensus protocols to message-passing consensus protocols that can tolerate $n - 1$ failures.

Specifically, we first define a *probabilistic single-writer/multi-reader atomic register* (or *probabilistic register* in short), which is a single-writer/multi-reader atomic register where reads may return stale values with error probability of ϵ. We do not make any assumption on the correlation of stale reads. Using a protocol similar to that in [4], we can implement such a probabilistic register under the witness model without requiring a majority of correct witnesses. A player writes a value into the register by sending the value to the witnesses using all m keys. The witnesses will then record the value. To read a value, the player first retrieves the value using all m keys and then confirms the value by writing it again to the witnesses. The second round in the read operation serves to achieve atomicity. The resulting probabilistic register has an error probability of P_{nc}. Next, we simply substitute registers with probabilistic registers in the **RandCons**() main consensus protocol (Fig. 1 of [28]) and the **SharedCoin**() sub-protocol (Fig. 4 of [28]) (which is invoked by **RandCons**() each round). The following theorem summarizes how stale reads affect the high-level guarantees of the protocol:

Theorem 3. *Suppose we use probabilistic registers with error probability of $\epsilon <$ $1/(4n^4)$ in the **RandCons**() protocol and **SharedCoin**() protocol. The resulting consensus protocol has expected time complexity of $O(n^2)$, message complexity of $O(n^3 m)$, and unsafety of $16n^2\epsilon$.*

Even though the previous randomized protocol is rather straightforward, we emphasize that our construction is non-trivial. Probabilistic registers are not applicable to all shared-memory protocols because of several subtle reasons. First, since stale reads may be arbitrarily correlated, they can qualitatively change the termination property of a shared-memory consensus protocol. For example, using probabilistic registers in the consensus protocol [2] by Aspnes and Herlihy will result in a non-zero probability of not terminating. Second, unsafety of a protocol is amplified by the number of rounds. To properly bound unsafety, this prevents us from applying probabilistic registers to protocols (such as Disk Paxos [16]) that only guarantee *eventual* termination. Finally, in analyzing the effects of stale reads on protocol properties, potentially correlated stale reads can introduce significant challenge. For example, it is yet unclear to us how stale reads affect the shared coin protocol in [3].

6.2   Consensus Protocols Assuming Initially Dead

Emulating a shared-memory is not the only way to use the witness model. This section presents two protocols that do not use the register abstraction. Both terminate deterministically but rely on the significant assumption of *initially dead*:

Assumption 3 Initially dead. *We assume that a player is strongly correct as long as it sends a single message during an execution. In other words, the only failure allowed is a failure before the player enters the protocol.*

```
For Players: % input: initial preference of this player
    for (int i = 1; i ≤ m; i++) {
        witness(key[i], request_permission);
        if (cannot reach key[i]) continue to next iteration;
        if (reply = denied) block until decision is received;
    }
    decide on input; repeatedly broadcast the decision value;
For Witnesses: % has_granted: initialized to false;
    On receiving a permission request:
        if (has_granted = false) {
            has_granted = true; return granted;
        } else return denied;
```

Fig. 8. Sequential witness protocol.

Even though such assumption is quite strong, these protocols can be combined with the randomized protocol to improve its performance.

Our first protocol is a sequential protocol (Fig. 8), which can be best explained with an analogy of acquiring m locks. Without witness mismatch, only one player is able to acquire all locks and become the winner. Other players will be "defeated" once they collide with the winner on any lock.

Theorem 4. *Assuming initially dead, the consensus protocol in Fig. 8 always terminates. Its time complexity is $O(m)$, message complexity is $O(nm)$, and unsafety is $\binom{n}{2} P_{nc}$.*

Due to space limitations, we omit discussion on the second protocol and present its properties directly:

Theorem 5. *Assuming initially dead, there exits a consensus protocol that always terminates with time complexity of $O(1)$, message complexity of $O(nm)$, and unsafety of $\binom{n}{2} P_{nc}$.*

6.3   Lower Bound and Discussion

We now show that the $\binom{n}{2} P_{nc}$ unsafety in the previous two protocols is actually optimal:

Theorem 6. *Whether we assume initially dead or not, a consensus protocol under the witness model has an unsafety of at least $\binom{n}{2} P_{nc}$.*

Our protocols clearly show that the witness model helps to overcome the majority barrier. However, the protocols cannot terminate deterministically (without assuming initially dead). With just two players, the witness model becomes similar to the failure detector of S [10], and deterministic termination is in fact possible. But with more than two players, it remains unclear whether the model is strong enough to allow deterministic termination.

7   Conclusions

The majority barrier in asynchronous systems prevents us from achieving consensus with more than $n/2$ fail-stop failures. This paper argues that such limitation severely impacts distributed system availability. To overcome the majority barrier, we propose a witness model that probabilistically strengthens the traditional asynchronous model. Through experimental validation, we show that such model is weak enough to be realistic in today's Internet. Our consensus protocol design further proves that the model is strong enough to overcome the barrier. We are currently incorporating the witness model into our peer-to-peer system prototype.

Acknowledgment. I would like to thank Amin Vahdat and Jeff Chase for raising the question of clean partitions; Ronald Parr for help on hypothesis testing; and Dahlia Malkhi for inspiring discussion on implementing probabilistic quorums and combining quorums with the witness model. Finally, the insightful comments of the anonymous reviewers greatly improved this paper.

References

1. D. Andersen, H. Balakrishnan, F. Kaashoek, and R. Morris. Resilient Overlay Networks. In *Proceedings of the 18th Symposium on Operating Systems Principles (SOSP)*, October 2001.
2. J. Aspnes and M. Herlihy. Fast Randomized Consensus Using Shared Memory. *Journal of Algorithms*, 11(3):441–461, 1990.
3. J. Aspnes and O. Waarts. Randomized Consensus in Expected $O(nlog^2n)$ Operations per Processor. *SIAM Journal on Computing*, 25(5):1024–1044, October 1996.
4. H. Attiya, A. Bar-Noy, and D. Dolev. Sharing Memory Robustly in Message-Passing Systems. *Journal of the ACM*, pages 124–142, January 1996.
5. H. Attiya, C. Dwork, N. Lynch, and L. Stockmeyer. Bounds on the Time to Reach Agreement in the Presence of Timing Uncertainty. *Journal of the ACM*, 41(1):122–152, January 1994.
6. D. Barbara and H. Garcia-Molina. The Vulnerability of Vote Assignments. *ACM Transactions on Computer Systems*, August 1986.
7. M. Ben-Or. Another Advantage of Free Choice: Completely Asynchronous Agreement Protocols. In *Proceedings of the 2nd Annual ACM Symposium on Principles of Distributed Computing*, pages 27–30, 1983.
8. G. Bracha and S. Toueg. Asynchronous Consensus and Broadcast Protocols. *Journal of the ACM*, pages 824–840, October 1985.
9. B. Chandra, M. Dahlin, L. Gao, and A. Nayate. End-to-End WAN Service Availability. In *Proceedings of the 3rd Usenix Symposium on Internet Technologies and Systems*, January 2001.
10. T. Chandra and S. Toueg. Unreliable Failure Detectors for Reliable Distributed Systems. *Journal of the ACM*, pages 225–267, March 1996.
11. B. Chor, A. Israeli, and M. Li. On Processor Coordination Using Asynchronous Hardware. In *Symposium on Principles of Distributed Computing*, pages 86–97, 1987.
12. R. Cohen, K. Erez, D. ben Avraham, and S. Havlin. Resilience of the Internet to Random Breakdowns. *Physical Review Letters*, 85(21), November 2000.
13. C. Dwork, N. Lynch, and L. Stockmeyer. Consensus in the Presence of Partial Synchrony. *Journal of the ACM*, 35(2):288–323, April 1990.

14. B. Englert and A. A. Shvartsman. Graceful Quorum Reconfiguration in a Robust Emulation of Shared Memory. In *Proceedings of the International Conference on Distributed Computer Systems*, pages 454–463, 2000.

15. M. Fischer, N. Lynch, and M. Paterson. Impossibility of Distributed Consensus with One Faulty Process. *Journal of the ACM*, pages 374–382, 1985.

16. E. Gafni and L. Lamport. Disk Paxos. In *Proceedings of the International Symposium on Distributed Computing*, pages 330–344, 2000.

17. I. Gupta, R. V. Renesse, and K. Birman. A Probabilistically Correct Leader Election Protocol for Large Groups. In *Proceedings of the International Symposium on Distributed Computing (DISC)*, October 2000.

18. J. Hennessy. The Future of Systems Research. *IEEE Computer*, 32(8):27–33, August 1999.

19. L. Lamport. The Part-Time Parliament. *ACM Transactions on Computer Systems*, 16:133–169, May 1998.

20. E. K. Lee and C. A. Thekkath. Petal: Distributed Virtual Disks. In *Proceedings of the 7th International Conference on Architectural Support for Programming Languages and Operating Systems*, October 1996.

21. N. Lynch. *Distributed Algorithms*. Morgan Kaufmann Publishers, 1997.

22. N. Lynch and A. Shvartsman. RAMBO: A Reconfigurable Atomic Memory Service for Dynamic Networks. In *Proceedings of the 16th International Symposium on Distributed Computing (DISC)*, October 2002.

23. D. Malkhi, M. Reiter, A. Wool, and R. Wright. Probabilistic Quorum Systems. *The Information and Computation Journal*, 170(2), November 2001.

24. A. Mostefaoui and M. Raynal. Unreliable Failure Detectors with Limited Scope Accuracy and an Application to Consensus. In *Proceedings of the 19th International Conference on Foundations of Software Technology and Theoretical Computer Science*, December 1999.

25. A. Muthitacharoen, R. Morris, T. Gil, and B. Chen. Ivy: A Read/Write Peer-to-peer File System. In *Proceedings of the 5th Symposium on Operating Systems Design and Implementation*, December 2002.

26. D. Peleg and A. Wool. The Availability of Quorum Systems. *Information and Computation*, pages 210–223, 1995.

27. A. Rowstron and P. Druschel. Pastry: Scalable, Distributed Object Location and Routing for Large-scale Peer-to-peer Systems. In *Proceedings of the 18th IFIP/ACM International Conference on Distributed Systems Platforms (Middleware 2001)*, November 2001.

28. M. Saks, N. Shavit, and H. Woll. Optimal Time Randomized Consensus – Making Resilient Algorithms Fast in Practice. In *Proceedings of the Second Symposium on Discrete Algorithms*, pages 351–362, January 1991.

29. S. Savage, T. Anderson, A. Aggarwal, D. Becker, N. Cardwell, A. Collins, E. Hoffman, J. Snell, A. Vahdat, G. Voelker, and J. Zahorjan. Detour: A Case for Informed Internet Routing and Transport. *IEEE Micro*, 19(1), January 1999.

30. I. Stoica, R. Morris, D. Karger, F. Kaashoek, and H. Balakrishnan. Chord: A Scalable Peer-To-Peer Lookup Service for Internet Applications. In *Proceedings of the ACM SIGCOMM 2001*, pages 149–160, August 2001.

31. H. Yu. Overcoming the Majority Barrier in Large-Scale Systems. Technical report, Duke University, 2003. Technical Report CS-2003-05. Available at `http://www.cs.duke.edu/~yhf/tr-2003-05.pdf`.

32. H. Yu and A. Vahdat. The Costs and Limits of Availability for Replicated Services. In *Proceedings of the 18th ACM Symposium on Operating Systems Principles (SOSP)*, October 2001.

Author Index